Gui

Guide to Good Practice

The Law Society

The Law Society

ISBN: 978-1-85328-734-3

Published in 2009 by the Law Society
113 Chancery Lane, London WC2A 1PL

Typeset by J&L Composition Limited, Scarborough, North Yorkshire
Printed by CPI Antony Rowe, Chippenham, Wiltshire

FSC
Mixed Sources
Product group from well-managed
forests and other controlled sources
Cert no. SGS-COC-2953
www.fsc.org
© 1996 Forest Stewardship Council

The paper used for the text pages of this book is FSC certified, FSC (the Forest Stewardship Council) is an international network to promote responsible management of the world's forests.

Contents

Foreword

It is difficult to over-emphasise the degree of change sweeping across the solicitors' profession. The revolution heralded by the passage of the Legal Services Act in 2007 has challenged traditional business practices and introduced new models for the provision of legal services. More is yet to come with the introduction of Alternative Business Structures in 2011.

In parallel with this, a better informed, results-focused consumer market demands greater value from the legal services within the context of widespread economic upheaval.

With so much for solicitors to consider regarding the future, the Law Society of England and Wales knows the importance of assisting solicitors in surmounting the problems of the present. The Law Society's practice notes have become beacons of best practice for all solicitors concerned with navigating new regulatory waters and changing economic circumstances. Similarly, the Law Society's Practice Advice Service provides invaluable expert advice for all solicitors at the end of the phone.

In collating the most frequently sought advice alongside the full range of practice notes, the *Guide to Good Practice* should occupy a prime position in the armoury of any practising solicitor.

I am confident that the profession faces a bright future. By understanding the challenges ahead we can ensure that we remain the most trusted, most successful and most widely-used providers of legal services. To do so however, we need to ensure that all solicitors remain informed and in step with the changes occurring both within and around the profession. I commend the *Guide to Good Practice* as an essential tool to ease the burden upon all solicitors in the current changing market.

Paul Marsh
President of the Law Society of England and Wales
May 2009

Introduction

This book is a unique compilation of questions frequently posed by practitioners to the Law Society's Practice Advice Service (PAS) together with answers to those questions. Now in its twentieth year, the PAS is part of a range of dedicated telephone based helplines available exclusively to solicitors and their staff. The service is staffed by solicitors and received over 35,000 enquiries in 2008. The PAS provides advice on a wide range of matters including anti-money laundering, costs, conveyancing, probate, tax, practice notes and Law Society policy. The PAS does not give legal advice.

This guide is aimed at fee earners at all levels working in law firms. The purpose of this book is to save you a considerable amount of time researching answers which can easily be found in the book. This comprehensive guide not only provides answers to frequently asked questions on practical issues such as 'My client has asked for my bill to be assessed. What do I have to do?' or 'In which areas of law is it possible to use a conditional fee agreement?', but also contains all current Law Society booklets on costs as well as relevant Law Society practice notes. Practice notes are issued by the Law Society for the use and benefit of its members. They represent the Law Society's view of good practice in a particular area. You are not required to follow them, but doing os will make it easier to account to oversight bodies for your actions. They do not constitute legal advice.

The book is a convenient, time saving tool which will be invaluable in any busy office. The questions and answers are listed under chapter headings with a detailed index at the back which should assist the reader to find what they are looking for quickly.

The PAS answers most queries over the telephone and can be contacted on 0870 606 2522 and practiceadvice@lawsociety.org.uk

The Law Society also operates the Pastoral Care Helpline (020 7320 5795) which refers solicitors with personal, professional or employment problems to the most suitable helpline to assist with their problems.

On 30 March 2009, the Law Society also set up Lawyerline (0870 606 2588) which provides advice to solicitors on client care and handling complaints made by their clients.

The content of this book is based on the information available at 15 April 2009.

1

Civil litigation

For information on funding, including contingency fee agreements and conditional fee agreements please see **Chapter 3, Costs and fees.**

I have been asked to administer an oath to a document intended for use in court proceedings in a foreign country. Can I do this?

It depends on the law of that country. Do not take it for granted that the country concerned will accept the signature of a commissioner authorised to take oaths under the law of England and Wales.

You should suggest that the prospective deponent makes enquiries with his lawyers abroad. In case of doubt, he can be referred to a notary public whose authority to administer oaths is recognised internationally.

Please see Anderson and Warner (2008) *Execution of Documents* (2nd Edition), Law Society Publishing.

Which pre-action protocols are currently in place?

At the time of writing there are 10 pre-action protocols in force; personal injury, clinical negligence, construction and engineering, defamation, professional negligence, judicial review, disease and illness, housing dis-repair cases, possession claims based on rent arrears and on mortgage or home plan arrears. Please also see the Ministry of Justice's website (**www.justice.gov.uk**).

I act for the claimant in civil litigation proceedings which are approaching trial. How many copies of the trial bundle are required?

You should supply identical trial bundles for the court, for each of the parties, and one for use by the witnesses at the trial (CPR PD 39, para.3.10). Originals of the documents, together with copies of any other court orders should be available for production at the trial (CPR PD 39, para.3.3).

I act for the claimant in civil litigation proceedings, and have just completed preparation of the trial bundles. Who bears the cost of this?

In the absence of any provision in the rules, the cost of preparing trial bundles is part of the claimant's general costs, the reasonable costs of which may be recoverable if your client goes on to win the case.

I am acting in a litigation matter for a client who no longer has the mental capacity to continue with the proceedings. Should I contact the Office of the Public Guardian or the Official Solicitor's office to ensure that the client's interests are protected?

You should contact the Official Solicitor's office which provides representation for minors or adults under a disability in county court or High Court proceedings in England and Wales. The telephone number is 020 7911 7127. The website address is **www.officialsolicitor.gov.uk.**

The Office of the Public Guardian provides property and financial protection services for clients who are not able to manage their financial affairs because of mental incapacity. The telephone number is 0845 330 2900. The website address is **www.publicguardian.gov.uk.**

My firm represents a claimant in relation to a personal injury claim and we have received the final order from the court today. There is an error in the order which makes its interpretation unclear. How can the order be amended? Do we need to inform the defendant's solicitors?

Clerical mistakes in judgments, or orders or errors arising from any accidental slip or omission, may at any time be corrected by the court (CPR 40.12)). A party may apply for a correction without notice. There is no time limit for such an application.

Do trainee solicitors have rights of audience in tribunals?

Yes. In the majority of tribunals, parties can be represented by an individual of their choice which need not be restricted to representation by a solicitor or barrister.

One of my clients wants some advice about a potential claim involving a defective drug. We do not specialise in litigation and are unable to assist him but would like to help him find a solicitor. Any ideas?

It is likely that a claim of this nature will fall within the category of a multi-party action. You should contact the Law Society's Multi-party Action Information Service (MPAIS) which is maintained by the Practice Advice Service (**www.lawsociety.org.uk/practiceadvice**). The Practice Advice Service holds a database of multi-party actions along with information about contemplated actions and participating firms.

Firms are invited to contact the MPAIS with information about current or contemplated actions. Once a group litigation order has been made, the MPAIS is reliant on firms supplying a copy of the order to the Law Society as stated in the Civil Procedure Rules, Practice Direction 19B, para.11.

Is there is a protocol for the instruction of experts in civil claims?

The *Protocol for the Instruction of Experts to give Evidence in Civil Claims* is available from the Ministry of Justice website, **www.justice.gov.uk** (CPR PD 35).

The purpose of this protocol is to provide clear guidance to those who instruct experts and experts themselves as to what they are expected to do in civil proceedings.

Where can I find a list of expert witnesses?

For information on expert witnesses, solicitors may refer to the Academy of Experts who produce an online directory (**www.academy-experts.org**). The Expert Witness Institute also publish a list, see **www.ewi.org.uk**.

Please note that these lists are not exhaustive and are not endorsed or verified by the Law Society.

For further information, please see Burn and Peysner (eds.) (2007) *Civil Litigation Handbook* (2nd Edition), Law Society Publishing.

I am instructed to act for a company in civil proceedings. Who may sign the statement of truth on behalf of the company in its statement of case?

One option is for a person holding a senior position in the company, such as a director, treasurer or chief executive, to sign on behalf of the company

(CPR PD 22.3.4). In addition to signing the statement of truth, the person must also state their position or role in the company and sign and print their own name (and not the name of the company they are signing on behalf of) (CPR PD 22.3.9).

Alternatively, as the company is legally represented, the legal representative may sign on the company's behalf.

Please see Anderson and Warner (2008) *Execution of Documents* (2nd Edition), Law Society Publishing.

I am seeking to recover costs from my client in the sum of £9,000. In which court do I commence proceedings?

You can only commence this action in the county court. Proceedings cannot be commenced in the High Court unless the value of the claim is more than £15,000 (see the Practice Direction supplementing CPR Part 7).

I am a solicitor and would prefer to conduct my own personal injury case in the county court and not instruct my firm to act for me. Would I be able to recover any of my costs in doing so?

Yes, a solicitor who is acting for himself is regarded as a litigant in person (see CPR 48.6(6)). The rule provides that a litigant in person may be awarded up to two thirds of the costs and all the disbursements which would have been allowed if the litigant in person had been represented by a legal representative. In quantifying the costs for time spent on the litigation, the litigant in person will be allowed his financial loss for doing the work on the case and a copy of the evidence proving financial loss must be served on the paying party at least 24 hours before the assessment hearing (see the Costs Practice Direction supplementing the CPR 43–48, para.52.2, available online at **www.justice.gov.uk**).

I understand that there is a pre-action protocol for possession claims based on rent arrears. Is this correct?

Yes. The pre-action protocol came into force on 2 October 2006 and it applies to residential possession claims by social landlords which are based solely on rent arrears.

It can be found on the Ministry of Justice website (**www.justice.gov.uk**) in the Civil Procedure Rules section.

I act for a group of claimants in relation to Multi-party Action. A group litigation order (GLO) has been granted. My colleague informs that we need to forward a copy to the Law Society. Is this correct?

Yes. Practice Direction 19B on Group Litigation, that supplements Section III of CPR Part 19, states that after a GLO has been made, a copy of the GLO should be supplied to:

(i) the Law Society (Practice Advice Service), 113 Chancery Lane, London WC2A 1PL; and

(ii) the Senior Master, Queen's Bench Division, Royal Courts of Justice, Strand, London WC2A 2LL.

The Practice Advice Service operates the Law Society's Multi-party Action Information Service (MPAIS). For further information please telephone 0870 606 2522.

My client requires after the event insurance for a personal injury matter. Where can I find out what products are available?

You may refer to the online version of the Practice Advice Service booklet *Payment by Results* which contains an extract from the *Litigation Funding* magazine detailing some of the products on the market which have been compared. This may be accessed via the Practice Advice section of the Law Society website (**www.lawsociety.org.uk/practiceadvice**).

Alternatively, you may refer to the most recent *Litigation Funding* magazine which is prepared by the Law Society as a bi-monthly publication. For subscription details, please call 020 7841 5523.

We are acting in a personal injury matter and need to obtain certain documents from the police. We have been informed by them that the charges in respect of supplying copy documents have increased. From where can I obtain details of the revised charges?

Charges for the provision by the Metropolitan Police Service of copy documentation in civil proceedings are available at **www.met.police.uk/fees/index.htm**.

Is there a lower age limit when a child may give evidence in civil proceedings?

No. Section 96 of the Children Act 1989 states:

(1) Subsection (2) applies where a child who is called as a witness in any civil proceedings does not, in the opinion of the court, understand the nature of an oath.

(2) The child's evidence may be heard by the court if, in its opinion –

(a) he understands that it is his duty to speak the truth; and

(b) he has sufficient understanding to justify his evidence being heard.

Thus the evidence of a child who, in the opinion of the court, does not understand the nature of an oath, may be heard if, he understands that it is his duty to speak the truth and has sufficient understanding to justify his evidence being heard.

Although section 96 does not expressly so provide, the clear implication is that in such circumstances the child will give evidence unsworn.

In order to proceed with my client's case, I need to access her GP and hospital health records, and understand that there is a form approved by the Law Society and the British Medical Association to request the records. From where can I get a copy of this form?

The consent form, which has been agreed by the BMA and the Law Society, can be obtained online (**www.lawsociety.org.uk**). The form is aimed at improving protection for the public when they agree to release their health records and will demonstrate that the patient's informed consent has been gained before health records are disclosed.

Annex 1A

Compensation Act 2006 practice note

20 February 2007

Status of this practice note

Practice notes are issued by the Law Society for the use and benefit of its members. They represent the Law Society's view of good practice in a particular area. They are not intended to be the only standard of good practice that solicitors can follow. You are not required to follow them, but doing so will make it easier to account to oversight bodies for your actions.

Practice notes are not legal advice, nor do they necessarily provide a defence to complaints of misconduct or of inadequate professional service. While care has been taken to ensure that they are accurate, up to date and useful, the Law Society will not accept any legal liability in relation to them.

For queries or comments on this practice note contact the Law Society's Practice Advice Service.

Do you receive claims referrals from a claims referrals company or a claims management company?

If you receive claims referrals from a claims referrals company, or a claims management company, you need to be aware of the new regulatory regime being introduced under the Compensation Act 2006.

From 6 April 2007, persons providing claims management services (this would include those who refer claims as well as those who represent clients) must be authorised under the Act to do so, or be exempted, or have the benefit of a waiver of the obligation to be authorised. Solicitors who provide these services through their law firms are exempt. Claims management/referrals companies which fail to meet these new requirements will not be permitted to trade, and any of those which do trade will be committing an offence. You should check that, where appropriate, any introducer is authorised or exempt under the new regulatory regime. If you don't, you may be aiding and abetting an offence – and such conduct could involve disciplinary sanctions against you. You can check the status of an introducer by visiting **www.claimsregulation.gov.uk/ search.aspx**.

You should also be sure that you act independently in your client's best interests, particularly if you receive a significant number of referrals from a single source. As with any referral arrangement, you must comply with your regulatory requirements. Visit **www.referrals.sra.org.uk** to view all the current regulatory requirements in relation to referrals and those which will be brought in when the new Solicitors' Code of Conduct is in force.

Is your website breaching your legal and professional obligations?

The new claims regulator is identifying a significant number of websites which link back to firms of solicitors, but which do not make it clear on the face of the website that they belong to a solicitors' firm that is regulated by the Solicitors Regulation Authority (SRA). Remember that you must comply with the provisions of the Electronic Commerce (EC Directive) Regulations 2002, which require you to display certain information on your firm's website, including your professional title, details of your professional body, and a means of accessing your professional rules (for example, a link to **www.guide-online.lawsociety.org.uk** will take you to the rules currently in force). You will also need to ensure that your website complies with the Solicitors' Publicity Code 2001. The new claims regulator will be reporting any concerns about solicitors' websites to the SRA and, where the site does not belong to a solicitors' firm nor a regulated claims management company, may prosecute under the Compensation Act 2006.

Do you have a separate business which is not run as part of your law firm and which undertakes relevant claims management services?

If you have a practice as a solicitor (or registered European lawyer), you can't do most activities which constitute claims management services through any business except your solicitor's (or REL's) practice. See section 3 of the Solicitors' Separate Business Code 1994. You can undertake activities such as marketing through a separate business, but not:

- work which is preparatory to a claim which could proceed to a court, tribunal or inquiry;
- legal advice;
- drafting legal documents.

Any activities which constitute claims management services which you undertake through the separate business will be subject to the new regulatory regime. This means that your separate business will need to be authorised by the claims regulator so that it can lawfully continue trading after 6 April 2007. For more information visit **www.claimsregulation.gov.uk**.

Annex 1B

Payment by results

September 2008

The purpose of this booklet is to provide solicitors with basic information on the ever changing and complex area of 'payment by results' which includes conditional fee agreements (CFAs), contingency fees, the indemnity principle and fixed costs.

Solicitors anticipating entering into a CFA should familiarise themselves in more detail with:

- s.58 Courts and Legal Services Act 1990 (as amended by s.27 of the Access to Justice Act 1999);
- the Civil Procedure (Amendment No.3) Rules 2000 (SI 2000/1317);
- the Practice Direction supplementing Parts 43 to 48 of the Civil Procedure Rules 1998;
- the Solicitors' Code of Conduct 2007.

Introduction

Solicitors face an increasingly competitive market. The restricted availability of public funding for contentious matters and new legislation has encouraged solicitors to be innovative in the methods used to charge clients.

This booklet provides basic information for solicitors on the different forms of payment by results for contentious matters. It is designed to be used in conjunction with the Law Society's Practice Advice Service Booklet entitled 'Contentious Costs'.

Further costs guidance booklets on Contentious and Non-Contentious Costs are available from the Law Society's Practice Advice Service, see **www.lawsociety.org.uk/practiceadvice** or telephone the Practice Advice Service on 0870 606 2522.

Conditional fee agreements

Conditional fee agreements ('CFAs') are used in matters where the level of fee depends upon a particular event, usually winning the case.

A CFA is a type of contingency fee which is permitted for contentious business providing it meets the requirements contained in section 58 of the Courts and Legal Services Act 1990 (CLSA) (as amended by section 27 of the Access to Justice Act 1999 (AJA)).

In making CFAs, solicitors must comply with the Solicitors' Code of Conduct 2007 ('the Code').

There are various types of CFAs including:

- CFA without success fee

  The client must pay ordinary costs if he wins and either no costs or reduced costs if he loses.

- CFA with success fee

  The maximum success fee that can be charged is 100% (often referred to as the amount of 'uplift'). The success fee is intended to cover two elements: the risk element and the deferred fee element. The client may be able to recover some or all of the risk element from an opposing party. However, the Civil Procedure Rules 1998 (CPR) provide that the deferment element cannot be recovered from the opposing party (CPR 44.3B(1)(a)).

- Collective CFA

  A Collective CFA does not refer to specific proceedings but, as and when instructions are given to the solicitor, they can be brought within the agreement. Trade unions or other bulk purchasers of legal services (such as legal insurers) commonly use these types of agreements.

CFAs were originally introduced in the 1990s to fill the gap between the few clients who qualify for legal aid and the few clients who can afford to access justice without it. For the vast majority of people, exposure to own solicitor costs and also potentially to those of the other side if the case is lost are a very real barrier to making claims for damages. The CFA regime was the government's response to this fundamental problem. Please see Appendix 1 [of this booklet].

Post 1 November 2005

The new CFA Regime

On 1 November 2005 the Conditional Fee and Collective Conditional Fee Regulations 2000 were revoked by the Conditional Fee Agreements (Revocation) Regulations (2005/2305). Please see Appendix 2 [of this booklet].

The new regime applies to all conditional fee agreements, collective or otherwise, entered into on or after 1 November 2005. The old regulations continue to have effect in relation to agreements entered into before 1 November 2005.

Solicitors still have to comply with the primary legislation, namely the mandatory requirements in s.58 of the Courts and Legal Services Act 1990 (CLSA) (as amended by s.27 of the Access to Justice Act 1999 (AJA)) and also with the new Solicitors' Code of Conduct as set out by the Solicitors Regulation Authority. Particular attention is drawn to rule 2.03(2). These rules came into effect on 1 July 2007. Please see Appendix 3 [of this booklet]. The Civil Procedure Rules also remain in force.

Solicitors should consider these provisions carefully when entering into a CFA. Further information on these is set out below.

The Law Society prepared a new model CFA for use from 1 November 2005. It is available on the Law Society website **www.lawsociety.org.uk** (search 'model conditional fee agreement') and is included in Appendix 4 [of this booklet]. The model CFA consists of a one page agreement and an attached leaflet entitled 'What you need to know about a CFA'. The agreement contains the statutory and basic requirements and the purpose of the leaflet is to explain the agreement. This format is designed to be clearer for the client and therefore, easier for the solicitor to use.

While the 'What you need to know about a CFA' leaflet addresses most of the information a solicitor is required to provide when using a CFA, a client care letter is still necessary. The Law Society has produced practice notes 'Complaints management' dated 9 April 2008, 'Initial interviews' dated 15 May 2008 and 'Client care letters' dated 3 July 2008 which are intended to assist solicitors with amongst other things client care letters and terms and conditions. The practice notes are available on our website **www.lawsociety.org.uk**.

Primary legislation

The requirements of s.58 of the CLSA 1990 (as amended by s.27 of the Access to Justice Act 1999) remain. If s.58 requirements are not met then the agreement is unenforceable, and, by virtue of the indemnity principle, the losing party is not liable to pay the winning party's costs.

Section 58 requires CFAs to:

- be in writing;
- not relate to criminal or family proceedings;
- [and in the case of a] success fee, to specify the percentage increase, which must not exceed that specified by the Lord Chancellor (currently set at 100%).

Before 1 November 2005, the CFA Regulations fell under s.58 and if these were breached in a material way, the agreement could have been deemed to be unenforceable in accordance with s.58(1).

The intention behind the 1 November 2005 changes is to strip away unnecessary regulation and bring balance to the CFA regime. In transferring CFA requirements from statutory regulation to the Law Society's Solicitors' Costs Information and Client Care Code and now the Client Relations rule 2.03(2) of the Solicitors' Code of Conduct, it reduces the possibility of draconian sanctions for minor breaches.

A positive indication of how the regime will be received is the recent Court of Appeal decision in *Garbutt* v *Edwards* [2005] EWCA Civ 1206 which was decided under the old CFA Regulations where the court held that a failure to provide clients with costs estimates did not mean the solicitors could not recover their costs. The court found that the Law Society client care rules are not in place 'to relieve paying parties of their obligations to pay costs which have been reasonably incurred'. The court went on to say that a failure to provide costs estimates should not render a retainer unenforceable.

This is an encouraging signal from the courts that breaches of the Solicitors' Code of Conduct should not be used to launch technical challenges. The court did, however, make it clear that it backed the use of estimates. If no proper estimate had been given the court would have to consider whether and to what extent that costs claimed would have been significantly lower if there had been an estimate.

The Law Society was recognised by the court as providing disciplinary sanction for breach of its rules.

Breach of a rule in 'the Code' is a matter that the Solicitors Regulation Authority takes seriously and solicitors may be subject to disciplinary action by the Authority if they do not comply with 'the Code'.

The new Solicitors' Code of Conduct 2007

The new emphasis on the Code of Conduct reflects the fact that the Solicitors Regulation Authority has taken up the role of primary regulator in the area of CFAs.

In particular, the new Client Relations rule 2 requires that solicitors give information about:

- client care;
- costs;
- complaints handling procedure;
- commission.

The new Client Relations rule 2.03(2)

The new Code of Conduct rule 2.03(2) replaces the Law Society's Solicitors' Costs Information and Client Care Code 1999 (as amended by the Solicitors' Practice (Client Care) Amendment Rule 2005).

It should be noted that paragraph 5(d)(iii) of the old code which dealt with declaring any interest a solicitor may have in recommending a particular policy or other funding has not been mirrored in the new rule 2.03(2). This is because it is already dealt with by the new rule 19 and solicitors should consider carefully how to comply with this. Brief details are set out below under 'Solicitor interest in CFAs – financial services issues'. If you have a CFA under the 2000 Regulations you should also note the case of *Garrett* v *Halton BC* [2006] EWCA Civ 1017 as set out in Appendix 1 [of this booklet].

Where a solicitor is acting for a client under a CFA or CCFA in addition to complying with rule 2.03(1), (2) and (5) and (6), solicitors should explain the following, both at the outset and, when appropriate, as the matter progresses:

(a) the circumstances in which your client may be liable for your costs and whether you will seek payment of these from the client, if entitled to do so;

(b) if you intend to seek payment of any or all of your costs from your client, you must advise your client of their right to an assessment of those costs; and

(c) where applicable, the fact that you are obliged under a fee sharing agreement to pay to a charity any fees which you receive by way of costs from the client's opponent or other third party.

Solicitor interest in CFAs – financial services issues

Solicitors should be aware that the Financial Services Authority ('the FSA') regulates contracts of insurance such as after the event insurance.

Under rule 19 of the Solicitors' Code of Conduct 2007, solicitors are able to enter into arrangements with third parties in connection with general insurance contracts. This means that solicitors can have an arrangement with a provider whereby they recommend one ATE insurance policy only.

In making such a recommendation, and in circumstances where the firm is not authorised by the FSA and relies instead on the exemption granted to professional firms under the Financial Services and Markets Act 2000, the firm must ensure it complies with the Solicitors' Financial Services (Scope) Rules 2001. For example, the firm must ensure that they account to the client for any pecuniary reward or other advantage which they receive from a third party (rule 4(c)) and it must be on the FSA's Exempt Professional Firms Register and appoint a compliance officer (rule 5(6)).

Solicitors must also comply with the Solicitors' Financial Services (Conduct of Business) Rules 2001 and, in respect of insurance mediation activities such as arranging and recommending an ATE insurance policy, must provide the information required at rule 3(3) and in Appendix 1. [Note: this is Appendix 1 of the 2001 Rules, not this booklet]

The Solicitors' Financial Services (Scope) Rules 2001 and the Solicitors' Financial Services (Conduct of Business) Rules 2001 are available on the SRA website (**www.sra.org.uk**).

The client's ability to pay – 2.03(1)(d) and (g)

Solicitors continue to have obligations in respect of their client's ability to pay and must discuss as set out in 2.03(1)(d):

(i) whether the client may be eligible and should apply for public funding; and

(ii) whether the client's own costs are covered by insurance or may be paid by someone else such as an employer or trade union.

Further 2.03(1)(g) states that solicitors must discuss with the client whether the client's liability for any other party's costs may be covered by existing insurance or whether specially purchased insurance may be obtained.

The wider funding issues remain relevant. The Civil Procedure Rules which govern the court's discretion in respect of recoverable costs are unchanged under the new regime.

Existing guidance in this area continues be applicable, including the Court of Appeal decision in *Sawar* v *Alam* [2001] EWCA Civ 1401. It is well documented that the Law Society was disappointed that the court did not accept the Society's contention that there is a strong public interest in maintaining the client's freedom of choice. Please see Appendix 1 [of this booklet] for guidance.

Civil Procedure Rules (CPR) and Practice Direction (PD)

The CPR continue to apply to the new CFA regime and solicitors should be mindful of these when entering into a CFA.

Parts 43–48 of the CPR and the accompanying PD contain a number of important matters for those intending to use CFAs. The following is only a summary and practitioners should read the Rules in detail:

CPR Part 43.2(3) where advocacy or litigation services are provided to a client under a CFA costs are recoverable under Parts 44 to 48 notwithstanding that the client is liable to pay his legal representative's fees and expenses only to the extent that sums are recovered in respect of the proceedings, whether by way of costs or otherwise. Some commentators are arguing that this does not alter the law but merely clarifies that you can have CFA lites, i.e. the client's liability for fees and expenses is limited to costs recovered from an opponent.

CPR Part 43.3A states that the court will not assess the success fee and insurance premium until the conclusion of proceedings. This is to ensure that the level of success fee does not become apparent to the other side before resolution of the case.

CPR Part 44.3B disallows recovery of the additional liability in a number of situations, the main one being that part of the success fee which relates to the solicitor's costs of funding the action through the postponement of his fees. It is important to note that the percentage of success fee which relates to the postponement of fees must be separately stated in the agreement and is not recoverable from an opponent.

CPR Part 44.15 is one of the most important provisions and it deals with the duty on practitioners to notify the existence of CFAs both to the court and to the other parties involved and the fact that additional liabilities are claimed from the other side. Notification is required in respect of the original agreement and any subsequent changes. Failure to comply with this duty could lead to an additional liability not being recovered under Part 43.3B.

CPR Part 44.12A makes provision for a new and vital procedure for costs to be assessed where the parties have settled the substantive dispute without proceedings but are unable to agree costs. The claim should be brought under Part 8 but the court must dismiss the claim if it is opposed and effectively can only act as arbiter if both sides agree. Practitioners may want to consider securing the opponent's consent to this procedure before concluding the settlement of the substantive claim.

The Practice Direction

The Practice Direction about costs supplementing Parts 43 to 48 of the Civil Procedure Rules can be found on the Ministry of Justice website **www.justice.gov.uk**. Below is a basic overview of the most relevant sections of the Practice Direction in the context of conditional fee agreements. Solicitors should study the relevant sections themselves in detail to ensure that they are in compliance.

Section 3 states that where there is an additional liability the court can on summary assessment assess either the base costs alone or together with any additional liability depending on the stage the case has reached. Generally it is unlikely the court will assess an additional liability before the end of a case, as to do so would divulge that party's view of the risk involved to the other side.

Section 4.17 states that the percentage of the success fee needs to be shown separately from base costs.

Section 6 states that 'estimates of costs' which are to be recovered from the other side are to be limited to an estimate of base costs and should not include additional liabilities.

Section 11 states that proportionality is applicable to base costs but not to additional liabilities which must be viewed on what was reasonable at the time they were agreed.

This section also sets out factors to be considered when deciding whether a success fee is reasonable, including the availability of other methods of funding.

Amongst other things there are at least 5 issues that the courts will consider when determining whether or not insurance premiums are reasonable:

(i)   where the insurance cover is not purchased in support of a CFA with a success fee, how its cost compares with the likely cost of funding the case with a CFA with a success fee and insurance cover;

(ii) the level and extent of cover provided;

(iii) the availability of any pre-existing insurance cover;

(iv) whether any part of the premium would be rebated in the event of early settlement;

(v)   the amount of commission payable to the receiving party or his legal representatives or other agents.

Appendix 6 of this booklet lists a table of some of the after-the-event insurance products that are available on the market for use with conditional fees.

Section 17 deals with the costs only procedure under rule 44.12A.

Section 19 deals with notification of funding arrangements, which is one of the most important aspects of the Practice Direction. If a solicitor is claiming an additional liability he must inform the other parties or potential parties to the claim that he is doing so.

A party will risk not recovering any additional liabilities for any period during which he failed to provide such information. Section 19(2) states that notification to the other side and to the court should be given:

(i)   on issuing proceedings; or

(ii) if defending an action or in Part 20 proceedings, in the solicitor's first act in the action e.g. when filing an acknowledgement of service; or

(iii) within 7 days if the client enters a CFA after proceedings have been commenced; or

(iv) if proceedings have not commenced, although the PD does not require practitioners to inform potential parties about funding arrangements before the commencement of proceedings, it is recommended that practitioners do so and such a provision may be required by a pre-action protocol. The Personal Injury Protocol suggests that notification should be given to potential parties. It is important to remember that the court is able to take into account pre-action conduct and if a practitioner does not comply with a pre-action protocol this can be taken into account by the court when dealing with the issue of costs.

Section 19.4 sets out the extent of information to be provided.

Section 20 deals with the situation where a practitioner wishes to recover from the client that part of the success fee which was disallowed or reduced on assessment under rule 44.16.

On *summary assessment*, the court must give a direction to enable the legal representative to apply for the disallowed percentage to be paid by the client.

The receiving solicitor should notify any counsel representing his client who must respond or is deemed to accept the reduction. The receiving solicitor must also notify the client and provide a written explanation of the points in dispute.

On *detailed assessment*, the court can decide there and then if the disallowed amount should be payable, or it can give directions for a later hearing date.

Collective conditional fee agreements (CCFAs)

Collective conditional fee agreements (CCFAs) are intended for bulk purchasers of legal services using CFAs such as trade unions and commercial organisations. They enable bulk purchasers to enter into a single agreement with solicitors to allow them to run their members' cases. The agreement does not have to refer to specific proceedings, but will provide for fees to be payable on a common basis in relation to a class of proceedings.

CCFAs are now 'funding arrangements' for the purposes of recovery of additional liabilities, such as the cost of membership (CPR r.43.2(1)).

Separate rules for CCFAs are no longer required under the new regime, and the Collective Conditional Fee Agreements Regulations 2000 (SI 2000/2988) have been revoked.

As the authority for the validity for CFAs comes from s.58 CLSA 1990 as amended by s.27 AJA 1999, the authority for CCFAs to exist is unchanged. CCFAs are just another form of CFAs and are allowed under the above Acts. Like other CFAs, CCFAs are subject to the Solicitors Regulation Authority's rules.

Contingency fees

The difference between a conditional fee under a CFA and a contingency fee is:

A 'contingency fee' is the generic term used to describe any fee arrangements between solicitors and clients where payment of the solicitor's fees is dependent upon the result of litigation or arbitration. A conditional fee is a statutory species of contingency fee and is governed by s.58 of the Courts and Legal Services Act.

Contingency fee agreements are traditionally known to be agreements where the solicitor's fee is calculated as a percentage of the moneys recovered. A conditional fee agreement differs in that the solicitor's fee is based on the amount of work done to secure that money.

Rule 2.04 of the Solicitors' Code of Conduct permits solicitors to use contingency fees for all *non-contentious* cases and in those contentious cases which are permitted by common law or statute. Generally, contingency fees are unenforceable in England and Wales in litigation because they are considered to be champertous arrangements, which are contrary to public policy and the common law. For court commentary, please refer to Appendix 7 [of this booklet].

Although contingency fees are mostly restricted to work which is defined as non-contentious, the definition of non-contentious is fairly broad and includes work before many tribunals.

This means contingency fees are a valid option for work done before Employment Tribunals but not in Employment Appeal Tribunal cases. To be valid, the agreement must be contained in a non-contentious business agreement as defined by s.57 Solicitors Act 1974 (see also s.58 CLSA, as amended by AJA 1999). Section 27 of AJA 1999 specifically states that conditional fee regulations do not apply to non-contentious business agreements.

There is an argument that it is also feasible to use contingency fees in a matter up to the stage of issuing court proceedings. However, it should be noted that if proceedings are subsequently issued, it is a moot point as to whether all the work on the case retrospectively becomes contentious. This could potentially mean that the agreement is unenforceable against the client and recovery of any costs from the other side would be a breach of the indemnity principle. Please see Appendix 8 [of this booklet] for examples of contentious and non-contentious business.

What is the future for contingency fees? The Civil Justice Council (CJC) has recommended 'in contentious business cases where contingency fees are currently disallowed, American style contingency fees requiring abolition of the fee shifting rule should not be introduced. However, consideration should be given to the introduction of contingency fees on a regulated basis along similar lines to those permitted in Ontario by the Solicitors Act 2002 particularly to assist Access to Justice actions and other complex cases where no other method of funding is available.' How this recommendation is received remains to be seen. The Law Society response to the report can be found at **www.lawsociety.org.uk/costs**.

Fixed costs

The fixed fees scheme for low value personal injury road traffic accident that settle pre-issue ('the RTA scheme') is set out in the CPR Part 45 and the accompanying Practice Direction about Costs (PD 43–48) at s.25A.

What is covered?

Part 45.7(2) of the Civil Procedure Rules deals with what is covered by the fixed recoverable costs scheme:

(2) This section applies where:

(a) the dispute arises from a road traffic accident;

(b) the agreed damages include damage in respect of personal injury, damage to property, or both;

(c) the total value of the agreed damages does not exceed £10,000; and

(d) if a claim had been issued for the amount of the agreed damages, the small claims track would not have been the normal track for that claim.

Directions relating to Part 45 – fixed costs – Section 25A provides as follows:

25A.1 Section II of Part 45 ('the Section') provides for certain fixed costs to be recoverable between the parties in respect of costs incurred in disputes which are settled prior to proceedings being issued. This Section applies to road traffic accident disputes as defined in rule 45.7(4)(a), where the accident which gave rise to the dispute occurred on or after 6 October 2003.

25A.2 The Section does not apply to disputes where the total agreed value of the damages is within the small claims limit or exceeds £10,000. . .

NB. The small claims limit is £1,000 in relation to personal injury but £5,000 otherwise. Thus either the damages for personal injury must exceed £1,000 or the settlement must exceed £5,000.

25A.3 Fixed recoverable costs are to be calculated by reference to the amount of agreed damages which are payable to the receiving party. In calculating the amount of these damages:

(a) account must be taken of both general and special damages and interest;

(b) any interim payments made must be included;

(c) where the parties have agreed an element of contributory negligence, the amount of damages attributed to that negligence must be deducted.

(d) any amount required by statute to be paid by the compensating party directly to a third party (such as sums paid by way of compensation recovery payments and National Health Service expenses) must not be included.

What is included in the Fixed Costs Scheme?

(a) **Damage only, no injury** – such claims are covered provided the small claims track limit of £5,000 is exceeded.

(b) **Credit hire** is covered subject to the appropriate small claims track unit of £5,000 being exceeded.

(c) **Children and patients** are defined in Part 21 of the Civil Procedure Rules. Rule 45.10 specifically allows recovery of certain disbursements if incurred under Part 21, namely counsel's fees and court fees on application to the court.

(d) **Motor Insurance Bureau claims**; Uninsured Drivers (PD supplementing Part 45, s.25A.4).

(e) **Multiple claimants** are covered and the solicitor receives a separate fixed fee in relation to each claimant. Provided each claimant's claim exceeds the small claims limit but does not exceed the £10,000 limit then all claims are covered. The fact that four people may have claims of £10,000 each, total £40,000, does not take the matter outside the fixed recoverable costs scheme. If some claims are within the terms of the scheme and some are not then that is how they will be treated, that is some will attract fixed costs but not others.

(f) **Multi-track claims**, a claim which may have been allocated to the multi-track is covered by the scheme. However in practice, it will be rare for the claim to satisfy the other conditions of the scheme but it is possible to do so. For example, an accident involving a large number of claimants may have been allocated to the multi-track but if the claims are settled pre-issue for £10,000 or less then the fixed recoverable costs scheme applies.

(g) **Jurisdiction**, only accidents occurring in the jurisdiction of England and Wales are covered (CPR r.45.7(4)(a)). Accidents in Scotland or Northern Ireland, or any other jurisdiction are not within the scheme.

What is not included in the scheme?

(a) **Litigants in person**.

(b) **Issued proceedings** – the scheme does not apply if proceedings have been issued, even if liability is admitted and it is only quantum that is in dispute.

(c) **Motor Insurance Bureau claim; Untraced Drivers**.

What disbursements are allowed under the scheme?

(a) Medical records.

(b) A medical report.

(c) A police report.

(d) An engineer's report.

(e) A search of the records of the Driver Vehicle Licensing Authority.

(f) An insurance premium as defined in rule 43.2(1)(m).

(g) Where the disbursements are incurred by the claimant who is a child or patient as defined in Part 21 counsel's fees and court fees on application are included.

(h) Any other disbursement that has arisen due to a particular feature of the dispute are allowed at the discretion of the court.

The effect of the indemnity principle is that any agreed fixed fee between a solicitor and client will also be the maximum that is recoverable from the other side.

CPR 48.8 requires that if a solicitor wants to charge his client in excess of what is recoverable from the other side he needs to include this in his terms of business.

Solicitors should refer to the CPR when using the provision in the Law Society model CFA for RTA cases.

What is the future of the RTA scheme? The Civil Justice Council has recommended that the predictable costs scheme (CPR Part 45 Section II), currently restricted to RTA cases below £10,000 should be extended to include all personal injury cases in the [increased level] fast track and should include fixed costs from the pre-action protocol stage through the post issue process and including trial with an escape route for exceptional cases. It recommends that fixed success fees, fixed/guideline ATE premiums and fixed/guideline disbursements should also be part of the scheme.

How this recommendation is received remains to be seen. The Law Society response to the CJC report can be found at **www.lawsociety. org.uk/costs**.

Indemnity principle

The indemnity principle is an entrenched principle of law. *Harold* v *Smith* [1860] 5 H&N 381 provided that costs between party and party are given by the law as an indemnity to the person entitled to them. They are not imposed as a punishment on the party who pays them, or given as a bonus to the party who receives them. The amount which the paying party has to pay cannot exceed the amount which the successful party has to pay to his own solicitor. This was reaffirmed in *Gundry* v *Sainsbury* [1910] 1 KB 645.

Therefore, if the solicitors representing the successful party have intimated that their client 'need not worry' about paying their fees, there is a possibility that the court will hold that the loser has no liability in costs. (See the House of Lords decision in *British Waterways Board* v *Norman* (1993) 26 HLR 232.)

There are six important exceptions to the indemnity principle:

1. Costs payable under conditional fee agreements (Courts and Legal Services Act 1990, s.58 as amended by the Access to Justice Act 1999).

2. Costs funded by the Legal Service Commission (Legal Aid Act 1988 s.31 and CLS (Costs) Regulations 2000 reg.15).

3. Sums payable to litigants in person (Litigants in Person (Costs and Expenses) Act 1975).

4. Fixed costs payable under CPR 45 (*Butt* v *Nizami* [2006] EWHC 159 (QB)).

5. Fixed sums in respect of fast track trial costs (CPR Part 46).

6. The allowance of costs in respect of an in-house solicitor or employed solicitor (*Re Eastwood (deceased)* [1975] Ch 112).

There have been many calls to abolish the indemnity principle. In May 1999, the government produced a consultative document called 'Controlling Costs'. The response of the Civil Justice Council to the consultation paper was to give clear recommendations for the indemnity principle not to be applied in costs assessment. They stated that 'the majority view of the Council is that the indemnity principle serves little or no purpose in improving access to justice and that the assessment of costs process is sufficient to ensure that solicitors do not claim in between the parties costs any amount as opposed to the actual cost to the client'.

To date, these recommendations have not been implemented and the indemnity principle remains in operation.

The Civil Justice Council has recommended 'between the parties costs should be payable on the basis of costs and disbursements reasonably and proportionately incurred and should be assessed at hourly rates determined from time to time by the Costs Council without prejudice to the ability of solicitors (and barristers) to agree other rates on a solicitor/client basis'.

The Law Society continues to press for the abolition of the indemnity principle.

Further reading

-   Solicitors' Code of Conduct 2007 available online at **www.sra.org.uk**. The Code took effect on 1 July 2007. The Code replaces almost all of the provisions found in *The Guide to the Professional Conduct of Solicitors* – 8th Edition 1999 except for the Solicitors' Accounts Rules and rules relating to professional indemnity and the Compensation Fund. The Code does not significantly alter solicitors' duties relating to the funding of litigation, but this booklet fully takes into account the new rules.

- *Cook on Costs 2008* by Michael J Cook published by Butterworths.
- *Conditional Fees, A Guide to CFAs and Litigation Funding* by Gordon Wignall published by The Law Society. Available from [**www.lawsociety.org.uk/bookshop**].
- Law Society's Model Conditional Fee Agreement for use in personal injury and clinical negligence cases. Available on the Law Society's website at **www.lawsociety.org.uk**.
- 'What you need to know about a CFA' available on the Law Society's website at **www.lawsociety.org.uk**.
- *Litigation Funding* which is a bi-monthly magazine published by the Law Society. For subscription details please call 020 7841 5523.
- The Practice Advice Service Frequently Asked Questions published in the *Gazette*. A selection of these is available on the Law Society's website at **www.lawsociety.org.uk/practiceadvice**.
- Updates and guidance on cases and general developments are provided by the Law Society as appropriate. Solicitors should regularly refer to the Law Society's website **www.lawsociety.org.uk**.
- The Civil Justice Council's report 'Improved Access to Justice – Funding Options and Proportionate Costs' (published in August 2005) which can be accessed at **www.civiljusticecouncil.gov.uk**. The report has significant and widespread implications for all users of the civil litigation system. The Law Society's response to the report can be accessed on the Law Society website.

Law Society Sections

There are four Law Society Sections – self-governing, committee-led, membership associations – offering practice-specific guidance, information and support to subscribing members. Benefits include regular magazines and electronic newsletters, interactive websites, CPD accredited events and discounts on a variety of products and services.

For further information about the Property Section, visit **www.propertysection.org.uk**, e-mail propertysection@lawsociety.org.uk or telephone 020 7320 5873.

For further information about the Probate Section, visit **www.probatesection.org.uk**, e-mail probatesection@lawsociety.org.uk or telephone 020 7316 5678.

For further information about the Law Management Section, visit **www.lms.lawsociety.org.uk**, e-mail lawmanagementsection@lawsociety.org.uk or telephone 020 7316 5707.

For further information about the Dispute Resolution Section, visit **www.lawsociety.org.uk**, e-mail drs@lawsociety.org.uk or telephone 020 7316 5668.

Appendix 1 – Before 1 November 2005

CFA developments

CFAs were first introduced in 1995 for personal injury, some insolvency work and cases before the European Commission of Human Rights and the European Court of Human Rights. In 1998, CFAs were extended to all types of proceedings except family and criminal.

Under these types of agreements, both the success fee and any after-the-event (ATE) insurance policy premium (which was purchased to protect the client against an adverse costs order) were payable by the solicitor's own client and were not recoverable from the other side. Inevitably, this meant that the client had to pay these out of any damages received.

In 2000, the regime changed when s.58 of the CLSA 1990 sanctioned the Conditional Fee Agreements Regulations 2000 (SI 2000/692) (the 2000 Regulations). These Regulations, along with the Conditional Fee Agreements Order 2000 (SI 2000/823), came into effect on 1 April 2000; they set out the requirements of an enforceable CFA.

The 2000 regime introduced recoverability of the success fee and ATE insurance premium which meant that as the losing party in the matter was liable to pay these 'additional liabilities', they now had an interest in how much was being charged for them.

The Law Society produced a model CFA for use in personal injury cases in July 2000. This model has now been superseded.

Conditional Fee Agreements (Miscellaneous Amendments) Regulations 2003

The government attempted to simplify the CFA regime by introducing further Regulations. The Conditional Fee Agreements (Miscellaneous Amendments) Regulations 2003 (SI 2003/1240) were brought in to effect on 2 June 2003. An agreement under these Regulation is often referred to as a 'CFA simple' or 'CFA lite'. For various reasons, the CFA lite was not widely adopted.

Further regulations were introduced in 2003 following discussions between the Law Society and the Department for Constitutional Affairs (DCA), covering outstanding issues such as the death or bankruptcy of a client. The Conditional Fee Agreements (Miscellaneous Amendments) (No.2) Regulations 2003 (SI 2003/3344), came into force on 2 February 2004.

The 'costs war'

The 2000 Regulations (and subsequent 2003 Regulations) were detailed and technical, and because of the link to s.58(1) of the CLSA 1990 solicitors were constantly faced with a very real threat that a breach would lead to unrecoverability of all costs. Conversely, for the paying party, the prospect of being relieved of the burden to pay the winning party's costs created an incentive to challenge the CFA on a technicality. The resulting flood of satellite cost litigation has been described by Michael Cook in *Cook on Costs* as 'trench warfare' based on 'spot the breach'.

The 2003 Court of Appeal decision in *Hollins* v *Russell* [2003] EWCA Civ 718 (in which the Law Society intervened) stemmed the flow of technical challenges by determining that validity of a CFA was not affected unless the breach was 'material' and 'adversely affected the client or the administration of justice'.

However, case law continued to develop – see below.

The new regime

In practice, the 2003 Regulations were unworkable, and added to the confusion of the 2000 regime. After pressure from the Law Society, the DCA agreed to try to simplify matters.

In June 2003, the DCA produced a consultation paper called 'Simplifying CFAs' (see **www.justice.gov.uk**). The focus was on the problems caused by the secondary legislation (in effect the 2000 Regulations). Various stakeholders were involved, including the Judiciary, the Law Society, Consumers Association and Association of British Insurers.

In June 2004, the DCA produced a document 'Making simple CFAs a reality – A summary of responses to the consultation paper simplifying conditional fee agreements and proposals for reform'. As a result of further feedback from stakeholders, a new 2005 regime was outlined in the DCA's final paper 'New Regulation for Conditional Fee Agreements'.

The Law Society strongly believed that it would be more sensible for regulatory requirements on solicitors to be in Law Society's rules, rather than Regulations. The DCA, with the support of the Judiciary and other stakeholders agreed and by revoking the Regulations on 1 November 2005 handed over responsibility to the Law Society.

Case law

The following cases are a sample of those available in this area. There are many other relevant cases; those mentioned below are just a selection which attracted interest. The Law Society has intervened in a number of influential cost cases.

In most situations the pre 1 November 2005 case law is likely to be relevant. While the 2000 Regulations have been repealed, similar obligations exist in the Solicitors' Code of Conduct 2007, with the CPR and section 58 of the CLSA 1990 continuing to apply. The effect of breaching Law Society rules is discussed earlier in this booklet with reference to the Court of Appeal decision *Garbutt* v *Edwards*.

Success fee – *Callery* v *Gray* – [2001] EWCA Civ 1117

The first major case under the 2000 Regulations was that of *Callery* v *Gray* in 2001 where the Court of Appeal upheld the legality of CFAs and set out some guidelines regarding success fees and after-the-event insurance (ATE) premiums. Although this matter went to the House of Lords, it declined to interfere with the Court of Appeal decision.

Before-the-event insurance – *Sawar* v *Alam* [2001] EWCA Civ 1401

Sawar v *Alam* dealt with the situation where despite there being before-the-event insurance (BTE) covering the claimant, he chose to use a CFA and after-the-event insurance (ATE) instead. This was an unusual case in that the BTE policy was that of the driver who was the other party in the proceedings. The court decided that a solicitor needs to check whether the client, his spouse or partner has a BTE policy before recommending a CFA and ATE. This follows the 2000 Regulations in that regulation 3 states that a solicitor has to cover in preliminary discussions whether the client is already covered for the costs of taking a claim by the terms of a pre-existing insurance policy or by membership of a scheme run by an organisation of which he is a member, such as a trade union.

The question, however, has to be how far does the solicitor have to go to make these checks. In *Sawar* v *Alam* the court suggested that any enquiries did not have to be extensive in a small case. It is well documented that the Law Society was disappointed that the court did not accept the Society's contention that there is a strong public interest in preserving the client's freedom of choice. This case was the subject of a lengthy article in the Law Society *Gazette* on 15 November 2001.

Regulation 4(2)(c) of Conditional Fee Agreements Regulations 2000 – BTE – *Culshaw* v *Goodliffe* [2003] Liverpool County Court 29 November

In the case of *Culshaw* v *Goodliffe* in 2003, the judge found that the solicitor's question to the client 'Do you have any legal expenses insurance?' was an inadequate approach to his obligation under regulation 4(2)(c) of the 2000 Regulations to 'consider' the insurance position of the client. He found that this failure to comply had materially affected both the client and the defendant so as to lead to the CFA being unenforceable. The client in fact had BTE cover under the motor policy covering the car involved in the accident. This case has not been reported or appealed. This case seems to place a significant duty on solicitors not only to check whether the client believes that he has a BTE policy, but also whether that belief is accurate.

Funding – *Bowen* v *Bridgend County Borough Council* [2004] SCCO 25 March

This issue that a solicitor also has to discuss with the client the most appropriate means of funding his claim, and any financial liabilities he may face in entering a CFA became a significant point in this case. Costs Judge O'Hare concluded that the client had not been advised about the availability of public funding for housing disrepair cases. As a result, he decided that the solicitors had not complied with the 2000 Regulations and therefore the CFA was unenforceable.

Unenforceability – *Hollins* v *Russell* [2003] EWCA Civ 718

A major decision on the CFA scheme was *Hollins* v *Russell* in 2003 when the Court of Appeal held that breaches of the 2000 Regulations had to be divided into those that were material and those that were not. Material breaches are those that affect the administration of justice or consumer protection. Only breaches that were both material and adversely affected the client or the administration of justice will cause the CFA to be unenforceable.

The court also stated that 'technical challenges' to CFAs should stop.

Stating postponement element – *Spencer* v *Wood* [2004] EWCA Civ 352

In the case of *Spencer* v *Wood* in 2004 a similarly constituted Court of Appeal held that where it could not be seen from the CFA document how much of the success fee was related to the postponement element, the breach of the regulations was material and the CFA was unenforceable.

Enforceability of the Law Society's CFA – *Ghannouchi* v *Houni* [2004] SCCO 4 March

In *Ghannouchi* v *Houni* in 2004, Costs Judge Seager Berry held that the wording of the Law Society's model CFA was in breach of the 2000 Regulations in respect of the parts relating to the inability of the solicitor to recover money from the client where the costs had been agreed or assessed at a lower level than claimed. However, he concluded that the breach was not material and the CFA was still enforceable.

Regulation 4(2)(c) of the 2000 Regulations – BTE – *Samonini* v *London General Transport Services Ltd* [2005] EWHC 90001 (Costs)

In *Samonini* v *London General Transport Services Ltd* 2005 the question was whether the Claimant's solicitor had complied with regulation 4(2)(c) of the 2000 Regulations. This regulation states that the solicitor has to inform the client: 'whether the legal representative considers that the client's risk of incurring liability for costs in respect of the proceedings to which the agreement relates is insured against under the existing contract of insurance'.

The client was a taxi driver who informed his claims management company representative that he did not have legal expenses insurance attached to his motor insurance. This should have put the solicitor on notice that the situation was unusual and indicated that further enquiry was required. The solicitor made little or no enquiry as to other insurance policies that might provide cover. Chief Costs Judge Hurst concluded that there had been a breach of the 2000 Regulations and that the breach was material (in the terms of *Hollins* v *Russell* 2003, see above) and that the costs under the CFA were irrecoverable.

Breach of regulation 4(2)(d) of the 2000 Regulations – Obligation to consider other funding options – *Traci Hughes* v *Newham London Borough Council* SCCO 28 July 2005

The court found that the solicitors had failed to inform the client properly of the availability of public funding in this housing disrepair case. The solicitors needed to do more than mention the possibility of legal aid funding to the client in order to comply with the Regulations and Practice Rule 15 (Solicitors' Costs Information and Client Care Code 1999). The breach of the Regulations had a materially adverse effect upon the protection provided to the client in this instance, therefore the court found the CFA to be unenforceable.

Third party funding – *Arkin* v *Borchard* [2005] EWCA Civ 655

This was a case about third party funding. The case had originally been publicly funded but this was withdrawn. Solicitor and counsel then acted under a CFA but the client could not afford the expert's fees and so the cost of this was provided by a third party funding company. The claim was dismissed and the claimant was impecunious. The trial judge refused the defendant's application that the funder should pay the costs and the defendant appealed. The Court of Appeal held it was 'unjust that a funder who purchases a stake in an action for a commercial motive should be protected from all liability for the costs of the opposing party if the funded party fails in the action'. The court found that the professional funder should be potentially liable to the extent of the funding it had provided. It is unclear whether the principles decided in the case are of general application or only when access to justice is an issue as was the situation in this particular case.

Regulation 4(2)(c) of Conditional Fee Agreements Regulations 2000 – BTE – *Myatt* v *National Coal Board* [2006] EWCA Civ 1017

The court found that the clients had been asked the wrong question in respect of the availability of BTE cover. The question asked was too restrictive to comply with the regulation as it placed too much of a burden of understanding of complex terms of insurance policies on the clients. Some general guidance on the scope of a solicitor's duty under regulation 4(2)(c) was given. The court also looked at the meaning of the *Hollins* v *Russell* 2003 judgment and found that the language of s.58 of the Courts and Legal Services Act 1990 was clear and uncompromising. They therefore found that as a statutory condition had been breached the CFA was unenforceable and the solicitor was not entitled to any costs despite the fact that the clients had suffered no detriment.

Regulation 4(2)(e)(ii) of Conditional Fee Agreements Regulations 2000 – Interest in recommending a contract of insurance – *Garrett* v *Halton BC* [2006] EWCA Civ 1017

The solicitors, who had failed to tell their clients that it was a term of their claims management panel membership that they should recommend a particular insurance policy, were in breach of regulation 4(2)(e)(ii). Continued panel membership was an indirect financial interest and needed to be declared in order to comply with the Regulations. Again the court looked at the meaning of the *Hollins* v *Russell* 2003 judgement and found that the language of s.58 of the Courts and Legal Services Act 1990 was clear and uncompromising.

They therefore found that as a statutory condition had been breached the CFA was unenforceable and the solicitor was not entitled to any costs despite the fact that the clients had suffered no detriment.

Appendix 2 – The Conditional Fee Agreements (Revocation) Regulations 2005

Made .... August 2005

Laid before Parliament .... August 2005

Coming into force .... 1st November 2005

The Secretary of State, in exercise of t (he powers conferred upon the Lord Chancellor by sections 58(3)(c), 58A(3), 119 and 120(3) of the Courts and Legal Services Act 1990[a] and now vested in him[b] makes the following Regulations:

Citation and commencement

1. These Regulations may be cited as the Conditional Fee Agreements (Revocation) Regulations 2005 and shall come into force on 1st November 2005.

Revocation

2. Subject to regulation 3, the Conditional Fee Agreements Regulations 2000[c] (the 'CFA Regulations'), the Collective Conditional Fee Agreements Regulations 2000[d] (the 'CCFA Regulations'), the Conditional Fee Agreements (Miscellaneous Amendments) Regulations 2003[e], and the Conditional Fee Agreements (Miscellaneous Amendments) (No. 2) Regulations 2003[f] are revoked.

Savings and transitional provisions

3. (1) The CFA Regulations shall continue to have effect for the purposes of a conditional fee agreement entered into before 1st November 2005.

(a) 1990 c.41. Section 58 was substituted and section 58A inserted by the Access to Justice Act 1999 (c.22), section 27. Section 119 is cited because of the definition of 'prescribed'.

(b) Article 4, Schedule 1 and paragraph 8(1)(c) of Schedule 2 of the Secretary of State for Constitutional Affairs Order 2003 (S.I. 2003/1887).

(c) S.I. 2000/692.

(d) S.I. 2000/2988.

(e) S.I. 2003/1240.

(f) S.I. 2003/3344.

(2) Paragraph (1) shall apply in relation to a collective conditional fee agreement as if there were substituted for a reference to the CFA Regulations a reference to the CCFA Regulations.

Signed

Name

Address Parliamentary Under Secretary of State

Date Department for Constitutional Affairs

EXPLANATORY NOTE

(This note is not part of the Regulations)

These Regulations revoke the Conditional Fee Agreements Regulations 2000 (S.I. 2000/692), the Collective Conditional Fee Agreements Regulations 2000 (S.I. 2000/2988), the Conditional Fee Agreements (Miscellaneous Amendments) Regulations 2003 (S.I. 2003/1240) and the Conditional Fee Agreements (Miscellaneous Amendments) (No. 2) Regulations 2003 (S.I. 2003/3344) in respect of conditional fee agreements and collective conditional fee agreements entered into on or after 1st November 2005.

Parties may enter into Conditional Fee Agreements and Collective Conditional Fee Agreements on or after that date based on the primary legislation.

Appendix 3 – Rule 2 of the Solicitors' Code of Conduct 2007

[NB Please check **www.sra.org.uk/rules** for any amendments to rules]

Client relations

2.01   Taking on clients

(1) You are generally free to decide whether or not to take on a particular client. However, you must refuse to act or cease acting for a client in the following circumstances:

(a) when to act would involve you in a breach of the law or a breach of the rules of professional conduct;

(b) where you have insufficient resources or lack the competence to deal with the matter;

(c) where instructions are given by someone other than the client, or by only one client on behalf of others in a joint matter, you must not proceed without checking that all clients agree with the instructions given; or

(d) where you know or have reasonable grounds for believing that the instructions are affected by duress or undue influence, you must not act on those instructions until you have satisfied yourself that they represent the client's wishes.

(2) You must not cease acting for a client except for good reason and on reasonable notice.

2.02 Client care

(1) You must:

(a) identify clearly the client's objectives in relation to the work to be done for the client;

(b) give the client a clear explanation of the issues involved and the options available to the client;

(c) agree with the client the next steps to be taken; and

(d) keep the client informed of progress, unless otherwise agreed.

(2) You must, both at the outset and, as necessary, during the course of the matter:

(a) agree an appropriate level of service;

(b) explain your responsibilities;

(c) explain the client's responsibilities;

(d) ensure that the client is given, in writing, the name and status of the person dealing with the matter and the name of the person responsible for its overall supervision; and

(e) explain any limitations or conditions resulting from your relationship with a third party (for example a funder, fee sharer or introducer) which affect the steps you can take on the client's behalf.

(3) If you can demonstrate that it was inappropriate in the circumstances to meet some or all of these requirements, you will not breach 2.02.

2.03   Information about the cost

(1) You must give your client the best information possible about the likely overall cost of a matter both at the outset and, when appropriate, as the matter progresses. In particular you must:

(a) advise the client of the basis and terms of your charges;

(b) advise the client if charging rates are to be increased;

(c) advise the client of likely payments which you or your client may need to make to others;

(d) discuss with the client how the client will pay, in particular:

(i) whether the client may be eligible and should apply for public funding; and

(ii) whether the client's own costs are covered by insurance or may be paid by someone else such as an employer or trade union;

(e) advise the client that there are circumstances where you may be entitled to exercise a lien for unpaid costs;

(f) advise the client of their potential liability for any other party's costs; and

(g) discuss with the client whether their liability for another party's costs may be covered by existing insurance or whether specially purchased insurance may be obtained.

(2) Where you are acting for the client under a conditional fee agreement, (including a collective conditional fee agreement) in addition to complying with 2.03(1) above and 2.03(5) and (6) below, you must explain the following, both at the outset and, when appropriate, as the matter progresses:

(a) the circumstances in which your client may be liable for your costs and whether you will seek payment of these from the client, if entitled to do so;

(b) if you intend to seek payment of any or all of your costs from your client, you must advise your client of their right to an assessment of those costs; and

(c) where applicable, the fact that you are obliged under a fee sharing agreement to pay to a charity any fees which you receive by way of costs from the client's opponent or other third party.

(3) Where you are acting for a publicly funded client, in addition to complying with 2.03(1) above and 2.03(5) and (6) below, you must explain the following at the outset:

(a) the circumstances in which they may be liable for your costs;

(b) the effect of the statutory charge;

(c) the client's duty to pay any fixed or periodic contribution assessed and the consequence of failing to do so; and

(d) that even if your client is successful, the other party may not be ordered to pay costs or may not be in a position to pay them.

(4) Where you agree to share your fees with a charity in accordance with 8.01(k) you must disclose to the client at the outset the name of the charity.

(5) Any information about the cost must be clear and confirmed in writing.

(6) You must discuss with your client whether the potential outcomes of any legal case will justify the expense or risk involved including, if relevant, the risk of having to pay an opponent's costs.

(7) If you can demonstrate that it was inappropriate in the circumstances to meet some or all of the requirements in 2.03(1) and (5), you will not breach 2.03.

2.04   Contingency fees

(1) You must not enter into an arrangement to receive a contingency fee for work done in prosecuting or defending any contentious proceedings before a court of England and Wales, a British court martial or an arbitrator where the seat of the arbitration is in England and Wales, except as permitted by statute or the common law.

(2) You must not enter into an arrangement to receive a contingency fee for work done in prosecuting or defending any contentious proceedings before a court of an overseas jurisdiction or an arbitrator where the seat of the arbitration is overseas except to the extent that a lawyer of that jurisdiction would be permitted to do so.

2.05   Complaints handling

(1) If you are a principal in a firm you must ensure:

(a) that the firm has a written complaints procedure and that complaints are handled promptly, fairly and effectively in accordance with it;

(b) that the client is told, in writing, at the outset:

   (i) that, in the event of a problem, the client is entitled to complain; and

   (ii) to whom the client should complain;

(c) that the client is given a copy of the complaints procedure on request; and

(d) that once a complaint has been made, the person complaining is told in writing:

   (i) how the complaint will be handled; and

   (ii) within what timescales they will be given an initial and/or substantive response.

(2) If you can demonstrate that it was inappropriate in the circumstances to meet some or all of these requirements, you will not breach 2.05.

(3) You must not charge your client for the cost of handling a complaint.

2.06   Commissions

If you are a principal in a firm you must ensure that your firm pays to your client commission received over £20 unless the client, having been told the amount, or if the precise amount is not known, an approximate amount or how the amount is to be calculated, has agreed that your firm may keep it.

2.07   Limitation of civil liability by contract

If you are a principal in a firm you must not exclude or attempt to exclude by contract all liability to your clients. However, you may limit your liability, provided that such limitation:

(a) is not below the minimum level of cover required by the Solicitors' Indemnity Insurance Rules for a policy of qualifying insurance;

(b) is brought to the client's attention; and

(c) is in writing.

Appendix 4 – The Law Society's
Model Conditional Fee Agreement November 2005

For use in personal injury and clinical negligence cases only.

This agreement is a binding legal contract between you and your solicitor/s. Before you sign, please read everything carefully. This agreement must be read in conjunction with the Law Society document 'What you need to know about a CFA'.

Agreement date

[...]

I/We, the solicitor/s [..]

You, the client [..]

What is covered by this agreement

- Your claim against [.......................................] for damages for personal injury suffered on [.......................................]. (*if either the name of the opponent or the date of the incident are unclear then set out here in as much detail as possible to give sufficient information for the client and solicitor to understand the basis of the claim being pursued*)
- Any appeal by your opponent.
- Any appeal you make against an interim order.
- Any proceedings you take to enforce a judgment, order or agreement.
- Negotiations about and/or a court assessment of the costs of this claim.

What is not covered by this agreement

- Any counterclaim against you.
- Any appeal you make against the final judgment order.

Paying us

If you win your claim, you pay our basic charges, our disbursements and a success fee. You are entitled to seek recovery from your opponent of part or all of our basic charges, our disbursements, a success fee and insurance premium as set out in the document 'What you need to know about a CFA'.

It may be that your opponent makes a Part 36 offer or payment which you reject on our advice, and your claim for damages goes ahead to trial where you recover damages that are less than that offer or payment. If this happens, we will [*not add our success fee to the basic charges*] [*not claim any costs*] for the work done after we received notice of the offer or payment.

If you receive interim damages, we may require you to pay our disbursements at that point and a reasonable amount for our future disbursements.

If you receive provisional damages, we are entitled to payment of our basic charges, our disbursements and success fee at that point.

If you lose you remain liable for the other side's costs.

The success fee

The success fee is set at [............]% of basic charges, where the claim concludes at trial; or [............]% where the claim concludes before a trial has commenced. In addition [............]% relates to the postponement of payment of our fees and expenses and can not be recovered from your opponent. The success fee inclusive of any additional percentage relating to postponement cannot be more than 100% of the basic charges in total.

Other points

The parties acknowledge and agree that this agreement is not a Contentious Business Agreement within the terms of the Solicitors Act 1974.

Signatures

Signed by the solicitor(s): ....

Signed by the client: ....

Appendix 5 – Conditional Fee Agreements: what you need to know leaflet (November 2005)

- What do I pay if I win?
- What do I pay if I lose?
- Ending this agreement
- Basic charges
- How we calculate our basic charges
- Road traffic accidents
- Success fee
- Value added tax (VAT)
- The insurance policy
- Law Society Conditions

- Our responsibilities
- Your responsibilities
- Dealing with costs if you win
- Payment for advocacy
- What happens when this agreement ends before your claim for damages ends?
- What happens after this agreement ends
- Explanation of words used

Definitions of words used in this document and the accompanying CFA are explained at the end of this document.

What do I pay if I win?

If you win your claim, you pay our basic charges, our disbursements and a success fee. The amount of these is not based on or limited by the damages. You can claim from your opponent part or all of our basic charges, our disbursements, a success fee and insurance premium.

It may be that your opponent makes a Part 36 offer or payment which you reject on our advice, and your claim for damages goes ahead to trial where you recover damages that are less than that offer or payment. Refer to the 'Paying Us' section in the CFA document to establish costs we will be seeking for the work done after we received notice of the offer or payment.

If you receive interim damages, we may require you to pay our disbursements at that point as well as a reasonable amount for our future disbursements.

If you receive provisional damages, we are entitled to payment of our basic charges, our disbursements and success fee at that point.

If you win overall but on the way lose an interim hearing, you may be required to pay your opponent's charges of that hearing.

If on the way to winning or losing you are awarded any costs, by agreement or court order, then we are entitled to payment of those costs, together with a success fee on those charges if you win overall.

What do I pay if I lose?

If you lose, you pay your opponent's charges and disbursements. You may be able to take out an insurance policy against this risk. If you lose, you do not pay our charges but we may require you to pay our disbursements.

Ending this agreement

If you end this agreement before you win or lose, you pay our basic charges and disbursements. If you go on to win, you also pay a success fee.

We may end this agreement before you win or lose.

Basic charges

These are for work done from now until this agreement ends. These are subject to review.

How we calculate our basic charges

These are calculated for each hour engaged on your matter. Routine letters and telephone calls will be charged as units of one tenth of an hour. Other letters and telephone calls will be charged on a time basis. The hourly rates are:

Grade of Fee Earner	Hourly Rate
1 Solicitors with over eight years' post qualification experience including at least eight years' litigation experience.	
2 Solicitors and legal executives with over four years' post qualification experience including at least four years litigation experience.	
3 Other solicitors and legal executives and fee earners of equivalent experience	
4 Trainee solicitors, paralegals and other fee earners.	

We review the hourly rate on [review date] and we will notify you of any change in the rate in writing.

Road traffic accidents

[If your claim is settled before proceedings are issued, for less than £10,000, our basic costs will be £800; plus 20% of the damages agreed up to £5,000; and 15% of the damages agreed between £5,000 and £10,000.] [If you live in London, these costs will be increased by 12.5%]. These costs are fixed by the Civil Procedure Rules.

Success fee

The success fee percentage set out in the agreement reflects the following:

(a) the fact that if you lose, we will not earn anything;

(b) our assessment of the risks of your case;

(c) any other appropriate matters;

(d) the fact that if you win we will not be paid our basic charges until the end of the claim;

(e) our arrangements with you about paying disbursements.

Value added tax (VAT)

We add VAT, at the rate (now [. . .]%) that applies when the work is done, to the total of the basic charges and success fee.

The insurance policy

In all the circumstances and on the information currently available to us, we believe, that a contract of insurance with [.......................................] is appropriate to cover your opponent's charges and disbursements in case you lose.

This is because

You do not have an existing or satisfactory insurance that would cover the costs of making this claim. The policy we recommend will pay:

(a) *the costs of the other party in the event that the claim fails, to a maximum of £X;*

(b) *all your disbursements if your claim fails.*

(c) *[add other key features where necessary such as, our costs and the other side's costs (without deduction from your damages) if you fail to beat an (Part 36) Offer to Settle your claim, which you rejected following our advice].*

or:

[We cannot identify a policy which meets your needs but our recommended policy is the closest that we can discover within the products that we have searched. It does not meet your needs in the following respects:

(a) *it has an excess of £Z*

(b) *the maximum cover is £ZZ]*

or:

[We cannot obtain an insurance policy at this stage but we shall continue to look for one and if we are successful in our search then we shall advise you at that stage of the benefits of the policy and purchasing it]

[NB. The italicised reasons set out are examples only. Your solicitor must consider your individual circumstances and set out the reasons that apply.]

Law Society Conditions

The Law Society Conditions below are part of this agreement. Any amendments or additions to them will apply to you. You should read the conditions carefully and ask us about anything you find unclear.

Our responsibilities

We must:

- always act in your best interests, subject to our duty to the court;
- explain to you the risks and benefits of taking legal action;
- give you our best advice about whether to accept any offer of settlement;
- give you the best information possible about the likely costs of your claim for damages.

Your responsibilities

You must:

- give us instructions that allow us to do our work properly;
- not ask us to work in an improper or unreasonable way;

- not deliberately mislead us;
- co-operate with us;
- go to any medical or expert examination or court hearing.

Dealing with costs if you win

- You are liable to pay all our basic charges, our disbursements and success fee.
- Normally, you can claim part or all of our basic charges, our disbursements, success fee and insurance premium from your opponent.
- If we and your opponent cannot agree the amount, the court will decide how much you can recover. If the amount agreed or allowed by the court does not cover all our basic charges and our disbursements, then you pay the difference.
- You will not be entitled to recover from your opponent the part of the success fee that relates to the cost to us of postponing receipt of our charges and our disbursements. This remains payable by you.
- You agree that after winning, the reasons for setting the success fee at the amount stated may be disclosed:

    (i) to the court and any other person required by the court;
    (ii) to your opponent in order to gain his or her agreement to pay the success fee.

- If the court carries out an assessment and reduces the success fee because the percentage agreed was unreasonable in view of what we knew or should have known when it was agreed, then the amount reduced ceases to be payable unless the court is satisfied that it should continue to be payable.
- If we agree with your opponent that the success fee is to be paid at a lower percentage than is set out in this agreement, then the success fee percentage will be reduced accordingly unless the court is satisfied that the full amount is payable.
- It may happen that your opponent makes an offer of one amount that includes payment of our basic charges and a success fee. If so, unless we consent, you agree not to tell us to accept the offer if it includes payment of the success fee at a lower rate than is set out in this agreement.
- If your opponent is receiving Community Legal Service funding, we are unlikely to get any money from him or her. So if this happens, you have to pay us our basic charges, disbursements and success fee.

As with the costs in general, you remain ultimately responsible for paying our success fee.

You agree to pay into a designated account any cheque received by you or by us from your opponent and made payable to you. Out of the money, you agree to let us take the balance of the basic charges; success fee; insurance premium; our remaining disbursements; and VAT.

You take the rest.

We are allowed to keep any interest your opponent pays on the charges.

If your opponent fails to pay

If your opponent does not pay any damages or charges owed to you, we have the right to take recovery action in your name to enforce a judgment, order or agreement. The charges of this action become part of the basic charges.

Payment for advocacy

The cost of advocacy and any other work by us, or by any solicitor agent on our behalf, forms part of our basic charges. We shall discuss with you the identity of any barrister instructed, and the arrangements made for payment.

Barristers who have a conditional fee agreement with us

If you win, you are normally entitled to recover their fee and success fee from your opponent.

The barrister's success fee is shown in the separate conditional fee agreement we make with the barrister. We will discuss the barrister's success fee with you before we instruct him or her. If you lose, you pay the barrister nothing.

Barristers who do not have a conditional fee agreement with us

If you win, then you will normally be entitled to recover all or part of their fee from your opponent. If you lose, then you must pay their fee.

What happens when this agreement ends before your claim for damages ends?

(a)   Paying us if you end this agreement

You can end the agreement at any time. We then have the right to decide whether you must:

- pay our basic charges and our disbursements including barristers' fees but not the success fee when we ask for them; or
- pay our basic charges, and our disbursements including barristers' fees and success fees if you go on to win your claim for damages.

(b)   Paying us if we end this agreement

(i) We can end this agreement if you do not keep to your responsibilities. We then have the right to decide whether you must:

- pay our basic charges and our disbursements including barristers' fees but not the success fee when we ask for them; or

- pay our basic charges and our disbursements including barristers' fees and success fees if you go on to win your claim for damages.

(ii) We can end this agreement if we believe you are unlikely to win. If this happens, you will only have to pay our disbursements. These will include barristers' fees if the barrister does not have a conditional fee agreement with us.

(iii) We can end this agreement if you reject our opinion about making a settlement with your opponent. You must then:

- pay the basic charges and our disbursements, including barristers' fees;

- pay the success fee if you go on to win your claim for damages.

If you ask us to get a second opinion from a specialist solicitor outside our firm, we will do so. You pay the cost of a second opinion.

(iv) We can end this agreement if you do not pay your insurance premium when asked to do so.

(c)   Death

This agreement automatically ends if you die before your claim for damages is concluded. We will be entitled to recover our basic charges up to the date of your death from your estate.

If your personal representatives wish to continue your claim for damages, we may offer them a new conditional fee agreement, as long as they agree to pay the success fee on our basic charges from the beginning of the agreement with you.

What happens after this agreement ends

After this agreement ends, we may apply to have our name removed from the record of any court proceedings in which we are acting unless you have another form of funding and ask us to work for you.

We have the right to preserve our lien unless another solicitor working for you undertakes to pay us what we are owed including a success fee if you win.

Explanation of words used

(a) Advocacy

Appearing for you at court hearings.

(b) Basic charges

Our charges for the legal work we do on your claim for damages.

(c) Claim

Your demand for damages for personal injury whether or not court proceedings are issued.

(d) Counterclaim

A claim that your opponent makes against you in response to your claim.

(e) Damages

Money that you win whether by a court decision or settlement.

(f) Our disbursements

Payment we make on your behalf such as:

- court fees;

- experts' fees;

- accident report fees;

- travelling expenses.

(g) Interim damages

Money that a court says your opponent must pay or your opponent agrees to pay while waiting for a settlement or the court's final decision.

(h) Interim hearing

A court hearing that is not final.

(i) Lien

Our right to keep all papers, documents, money or other property held on your behalf until all money due to us is paid. A lien may be applied after this agreement ends.

(j) Lose

The court has dismissed your claim or you have stopped it on our advice.

(k) Part 36 offers or payments

An offer to settle your claim made in accordance with Part 36 of the Civil Procedure Rules.

(l) Provisional damages

Money that a court says your opponent must pay or your opponent agrees to pay, on the basis that you will be able to go back to court at a future date for further damages if:

- you develop a serious disease; or

- your condition deteriorates;

in a way that has been proved or admitted to be linked to your personal injury claim.

(m) Success fee

The percentage of basic charges that we add to your bill if you win your claim for damages and that we will seek to recover from your opponent.

(n) Trial

The final contested hearing or the contested hearing of any issue to be tried separately and a reference to a claim concluding at trial includes a claim settled after the trial has commenced or a judgment.

(o) Win

Your claim for damages is finally decided in your favour, whether by a court decision or an agreement to pay you damages or in any way that you derive benefit from pursuing the claim.

'Finally' means that your opponent:

- is not allowed to appeal against the court decision; or

- has not appealed in time; or

- has lost any appeal.

Appendix 6 – The Litigation Funding Table

[The] table which appeared in the August edition of Litigation Funding represents a snapshot of the ATE market as at August 2008. The ATE market is constantly changing and evolving, and each entry in the table is checked and updated in every issue and new entrant to the market added. To [see the most recent table you can] subscribe to Litigation Funding a bi-monthly magazine please contact subscriptions on 020 7841 5523.

[. . .]

Appendix 7 – Case law

Kilby v *Gawith* **[2008] EWCA Civ 812**

The appellant (G) appealed against a costs decision made in favour of the respondent (K). G and K had been involved in a road traffic accident. G admitted liability and K, who had the benefit of before-the-event insurance, entered into a CFA with her solicitor. Quantum was agreed and G agreed to pay costs but disputed the success fee fixed at 12.5% of the fixed recoverable costs by virtue of rule 45.11(2) of the Civil Procedure Rules. K issued costs proceedings and G contended that the court had a discretion whether or not to allow a success fee and at what level. The costs judge ruled that rule 45.11(2) was not discretionary.

A district judge dismissed G's appeal.

The Court of Appeal held that the costs judge and district judge had reached the correct conclusion. Rule 45.11 had to be construed by reference to its ordinary natural meaning in the context of the rules as a whole. While rule 45.11(1) provided that a claimant 'may recover a success fee' the natural meaning was that a claimant was entitled to claim a success fee.

Rule 45.11(2) provided that the amount of the success fee 'shall be' 12.5%, which meant that where a success fee was recovered it had to be 12.5%. If the draftsman had meant for there to be a discretion to grant a success fee he would not have fettered that discretion by specifying the amount. The purpose of the rules was to provide fixed levels of remuneration, *Nizami* v *Butt* [2006] EWHC 159 QB, [2006] 1 WLR 3307 and *Lamont* v *Burton* [2007] EWCA Civ 429, [2007] 1 WLR 2814 applied. The approach to before-the-event insurance in *Sarwar* v *Alam* [2001] EWCA Civ 1401, [2002] 1 WLR 125 did not lead to the conclusion that rule 45.11(2) should be construed any differently, *Sarwar* applied.

Times Newspapers Limited v *Keith Burstein* **[2002] EWCA Civ 1739**

The Court of Appeal held that there was no principle of law which precluded a solicitor from continuing to act for a client whenever he became aware that the client was no longer able to pay his costs. The newspaper contended that a retainer was or became champertous if a solicitor became aware that the client could not possibly meet costs payable under it. When it came to the issue of permission to appeal and costs, the Master of Rolls stated: 'This submission presupposed that maintenance and champerty were matters of general public importance whereas the Access to Justice Act 1999 had largely swept away those principles.'

King v Telegraph [2004] EWCA Civ 613

In a case where a success fee of 100% was claimed on the basis that the case had a prospect of no better than 50%, the defendant sought security for costs because no after the event insurance had been notified. The court declined and Eady J. said there was nothing inconsistent with the intention of the legislature in lawyers agreeing to support a claim by means of a CFA even where a cold dispassionate assessment of the likely outcome would lead them to the conclusion that the claim is unlikely to succeed. 'It is not for this court to thwart the wish of Parliament that lit-igants should be able to bring actions to vindicate their reputations under a CFA, and that they should not be obliged to obtain ATE cover before they do so.

R (on the application of Factortame) v Secretary of State for Transport [2002] All ER (D) 41

This judgment concerned fees paid by the successful claimants to a firm of accountants, Grant Thornton. The claimants had agreed to pay Grant Thornton 8% 'of the final settlement received'. This was to constitute payment for Grant Thornton's accountancy and back-up services in relation to the assessment of quantum and for the retention and pay-ment by Grant Thornton of independent expert witnesses. The defendant challenged the claimants' right to recover this payment as costs on the ground that the agreement in question was champertous and unenforce-able. The court rejected this argument. Relevant to its decision was that Grant Thornton did not attempt to exert any influence upon the conduct of this phase of the litigation, the fact that the 8% recovery did not exceed what would have been fair remuneration for Grant Thornton's services, indeed it acted as a cap on their fees, and the fact that the agreement to remunerate Grant Thornton had been necessary in order to procure for the claimants access to justice.

The court observed that the introduction of CFAs evidenced a radi-cal shift in the attitude of public policy to the practice of conducting litigation on terms that the obligation to pay fees would be contingent on success.

Hamilton v Fayed (Costs) [2002] 3 All ER 641

Chadwick LJ at pages 665–6 did not contemplate any legal bar to experts acting directly under a 'no win, no fee' arrangement. However, Lord Phillips observed in Factortame at p.1128 para.73 that 'as a general proposition, such an interest is highly undesirable. In many cases the expert will be giving an authoritative opinion on issues that are critical to the outcome of the case. We consider that it will be a very rare case indeed that the court will be prepared to consent to an expert being instructed under a contingency fee agreement.'

The Eurasian Dream (No.2) [2002] Lloyd's Rep. 692

A marine claims recovery agent acted on a 5% 'no cure, no pay' basis. Solicitors subsequently instructed were allowed to recover that item as costs. It was held not to be champertous on various grounds including the fact that the agreement was not exclusively concerned with litigation and that the majority of claims of this sort were compromised without lawyers.

Kenneth Kellar (2), Carib West Ltd v Stanley A Williams [2004] UKPC 30

Their lordships stated that 'the content of public policy can change over the years, and it may now be time to reconsider the accepted prohibition in light of modern practising conditions'. They would point only to the views expressed by Millet LJ giving the judgment of the Court of Appeal in *Thai Trading Co v Taylor* [1998] QB 781 and by May LJ in *Awwad v Geraghty & Co* [2001] QB 570.

Arkin v Borchard Lines and Others [2005] EWCA Civ 655

In this decision the Court of Appeal treated as non-champertous a clear contingency fee arrangement where the funder had not sought to control the litigation and where the percentage share did not exceed what would have been fair remuneration for services and served to act as a cap on the fees payable.

Appendix 8 – Examples of contentious and non-contentious matters

* If proceedings are subsequently issued, it is a moot point whether all prior work leading to the action automatically becomes contentious. Please see obiter comment of Lord Justice Brooke in *Crosbie* v *Munroe* [2003] EWCA Civ 350.

Contentious	Non-contentious
1. Proceedings actually begun in the County Court, High Court, Magistrates' Court, Crown Court and the Court of Protection.	Proceedings before all tribunals other than the Lands Tribunal and the Employment Appeal Tribunal.
2. Proceedings actually begun before the Lands Tribunal and the Employment Appeal Tribunal.	Planning and other public enquiries including Coroner's Court work.
3. Contentious probate proceedings actually begun.	Non-contentious or common form probate business.
4. Proceedings on appeal to the Court of Appeal, Privy Council and House of Lords.	Conveyancing, company acquisitions and mergers, the administration of estates and trusts out of court, the preparation of wills, statements and contracts, and any other work not included in the 'contentious' column.
5. Proceedings in arbitration.	Criminal Injuries Compensation Board.
6. Motor Insurers Bureau Uninsured drivers' claims (proceedings issued).	Motor Insurers Bureau Untraced drivers' claims. Motor Insurers Bureau Uninsured drivers' claims (proceedings not issued).
7. Work done preliminary to proceedings covered by 1–5 above including advice, preparation and negotiations provided the proceedings are subsequently begun (although see note below*).	Work done preliminary to the proceedings included in the 'contentious' column if such proceedings are not subsequently begun.
8. Licensing (appeals to Magistrates' Court).	Licensing (administered by Local Authority).

* If proceedings are subsequently issued, it is a moot point whether all prior work leading to the action automatically becomes contentious. Please see obiter comment of Lord Justice Brooke in *Crosbie* v *Munroe* [2003] EWCA Civ 350.

2

Conveyancing and property

I act for the purchaser in a conveyancing transaction which has just completed. The seller's solicitor says he has posted the title deeds to me, but it appears that they have become lost in transit. We had agreed to use the Law Society's Code for Completion by Post. Who is responsible for the cost of replacing the deeds?

You are. Under paragraph 10(ii)(b) of the Law Society's Code for Completion by Post, the seller's solicitor undertakes to send the deeds by first class post or document exchange to the buyer's solicitor as soon as possible after completion, and in any event on the same day. This is done at the risk of the buyer's solicitor.

Can a solicitor sign the contract for sale in a conveyancing transaction on behalf of a client?

The case of *Suleman* v. *Shahsavari* [1989] 2 ALL ER 460 confirmed that a solicitor needs his client's express authority to sign the contract on behalf of the client.

Unless the solicitor holds a valid power of attorney it is recommended that such an authority be obtained from the client in writing, the client previously having been informed of the legal consequences of giving such authority including that the signature implies authority to proceed to exchange, and exchange creates a binding contract. A solicitor should never sign a contract on behalf of a client without being certain that the client accepts all the terms of the contract.

Particular care should be taken when there are joint purchasers or co-owners involved. It is recommended that express authority is obtained from each party and that the solicitor ensures that each party understands the legal consequences of the authority and accepts the terms of the contract.

Failure to obtain authority may render the solicitor liable in damages for breach of warranty of authority. See Silverman (ed.) (2008) *Conveyancing Handbook* (15th edition), Law Society Publishing.

I am acting for a buyer in a residential conveyancing transaction. I have just received the contract package from the seller's solicitor and in the covering letter it states that he 'expects such papers to be returned to his firm on request if the transaction does not proceed to exchange.' I have never come across this before, is this correct?

Yes, this has been included in the covering letter in case the transaction is aborted. A draft contract along with the other papers supplied by the seller's solicitor to the buyer's solicitor in the contract package belong to the seller until contracts are exchanged. If the transaction is aborted before exchange takes place, the buyer's solicitor should comply with a request for return of those papers made by the seller's solicitor. This is notwithstanding any contrary instructions issued by the buyer to his own solicitor. For the avoidance of doubt, it is suggested that the seller's solicitor indicates in his covering letter to the buyer's solicitor that he expects such papers to be returned to him on request if the transaction does not proceed to exchange, just as your seller's solicitor has done. See the *Conveyancing Handbook* (15th Edition).

Where can I obtain a copy of the current edition of the Council of Mortgage Lenders' Handbook?

The handbook is available online only, on the Council of Mortgage Lenders' website (**www.cml.org.uk**).

My client intends to buy a property in Cornwall. I understand I should make tin-mining and clay-mining searches. Who do I contact in order to do this?

For a tin-mining search you could contact:

Cornwall Consultants Ltd
Parc Vean House
Coach Lane
Redruth
Cornwall
TR15 2TT
Tel: 01209 313 511
Fax: 01209 313 512
www.cornwallconsultants.co.uk

For a clay-mining search you could contact:

Kaolin and Ball Clay Association Ltd
Par Moor Centre

Par Moor
Par
Cornwall
PL24 2SQ
Tel: 01726 811 328
Fax: 01726 811 200
www.kabca.org

Alternatively, searches may also be conducted using the National Land Information Service (**www.nlis.org.uk**).

For further guidance and details of some of the other less usual searches, see *Conveyancing Handbook* (15th edition).

What is NLIS?

The National Land Information Service (NLIS) is a joint initiative between central and local government and delivers land and property information held by many different organisations. NLIS is a complete 'one stop shop', which delivers integrated land and property information search facilities and assists the conveyancing process through quicker and more accurate property identification available by using the National Land and Property Gazetteer.

Conveyancing searches are requested and delivered, where possible, electronically. Solicitors and licensed conveyancers can retrieve land and property information from the Land Registry and conduct local authority searches, as well as searching for other information such as coal mining activity, utility services or environmental data relating to the property.

There are three channels licensed by government to provide NLIS services to solicitors and licensed conveyancers. See the NLIS website for details (**www.nlis.org.uk**). See also the *Conveyancing Handbook* (15th edition).

Can I reproduce the Local Authority CON29R (2007) and the Optional enquiries of a Local Authority CON29O (2007) on a word processor?

A general licence has been granted to solicitors to reproduce only the front sheets (not the actual enquiries on the reverse of the forms) on word processors, provided that:

- the quality of the form produced is of a standard acceptable to local authorities;
- the format of the printed form is followed as closely as is possible;
- the Law Society coat of arms is not reproduced;

- a covering note explains that only the front sheets are reproduced under a general licence from the Law Society.

Word processed forms should be on A4 size paper of no less than 80gsm weight at a resolution of no less than 300 dpi, in 12 point Roman typeface. The Local Authority may reject a form which does not meet an acceptable standard of reproduction.

The Law Society suggests using electronic forms through NLIS channels (**www.nlis.org.uk**) or a professionally produced version of the form from any of the following suppliers:

- IRIS Software and Services (IRIS Laserform) – **www.iris.co.uk**
- LexisNexis (Everyform) – **www.lexisnexis.co.uk**
- Oyez Straker – **www.oyezstraker.co.uk**
- PEAPOD LEGALOffice Ltd – **www.peapod-legal.co.uk**
- Shaw & Sons Ltd – **www.shaws.co.uk**

Can I exchange contracts by fax?

The main use of fax is to transmit the messages which activate the Law Society's formulae for exchanging contracts by telephone, fax or telex. In this context, fax is merely a substitute for using the telephone. Standard Condition of Sale (4th Edition) 1.3.3 and Standard Commercial Property Condition (2nd Edition) 1.3.3 do not permit fax to be used as a valid method of service of a document where delivery of the original document is essential (as it is with the contract), thus effectively ruling out an exchange by this method, although there is no objection to the parties using fax in order to activate the Law Society's formulae.

A physical exchange of documents must follow the faxed messages. If this were never to happen, a party seeking enforcement of the contract would have difficulty in demonstrating that the requirements of the Law of Property (Miscellaneous Provisions) Act 1989, s.2 have been satisfied. See the case of *Milton Keynes Development Corporation* v. *Cooper* [1993] EGCS 142, where an exchange of faxes was not held to be an exchange of contracts. See the *Conveyancing Handbook* (15th Edition).

A colleague has informed me that I must personally complete the stamp duty land tax (SDLT) forms on behalf of my client. Is this true?

The current stamp duty regime became effective on 1 December 2003. Although it is not mandatory, the Law Society advises that it is good practice for solicitors to complete the form on behalf of the client as most clients are likely to require guidance when completing it themselves and may go to accountants instead for assistance. Clients are however responsible for signing the returns. Furthermore, if you are also acting on behalf of a lender, then the lender is likely to insist that you take responsibility for completing the form. The Law Society recommends that you charge the client for time spent completing the form.

If you choose to complete the content of the form on behalf of your client, then you should inform him that it is his obligation to notify 'liability to tax' within the defined period (i.e. within 30 days from the effective date of transaction) and pay the tax due. You should inform the client that he remains ultimately responsible for the accuracy of the information and for the consequences of delay on his part and the implications for registering the property as a result. Where you are acting for the lender, you should be aware that the failure of the client to co-operate in completing the form could lead to a conflict of interest. It is advisable to inform your client of the penalties which may be incurred if the form is returned late.

I am proposing to use the Standard Commercial Property Conditions of Sale in a transaction. Which is the current edition and where can I obtain them from?

The current edition of the Standard Commercial Property Conditions is the second edition which took effect on 1 June 2004. The conditions are available from the following suppliers:

- IRIS Software and Services (IRIS Laserform) – **www.iris.co.uk**
- LexisNexis (Everyform) – **www.lexisnexis.co.uk**
- Oyez Straker – **www.oyezstraker.co.uk**
- PEAPOD LEGALOffice Ltd – **www.peapod-legal.co.uk**
- Shaw & Sons Ltd – **www.shaws.co.uk**

For more information regarding the conditions, please see the *Conveyancing Handbook* (15th edition).

How can I find some information on salaries for a two and a half year qualified solicitor practising residential conveyancing?

The Law Society does not produce any guidelines on recommended salaries for qualified solicitors. However, the Strategic Research Unit at the Law Society has published a factsheet entitled 'Private Practice Solicitors' Salaries' based on a survey conducted in 2007 which is available online at **www.research.lawsociety.org.uk**. Alternatively, you may wish to contact a local legal recruitment agency.

I act for clients in a conveyancing matter. The office copies show a charge in favour of the Law Society. Who do I contact to get this discharged?

In April 1989 responsibility for the administration of the legal aid scheme transferred from the Law Society to the Legal Aid Board (now the Legal Services Commission). You therefore need to contact the Land Charges Department at the Legal Services Commission, DX 100170 Docklands 2 or by telephone (020 7783 7000).

I am acting for the buyer in a residential conveyancing matter. Contracts have not yet been exchanged. The seller's solicitor is not in the same locality as my firm and I am hoping that he will agree to complete by post and adopt the Law Society's Code for Completion by Post. Can I insist that he do so and at what stage should I make the proposal?

Arrangements for completion may be set out in the draft contract. In the absence of any specific contractual provision the seller's solicitor is not obliged to adopt the Law Society's Code for Completion by Post, although its use would be recommended in these circumstances. It is therefore advisable to approach the seller's solicitor on this matter as early as possible in the transaction, perhaps raising this as a preliminary enquiry, but at the latest at the Requisitions on Title stage. Furthermore it is courteous to do so as soon as possible in the transaction because the seller's solicitor may need to obtain the consent of his client's lender's solicitors to this arrangement. Variations of the Code should be agreed in writing between the solicitors well in advance of completion.

For further guidance see the *Conveyancing Handbook* (15th edition).

I am acting for the seller in the sale of a leasehold residential property and the buyer's solicitor has agreed to adopt the National Conveyancing Protocol. I have forwarded the TA6 Property Information Form and the TA7 Leasehold Information Form fully completed to this solicitor but he has now raised a large quantity of additional enquiries, some of which are in standard form, and some of which have been answered by the information already supplied. How should I deal with these extra enquiries?

There is no restriction on users of the protocol raising relevant additional enquiries particularly those arising out of the documents provided with the draft contract. However, a buyer's solicitor who sends a sheet of standard additional enquiries is not adhering to the terms and spirit of the protocol. The main aim of the protocol is to streamline procedures in domestic conveyancing. Practitioners are urged to raise only those additional enquiries that are needed in each particular transaction or locality and to resist the temptation to ask additional enquiries especially those relating to the state and condition of the property. If a solicitor, having agreed to adopt the protocol, departs from its provisions he or she should give notice to the solicitor acting for the other party.

For further guidance see The Law Society (2005) *A Guide to the National Conveyancing Protocol* (5th Edition), Law Society Publishing.

I act for the directors of a company in the purchase of a property, and we are due to exchange contracts soon. Do all the directors have to sign the contract?

No. Provided that the transaction has been authorised by the company, an officer of the company (usually a director or the secretary) may be authorised to sign the contract on behalf of the company. See the *Conveyancing Handbook* (15th edition).

I have been told that there is a Land Registry requirement that all leases should contain a front sheet summarising the contents of the lease. Where can I find more information?

Under the Land Registration (Amendment) (No 2) Rules 2005, SI 2005/1982 (as amended by the Land Registration (Amendment) Rules 2008, SI 2008/1919), a requirement was introduced for most new leases of any type of property which are registerable under the Land Registration Act 2002. These leases must have a front sheet setting out 'prescribed information' containing details such as the date of the lease, the term, the premium and other relevant information. The use of these 'prescribed clauses leases' become compulsory for leases dated on or after 19 June 2006.

For additional information, you may also wish to obtain a copy of the Land Registry Practice Guide 64 and addendum which is available on the Land Registry website (**www.landregistry.gov.uk**).

My client is buying a house and has asked me to complete the Stamp Duty Land Tax form on his behalf. Must I obtain his National Insurance (NI) number to enable me to complete the form?

No, the NI number is not essential. HM Revenue and Customs has produced some useful guidance entitled 'How to complete your Land Transaction Return' (see paragraph 50) which is available at **www.hmrc.gov.uk/sdlt6/index.htm**

My client is buying the ground floor flat of a house containing two flats in Newcastle. The freehold of my client's flat is owned by the lessee of the first floor flat. Similarly, on completion my client will own the freehold of the first floor flat. I was concerned by this situation but I have been told by a local solicitor that this arrangement is recognised by the local land registry. Is this correct?

The type of arrangement you describe is known locally as a 'Tyneside flat' scheme and is understood to be in common use by practitioners in the Newcastle area in relation to particular properties in north Tyneside that are divided into two flats on a 'one up, one down' basis. Since the freehold that your client would be acquiring in the upper flat lies above ground floor level, it would constitute a flying freehold. So, in relation to the acceptability of the arrangements for the purposes of any particular lender that is a member of the Council of Mortgage Lenders, you would need to observe the requirements of the Council's Handbook as they apply to flying freeholds.

The Durham (Southfield) office of the Land Registry is the proper office for the north Tyneside area. It will process the registration of the lease of the ground floor flat and the transfer of the freehold to the upper flat in the same way as any other lease or transfer, provided the forms used and the applications lodged comply with the normal registration requirements.

I understand the Law Society has prepared a standard business lease. Where can I find more information?

The documents are:

- The Law Society Business Lease (Part of Building) (Unregistered) 2008
- The Law Society Business Lease (Part of Building) (Registered) 2008
- The Law Society Business Lease (Whole of Building) (Unregistered) 2008
- The Law Society Business Lease (Whole of Building) (Registered) 2008

The forms are available from:

- LexisNexis (Everyform) – **www.lexisnexis.co.uk**
- Oyez Straker – **www.oyezstraker.co.uk**
- PEAPOD LEGALOffice Ltd – **www.peapod-legal.co.uk**
- Shaw & Sons Ltd – **www.shaws.co.uk**

Does the Law Society produce any information to assist solicitors when calculating apportionment of rent in leasehold properties?

Yes. The Conveyancing and Land Law Committee has prepared an 'Apportionment of Rent Formula' and this is contained in the *Conveyancing Handbook* (15th edition).

I am a sole practitioner specialising in conveyancing and am extremely concerned about the issue of mortgage fraud. Are there any warning signs that may assist in alerting me to a potential problem?

Criminal methodologies are continually changing. However, there are several known warning signs:

Identity and ownership

- The client or the property involved is located a long distance from your firm.
- The client seems unusually disinterested in their purchase.
- The seller is a private company or they have recently purchased the property from a private company.
- The client does not usually engage in property investment of this scale.
- The current owner has owned the property for under six months.
- The client's credit history is shorter than you would expect for their age, when you run an electronic identity check, which may include credit history information.
- There are plans for a sub-sale or back-to-back transaction.
- There is a last minute change of representative on the other side.
- The property has a history of being re-sold quickly or mortgages settled quickly.
- A transfer of title to land is requested with respect to only some of the seller's holdings and the properties are not grouped together.
- Finance is sought after the property has been registered to an owner for a significant period of time and the owner does not appear to be of an age to have held the land for that length of time.
- The other conveyancer or solicitor allegedly involved in the transaction has an email address from a large-scale web provider.
- There is a county court judgment against the property.
- The land is transferred following a court order, but the mortgage is sought some time later.

Value

- The value of the property has significantly increased in a short period of time out of line with the market in the area.
- The mortgage is for the full property value.
- The seller or developer has provided incentives, allowances or discounts.
- The deposit is being paid by someone other than the purchaser.
- The purchaser has paid the deposit directly to the seller.
- There is money left over from the mortgage after the purchase price has been paid, and you are asked to pay this money to the account of someone you do not know, or to the introducer.
- You are asked to enter a price on the title register that is greater than you know was paid for the property.
- There has been a recent transfer of land where no money has changed hands or the price was significantly less than the full market value.

For further information see the Law Society's practice note on mortgage fraud (**Annex 2C**).

I am acting for sellers in a conveyancing transaction and have exchanged contracts. The buyer has now unfortunately died and I must serve a notice to complete. Where do I serve the notice?

If it is necessary to serve a notice to complete in a situation where the delay is caused by the death of one of the contracting parties, the notice should be addressed to the deceased and his personal representatives at the deceased's last known address. A further copy of the notice should be served on the Public Trustee, please see **www.officialsolicitor.gov.uk**. See also, the *Conveyancing Handbook* (15th Edition).

I am acting on behalf of the buyer in a conveyancing transaction and I suspect that he may be involved in some element of mortgage fraud. If I discuss the matter with the lender would I be guilty of 'tipping off' under the Proceeds of Crime Act 2002 (PoCA 2002)?

Solicitors are often concerned about tipping off offences under PoCA 2002 when talking to the lender, insurer, or your purchaser client.

A key element of these offences is the likelihood of prejudicing an investigation under PoCA 2002, s.342(1). The risk of this is small when disclosing to a reputable lender or your insurer. They are also regulated for the purposes of anti-money laundering and subject to the same obligations. There is also a specific defence of making a disclosure for the purposes of preventing a money laundering offence.

In relation to asking further questions of your client and discussing the implications of the Act, there is a specific defence for tipping off for legal advisors who are seeking to dissuade their client from engaging in a money laundering offence.

For further advice on avoiding tipping off, see Chapter 5 of the Law Society's Anti-money laundering practice note (**Annex 5A**).

For further information and to discuss the risk of tipping off in a particular case, contact the Serious Organised Crime Agency's Financial Intelligence Helpdesk on 020 7238 8282.

I am acting for a seller in a conveyancing transaction. The buyers' solicitor has sent me the old transaction forms. Is it compulsory to use the most recent Law Society TA forms?

Although it is not compulsory to use the most recent TA forms, the Law Society suggests that it is good practice to do so and indeed, the old forms are no longer available to purchase.

Where can I find more guidance on Home Information Packs (HIPs)?

Please see the questions and answers set out below. For further information see **www.hips.lawsociety.org.uk**. Additional resources include the Law Society publication, 'Handling HIPs', which is available free of charge to members of the Property Section (£25.00 to non-members) at **www.propertysection.org.uk**. Also, see the *Conveyancing Handbook* (15th Edition).

Our firm is considering becoming a Home Information Pack provider. Do the Money Laundering Regulations 2007 apply to the provision of this service?

No. The regulations which came into force on 15 December 2007 contain a specific exclusion in reg.4(1)(f) regarding HIPs, which states: 'these regulations do not apply to . . . a person, when he prepares a HIP or a document or information for inclusion in a home information pack.' Please see Chapter 1 of the Anti-money laundering practice note which is reproduced in its entirety at **Annex 5A**.

What are the general penalties and potential redress for a breach of the Home Information Pack Regulations (No.2) 2007?

Practitioners can face a penalty notice of £200.00 for breach of the HIP Regulations. The duties imposed by the regulations will be enforced by the local authority Trading Standards Officers under a civil sanctions regime.

Under the Home Information Pack (Redress Scheme) Order 2007, SI 2007/560, all estate agents must, for matters relating to HIPs, belong to a compulsory redress scheme. The Consumer Estate Agents and Redress Act (CEARA) received Royal Assent on 19 July 2007. The Estate Agents (Redress Scheme) Order 2008, SI 2008/1712 came into force on 1 October 2008. It is now compulsory for all estate agents to belong to a redress scheme and establish complaint handling procedures in relation to all estate agency work. Part 3 of CEARA also provides for records to be maintained and to be made available for inspection by enforcement officers.

In respect of HIPs, the Ombudsman for Estate Agents' HIPs Redress Scheme and the RICS Surveyors' Ombudsman Scheme are the only recognised schemes for estate agents. Solicitor property sellers will be bound by an amendment to rule 18 of the Solicitors' Code of Conduct 2007 concerning the conduct of property sellers which to similar effect makes them accountable for complaints. It is recommended that you check at **www.sra.org.uk/rules** for the up to date position.

I am acting in the sale of a residential property and my client has asked me to prepare the Home Information Pack. Do I have to provide a paper copy of the HIP to any potential buyer? I would prefer to provide this information online.

A copy of the pack only needs to be provided to a potential buyer when he asks for one. If the potential buyer is happy to have an electronic copy, that is fine but otherwise a paper copy must be provided. Where the potential buyer insists on a paper copy, the seller is entitled to make a reasonable charge to cover postage, please see the Housing Act 2004, s.156(8).

I act for a tenant who is purchasing a property from a local authority. Is there any requirement for the seller to produce a Home Information Pack?

No. Properties being purchased under 'Right to Buy' schemes or where a tenant buys the property in which she lives fall outside the HIP legislation as the property is not being sold with vacant possession and presumably would not have been 'marketed'.

I am acting for a son who is administering the estate of his late mother. In view of the Home Information Pack Regulations, can he market her house before probate is granted?

Yes. The Home Information Pack Regulations (No 2) 2007 are not intended to delay any transactions. A HIP is required and the sale statement should explain why the seller is different from the registered owner.

My clients wish to sell the detached garage at the end of their garden to their next door neighbour. Do I need to prepare a Home Information Pack for the sale of this piece of land?

No. Under s.148 of the Housing Act 2004, HIPs are only required for premises consisting of a single dwelling house, including any ancillary land. Under s.177 of that Act, ancillary land means 'in relation to a dwelling house, any land intended to be occupied and enjoyed with that dwelling house'. It follows that the sale of the garage as ancillary land would not require a HIP.

My clients wish to sell their static mobile home which they refer to as a 'park home'. Does the sale of this property require a Home Information Pack?

No. Under s.148 of the Housing Act 2004, HIPs are required only for 'premises consisting of a single dwelling house including any ancillary land'. 'Dwelling house' is defined as 'a building or part of a building occupied or intended to be occupied as a separate dwelling'. This definition of building does not cover a static mobile home although obviously flats forming part of a building are covered and would require HIPs.

Are Energy Performance Certificates (EPCs) now required for the sale of commercial properties?

Yes. The Energy Performance of Buildings (Amendment) Regulations 2007, SI 2007/1669, set out the phased introduction of the requirement to provide an EPC for both commercial and residential property. Since 1 October 2008, EPCs are required on the sale or rent of all buildings.

For further information, please refer to the *Conveyancing Handbook* (15th Edition).

A seller is acting in person and has provided us with a Home Information Pack. What qualifications does a person need to compile a HIP?

A person does not need any qualifications to compile a HIP. However certain components of a HIP must be prepared by qualified persons, for example, only qualified Domestic Energy Assessors or registered Home Inspectors may provide an Energy Performance Certificate (a compulsory part of the pack). Only registered Home Inspectors may carry out a Home Condition Report (an optional part of the pack). For more information see the section on HIPs in the Health, Safety and Premises section of **www.businesslink.gov.uk**.

If a property is taken off the market and then put back on the market is another Home Information Pack required?

The HIP must be available before the 'first point of marketing', that is the date on which the duty arises under s.155(1) of the Housing Act 2004.

If the property is taken off the market and then put back on the market within a year of the 'first point of marketing', no further 'first point of marketing' arises (Regulation 3(3) of the Home Information Pack (No.2) Regulations 2007) so the original HIP can be used.

If the property is taken off the market and is put back on the market after the end of one year from the 'first point of marketing', then another 'first point of marketing' will arise and the HIP must be up to date to that point (reg.3(4)). When a property is taken off the market because a buyer has been found and is put back on the market within 28 days of the offer being withdrawn, no further 'first point of marketing' will arise and the existing HIP can still be used.

This means that the HIP has a shelf life of at least one year for the seller. For more information see the *Conveyancing Handbook* (15th Edition).

Annex 2A

House competitions practice note

30 October 2008

1. Introduction

1.1 Who should read this practice note?

All solicitors and employees involved in conveyancing transactions and the provision of advice in relation to the sale or purchase of homes.

1.2 What is the issue?

In an economic downturn, mortgages are harder to obtain and home owners find it harder to sell their houses. A small but increasing number of home owners are attempting to increase the likelihood of a sale by organising some kinds of competition in which participants can pay for the opportunity to win the property.

This practice note provides advice for solicitors who are asked to advise or assist with such transactions, and highlights risks relating to illegal lotteries, fraud and money laundering.

1.3 Professional conduct

The following sections of the Solicitors' Code of Conduct 2007 [**www.rules.sra.org.uk**] are relevant to this issue:

- Rule 1.01 Justice and the rule of law
- Rule 1.05 Standard of service
- Rule 1.06 Public confidence
- Rule 3 Conflict of interests

1.4   Legal and other requirements

Several pieces of legislation impose obligations on you with respect to this type of property transaction. If these obligations are breached, criminal sanctions can follow.

- Gambling Act 2005
- Fraud Act 2006
- Proceeds of Crime Act 2002 as amended
- Money Laundering Regulations 2007

[. . .]

1.5   Status of this practice note

Practice notes are issued by the Law Society as a professional body for the benefit of its members. They represent the Law Society's view of good practice in a particular area. They are not intended to be the only standard, nor do they necessarily provide a defence to complaints of misconduct or of inadequate professional service. Solicitors are not required to follow them, but doing so will make it easier to account to oversight bodies for their actions.

They do not constitute legal advice and, while care has been taken to ensure that they are accurate, up to date and useful, the Law Society will not accept any legal liability in relation to them.

For queries or comments on this practice note contact the Law Society's Practice Advice Service.

1.6   Terminology in this practice note

Must – a specific requirement in the Solicitors' Code of Conduct or legislation. You must comply, unless there are specific exemptions or defences provided for in the code of conduct or relevant legislation.

Should – good practice for most situations in the Law Society's view. If you do not follow this, you should be able to justify to oversight bodies why the alternative approach you have taken is appropriate, either for your practice, or in the particular retainer.

May – a non-exhaustive list of options for meeting your obligations. Which option you choose is determined by the risk profile of the individual practice, client or retainer. You must be able to justify why this was an appropriate option to oversight bodies.

1.7 More information and products

1.7.1 Law Society

- Practice Advice Service [www.lawsociety.org.uk/practiceadvice]
- Anti-money laundering practice note [www.lawsociety.org.uk/practicenotes]
- Property Section [www.propertysection.org.uk]

1.7.2 Other

- SRA Professional Ethics Helpline [www.sra.org.uk/sra/contactus]
- Gambling Commission [www.gamblingcommission.gov.uk]

2. Overview of selling a house by competition

2.1 General stages

There are a number of different variations on the process of selling a house by competition, but the general stages are:

1. The house is valued at £X.

2. The seller advertises tickets for a nominal value by comparison to the value of the house (for example £25 or £125).

3. The value of the total number of tickets available for sale exceeds the house valuation.

4. A minimum number of tickets are sold in order for the winner to be transferred ownership in the house.

The seller may also offer to donate proceeds above a certain value to charity if the sale completes.

2.2 Who holds the money?

The seller may hold the proceeds of the ticket sales in their bank account, or may ask you to hold the monies in your client account.

2.3 What if there aren't enough tickets sold?

You should manage your client's expectations on the likely success of this strategy for selling their house. Generally, if the minimum number is not sold, the seller can either:

- transfer the property anyway;
- provide the winner with a stated percentage of the proceeds of the ticket sales, keeping both the house and the remaining proceeds.

If the seller doesn't receive enough interest in the sale they run the risk of not selling enough tickets to warrant the transfer of the house, or even to cover their costs. You should ensure that they understand the risk of this happening.

3.   Is the scheme legal?

There is legislative control over the types of competitions which can be run in England and Wales.

For more information see the Gambling Commission website [**www. gamblingcommission.gov.uk**].

3.1   Illegal lotteries

You must determine if the proposed house competition is in fact a lottery. The Gambling Commission issued guidance on their website on the boundary between prize competitions, free draws and lotteries in November 2007.

A scheme will be a simple lottery if the following criteria are met:

- a person is required to pay to participate;
- one or more prizes are allocated;
- the allocation of the prize relies wholly on chance.

Under the Gambling Act 2005 lotteries remain the preserve of good causes and therefore cannot be operated for commercial or private gain. Lotteries must be licensed by the Gambling Commission, unless they qualify in one of the exempt categories. Unregistered lotteries are illegal and any funds received from them will be considered the proceeds of crime.

3.2   Prize competitions

In an increasing attempt to avoid the need for registration of a lottery, many schemes for selling a house by competition are seeking to include a skills element, so that the scheme becomes a prize competition.

Generally, prize competitions are those in which success depends on the exercise of skill, judgement or knowledge by the participants rather than by chance alone. Genuine prize competitions are free of statutory control under the Gambling Act.

A failure to satisfy the skills, knowledge or judgement element may result in prosecution. This is a question of law for the court, so the Gambling Commission cannot give clearance to individual schemes.

3.2.1   The skill, knowledge or judgement element

The level of skill, knowledge of judgement to be demonstrated by participants must be high enough to satisfy the test in the Gambling Act. You should warn clients that if their scheme fails to meet the test they risk committing a criminal offence by offering an illegal lottery.

Meeting the skills element of the competition may however reduce the number of people willing to enter. This may prevent the seller from selling enough tickets to raise an amount equivalent to the value of the house.

4.   Fraud and money laundering

There may be other risks posed to you through these transactions, even where the scheme is a legally recognised prize competition.

4.1   Opportunities for fraud

Fraud will arise where the seller is actively complicit in one or more of the following:

- not owning the house they are offering as a prize;
- failing to abide by the terms and conditions of the competition;
- keeping proceeds from ticket sales without providing any prize;
- failing to include all of the eligible entrants in the draw;
- providing the answer to the competition question to one or more of the entrants;
- manipulating the draw in favour of a specific entrant;
- obtaining a new, or further mortgage over the property before the draw, without advising the winner;
- failing to declare problems with the title to the house or structural problems which would dramatically reduce the value of the property;
- not paying relevant tax.

4.2   Consequences of fraud

If a fraud occurs, the money received from the tickets will become criminal property. If the winner was complicit in the fraud, the house and/or any funds returned from ticket sales will become criminal property.

You should consider your risk of being complicit in any fraud or in dealing with criminal property. This risk will depend on your level of knowledge and the extent of your involvement in the transaction.

4.3   Money laundering

Criminal activity will often generate large amounts of cash in smaller denominations. Integrating this cash into the mainstream financial system often poses a challenge for criminals. In house-selling competitions, often the price of the raffle tickets is low (under £100) and the number of tickets is very high (in the thousands). A criminal could use this opportunity to launder money by purchasing a large number of tickets either:

- under their own name;
- through money-mules;
- under aliases.

This would place criminally derived cash into the financial system either through the seller's account or your client account.

4.3.1   Laundering through refunds

A raffle does not need to proceed to a draw in order for money laundering risks to materialise. If the competition is called-off under the pretext of non-compliance with the law, payments must be refunded. If the refund is by bank transfer, the funds remain in the mainstream financial system and look legitimate. If the refund is by way of cheque, the criminal receives funds which look legitimate to place into their own bank accounts.

4.3.2   Laundering through fixed-outcome draws

If the competition goes ahead with the seller manipulating the draw in the criminal's favour, funds could be laundered. This will be effective whether the draw is for a proportion of the ticket sales or for the actual house.

For more information see our anti-money laundering practice note [**www.lawsociety.org.uk/practicenotes**].

4.4   Criminal liability

You should consider the risk of being complicit in a criminal offence. This risk will depend on the extent of your involvement with the transaction and/or any money deposited in client accounts.

You do not actually have to touch the criminal property in order for a money laundering offence to have occurred. Even if the funds do not enter your client account, and depending on your knowledge or suspicion with respect to the criminal property you may still be at risk of both:

- entering into an arrangement to facilitate money laundering;
- committing a non-disclosure offence.

5. Acting on behalf of the winner

It is highly unlikely that a ticket purchaser will have received legal advice prior to the competition draw. If you are instructed by a ticket purchaser/winner to assist with the transfer of the title you should ensure that they are aware of any legal requirements and risks associated with the transaction.

5.1   Where you are also acting for the seller

If you are also acting for the seller, you must consider rule 3 of the code of conduct before acting on behalf of both parties in the transfer of the title after the draw.

5.2   Where you have no prior involvement

You should consider the following risks and issues to help protect both your client and yourself from potential risks:

- The competition was an illegal lottery.
- There is an unregistered mortgage or charge on the house.
- There are no instructions for the removal of the current mortgage or charge on the house prior to the transfer.
- Structural problems, environmental contamination, planning issues or other defects to the house or title may exist.
- Ownership may not be correctly registered if the ticket was purchased by co-habitees or a group of people.
- It may not be clear what purchase price should be listed on the transfer document – the price of the single ticket or the price of all of the tickets sold.
- Insufficient stamp duty land tax or land registry fees may be paid on the transaction.

6. Protecting your practice

You should consider carefully the risks involved in accept a retainer relating to the sale of a house by way of prize competition, whether you are acting for the seller or the winner.

Where you have accepted a retainer of this type you should take the following steps to assist in protecting your firm and avoiding any breach of the law.

6.1 Establish appropriate client acceptance protocols

You should ensure that senior management approves the acceptance of any retainers of this nature to reflect the risks posed to the firm. This may involve:

- sign off by the managing partner;
- sign off by a partner and the head of compliance, client acceptance or similar position;
- sign off by two partners.

6.2 Ensure you have sufficient legal expertise

If you are not an expert in gambling law and conveyancing law, you should consider both:

- taking legal advice from an expert in gambling law;
- contacting the Gambling Commission for guidance on lotteries and prize competitions.

6.3 Know your client

For the purposes of the Money Laundering Regulations 2007, where you have been instructed by the seller your client due diligence obligations relate directly to them. However, knowing your client means more than just identifying them in accordance with the regulations.

Other relevant information may include:

The seller:
- whether they have title to the house;
- why they want to sell the house in this way;
- whether or not they are worried by the prospect of not finding enough participants;
- how long the house has already been on the market, if at all;
- the source of the valuation of the house.

The winner:
- how many tickets they purchased;
- what the source of the funds for the ticket purchases was;
- whether the winning ticket was purchased jointly with others.

6.4   Know the transaction

You should thoroughly understand the process of the scheme to mitigate the risks of fraud and money laundering. If any of the relevant aspects of the transaction give rise to a suspicion of fraud or money laundering, you should consider whether you can continue to act or whether you need to make a suspicious activity report.

Relevant aspects of the transaction include:

- how entrants are able to purchase tickets and the information they have to provide when they do so;
- where the money from the tickets will be held and who can authorise any withdrawal;
- who will judge the eligibility of entrants;
- the processes in place to ensure that all eligible entries are included in the draw;
- how the draw will take place;
- whether the title is unencumbered, and if not, whether there are instructions from the seller to redeem the mortgage(s);
- whether the terms and conditions of entry incorporate the terms of the Standard Conditions of Sale or similar conditions to enable the winner to see the terms on which the property will be transferred.

6.5   Protect your client account

Where funds are being paid directly to your client account, you may consider the following options to help minimise the risk of money laundering:

- identify and verify all entrants;
- require identity information such as name, address and/or date of birth from all entrants and electronically verify a sample of these;
- require all tickets to be purchased via an electronic transfer from a UK bank account held in the same name as the entrant.

See also section 11.2.3 of our anti-money laundering practice note.

6.6 Oversee the draw

When acting for the seller, you should review the actual conduct of the draw and verify the identity of the winner.

6.7 Register the new ownership

When acting for the winner you should register the new ownership promptly and in a way which accurately reflects any joint ownership.

You should discuss with the Land Registry the correct sale price to be entered on the register.

You should ensure that the correct level of Stamp Duty Land Tax and Land Registry Fees are paid.

Annex 2B

Identity evidence for Land Registry practice note

4 December 2008

1. Introduction

1.1 Who should read this practice note?

Solicitors dealing with conveyancing matters involving the Land Registry (LR).

1.2 What is the issue?

From 24 November 2008 the Land Registry requires most applicants to give details of the conveyancers acting for all the other parties to the transaction and, where a party is unrepresented, to provide evidence of that party's identity. The requirement has been introduced to help combat fraud.

This practice note provides advice on managing the process and highlights areas of risk.

1.3 Legal and other requirements

- Land Registration Rules 2008 (as amended) (LRR)
- Land Registration Act 2002 (as amended) (LRA)
- Land Registration Rules 2003 (as amended) (LRR)
- Fraud Act 2006
- Money Laundering Regulations 2007
- Proceeds of Crime Act 2002 (as amended)
- CML Handbook [www.cml.org.uk]

1.4 Rules of professional conduct

The following sections of the Solicitors' Code of Conduct 2007 (code of conduct) are relevant to issues relating to identity:

- Rule 1.01 Justice and the rule of law
- Rule 2 Client relations
- Rule 3 Conflict of interest
- Rule 3 Acting for lender and borrower in conveyancing transactions
- Rule 4.01 Duty of confidentiality
- Rule 4.02 Duty of disclosure

1.5   Status of this advice

Practice notes are issued by the Law Society for the use and benefit of its members. They represent the Law Society's view of good practice in a particular area. They are not intended to be the only standard of good practice that solicitors can follow. You are not required to follow them, but doing so will make it easier to account to oversight bodies for your actions.

Practice notes are not legal advice, nor do they necessarily provide a defence to complaints of misconduct or of inadequate professional service. While care has been taken to ensure that they are accurate, up to date and useful, the Law Society will not accept any legal liability in relation to them.

For queries or comments on this practice note contact the Law Society's Practice Advice Service.

1.6   Terminology in this advice

Must – a specific requirement in the Solicitor's Code of Conduct or legislation. You must comply, unless there are specific exemptions or defences provided for in the code of conduct or relevant legislation.

Should – good practice for most situations in the Law Society's view. If you do not follow this, you must be able to justify to oversight bodies why this is appropriate, either for your practice, or in the particular retainer.

May – a non-exhaustive list of options for meeting your obligations. Which option you choose is determined by the risk profile of the individual practice, client or retainer. You must be able to justify why this was an appropriate option to oversight bodies.

ID – identification.

1.7   More information

1.7.1   Practice Advice Service

The Law Society provides support for solicitors on a wide range of areas of practice. Practice Advice Service can be contacted on 0870 606 2522 from 9am to 5pm on weekdays.

1.7.2 Land Registry

- Land Registry Practice Guide 67 [**www1.landregistry.gov.uk/assets/ library/documents/lrpg067.pdf**]
- Land Registry Public Guide 20 [**www1.landregistry.gov.uk/assets/ library/documents/public_guide_020.pdf**]

1.7.3 Other practice notes and Law Society materials

- Mortgage fraud practice note
- Anti-money laundering practice note
- Legal Complaints Service short guidance on mortgage fraud
- Property Section
- The Law Society's *Conveyancing Handbook* 15th edition

2. Changes to registration requirements

New versions of forms API, DS2 and FR1 require that the application for land registration must include details of both:

- registered conveyancers acting for any other parties to the transaction;
- any unrepresented parties involved in the transaction.

The 'parties' include:

- the seller;
- the seller's lender;
- the buyer; and
- the buyer's lender.

The identification requirement should be addressed at an early stage in the transaction and, where possible, be fulfilled prior to completion.

2.1 Transactions affected

You must apply the requirements to the following transactions if the property is worth more than £5,000:

- transfers, whether for the full value or not, including changes of trustee;
- registration of leases, whether or not for the full value;
- surrender of leases;
- registration of charges, whether or not for the full value;
- discharge paper (DS1);

- DS3 releases of part;
- applications for compulsory first registration;
- applications for voluntary first registration where the title deeds have been lost or destroyed.

The requirement does not apply to:

- transactions where the value is £5,000 or less. Evidence must be provided where this is the case;
- noting of leases or charges;
- assents;
- statutory vestings;
- voluntary applications for first registration where title deeds are available;
- transactions where an Electronic Notice of Discharge (END) or an Electronic Discharge (ED) has been transmitted directly from the relevant lender, see section 4.4.5 [of this practice note] 'Exemptions'.

2.2   Exceptions

Identity evidence is not required for some parties, for example:

- receivers;
- liquidators;
- Mental Capacity Act deputies.

For details see Land Registry Practice Guide 67.

2.3   Rejection of LR application

Applications are at risk of rejection by the LR if the ID forms are insufficiently completed and you may lose priority by the time the issues are resolved. You should assess at an early stage whether it is better for your client to delaying lodging the application in order to fulfil the ID requirement than to risk rejection.

For more information about the risks of not obtaining registrations within the priority period see section 7.1 of the Land Registry Practice Guide 67.

You should check with the LR at an early stage in the transaction if you are proposing to comply with the requirements by letter, or where the LR has discretion – see section 6, below.

2.4   Your obligations

You are not legally obliged to guarantee that information provided to you is genuine. LR state that they regard you as being satisfied with the validity of any identity details included in an application, whether or not you have personally verified the information given. The extent of this obligation may be a matter for the courts to decide.

You should therefore both:

1.   assess the risks involved in providing details;

2.   develop adequate policies for staff who are completing these forms.

3.   Identifying the conveyancer

You should provide details of any conveyancers acting within the transaction and check that the details given are genuine.

3.1   Who is a 'conveyancer'?

A 'conveyancer' is defined by rule 217(1) (as amended) LRR 2003 as being one of the following:

- solicitor;
- licensed conveyancer;
- legal executive;
- notary public;
- barrister;
- registered European lawyer.

The conveyancer may also be from an in-house legal department, for example those representing a developer, lender or local authority.

3.2   Risk of false identities

Fraud has been reported where the 'conveyancer' has attempted to:

- falsely claim to be a solicitor;
- assume the identity of professionals who do exist and whose details appear in a recognised directory;
- use the address of an existing practice.

You should therefore consider the following to establish whether the details are genuine:

- Does the 'conveyancer' actually exist?
- Are they authorised by an appropriate professional body?
- If they do exist and are authorised, can they confirm that their details are not being given fraudulently?

See also the Law Society's mortgage fraud practice note.

3.2.1 Checking professional registers

You may check details against the registers of professional bodies. Be aware that directories may only list whether or not the firm exists, not whether the person you are dealing with works for that practice.

You should also check that the information in the directory matches both:

- the practice details; and
- the final destination of documents and funds.

You can check the Law Society's roll of registered solicitors by using the Find a solicitor search.

For further information about the ID requirement for conveyancers who are unknown to you see section 3.2 in the CML Lenders' Handbook.

4. Identifying unrepresented parties

You must gather evidence and provide certified details of any unrepresented parties. Failure to provide details of unrepresented parties will result in rejection of the application to register the transaction.

You can provide the details in one of the following three ways:

1. Declare that you are satisfied that sufficient steps have been taken to verify the identity of the unrepresented parties. You should exercise caution in taking this option if you have not supplied the verification yourself and you may choose only to confirm satisfaction where you have evidence that verification has been carried out by another conveyancer.

2. Enclose verified Land Registry forms ID1 or ID2 as evidence of the unrepresented parties' identity.

3. Request that unrepresented parties attend the Land Registry in person when the application is made so that an official can complete ID1 or ID2 for them.

The evidence must be provided in accordance with any current direction made by the Chief Land Registrar, under s.100(4) LRA for the purposes of confirming identity.

4.1   Using form ID1 – identity of individuals

The ID1 form is in two parts. Section A must be completed by the individual and provides certain basic information including:

*   name;
*   address;
*   telephone number;
*   date of birth.

Section B must be completed by the conveyancer. This requires evidence of identity which may include:

*   passport;
*   photocard driving licence;
*   utility bills
*   mortgage statement;
*   credit or debit card;
*   Council tax bill.

The individual must also supply a passport size photograph.

A conveyancer must verify that they have seen the evidence provided in the ID1 form and that the photograph is of the person who produced it.

4.2   Using form ID2 – identity of corporate bodies

Confirming the identity of a corporate body or company using form ID2 is more complicated.

The company must nominate an individual as their representative. This person must then provide evidence that:

*   the corporate body they represent and the registered proprietor, or body entitled to be registered as proprietor, are one and the same;
*   the corporate body still exists;
*   the nominee has authority to act as its representative.

4.2.1   Does the corporate body exist?

A company search will provide evidence of this for a UK company. The search may also provide information indicative of fraud. For example, the date of the company's registration may indicate that it cannot be the registered proprietor.

4.2.2   Overseas companies

Overseas corporations must also provide evidence that they are the same as the registered proprietor of the estate or charge. This may be provided as an opinion letter from a lawyer qualified in the relevant jurisdiction, confirming the corporation still exists and that the representative is authorised to act on its behalf.

The Land Registry Public Guide 20 does not mention the need for an opinion letter for foreign companies, so you may need to explain this requirement to someone who is not your client. You should take care that you do not get drawn into giving advice in these circumstances.

For information on the types of evidence which may be used to verify the identity of corporate entities both within the UK and overseas, see the Law Society's practice note on anti-money laundering.

4.3   Who can verify ID?

Details can be verified by amongst others any licensed conveyancer, solicitor or European lawyer who is fully qualified and registered in the UK. This person does not have to be acting in the transaction.

Frauds have been perpetrated using fictitious solicitor's details. If you are not completing the verification information yourself you should check that:

1.   the solicitor who has provided the information actually exists;

2.   they hold appropriate qualifications;

3.   they can confirm that that they signed the form you have in your possession.

4.4   The seller's lender

The new AP1 form requires you to provide details of the lender who is discharging the seller's mortgage. You must state whether the discharging lender was represented, and if not, you must take the steps described above to provide details of their identity.

4.4.1   Requesting ID forms

You may request ID forms directly from the lender, but be aware that they may not be under any obligation to provide these details.

Alternatively, you may request them from the seller's solicitor who may be in a good position to provide this information. The seller's solicitor generally doesn't act for the discharging lender but will deal with the lender without a retainer, for example, by obtaining redemption statements.

You may be able to confirm that the seller's solicitor is also representing the lender for ID purposes. In order to do this you will need a statement to this effect from the seller's solicitor.

It is anticipated that the requirements will usually be satisfied by the seller's solicitor providing a DS2 (or AP1or a DS3) rather than by providing a form ID1 or ID2.

4.4.2   Pre-contract requests and contractual provisions

You may do any of the following prior to the exchange of contracts, where possible, to help meet the ID requirements for the seller's lender:

- Ask in preliminary enquiries how the seller proposes to satisfy the new ID requirements.
- Request that lenders provide ID and an indicative redemption statement to the seller's solicitor at an early stage in the transaction.
- Add contractual obligations which require the seller's solicitor to provide evidence of ID via the DS2 or relevant ID form.

Remember that new charges may be registered during the course of a transaction.

You should however advise your client that contractual provisions relating to ID requirements may be difficult to enforce and you may be unable to complete the transaction if they are not met.

4.4.3   Evidence of discharge (DS2)

You may request that the seller's solicitor provides the information in a DS2 form, alongside the Evidence of Discharge form (DS1).

You should be aware that if you submit the lender's DS2 and DS1 forms along with an AP1, the LR will:

1.   regard this as comprising two separate applications;

2.   process the discharge application before the AP1 application;

3.   assume that you are satisfied with the details of the lender's identity.

Point number 3 above may expose you to risk if the issue is litigated. This risk is reduced if the DS2 is provided by the seller's solicitor.

4.4.4 Banks and building societies

UK banks or building societies which send a DS2 and DS1 discharge or DS3 release direct to LR do not have to lodge form ID2 as well. They should however declare their role as a conveyancer or non-conveyancer within the transaction on the DS2, and complete the sections of the form relevant to that role.

4.4.5 Exemptions

There is a general exemption to the ID requirement for lenders who have submitted details through either:

- electronic discharge (ED);
- electronic notification of discharge (END).

Information about exemptions regarding lenders is available under s.100(4) of the LRA.

You should still however comply with identity requirements as lenders who have indicated that they intend to use ED or END may use a DS1 after the redemption monies have been paid, without notifying you until a late stage in the transaction. It will usually be too late by this point for you to provide the necessary ID details unless you have collected them in advance.

5. Obtaining ID evidence in difficult circumstances

5.1 Transfers of shares of property where there are joint owners

To avoid intra-family fraud, transfers of shares are now also subject to the LR identity requirements. It is not uncommon for one joint owner to be unrepresented in a transfer of their share in a property, typically when the transfer is the result of a court order following the breakdown of a relationship.

It may be difficult in these situations to obtain the requisite completion of AP1, FR1 and ID1 and you should address the issue of ID early on in the proceedings. Where one of the owners is unrepresented you must take the required steps to confirm their identity as an unrepresented party.

5.1.1   Potential problems

As these transfers often involve personal relationships between clients you should also be aware of the potential for:

- duress;
- undue influence;
- signature forgery.

You should ask for separate representation and completion of an ID1 form where, for the above or any other reasons, you consider it appropriate.

5.1.2   Confirming details for the other party

You may be asked to confirm the ID of an unrepresented transferor whilst acting for the transferee, but you are not obliged to do so.

You must make it clear if you do provide confirmation that you are not providing any advice to but are acting on a limited retainer for ID purposes only. Your instructions are therefore limited to checking his or her identity to facilitate the transfer and you must be alert to any potential conflict of interests.

You should keep records evidencing your actions where you act for ID purposes only.

5.1.3   Reluctant parties

Owners may refuse to be represented, or to sign the transfer because they feel they are being forced to give up their interest in a property against their wishes. Where the judge has made an order nominating a person to sign the transfer on behalf of a refusing party, you should provide a covering letter explaining why it is not possible to provide ID information for the other owner, with the application.

The LR will decide if they need to investigate the matter before completing the registration.

5.2   Owners requesting verification by the Land Registry

You may encounter situations where an unrepresented owner prefers to have their identity verified by Land Registry. You may therefore attend the LR with the owner to lodge the application, as the officials will not verify identity in advance.

You should be aware of the risk that the unrepresented party will not attend, thus preventing you from submitting your application. This may expose your client to the risk of not obtaining registration within the priority period or at all.

5.3 Surrenders of lease

It is common for a tenant to be unrepresented when surrendering their registered lease to their landlord. You must provide confirmation of the tenant's identity in applications to register the surrender. You may insert a provision in the contract to provide for this, which requires the tenant to provide the relevant ID form on or before completion of the surrender.

5.4 Powers of attorney

Where neither the donor nor the donee are represented:

- you must provide evidence of identity for the donor and the donee;
- overseas donors must provide ID1 or ID2 forms verified before a British consular official or by a foreign notary.

6. Situations in which ID requirements should be addressed at an early stage

There will be situations where it will not possible to obtain adequate evidence. The LR accepts this and has discretion in applying the requirement. For example, for an elderly person in residential care who is unable to sign an ID form.

You must enclose an explanatory letter with your application in these situations.

You should however be aware that the LR will challenge any reason for using a covering letter that they consider frivolous. You should contact LR at an early stage in the transaction to establish the correct approach, before exchanging contracts, to avoid lodging an application which cannot proceed.

6.1 Valuation issues

If the value of a property or share thereof is £5,000 or less you do not need to verify ID for other parties to the transaction, but you must evidence this valuation. You should check in advance what kind of evidence LR requires. This avoids costly formal valuations unless they are considered necessary to satisfy the requirement.

For example, where you are acting for the purchaser of a leasehold flat plus a share in the freehold reversion, the LR will accept a letter stating the value of the freehold reversion if this is £5,000 or less. This means that ID information is not required for all of the other leaseholders who own the freehold reversion.

6.2   Unregistered DS1

You may find completed but unregistered DS1 forms with the deeds. You should enclose a covering letter to accompany the application which explains the situation in these circumstances. You should also check whether LR has further requirements before lodging the application.

6.3   ID information that is not current

This information is only correct at a particular point in time. The relevant time is the time of the transaction. If there is a long delay between the completion of the forms and application for registration you may need to prove further confirmation. You should refer to the LR to establish their requirements.

7.   Issues to consider when asked to verify the identity of non-clients

7.1   Must I verify ID?

This is a matter for individual practices to decide. You are under no obligation to provide any sort of service to someone who is not your client. You may however decide that this is part of the service that you provide to your client where you are taking part in the transaction, for example by establishing the seller's lender's identity when you are acting on behalf of the seller.

You should consider the risk of liability if you are deceived by any forged documents provided as evidence.

7.1.1   Verifying ID for individuals

You may be approached by unknown individuals who request that you verify their identity for transactions in which you are not acting.

The ID1 form asks whether or not you have known the individual for two years, but you are not requested to state in which capacity. You must decide whether your knowledge of this person is sufficient to vouch for them on these terms. You may still verify identity even if the person is a complete stranger.

For more information about verifying a person's identity see the sections on 'ID for natural person' and 'enhanced due diligence' in the Law Society's practice note on anti-money laundering.

7.1.2   Verifying ID for companies

You should satisfy yourself that the corporation and the registered pro-prietor are one and the same person. This process goes further than the identity checks required of a solicitor's own client under the anti-money laundering rules. For example, as the verifying solicitor you should see the title register.

You should also make reasonable checks of the nominated person's authority to act. Evidence should be reasonably recent. For example, you do not have to provide further verification if the person produces a power of attorney less than 12 months old and confirms that it has not been revoked.

For information on the types of evidence which may be used for com-panies, see the Law Society's practice note on anti-money laundering.

7.2   Fees

You are entitled to charge for dealing with verification. There is no fixed fee, but you should consider the degree of risk and responsibility you are undertaking. Any charges are subject to regulatory requirements includ-ing service of Terms of Business, rule 2 requirements and payment of VAT where applicable.

7.3   Exempt information document status

For fraud-prevention reasons, ID1 and ID2 are not open to public inspec-tion and there is no need to apply for exempt information document status for them.

7.4   Records

You should record the steps you have carried out in relation to checking ID for your own protection. This could include keeping a long-term record of verification details, subject to any data protection requirements.

Annex 2C

Mortgage fraud practice note

15 April 2009

1. Introduction

1.1   Who should read this practice note?

All solicitors who do conveyancing work involving a mortgage.

1.2   What is the issue?

Criminals will exploit weaknesses in lending and conveyancing systems to gain illegitimate financial advantage from the UK property market. This can be either:

*   opportunistic action using misrepresentation of income or property value to obtain greater loans than a person is entitled to
*   organised crime syndicates overvaluing properties, using false identities and failing to make any mortgage repayments

A solicitor will be involved in most property transactions undertaken in the UK. You can find yourself criminally liable if your client commits mortgage fraud, because of the extension of the definition of fraud in the Fraud Act 2006 and the anti-money laundering regime in the UK. You can be liable even if you were not aware of the fraud or actively participated in it.

Courts will assume a high level of knowledge and education on your part. They will often be less willing to accept claims that you were unwittingly involved if you have not applied appropriate due diligence.

This practice note highlights the warning signs of mortgage fraud and outlines how you can protect yourself and your firm from being used to commit mortgage fraud.

1.3   Professional conduct

The following sections of the Solicitors' Code of Conduct 2007 (code of conduct) are relevant to mortgage fraud:

- Rule 1.01 Justice and the Rule of Law
- Rule 3.16 Acting for lender and borrower in conveyancing transactions
- Rule 4.01 Duty of confidentiality
- Rule 4.02 Duty of disclosure

1.4   Legal and other requirements

Several pieces of legislation impose obligations on you with respect to property transactions. If these obligations are breached, criminal sanctions can follow.

- Fraud Act 2006
- Proceeds of Crime Act 2002 (as amended)
- Money Laundering Regulations 2007

All links to legislation in this practice note will take you to the Statute Law Database website. The legislation contained in this database may not contain the most current amendments and you should take your own action to ensure you have the most up-to-date version of the legislation.

1.5   Status of this practice note

Practice notes are issued by the Law Society for the use and benefit of its members. They represent the Law Society's view of good practice in a particular area. They are not intended to be the only standard of good practice that solicitors can follow. You are not required to follow them, but doing so will make it easier to account to oversight bodies for your actions.

Practice notes are not legal advice, nor do they necessarily provide a defence to complaints of misconduct or of inadequate professional service. While care has been taken to ensure that they are accurate, up to date and useful, the Law Society will not accept any legal liability in relation to them.

For queries or comments on this practice note contact the Law Society's Practice Advice Service: **www.lawsociety.org.uk/practiceadvice**.

1.6   Terminology in this practice note

Must – a specific requirement in the Solicitors' Code of Conduct or legislation. You must comply, unless there are specific exemptions or defences provided for in the code of conduct or relevant legislation.

Should – good practice for most situations in the Law Society's view. If you do not follow this, you should be able to justify to oversight bodies why the alternative approach you have taken is appropriate, either for your practice, or in the particular retainer.

May – a non-exhaustive list of options for meeting your obligations. Which option you choose is determined by the risk profile of the individual practice, client or retainer. You must be able to justify why this was an appropriate option to oversight bodies.

1.7   More information and products

- best practice training
- the Law Society's anti-money laundering practice note
- the Council of Mortgage Lenders' Handbook – what's expected of you when working with lenders.
- the Law Society's Property Section – join for support and training
- other Law Society publications – order from our [online] bookshop

    – *Solicitors and Money Laundering Handbook* – 3rd edition
    – *Conveyancing Handbook* – 15th edition

- the Solicitors Regulation Authority's *Professional Ethics Helpline* for advice on conduct issues

2.   How does mortgage fraud occur?

2.1   What is mortgage fraud?

Mortgage fraud occurs where individuals defraud a financial institution or private lender through the mortgage process.

The definition of fraud in the Fraud Act 2006 covers fraud by false representation and by failure to disclose information where there is a legal duty to disclose. False representations can be made explicitly or implicitly and may occur even where you know only that the representation might be misleading or untrue.

The value of a mortgage obtained through fraud is the proceeds of crime. Under the Proceeds of Crime Act 2002, you risk committing a money laundering offence if you acquire, use, have possession of, enter into an arrangement with respect to, or transfer this criminal property.

Read the relevant legislation and the anti-money laundering practice note, Chapter 5.

2.2   Opportunistic mortgage fraud

2.2.1   General methodology

Individual purchasers can commit mortgage fraud by obtaining a higher mortgage than they are entitled to by providing untrue or misleading information or failing to disclose required information. This may include providing incorrect information about:

* identity
* income
* employment
* other debt obligations
* the sources of funds other than the mortgage for the purchase
* the value of the property
* the price to be paid and whether any payments have been, or will be made, directly between the seller and the purchaser

2.2.2   Use of professionals

Opportunistic fraudsters will not usually attempt to include their solicitor in the original fraud. However, you may become aware of information conflicting with that provided to the lender as you progress the conveyance.

Clients engaged in opportunistic fraud may be evasive when questioned on the conflict and may try to dissuade you from conducting relevant checks or advising the lender.

2.3   Large scale mortgage fraud

2.3.1   General methodology

Large scale mortgage fraud is usually more sophisticated and involves several properties. It may be committed by criminal groups or individuals, referred to hereon as fraudsters. The buy-to-let market is particularly vulnerable to mortgage fraud, whether through new-build apartment complexes or large scale renovation projects. Occasionally commercial properties will be involved. The common steps are:

- The nominated purchasers taking out the mortgage often have no beneficial interest in the property, and may even be fictitious.
- The property value is inflated and the mortgage will be sought for the full inflated valuation.
- Mortgage payments are often not met and the properties are allowed to deteriorate or used for other criminal or fraudulent activities, including drug production, unlicensed gambling and prostitution.
- When the bank seeks payment of the mortgage, the fraudsters raise mortgages with another bank through further fictitious purchasers and effectively sell the property back to themselves, but at an even greater leveraged valuation.
- Because the second mortgage is inflated, the first mortgage and arrears are paid off, leaving a substantial profit. This may be repeated many times
- Eventually a bank forecloses on the property, only to find it in disrepair and worth significantly less than the current mortgage and its arrears.

2.3.2   Use of non-bank lenders

Fraudsters may use private sources of funding such as property clubs, especially when credit market conditions tighten. These lenders often have lower safeguards than institutional lenders, leaving them vulnerable to organised fraud. Property clubs can be targeted particularly in relation to overseas properties where the property either does not exist, or it is a vacant piece of land, not a developed property.

2.3.3   Use of corporate structures

Sometimes fraud is achieved by selling the property between related private companies, rather than between fictitious individuals. The transactions will involve inflated values, and will not be at arm's length.

Increasingly, off-shore companies are being used, with the property sold several times within the group before approaching a lender for a mortgage at an inflated value.

You may be asked to act for both the seller and the purchaser in these transactions.

2.3.4   Flipping and back-to-back transactions

Investors will always look to re-sell a property at a profit. However, fraudsters may seek to re-sell a property very quickly for a substantially increased price. This process is called flipping, and will usually involve back-to-back sales of the property to limit the time between sales. Variations on this fraud include:

- The first mortgage is not registered against the property, and not redeemed upon completion of the second sale.
- The second purchaser may be fictitious, using a false identity or be someone vulnerable to pressure from the fraudster.
- A mortgage may only be obtained by the second purchaser and for an amount significantly higher than the value of the property. The profit goes to the fraudster.

2.3.5   Use of professionals

Fraudsters will usually use at least one professional at the core of the fraud, to direct and reassure other professionals acting at the periphery. Mortgage brokers and introducers have been used in this role in the past.

Mortgage lenders often rely on other professionals to verify the legitimacy of a transaction and safeguard their interests. Lenders may not extensively verify information they receive, especially in a rising market. Institutional lenders will subscribe to the Council of Mortgage Lenders' Handbook and expect solicitors to comply with these guidelines. Private investors will rely on compliance with the Solicitors' Code of Conduct to protect their lending.

You may be approached in any of the following ways:

- You may be asked to complete the transaction and simply transfer the title in accordance with already exchanged contracts. A lender who has received the loan applications and already approved the loan may approach you with packaged transactions and completed paper work.
- You may be encouraged to alter the value on the Certificate of Title given to the lender.
- You may be encouraged not to comply with obligations in the CML Handbook.
- You may be offered continued work at a higher margin to encourage less diligent checks.
- Fraudsters may attempt to recruit you into the fraud, especially if you have unwittingly assisted previously, or have developed an especially close relationship with other participants in the scheme.

2.4   Other methodologies

Fraud methodologies regularly evolve, particularly in changing economic circumstances.

2.4.1   Foreclosure fraud

In difficult economic times, clients may struggle to meet mortgage repayments, and turn to a foreclosure rescue scheme, to be able to remain in their homes. This scheme sees home owners receiving an offer from a third party to purchase the property while the home owner is allowed to rent the property. The home owner is given the option to purchase the property back when their financial position improves.

However, criminal involvement can result in the following:

1. The home owner sells the property to someone who is actually a member of the criminal syndicate, a mortgage mule, or an entirely fictitious person.

2. A mortgage will be taken out by this investor for an inflated value against the property.

3. The original loan will be paid out and the money representing the equity in the home will be taken by the criminal syndicate. No payments will be made towards the mortgage.

4. The original home owner will be unaware of the lack of payments being made until the bank seeks to foreclose and evicts them a mere tenant.

5. The value of the mortgage will be far greater than the original mortgage and it will be impossible for the original owner to purchase the property back.

2.4.2   Application hijack

Application hijacking involves criminals intervening before completion of a mortgage, falsely claiming to be the new representatives for the purchaser. They thereby obtain the mortgage advance in place of the real purchaser.

The lender is contacted later by the real representatives looking to complete the transaction, only to find the funds have already been paid away and have now disappeared.

The criminals will generally pose as solicitors or conveyancers, taking the details of someone who is on the professional register. They will then use fake or cloned letterhead to write to the lender as the representative, providing their own account details for the client account.

Solicitors who have unknowingly undertaken work for criminal syndicates previously may find that they are at greater risk of this type of fraud as the syndicate will have access to their genuine letter head and standard mortgage correspondence.

2.4.3   After the event mortgaging

While re-mortgaging and re-financing may be common during an economic down turn, the use of apparent equity to access mortgage funds is an avenue also exploited by criminals.

1. Fraudsters will use private funds, often of criminal origin, to purchase a property. Often the purchase will be through an auction and may involve repossessed properties, to ensure a discounted purchase price.

2. After the purchase is completed, and usually within 12 months, the fraudster will seek external funding against the property.

3. They then take the mortgage advance and disappear, failing to make any payments.

Another variation on this methodology is that the fraudster will pose as a property developer and will seek bridging loans to cover the purchase of a number of properties. These may be properties which the fraudsters previously used as part of a flipping scheme and have finally been reposed by the bank. The bridging loan is only sought after the purchase has been registered and possession has been taken of the property.

2.4.4   Claiming deceased estates

Criminals will make use of the notices section of their local papers to identify deceased estates that can be exploited for criminal gain, either because there are no known heirs or probate has been delayed. They will seek to either falsely establish their identity as a long lost heir or will pose as the deceased person. In both scenarios they will seek a mortgage over the existing equity in the property and then disappear with the funds.

2.4.5   Court orders for sale

In an economic downturn, more properties are repossessed or are unable to be sold. They are then left unoccupied and boarded up.

1. Criminals will seek out these properties and details of the owners.

2. They will then apply to the County Court for a judgement against the owner over a non-existent debt.

3. They will not actually give the owner notice of this application.

4. Once obtained, this judgement is converted into an order for sale.

5. The property is sold either directly to the person claiming the debt or to one of their associates at an inflated price, using criminal money.

6. A mortgage will be obtained over the property at the inflated value.

7. The mortgage advance will be taken and no payments will be made.

3. Warning signs

Criminal methodologies are continually changing. However, there are several known warning signs, which may be indicators of mortgage fraud.

You should remain alert to warning signs in the information and documentation which are in your possession. You should pay particular attention to transactions which exhibit a number of warning signs.

3.1 Identity and ownership

- The client or the property involved is located a long distance from your firm. If bulk long distance instructions are not in your normal work, you may ask why they chose your firm, especially if they are a new client.
- The client seems unusually uninterested in their purchase. You should look for other warning signs suggesting they are not the real purchaser.
- The seller is a private company or they have recently purchased the property from a private company. You should consider whether the office holders or shareholders of the private company are otherwise connected with the transaction you are undertaking, and whether this is an arms length commercial transaction.
- The client does not usually engage in property investment of this scale. You should ask why they are undertaking this new venture and where they are getting the financial backing from.
- The current owner has owned the property for under six months. You should ask them to explain why they are selling so quickly.
- The client's credit history is shorter than you would expect for their age, when you run an electronic identity check, which may include credit history information. Fraudsters will often run a fake identity for a few months to give it legitimacy. You should ask your client about this.
- There are plans for a sub-sale or back-to-back transactions. You should ask your client why they are structuring the transaction this way and seek information on the identities of the second purchaser, their solicitor and the lender.
- There is a last minute change of representative on the other side.
- The property has a history of being re-sold quickly or mortgages settled quickly.
- A transfer of title to land is requested with respect to only some of the seller's holdings and the properties are not grouped together.
- Finance is sought after the property has been registered in the buyer's name.

- The property has been registered to an owner for a significant period of time and the person claiming to be the owner does not appear to be of an age to have held the land for that length of time.
- The other conveyancer or solicitor allegedly involved in the transaction has an e-mail address from a large-scale web based provider.
- There is a County Court judgement against the property.
- The land is transferred following a court order, but the mortgage is sought some time later.

3.2   Value

- The property value has significantly increased in a short period of time out of line with the market in the area
- The mortgage is for the full property value. While this is less likely in tighter credit conditions, you should consider it in light of the other warning signs.
- The seller or developer have provided incentives, allowances or discounts. These may include cash back, free holidays, household fittings, payment of legal fees, help with mortgage repayments or rental guarantees, among others. You should consider whether this information has been properly disclosed to the lender.
- The deposit is being paid by someone other than the purchaser. You should ask why, where the money is coming from, and whether this information has been properly disclosed to the lender.
- The purchaser has paid the deposit directly to the seller or a developer. You should ask for evidence of the payment and consider whether this information has been properly disclosed to the lender.
- There is money left over from the mortgage after the purchase price has been paid, and you are asked to pay this money to the account of someone you do not know, or to the introducer. You should ask why, and remember that you must not use your client account as a mere banking facility. See note ix to Rule 15 of the Solicitors Accounts Rules 1998.
- You are asked to enter a price on the title that is greater than you know was paid for the property. You should ask why the prices are different. Read more about recording property value in the anti-money laundering practice note, Chapter 4.6.
- There has been a recent transfer of land where no money has changed hands or the price was significantly less than the full market value.

4. Protecting your firm

4.1 Ask questions

You should ask questions if you receive unusual instructions from your client, if any of the warning signs are present or there are inconsistencies in the retainer. You will better understand your instructions and be able to effectively assess the risk of the retainer to your firm.

Criminal methodologies change constantly, so you should remain alert to transactions that are unusual for a normal residential or commercial conveyance.

4.2 Identify and verify the client

You must find out and verify the identity of your client and where relevant, any beneficial owners. This is important whether you are acting for the purchaser or the seller. You are not expected to be experts in forged documents, but you should ensure the identities you have been given correspond with the information on the mortgage documents and the bank accounts relating to the transaction.

If you have concerns about a person's identity, you should consider checking whether the person is listed on a negative database, such as the register of deaths or a list of known fraudsters.

Where a private company is the seller, or the seller has purchased from a private company in the recent past, and you are concerned that the sale may not be an arms length transaction, you should conduct a search of the Companies Register. You should find out the names and addresses of the office holders and the shareholders, which can be cross referenced with the names of those connected with the transaction, the seller and the buyer.

You should consider the anti-money laundering practice note, the identity evidence for land registry practice note and the CML Handbook when deciding what information needs to be obtained to identify and verify the client and others.

4.2.1 Enhanced due diligence

Many mortgage fraudsters provide only paperwork and try to avoid meetings, particularly with the named purchasers. If you do not meet your client in a property transaction, you must undertake enhanced due diligence, as required under the Money Laundering Regulations 2007.

Read about enhanced due diligence in our anti-money laundering practice note, Chapter 4.9.

4.2.2 Reliance

Fraudsters will try to limit scrutiny of their identity and the transaction. They may ask you to use the reliance provisions under the Money Laundering Regulations 2007 to minimise the number of due diligence checks that you conduct.

You should consider reliance as a potential risk in itself. You remain liable for any breach of the regulations if the checks you rely on have not been conducted properly. To protect your firm, you should ask the following questions of the firm or individual you are being asked to rely on:

- Are they regulated for anti-money laundering purposes? Mortgage brokers are currently not regulated under the Money Laundering Regulations 2007.
- Have you done business with them previously?
- Are they from an established firm?
- What is their reputation? A general web search may reveal this.
- Are they able to provide you with the client due diligence material they have?

You should ask for copies of the due diligence conducted, so that you can cross reference documents within the retainer and satisfy yourself as to the identity of the purchaser and, where relevant, beneficial owners.

Read more about reliance in our anti-money laundering practice note, Chapter 4.3.4.

4.3 Identify other solicitors or conveyancers

Fraudsters may pose as a solicitor or a conveyancer acting for either party to add greater legitimacy to the transaction. If you do not know them, you should check the recognised directory of their professional body.

- Find a Solicitor [Law Society's online directory]
- Directory of Licensed Conveyancers

You can also check a solicitor's details with the SRA over the telephone. Their contact number is 0870 606 2555.

Some fraudsters will try to assume the identity of professionals who actually exist. You should check that both the details and the final destination of documents match the details in the directory. You may consider contacting the firm directly by the contact details on the registry if you have concerns about the bona fides of the representatives on the other side to the transaction, particularly if there is a last minute change of representative.

4.4   Consider all information on the retainer

4.4.1   Sources of information

The following information may be relevant in assessing the risk of a retainer, in monitoring of the retainer, and in resolving concerns when mortgage fraud risks appear:

- documents involved in the retainer
- comments by the client in interviews
- correspondence or telephone conversations
- comments by other parties to the transaction or their representatives
- previous retainers for the client

4.4.2   Does it all add up?

You should consider whether the property and mortgage are consistent with what you know about the financial position and sources of income available to the client.

Example

You may have prepared a will for a client and done conveyancing on the purchase of a modest family home. If, a few years later, they then instruct you in the purchase of a holiday home that appears to be beyond their means according to earlier retainers, this would warrant closer inspection of the mortgage application. You should ask questions of the client to verify this information.

You should check all mortgage and contractual documentation carefully. Seek explanations from the client for any discrepancies in the document. It may be a simple misunderstanding of the documents or an inadvertent error needing correction.

You should consider whether the identity you have been given is consistent with the actual presentation of the client and the transaction as a whole.

4.4.3   Ensure documents are fully completed

You may receive contract documents that are not fully completed. For example, dates may be missing, the identities of parties not fully described, or financial details not fully stated. You should ensure all relevant sections of documents are completed before your client signs them, to avoid incorrect or fraudulent information being added later.

4.5 Signatures

You must ensure that you and your staff only witness signatures where you have actually seen the person signing the document. If any contract or mortgage documents have been pre-signed, you must either:

- verify it was pre-signed in the presence of a witness
- have the documents re-signed in your presence

You should take note of all signatures on transaction documents and consider examining and comparing signatures with other available documentation if:

- you notice a discrepancy between signatures on the documentation
- you have concerns about the identity of any of the parties to the transaction
- the transaction is higher risk because it exhibits a number of the warning signs of mortgage fraud

4.6 Recording the property value

You should ascertain the true net cash price to be paid, to comply with the CML handbook and Land Registry requirements. You should consider any direct payments, allowances, incentives or discount in ascertaining this price.

You should state this amount as the consideration in all of the following documents:

- contract
- transfer documents
- mortgage instructions
- certificate on title to the lender
- Land Registry forms

You should seek to understand any discrepancy between the value recorded in any of these documents, or if you are asked to enter a different value.

If you discover discrepancies in the valuation of the property between any of the relevant documents, you should consider your obligations to disclose this information to the lender.

Part one of the CML Handbook says you must report such changes to the lender. However, individual lenders may vary this obligation, either by using part two of the handbook, or through the specific instructions they provide.

Also consider your obligation to the lender to disclose any direct payments between the buyer and seller either already made, or proposed, that are not included in the mortgage instructions.

4.7   Changes to the retainer

You should stay alert to any changes in the circumstances of the retainer that may affect the agreed basis of the mortgage provision. These may include changes to the purchase price or previously undisclosed allowances, incentives or discounts.

Such arrangements may mean that the purchase price is different to that in the lender's instructions. In general, lenders will reasonably expect to receive such information, as it may affect their decision to grant the mortgage, or the terms of granting the mortgage.

You should ask questions to understand any changes. You should consult the lenders instructions or the *CML Handbook* part two, to assess your obligations to disclose this information to the lender.

5.   Confidentiality and disclosure

5.1   Code of conduct obligations

5.1.1   *Rule 3.16*

You must not act for a buyer and a lender if a conflict of interest exists or arises between them. You have a conflict of interest if you have information about the conveyance that the lender would consider relevant to granting the loan, but the client does not want you to tell the lender.

5.1.2   *Rule 4.02*

You must disclose relevant information to the lender client. Any change to the purchase price, or information reasonably expected to be important to the decision to grant the mortgage, will be relevant to the lender.

However this obligation of disclosure to the lender client is overridden by your duty of confidentiality to the purchaser client in *Rule 4.01*. This duty of confidentiality can only be waived with the consent of the purchaser client, or if it is required or permitted by law.

While you should always seek clarification from your client if you discover any discrepancies in relevant information, you may wish to streamline the consent process. You may include a section in your standard terms and conditions for conveyancing clients, which provides that you will advise the lender client of any relevant information arising during the retainer. To rely on this approach for consent, you should:

- specifically bring this term to the client's attention at the outset of the retainer
- have them sign to signify acceptance of the terms and conditions

5.2 When can you tell the lender?

Where you believe a purchaser client has provided incorrect or incomplete information to a lender during the mortgage process, you must seek consent from them to provide the correct information to the lender. If your purchaser client refuses, you must refuse to continue to act for them and the lender.

You must still consider legal professional privilege and your duty of confidentiality before passing information to the lender, even after you have ceased to act for a client.

You are only released from your duty of confidentiality where you are satisfied of a strong prima facie case that the client, or third party, was using you to further a fraud or other criminal purpose. This test may be satisfied if a client has made deliberate misrepresentations on their mortgage application.

If you are not released from the duty of confidentiality, you should simply return the mortgage documents to the lender and advise that you are ceasing to act due to professional reasons, without providing any further information.

For further advice on whether you need to cease to act in a matter and whether you can provide information to the lender, contact the SRA's Professional Ethics Helpline, or seek independent legal advice.

5.3 When can you tell law enforcement?

You must consider the money laundering risk if you discover or suspect that a mortgage has been obtained fraudulently, and the funds have been received by the client, either into their account, or your client account.

You must consider making a disclosure to the Serious Organised Crime Agency. You must also consider your duty of confidentiality and legal professional privilege before you do so.

Importantly, making a disclosure to SOCA is merely a defence to money laundering offences. It is not a crime report. You may also make a report to your local police if you feel an investigation is warranted.

For further information on money laundering offences and making disclosures to SOCA, see the anti-money laundering practice note.

For further information on whether legal professional privilege prevents you from making a disclosure to either SOCA or the lender you may take legal advice. You can find a list of solicitors offering such advice in the Law Society's AML directory.

For further advice on whether you need to cease to act in a matter, contact the SRA's *Professional Ethics Helpline*.

5.4 Alerting your insurer

Banks are increasingly trying to recover mortgage fraud losses from professionals involved in conveyancing. If you suspect mortgage fraud has occurred, you should consider your obligations to your professional indemnity insurer. For further information on possible civil liability see the anti-money laundering practice note, Chapter 10.

5.5 Tipping off

You may be concerned about tipping off offences under the Proceeds of Crime Act 2002, in talking to the lender, insurer, or your purchaser client.

A key element of these offences is the likelihood of prejudicing an investigation. The risk of this is small when disclosing to a reputable lender or your insurer. They are also regulated for the purposes of anti-money laundering and subject to the same obligations. There is also a specific defence of making a disclosure for the purposes of preventing a money laundering offence.

In relation to asking further questions of your client and discussing the implications of the Proceeds of Crime Act 2002, there is a specific defence for tipping off for legal advisors who are seeking to dissuade their client from engaging in a money laundering offence.

For further advice on tipping off, see anti-money laundering practice note, Chapter 5.8.

For further information about avoiding tipping off in a particular case, contact SOCA's Financial Intelligence Helpdesk on 020 7238 8282.

Annex 2D

Mortgage possession claims practice note

13 February 2009

1. Introduction

1.1 Who should read this practice note?

All solicitors who act for lenders and borrowers in mortgage possession claims brought in relation to residential property.

1.2 What is the issue?

This practice note provides advice to solicitors who are asked to advise borrowers whose mortgages are in arrears and are facing mortgage possession proceedings and the loss of their homes.

The Pre-action Protocol for Possession Claims Based on Mortgage Arrears in Respect of Residential Properties came into force on 19 November 2008 [**www.justice.gov.uk/civil/procrules_fin/contents/ protocols/prot_mha.htm**]. The protocol aims to make proceedings for residential possession claims a last resort.

Two major issues arise for solicitors from the introduction of the protocol:

- It does not apply to all the ways lenders seek to realise their security, so it does not protect all borrowers whose mortgage accounts are in arrears.
- Borrowers may not be aware of the relevant Court of Appeal decisions concerning what is a reasonable period for borrowers to pay mortgage arrears. This leaves many borrowers unnecessarily vulnerable to losing their homes.

This practice note gives advice on:

- what to look for if advising a borrower whose lender has started to seek payment of mortgage arrears, to satisfy yourself that the lender is complying with the protocol;
- how to advise a borrower whose lender has appointed a receiver.

Major lenders agreed with the government on 24 November 2008 that they would not start mortgage possession proceedings in relation to residential property unless the borrower had accrued three months' arrears. This should give parties sufficient time to comply with the protocol and should give borrowers an opportunity to seek advice before mortgage possession proceedings have been issued.

2.   The protocol

2.1   Aims of the protocol

Paragraph 2 of the protocol describes its aims as to encourage:

- lenders and borrowers to act fairly and reasonably with each other and resolve disputes over any matter concerning mortgage or home purchase plan arrears;
- more pre-action contact between lenders and borrowers to seek agreement so that if court proceedings become necessary, the court's time and resources may be used efficiently.

Paragraph 2.2 of the protocol states that where it requires the borrower or lender to communicate and provide information to the other, that party should take reasonable steps to do so in a way that is clear, fair and not misleading. This aims to ensure that the communications between the lender and the borrower are meaningful.

The lender will bear the principal burden to provide information, since the greater obligations to provide information are imposed on them. Also, if the lender is aware that the borrower may have difficulties in reading or understanding the information provided, the lender should take reasonable steps to communicate that information in a way that the borrower can understand.

2.2   Status of the protocol

The protocol does not alter the substantive law, and it does not alter the parties' rights or obligations. It describes the behaviour the court will normally expect of the parties before the start of a mortgage possession claim.

The court may take into account whether a party to proceedings has complied with a protocol when it gives directions for the management of the case and when it makes orders for costs.

The court may impose a sanction on a party that fails to comply with a protocol where that failure either:

- caused proceedings to be commenced which would otherwise have been unnecessary;
- led to costs being incurred in proceedings which might not otherwise have been incurred.

If a party does not comply with the protocol but there are no court proceedings, no sanction will arise.

Paragraph 9.1 of the protocol states that lenders and borrowers should be able to explain the actions they took to comply with the protocol, if requested by the court.

2.3   Scope of the protocol

The protocol does not apply to mortgage possession claims issued before 19 November 2008.

The protocol applies to arrears which arise on:

- first charge residential mortgages and home purchase plans regulated by the Financial Services Authority [**www.fsa.gov.uk**] under the Financial Services and Markets Act 2000;
- second charge mortgages over residential property and other secured loans regulated under the Consumer Credit Act 1974 on residential property;
- unregulated residential mortgages.

Paragraph 4.1(2) of the protocol defines a home purchase plan as a method of purchasing a property by way of a sale and lease arrangement that does not require the payment of interest.

The protocol only governs the behaviour of parties where the lender is enforcing its rights through possession proceedings. Lenders may use other means to enforce their security, such as appointing a receiver or exercising their contractual power of sale.

Where a potential claim includes a money claim and a claim for possession, the protocol applies to both.

3.   Requirements of the protocol

3.1   Information lenders must give borrowers

Paragraph 5 of the protocol obliges the lender to provide the borrower with the following information when the mortgage falls into arrears:

- the total amount of arrears the borrower owes;
- the total outstanding amount owed under the mortgage;
- whether interest or charges will be added;
- where appropriate, the required regulatory information sheet or the National Homelessness Advice Service booklet on mortgage arrears.

It would also be sensible for lenders to give borrowers a copy of the protocol when they supply this information, since the protocol sets out how the court will expect borrowers to behave once they have received this information. However, the protocol does not require lenders to do so.

3.2   Discussion between lenders and borrowers

After the lender has supplied the borrower with this information, the lender and the borrower should take reasonable steps to discuss with each other, or their representatives, the following matters:

- the cause of the borrower's arrears;
- the borrower's financial circumstances;
- the borrower's proposals for repayment of the arrears.

Paragraph 5.2 of the protocol states that these discussions will include consideration of whether:

- the causes of the arrears are temporary or long term;
- the borrower may be able to pay the arrears in a reasonable time.

Paragraph 7.1 of the protocol states that any discussion between the lender and the borrower may include options such as:

- extending the term of the mortgage;
- changing the type of a mortgage;
- deferring payment of interest due under the mortgage;
- capitalising the arrears.

The purpose of these discussions is to avoid court proceedings by the lender reaching an agreement with the borrower over paying the mortgage arrears.

To make these discussions meaningful, the borrower should communicate to the lender their financial circumstances and proposals for repayment of the arrears.

If intending to sell the property, the borrower should:

- demonstrate they are taking steps to market the property;
- provide the lender with:

    - a copy of the particulars of sale;
    - the home information pack;
    - any details of purchase offers;
    - details of the estate agent and conveyancer instructed to deal with the sale.

Paragraph 5.6 of the protocol states that if the lender submits a proposal for payment, the borrower should be given a reasonable period of time in which to consider such proposals. The lender should set out the proposal in sufficient detail to enable the borrower to understand the implications of the proposal.

Paragraph 5.5 of the protocol states that if the borrower submits a proposal for payment, the lender should respond promptly to it. If the lender does not agree to the proposal it should give reasons in writing to the borrower within 10 business days of the proposal.

3.2.1   Lenders considering borrowers' offers to pay the arrears

The protocol does not state what is a reasonable period for payment of mortgage arrears. Some lenders might not view as reasonable a request by a borrower to spread the payment of arrears over a long period of time, as lenders generally require borrowers to pay their arrears over a short period.

Although it is in the borrower's interests to discharge the mortgage arrears as soon as possible to minimise the amount of interest the lender can charge on the arrears, the borrower will want to offer a repayment plan which they can afford to comply with, and should not be pressurised by the lender into agreeing an unaffordable repayment plan.

To determine whether a borrower's offer to pay arrears is reasonable and would be acceptable to the court, you should refer to the guidance set out in:

- *Cheltenham and Gloucester Building Society* v *Norgan* [1996] 1 All ER 449 for mortgages not regulated by the Consumer Credit Act 1974;

- *Southern and District Finance* v *Barnes* (1995) 27 HLR 691 for mortgages regulated by that Act.

In *Cheltenham and Gloucester Building Society* v *Norgan*, the court held that the starting point for assessing what was a reasonable period in which the borrower should pay the mortgage arrears was the remainder of the term of the mortgage. In *Southern and District Finance* v *Barnes*, the court held that the total indebtedness secured by the charge on the property could be subject to an order to allow more time to pay a loan agreement.

3.2.2   Requests for change in payments

Paragraph 5.4 of the protocol states that the lender should consider a reasonable request from a borrower to change the date of regular payment or the method by which the payment is made. If the lender refuses such a request, it should give the borrower a written explanation of its reasons for the refusal within a reasonable period of time.

3.3   Referral to other agencies

Paragraph 5.3 of the protocol states that lenders should advise borrowers to contact their local authority's housing department and, where necessary, refer borrowers to agencies that provide debt advice.

4.   When can the lender start a possession claim?

Paragraph 5.7 of the protocol states what a lender should do if the borrower fails to comply with an agreement. The lender should warn the borrower by giving them 15 business days' notice in writing of its intention to start a possession claim unless the borrower remedies the breach.

A lender can start a possession claim if it has not been possible to reach an agreement with the borrower about the payment of mortgage arrears. However, paragraph 7.1 of the protocol states that the lender should not normally start a possession claim while the parties are still discussing ways of addressing the arrears.

4.1   Postponing the start of a possession claim

Lenders should consider not starting a possession claim in certain circumstances including:

- where a borrower can demonstrate to a lender that they have submitted a claim to an insurer under a mortgage payment protection policy and:

- has provided all the evidence required to process a claim;
- has a reasonable prospect of eligibility of payment from the insurer;
- is able to pay a mortgage instalment which is not covered by the insurance;

- where a borrower can demonstrate that they have taken reasonable steps to market the property at an appropriate price in accordance with reasonable professional advice.

If the lender agrees to postpone taking possession proceedings because the borrower is marketing the property, the borrower:

- must continue to take all reasonable steps to actively market the property;
- should provide the lender with:

  - a copy of the particulars of sale;
  - the Home Information Pack;
  - where relevant, details of purchase offers received within a reasonable period of time specified by the lender;
  - details of the estate agent and the conveyancer instructed to deal with the sale;

- should authorise the estate agent and the conveyancer to communicate with the lender about the progress of the sale and the borrower's conduct during the process.

Paragraph 6.4 of the protocol states that where the lender decides not to postpone the start of a possession claim it should inform the borrower of the reasons for this decision at least 5 business days before starting proceedings.

5. Enforcement of the protocol

The Civil Procedure Rules (CPR) enable the court to take into account a party's compliance or non-compliance with a pre-action protocol when:

- giving directions for the management of proceedings – see CPR 3.1(4) and (5) and 3.9(e);
- making orders for costs, when it will have regard to the conduct of the parties – see CPR 44.3(4)(a).

CPR 44.3(5)(a) states that such conduct includes conduct before as well as during the proceedings.

The court will expect all parties to be able to explain the actions that they have taken to comply if requested to do so. See CPR Practice Direction – Protocols paragraph 2.2. The court will look at the effect of non-compliance on the other party when deciding to impose sanctions. This has implications for both the lender and the borrower.

5.1   Possible consequences of non-compliance

If proceedings are commenced and the court finds that a party has not complied with the protocol, the court may order both that:

- the party pays the full amount or part of the costs of the proceedings of the other party or parties;
- the party pays those costs on an indemnity basis.

See CPR Practice Direction paragraph 2.3.

The court can vary the level of interest payable on specified sums, depending on the compliance of either the borrower or the lender.

If the borrower is found to have not complied with the protocol and an order is made for the payment to the lender of a specified sum, such as the mortgage arrears, the court may award the lender interest on that sum for a period specified by the court at a higher rate than that which would otherwise have been awarded. This will not be more than 10 per cent above the base rate – PD Protocols paragraph 2.3(4).

If the lender is found to have not complied with the protocol and an order is made for the payment to it of a specified sum, such as mortgage arrears, the court may make an order depriving the lender of interest on such sum and for such a period as the court may specify and/or awarding the lender interest at a lower rate than that at which interest would otherwise have been awarded (PD Protocols paragraph 2.3(3)).

5.2   Costs

Lenders do not normally seek an order for costs against borrowers in mortgage possession claims. This is because most mortgage deeds contain a clause stating that the borrower will indemnify the lender against all costs incurred in enforcing the security. It is advantageous for lenders to rely on this contractual provision because courts usually award costs on the standard basis, either by adding them to the security or making no order for costs. The standard provision that there should be a summary assessment of costs after a hearing lasting less than a day does not apply to mortgage possession cases, according to PD Protocol 44, paragraph 13.3.

Contractual liability to pay the lender's costs affects borrowers in two ways:

1.   They are liable even if they successfully defend mortgage possession proceedings.

2.   They are liable even if the lender unreasonably incurs costs. For example, if the parties negotiate before proceedings are begun and the lender refuses to allow the borrower the remaining period of the mortgage to pay the arrears claimed when full disclosure of the borrower's finances has been made and the lender's security is amply safeguarded, thus satisfying the test in *Cheltenham and Gloucester Building Society* v *Norgan.*

5.2.1   Court assessment

A court may disallow all or part of the costs payable under a contract such as a mortgage if it is satisfied that those costs were unreasonably incurred or are unreasonable in amount. This is stated in PD 48 paragraph 50.1. However, the presumption is that such costs will be allowed, and court orders should normally reflect the contractual right to costs under PD 48 paragraph 50.3(2).

The court's discretion when considering costs arises from PD 48 paragraph 50.3(1). CPR 44.5 states that in deciding the amount of costs, the courts must consider the parties' conduct and the skill, effort, specialised knowledge and responsibility involved.

If the lender has not complied with the protocol or unreasonably refused a borrower's offer, you should ask the court to order that:

*   the lender pays the borrower's costs; and
*   the lender be forbidden from adding the costs it has incurred in the proceedings, including its liability to pay the borrower's costs, to the security.

5.2.2   Knowing the lender's costs and disputing them

Neither the borrower nor the court usually knows the amount of costs a lender has incurred and will be added to the security, because the normal summary assessment of costs does not take place after a mortgage possession hearing.

The borrower can apply to the court for a direction that an account of the lender's costs be taken, if the mortgage deed either:

*   allows the lender to add the costs of the litigation to the sum secured by the mortgage;

- requires the borrower to pay those costs.

The borrower may then challenge items incurred by the lender under PD 48 paragraph 50.4 on the basis that they have been unreasonably incurred or are unreasonable in amount. The court may then order that the disputed costs are assessed under CPR 48.3.

6.   Contractual right to enforce security

Instead of seeking a court order for possession, a lender may exercise a contractual right to enforce its security by selling the property. This may appeal to lenders because the mortgage arrears protocol will not apply and the borrower will forfeit their equity of redemption.

The lender would formally demand payment of the sum due under the mortgage. If the borrower fails to comply, the lender can appoint receivers and/or sell the property as an alternative to seeking a court order for possession. For more information, see *Ropaigealach* v *Barclays Bank* [1999] 4 All ER 235.

The court has no discretion under the Administration of Justice Acts 1970 and 1973 to protect the borrower in a possession claim that has been brought by the new owner of the property. In *Horsham Properties Group* v *Clark and Beech* [2008] EWHC 2327 (Ch), the lender enforced its security by exercising its contractual right to appoint a receiver who sold the property using the lender's contractual right to sell. In these circumstances, a borrower will lose their equity of redemption and if they remain in occupation will become a trespasser.

You should note that there is a clause in almost every mortgage allowing lenders to demand that a mortgage is repaid at short notice. However the Council of Mortgage Lenders states that this is only meant to cover exceptional circumstances. It is unclear whether exceptional circumstances may include the financial circumstances of the lender in a recession, regardless of whether the borrower is in arrears or not.

7.   Use of Part 36 offers

When acting for a borrower you may use the procedure set out in CPR Part 36 to persuade lenders to agree payment terms without obtaining a court order.

Under CPR 36.3(2), a Part 36 offer can be made at any time, including before the commencement of proceedings. CPR 44.3(4)(c) states that a court must have regard to all the circumstances, including a borrower's offer to settle, whether or not that offer complies with Part 36, when deciding what costs order to make.

The advantages of making a Part 36 offer are as follows:

- If the lender accepts the offer before proceedings are started, there will be no court action unless the borrower fails to comply with the agreement.
- If the lender accepts the offer after proceedings have begun, the claim for possession will be stayed and there will be no order for possession unless the stay is lifted because the borrower has failed to comply with the agreement.
- If the lender refuses the offer, and fails to obtain a more advantageous judgment, the court will order that the borrower is entitled to their costs unless it is unjust to do so. It will order costs with interest from the date on which the relevant period expired. See CPR 36.14(2).

If the lender accepts the Part 36 offer within the relevant period, they will be entitled to the costs of enforcing the mortgage, but they are entitled to this as a matter of contract anyway.

8.   The Mortgage Rescue Scheme

The Mortgage Rescue Scheme was introduced on 16 January 2009 to help home owners in financial difficulty and at risk of repossession and threatened with homelessness. The scheme enables social landlords to acquire the homes of eligible people, and rent them back to them. The scheme will run for two years in England, and a similar scheme has been in place in Wales since June of 2008.

Households at risk should be referred to their local housing authority. The authority will assess their eligibility for the scheme in the same way as for homelessness assistance, using the criteria for homelessness set out in the Housing Act 1996 and Priority Needs Order 2001. These stipulate that the household must include at least one person in priority need, as follows:

- a pregnant woman or a person with whom she resides or might reasonably be expected to reside;
- a person with whom dependent children reside or might reasonably be expected to reside;
- a person who is vulnerable as a result of old age, mental illness or a handicap or physical disability or other special reason, or with whom such a person resides or might reasonably be expected to reside.

Further criteria for the scheme include:

- The owners of the property agree to be considered for the scheme.

- There must be sufficient equity in the scheme to cover priority debts.
- Living in the property must be sustainable after mortgage rescue.
- The household must demonstrate a clear need to stay in the area.
- The property must be suitable for the needs of the household, e.g. not overcrowded.
- The household income must be less than £60,000 per annum.
- Applicants must not have a second home, including abroad.
- Owners must have sought debt counselling and advice, agreed to debt rescheduling and discussed alternative options with mortgage lenders before admission to the scheme.
- Caps will be set on the value of the property, at regional level, and on the household's income level.

The scheme also assists those with second charges on their homes.

Once a household's eligibility is determined by the local authority the lender will be alerted and money advisors engaged. The money advisor will assess the household's realistic affordable housing costs and draw up a debt management plan or other financial solution.

Following this, a registered social landlord (RSL) will be engaged. They will assess the property to ensure it is structurally sound. The RSL will then decide the suitability of either:

- a shared equity option, where the mortgage is reduced to a sustainable level;
- a mortgage to rent scheme where the debt is cleared entirely.

9. Changes to income support rules

Additional assistance is now available to those out of work, following temporary amendments to the rules for claiming assistance with mortgage payments through income support.

The Social Security (Housing Costs Special Arrangements) (Amendment and Modification) Regulations 2008 amend and modify the:

- Employment and Support Allowance Regulations 2008;
- Income Support Regulations;
- Jobseeker's Allowance Regulations.

The following changes were introduced:

- reduction of the waiting period before mortgage interest can be paid from 39, to 13 weeks;
- reduction of the waiting period before mortgage interest can be paid from 26 to 13 weeks if:

- the mortgage was taken out before 2 October 1995;
- the claimant is a carer, or has a child and claims income support;
- the claimant is in custody pending trial or sentence;
- the claimant has been refused payment under a mortgage protection policy either because the claimant has AIDS or has a medical condition which existed at the time the policy was taken out;

- increasing the capital limit up to which mortgage interest can be paid to £200,000;
- introducing a two-year limit on payment of mortgage interest for Job Seeker's Allowance only;
- modifying the State Pension Credit Regulations so that in some cases the increased capital limit can apply to pensioners;
- changing the standard interest rate payable for claims to 6.08 per cent.

These changes are temporary and will be reviewed when housing market conditions are more favourable.

10.   Regulation of the mortgage industry

The Financial Services Authority (FSA) is the statutory regulator of the mortgage industry. The FSA's Handbook contains the Mortgages: Conduct of Business (MCOB) rules which govern the way that residential mortgages are sold and administered in the UK. The MCOB replaced the Mortgage Code on 31 October 2004.

10.1   Dealing with customers in arrears

Section 13.5 of the MCOB outlines the way in which mortgage lenders should deal with a customer in arrears. Where a borrower is in arrears, the lender must provide the borrower with a regular written statement at least once a quarter, containing:

- the payments due;
- the actual payment shortfall;
- the charges incurred;
- the debt.

Lenders must not put pressure on a borrower in arrears through excessive telephone calls or correspondence, or by contact at an unreasonable hour. Putting pressure on a borrower includes sending them letters that resemble a court summons or other official document.

10.2 The Mortgage Code – mortgages sold before 31 October 2004

The Mortgage Code applies to mortgages sold prior to 31 October 2004. It states that lenders should co-operate and develop a plan with borrowers to deal with financial difficulties and that possession of a property will only be sought as a last resort.

10.3 The Financial Ombudsman Service

The Financial Ombudsman Service deals with consumer complaints relating to the sale of mortgages under the provisions set out in MCOB. It also deals with consumer complaints relating to mortgages sold prior to the introduction of MCOB, under the Mortgage Code.

11. More information

11.1 Professional conduct

The following sections of the Solicitors' Code of Conduct 2007 are relevant to this issue:

- Rule 1 Core duties
- Rule 2 Client relations

11.2 Legal and other requirements

- Administration of Justice Acts 1970 and 1973
- Financial Services and Markets Act 2000
- Consumer Credit Act 1974
- Civil Procedure Rules 1998 Parts 35 and 55 and PD 55

11.3 Status of this practice note

Practice notes are issued by the Law Society for the use and benefit of its members. They represent the Law Society's view of good practice in a particular area. They are not intended to be the only standard of good practice that solicitors can follow. You are not required to follow them, but doing so will make it easier to account to oversight bodies for your actions.

Practice notes are not legal advice, nor do they necessarily provide a defence to complaints of misconduct or of inadequate professional service. While care has been taken to ensure that they are accurate, up to date and useful, the Law Society will not accept any legal liability in relation to them.

For queries or comments on this practice note contact the Law Society's Practice Advice Service.

11.4 Terminology in this practice note

Must – a specific requirement in the Solicitors' Code of Conduct or legislation. You must comply, unless there are specific exemptions or defences provided for in the code of conduct or relevant legislation.

Should – good practice for most situations in the Law Society's view. If you do not follow this, you must be able to justify to oversight bodies why this is appropriate, either for your practice, or in the particular retainer. Courts will take into account compliance or non-compliance with a protocol when giving directions for the management of the case and making costs orders.

May – a non-exhaustive list of options for meeting your obligations. Which option you choose is determined by the risk profile of the individual practice, client or retainer. You must be able to justify why this was an appropriate option to oversight bodies.

You – a solicitor.

11.5 Further products and support

11.5.1 Practice Advice Service

The Law Society provides support for solicitors on a wide range of areas of practice. The Practice Advice Service can be contacted on 0870 606 2522 from 9am to 5pm on weekdays.

www.lawsociety.org.uk/practiceadvice

11.5.2 Publications

Burn, S. (Ed.) (2007) *Civil Litigation Handbook*, 2nd edition, Law Society Publishing, London

Madge, N., McConnell, D., Gallagher, J. & Luba, J. (2006) *Defending Possession Proceedings*, 6th edition, LAG Books, London

Sime, S. & French, D. (2008) *Blackstone's Civil Practice 2009*, 2009 edition, Oxford University Press

www.lawsociety.org.uk/bookshop

Costs and fees

How much should I charge for swearing an oath and is this charge mandatory?

Section 2 of The Commissioners for Oaths (Fees) Order 1993 states that the following fees 'shall' be charged: £5.00 for taking an affidavit, declaration or affirmation, for each person making the same and, in addition, £2.00 for each exhibit or schedule referred to. Please see Anderson and Warner (2008) *Execution of Documents*, 2nd Edition, Law Society Publishing.

Where can I find the specimen information for entitled persons under the Solicitors' (Non-Contentious Business) Remuneration Order 1994?

This is set out in Appendix 1 of the Practice Advice Service booklet *Non-contentious Costs* (November 2008) which is reproduced at **Annex 3C**. The specimen information for the entitled person is not part of the Order and solicitors may use any form of words which comply with the Solicitors' (Non-Contentious Business) Remuneration Order 1994. Please see below:

Remuneration certificate

(1) If you are not satisfied with the amount of our fee you have the right to ask us to obtain a remuneration certificate from the Law Society.

(2) The certificate will either say that our fee is fair and reasonable, or it will substitute a lower fee.

(3) If you wish us to obtain a certificate you must ask us to do so within a month of receiving this notice.

(4) We may charge interest on unpaid bills and we will do so at [the rate payable on judgement debts, from one month after delivery of our bill].

(5) (i) If you ask us to obtain a remuneration certificate, then unless we already hold the money to cover these, you must first pay:

– half our fee shown in the bill;

– all the VAT shown in the bill;

> – all the expenses we have incurred shown in the bill – sometimes called 'paid disbursements'

> (ii) However, you may ask the Legal Complaints Service at 8 Dormer Place, Leamington Spa, Warwickshire CV32 5AE to waive this requirement so that you do not have to pay anything for the time being. You would have to show that exceptional circumstances apply in your case.

> (6) Your rights are set out more fully in the Solicitors' (Non Contentious Business) Remuneration Order 1994.

Assessment

You may be entitled to have our charges reviewed by the Court. This is called 'assessment'. The procedure is different from the remuneration certificate procedure and is set out in ss.70, 71 and 72 of the Solicitors Act 1974.

For further information, see the Practice Advice Service *Non-Contentious Costs* booklet (**Annex 3C**).

My client has requested a remuneration certificate, and the bill has been paid in full by way of deduction from monies received on account. Is he still entitled to a certificate?

Yes. If a solicitor deducts his costs from monies held on account and the client objects in writing to the amount of those costs within the 'prescribed time' (three months or lesser time specified by the solicitor which cannot be less than one month) the solicitor must immediately inform the client in writing of his right to obtain a remuneration certificate or to apply for assessment. The client then has one month in which to ask the solicitor to apply for a remuneration certificate. If a solicitor wishes to speed up the process, he should send the necessary information to the client with the bill. The client then has one month from that time to ask the solicitor to apply for a certificate. See the Solicitors' (Non-Contentious Business) Remuneration Order 1994.

My firm are acting for a client in relation to a conveyancing matter. We issued our final bill over two months ago which still remains unpaid. My firm now wishes to take steps to recover the outstanding fees. There was no agreement with regard to charging interest in our retainer letter. Are we still entitled to charge interest and if so at what rate?

Article 14 of the Solicitors' (Non-Contentious Business) Remuneration Order 1994 deals with interest payable on unpaid costs in non-contentious matters and entitles solicitors to charge interest from one month from the delivery of the bill of costs provided that the prescribed information under Article 8 of the aforementioned order has been given to the client. The prescribed information details notification by the solicitor to the client of their right to obtain a remuneration certificate, waiver of payment of a sum towards the costs, the right in relation to assessment and the solicitor's right to charge interest on an unpaid bill.

As you did not agree the rate of interest with the client the rate will be 8 per cent per annum. This has been the interest rate on judgment debts since 1 April 1993.

My client has requested a remuneration certificate and is refusing to pay any of my firm's costs. Is it correct that no payment is required until the remuneration certificate procedure has been completed?

No. Article 11 of the Solicitors' (Non-Contentious Business) Remuneration Order 1994 provides that the client must pay one half of the costs together with all the VAT and all the paid disbursements before the solicitor is required to make the application for a remuneration certificate, unless either the solicitor or the Legal Complaints Service waives the requirement. The solicitor is not obliged to make the application if the client does not pay the required amount and has not applied for a waiver.

I am acting as executor in the administration of an estate where the only residuary beneficiary is a charity. The charity is unhappy with my firm's costs and has requested a remuneration certificate. I have provided the charity with a client care letter and information on costs, even though they are strictly speaking not my 'clients'. Am I obliged to comply with their request? My final bill of costs is less than £50,000.

Yes. As the charity is an entitled third party, Article 2 of the Solicitors' (Non-Contentious Business) Remuneration Order 1994 permits a residuary beneficiary absolutely and immediately (not contingently) entitled to an inheritance to request a remuneration certificate where the only personal representatives are:

- solicitors (whether or not acting in a professional capacity); or
- solicitors acting jointly with partners or employees in a professional capacity.

I am acting for the tenant in a transaction in which my client is required to pay the costs of the landlord's solicitor. I have just received details of these costs, which are excessive. What can I do?

The tenant is not entitled to ask the landlord's solicitors to obtain a remuneration certificate because he is not their client. However, the tenant can ask the landlord to request a remuneration certificate from his solicitors, although there is no obligation on him to do so. As a matter of practice the Law Society will accept an application for a remuneration certificate in such circumstances, but only if the landlord consents. In appropriate cases, the Council would hope that landlords' solicitors will encourage their clients to give such consent.

If the landlord is unwilling to give such consent, the tenant is entitled to apply to the High Court for assessment of the bill under s.71 of the Solicitors Act 1974.

Please note the Leasehold Valuation Tribunal can determine costs payable by tenants and landlords in a variety of cases.

My client has requested a remuneration certificate. The basis of our retainer is a section 57 non-contentious business agreement. Do I need to comply with the request?

No, the client should be advised at the outset that the provisions of the Solicitors' (Non-Contentious Business) Remuneration Order 1994 do not apply to a s.57 agreement (see *Walton* v. *Egan* [1982] 3 ALL ER 849). Therefore the client is unable to obtain a remuneration certificate. Please see the Practice Advice Service booklet *Non-contentious Costs* (**Annex 3C**).

When can I start charging interest on unpaid costs?

If the matter is non-contentious, Article 14 of the Solicitors' (Non-Contentious Business) Remuneration Order 1994 entitles the solicitor to charge interest from one month after delivery of the bill of costs, provided that the prescribed information under Article 8 has been given to the client, namely, written notice of the right to request a remuneration certificate and of the right to seek assessment of the bill by the court.

If the matter is contentious, there is no statutory authority for a solicitor to charge interest on outstanding contentious costs. However, interest may be charged in the following circumstances:

- if the right to charge interest has been expressly reserved in the original retainer agreement, or
- if the client later agrees for a contractual consideration to pay interest, or

- where the solicitor has sued the client and claimed interest under s.35A of the Supreme Court Act 1981 or s.69 of the County Courts Act 1984.

What is the difference between an interim bill and an interim statute bill?

Interim bills are simply requests for payments on account of a final bill to be delivered at a later date. It is not possible to sue on this type of bill and a client cannot apply for assessment of it.

However, interim bills should be distinguished from interim statute bills. The latter comply with all the requirements of the Solicitors Act 1974 and result in all the consequences which flow from such compliance. The solicitor can sue on them and the client can apply for assessment of them. They are final bills in respect of the work covered and cannot be adjusted at a later date.

Interim statute bills are not widely used and can arise in two ways. Firstly, a natural break, however the Law Society's advice is not to rely on this ground except in the clearest circumstances. See *Chamberlain* v. *Boodle and King* [1982] 3 All ER 188, CA for further guidance. Secondly, by agreement with the client. Practitioners should however make it absolutely clear in their retainer letter that they propose to deliver interim statute bills in the event of protracted work.

For further information see Practice Advice Service booklet *Contentious Costs* (**Annex 3B**).

Is licensing work regarded as non-contentious business or contentious business?

Where licensing work is administered by the Local Authority then it is regarded as non-contentious business. However, if an appeal is made to the magistrates court then this will be regarded as contentious work.

For further information please see Hayden and Hanney (2005) *Licensing for Conveyancers: A Practical Guide*, Law Society Publishing.

For further guidance see the Practice Advice Service booklets, *Payment by Results*, *Contentious Costs* and *Non-contentious Costs*.

Can a bill of costs include unpaid disbursements?

Yes, but only if the unpaid disbursements are described in the bill as not yet paid. The deficiency can lead to difficulties with these items if they are challenged on a later assessment. One solution in such an instance would be to ask the costs judge for an adjournment, apply to the court for leave to withdraw the entire bill and redeliver it (but there is a risk that you may be ordered to pay all the costs thrown away) and deliver a fresh bill (Solicitors Act 1974, s.67). It should be noted that in *Tearle & Co* v. *Sherring* (29 Oct 1993, unreported, QBD), Wright J. held that where a solicitor has acted in good faith but has inadvertently omitted to describe the disbursements as unpaid, the court not only had the power to give him leave to withdraw his bill and deliver another one, to save costs it could in an appropriate case give leave to amend his bill by adding the words 'unpaid'. However, you should err on the side of caution and describe unpaid disbursements as 'unpaid' in the bill.

A former client has made an application for an assessment of our firm's costs under section 70 of the Solicitors' Act 1974. How are the costs of the assessment hearing dealt with?

The costs of the assessment hearing usually follow the event. Section 70(9) of the Solicitors' Act 1974 states if your bill is reduced by one fifth or more, then you will bear the costs of the hearing. If the bill is reduced by less than one fifth or is not reduced, the former client will pay the costs.

I have issued a gross sum bill to my client. He has now requested a further detailed breakdown. Must I supply this?

In contentious matters, where a solicitor has issued a gross sum bill, the client may request a detailed breakdown of costs in lieu of the original bill within 3 months of receiving the bill. This does not apply if the solicitor has issued proceedings for payment of the bill or if the costs are subject to a Contentious Business Agreement (see Solicitors Act 1974, s.64(2)).

However, you might wish to explain to your client that his request has the dramatic effect of cancelling the original gross sum bill. If, when going through your file, you consider you did not include all of your costs in the original bill, you are free to draw up a bill for the higher amount.

The position differs in non-contentious matters as the client has the right to ask for a remuneration certificate (see Article 4 of the Solicitors' (Non-Contentious Business) Remuneration Order 1994) if he is unhappy with the amount charged. In this case, the solicitor is not obliged to provide a further detailed breakdown after providing a gross sum bill. If the client wishes to receive a further breakdown, the solicitor can make a charge for the further work involved as long as the client is informed in advance of this additional cost.

My client has asked for my bill to be assessed. What do I have to do?

You should advise him to make his own application. Although you may issue an application to have your own costs assessed it is inadvisable unless there are very unusual circumstances. Unless the client attends the assessment hearing, or the costs judge certifies that there are special circumstances the court will not make an order for the costs of the assessment proceedings (Solicitors Act 1974, s.70(9)(a) and (b)). Also the order made at the hearing will not include an order for payment of the assessed costs by the client, so that if the client does not pay the bill after the assessment you will have to commence separate proceedings for payment.

My costs are about to be assessed. Is there any information available on the hourly rates allowed on assessment in my local county court?

The Courts Service provides details of guideline hourly charging rates. At the time of writing the most recent were published in January 2009 and are available on the Courts Service website **www.hmcourts-service.gov. uk/publications/guidance/scco** at guideline rates. There is a model solicitor–client costs breakdown in the schedule of costs precedents attached to the Civil Procedure Rules. This is the recommended format if the matter goes to assessment.

I am a solicitor and would prefer to conduct my own personal injury case in the county court and not instruct my firm to act for me. Would I be able to recover any of my costs in doing so?

Yes, a solicitor who is acting for himself is regarded as a litigant in person (see CPR 48.6(6)). The rule provides that a litigant in person may be awarded up to two thirds of the costs and all the disbursements which would have been allowed if the litigant in person had been represented by a legal representative. In quantifying the costs for time spent on the litigation, the litigant in person will be allowed his financial loss for doing the work on the case and a copy of the evidence proving financial loss must be served on the paying party at least 24 hours before the assessment hearing (see the Costs Practice Direction supplementing CPR 43–48 paragraph 52.2, available online at **www.justice.gov.uk**).

I am aware of the requirement in Rule 2.02 of the Solicitors' Code of Conduct 2007 that firms give clients details of the status of the fee earner who is dealing their particular matter, but I would also like to know the name of the case that states this?

The case is *Pilbrow* v. *Pearless de Rougement* [1999] 3 All ER 355. For a copy of the case please contact the Law Society Library Enquiry Service on 0870 606 2511.

I am seeking to recover costs from my client in the sum of £9,000. In which court do I commence proceedings?

You can only commence this action in the county court. Proceedings cannot be commenced in the High Court unless the value of the claim is more than £15,000 (see the Practice Direction supplementing CPR Part 7).

Are there any guideline rates for summary assessment in relation to counsel's fees?

Yes, you can find them at **www.hmcourts-service.gov.uk**. It is emphasised that these figures are not recommended rates but it is hoped that they may provide a helpful starting point for judges when assessing counsel's fees.

What are the categories of fee earner as outlined in the Supreme Court Costs Office (SCCO) Guide to Summary Assessment of Costs.

The grades of fee earner have been agreed between representatives of the SCCO, the Association of District Judges and the Law Society. There are four grades of fee earner:

1. Solicitors with over eight years' post qualification experience including at least eight years' litigation experience.

2. Solicitors and legal executives with over four years' post qualification experience including at least four years' litigation experience.

3. Other solicitors and legal executives and fee earners of equivalent experience.

4. Trainee solicitors, paralegals and other fee earners.

Note: 'legal executive' means a Fellow of the Institute of Legal Executives.
    See the Supreme Court Costs Office Guide on the Courts Service website (**www.hmcourts-service.gov.uk**).

Does the Law Society recommend a fee we should charge for certifying copies of documents?

No. There are no specific rules that apply to the certification of documents in the same way as there are for the swearing of oaths, affirmations and declarations. It is therefore entirely up to you how you charge. You may wish to charge the equivalent of the fee which is prescribed for the swearing of affidavits, declarations and affirmations, which is £5.00, or you may wish to charge purely on a time basis or other fixed fee basis. However, your charge should be fair and reasonable in all the circumstances.

I am a trainee solicitor assisting in the preparation of a bill of costs in a contentious matter. My firm's cost draftsperson tells me that I cannot make a charge for incoming letters in my bill of costs. Is this correct?

Yes. The unit charge for letters out will include perusing and considering the relevant letters in and no separate charge should be made for incoming letters (see section 4.16(1) of the Costs Practice Direction relating to Part 43 of the Civil Procedure Rules 1998), although the terms of your retainer may allow recovery of this from your client.

I am a trainee solicitor, preparing a bill of costs on a contentious matter for the purposes of detailed assessment. Can I claim for my time spent preparing the bill of costs?

Yes, a claim may be made for the reasonable costs of preparing and checking the bill of costs (see section 4.18 of the Costs Practice Direction relating to CPR Part 43). See at **www.justice.gov.uk** under the Civil Procedure Rules.

My firm have set up a new computer system which enables us to use electronic signatures. Can bills be signed using an electronic signature?

Yes. Schedule 16 to, and s.64(3) of, the Legal Services Act 2007 which came into force in March 2008 amends s.69 of the Solicitors Act 1974 to enable electronic billing.

For further guidance see the Practice Advice Service booklet *Contentious Costs*.

What is the current judgment debt rate?

Since 1 April 1993, the rate of interest payable on judgment debts has been 8 per cent per annum. See Judgment Debts (Rates of Interest) Order 1993, SI 1993/564.

When does a legatee have a right to interest on a pecuniary legacy under a will and what rate of interest is payable?

Legacies should be paid with due diligence and usually within the executor's year. Paragraph 15 of Practice Direction 40 of the Civil Procedure Rules states:

> Where an account of legacies is directed by any judgement, then, subject to–
>
> (a) any directions contained in the will or codicil in question;

(b) and any order made by the court,

interest shall be allowed on each legacy at the basic rate payable for the time being on funds in court or at such other rate as the court shall direct, beginning one year after the testator's death

The current rate payable on legacies can be checked on the Court Funds Office website (**www.officialsolicitor.gov.uk/cfo/investments_interest.htm**).

In light of the practice note on telegraphic transfer (TT) fees, would I comply with best practice if it was stated in the bill to my client that the charge is £35 + VAT under the profit costs column? My view is that if I absorb the £5 bank charge within my firm's overhead, it is not necessary to inform the client of the actual bank charge as he is not paying for it.

The Law Society has produced a practice note to highlight the fact that profit cost cannot be added on top of a disbursement and then charged solely as a disbursement; following the decision of the Solicitors' Disciplinary Tribunal in the case of Anton Howse, Peter Jones (and others) (see Law Society *Gazette* 12 June 2008 (**www.lawsociety.org.uk/archive.law**)).

You may roll the TT fees into profit costs but you should adopt a precautionary approach. It is suggested that you are transparent as to what is profit cost and what is a disbursement both in your client care letter and your bill.

Therefore, in your example, the client care letter should make reference to the fact that a charge will be made for dealing with the telegraphic transfer. The bill should show £30 under the profit costs column and the bank charge of £5 under the disbursements column.

For further information, please see the Law Society's Telegraphic Transfer Fees Practice Note (**Annex 3A**).

Conditional/contingency fee agreements

What is the difference between a contingency fee agreement and a conditional fee agreement?

The term 'contingency fee' is generic in that it covers all agreements where the fee (whether fixed, or calculated either as a percentage of the proceeds or otherwise howsoever) is payable only in the event of success.

However, 'contingency fee agreements' are traditionally known to be agreements whereby the fee is calculated as a percentage of the proceeds recovered. Such contingency fee agreements are only permissible in non-contentious matters (see Solicitors' Code of Conduct 2007, Rule 2.04)

A conditional fee agreement is a statutory species of contingency fee.

Conditional fee agreements are agreements where the fee charged depends on whether you win or lose the case. They are commonly known as 'no win, no fee' agreements, The fee may consist of basic or reduced costs or basic costs plus a success fee of anything up to 100 per cent of the basic costs, although the wording of s.27 of the Access to Justice Act 1999 is wide, and covers any arrangement where certain fees are payable only in specified circumstances.

If you are considering entering into a conditional fee agreement, you should familiarise yourself with the following:

- section 58 of the Courts and Legal Services Act 1990 (as amended by s.27 of the Access to Justice Act 1999);
- the Civil Procedure Costs Rules 2000 (SI 2000/1317.L.11);
- the Practice Direction (PD) supplementing Parts 43 to 48 of the Civil Procedure Rules (CPR) 1998; and
- the Solicitors' Code of Conduct 2007.

General guidance on contingency fee agreements and conditional fee agreements is also available in our booklet *Payment by Results* (**Annex 1B**).

Has the Law Society produced a model conditional fee agreement (CFA) in light of the regime that came into force on 1 November 2005?

Yes. The model agreement may be used in both personal injury and clinical negligence matters. There is also an information leaflet for clients called *Conditional Fee Agreements: What you need to know*. Please also see the Practice Advice Service booklet *Payment by Results* (**Annex 1B**).

Once my client and I have agreed to enter into the Law Society's current CFA should I recommend that he seek independent legal advice before signing the agreement?

No. There is no requirement that the client take independent legal advice before signing the CFA. This assumes that by using the plain English version of the model, its terms will have been fully explained. It is, therefore, reasonable to expect the client to be able to determine unaided whether to go ahead. If you use a different version, other than the Law Society's model agreement, particularly one that is not in plain English, then you should consider whether the client can make an informed decision about its terms without independent advice.

In which areas of law is it possible to use a conditional fee agreement (CFA)?

Section 58A of the Courts and Legal Services Act 1990 as substituted by s.27 of the Access to Justice Act 1999 states that 'the proceedings which cannot be the subject of an enforceable CFA are (a) criminal proceedings, apart from those under s.82 of the Environmental Protection Act 1990 and (b) family proceedings', the definition of family proceedings can also be found in this section. The Conditional Fee Agreement Order 2000 allows all such agreements to provide for success fees except for proceedings under s.82 of the Environmental Protection Act 1990 where success fees are not permissible (s.3).

Can I use a conditional fee agreement in housing disrepair cases?

Yes. Section 58A of the Courts and Legal Services Act 1990 (which was introduced by s.27 of the Access to Justice Act 1999) allows proceedings under s.82 of the Environmental Protection Act 1990 to be prosecuted under a conditional fee agreement although they cannot provide for a success fee. Section 82 cases are statutory nuisance cases and this is the criminal provision relating to housing disrepair cases.

Has the Law Society any information on backdating conditional fee agreements (CFAs)?

Whether CFAs can be backdated or given retrospective effect is a contractual question. The issues have been discussed in several cases including *Birmingham City Council* v. *Forde* [2009] EWHC 12 (QB), 13 January 2009; *Holmes* v. *Alfred McAlpine Homes (Yorkshire) Ltd* [2006] EWCA 110, 7 February 2006; *Musa King* v. *Telegraph Group Limited* [2005] EWHC 90015 (Costs), 2 December 2005 and *Kenneth Kellar* v. *Stanley Williams (Turks and Caicos Islands)* [2004] UKPC 30, 24 June 2004 (although the relevance of this case to English and Welsh CFAs is doubtful).

Please also see Wignall (2008) *Conditional Fees: A Guide to CFAs and Litigation Funding*, 3rd Edition, Law Society Publishing.

Has the Law Society produced a model CFA agreement for use in non-personal injury cases?

No. The model agreement is specifically for use in personal injury and clinical negligence cases only. The current version was published for use from 1 November 2005 following the introduction of the new CFA regime. See the Practice Advice booklet *Payment by Results* (**Annex 1B**).

I am a solicitor representing a client in an employment case before the Employment Tribunal. Can I enter into a contingency fee agreement?

Yes. Rule 2.04 of the Code of Conduct 2007 allows solicitors to enter contingency fee arrangements in non-contentious matters. Proceedings before all tribunals other than the Lands Tribunal and Employment Appeals Tribunal are deemed to be non-contentious business.

Please see the Practice Advice Service booklet *Non-Contentious Costs* (**Annex 3C**).

In a family matter, with the agreement of my client at the outset, can I charge extra if she is awarded a financial settlement which exceeds her expectations?

No. This arrangement would constitute a conditional fee agreement which is prohibited in family matters under s.58A of the Courts and Legal Services Act 1990 as substituted by s.27 of the Access to Justice Act 1999.

I represent a client in a commercial litigation matter. I would like to instruct counsel on a CFA basis. Are there any precedent agreements available?

One is the joint Association of Personal Injury Lawyers (APIL)/Personal Injuries Bar Association (PIBA) agreement for use in personal injury (PI)/clinical negligence cases and the other is the Chancery Bar Association terms of engagement.

The first represents a compromise reached between PI solicitors and barristers. APIL/PIBA 6 was drafted specifically with PI and clinical negligence proceedings in mind where the solicitor is also working under terms with his client (on the Law Society model agreement). It is an industry-wide agreement and there is little prospect of a prudent PI solicitor departing from its key clauses.

The Chancery Bar Association agreement is a much more flexible instrument and is more effective at protecting the interests of barristers. In particular it contains express provision allowing the CFA to be treated as a contractual retainer and it allows doe fees to be agreed on a differential basis (reduced fees rather than no fees in the event of failure). The Chancery Bar Association terms of engagement can be easily adapted to cover a very wide range of circumstances.

Annex 3A

Telegraphic transfer fees practice note

30 July 2008

1. Introduction

1.1   Who should read this practice note?

All solicitors who arrange telegraphic transfers of funds on behalf of clients in the course of their business.

1.2   What is the issue?

A recent Solicitors Disciplinary Tribunal (SDT) decision found against the partners of a practice for concealing profit costs from their clients by referring to a telegraphic transfer fee as a disbursement.

1.3   Professional conduct

The following sections of the Solicitors' Code of Conduct 2007 (code of conduct) [**www.rules.sra.org.uk**] are relevant:

*   1.01 Justice and the rule of law
*   1.02 Integrity
*   1.04 Best interests of clients
*   1.05 Standard of service
*   1.06 Public confidence
*   2.03 Information about the cost

1.4   Status of this practice note

Practice notes are issued by the Law Society for the use and benefit of its members. They represent the Law Society's view of good practice in a particular area. They are not intended to be the only standard of good practice that solicitors can follow. You are not required to follow them, but doing so will make it easier to account to oversight bodies for your actions.

Practice notes are not legal advice, nor do they necessarily provide a defence to complaints of misconduct or of inadequate professional service. While care has been taken to ensure that they are accurate, up to date and useful, the Law Society will not accept any legal liability in relation to them.

For queries or comments on this practice note contact the Law Society's Practice Advice Service: **www.lawsociety.org.uk/practiceadvice**.

1.5   Terminology in this practice note

Must – a specific requirement in the Solicitors' Code of Conduct or legislation. You must comply, unless there are specific exemptions or defences provided for in the code of conduct or relevant legislation.

Should – good practice for most situations in the Law Society's view. If you do not follow this, you should be able to justify to oversight bodies why the alternative approach you have taken is appropriate, either for your practice, or in the particular retainer.

May – a non-exhaustive list of options for meeting your obligations. Which option you choose is determined by the risk profile of the individual practice, client or retainer. You must be able to justify why this was an appropriate option to oversight bodies.

SDT – Solicitors Disciplinary Tribunal.

TT – Telegraphic transfer.

2.   Charging for telegraphic transfers

2.1   What is a disbursement?

The Solicitors' Accounts Rules define a disbursement as 'an expense'.

2.2   Is a telegraphic transfer fee a disbursement?

A TT fee is an expense but some practices charge more than the cost of the transfer under the heading disbursement, thereby concealing profit costs from clients.

The SDT has found that this clearly breaches rule 1 of the code of conduct, particularly in relation to the solicitor's duty to act with integrity and in the best interests of the client.

This conduct is also likely to be in breach of rule 2, client care, if any amount over the cost of the transfer is not explicitly declared to the client as profit costs.

2.3   How should telegraphic transfers be charged?

You must advise the client of the basis and terms of your charges.

You should tell your client that you are charging them the fee that has been charged to the practice by the financial institution executing the telegraphic transfer, and that this fee is a disbursement.

You must charge VAT on the fee that has been charged to the practice by the financial institution executing the telegraphic transfer, even if no VAT is charged to you. For more information see VAT on incidental expenses to clients; disbursements on the HM Revenue and Customs website [**www.hmrc.gov.uk/vat/charge-disbursements**].

You must not include any profit cost element as a disbursement. For example, you must not include a fixed monthly charge by the bank for having an in-house terminal, or any internal staff costs.

If you charge the client an administration fee for arranging the telegraphic transfer you must inform the client and charge it as profit cost.

3.   The Solicitors Disciplinary Tribunal (SDT) ruling

An SDT case reported in June 2008 clearly demonstrates the implications of referring to a mixed charge partially comprising a profit costs element and including a telegraphic transfer fee as 'a disbursement'.

3.1   The facts

The practice charged the client £30 plus VAT for a TT as a disbursement. The practice only paid £10 to its bank for each TT.

The client care letter sent to clients under rule 15 (now rule 2 of the code of conduct) did not explain that the practice would only pay on £10 and that the balance amounted to profit costs for the practice.

It did not explain that the additional fee related to work undertaken in arranging the TT.

3.2   The allegations

Claiming the TT fee as a disbursement of £30 was misleading to the client. The balance over the actual disbursement was additional income and profit to the practice.

3.3   The findings

- The respondents had acted in breach of rule 1 and rule 2 of the code of conduct.

- The practice's invoices did not reflect the telegraphic transfer fee and the true position was not addressed in the letters addressed to the clients. The clients had therefore been misled.
- A fee charged to the client by the practice had been described as a disbursement met by the practice which was inaccurate. This hid the fee for handling a transfer in addition to the bank's charges.
- In all of the circumstances of the case, the SDT considered it appropriate and proportionate to fine each respondent £1,500.

Annex 3B

Contentious costs – Practice Advice Service

November 2008

Introduction

This booklet, prepared by the Practice Advice Service, is not intended to be a fully comprehensive guide to contentious costs but attempts to cover those areas that generate the most frequent enquiries from solicitors. The booklet provides information on charging in contentious matters. It discusses billing generally and the procedures available to clients who wish to challenge solicitors' costs.

This booklet refers to various cases. Practitioners requiring copies of the relevant cases or information on case law may wish to contact the Law Society library which provides a photocopying service, please telephone 0870 606 2511 or e-mail library@lawsociety.org.uk for further details.

Solicitors should familiarise themselves in more detail with:

- Solicitors' Code of Conduct 2007 [NB: Updated 31 March 2009], in particular rule 2 which deals with Client Relations;
- Parts 43 to 48 of the Civil Procedure Rules 1998 ('CPR') and supplementing Practice Direction.

Throughout this booklet, reference is made to various procedures available under the CPR. The court fees applicable to each procedure may be accessed at **www.hmcourts-service.gov.uk**.

It is intended to update this booklet from time to time. When this edition is revised, a note will be inserted on the Law Society website and copies may be downloaded from **www.pas.lawsociety.org.uk**.

Booklets on non-contentious costs (entitled 'Non-contentious Costs') and conditional fee agreements (entitled 'Payment by Results') are also available. For advice on solicitors' costs generally, please telephone the Practice Advice Service on 0870 606 2522 or e-mail practiceadvice@lawsociety.org.uk.

Contentious costs – what are they?

Contentious costs in this booklet are defined as monies payable in connection with legal services which relate to matters where proceedings have actually:

a. begun before a court or before an arbitrator; and are

b. not business which falls within the definition of non-contentious or common form probate business contained in s.128 of the Supreme Court Act 1981.

This definition is found in s.87(1) of the Solicitors Act 1974 (as amended by s.107(2), Sched.4 to the Arbitration Act 1996 and s.8 Sched.1 para.12(A) to the Access to Justice Act 1985).

Work prior to proceedings being issued is regarded as non-contentious provided proceedings are not subsequently begun. For example, if a solicitor takes instructions on a personal injury matter and the parties reach settlement before proceedings are issued, the work is regarded as non-contentious.

Examples of contentious and non-contentious matters

Contentious	Non-contentious
1. Proceedings actually begun in the County Court, High Court, Magistrates' Court, Crown Court and the Court of Protection.	Proceedings before all tribunals other than the Lands Tribunal and the Employment Appeal Tribunal.
2. Proceedings actually begun before the Lands Tribunal and the Employment Appeal Tribunal.	Planning and other public enquiries including Coroner's Court work.
3. Contentious probate proceedings actually begun.	Non-contentious or common form probate business.
4. Proceedings on appeal to the Court of Appeal, Privy Council and House of Lords.	Conveyancing, company acquisitions and mergers, the administration of estates and trusts out of court, the preparation of wills, statements and contracts, and any other work not included in the 'contentious' column.
5. Proceedings in arbitration.	Criminal Injuries Compensation Board.
6. Motor Insurers Bureau Uninsured drivers' claims (proceedings issued).	Motor Insurers Bureau Untraced drivers' claims. Motor Insurers Bureau Uninsured drivers' claims (proceedings not issued).

Contentious	Non-contentious
7. Work done preliminary to proceedings covered by 1–5 above including advice, preparation and negotiations provided the proceedings are subsequently begun (although see note below*).	Work done preliminary to the proceedings included in the 'contentious' column if such proceedings are not subsequently begun.
8. Licensing (appeals to Magistrates' Court).	Licensing (administered by Local Authority).

* If proceedings are subsequently issued, it is a moot point whether all prior work leading to the action automatically becomes contentious. Please see obiter comment of Lord Justice Brooke in *Crosbie* v *Munroe* [2003] EWCA Civ 350.

Costs information and client care

Practitioners are referred to the Solicitors' Code of Conduct 2007 ('the Code') which is of general application to solicitors practising contentious and non-contentious business [NB: Updated 31 March 2009].

Rule 2 (Client relations) is designed to help solicitors and their clients understand each other's expectations and responsibilities. In particular, the purpose of subrules 2.02 (Client care) and 2.03 (Information about the cost) is to ensure clients are given the information necessary to enable them to make appropriate decisions about if and how their matter should proceed.

When considering the options available to the client, if the matter relates to a dispute between the client and a third party, a solicitor should discuss whether mediation or some other alternative dispute resolution (ADR) procedure may be more appropriate than litigation, arbitration or other formal processes. There may be a costs sanction if a party refuses ADR, please see *Halsey* v *Milton Keynes Trust* [2004] EWCA Civ 576.

The rules in the Code are backed by guidance to aid understanding and compliance. Although the guidance is not mandatory, solicitors who do not follow the guidance may be required to demonstrate how they have nevertheless complied with the rule.

For ease of reference, rule 2 and the accompanying guidance are reproduced at Appendix 1 [of this booklet]. The Code in its entirety may be viewed at **www.sra.org.uk**.

Written retainer – why is this important?

In every contentious matter, a solicitor should ensure that his client signs a written agreement as to his terms of business. CPR r.48.8(1) and (1A) provide:

(1) This rule applies to every assessment of a solicitor's bill to his client except a bill which is to be paid out of the Community Legal Service Fund under the Legal Aid Act 1988 or the Access to Justice Act 1999 – and

(1A) Section 74(3) of the Solicitors Act 1974 applies unless the solicitor and client have entered into a written agreement which expressly permits payment to the solicitor of an amount of costs greater than that which the client could have recovered from another party to the proceedings.

If a solicitor fails to ensure that his client signs such written agreement, then s.74(3) of the Solicitors Act 1974 provides that:

> The amount which may be allowed on the taxation of any costs or bill of costs in respect of any item relating to proceedings in a county court shall not, except in so far as rules of court may otherwise provide, exceed the amount which could have been allowed in respect of that item as between party and party in those proceedings, having regard to the nature of those proceedings and the amount of the claim and any counterclaim.

The practical effect of rule 48.8 is that in every contentious matter a solicitor should ensure that the client signs a written agreement as to his terms of business, without which on the assessment of any item in county court proceedings the solicitor will not be able to recover any more from his client than he would have recovered from the other side.

Methods of charging

A client and his solicitor may agree whatever terms they consider appropriate about the payment of the solicitor's charges for his services under CPR r.48.8.

If, however, the costs are of an unusual nature (either in amount or in the type of costs incurred) those costs will be presumed to have been unreasonably incurred unless the solicitor satisfies the court that he informed the client that they were unusual and, where the costs relate to litigation, that he informed the client they might not be allowed on an assessment of costs between the parties. That information must have been given to the client before the costs were incurred (CPR r.44.8).

Solicitors are also required to adhere to the Code. Subrule 2.03 directs solicitors to advise clients about the range of funding options which may be available for their case and when costs are to be met.

The different charging options dealt with in this booklet are:

- hourly rate;
- fixed fee;
- contingency fee agreement;

- conditional fee agreement;
- public funding.

Information on contentious business agreements is contained in Appendix 2 [of this booklet].

Hourly rate

Traditionally, privately paying clients paid for work as it was carried out. This was on the basis of (i) the cost per hour of the time spent by a solicitor on a matter having regard to the overhead expenses of that solicitor's firm (the 'A' rate) and (ii) the mark-up for care and conduct, usually at 50 per cent of the A rate (the 'B' rate).

It has become more common for solicitors to charge for their services on the basis of an hourly rate which is inclusive of the mark-up for care and conduct. This is also recognised by the courts in relation to assessment of costs between the parties. The starting point assumes that the hourly rate comprises a standard 50 per cent mark-up for care and conduct in ordinary cases, which the court may increase or decrease having regard to those factors contained in CPR r.44.5(3).

In view of the above, and in light of cases such as *General of Berne Insurance Company* v *Jardine Reinsurance Management Limited* [1998] 2 All ER 301 (CA) and *Nederlandse Reassurantie Group Holding NV* v *Bacon and Woodrow (No.4)* [1988] 2 Costs LR 32 (QBD), it is now recommended that hourly rates should be inclusive of the care and conduct mark-up with the addition of a 'slip clause' permitting solicitors to charge an additional percentage in the final bill in certain circumstances to cover the General of Berne item-by-item approach.

For assistance in calculating the time element of the hourly rate, please see the [out of print] Law Society publication *The Expense of Time* (5th edition), a copy of which can be obtained from the Law Society's Library (telephone 0870 606 2511).

Fixed fee

Costs that are recoverable from another party (e.g. unsuccessful opposing party) are fixed for cases taken on the fast track or under the road traffic accident scheme (CPR r.46 and r.45). The effect of the indemnity principle is that any agreed fixed fee between a solicitor and client will also be the maximum that is recoverable from the other side.

As mentioned earlier under 'Costs information and client care', the practical effect of CPR rule 48.8 is that in every contentious matter a solicitor should ensure that the client signs a written agreement as to his terms of business, without which on the assessment of any item in county court proceedings the solicitor will not be able to recover any more from his client than he would have recovered from the other side.

Contingency fees

Rule 24 of the Code defines a contingency fee as meaning 'any sum (whether fixed, or calculated either as a percentage of the proceeds or otherwise) payable only in the event of success' in the prosecution of any other contentious proceeding.

Rule 2.04(1) of the Code prohibits a solicitor from entering into a contingency fee agreement for contentious proceedings before a court in England and Wales, a British court martial or an arbitrator where the seat of the arbitration is in England or Wales except where permitted by statute or the common law.

Rule 2.04(2) prohibits a solicitor from entering into a contingency fee agreement in contentious proceedings before the court of an overseas jurisdiction or an arbitrator where the seat of the arbitration is overseas except to the extent that a lawyer of that jurisdiction would be permitted to do so.

Practitioners are reminded that there is no prohibition against doing non-contentious work on a contingency fee basis. For further information, please refer to the chapter on Contingency Fees contained in 'Non-Contentious Costs' produced by the Practice Advice Service, which is available at **www.pas.lawsociety.org.uk**.

Conditional fee agreement

A conditional fee agreement ('CFA') is a type of contingency fee agreement that is permitted for contentious business, providing it meets the requirements contained in section 58 of the Courts and Legal Services Act 1990 (as amended by section 27 of the Access to Justice Act 1999).

A new regime for conditional fee agreements and collective conditional fee agreements commenced on 1 November 2005. From that date, the Conditional Fee Agreements Regulations 2000 and the Collective Conditional Fee Agreements Regulations 2000 were revoked and the Law Society is now responsible for providing disciplinary sanctions for breaches of the Code.

CFAs are beyond the subject matter of this booklet. The Practice Advice Service has produced a separate booklet on conditional fees entitled 'Payment by Results', which is available to download from **www.pas.lawsociety.org.uk**. For further guidance on costs, including the Law Society's model CFA for personal injury and clinical negligence cases, see **www.costs.lawsociety.org.uk** or contact the Practice Advice Service (telephone 0870 606 2522).

Public funding

Public funding as a means of charging for contentious costs is included in this section for the purpose of completeness. Subrule 2.03(1)(d) of the Code requires the solicitor to consider whether the client may be eligible and should apply for public funding and 2.03(3) sets out further information which should be given to the client in a publicly funded matter, please see Appendix 1 [of this booklet].

Billing your client

This section deals with the following types of bills:

* interim bills on account;
* interim statute bills;
* final bills.

Interim bills

It is perfectly acceptable for a solicitor to request interim payments for work, particularly when the work is protracted. The client can appreciate knowing the costs that they have incurred to date and the solicitor can avoid the burden of financing the entire work. However, the solicitor should make his right to request interim payments an express condition of his written retainer i.e. at the very outset of a particular matter.

Interim bills on account

These bills are requests for payments on account of a 'final bill' to be delivered at a later date. It is not possible to sue on this type of bill and a client is not entitled to an assessment of it.

However, a solicitor may at the outset of a retainer require a client to make payments on account of costs and disbursements. Section 65(2) of the Solicitors Act 1974 allows a solicitor conducting contentious business to terminate a retainer within a reasonable time if a client fails to pay an interim bill on account.

If the client disagrees with the amount of the bill he can ask the solicitor to provide an interim statute bill which can then be assessed. Section 68 enables the court to require a solicitor to provide such a bill.

Interim statute bills

These bills are termed statute bills because they comply with all the requirements of the Solicitors Act 1974 and result in all the consequences that flow from such compliance. A solicitor may sue on them and a client may apply for assessment of them. These bills are final bills in respect of the work covered and cannot be adjusted at a later date.

Interim statute bills can arise in two ways:

(i) **Natural break**: The Law Society's advice is not to rely on this ground except in the clearest circumstances. For guidance on what constitutes a natural break, see *Chamberlain* v *Boodle and King* [1982] 3 All ER 188 (CA).

(ii) **Agreement**: Solicitors should make it expressly clear in their terms of business letter that they propose to deliver interim statute bills in the event of protracted work. For guidance on the distinction between interim statute bills and requests for payment on account generally, see the Court of Appeal judgments in *Davidson* v *Jones-Fenleigh* (*The Times* 11 March 1980) and *O Palomo SA* v *Turner and Co* [2000] 1 WLR 37.

Final bills

Final bills may be rendered in the following circumstances:

* where a client has agreed to, or asked for delivery of a final bill;
* at the conclusion of a matter;
* on the termination of a retainer;
* on an order made by the High Court for the delivery by a solicitor of a bill of costs (see s.68 of the Solicitors Act 1974).

Where interim bills on account have been rendered pursuant to s.65(2) of the Solicitors Act 1974, these should be disregarded for the purposes of the final bill and treated as requests for payment of money on account. The final bill should therefore cover the total amount of the solicitor's charges and disbursements with any additional mark up on the interim bills and should give credit for all payments received as a result of interim bills on account.

Content of bill

Schedule 16, s.64(3) of the Legal Services Act 2007 which came into force on 7 March 2008 amended s.69 of the Solicitors Act 1974. This amendment allows solicitors to deliver their bills electronically, please see Appendix 4 [of this booklet] for further information. A solicitor's bill of costs should contain sufficient information to identify the matter and period of time to which it relates.

The bill must also comply with s.69(2) of the Solicitors Act 1974 which requires that the bill must be:

(a) signed in accordance with subsection (2A), and

(b) delivered in accordance with subsection (2C).

(2A) A bill is signed in accordance with this subsection if it is –

(a) signed by the solicitor or on his behalf by an employee of the solicitor authorised by him to sign, or

(b) enclosed in, or accompanied by, a letter which is signed as mentioned in paragraph (a) and refers to the bill.

(2B) For the purposes of subsection (2A) the signature may be an electronic signature.

(2C) A bill is delivered in accordance with this subsection if –

(a) it is delivered to the party to be charged with the bill personally,

(b) it is delivered to that party by being sent to him by post to, or left for him at, his place of business, dwelling-house or last known place of abode, or

(c) it is delivered to that party –

(i) by means of an electronic communications network, or

(ii) by other means but in a form that nevertheless requires the use of apparatus by the recipient to render it intelligible,

and that party has indicated to the person making the delivery his willingness to accept delivery of a bill sent in the form and manner used.

If the bill is not properly signed, it is still valid but will be unenforceable in the courts.

The bill should show disbursements separately from the solicitor's fees, see s.67 of the Solicitors Act 1974.

In order to comply with the VAT regulations, when a third party is paying the solicitor's costs, the bill must be made out to the client, but it should state that the bill is payable by a third party. Please see Value Added Tax Regulations 1995. Part III deals with VAT invoices and other invoicing requirements. Para.13 provides that where the registered person (i.e. the solicitor) makes a taxable supply to a taxable person (i.e. someone resident in the UK) then he shall supply them with an invoice. Para.14 sets out the required contents of an invoice which includes the name and address of the person to whom the goods and services are supplied.

Gross sum and detailed itemised bills

It is for the solicitor to decide whether to deliver a gross sum bill or one containing detailed items, provided that the costs are not subject to a contentious business agreement under the Solicitors Act 1974 which may specify the form of bill to be rendered.

In a contentious matter, a client who has received a gross sum bill may, before he is served with proceedings and within three months of the date on which the bill was delivered, require a solicitor to deliver a detailed itemised bill to replace the original bill, see s.64(2) of the Solicitors Act 1974. In these circumstances, the solicitor will not be restricted to the amount of the gross sum bill and, if justified after recalculation, may deliver a detailed bill for a higher amount.

Recovering your costs from your client

Provided that a solicitor's bill complies with the requirements of s.69(2) of the Solicitors Act 1974 (as set out under the heading 'Content of Bill') recovery proceedings for costs may be commenced after one month has elapsed from the date of delivery of the final or interim statute bill. However, in circumstances where the client is about to quit England and Wales, to be declared bankrupt or to compound with his creditors or do any other act which tends to prevent or delay the solicitor obtaining payment, a solicitor may seek leave to issue proceedings within a month, see s.69(1) of the Solicitors Act 1974.

It should be noted that a solicitor will be prevented from issuing recovery proceedings for costs where the client has made an application to the court for detailed assessment of the costs within one month of delivery of the bill or where he has obtained an order for the bill to be assessed – see s.70(1) and (2) of the Solicitors Act 1974.

Rule 2.03(2) of the Code of Conduct requires solicitors to notify clients of their right to assessment in CFA cases. The Law Society, however, recommends that a solicitor informs a client of the assessment procedure in all matters before beginning recovery proceedings. This avoids confusion and may prevent the case being adjourned at a later date to allow the assessment to take place.

Interest on costs

There is no statutory authority for a solicitor to charge interest on outstanding contentious costs. However, interest may be charged in the following circumstances:

- if the right to charge interest has been expressly reserved in the original retainer agreement; or

- if the client later agrees for a contractual consideration to pay interest; or
- where the solicitor has sued the client and claimed interest under s.35A of the Supreme Court Act 1981 or s.69(1) of the County Courts Act 1984.

Unless otherwise agreed with the client, the rate of interest will be equal to the interest rate on judgment debts, which at the date of publication is 8% per annum (see the Judgment Debts (Rate of Interest) Order 1993, SI 1993/564).

Service of a statutory demand

A solicitor may serve a statutory demand within one month of delivering a bill and can, after the expiration of one month from the delivery of the bill, issue a bankruptcy petition provided 21 days have expired from service of the statutory demand.

A petition, but not a statutory demand, is an 'action' within the meaning of s.69 of the Solicitors Act 1974 (which prohibits solicitors bringing an action to recover costs within one month of delivery of the bill without special leave from the court).

In general, solicitors should be wary of following this route as there is a power to set aside a statutory demand on the grounds of injustice. See *Re a Debtor (No.88 of 1991)*; *Marshalls (A Firm)* v *A Debtor* [1993] Ch 286 (also reported in *The Independent* 10.07.1992) and *Shalston* v *DF Keane Ltd* [2003] EWHC 599.

Solicitors should also be mindful of the decision in *Turner & Co (A Firm)* v *O Palomo SA* [1999] 4 All ER 353, CA, which may have the affect of outlawing statutory demands on the basis that the amount on a solicitor's bill is still subject to assessment by the court if there are proceedings. As it is not a liquidated demand, there is no right to serve a statutory demand. An application for this case to be heard by the House of Lords was refused.

See also 'Fees by Statutory Demand' by Angharad J. T. Start, *New Law Journal* 7 August 1992.

Assessment of solicitor and client costs

A client can apply for an assessment of his solicitor's costs under section 70 of the Solicitors Act 1974. He has a right to assessment within one month from the date of the delivery of the bill.

If the application is made after one month but before twelve months from the date of delivery of the bill, the court's permission is required for the bill to be assessed.

Except in special circumstances, no order for assessment will be made:

(i) after twelve months from the delivery of the bill; or

(ii) after a judgment has been obtained for the recovery of the costs covered by the bill; or

(iii) after the bill has been paid, but before the expiration of 12 months from the payment of the bill.

In relation to the application of section 70, practitioners should also have regard to the Court of Appeal decisions in *Thomas Watts & Co (A Firm)* v *Smith (Malcolm Davies)* [1998] Costs LR 59 and *Turner* v *Palomo* [2000] 1 WLR 37. Both of these decisions appear to allow the client a common law means to challenge a solicitor's bill outside the statutory limitations of s.70. The practical effect of this means that where a solicitor sues for non-payment of fees, any summary judgment will be for assessment of damages and not for a liquidated amount.

Also note the House of Lords decision in *Harrison* v *Tew* [1990] 2 AC 532 which stated that the court had no power to order taxation under s.70 outside the statutory period. This decision was distinguished in *Turner* v *Palomo*. An application for *Turner* v *Palomo* to be heard by the House of Lords was refused (see the Law Society's *Gazette* 8 September 1999 page 32).

Detailed assessment of solicitors' contentious costs payable by a client

CPR r.48.8 sets out the basis for assessment of solicitors' costs payable by a client and CPR r.48.10 sets out the procedure for assessment. These Rules should be read in conjunction with the Practice Direction supplementing CPR Parts 43–48. All references below to 'Precedents' are to the Schedule of Costs Precedents found in CPR Parts 43–48.

Procedure

- The client applies for an order for assessment (Precedent L) by initiating a claim form under CPR Part 8 (Precedent J).
- The solicitor must serve a breakdown of costs (Precedent P) within 28 days of the order for costs to be assessed.
- The client must serve points of dispute within 14 days after service on him of the breakdown of costs.
- If the solicitor wishes to serve a reply, he must do so within 14 days of service on him of the points of dispute.

- Either party may file a request for a hearing date after points of dispute have been served, but no later than 3 months after the date of the order for the costs to be assessed.

This procedure applies subject to any contrary order made by the court.

Where to apply?

CPR r.47.4 deals with the appropriate venue for detailed assessment proceedings. This should be read in conjunction with s.69(3) of the Solicitors Act 1974.

Who should apply?

It is usual for the client to apply for assessment although it is possible for a solicitor to apply to have his own costs assessed (see CPR r.48.10(5)). The latter is inadvisable because the solicitor will generally be unable to recover his costs for attending the hearing if the client fails to attend (see s.70(9) of the Solicitors Act 1974).

Costs of assessment

The costs of assessment will follow the event. If a solicitor's bill is reduced by one fifth or more, then the solicitor will bear the costs of the assessment. If the bill is reduced by less than one fifth or is not reduced at all, the party chargeable will pay the costs (see s.70(9) of the Solicitors Act 1974). The one fifth figure is calculated on the total of the bill excluding VAT.

Assessment of solicitors' contentious costs payable by the other side

The starting point is that each party is primarily responsible for their own solicitor's costs. That said, the general rule is that the unsuccessful party will be ordered to pay the costs of the successful party, provided that these costs have been reasonably incurred, are of a reasonable amount and are proportionate to the matters in issue (CPR r.44.3 and r.44.4).

The court has the discretion to make any order it chooses in relation to the payment of costs between the parties (CPR r.44.3(2)(b)). CPR r.44.5 sets out factors that can affect the amount one party can recover from the other.

Under rule 2.03 of the Code, a solicitor must advise his client of any potential liability for paying the costs of any other party. Where appropriate solicitors are advised to obtain a fixed figure or agree a cap on a third party's costs, please see Appendix 1 [of this booklet].

The costs rules (see CPR Parts 43–48 inclusive) provide four main ways by which the amount of costs payable by one party to another may be ascertained:

(i)   fixed costs (CPR Part 45);

(ii) fast track trial costs (CPR Part 46);

(iii) summary assessment (CPR Part 44);

(iv) detailed assessment (CPR Part 47).

(i)   Fixed costs

Cases involving fixed costs mean that the contentious costs payable by another party (e.g. the unsuccessful party) will be automatically fixed at a specified sum depending on the nature of the case. CPR Part 45 prescribes the sums allowed. There is also a specific scheme for road traffic accidents ('RTAs') set out in Section II of CPR Part 45. Solicitors should note the relevance of CPR r.48.8(1) and (1A) as set out earlier in this booklet.

(ii)   Fast track trial costs

Costs recoverable from another party (e.g. the unsuccessful party) of a trial on the fast track are subject to fixed costs under CPR Part 46.

(iii)   Summary assessment

The general rule is that a court will make a summary assessment for a case dealt with on the fast track or at the end of a hearing that has lasted a day or less in the Court of Appeal to which paragraph 14 of the Practice Direction supplementing Part 52 (Appeals) applies, unless there is good reason not to. There are exceptions to this general rule. (Please refer to CPR r.43.3, sections 13 and 14 of the Practice Direction.)

CPR r.43.3 defines summary assessment as 'the procedure by which the court, when making an order about costs, orders payment of a sum of money instead of fixed costs or detailed assessment'.

Each party intending to claim summarily assessed costs must serve a statement of costs at least 24 hours before the date fixed for the hearing (section 13.5(4) of the Costs Practice Direction). The statement of costs should follow form N260 as closely as possible (section 13.5(3) of the Costs Practice Direction). In deciding what figure to allow, the court will hear argument from both parties and will focus on the statement of costs incurred by the party in question.

Solicitors should ensure that where a summary assessment of costs is a possibility they provide the required statement of costs within the requisite timescale. If they do not, they run the risk of the court deciding that no sums be paid and the solicitor will not be able to claim the cost of the work done for that hearing on a subsequent detailed assessment.

Guideline hourly rates for the summary assessment of costs may be found on the court service website: **www.hmcourts-service.gov.uk/ publications/guidance/scco/appendix_2.htm**.

(iv)   Detailed assessment

Detailed assessment is defined in CPR r.43.4 as 'the procedure by which the amount of costs is decided by a costs officer in accordance with Part 47'. The detailed assessment procedure is distinct from the main case in which substantive issues are considered and is concerned only with the costs element of the main case. It is generally carried out when the substantive proceedings have been concluded.

Solicitors should familiarise themselves with the procedures set out in Part 47. In particular, solicitors should abide by the timetable set for these proceedings because of the default provisions incorporated into the rules which, once triggered, may mean that the paying party is ordered to pay immediately a proportion of the receiving party's costs.

There are special provisions dealing with the detailed assessment procedure for the costs of a publicly funded client or an assisted person where the costs are payable out of the community legal service fund or another fund, see CPR r.47.17 and r.47.17A.

There are also various default provisions under Part 47, which are dealt with in CPR r.47.11 and r.47.12.

Unless the court makes a contrary order, the procedure for the detailed assessment of costs payable by one party to another is as follows:

- The receiving party serves on the paying party (i) notice of commencement by using form N252 and (ii) a copy of the bill of costs.
- After service of the notice of commencement and accompanying bill of costs, the paying party may, within 21 days, dispute any item on the bill of costs by serving points of dispute.
- If the paying party and the receiving party agree the amount of costs, either party may apply for a costs certificate, see CPR r.47.10, r.47.15 and r.47.16.
- Where points of dispute are served, the receiving party may serve a reply within 21 days after service on them of the points of dispute to which their reply relates.
- The receiving party must file a request for a detailed assessment hearing within 3 months of the expiry of the period for commencing detailed assessment proceedings, see CPR r.47.7 and r.47.14.

Deadline for commencement

Detailed assessment proceedings should be commenced within 3 months after the event giving rise to the right to detailed assessment, see CPR r.47.7.

Where should you apply?

CPR r.47.4 deals with the appropriate venue for detailed assessment proceedings. This should be read in conjunction with s.69(3) of the Solicitors Act 1974.

Costs of the assessment

The receiving party is entitled to their costs of the detailed assessment proceedings except where the court makes some other order in relation to all or part of the costs or where the provisions of the CPR or legislation provide otherwise (see CPR r.47.18).

A claim may also be made for the reasonable costs of preparing and checking the bill of costs (section 4.18 of the Costs Practice Direction). The bill of costs may be prepared by the solicitor or a costs draftsman, whether independent or an employee of the firm, see *Smith Graham (A Firm)* v *Lord Chancellor's Department* [1999] NLJR 1443, QBD and *Crane* v *Canons Leisure Centre* [2007] EWCA Civ 1352. For further information on the category of fee earner a costs draftsman will fall under, please see *Cook on Costs 2008*, pp.407–8.

Enforcement of an order for costs

When an order for the payment of costs is made, a solicitor may expect payment by the time specified in the order. Where payment is not forthcoming, there are various ways of enforcing an order for costs which are potentially available to the unpaid solicitor who is seeking to recover costs from his client, or to the successful party who is seeking to recover his costs from the other side. Such methods include a writ of *fieri facias*, a warrant of execution, a third party debt order, a charging order, a stop order or stop notice, an attachment of earnings order, the appointment of a receiver or an order for committal. These options are mentioned as possibilities for enforcement by way of completeness, and the appropriateness of each method will depend on individual circumstances. To that end, solicitors are referred to CPR Part 70 on enforcement generally, and in particular CPR r.70.2 and sections 1.1 and 1.2 of the Practice Direction supplementing CPR Part 70.

Further reading

- Law Society Practice Notes which are available at **www.lawsociety. org.uk**.
- The Solicitors' Code of Conduct 2007 came into force on 1 July 2007 and is available online at **www.sra.org.uk**. The Code replaces almost all of the provisions found in *The Guide to the Professional Conduct of Solicitors* (8th edition 1999) except the Solicitors' Accounts Rules and the rules relating to professional indemnity, financial service(s) and the Compensation Fund [NB: Updated 31 March 2009].
- *Cook on Costs 2008* by Michael J. Cook, published by Butterworths.
- *The Expense of Time* (5th edition), published by the Law Society. A concise guide to calculating the annual expense and hourly expense of fee-earners in a solicitor's firm. Photocopies are available from the Law Society Library (telephone 0870 606 2511).
- *Civil Litigation Handbook* (2nd edition) general editor Suzanne Burn, published by the Law Society in 2007. Available from the Law Society Bookshop (telephone 0207 320 5640).
- *Civil Costs Assessment Handbook* (2nd edition), by Peter Burdge. Available from the Law Society Bookshop.
- Practice Advice Service Frequently Asked Questions, which are regularly published in the Law Society's *Gazette*. A selection of questions is reproduced in Appendix 3 [of this booklet].

Updates and guidance on cases and general developments are provided by the Law Society as appropriate. Solicitors should regularly refer to the Law Society website at **www.lawsociety.org.uk**.

Special interest groups

International

For law firms, solicitors, and foreign lawyers seeking to develop their international business and build global relationships and profile, our innovative International Division provides the contacts, tools and information your firm needs and opportunities to progress your international career.

www.lawsociety.org.uk/international

Junior lawyers

Launched in January 2008, the Junior Lawyers Division provides a clear voice for student members of the Law Society enrolled through the SRA, trainees, and solicitors with up to five years' active PQE.

www.lawsociety.org.uk/juniorlawyers

Law management

Established in 1998, the Law Management Section focuses on the full range of practice management disciplines, including HR, finance, marketing, IT, business development, client care, quality and risk.

www.lawsociety.org.uk/lawmanagement

Probate

Established in 1997, the Probate Section focuses on wills, financial planning, trusts, tax planning, Court of Protection, care planning and estate administration.

www.lawsociety.org.uk/probate

Property

The Property Section focuses on areas including e-conveyancing, home information packs, housing, land registration, money laundering, planning and environment, as well as tax and revenue.

www.lawsociety.org.uk/property

Dispute resolution

The Dispute Resolution Section focuses on all areas of dispute resolution including arbitration, litigation and mediation.

www.lawsociety.org.uk/disputeresolution

Other groups

We also maintain a list of useful practitioner associations and groups.

Appendix 1 – Solicitors' Code of Conduct 2007
rule 2 Client relations

[Please see **sra.org.uk/rules** for any amendments].

Introduction

Rule 2 is designed to help both you and your clients understand each other's expectations and responsibilities. In particular, the purpose of 2.02 (Client care) and 2.03 (Information about the cost) is to ensure that clients are given the information necessary to enable them to make appropriate decisions about if and how their matter should proceed. [. . .]

Rule

2.01   Taking on clients

(1) You are generally free to decide whether or not to take on a particular client. However, you must refuse to act or cease acting for a client in the following circumstances:

(a) when to act would involve you in a breach of the law or a breach of the rules of professional conduct;

(b) where you have insufficient resources or lack the competence to deal with the matter;

(c) where instructions are given by someone other than the client, or by only one client on behalf of others in a joint matter, you must not proceed without checking that all clients agree with the instructions given; or

(d) where you know or have reasonable grounds for believing that the instructions are affected by duress or undue influence, you must not act on those instructions until you have satisfied yourself that they represent the client's wishes.

(2) You must not cease acting for a client except for good reason and on reasonable notice.

2.02   Client care

(1) You must:

(a) identify clearly the client's objectives in relation to the work to be done for the client;

(b) give the client a clear explanation of the issues involved and the options available to the client;

(c) agree with the client the next steps to be taken; and

(d) keep the client informed of progress, unless otherwise agreed.

(2) You must, both at the outset and, as necessary, during the course of the matter:

(a) agree an appropriate level of service;

(b) explain your responsibilities;

(c) explain the client's responsibilities;

(d) ensure that the client is given, in writing, the name and status of the person dealing with the matter and the name of the person responsible for its overall supervision; and

(e) explain any limitations or conditions resulting from your relationship with a third party (for example a funder, fee sharer or introducer) which affect the steps you can take on the client's behalf.

(3) If you can demonstrate that it was inappropriate in the circumstances to meet some or all of these requirements, you will not breach 2.02.

2.03   Information about the cost

(1) You must give your client the best information possible about the likely overall cost of a matter both at the outset and, when appropriate, as the matter progresses. In particular you must:

(a) advise the client of the basis and terms of your charges;

(b) advise the client if charging rates are to be increased;

(c) advise the client of likely payments which you or your client may need to make to others;

(d) discuss with the client how the client will pay, in particular:

(i) whether the client may be eligible and should apply for public funding; and

(ii) whether the client's own costs are covered by insurance or may be paid by someone else such as an employer or trade union;

(e) advise the client that there are circumstances where you may be entitled to exercise a lien for unpaid costs;

(f) advise the client of their potential liability for any other party's costs; and

(g) discuss with the client whether their liability for another party's costs may be covered by existing insurance or whether specially purchased insurance may be obtained.

(2) Where you are acting for the client under a conditional fee agreement, (including a collective conditional fee agreement) in addition to complying with 2.03(1) above and 2.03(5) and (6) below, you must explain the following, both at the outset and, when appropriate, as the matter progresses:

   (a) the circumstances in which your client may be liable for your costs and whether you will seek payment of these from the client, if entitled to do so;

   (b) if you intend to seek payment of any or all of your costs from your client, you must advise your client of their right to an assessment of those costs; and

   (c) where applicable, the fact that you are obliged under a fee sharing agreement to pay to a charity any fees which you receive by way of costs from the client's opponent or other third party.

(3) Where you are acting for a publicly funded client, in addition to complying with 2.03(1) above and 2.03(5) and (6) below, you must explain the following at the outset:

   (a) the circumstances in which they may be liable for your costs;

   (b) the effect of the statutory charge;

   (c) the client's duty to pay any fixed or periodic contribution assessed and the consequence of failing to do so; and

   (d) that even if your client is successful, the other party may not be ordered to pay costs or may not be in a position to pay them.

(4) Where you agree to share your fees with a charity in accordance with 8.01(k) you must disclose to the client at the outset the name of the charity.

(5) Any information about the cost must be clear and confirmed in writing.

(6) You must discuss with your client whether the potential outcomes of any legal case will justify the expense or risk involved including, if relevant, the risk of having to pay an opponent's costs.

(7) If you can demonstrate that it was inappropriate in the circumstances to meet some or all of the requirements in 2.03(1) and (5), you will not breach 2.03.

2.04   Contingency fees

(1) You must not enter into an arrangement to receive a contingency fee for work done in prosecuting or defending any contentious proceedings before a court of England and Wales, a British court martial or an arbitrator where the seat of the arbitration is in England and Wales, except as permitted by statute or the common law.

(2) You must not enter into an arrangement to receive a contingency fee for work done in prosecuting or defending any contentious proceedings before a court of an overseas jurisdiction or an arbitrator where the seat of the arbitration is overseas except to the extent that a lawyer of that jurisdiction would be permitted to do so.

2.05   Complaints handling

(1) If you are a principal in a firm you must ensure:

   (a) that the firm has a written complaints procedure and that complaints are handled promptly, fairly and effectively in accordance with it;

   (b) that the client is told, in writing, at the outset:

      (i) that, in the event of a problem, the client is entitled to complain; and

      (ii) to whom the client should complain;

   (c) that the client is given a copy of the complaints procedure on request; and

   (d) that once a complaint has been made, the person complaining is told in writing:

      (i) how the complaint will be handled; and

      (ii) within what timescales they will be given an initial and/or substantive response.

(2) If you can demonstrate that it was inappropriate in the circumstances to meet some or all of these requirements, you will not breach 2.05.

(3) You must not charge your client for the cost of handling a complaint.

2.06   Commissions

If you are a principal in a firm you must ensure that your firm pays to your client commission received over £20 unless the client, having been told the amount, or if the precise amount is not known, an approximate amount or how the amount is to be calculated, has agreed that your firm may keep it.

2.07 Limitation of civil liability by contract

If you are a principal in a firm you must not exclude or attempt to exclude by contract all liability to your clients. However, you may limit your liability, provided that such limitation:

(a) is not below the minimum level of cover required by the Solicitors' Indemnity Insurance Rules for a policy of qualifying insurance;

(b) is brought to the client's attention; and

(c) is in writing.

Guidance to rule 2 – Client relations

General

1. The requirements of rule 2 do not exhaust your obligations to clients. As your client's trusted adviser, you must act in the client's best interests (see 1.04) and you must not abuse or exploit the relationship by taking advantage of a client's age, inexperience, ill health, lack of education or business experience, or emotional or other vulnerability.

2. It is not envisaged or intended that a breach of 2.02, 2.03 or 2.05 should invariably render a retainer unenforceable. As noted in the introduction to this rule, the purpose of 2.02 and 2.03 is to ensure that clients are given the information necessary to enable them to make appropriate decisions about if and how their matter should proceed. These parts of the rule together with 2.05 require you to provide certain information to your client. Subrules 2.02(3), 2.03(7) and 2.05(2) recognise that it is not always necessary to provide all this information to comply with the underlying purpose of the rule. Similarly, the information you are required to give to your client varies in importance both inherently and in relation to the individual client and the retainer. Consequently, the rule will be enforced in a manner which is proportionate to the seriousness of the breach. For example, if you were to fail to tell your client that they would be liable to pay another party's costs in breach of 2.03(1)(f), this is likely to be treated as a more serious breach than your failure to advise your client about your right to exercise a lien for unpaid costs in breach of 2.03(1)(e).

You should note that a breach of rule 2 may provide evidence against a solicitor, an REL or a recognised body of inadequate professional services under section 37A of the Solicitors Act 1974. The powers of the Legal Complaints Service on a finding of an inadequate professional service include disallowing all or part of the solicitor's or REL's costs and directing the solicitor or REL to pay compensation to the client. Section 37A does not apply to you if you are an RFL. Solicitor and REL partners in a multi-national partnership (MNP) are subject to section 37A in respect of services provided by the MNP.

Taking on clients – 2.01

3. Subrule 2.01 identifies some situations where you must refuse to act for a client or, if already acting, must stop doing so.

   The retainer is a contractual relationship and subject to legal considerations. You should be sure of your legal position as to who is your client if you contract to provide services to a third party. For example, if you agree to provide all or part of a Home Information Pack to an estate agent or Home Information Pack provider for the benefit of a seller, you should ensure there is an agreed understanding as to whether the estate agent/pack provider or the seller is your client.

4. Your right to decide not to accept instructions is subject to restrictions, including the following:

   (a) You must not refuse for a reason that would breach rule 6 (Equality and diversity).

   (b) Rule 11 (Litigation and advocacy), governing a solicitor or REL acting as an advocate, contains restrictions on when the solicitor or REL may refuse instructions.

   (c) Be aware of restrictions on when you can refuse to act or cease acting for a publicly funded client in a criminal matter.

5. If you are an in-house solicitor or in-house REL you are already in a contractual relationship with your employer who is, for the purpose of these rules, your client. You are not therefore necessarily as free as a solicitor or REL in a firm to refuse instructions, and will need to use your professional judgement in applying 2.01.

6. Subrule 2.01 sets out situations in which you must refuse instructions or, where appropriate, cease acting. These might include the following:

   (a) Breach of the law or rules

      (i) where there is a conflict of interests between you and your client or between two or more clients – see rule 3 (Conflict of interests);

(ii) where money laundering is suspected, your freedom to cease acting is curtailed (see the Proceeds of Crime Act 2002, the Money Laundering Regulations 2003 (SI 2003/3075), other relevant law and directives, and guidance issued by the Board of the Solicitors Regulation Authority on this subject); and

(iii) where the client is a child or a patient (within the meaning of the Mental Health Act 1983), special circumstances apply. You cannot enter into a contract with such a person and, furthermore, if your client loses mental capacity after you have started to act, the law will automatically end the contractual relationship. However, it is important that the client, who is in a very vulnerable situation, is not left without legal representation. Consequently, you should notify an appropriate person (e.g. the Court of Protection), or you may look for someone legally entitled to provide you with instructions, such as an attorney under an enduring power of attorney, or take the appropriate steps for such a person to be appointed, such as a receiver or a litigation friend. This is a particularly complex legal issue and you should satisfy yourself as to the law before deciding on your course of action.

(b) Insufficient resources

Before taking on a new matter, you must consider whether your firm has the resources – including knowledge, qualifications, expertise, time, sufficient support staff and, where appropriate, access to external expertise such as agents and counsel – to provide the support required to represent the client properly. The obligation is a continuing one, and you must ensure that an appropriate or agreed level of service can be delivered even if circumstances change.

(c) Duress or undue influence

It is important to be satisfied that clients give their instructions freely. Some clients, such as the elderly, those with language or learning difficulties and those with disabilities are particularly vulnerable to pressure from others. If you suspect that a client's instructions are the result of undue influence you need to exercise your judgement as to whether you can proceed on the client's behalf. For example, if you suspect that a friend or relative who accompanies the client is exerting undue influence, you should arrange to see the client alone or if appropriate with an independent third party or interpreter. Where there is no actual evidence of undue influence but the client appears to want to act against their best interests, it may be sufficient simply to explain the consequences of the instructions the client has given and confirm that the client wishes to proceed. For evidential purposes, it would be sensible to get this confirmation in writing.

7. As a matter of good practice you should not act for a client who has instructed another firm in the same matter unless the other firm agrees. If you are asked to provide a second opinion, you may do so but you should satisfy yourself that you have sufficient information to handle the matter properly.

Ceasing to act

8. A client can end the retainer with you at any time and for any reason. You may only end the relationship with the client if there is a good reason and after giving reasonable notice. Examples of good reasons include where there is a breakdown in confidence between you and the client, and where you are unable to obtain proper instructions.

9. If there is good reason to cease acting, you must give reasonable notice to the client. What amounts to reasonable notice will depend on the circumstances. For example, it would normally be unreasonable to stop acting to find alternative representation. In such a case, if there is no alternative but to cease acting immediately, you should attend and explain the circumstances to the court – see rule 11 (Litigation and advocacy). There may be circumstances where it is reasonable to give no notice.

10. The relationship between you and your client can also be ended automatically by law, for example by the client's bankruptcy or mental incapacity (see note 6(a)(iii) above).

11. When you cease acting for a client, you will need to consider what should be done with the paperwork. You must hand over the client's files promptly on request subject to your right to exercise a lien in respect of outstanding costs. You should try to ensure the client's position is not prejudiced, and should also bear in mind his or her rights under the Data Protection Act 1998. Undertakings to secure the costs should be used as an alternative to the exercise of a lien if possible. There may be circumstances where it is unreasonable to exercise a lien, for example, where the amount of the outstanding costs is small and the value or importance of the matter is very great. In any dispute over the ownership of documents you should refer to the law. Further advice about the law of lien or the ownership of documents can be found in *Cordery on Solicitors* or other reference books on the subject.

Client care – 2.02

12. The purpose of 2.02 is to set out the type of information that must normally be given to a client. This information must be provided in a clear and readily accessible form.

13. Subrule 2.02 is flexible about the extent of the information to be given in each individual case. Over-complex or lengthy terms of business letters may not be helpful.

14. The 'level of service' to be provided should be agreed at the outset. For example, the client may want regular written reports. Alternatively, the client may want to provide initial instructions then to hear no more until an agreed point has been reached. This will affect the projected costs of the matter.

15. When considering the options available to the client (2.02(1)(b)), if the matter relates to a dispute between your client and a third party, you should discuss whether mediation or some other alternative dispute resolution (ADR) procedure may be more appropriate than litigation, arbitration or other formal processes. There may be costs sanctions if a party refuses ADR – see *Halsey* v *Milton Keynes NHS Trust and Steel and Joy* [2004] EWCA (Civ) 576. More information may be obtained from the Law Society's Practice Advice Service.

16. Subrule 2.02(2)(e) requires you to explain limitations or conditions on your acting arising from your relationship with a third party. Where such a relationship involves sharing any client information with a third party, you must inform the client and obtain their consent. Failure to do so would be a breach of client confidentiality (see rule 4 – Confidentiality and disclosure) and possibly also a breach of the Data Protection Act 1998. Some arrangements with third parties, such as introducers under rule 9 (Referrals of business) or fee sharers under rule 8 (Fee sharing), may constrain the way in which you handle clients' matters.

17. The constraints that such arrangements impose may fall into one of the following categories:

    (a) Constraints which are proper and do not require disclosure to the client. These normally relate to service standards such as dealing with client enquiries within a specified time, the use of specified computer software, telecommunications systems, a particular advertising medium, or particular training provision.

    (b) Constraints which are proper but require disclosure to the client. Some third parties may have a legitimate interest in the progress of the client's matter and the way it is dealt with – for instance, third parties who fund a client's matter, and insurers. Constraints that they impose, e.g. that you will not issue proceedings without the authority of the funder are proper provided they do not operate against the client's best interests, but should be disclosed to the client.

(c) Constraints which are improper cannot be remedied by disclosing them to the client. These are constraints which impair your independence and ability to act in the client's best interests. You cannot accept an arrangement which involves such constraints. They might include, for instance, requirements that you do not disclose information to the client to which the client is entitled, or give advice to the client which you know is contrary to the client's best interests, or with which you disagree, or that you act towards the court in a deceitful manner or lie to a third party.

18. You must give the required information to the client as soon as possible after you have agreed to act. You must then keep the client up to date with the progress of the matter and any changes affecting the original agreement.

19. The status of the person dealing with your client must be made absolutely clear, for legal and ethical reasons. For example, a person who is not a solicitor must not be described as one, either expressly or by implication. All staff having contact with clients, including reception, switchboard and secretarial staff, should be advised accordingly.

20. All clients affected by a material alteration to the composition of the firm must be informed personally. Where the person having conduct of a matter leaves a firm, the client in question must be informed, preferably in advance, and told the name and status of the person who is to take over their matter.

21. Subrule 2.02(2)(d) refers to the person responsible for the overall supervision of a matter. Supervision requirements are dealt with in rule 5 (Business management) and guidance about who can supervise matters may be found there.

22. There may be circumstances when it would be inappropriate to provide any or all of the information required by 2.02. It will be for you to justify why compliance was not appropriate in an individual matter. For example, where you are asked for one-off advice, or where you have a long-standing client who is familiar with your firm's terms of business and knows the status of the person dealing with the matter, this information may not need to be repeated. However, other aspects of 2.02 must be complied with and the client must be kept up to date and informed of changes.

23. If you are an in-house solicitor or in-house REL much of 2.02 will be inappropriate when you are acting for your employer. However, it may be necessary for you to comply with aspects of 2.02 when you are acting for someone other than your employer in accordance with rule 13 (In-house practice).

24. If you receive instructions from someone other than your client, you must still give the client the information required under 2.02. There are, however, exceptions to this. For example, where your client is represented by an attorney under a power of attorney or where a receiver has been appointed because the client has lost mental capacity, the information required by 2.02 should be given to the attorney or receiver.

25. In order to provide evidence of compliance with 2.02, you should consider giving the information in writing even though this is not a requirement.

26. Where you are, in effect, your firm's client – for example, as an executor administering a deceased's estate or a trustee of a trust – you should consider what information, if any, should be given to interested parties. There is no requirement, for example, that beneficiaries under a will or trust should be treated as though they were clients. It may, however, be good practice to provide some information – for example, about the type of work to be carried out and approximate timescales.

Information about the cost – 2.03

27. The purpose of 2.03 is to ensure that the client is given relevant costs information and that this is clearly expressed. Information about costs must be worded in a way that is appropriate for the client. All costs information must be given in writing and regularly updated.

28. Subrule 2.03 recognises that there may be circumstances where it would be inappropriate to provide any or all of the information required. It will be for you to justify why compliance was not appropriate in an individual matter. For example, your firm may regularly do repeat work for the client on agreed terms and the client might not need the costs information repeated. However, the client should be informed, for example, of any changes in a firm's charging rates.

29. If you are an in-house solicitor or REL, much of 2.03 will be inappropriate if you are acting for your employer.

30. This guidance does not deal with the form a bill can take, final and interim bills, when they can be delivered and when and how a firm can sue on a bill. All these matters are governed by complex legal

provisions, and there are many publications that provide help to firms and clients. Advice on some aspects of costs is available from the Law Society's Practice Advice Service. This guidance does not deal with the form a bill can take, final and interim bills, when they can be delivered and when and how a firm can sue on a bill. All these matters are governed by complex legal provisions, and there are many publications that provide help to firms and clients. Advice on some aspects of costs is available from the Law Society's Practice Advice Service.

31. You will usually be free to negotiate the cost and the method of payment with your clients. It will not normally be necessary for the client to be separately advised on the cost agreement. Different cost options may have different implications for the client – for example, where the choice is between a conditional fee agreement and an application for public funding. In those circumstances clients should be made aware of the implications of each option.

32. The rule requires you to advise the client of the circumstances in which you may be entitled to exercise a lien for unpaid costs. For more information see note 11 above.

33. Clients may be referred to you at a stage when they have already signed a contract for a funding arrangement – see also rule 9 (Referrals of business). You should explain the implications of any such arrangement fully including the extent to which the charges associated with such an arrangement may be recovered from another party to the proceedings.

34. There may be some unusual arrangements, however, where it should be suggested that the client considers separate advice on what is being proposed – for example, where you are to receive shares in a new company instead of costs. See also rule 3 (Conflict of interests) and 9.02(g) for details about your obligations to clients who have been referred to you.

35. Subrule 2.03 does not cover all the different charging arrangements possible or the law governing them. However, it does require that the chosen option is explained as fully as possible to the client. It also requires that if you have agreed to pay all, or part, of your fees to a charity in accordance with rule 8 (Fee sharing) the client must be informed at the outset of the name of that charity.

36. It is often impossible to tell at the outset what the overall cost will be. Subrule 2.03 allows for this and requires that you provide the client with as much information as possible at the start and that you keep the client updated. If a precise figure cannot be given at the outset, you should explain the reason to the client and agree a ceiling figure or review dates.

37. Particular information will be of relevance at particular stages of a client's matter. You should, for example, ensure that clients understand the costs implications of any offers of settlement. Where offers of settlement are made, clients must be fully informed of the amount to be deducted in respect of costs and how this figure is calculated. You should advise clients of their rights to assessment of your costs in such circumstances.

38. When a potential client contacts you with a view to giving you instructions you should always, when asked, try to be helpful in providing information on the likely costs of their matter.

Work under a conditional fee agreement or for a publicly funded client

39. Subrules 2.03(2) and (3) set out additional information which must be explained to the client when work is done under a conditional fee agreement or on a publicly funded basis. Conditional fee agreements are subject to statutory requirements and all agreements must conform to these. Where you are acting under a conditional fee agreement and you are obliged under a fee sharing agreement to pay to a charity any fees which you receive by way of costs from the client's opponent or other third party, the client must be informed at the outset of the name of that charity.

Payments to others

40. You must explain at the outset to your client any likely payments they will have to make. These could include court fees, search fees, experts' fees and counsel's fees. Where possible, you should give details of the probable cost and if this is not possible you should agree with the client to review these expenses and the need for them nearer the time they are likely to be incurred.

Contingency fees – 2.04

41. A 'contingency fee' is defined in rule 24 (Interpretation) as any sum (whether fixed, or calculated either as a percentage of the proceeds or otherwise) payable only in the event of success.

42. If you enter into an arrangement for a lawful contingency fee with a client, what amounts to 'success' should be agreed between you and your client prior to entering into the arrangement.

43. Under rule 24 (Interpretation), 'contentious proceedings' is to be construed in accordance with the definition of 'contentious business' in section 87 of the Solicitors Act 1974.

44. Conditional fees are a form of contingency fees. In England and Wales a conditional fee agreement for certain types of litigation is permitted by statute. See section 58 of the Courts and Legal Services Act 1990 (as amended by section 27 of the Access to Justice Act 1999) and 2.03(2) above for more information.

45. It is acceptable to enter into a contingency fee arrangement for non-contentious matters (see section 87 of the Solicitors Act 1974 for the definition of 'non-contentious business') but you should note that to be enforceable the arrangement must be contained in a non-contentious business agreement.

46. An otherwise contentious matter remains non-contentious up to the commencement of proceedings. Consequently, you may enter into a contingency fee arrangement for, for example, the receipt of commission for the successful collection of debts owed to a client, provided legal proceedings are not started.

Complaints handling – 2.05

47. The purpose of 2.05 is to encourage complaints to be properly and openly dealt with. There are huge benefits in terms of time, money and client satisfaction if complaints can be dealt with effectively at firm level.

48. The content of your firm's complaints handling procedure is a matter for the firm, but the procedure must be in writing, clear and unambiguous. If a complaint is made to the Legal Complaints Service (LCS) or the Solicitors Regulation Authority the firm will need to be able to demonstrate compliance. Everyone in the firm will need to know about this obligation to ensure that clients know who to contact if they have a problem, the information to give the client when a complaint is made, and the importance of recording the stages of the complaint and the final outcome. When you acknowledge the complaint, your letter should contain details of the Legal Complaints Service, with the post and web addresses of that organisation. You should also explain that the client(s) can ask the LCS to become involved at the end of the firm's own complaints procedure if they are unhappy with the outcome. It is important to advise of the time limit, which is generally 6 months from the end of the firm's procedure, and can be checked by looking at the LCS website or by telephoning the LCS.

49. Your firm's arrangements for dealing with complaints must be fair and effective. Any investigation must be handled within an agreed timescale. Any arrangements must also comply with rule 6 (Equality and diversity).

50. Subrule 2.05(3) prevents you charging your client for the cost of handling a complaint. Dealing properly with complaints is an integral part of any professional business. The associated costs are part of the firm's overheads, and complainants must not be charged separately.

51. Subrule 2.05(2) allows for situations where it may be inappropriate to give all the information required.

Commissions – 2.06

52. Subrule 2.06 reflects the legal position, preventing a solicitor making a secret profit arising from the solicitor–client relationship.

53. A commission:

   (a) is a financial benefit you receive by reason of and in the course of the relationship of solicitor and client; and

   (b) arises in the context that you have put a third party and the client in touch with one another. (See *The Law Society* v *Mark Hedley Adcock and Neil Kenneth Mocroft* [2006] EWHC 3212 (Admin).)

54. Examples of what amounts to a commission include payments received from a stockbroker on the purchase of stocks and shares, from an insurance company or an intermediary on the purchase or renewal of an insurance policy, and from a bank or building society on the opening of a bank account. Also, a payment made to you for introducing a client to a third party (unless the introduction was unconnected with any particular matter which you were currently or had been handling for the client) amounts to a commission.

55. On the other hand, a discount on a product or a rebate on, for example, a search fee would not amount to a commission because it does not arise in the context of referring your client to a third party. Such payments are disbursements and the client must get the benefit of any discount or rebate.

56. A client can give informed consent only if you:

   (a) provide details concerning the amount; and

   (b) make it clear that they can withhold their consent and, if so, the commission will belong to them when it is received by you.

57. Commission received may be retained only if the conditions within 2.06 are complied with and the arrangement is in your client's best interests – either:

(a) it is used to offset a bill of costs; or

(b) you must be able to justify its retention – for example, the commission is retained in lieu of costs which you could have billed for work done in placing the business, but were not so billed.

58. It cannot be in the best interests of the client for you to receive the commission as a gift. There must be proper and fair legal consideration, such as your agreement to undertake legal work. In consequence, except where the commission is to be offset against a bill of costs:

(a) it is important that consent is obtained prior to the receipt of the commission (and preferably before you undertake the work leading to the paying of the commission);

(b) for the purposes of complying with 2.06 you may not obtain your client's consent to retain the commission after you have received it. If consent is not given beforehand, there can be no legal consideration and so the money belongs to the client; and

(c) if you have obtained consent but the amount actually received is materially in excess of the estimate given to your client, you cannot retrospectively obtain consent to retain the excess. The excess belongs to your client and should be handled accordingly.

59. In order to minimise possible confusion and misunderstanding, and to protect both you and your client, it is recommended that the agreement containing the details about the commission be in writing.

60. If it is your intention from the outset to use the commission to offset a bill of costs, it should be (subject to there being no specific instructions concerning the use of the commission):

(a) paid into client account as money on account of costs, if received before the bill has been submitted; or

(b) paid straight into office account if the bill has already been submitted.

61. Where you intend to retain the commission in lieu of costs and your client has provided their consent in accordance with 2.06, the money may be paid into office account as soon as it is received. Where you have requested your client's consent and it has been refused, the commission will belong to the client on receipt and must be paid into client account. It may then be paid to the client or used to offset a bill subject to note 60. See the Solicitors' Accounts Rules 1998 for more information.

62. Where you are a sole trustee or attorney or a joint trustee or attorney only with other solicitors, you cannot give proper consent to your retaining commission by purporting to switch capacities. Furthermore, you are very likely to be acting contrary to your fiduciary obligations at law.

63. For further information about dealing with commission see the Solicitors' Financial Services (Scope) Rules 2001.

Limitation of civil liability by contract – 2.07

64. For the qualifying insurance cover currently required see the Solicitors' Indemnity Insurance Rules.

65. The details of any limitation must be in writing and brought to the attention of the client. Because such a limitation goes to the heart of the agreement between you and your client, you should ensure that your client knows about the limitation and, in your opinion, understands its effect. Consequently, it would not be appropriate to include the limitation within a 'terms of business' letter without specifically drawing your client's attention to it.

66. Where you are preparing a trust instrument for a client and that instrument includes a term or terms which has or have the effect of excluding or limiting liability in negligence for a prospective trustee, you should take reasonable steps before the trust is created to ensure that your client is aware of the meaning and effect of the clause. Extra care will be needed if you are, or anyone in or associated with your firm is, or is likely later to become, a paid trustee of the trust.

67. Where you or another person in, or associated with, your firm is considering acting as a paid trustee you should not cause to be included a clause in a trust instrument which has the effect of excluding or limiting liability for negligence without taking reasonable steps before the trust is created to ensure that the settlor is aware of the meaning and effect of the clause.

    It would be prudent to ensure both that:

    (a) there is evidence that you have taken the appropriate steps; and

    (b) that evidence is retained for as long as the trust exists and for a suitable period afterwards.

68. Subrule 2.07 is subject to the position in law. The points which follow should be noted. The Solicitors Regulation Authority is entitled to expect you to undertake your own research and/or take appropriate advice as to the general law in this area. Relying upon this guidance alone may not be sufficient to ensure compliance with the law.

(a) Liability for fraud or reckless disregard of professional obligations cannot be limited.

(b) Existing legal restraints cannot be overridden. In particular, the courts will not enforce in your favour an unfair agreement with your client.

(c) Under section 60(5) of the Solicitors Act 1974 and paragraph 24 of Schedule 2 to the Administration of Justice Act 1985, a provision in a contentious business agreement that a firm shall not be liable for negligence, or shall be relieved from any responsibility which would otherwise apply is void.

(d) By section 2(2) of the Unfair Contract Terms Act 1977, a contract term which seeks to exclude liability for negligence is of no effect except insofar as it satisfies the requirement of reasonableness set out in section 11 of the Unfair Contract Terms Act. Section 11 specifies that the contract term must be fair and reasonable having regard to the circumstances which were or ought reasonably to have been known to, or in the contemplation of, the parties when the contract was made. Schedule 2 to the Unfair Contract Terms Act sets out guidelines as to the factors to be taken into account in considering whether the contract term meets the test of reasonableness.

(e) Section 11(4) of the Unfair Contract Terms Act 1977 provides that where a contractual term seeks to restrict liability to a specified sum of money, the question of whether the requirement of reasonableness has been satisfied must also take into account the resources available to you for the purpose of meeting the liability, and the extent to which insurance is available.

(f) The Unfair Terms in Consumer Contracts Regulations 1999 (SI 1999/2083) have a comparable effect to the Unfair Contract Terms Act 1977 as to limitation or exclusion of liability, where your client is a consumer and the term in question has not been individually negotiated. Regulation 3(1) of the 1999 Regulations defines a consumer as any natural person who, in contracts covered by those Regulations, is acting for purposes which are outside their trade, business or profession. Regulation 5(2) states that a term shall always be regarded as not having been individually negotiated where it has been drafted in advance and the consumer has therefore not been able to influence the substance of the term. Regulation 5(1) provides that a term is unfair if, contrary to the requirements of good faith, it causes a significant imbalance in the parties' rights and obligations. Schedule 2 to the Regulations contains an indicative, non-exhaustive list of contract terms which may be regarded as unfair. The test of fairness under these Regulations is not identical to the test of reasonableness under the Unfair Contract Terms Act 1977.

(g) When the retainer may be affected by foreign law, such matters may need to be considered according to the law applicable to the contract.

69. You should also note that if you want to limit your firm's liability to a figure above the minimum level for qualifying insurance but within your firm's top-up insurance cover, you will need to consider whether the top-up insurance will adequately cover a claim arising from the matter in question. For example:

(a) If your firm agrees with a client that its liability will not exceed £4 million, and the top-up insurance is calculated on an aggregate yearly basis, there is no guarantee that the amount of the top-up cover would be sufficient where there have been multiple claims already.

(b) Because insurance cover available to meet any particular claim is usually ascertained by reference to the year in which the claim itself is first made, or notice of circumstances which may give rise to a claim is first brought to the attention of insurers, the top-up cover when the claim is brought (or notice of circumstances given) may not be the same as it was when the contract was made.

70. You will not breach 2.07 by agreeing with your client that liability will rest with your firm and not with any employee, director, member or shareowner who might otherwise be liable. However, any such agreement is subject to section 60(5) of the Solicitors Act 1974, the Unfair Contract Terms Act 1977 and the Unfair Terms in Consumer Contracts Regulations 1999.

71. Subrule 2.07 does not apply in relation to your overseas practice. However, if you are a principal or a recognised body 15.02(3) prohibits you from seeking to limit your civil liability below the minimum level of cover you would need in order to comply with 15.26 (Professional indemnity).

72. You will not breach 2.07 by a term limiting or excluding any liability to persons who are not your client under the principle in *Hedley Byrne & Co Ltd* v *Heller & Partners Ltd* [1964] AC 465. However, any such term will be subject to section 60(5) of the Solicitors Act 1974, the Unfair Contract Terms Act 1977 and the Unfair Terms in Consumer Contracts Regulations 1999, where appropriate.

Appendix 2 – Contentious business agreements

Section 59(1) of the Solicitors Act 1974 (as amended by s.98(5) of the Courts and Legal Services Act 1990) provides that '. . . a solicitor may make an agreement in writing with his client as to his remuneration . . . providing that he shall be remunerated by a gross sum or by reference to an hourly rate, or by a salary, or otherwise . . .'.

Such an agreement made under the Solicitors Act is called a 'contentious business agreement' for the purposes of that Act. Sections 59–63 of the Solicitors Act 1974 (as amended) contain provisions which regulate the making and enforcement of 'contentious business agreements'.

Form of the agreement

The agreement must:

- be in writing and signed by the client;
- show all the terms – see *Chamberlain* v *Boodle and King* [1982] 3 All ER 188 (CA).

The agreement should expressly state that it is a contentious business agreement and be certain as to the charging and review mechanism. The majority of these types of agreements that are not upheld tend to fail on lack of certainty in this regard.

Effect of a contentious business agreement

The assessment of contentious business agreements is governed by section 60 of the Solicitors Act. The effect of the agreement is that clients cannot apply for assessment of costs except where the contentious business agreement provides for hourly rates. The reference to hourly rates was added by section 98 of the Courts and Legal Services Act 1990.

Clients can apply under s.61(3) of the Solicitors Act 1974 for the agreement to be examined by a taxing officer. The taxing officer will either allow it or require the opinion of the court to be taken on it. By s.61(4) of the Act 'the court may allow the agreement or reduce the amount payable under it, or set it aside and order the costs covered by it to be taxed as if it had never been made'. Clients can also apply under section 61(1) to have the agreement set aside. An application under section 61(3) does not preclude a client from making an application under section 61(1) to have the agreement set aside.

Enforcing a contentious business agreement

Section 61 of the Solicitors Act 1974 deals with the enforcement of contentious business agreements. A solicitor seeking to rely on a contentious business agreement must obtain the permission of the court to enforce it.

Appendix 3 – Frequently asked questions

1. My client has asked for my bill to be assessed. What do I have to do?

You should advise him to make his own application. Although you may issue an application to have your own costs assessed, it is inadvisable unless there are very unusual circumstances. Unless the client attends the assessment hearing, or the costs judge certifies that there are special circumstances, the court will not make an order for the costs of the assessment proceedings (s.70(9)(a) and (b) Solicitors Act 1974). Also, the order made at the hearing will not include an order for payment of the assessed costs by the client, so that if the client does not pay the bill after the assessment you will have to commence separate proceedings for payment.

2. I have issued a gross sum bill to my client. He has now requested a further detailed breakdown. Must I supply this?

In contentious matters, where a solicitor has issued a gross sum bill, the client may request a detailed breakdown of costs in lieu of the original bill within 3 months of receiving the bill. This does not apply if the solicitor has issued proceedings for payment of the bill or if the costs are subject to a Contentious Business Agreement (see Solicitors Act 1974 s.64(2)).

However, you might wish to explain to your client that his request has the dramatic effect of cancelling the original gross sum bill. If, when going through your file, you consider you did not include all of your costs in the original bill, you are free to draw up a bill for the higher amount.

The position differs in non-contentious matters as the client has the right to ask for a Remuneration Certificate (see article 4 of the Solicitors' (Non-Contentious Business) Remuneration Order 1994) if he is unhappy with the amount charged. In this case, the solicitor is not obliged to provide a further detailed breakdown after providing a gross sum bill. If the client wishes to receive a further breakdown, the solicitor can make a charge for the further work involved as long as the client is informed in advance of this additional cost.

3. **My costs are about to be assessed. Is there any information available on the hourly rates allowed on assessment in my local county court?**

The Court Service provides details of guideline hourly charging rates. The most recent are available on the Court Service website **www.hmcourts-service.gov.uk/publications/guidance/scco** at appendix 2. There is a model solicitor–client costs breakdown in the schedule of costs precedents attached to the Civil Procedure Rules. This is the recommended format if the matter goes to assessment.

4. **Are there any guideline rates for summary assessment in relation to counsel's fees?**

Yes, you can find them at **www.hmcourts-service.gov.uk**. It is emphasised that these figures are not recommended rates but it is hoped that they may provide a helpful starting point for judges when assessing counsel's fees.

5. **I act for the claimant in civil litigation proceedings, and have just completed preparation of the trial bundles. Who bears the cost of this?**

In the absence of any provision in the rules, the cost of preparing trial bundles is part of the claimant's general costs, the reasonable costs of which may be recoverable if your client goes on to win the case (see *Blackstone's Civil Practice 2008*, p.764).

6. **A former client has made an application for an assessment of our firm's costs under s.70 Solicitors Act 1974. How are the costs of the assessment hearing dealt with?**

The costs of the assessment hearing usually follow the event. Section 70(9) Solicitors Act 1974 states if your bill is reduced by one fifth or more, then you will bear the costs of the hearing. If the bill is reduced by less than one fifth or is not reduced, the former client will pay the costs.

7. **I have issued a gross sum bill to my client. He has now requested a further detailed breakdown. Must I supply this?**

In contentious matters, where a solicitor has issued a gross sum bill, the client may request a detailed breakdown of costs in lieu of the original bill within 3 months of receiving the bill. This does not apply if the solicitor has issued proceedings for payment of the bill or if the costs are subject to a Contentious Business Agreement (see Solicitors Act 1974 s.64(2)).

However, you might wish to explain to your client that his request has the dramatic effect of cancelling the original gross sum bill. If, when going through your file, you consider you did not include all of your costs in the original bill, you are free to draw up a bill for the higher amount.

8.   Can a bill of costs include unpaid disbursements?

Yes, but only if the unpaid disbursements are described in the bill as not yet paid. The deficiency can lead to difficulties to these items if they are challenged on a later assessment. One solution in such an instance would be to ask the costs judge for an adjournment, apply to the court for leave to withdraw the entire bill and redeliver it (but there is a risk that you may be ordered to pay all the costs thrown away) and deliver a fresh bill, Solicitors Act 1974 s.67. It should be noted that in *Tearle & Co* v *Sherring* (29 October 1993, unreported, QBD), Wright J held that where a solicitor has acted in good faith but has inadvertently omitted to describe the disbursements as unpaid, the court not only had the power to give him leave to withdraw his bill and deliver another one, to save costs it could in an appropriate case give leave to amend his bill by adding the words 'unpaid'. However, you should err on the side of caution and describe unpaid disbursements as 'unpaid' in the bill.

Appendix 4 – Amendments to s.69 Solicitors Act 1974

Action to recover solicitor's costs

(1)   Subject to the provisions of this Act, no action shall be brought to recover any costs due to a solicitor before the expiration of one month from the date on which a bill of those costs is delivered in accordance with the requirements mentioned in subsection (2); but if there is probable cause for believing that the party chargeable with the costs –

   (a)   is about to quit England and Wales, to become bankrupt or to compound with his creditors, or

   (b)   is about to do any other act which would tend to prevent or delay the solicitor obtaining payment,

   the High Court may, notwithstanding that one month has not expired from the delivery of the bill, order that the solicitor be at liberty to commence an action to recover his costs and may order that those costs be taxed [assessed].

[(2)   The requirements referred to in subsection (1) are that the bill must be –

(a) signed in accordance with subsection (2A), and

(b) delivered in accordance with subsection (2C).

(2A) A bill is signed in accordance with this subsection if it is–

(a) signed by the solicitor or on his behalf by an employee of the solicitor authorised by him to sign, or

(b) enclosed in, or accompanied by, a letter which is signed as mentioned in paragraph (a) and refers to the bill.

(2B) For the purposes of subsection (2A) the signature may be an electronic signature.

(2C) A bill is delivered in accordance with this subsection if –

(a) it is delivered to the party to be charged with the bill personally,

(b) it is delivered to that party by being sent to him by post to, or left for him at, his place of business, dwelling-house or last known place of abode, or

(c) it is delivered to that party –

(i) by means of an electronic communications network, or

(ii) by other means but in a form that nevertheless requires the use of apparatus by the recipient to render it intelligible,

and that party has indicated to the person making the delivery his willingness to accept delivery of a bill sent in the form and manner used.

(2D) An indication to any person for the purposes of subsection (2C)(c) –

(a) must state the address to be used and must be accompanied by such other information as that person requires for the making of the delivery;

(b) may be modified or withdrawn at any time by a notice given to that person.

(2E) Where a bill is proved to have been delivered in compliance with the requirements of subsections (2A) and (2C), it is not necessary in the first instance for the solicitor to prove the contents of the bill and it is to be presumed, until the contrary is shown, to be a bill bona fide complying with this Act.

(2F) A bill which is delivered as mentioned in subsection (2C)(c) is to be treated as having been delivered on the first working day after the day on which it was sent (unless the contrary is proved).]

(3) Where a bill of costs relates wholly or partly to contentious business done in a county court and the amount of the bill does not exceed [£5,000], the powers and duties of the High Court under this section and sections 70 and 71 in relation to that bill may be exercised and performed by any county court in which any part of the business was done.

[(4) ...]

[(5) In this section references to an electronic signature are to be read in accordance with section 7(2) of the Electronic Communications Act 2000 (c 7).

(6) In this section –

'electronic communications network' has the same meaning as in the Communications Act 2003 (c 21);

'working day' means a day other than a Saturday, a Sunday, Christmas Day, Good Friday or a bank holiday in England and Wales under the Banking and Financial Dealings Act 1971 (c 80).]

Annex 3C

Non-contentious costs – Practice Advice Service

November 2008

Introduction

This booklet, prepared by the Practice Advice Service, is not intended to be a fully comprehensive guide to non-contentious costs but attempts to cover those areas that generate the most frequent enquiries from solicitors. The booklet provides information on charging in non-contentious matters. It also discusses billing generally and the procedures available to clients who may wish to challenge solicitors' costs.

This booklet refers to various cases. Practitioners requiring copies of the relevant cases or information on case law may wish to contact the Law Society library which provides a photocopying service, telephone 0870 606 2511 or e-mail library@lawsociety.org.uk for further details.

Solicitors should in particular familiarise themselves in more detail with:

- Solicitors' (Non-Contentious Business) Remuneration Order 1994;
- Solicitors' Code of Conduct 2007 [NB: Updated 31 March 2009], in particular rule 2 which deals with Client Relations;
- section 57 of the Solicitors Act 1974;
- rule 48.10 of the Civil Procedure Rules.

It is intended to update this booklet from time to time. When this edition is revised, a note will be inserted in the Law Society's *Gazette* and the updated version will be available on request from the Practice Advice Service. Alternatively, copies may be downloaded from the Law Society's website [**www.lawsociety.org.uk**].

Booklets on contentious costs and payment by results are also available. For advice on costs generally, telephone the Practice Advice Service on 0870 606 2522 or e-mail practiceadvice@lawsociety.org.uk.

What is non-contentious business?

Non-contentious business is defined in s.87(1) Solicitors Act 1974 as 'any business done as a solicitor which is not contentious business'.

Work done preliminary to proceedings is non-contentious provided proceedings are not subsequently begun. The keyword is 'begun'. So, for example, if a solicitor takes instructions on a personal injury matter and the parties reach settlement before proceedings are issued, the work is regarded as non-contentious.

Please note * When proceedings have been issued, it is a moot point as to whether all prior work leading to the action automatically becomes contentious. Please see obiter comment of Lord Justice Brooke in *Crosbie* v *Munroe* [2003] EWCA Civ 350.

If solicitors in England and Wales are involved in work where proceedings are issued abroad, the work will be regarded as non-contentious. But please note rule 2.04(2) of the Solicitors' Code of Conduct 2007 (see Appendix 2 of this booklet) in regard to fee arrangements.

Examples of contentious and non-contentious business

Contentious	Non-contentious
1. Proceedings actually begun in the County Court, High Court, Magistrates' Court, Crown Court and the Court of Protection.	Proceedings before all tribunals other than the Lands Tribunal and the Employment Appeal Tribunal.
2. Proceedings actually begun before the Lands Tribunal and the Employment Appeal Tribunal.	Planning and other public enquiries including Coroner's Court work.
3. Contentious probate proceedings actually begun.	Non-contentious or common form probate business.
4. Proceedings on appeal to the Court of Appeal, Privy Council and House of Lords.	Conveyancing, company acquisitions and mergers, the administration of estates and trusts out of court, the preparation of wills, statements and contracts, and any other work not included in the 'contentious' column.
5. Proceedings in arbitration.	Criminal Injuries Compensation Board.
6. Motor Insurers Bureau Uninsured drivers' claims (proceedings issued).	Motor Insurers Bureau Untraced drivers' claims. Motor Insurers Bureau Uninsured drivers' claims (proceedings not issued).

Contentious	Non-contentious
7. Work done preliminary to proceedings covered by 1–5 above including advice, preparation and negotiations provided the proceedings are subsequently begun (although see note above*).	Work done preliminary to the proceedings included in the 'contentious' column if such proceedings are not subsequently begun.
8. Licensing (appeals to Magistrates' Court).	Licensing (administered by Local Authority).

Basis of charging in non-contentious business

When charging for non-contentious work, consideration must be given to article 3 of the Solicitors' (Non-Contentious Business) Remuneration Order 1994 (SI 1994/2616).

Article 3 states:

A solicitor's costs shall be such sum as may be fair and reasonable to both solicitor and entitled person*, having regard to all the circumstances of the case and in particular to:

(a) the complexity of the matter or the difficulty or novelty of the questions raised;

(b) the skill, labour, and specialised knowledge and responsibilities involved;

(c) the time spent on the business;

(d) the number and importance of the documents prepared or perused without regard to length;

(e) the place where and the circumstances in which the business or any part thereof is transacted;

(f) the amount or value of any money or property involved;

(g) whether any land involved is registered land;

(h) the importance of the matter to the client; and

(i) the approval (express or implied) of the entitled person* or the express approval of the testator to:

(i) the solicitor undertaking all or any part of the work giving rise to the costs or

(ii) the amount of the costs.

Practitioners are referred to rule 2 of the Solicitors' Code of Conduct 2007 within Appendix 2 of this booklet and particularly to the information relating to charging rates. Best modern practice is to use an inclusive charging rate (including care and conduct) rather than to show the hourly rate separately from the care and conduct element.

Article 3 above contains those factors that need to be considered when calculating the care and conduct element of the charging rate.

For assistance in calculating the time element of the charging rate please see the Law Society publication *The Expense of Time* (details at the [end] of this booklet).

* Entitled person as defined by article 2 means the client and certain residuary beneficiaries (see article 2 of the Solicitors' (Non-Contentious Business) Remuneration Order 1994 at Appendix 1 of this booklet).

Value element

In certain areas of work, such as probate, mortgages, commercial leases and domestic conveyancing amongst others, it may be appropriate to include a value element in the method of charging. Information on these specific areas is discussed in the subject areas below.

However, the question of whether a value element is used is a matter for agreement between the solicitor and the client; it is not mandatory. Where a value element is used, practitioners may wish to use the guidance that follows, which has been distilled from the decisions made by assessors in dealing with applications for remuneration certificates.

Where no specific information is given in the individual subject areas, the table below may assist:

Value band	Percentage
Up to £400,000	0.5%
On next £600,000 (maximum value £1 million)	0.375%
On next £1,500,000 (maximum value £2.5 million)	0.25%
On next £2,500,000 (maximum value £5 million)	0.125%
On next £5,000,000 (maximum value £10 million)	0.1%

Client relations

Rule 2 of the Solicitors' Code of Conduct 2007 came into effect on 1 July 2007. A key part of the Code relates to providing costs information to clients. The text of the rule can be found at Appendix 2 of this booklet.

Charging in probate and in the administration of estates

Fair and reasonable

In all cases the overall consideration must be that the charges are fair and reasonable, having regard to all the circumstances of the matter. The figures below should not be regarded as scale charges in any way and must always be exercised with discretion. In *Jemma Trust* v *Liptrott* [2003] EWCA Civ 1476, the Court of Appeal stated that it would be best practice to agree the charging regime in advance not only with the executors but also, where appropriate, with any residuary beneficiary who is an entitled third party under the Solicitors' (Non-Contentious Business) Remuneration Order 1994. The Court of Appeal held that a value charge can either be made in addition to an hourly rate, or it can be included in the hourly rate, but the value element must not be reflected in both charges. The comments of the court are reproduced in Appendix 5 below but it is recommended that practitioners read the *Jemma Trust* judgment in its entirety.

Where appropriate, charges may consist of two elements:

(a) Hourly rate

This should be an inclusive figure incorporating the fee earner's expense rate and any appropriate care and conduct uplift.

(b) Value element

Account may be taken of the value of the assets in the estate. In calculating the value element of the charge, the following approach may be helpful:

Consider the value nature and number of assets

It is usual to divide the estate (i.e. total value of the assets left after death) into two parts:

(i) The deceased's residence

   The value of the deceased's home, or as much of it as he or she owned, if it was shared with another person. For example, where the property is jointly owned, the value is reduced by half.

(ii) Value of rest of the estate

Apply an appropriate percentage

An appropriate percentage should be considered in the light of the circumstances of the case but the following may be helpful.

Solicitor not acting as an executor

Value of gross estate less residence	1%
Value of residence	0.5%

WORKED EXAMPLE 1 – SOLICITOR NOT ACTING AS EXECUTOR

So for example if the residence was valued at £200,000 and was owned by the deceased alone this would be calculated as follows: £200,000 × 0.5% = £1,000.

Then consider the value of the rest of the estate, which is say, £50,000 ignoring the value of the residence then apply 1%. The remaining calculation therefore is:

Rest of estate is £50,000 then apply 1% = £500

Therefore total value element 5 £1,000 + £500 = £1,500.

Solicitor acting as sole executor or joint executor with another person

Value of gross estate less residence	1.5%
Value of residence	0.75%

WORKED EXAMPLE 2 – SOLICITOR ACTING AS EXECUTOR

So for example if the residence was valued at £200,000 and was owned by the deceased as a joint tenant this would be calculated as follows:

Value of residence (£200,000 divided by 2) = £100,000 × 0 .75% = £750. Note the value of the residence is reduced by half as the deceased owned it jointly with another person.

Then consider the value of rest of the estate which is say £50,000 ignoring the value of the residence then apply 1.5%.

The remaining calculation is therefore:

Rest of the estate is £50,000 then apply 1.5% = £750

Therefore total value element = £750 + £750 = £1,500

SOLICITOR NOT ACTING AS AN EXECUTOR BUT
ACTING FOR A CORPORATE EXECUTOR

	General conduct of matter	Probate application only
Gross estate less residence	0.5%	0.06%
Residence	0.25%	0.12%

SOLICITOR ACTING AS A JOINT EXECUTOR WITH
A CORPORATE EXECUTOR

Value of gross estate less residence	0.75%
Value of residence	0.375%

High value estates

When dealing with high value estates, consideration should be given to reducing the value element percentage charged in order to ensure that the overall level of charge is fair and reasonable. For general guidance on this point, see the case of *Jemma Trust* v *Liptrott* [2003] EWCA Civ 1476. In that case the Court of Appeal held that an appropriate charging regime was as set out in Appendix 4 of this booklet.

In the case of *Jemma Trust*, the Court of Appeal also noted that in the appropriate circumstances a regressive scale may also need to be applied to the value element related to the principal residence.

It is for individual practitioners to exercise their own professional judgment as to whether or not to apply the value element when charging for the administration of an estate.

Charging in property work

The following methods of charging may be appropriate.

Domestic conveyancing

Two methods are suggested:

(i) Calculate hourly expense rate

Add value element outlined in the table on page [184] of this booklet

or

(ii)   Take a broad look at the circumstances of the transaction

Calculate a single charging figure incorporating the time spent and what is fair and reasonable in all the circumstances. This single charging figure may comprise a fixed fee or an estimate. If an estimate is provided consideration should be given to updating costs information regularly. See rule 2.03 of the Solicitors' Code of Conduct 2007 at Appendix 2 of this booklet.

In practice the second method is more commonplace.

Leasehold work

Hourly rate

This should be a single figure incorporating the time spent together with what is fair and reasonable in all the circumstances.

Value element

The suggested formula for calculating the value element of charges for leasehold work is as follows:

(i)   Take half the yearly rent.

(ii) Multiply it by the unexpired term of the lease (limited to 20 years).

(iii) Add any premium payable by the lessee and deduct any payable by the lessor.

(iv) Apply the following regressive scale to the value as calculated:

Value band	Percentage
Up to £400,000	½% (0.5%)
On next £600,000 (maximum value £1 million)	⅜% (0.375%)
On next £1,500,000 (maximum value £2.5 million)	¼% (0.25%)
On next £2,500,000 (maximum value £5 million)	⅛% (0.125%)
On next £5,000,000 (maximum value £10 million)	⅒% (0.1%)

Is the formula applicable to an assignment as well as a grant of a lease?

In 'An Approach to Non-Contentious Costs' the above formula is described as a formula for establishing a capital value. It does not discuss whether or not a value element is applicable. If on an assignment the circumstances suggest a value element is justifiable, the formula can be used to calculate it.

Fair and reasonable

Please note that these figures do not constitute a recommended scale. The final figure should still be reviewed to ensure that the charges are fair and reasonable having regard to all the circumstances.

Calculating a value element when acting on a mortgage or re-mortgage

Where the lender does not have its own scale of charges, the following percentages of value may be appropriate:

When acting for purchaser/mortgagor	0.25%
When acting for purchaser/mortgagor and the mortgagee	0.25%
When acting for the mortgagee alone	0.5%
When acting for the mortgagor alone	0.5%

These percentages should be reduced if dealing with high values.

Non-contentious business agreements

Section 57 of the Solicitors Act 1974 as amended by section 98 of the Courts and Legal Services Act 1990 allows a solicitor to enter into an agreement with the client for remuneration of non-contentious work.

Form of the agreement

The agreement MUST:

- be in writing – s.57(3);
- be signed by the person to be bound by it or by his/her agent – s.57(3);
- have all the terms contained within the document.

See *Chamberlain* v *Boodle and King* [1982] 3 All ER 188.
The agreement MAY:

(i) be entered into before, after or in the course of the transaction – s.57(1);

(ii) provide for remuneration by a gross sum, or by reference to an hourly rate, or by a commission, or percentage, or by a salary, or otherwise – s.57(2). The reference to hourly rate was added by s.98 of the Courts and Legal Services Act 1990 which came into force on 1 March 1991;

(iii) include all or any disbursements made by the solicitor in respect of searches, plans, travelling, stamps, fees, or other matter s.57(2).

Effect of a non-contentious business agreement

The provisions of the Solicitors' (Non-Contentious Business) Remuneration Order 1994 do not apply to a s.57 agreement (see *Walton* v *Egan* [1982] 3 All ER 849). Therefore the client is not entitled to seek a Remuneration Certificate.

A s.57 agreement can be referred for assessment if the solicitor seeks to rely on the agreement and the client objects on the grounds that it is unfair and unreasonable. The court has the power to enquire into the facts and may set aside or vary the agreement if it is found to be unfair or unreasonable – s.57(5).

If a s.57 agreement as to hourly rates is referred to assessment and the client objects to the amount of costs and not that the agreement is unfair or unreasonable, the agreed hourly rate will not be open to challenge but the court may consider the number of hours worked and whether they were excessive – s.57(7).

Enforcing a non-contentious business agreement

Simple debt recovery proceedings can be commenced – s.57(4).

Section 69 of the Solicitors Act 1974 must still be complied with before an action for recovery is brought by a solicitor. See page [199] of this booklet for further details.

Contingency fees

Rule 2 of the Solicitors' Code of Conduct 2007 prohibits a solicitor from entering into a contingency fee agreement for contentious work except where permitted under statute or by the common law (see rule 2.04 of the Code of Conduct 2007). Contingency fees are permissible in non-contentious cases. For a definition and examples of non-contentious business, please see page [182].

The term 'contingency fee' is generic in that it covers all agreements where the fee (whether fixed, or calculated either as a percentage of the proceeds or otherwise) is payable only in the event of success. However, 'contingency fee agreements' are traditionally regarded as arrangements whereby the fee is calculated as a percentage of the proceeds recovered.

Conditional fee agreements (CFAs) are a form of contingency fee permitted under statute. They can be used for all non-contentious work except for family matters.

However, CFAs are not commonly used in non-contentious matters as they are best suited to cases where costs are recoverable from the other side. CFAs could be considered in matters where it is possible that proceedings could be issued.

At the outset of a matter in which it is likely that proceedings could be issued (e.g. a personal injury matter), a solicitor could either:

- use a contingency fee arrangement contained in a Non-Contentious Business Agreement until proceedings are issued. At that stage, the retainer could not continue on that basis (see rule 2 above), and the arrangement would have to be changed to an alternative fee arrangement. Solicitors should be aware that it is a moot point as to whether all work done for the client automatically becomes contentious once proceedings are issued. If this view is taken there is doubt as to whether the solicitor would be able to recover his pre issue costs;
- use a CFA from the outset, or
- use some other type of fee arrangement (e.g., hourly rate, fixed cost, etc.) from the outset.

For guidance on conditional fee agreements see the Practice Advice Service booklet 'Payment by Results' which can be downloaded from the Law Society website at **www.lawsociety.org.uk**.

Billing the client

Interim bills

Interim bills on account

These are in fact merely requests for payments on account of a 'final bill' to be delivered at a later date. It is not possible to sue on this type of bill and a client cannot apply for assessment of it.

In non-contentious matters, a solicitor must make any requirement for a payment on account of costs a condition of accepting instructions. Without this condition (or the client's subsequent agreement), a solicitor cannot terminate the retainer if the client refuses to make such a payment. This is something that should be considered at the outset of the retainer when terms of business are being agreed.

Interim statute bills

These are termed statute bills because they comply with all the requirements of the Solicitors Act 1974 and result in all the consequences that flow from such compliance. The solicitor can sue on them and the client can apply for assessment of them. They are final bills in respect of the work covered and cannot be adjusted in light of the outcome of the case. Interim statute bills can arise in two ways:

(i) **Natural break**: The Law Society's advice is not to rely on this ground except in the clearest circumstances. For limited guidance on what constitutes a natural break, practitioners should see *Chamberlain* v *Boodle and King* [1982] 3 All ER 188 (CA).

(ii) **Agreement**: Practitioners should make it expressly clear in their terms of business letter that they propose to deliver interim statute bills in the event of protracted work. See the Court of Appeal judgments in *Davidsons* v *Jones-Fenleigh* [1997] Costs LR (Core Vol.) 70 and *Palomo* v *Turner* [2000] 1 WLR 37 regarding the distinction between statute bills and requests for payment on account generally.

Final bills

These can be rendered in the following circumstances:

(i)   where the client has agreed to, or asked for, delivery of a final bill;

(ii) at the conclusion of the matter;

(iii) on the termination of the retainer;

(iv) on an application to the High Court under s.68 of the Solicitors Act 1974 to order the solicitor to deliver a bill.

Where interim bills on account have been rendered pursuant to s.65(2) of the Solicitors Act 1974, these should be disregarded for the purposes of the final bill and treated as requests for payment of money on account. The final bill should therefore set out the total amount of the solicitor's charges and disbursements with any additional mark up on the interim bills and should give credit for all payments received as a result of bills on account.

Content of bill

Schedule 16, s.64(3) of the Legal Services Act 2007 which came into force in March 2008 amended s.69 of the Solicitors Act 1974. This amendment allows solicitors to deliver their bills electronically, please see Appendix 6 [of this booklet] for further information. A solicitor's bill of costs should contain sufficient information to identify the matter and period of time to which it relates.

The bill must also comply with s.69(2) of the Solicitors Act 1974 which requires that:

. . . the bill must be –

   (a) signed in accordance with subsection (2A), and

   (b) delivered in accordance with subsection (2C).

(2A) A bill is signed in accordance with this subsection if it is –

   (a) signed by the solicitor or on his behalf by an employee of the solicitor authorised by him to sign, or

   (b) enclosed in, or accompanied by, a letter which is signed as mentioned in paragraph (a) and refers to the bill.

(2B) For the purposes of subsection (2A) the signature may be an electronic signature.

(2C) A bill is delivered in accordance with this subsection if –

   (a) it is delivered to the party to be charged with the bill personally,

   (b) it is delivered to that party by being sent to him by post to, or left for him at, his place of business, dwelling-house or last known place of abode, or

   (c) it is delivered to that party –

      (i) by means of an electronic communications network, or

      (ii) by other means but in a form that nevertheless requires the use of apparatus by the recipient to render it intelligible, and that party has indicated to the person making the delivery his willingness to accept delivery of a bill sent in the form and manner used.

If the bill is not properly signed, it is still valid but will be unenforceable in the courts.

The bill should show disbursements separately from the solicitor's fees, see s.67 of the Solicitors Act 1974.

In order to comply with the VAT regulations, when a third party is paying the solicitor's costs, the bill must be made out to the client, but it should state that the bill is payable by a third party. Please see Value Added Tax Regulations 1995. Part III deals with VAT invoices and other invoicing requirements. Para.13 provides that where the registered person (i.e. the solicitor) makes a taxable supply to a taxable person (i.e. someone resident in the UK) then he shall supply them with an invoice. Para.14 sets out the required contents of an invoice which includes the name and address of the person to whom the goods and services are supplied.

Gross sum and detailed itemised bills

It is for the solicitor to decide whether to deliver a gross sum bill or one containing detailed items.

In a contentious matter, a client who has received a gross sum bill has the right to require a solicitor to deliver a detailed itemised bill to replace the original bill, see s.64(2) Solicitors Act 1974. This right does not apply in non-contentious work. The client does however have the right to seek a remuneration certificate from the Law Society under the provisions of the Solicitors' (Non-Contentious Business) Remuneration Order 1994 as well as a general right to have the bill assessed by the court. See *Walton* v *Egan* [1982] 3 All ER 849 cited above in respect of non-contentious business agreements.

Remuneration certificates

Article 4 of the Solicitors' (Non-Contentious Business) Remuneration Order 1994 ('the Order') provides that in a non-contentious matter the client may require the solicitor to obtain a remuneration certificate from the Legal Complaints Service stating that in its opinion the sum charged is fair and reasonable or, as the case may be, what other sum would be fair and reasonable.

The client is entitled to seek a remuneration certificate:

(i)   within one month from being notified by the solicitor in writing of the right;

(ii) before the bill has been paid;

(iii) provided the court has not ordered the bill to be assessed;

(iv) provided the costs in the bill do not exceed £50,000 (excluding VAT and disbursements);

(v)   provided a valid non-contentious business agreement has not been entered into.

The request for the certificate is made by the client to the solicitor. The solicitor must obtain an application form from the Legal Complaints Service and forward a copy of the completed form to the client, requesting comments as to why the client considers the costs to be excessive. The form is then sent to the remuneration certificate department by the solicitor together with the file of papers. The remuneration certificate procedure is free of charge.

Costs paid by deduction

If a bill has been paid by deduction from money held on account, the entitled person will still have the right to seek a remuneration certificate if he objects to the amount of the costs within a prescribed time (article 7).

Requirement to pay a sum towards the costs

The remuneration certificate assessment is free for the client. Article 11 of the Order provides that the client must pay one half of the costs together with all the VAT and all the paid disbursements before the solicitor makes the application unless either the solicitor or the Legal Complaints Service waives this requirement. The solicitor is not obliged to make an application for a certificate if the client does not pay the required amount.

Refunds

Article 13 of the Order provides that if a solicitor receives all or part payment of the costs and if a remuneration certificate is issued for a sum smaller than that already received, the solicitor must make the refund to the client immediately. The refund need not be made if the solicitor applies for assessment of the bill within one month of receipt of the remuneration certificate. Interest may be due to the client on the amount refunded.

Residuary beneficiaries

Under the Solicitors' (Non-Contentious Business) Remuneration Order 1994 article 2, a residuary beneficiary absolutely and immediately (not contingently) entitled to an inheritance is entitled to a remuneration certificate where the only personal representatives are:

(i)   solicitors (whether or not acting in a professional capacity);

(ii) solicitors acting jointly with partners or employees in a professional capacity.

A residuary beneficiary may also be entitled to apply for assessment to the court under section 71 of the Solicitors Act 1974, see below.

Further information

The full text of the Solicitors' (Non-Contentious Business) Remuneration Order 1994 is set out in Appendix 1 of this booklet.

For application forms and explanatory leaflets on the remuneration certificate procedure, please contact:

Legal Complaints Service
The Law Society
Victoria Court
8 Dormer Place
Leamington Spa
Warwickshire CV32 5AE
DX 292320 LEAMINGTON SPA 4
Tel 0845 608 6565

Assessment of third party costs

Section 71(1) of the Solicitors' Act 1974 provides:

> (1) Where a person other than the party chargeable with the bill for the purposes of section 70 has paid, or is or was liable to pay, a bill either to the solicitor or to the party chargeable with the bill, that person, or his executors, administrators or assignees may apply to the High Court for an order for the assessment of the bill as if he were the party chargeable with it, and the court may make the same order (if any) as it might have made if the application had been made by the party chargeable with the bill.

The practical effect of this section is that if a client is required to pay a third party's solicitor's costs, he may be entitled to have the bill of costs assessed as if he were the party chargeable.

This provision may for example be useful in the following situations:

(i) Residuary beneficiaries may apply for assessment of the costs of the solicitor who is administering an estate whether or not the solicitor is an executor of the estate.

(ii) A mortgagor who would like the costs of the mortgagee's solicitor assessed.

(iii) A tenant required to pay a landlord's solicitor's charges.

Information on precautions which a lessee's solicitors can take to prevent a dispute arising over a landlord's solicitor's bill is contained in a Law Society Council statement printed in the *Gazette* on 19 December 1984 and reprinted in the Law Society publication *An Approach to Non-Contentious Costs* (see details at the [end] of this booklet [under 'Further reading']).

In rule 2 of the Solicitors' Code of Conduct 2007 (see Appendix 2 [of this booklet]), the solicitor must advise the client of their potential liability for any other party's costs. Where appropriate, solicitors are advised to obtain a fixed figure or agree a cap on a third party's costs.

Where an undertaking is given as to costs, it is an undertaking to pay 'proper costs' unless otherwise stated. This enables the giver of the undertaking to apply for assessment of the bill and, provided that the recipient is notified of this promptly, the undertaking will take effect on the bill as assessed. See Guidance to rule 10 paragraph 32 of the Solicitors' Code of Conduct 2007. The application for assessment is under section 71 of the Solicitors Act 1974.

A tenant cannot request a remuneration certificate of the costs of the landlord's solicitor because he is not the solicitor's client. The tenant can however ask the landlord to seek a remuneration certificate although there is no obligation on the landlord to do so.

The landlord's solicitor should inform his client that he may look to him for payment if the tenant does not pay his costs.

Assessment of solicitor and client costs

There are two bases for the assessment of costs, the standard basis and the indemnity basis, and on neither basis will the court allow costs which have been unreasonably incurred or are unreasonable in amount (Rule 44.4(1)).

On an assessment on the indemnity basis, there is no reference to proportionality and any doubts as to whether costs were reasonably incurred or were reasonable in amount is resolved in favour of the receiving party. However, on an assessment on the standard basis, the court will only allow costs which are proportionate to the matters in issue and will resolve any doubt which it may have about whether costs were reasonably incurred or reasonable and proportionate in amount in favour of the paying party.

Non-contentious costs are always to be assessed on the indemnity basis (Rule 48.8(2)) while Rule 44.4 prescribes that contentious costs may be awarded on either basis.

The client can apply for an assessment of his/her solicitor's costs under section 70 of the Solicitors Act 1974.

Time limits under section 70 of Solicitors Act

The client has a right to assessment within one month from the date of the delivery of the bill.

If the application is made after one month but before twelve months from the date of delivery of the bill, the court's permission is required for the bill to be assessed.

Except in special circumstances, no order for assessment will be made:

(i)   after twelve months from the delivery of the bill; or

(ii) after a judgment has been obtained for the recovery of the costs covered by the bill; or

(iii) after the bill has been paid, but before the expiration of 12 months from the payment of the bill.

In relation to the application of section 70, practitioners should also have regard to the Court of Appeal decisions in *Thomas Watts & Co (A Firm)* v *Smith (Malcolm Davies)* [1998] Costs LR 59 and *Turner* v *Palomo* [2000] 1 WLR 37. Both of these decisions appear to allow the client a common law means to challenge a solicitor's bill outside the statutory limitations of s.70. The practical effect of this means that where a solicitor sues for non-payment of fees, any summary judgment will be for assessment of damages and not for a liquidated amount.

Also note the House of Lords decision in *Harrison* v *Tew* [1990] 2 AC 532 which stated that the court had no power to order assessment under s.70 outside the statutory period. This decision was distinguished in *Turner* v *Palomo*. An application for *Turner* v *Palomo* to be heard by the House of Lords was refused (see The Law Society's *Gazette* 8 September 1999 page 32).

Assessment procedure

Rule 48.10 of the Civil Procedure Rules sets out the procedure to be followed where the court has made an order under Part III of the Solicitors Act 1974 for the assessment of costs payable to a solicitor by his client and is as follows:

The solicitor must serve a breakdown of costs within 28 days of the order for costs to be assessed.

The client must serve points of dispute within 14 days after service on him of the breakdown in costs.

If the solicitor wishes to serve a reply, he must do so within 14 days of service on him of the points of dispute.

Either party may file a request for a hearing date:

(i)   after points of dispute have been served; but

(ii) no later than 3 months after the date of the order for the costs to be assessed.

This procedure applies subject to any contrary order made by the court.

Precedent P showing the breakdown of costs is annexed to the Practice Direction accompanying Rule 48.10. This Practice Direction also deals generally with the practicalities of the assessment process.

Where to apply

Rule 47.4 deals with the appropriate venue for detailed assessment proceedings. This should be read in conjunction with s.69(3) of the Solicitors Act 1974.

Who should apply?

It is usual for the client to apply for assessment although it is possible for a solicitor to apply to have his own costs assessed (see Rule 48.10(5)). The latter is inadvisable because the solicitor will generally be unable to recover his costs for attending the hearing if the client fails to attend.

Costs of assessment

The costs of assessment will follow the event. If a solicitor's bill is reduced by one fifth or more, then the solicitor will bear the costs of the assessment. If the bill is reduced by less than one fifth or is not reduced, the party chargeable will pay the costs. See Solicitors Act 1974, s.70(9).

The one fifth figure is calculated on the total of the bill excluding VAT.

If non-contentious costs are reduced by more than half, the Costs Officer is under an obligation to refer the matter to the Council of the Law Society – see article 5 of the Solicitors' (Non-Contentious Business) Remuneration Order 1994.

Recovering your costs

Before you sue

Provided that a solicitor's bill complies with the requirements of s.69(2) of the Solicitors Act 1974 (as set out on [. . .] under the heading 'Content of Bill') recovery proceedings for costs may be commenced after one month has elapsed from the date of delivery of the final or interim statute bill. However, in circumstances where the client is about to quit England and Wales, to be declared bankrupt or to compound with his creditors or do any other act which tends to prevent or delay the solicitor obtaining payment, a solicitor may seek leave to issue proceedings within a month, see s.69(1) of the Solicitors Act 1974.

It should be noted that a solicitor will be prevented from issuing recovery proceedings for costs where the client has made an application to the court for detailed assessment of the costs within one month of delivery of the bill or where he has obtained an order for the bill to be assessed – see s.70(1) and (2) of the Solicitors Act 1974.

Articles 6 and 8 of the Solicitors' (Non-Contentious Business) Remuneration Order 1994 state that before the solicitor can bring proceedings to recover costs on a bill for non-contentious business, he must, unless the costs have been assessed, have informed the client in writing of:

(i)   his right to assessment by the court;

(ii) the solicitor's right to charge interest on the outstanding amount of the bill.

Where the costs are less than £50,000 (excluding VAT and disbursements) the client should also be informed in writing of his right:

(i)   to require the solicitor to obtain a remuneration certificate;

(ii) to apply to the Legal Complaints Service for a waiver of the requirement to pay half the costs plus VAT and disbursements.

Please see Appendix [1] for a specimen notice of information under the Solicitors' (Non-Contentious Business) Remuneration Order 1994.

Interest on costs

Article 14 of the Solicitors' (Non-Contentious Business) Remuneration Order 1994 deals with interest payable on unpaid costs in non-contentious matters and entitles the solicitor to charge interest from one month from the delivery of the bill of costs provided that the prescribed information under article 8 has been given to the client.

Unless otherwise agreed with the client, the rate of interest will be 8% per annum. This has been the interest rate on judgment debts since 1 April 1993 (see Judgment Debts (Rate of Interest) Order 1993, SI 1993/ 564). See also 'Costs: Some Interesting Comparisons' – William Gibson *New Law Journal* 20 September 2002.

Service of a statutory demand

A solicitor can serve a statutory demand shortly after delivery of a bill and can, after the expiration of one month from the delivery of the bill, issue a bankruptcy petition provided 21 days have expired from service of the statutory demand.

A petition, but not a statutory demand, is an 'action' within the meaning of s.69 of the Solicitors Act 1974.

In general solicitors should be wary of following this route as there is a power to set aside a statutory demand on the grounds of injustice. See *Re a Debtor (No 88 of 1991)* [1992] 4 All ER 301.

Note also the decision in *Turner* v *Palomo* which may have the effect of outlawing statutory demands on the basis that the amount on a solicitor's bill is still subject to assessment by the court if there are proceedings. As it is not a liquidated demand there is no right to serve a statutory demand. An application for this case to be heard by the House of Lords was refused.

See also 'Fees by Statutory Demand' – Angharad J.T. Start *New Law Journal* 7 August 1992.

Further reading

- Law Society Practice Notes which are available at **www.lawsociety.org.uk**.
- The Solicitors' Code of Conduct 2007 came into force on 1 July 2007 and is available online at **www.sra.org.uk**. The Code replaces almost all of the provisions found in *The Guide to the Professional Conduct of Solicitors* (8th edition 1999) except the Solicitors' Accounts Rules and the rules relating to professional indemnity, financial services and the Compensation Fund.
- *Cook on Costs 2008* by Michael J. Cook published by Butterworths.
- *The Expense of Time* (5th edition) – A concise guide to calculating the annual expense and hourly expense of fee-earners in your firm. Photocopies are available from the Law Society library.
- *An Approach to Non-Contentious Costs* (1st edition, revised 1995) – A guide to the key aspects of non-contentious costs. Includes detailed guidance on the Solicitors' (Non-Contentious Business) Remuneration Order 1994. Photocopies are available from the Law Society library.
- *Fixed Costs* – Kerry Underwood (2nd edition).
- Practice Advice Service Frequently Asked Questions which are regularly published in the Law Society's *Gazette*. A selection of questions is reproduced in Appendix 3 [of this booklet].

Updates and guidance on cases and general developments are provided by the Law Society as appropriate. Solicitors should regularly refer to the Law Society's website at **www.lawsociety.org.uk**.

Special interest groups

International

For law firms, solicitors, and foreign lawyers seeking to develop their international business and build global relationships and profile, our innovative International Division provides the contacts, tools and information your firm needs and opportunities to progress your international career.

www.lawsociety.org.uk/international

Junior lawyers

Launched in January 2008, the Junior Lawyers Division provides a clear voice for student members of the Law Society enrolled through the SRA, trainees, and solicitors with up to five years' active PQE.

www.lawsociety.org.uk/juniorlawyers

Law management

Established in 1998, the Law Management Section focuses on the full range of practice management disciplines, including HR, finance, marketing, IT, business development, client care, quality and risk.

www.lawsociety.org.uk/lawmanagement

Probate

Established in 1997, the Probate Section focuses on wills, financial planning, trusts, tax planning, Court of Protection, care planning and estate administration.

www.lawsociety.org.uk/probate

Property

The Property Section focuses on areas including e-conveyancing, home information packs, housing, land registration, money laundering, planning and environment, as well as tax and revenue.

www.lawsociety.org.uk/property

Dispute resolution

The Dispute Resolution Section focuses on all areas of dispute resolution including arbitration, litigation and mediation.

www.lawsociety.org.uk/disputeresolution

Other groups

We also maintain a list of useful practitioner associations and groups.

Appendix 1 – The Solicitors' (Non-Contentious Business) Remuneration Order 1994

Made .... 5th October 1994

Laid before Parliament .... 10th October 1994

Coming into force .... 1st November 1994

The Lord Chancellor, the Lord Chief Justice, the Master of the Rolls, the President of the Law Society, the president of Holborn law society and the Chief Land Registrar (in respect of business done under the Land Registration Act 1925[1]), together constituting the committee authorised to make orders under section 56 of the Solicitors Act 1974[2], in exercise of the powers conferred on them by that section and having complied with the requirements of section 56(3), hereby make the following Order:

Citation, Commencement and Revocation

1.– (1) This Order may be cited as the Solicitors' (Non-Contentious Business) Remuneration Order 1994.

(2) This Order shall come into force on 1st November 1994 and shall apply to all non-contentious business for which bills are delivered on or after that date.

(3) The Solicitors' Remuneration Order 1972[3] is hereby revoked except in its application to business for which bills are delivered before this Order comes into force.

---

[1] 1925 c. 21.
[2] 1974 c. 47, as modified by the Administration of Justice Act 1985 (c. 61), Schedule 2, paragraphs 22 and 23.
[3] S.I. 1972/1139.

Interpretation

2. In this Order:

    'client' means the client of a solicitor;

    'costs' means the amount charged in a solicitor's bill, exclusive of disbursements and value added tax, in respect of non-contentious business or common form probate business;

    'entitled person' means a client or an entitled third party;

    'entitled third party' means a residuary beneficiary absolutely and immediately (and not contingently) entitled to an inheritance, where a solicitor has charged the estate for his professional costs for acting in the administration of the estate, and either

    (a) the only personal representatives are solicitors (whether or not acting in a professional capacity); or

    (b) the only personal representatives are solicitors acting jointly with partners or employees in a professional capacity;

    'paid disbursements' means disbursements already paid by the solicitor;

    'recognised body' means a body corporate recognised by the Council under section 9 of the Administration of Justice Act 1985[4];

    'remuneration certificate' means a certificate issued by the Council pursuant to this Order;

    'residuary beneficiary' includes a person entitled to all or part of the residue of an intestate estate;

    'solicitor' includes a recognised body;

    'the Council' means the Council of the Law Society.

Solicitors' costs

3. A solicitor's costs shall be such sum as may be fair and reasonable to both solicitor and entitled person, having regard to all the circumstances of the case and in particular to:

    (a) the complexity of the matter or the difficulty or novelty of the questions raised;

    (b) the skill, labour, specialised knowledge and responsibility involved;

---

[4] 1985 c. 61.

(c) the time spent on the business;

(d) the number and importance of the documents prepared or perused, without regard to length;

(e) the place where and the circumstances in which the business or any part thereof is transacted;

(f) the amount or value of any money or property involved;

(g) whether any land involved is registered land;

(h) the importance of the matter to the client; and

(i) the approval (express or implied) of the entitled person or the express approval of the testator to:

    (i) the solicitor undertaking all or any part of the work giving rise to the costs or

    (ii) the amount of the costs.

Right to certification

4.– (1) Without prejudice to the provisions of sections 70, 71, and 72 of the Solicitors Act 1974 (which relate to taxation of costs), an entitled person may, subject to the provisions of this Order, require a solicitor to obtain a remuneration certificate from the Council in respect of a bill which has been delivered where the costs are not more than £50,000.

(2) The remuneration certificate must state what sum, in the opinion of the Council, would be a fair and reasonable charge for the business covered by the bill (whether it be the sum charged or a lesser sum). In the absence of taxation the sum payable in respect of such costs is the sum stated in the remuneration certificate.

Disciplinary and other measures

5.– (1) If on a taxation the taxing officer allows less than one half of the costs, he must bring the facts of the case to the attention of the Council.

(2) The provisions of this Order are without prejudice to the general powers of the Council under the Solicitors Act 1974.

Commencement of proceedings against a client

6. Before a solicitor brings proceedings to recover costs against a client on a bill for non-contentious business he must inform the client in

writing of the matters specified in article 8, except where the bill has been taxed.

Costs paid by deduction

7.– (1) If a solicitor deducts his costs from monies held for or on behalf of a client or of an estate in satisfaction of a bill and an entitled person objects in writing to the amount of the bill within the prescribed time, the solicitor must immediately inform the entitled person in writing of the matters specified in article 8, unless he has already done so.

(2) In this article and in article 10, 'the prescribed time' means:

(a) in respect of a client, three months after delivery of the relevant bill, or a lesser time (which may not be less than one month) specified in writing to the client at the time of delivery of the bill, or

(b) in respect of an entitled third party, three months after delivery of notification to the entitled third party of the amount of the costs, or a lesser time (which may not be less than one month) specified in writing to the entitled third party at the time of such notification.

Information to be given in writing to entitled person

8. When required by articles 6 or 7, a solicitor must inform an entitled person in writing of the following matters:

(a) where article 4(1) applies –

(i) that the entitled person may, within one month of receiving from the solicitor the information specified in this article or (if later) of delivery of the bill or notification of the amount of the costs, require the solicitor to obtain a remuneration certificate; and

(ii) that (unless the solicitor has agreed to do so) the Council may waive the requirements of article 11(1), if satisfied from the client's written application that exceptional circumstances exist to justify granting a waiver;

(b) that sections 70, 71 and 72 of the Solicitors Act 1974 set out the entitled person's rights in relation to taxation;

(c) that (where the whole of the bill has not been paid, by deduction or otherwise) the solicitor may charge interest on the outstanding amount of the bill in accordance with article 14.

Loss by client of right to certification

9. A client may not require a solicitor to obtain a remuneration certificate:

    (a) after a bill has been delivered and paid by the client, other than by deduction;

    (b) where a bill has been delivered, after the expiry of one month from the date on which the client was informed in writing of the matters specified in article 8 or from delivery of the bill if later;

    (c) after the solicitor and client have entered into a non-contentious business agreement in accordance with the provisions of section 57 of the Solicitors Act 1974;

    (d) after a court has ordered the bill to be taxed;

    (e) if article 11(2) applies.

Loss by entitled third party of right to certification

10. An entitled third party may not require a solicitor to obtain a remuneration certificate:

    (a) after the prescribed time (within the meaning of article 7(2)(b)) has elapsed without any objection being received to the amount of the costs;

    (b) after the expiry of one month from the date on which the entitled third party was (in compliance with article 7) informed in writing of the matters specified in article 8 or from notification of the costs if later;

    (c) after a court has ordered the bill to be taxed.

Requirement to pay a sum towards the costs

11.–(1) On requiring a solicitor to obtain a remuneration certificate a client must pay to the solicitor the paid disbursements and value added tax comprised in the bill together with 50% of the costs unless:

    (a) the client has already paid the amount required under this article, by deduction from monies held or otherwise; or

    (b) the solicitor or (if the solicitor refuses) the Council has agreed in writing to waive all or part of this requirement.

(2) The Council shall be under no obligation to provide a remuneration certificate, and the solicitor may take steps to obtain payment of his bill, if the client, having been informed of his right to seek a waiver of the requirements of paragraph (1), has not:

(a) within one month of receipt of the information specified in article 8, either paid in accordance with paragraph (1) or applied to the Council in writing for a waiver of the requirements of paragraph (1); or

(b) made payment in accordance with the requirements of paragraph (1) within one month of written notification that he has been refused a waiver of those requirements by the Council.

Miscellaneous provisions

12.–(1) After an application has been made by a solicitor for a remuneration certificate the client may pay the bill in full without invalidating the application.

(2) A solicitor and entitled person may agree in writing to waive the provisions of sub-paragraphs (a) or (b) of articles 9 or 10.

(3) A solicitor may take from his client security for the payment of any costs, including the amount of any interest to which the solicitor may become entitled under article 14.

Refunds by solicitor

13.–(1) If a solicitor has received payment of all or part of his costs and a remuneration certificate is issued for less than the sum already paid, the solicitor must immediately pay to the entitled person any refund which may be due (after taking into account any other sums which may properly be payable to the solicitor whether for costs, paid disbursements, value added tax or otherwise) unless the solicitor has applied for an order for taxation within one month of receipt by him of the remuneration certificate.

(2) Where a solicitor applies for taxation, his liability to pay any refund under paragraph (1) shall be suspended for so long as the taxation is still pending.

(3) The obligation of the solicitor to repay costs under paragraph (1) is without prejudice to any liability of the solicitor to pay interest on the repayment by virtue of any enactment, rule of law or professional rule.

Interest

14.–(1) After the information specified in article 8 has been given to an entitled person in compliance with articles 6 or 7, a solicitor may charge interest on the unpaid amount of his costs plus any paid disbursements and value added tax, subject to paragraphs (2) and (3) below.

(2) Where an entitlement to interest arises under paragraph (1), and subject to any agreement made between a solicitor and client, the period for which interest may be charged may run from one month after the date of delivery of a bill, unless the solicitor fails to lodge an application within one month of receipt of a request for a remuneration certificate under article 4, in which case no interest is payable in respect of the period between one month after receiving the request and the actual date on which the application is lodged.

(3) Subject to any agreement made between a solicitor and client, the rate of interest must not exceed the rate for the time being payable on judgment debts.

(4) Interest charged under this article must be calculated, where applicable, by reference to the following:

(a) if a solicitor is required to obtain a remuneration certificate, the total amount of the costs certified by the Council to be fair and reasonable plus paid disbursements and value added tax;

(b) if an application is made for the bill to be taxed, the amount ascertained on taxation;

(c) if an application is made for the bill to be taxed or a solicitor is required to obtain a remuneration certificate and for any reason the taxation or application for a remuneration certificate does not proceed, the unpaid amount of the costs shown in the bill or such lesser sum as may be agreed between the solicitor and the client, plus paid disbursements and value added tax.

Application by solicitor

15. A solicitor, when making an application for a remuneration certificate in accordance with the provisions of this Order, must deliver to the Council the complete relevant file and working papers, and any other information or documentation which the Council may require for the purpose of providing a remuneration certificate.

Mackay of Clashfern, C.
Taylor, C.J.
Bingham, M.R.
R C Elly
J Lewis
J Manthorpe
Dated 5th October 1994

EXPLANATORY NOTE

(This note is not part of the Order)

Section 56 of the Solicitors Act 1974 establishes a Committee with power to make general orders regulating the remuneration of solicitors in respect of non-contentious business. Paragraph 22(2) of Schedule 2 to the Administration of Justice Act 1985 modifies the section so that references to solicitors include references to recognised bodies (solicitors' incorporated practices recognised under section 9 of the Administration of Justice Act 1985). This Order sets out the rights of solicitors' clients and residuary beneficiaries of certain estates to require the solicitor charging the client or estate to obtain a certificate from the Law Society as to the reasonableness of his costs. The Order prescribes requirements in relation to information to be given in writing to clients and beneficiaries who are entitled to require a solicitor to obtain a certificate, and lays certain obligations on clients, beneficiaries and solicitors.

The Solicitors' (Non-Contentious Business) Remuneration Order 1994 is reproduced under the terms of Crown Copyright guidance issued by HMSO.

Guidance – specimen information for entitled persons under the Solicitors' (Non-Contentious Business) Remuneration Order 1994

Remuneration certificates

The specimen information for the entitled person is not part of the Order and solicitors may use any form of words which complies with the requirements of the Order.

(1) If you are not satisfied with the amount of our fee you have the right to ask us to obtain a remuneration certificate from the Law Society.

(2) The certificate will either say that our fee is fair and reasonable, or it will substitute a lower fee.

(3) If you wish us to obtain a certificate you must ask us to do so within a month of receiving this notice.

(4) We may charge interest on unpaid bills and we will do so at [the rate payable on judgment debts, from one month after delivery of our bill].

(5) (i) If you ask us to obtain a remuneration certificate, then unless we already hold the money to cover these, you must first pay:

- half our fee shown in the bill;

- all the VAT shown in the bill;

- all the expenses we have incurred shown in the bill – sometimes called 'paid disbursements'.

(ii) However, you may ask the Legal Complaints Service at 8 Dormer Place, Leamington Spa, Warwickshire CV32 5AE to waive this requirement so that you do not have to pay anything for the time being. You would have to show that exceptional circumstances apply in your case.

(6) Your rights are set out more fully in the Solicitors' (Non-Contentious Business) Remuneration Order 1994.

Assessment

You may be entitled to have our charges reviewed by the court. This is called assessment. The procedure is different from the remuneration certificate procedure and it is set out in sections 70, 71 and 72 of the Solicitors Act 1974.

Appendix 2 – Rule 2 of the Solicitors' Code of Conduct 2007

[Please see **sra.org.uk/rules** for any amendments]

Client relations

2.01   Taking on clients

(1) You are generally free to decide whether or not to take on a particular client. However, you must refuse to act or cease acting for a client in the following circumstances:

(a) when to act would involve you in a breach of the law or a breach of the rules of professional conduct;

(b) where you have insufficient resources or lack the competence to deal with the matter;

(c) where instructions are given by someone other than the client, or by only one client on behalf of others in a joint matter, you must not proceed without checking that all clients agree with the instructions given; or

(d) where you know or have reasonable grounds for believing that the instructions are affected by duress or undue influence, you must not act on those instructions until you have satisfied yourself that they represent the client's wishes.

(2) You must not cease acting for a client except for good reason and on reasonable notice.

2.02   Client care

(1) You must:

(a) identify clearly the client's objectives in relation to the work to be done for the client;

(b) give the client a clear explanation of the issues involved and the options available to the client;

(c) agree with the client the next steps to be taken; and

(d) keep the client informed of progress, unless otherwise agreed.

(2) You must, both at the outset and, as necessary, during the course of the matter:

(a) agree an appropriate level of service;

(b) explain your responsibilities;

(c) explain the client's responsibilities;

(d) ensure that the client is given, in writing, the name and status of the person dealing with the matter and the name of the person responsible for its overall supervision; and

(e) explain any limitations or conditions resulting from your relationship with a third party (for example a funder, fee sharer or introducer) which affect the steps you can take on the client's behalf.

(3) If you can demonstrate that it was inapppropriate in the circumstances to meet some or all of these requirements, you will not breach 2.02.

2.03 Information about the cost

(1) You must give your client the best information possible about the likely overall cost of a matter both at the outset and, when appropriate, as the matter progresses. In particular you must:

    (a) advise the client of the basis and terms of your charges;

    (b) advise the client if charging rates are to be increased;

    (c) advise the client of likely payments which you or your client may need to make to others;

    (d) discuss with the client how the client will pay, in particular:

        (i) whether the client may be eligible and should apply for public funding; and

        (ii) whether the client's own costs are covered by insurance or may be paid by someone else such as an employer or trade union;

    (e) advise the client that there are circumstances where you may be entitled to exercise a lien for unpaid costs;

    (f) advise the client of their potential liability for any other party's costs; and

    (g) discuss with the client whether their liability for another party's costs may be covered by existing insurance or whether specially purchased insurance may be obtained.

(2) Where you are acting for the client under a conditional fee agreement, (including a collective conditional fee agreement) in addition to complying with 2.03(1) above and 2.03(5) and (6) below, you must explain the following, both at the outset and, when appropriate, as the matter progresses:

    (a) the circumstances in which your client may be liable for your costs and whether you will seek payment of these from the client, if entitled to do so;

    (b) if you intend to seek payment of any or all of your costs from your client, you must advise your client of their right to an assessment of those costs; and

    (c) where applicable, the fact that you are obliged under a fee sharing agreement to pay to a charity any fees which you receive by way of costs from the client's opponent or other third party.

(3) Where you are acting for a publicly funded client, in addition to complying with 2.03(1) above and 2.03(5) and (6) below, you must explain the following at the outset:

(a) the circumstances in which they may be liable for your costs;

(b) the effect of the statutory charge;

(c) the client's duty to pay any fixed or periodic contribution assessed and the consequence of failing to do so; and

(d) that even if your client is successful, the other party may not be ordered to pay costs or may not be in a position to pay them.

(4) Where you agree to share your fees with a charity in accordance with 8.01(k) you must disclose to the client at the outset the name of the charity.

(5) Any information about the cost must be clear and confirmed in writing.

(6) You must discuss with your client whether the potential outcomes of any legal case will justify the expense or risk involved including, if relevant, the risk of having to pay an opponent's costs.

(7) If you can demonstrate that it was inappropriate in the circumstances to meet some or all of the requirements in 2.03(1) and (5), you will not breach 2.03.

2.04   Contingency fees

(1) You must not enter into an arrangement to receive a contingency fee for work done in prosecuting or defending any contentious proceedings before a court of England and Wales, a British court martial or an arbitrator where the seat of the arbitration is in England and Wales, except as permitted by statute or the common law.

(2) You must not enter into an arrangement to receive a contingency fee for work done in prosecuting or defending any contentious proceedings before a court of an overseas jurisdiction or an arbitrator where the seat of the arbitration is overseas except to the extent that a lawyer of that jurisdiction would be permitted to do so.

2.05   Complaints handling

(1) If you are a principal in a firm you must ensure:

(a) that the firm has a written complaints procedure and that complaints are handled promptly, fairly and effectively in accordance with it;

(b) that the client is told, in writing, at the outset:

(i) that, in the event of a problem, the client is entitled to complain; and

(ii) to whom the client should complain;

(c) that the client is given a copy of the complaints procedure on request; and

(d) that once a complaint has been made, the person complaining is told in writing:

(i) how the complaint will be handled; and

(ii) within what timescales they will be given an initial and/or substantive response.

(2) If you can demonstrate that it was inappropriate in the circumstances to meet some or all of these requirements, you will not breach 2.05.

(3) You must not charge your client for the cost of handling a complaint.

2.06 Commissions

If you are a principal in a firm you must ensure that your firm pays to your client commission received over £20 unless the client, having been told the amount, or if the precise amount is not known, an approximate amount or how the amount is to be calculated, has agreed that your firm may keep it.

2.07 Limitation of civil liability by contract

If you are a principal in a firm you must not exclude or attempt to exclude by contract all liability to your clients. However, you may limit your liability, provided that such limitation:

(a) is not below the minimum level of cover required by the Solicitors' Indemnity Insurance Rules for a policy of qualifying insurance;

(b) is brought to the client's attention; and

(c) is in writing

Appendix 3 – Frequently asked questions

[Please see **Chapter 3**].

Appendix 4 – High value probate cases

In *Jemma Trust* v *Liptrott* [2003] EWCA Civ 1476, the Court of Appeal held that there should be a regressive charging regime in respect of high value non-contentious cases and that the following bands would be applicable to cases such as this in 1993 (see paragraph 31):

(1) Up to £750,000

(2) £750,000 – £3 million

(3) £3 million – £6 million

(4) Above £6 million

That would suggest that the appropriate figures for bills rendered for work done in 2003 would be:

(1) Up to £1 million 1.5%

(2) £1 million – £4 million 0.5%

(3) £4 million – £8 million 0.1666%

(4) £8 million – £12 million 0.0833%

(5) Over £12 million 0.0416%

The appropriate percentages should be 1½%, ½%, ⅙% ¹⁄₁₂% and ¹⁄₂₄% (1.5%; 0.5%; 0.1666%; 0.0833% and 0.0416%).

Thus for an estate worth £11,500,000 in 2003, the appropriate value element would be:

£1 million × 1.5% = £15,000

£3 million × 0.5% = £15,000

£4 million × 0.1666% = £ 6,664

£3.5 million × 0.08333% = £ 2,915.50

Thus total value element = £39,579.50

Solicitors calculating all or part of their bill on a value basis should, therefore, ensure that they calculate the amount using appropriate bandings for the year in which the work was done.

Appendix 5 – Extract from Jemma Trust v Liptrott

In *Jemma Trust* v *Liptrott* [2003] EWCA Civ 1476, the Court of Appeal said at paragraph 33 of the judgment:

THE FUTURE

33. We have been asked to give the profession such guidance as we can for the future in the light of the issues to which the appeal has given rise. This is difficult and, for our part, we cannot do better than to suggest that it would be appropriate for solicitors to adhere to the following principles:

   1. Much the best practice is for a solicitor to obtain prior agreement as to the basis of his charges not only from the executors but also, where appropriate, from any residuary beneficiary who is an entitled third party under the 1994 Order. This is encouraged in the 1994 booklet [An Approach to Non-Contentious Costs] and letter 8 of Appendix 2 to the 1999 booklet [Practice Advice Service booklet called Non-Contentious Costs] provides a good working draft of such agreement. We support that encouragement;

   2. in any complicated administration, it will be prudent for solicitors to provide in their terms of retainer for interim bills to be rendered for payment on account; this is, of course, subject to the solicitor's obligation to review the matter as a whole at the end of the business so as to ensure that he has claimed no more than is fair and reasonable, taking into account the factors set out in the 1994 Order [Solicitors' (Non-Contentious Business) Remuneration Order 1994];

   3. there should be no hard and fast rule that charges cannot be made separately by reference to the value of the estate; value can, by contrast, be taken into account as part of the hourly rate; value can also be taken into account partly in one way and partly in the other. What is important is that

      a) it should be transparent on the face of the bill how value is being taken into account; and

      b) in no case, should it be taken into account more than once;

   4. in many cases, if a charge is separately made by reference to the value of the estate, it should usually be on a regressive scale. The bands and percentages will be for the costs judge in each case; the suggestions to the costs judge set out in paragraph 30 may be thought by him to be appropriate for this case but different bands and percentages will be appropriate for other cases and the figures set out in paragraph 30 cannot be any more than a guideline;

   5. it may be helpful at the end of the business for the solicitor or, if there is an assessment, for the costs judge, when a separate element

of the bill is based on the value of the estate, to calculate the number of hours that would notionally be taken to achieve the amount of the separate charge. That may help to determine whether overall the remuneration claimed or assessed is fair and reasonable within the terms of the 1994 Order.

6. it may also be helpful to consider the Law Society's Guidance in cases where there is no relevant and ascertainable value factor which is given in the 1994 booklet at paragraph 13.4. If the time spent on the matter is costed out at the solicitors' expense rate (which should be readily ascertainable from the Solicitors' Expense of Time calculations) the difference between that sum (the cost to the solicitor of the time spent on the matter) and the final figure claimed will represent the mark-up. The mark-up (which should take into account the factors specified in the 1994 Order including value) when added to the cost of the time spent must then be judged by reference to the requirement that this total figure must represent 'such sum as may be fair and reasonable to both solicitor and entitled person'.

Appendix 6 – Amendments to s.69 Solicitors Act 1974

Action to recover solicitor's costs

(1) Subject to the provisions of this Act, no action shall be brought to recover any costs due to a solicitor before the expiration of one month from the date on which a bill of those costs is delivered in accordance with the requirements mentioned in subsection (2); but if there is probable cause for believing that the party chargeable with the costs –

(a) is about to quit England and Wales, to become bankrupt or to compound with his creditors, or

(b) is about to do any other act which would tend to prevent or delay the solicitor obtaining payment,

the High Court may, notwithstanding that one month has not expired from the delivery of the bill, order that the solicitor be at liberty to commence an action to recover his costs and may order that those costs be *taxed* [*assessed*].

[(2) The requirements referred to in subsection (1) are that the bill must be –

(a) signed in accordance with subsection (2A), and

(b) delivered in accordance with subsection (2C).

(2A) A bill is signed in accordance with this subsection if it is –

(a) signed by the solicitor or on his behalf by an employee of the solicitor authorised by him to sign, or

(b) enclosed in, or accompanied by, a letter which is signed as mentioned in paragraph (a) and refers to the bill.

(2B) For the purposes of subsection (2A) the signature may be an electronic signature.

(2C) A bill is delivered in accordance with this subsection if –

(a) it is delivered to the party to be charged with the bill personally,

(b) it is delivered to that party by being sent to him by post to, or left for him at, his place of business, dwelling-house or last known place of abode, or

(c) it is delivered to that party –

(i) by means of an electronic communications network, or

(ii) by other means but in a form that nevertheless requires the use of apparatus by the recipient to render it intelligible,

and that party has indicated to the person making the delivery his willingness to accept delivery of a bill sent in the form and manner used.

(2D) An indication to any person for the purposes of subsection (2C)(c) –

(a) must state the address to be used and must be accompanied by such other information as that person requires for the making of the delivery;

(b) may be modified or withdrawn at any time by a notice given to that person.

(2E) Where a bill is proved to have been delivered in compliance with the requirements of subsections (2A) and (2C), it is not necessary in the first instance for the solicitor to prove the contents of the bill and it is to be presumed, until the contrary is shown, to be a bill bona fide complying with this Act.

(2F) A bill which is delivered as mentioned in subsection (2C)(c) is to be treated as having been delivered on the first working day after the day on which it was sent (unless the contrary is proved).]

(3) Where a bill of costs relates wholly or partly to contentious business done in a county court and the amount of the bill does not exceed [£5,000], the powers and duties of the High Court under this section

and sections 70 and 71 in relation to that bill may be exercised and performed by any county court in which any part of the business was done.

[(4) . . .]

[(5) In this section references to an electronic signature are to be read in accordance with section 7(2) of the Electronic Communications Act 2000 (c 7).

(6) In this section –

'electronic communications network' has the same meaning as in the Communications Act 2003 (c 21);

'working day' means a day other than a Saturday, a Sunday, Christmas Day, Good Friday or a bank holiday in England and Wales under the Banking and Financial Dealings Act 1971 (c 80).]

4

Crime

I need to write to my client, who is presently on remand in Wormwood Scrubs. How can I be sure my letters reach him without being opened?

A solicitor's letter should not be opened and read by the prison authorities if it is posted inside a double envelope. The outer envelope should be addressed as normal to your client; the inner unstamped envelope should be marked clearly 'Prison Rule 39' (or YOI (Young Offender's Institute Rule 14 if addressed to a young offender). The inner envelope should also be marked with the client's name and prison number, if known, address and telephone number of the solicitor's office; a reference number, if possible and the signature of the solicitor. Mail clearly marked in this way will be regarded as legally privileged and passed to your client unopened unless a governor suspects that it is not actually privileged. See Ede and Edwards (2008) *Criminal Defence* (3rd Edition), Law Society Publishing.

I am looking for up-to-date information on sentencing guidelines. Where can I find this?

The Sentencing Guidelines Council has identified and collated all existing sentencing guidelines and guidance cases into one compendium which is available online at **www.sentencing-guidelines.gov.uk**. Please also see Edwards and Savage (2009) *Sentencing Handbook*, Law Society Publishing.

I am a solicitor practicing criminal law. I have higher rights of audience. Where can I find information about court dress?

With effect from 2 January 2008 Practice Direction (Court Dress) (No 4) applies throughout the Supreme Court of England & Wales, including Crown Court, in county courts and in magistrates court. The Practice Direction can be found at **www.hmcourts-service.gov.uk/cms/files/PD-Court-dress-3.doc**.

I am considering withdrawing from a criminal case. What are 'compelling' reasons?

You must withdraw from a case if you conclude that you are professionally embarrassed by continuing to act, in accordance with the Solicitors' Code of Conduct, and the professional obligations you owe to your client, and/or to the court.

This is to avoid breaching the code, and also prevent risk of punishment by the court, whether through a wasted costs order or, in more serious cases, prosecution for an offence against public justice.

When considering withdrawing from a criminal case who determines whether there are compelling reasons?

The decision about whether compelling reasons to withdraw exist lies with you, not the court.

The Court in *R v Ulcay* agreed with the observations of Rose LJ in *R v G and B* when he said, at paragraph 14 of that case: 'We think it right, both in principle and pragmatically, that whether a solicitor or barrister can properly continue to act is a matter for him or her not the court, although of course the court can properly make observations on the matter.'

In *R v Ulcay* Judge LJ stated, at paragraph 30: 'The principle . . . remains clear. The court cannot oblige the lawyer to continue to act when he has made a professional judgement that he is obliged, for compelling reasons, to withdraw from the case'.

How does compliance with a court order affect your professional obligation to your client?

Complying with a court order which makes it impossible or difficult to achieve your normal standard of competence in looking after your client's interests does not put you in breach of the Solicitors' Code of Conduct, nor are you acting improperly or negligently.

I am a partner in a firm of solicitors and have been summoned for jury service my understanding is that solicitors are exempt from this particular civic duty. Is this correct?

No. Pursuant to section 321 (Schedule 33) of the Criminal Justice Act 2003 and the Criminal Justice Act 2003 (Commencement No.3 and Transitional Provisions) Order 2004 which commenced on 5 April 2004 solicitors are now eligible for jury service.

Jury service which usually lasts for up to ten working days is compulsory for all registered electors in England and Wales, aged between 18 and 70, who have lived in the UK, Channel Islands or Isle of Man for a continuous period of at least five years since the age of 13.

The Law Society has issued guidance which can be found in the Criminal Practitioner's Newsletter, Issue 62, October 2005. This can be found on the Law Society website (**www.lawsociety.org.uk**) under News/ Newsletters.

Annex 4A

Criminal Procedure Rules – Impact on solicitors' duties to the client practice note

31 March 2008

Status of this practice note

Practice notes are issued by the Law Society for the use and benefit of its members. They represent the Law Society's view of good practice in a particular area. They are not intended to be the only standard of good practice that solicitors can follow. You are not required to follow them, but doing so will make it easier to account to oversight bodies for your actions.

Practice notes are not legal advice, nor do they necessarily provide a defence to complaints of misconduct or of inadequate professional service. While care has been taken to ensure that they are accurate, up to date and useful, the Law Society will not accept any legal liability in relation to them.

For queries or comments on this practice note contact the Law Society's Practice Advice Service.

Introduction

The Court of Appeal in *R* v *K* has recently underlined the importance of the Criminal Procedure Rules 2005, making it clear that the rules:

> impose duties and burdens on all the participants in a criminal trial, including the judge, and the preparation and conduct of criminal trials is dependent on, and subject to, these rules . . .[1]

The purpose of this practice note is to provide assistance to the profession in seeking to define the extent of these duties and burdens, and to identify

---

[1]   [2006] EWCA Crim 724 at paragraph 6, [2006] 2 All ER (Note) 552.

and address the ethical problems that are likely to arise from their imposition. It will examine the following:

1. The solicitor's duty to the court.

2. The solicitor, the client and the court – 'a divided loyalty'.

3. The Criminal Procedure Rules ('CPR').

4. The approach of the court towards solicitors under CPR.

1.   The solicitor's duty to the court

Solicitors are officers of the court and have therefore always owed duties to the court. The introduction of the CPR has 'effected a sea change in the way in which cases should be conducted'[2] by imposing extra duties and burdens upon the criminal practitioner. The rules define with precision the full extent, not only of the duties already owed to the court by solicitors involved in the preparation and conduct of criminal trials, but also those now imposed by the CPR.

The nature of those obligations was described by the House of Lords in *Arthur J.S. Hall and Co.* v *Simons (AP)*.[3] Lord Hope's comments, whilst specifically referring to advocates, are of wider application:

> ... it is necessary to appreciate the extent of that duty and the extent to which the efficiency of our systems of criminal justice depends on it. The advocate's duty to the court is not just that he must not mislead the court, that he must ensure that the facts are presented fairly and that he must draw the attention of the court to the relevant authorities even if they are against him. *It extends to the whole way in which the client's case is presented, so that time is not wasted and the court is able to focus on the issues as efficiently and economically as possible.*[4] (emphasis added)

The Solicitors' Code of Conduct

The recently issued Solicitor's Code of Conduct effectively mirrors the earlier professional rules governing the solicitor's duty to the court.[5] Of particular relevance is the following rule [see **sra.org.uk/rules** for updates as of 31 March 2009]:

---

[2]   Per Thomas LJ in *R (on the application of the DPP)* v *Chorley Justices & Anor* [2006] EWHC 1795 at paragraph 24.
[3]   [2000] UKHL 38, [2002] 1 AC 615.
[4]   Per Lord Hope at page 715.
[5]   The new Solicitors' Code of Conduct entered force on 1 July 2007.

Rule 11 – Litigation and advocacy

11.02 Obeying court orders:

You must comply with any court order requiring you or your firm to take, or refrain from taking, a particular course of action.

The relevant guidance, entitled 'Obeying court orders 11.02', states:

19. You have a responsibility to ensure that you comply with any court order made against you. Similarly, you must advise your clients to comply with court orders made against them. If you are the recipient of a court order which you believe to be defective you must comply with it unless it is revoked by the court. If your client is the recipient of an order you believe to be defective you must discuss with the client the possibility of challenging it and explain to the client the client's obligation to comply if the order is not overturned.

The general guidance to Rule 11 also indicates, in paragraph 5:

If you are a solicitor you are an officer of the court and you should take all reasonable steps to assist in the smooth running of the court but only insofar as this is consistent with your duties to your client.

2.   The solicitor, the client and the court: 'A divided loyalty'[6]

Dual duties

The role of the solicitor when acting on behalf of a client who is actually or potentially the subject of criminal proceedings can be a complex one. As a lawyer the solicitor owes professional duties to his or her client, as well as – as one of its officers – to the court. On occasions these various duties may conflict with each other.

Whilst the court is entitled to expect the solicitor to act towards it with integrity, neither misleading nor deceiving it, the court should not demand that the solicitor in so acting should breach professional duties owed by the solicitor towards his or her client(s). Indeed, as explained below, the solicitor's proper discharge of the duty to their client should not cause him or her to be accused of being in breach of their duty to the court.[7]

---

[6]   See Lord Hoffmann in *Arthur J.S. Hall and Co.* v *Simons (AP)* [2000] UKHL 38, [2002] 1 AC 615 at page 686.

[7]   See *Medcalf* v *Mardell* [2002] UKHL 27 and [2003] 1 AC 120 per Lord Hobhouse at paragraph 55.

The solicitor's core duties

The core duties of a solicitor set the standards that will meet the needs of both clients and society. In balancing their allegiance to the rule of law and the proper administration of justice on the one hand, and working in partnership with a client on the other, criminal solicitors must have in mind the core duties which are set out in rule 1 of the Solicitors' Code of Conduct [see **sra.org.uk/rules** for amendments as of 31 March 2009]:

RULE 1 – CORE DUTIES

1.01   Justice and the rule of law

You must uphold the rule of law and the proper administration of justice.

1.02   Integrity

You must act with integrity.

1.03   Independence

You must not allow your independence to be compromised.

1.04   Best interests of clients

You must act in the best interests of each client.

1.05   Standard of service

You must provide a good standard of service to your clients.

1.06   Public confidence

You must not behave in a way that is likely to diminish the trust the public places in you or the profession.

Two specific professional obligations require comment. They are the duty to maintain client confidentiality, and the need to avoid a conflict of interest between clients.

Confidentiality

A solicitor is under a professional and legal obligation to keep the affairs of clients confidential and to ensure that all members of his or her staff do likewise.[8] This duty of confidence is fundamental to the fiduciary relationship that exists between solicitor and client. It extends to all matters divulged to a solicitor by a client, or on his or her behalf, from whatever

---

[8]   At the time of writing, Practice Rule 16E of the Solicitors' Practice (Confidentiality and Disclosure) Amendment Rule 2004, in effect since April 2006, applies. From 1 July 2007, when the new Solicitors' Code of Conduct comes into effect, this will become rule 4.01.

source. The provisions for dealing with the protection of clients' confidential information are set out in rule 4 of the new Solicitor's Code of Conduct.

Confidentiality and legal professional privilege

Certain confidential communications, however, can never be revealed without the consent of the client; they are privileged against disclosure. This protection is called legal professional privilege ('LPP').

What communications are privileged?

Not everything that lawyers have a duty to keep confidential is privileged. Only those confidential communications falling under either of the two heads of privilege – 'advice privilege' or 'litigation privilege' – are protected by LPP.

Advice privilege

Communications between a lawyer (acting in his or her capacity as a lawyer) and a client are privileged if they are confidential and for the purpose of seeking legal advice from a lawyer or providing legal advice to a client.

Merely because a client is speaking or writing to his or her solicitor does not make that communication privileged – it is only those communications between the solicitor and the client relating to the matter in which the solicitor has been instructed for the purpose of obtaining legal advice that will be privileged. Such communications do not need to 'contain advice on matters of law and construction, provided that they are directly related to the performance by the solicitor of his professional duty as legal adviser of his client'.[9]

Litigation privilege

Under this head the following are privileged:

Confidential communications made, after litigation has started, or is 'reasonably in prospect', between:

- a lawyer and a client;
- a lawyer and an agent (whether or not that agent is a lawyer); or
- a lawyer, or his or her client, and a third party

---

[9]   Per Lord Carswell in *Three Rivers District Council* v *Governor of the Bank of England* (No 6) [2004] UKHL 48, at paragraph 111, and [2005] 1 AC 610 at page 680.

for the sole or dominant purpose of litigation, whether:

- for seeking or giving advice in relation to it; or
- for obtaining evidence to be used in it; or
- for obtaining information leading to obtaining such evidence.

The importance of the solicitor's role in the criminal justice system was emphasised by the House of Lords when considering the nature and extent of LPP. In *R* v *Derby Magistrates' Court*, ex p. *B* Lord Taylor of Gosforth CJ said:

> The principle which runs through all these cases . . . is that a man must be able to consult his lawyer in confidence, since otherwise he might hold back half the truth. The client must be sure that what he tells his lawyer will never be revealed without his consent. Legal professional privilege is thus much more than an ordinary rule of evidence, limited in its application to the facts of a particular case. It is a fundamental condition on which the administration of justice as a whole rests.[10]

In *R (Morgan Grenfell & Co Ltd)* v *Special Commissioner of Income Tax* Lord Hoffmann describes LPP as:

> . . . a fundamental human right long established in the common law. It is a necessary corollary of the right of any person to obtain skilled advice about the law. Such advice cannot be effectively obtained unless the client is able to put all the facts before the adviser without fear that they may be afterwards disclosed and used to his prejudice.[11]

Conflict of interest

Rule 3 of the new Conduct Rules sets out clearly the provisions for dealing with conflicts of interest. Detailed guidance with specific regard to criminal practitioners is included in the Guidance to rule 3, which was drafted by the Law Society after close consultation with the Department for Constitutional Affairs and the Legal Services Commission.[12] This guidance recognises the need to balance the solicitor's duty to the proper administration of justice carefully with his or her duty towards the client, and sets out how to avoid conflicts from arising.

---

[10] [1996] AC 487 at page 507.
[11] [2002] UKHL 21 at paragraph 7, and [2003] 1 AC 563 at page 606.
[12] See Guidance to Rule 3 – Conflict, Co-defendants, paragraph 24–36. This was also published by the Law Society in the Criminal Practitioners' Newsletter, no.61, July 2005.

How can a solicitor's professional duties to his client conflict with his duty to the court?

A few examples may serve to illustrate the point:

1. If a conflict of interest arises during criminal proceedings between two or more clients represented by the same solicitor, the solicitor must withdraw from one or more clients. This is bound to cause inconvenience to the court and to other parties with consequent financial loss (normally to the legal aid fund).

2. A solicitor may hold factual information (for instance the name and address of a possible witness) which is of crucial importance to a party to the proceedings. When requested, or served with a witness summons, to produce this information the solicitor declines to do so.[13]

3. Professionally proper advice may be given by a solicitor at a police interview which may later be viewed by a court, in changed circumstances, as 'unhelpful', 'obstructive' or 'ill advised'.[14]

Whilst, understandably, the court when confronted with one of these problems, may consider itself entitled to an explanation, and frustrated by its absence, in the majority of cases, the court should understand that the solicitor's duty of confidentiality to his or her client absolutely forbids the provision of reasons, because the information sought by the court will be privileged. At most, the solicitor can only inform the court that his or her professional duties prevent their continuing to act and/or providing the information sought. As was recently underlined by Lord Justice Rose in *R v G & B*:

> We think it right, both in principle and pragmatically, that whether a solicitor or barrister can properly continue to act is a matter for him or her, not the court, although of course the court can properly make observations on the matter. ... Absent exceptional circumstances, such as an obvious attempt by a defendant to abuse the system by repeated applications, we think it is unlikely that, if leading counsel tells a judge that he is embarrassed to continue acting, the judge will not permit a change of representation.[15]

---

[13] In *R v Derby Magistrates*, ex p. *B* [1996] AC 487 Lord Nicholls of Birkenhead said, at page 510, 'subject to recognised exceptions, communications seeking professional legal advice, whether or not in connection with pending court proceedings, are absolutely and permanently privileged from disclosure even though, in consequence, the communications will not be available in court proceedings in which they might be important evidence'.

[14] See PACE Code C paragraph 6D.

[15] [2004] EWCA Crim 1368, and [2004] 2 Cr App R 37.

3.   The Criminal Procedure Rules

In the *Chorley Justices* case Lord Justice Thomas said:

> In April 2005 the Criminal Procedure Rules came into effect. By 15th April they were in force. They have effected a sea change in the way in which cases should be conducted . . . The rules make clear that the overriding objective is that criminal cases be dealt with justly; that includes acquitting the innocent and convicting the guilty, dealing with the prosecution and defence fairly, respecting the interests of witnesses, dealing with the case efficiently and expeditiously, and also, of great importance, dealing with the case in a way that takes into account the gravity of the offence, the complexity of what is in issue, the severity of the consequences to the defendant and others affected and the needs of other cases. Rule 1.2 imposes upon the duty of participants in a criminal case to prepare and conduct the case in accordance with the overriding objective, to comply with the rules and, importantly, to inform the court and all parties of any significant failure, whether or not the participant is responsible for that failure, to take any procedural step required by the rules.

> Rule 3.2 imposes upon the court a duty to further that overriding objective by actively managing the case.[16]

What do the CPR say?

1.1   The overriding objective:

(1)   The overriding objective of this new code is that criminal cases be dealt with justly.

(2)   Dealing with a criminal case justly includes –

    (a)   acquitting the innocent and convicting the guilty;

    (b)   dealing with the prosecution and the defence fairly;

    (c)   recognising the rights of a defendant, particularly those under Article 6 of the European Convention on Human Rights;

    (d)   respecting the interests of witnesses, victims and jurors and keeping them informed of the progress of the case;

    (e)   dealing with the case efficiently and expeditiously;

    (f)   ensuring that appropriate information is available to the court when bail and sentence are considered; and

    (g)   dealing with the case in ways that take into account –

---

[16]   *R (on the application of the DPP)* v *Chorley Justices & Anor* [2006] EWHC 1795 at paragraph 24.

    (i)   the gravity of the offence alleged,

    (ii) the complexity of what is in issue,

    (iii) the severity of the consequences for the defendant and others affected, and

    (iv) the needs of other cases.

1.2   The duty of the participants in a criminal case:

(1) Each participant, in the conduct of each case, must –

    (a) prepare and conduct the case in accordance with the overriding objectives;

    (b) comply with these Rules, practice directions and directions made by the court; and

    (c) at once inform the court and all parties of any significant failure (whether or not that participant is responsible for that failure) to take any procedural step required by these Rules, any practice direction or any direction of the court. A failure is significant if it might hinder the court in furthering the overriding objective.

Keeping the court informed whilst protecting the client's rights

It is essential to appreciate that the purpose of Rule 1.2(1)(c) is to enable the court to control the preparation process and avoid ineffective and wasted hearings. When something goes wrong because of a failure of a defendant to co-operate with his or her solicitors the court should be aware of this and if the solicitor fails to keep the court informed, he or she risks breaching their duty to the court under the provisions of the Rules.

> Lawyers conducting litigation owe a divided loyalty. They have a duty to their clients, but they may not win by every means. They also owe a duty to the court and the administration of justice. . . . Sometimes the performance of these duties to the court may annoy the client.[17]

The concept of the solicitor apparently putting the court's interests above those of the client has caused many solicitors to question where their duty lies. The answer is to be found in Rule 1.1(2)(c) which indicates that one of the requirements of the overriding objective is 'to recognise the rights of a defendant, particularly those under Article 6 of the ECHR European Convention on Human Rights'.

The relevant rights of a defendant in this context are:

---

17   *Arthur J S Hall & Co.* v *Simons* [2000] UKHL 38, and [2002] 1 AC 615 per Lord Hoffmann at page 686.

- the presumption of innocence;
- the right to silence and privilege against self-incrimination;
- the 'fundamental human right'[18] to legal professional privilege.

This is explicitly explained in the note of the Lord Chief Justice to the Rules where it is stated:

> The presumption of innocence and a robust adversarial process are essential features of the English legal tradition and of the defendant's right to a fair trial. The overriding objective acknowledges those rights. It must not be read as detracting from a defendant's right to silence or from the confidentiality properly attaching to what passes between a lawyer and his client.

The last of these rights means that a court cannot ask a solicitor to reveal what a defendant has told him or her if it is privileged, unless the defendant consents. Rather, he or she has a duty to the client not to reveal it.

However solicitors *can* clearly be required by the CPR, or by a direction of the court made under its case management duties arising from the CPR, to provide information that will enable the court process to proceed efficiently and expeditiously, but only if in so doing none of the defendant's rights listed above, is encroached upon.

Informing the client

R v *K*[19] makes it clear that the CPR impose duties and burdens upon solicitors in a criminal trial and that their preparation for and conduct of criminal trials is dependent upon and subject to the CPR.

It is important that clients should be made aware of these duties and the Law Society would advise solicitors to explain to their clients at the outset, and also in the terms of business/retainer letter, that whilst privileged communications can never be divulged to the court without the client's authority, solicitors are under a duty to provide information to the court which is not privileged and which enables the court to further the overriding objective by actively managing the case.

Informing the court

Therefore, if a solicitor is aware of any significant failure (whether or not the defendant is responsible for that failure) to take any procedural step required by the CPR or any practice direction or any direction of the court, it is neither a breach of the defendant's right to silence, nor legal

---

[18]   As per Lord Hoffmann in Morgan Grenfell, above.
[19]   [2006] EWCA Crim 724 at paragraph 6, [2006] 2 All ER (Note) 552.

professional privilege, for the solicitor to reveal that he or she has been unable to comply with the court's order.

It would not involve a breach of legal professional privilege for the court to ask the defendant or his or her lawyer to reveal whether instructions have been given, for the purpose of allowing the court to ensure that the case is ready to proceed.[20] It would be a breach, of course, for the court to ask what has been said between them. Courts should be aware that there are difficulties in asking a solicitor to confirm any more than this, for example, whether or not the solicitor has prepared a proof of evidence.

Particular difficulties will arise if a client changes his or her instructions in circumstances where it is proper for the solicitor to continue acting.[21] If the change in instructions will cause delay, whilst the solicitor must inform the court of the likelihood of delay, privilege will prevent disclosure of the reason for it.[22]

Identifying the issues in a case

Both before the coming into force of the CPR, in *R v Gleeson*[23] and since, in the *Chorley Justices* case,[24] the Court of Appeal and the Divisional Court have emphasised the duty upon practitioners to identify the real issues in a case early. It has been held that to do so does not offend the right of silence nor the privilege against self-incrimination (*Gleeson*); if a defendant refuses to do so, he can derive no advantage from this, nor 'attempt an ambush at trial':

> The duty of the court is to see that justice is done. That does not involve allowing people to escape on technical points or by attempting, as happened here, an ambush. It involves the courts in looking at the real justice of the case and seeing whether the rules have been complied with by 'cards being put on the table' at the outset and the issues being clearly identified.[25]

---

20 See *R v Cowan* [1996] 1 Cr App R 1 at page 9. The Court of Appeal ruled that for counsel to be asked by the trial judge (in accordance with paragraph 3 of the *Practice Direction (Crown Court: Defendant's Evidence)* [1995] 2 Cr App R 192) if he had advised the defendant concerning adverse inferences in the event of him not giving evidence, did not breach privilege as it did not concern anything confidential.

21 Of course if the change of instructions is such that the solicitor has to withdraw, privilege will prevent him or her disclosing the reasons.

22 If the change of instructions identifies fresh issues in the case, then of course the solicitor has an obligation under the CPR to identify these to the court – see below.

23 [2003] EWCA Crim 3357 at paragraph 36, (2004) Cr App R 29.

24 *R (on the application of the DPP) v Chorley Justices & Anor* [2006] EWHC 1795. See also *Malcolm v DPP* [2007] EWHC 363 (Admin).

25 Per Thomas LJ in *Chorley Justices* at paragraph 27.

Defence witnesses

Can a court order the defence solicitor or the defendant to disclose the identity and other details of non-alibi defence witnesses?

Sections 6C and 11 of the Criminal Procedure and Investigations Act 1996 (as amended by s.35 Criminal Justice Act 2003) which specifically require disclosure by the accused to the court and prosecution of defence witness details, at the risk of adverse comment and inference, have yet to be brought into force.

In *R (on the application of Kelly)* v *Warley Magistrates Court (the Law Society intervening*[26] Lord Justice Laws stated:

> . . . it is clear that litigation privilege attaches to the identity and other details of witnesses intended to be called in adversarial litigation, civil or criminal, whether or not their identity is the fruit of legal advice.[27]

The Court emphasised the need for a litigant to be able protect the confidentiality of the material he or she, or his or her lawyer, prepares for the presentation of a case, and this need for protection is the rationale for advice and litigation privilege.

> If there were no confidentiality such as both rights protect, and every litigant were liable to disclose the building blocks of his case stage by stage as they were developed, the scope for witnesses being discouraged, false points being taken, and the truth being distorted would surely be very greatly increased.[28]

The Court held the CPR had no authority to allow a court to override LPP unless the main legislation containing the CPR's *vires* conferred such authority expressly or by necessary implication. The relevant provision, s.69 of the Courts Act 2003, contained nothing of the kind and therefore a court had no power to make an order for a defendant to reveal the identity and/or other details of witnesses he or she intends to call.

Sanctions for non-compliance

In reaching its decision in *Kelly*, the Court was influenced by the nature of the original direction for disclosure of defence witness details and the open ended form of the relevant CP Rule. The absence of any sanction for failure to comply with the case management order for disclosure rendered the original order to disclose an *unconditional* order which, as such, infringed LPP.

---

[26] [2007] EWHC 1836.
[27] paragraph 20.
[28] paragraph 22.

If the Rules had contained provisions which set conditions upon the right to call live evidence, the privilege attaching to the material would be unaffected. The Court by making such an order would merely be making it a condition of a party's ability to call live evidence at trial, that prior notice of such evidence be provided. It would not mean that the party could be compelled to disclose LPP material – only if he or she wanted to use such material as falls within the order as evidence would the party be required as a precondition to disclose it in advance.

As a consequence of the decision in *Kelly*, the CPR have been amended.[29] As the Explanatory Note to the new Rule explains:

> 7.3 Part 3 of the Criminal Procedure Rules 2005 sets out the general duties and powers of the court, and the duties of the parties, relevant to the pre-trial preparation of a criminal case; and the rules in that Part set out the specific powers that the court may exercise for that purpose. However, the rules in that Part of the Criminal Procedure Rules 2005 contained no sanctions for a party's failure to comply with a procedure rule or with a case management direction made by the court. The court's powers to make a costs order in consequence of such a failure, to adjourn the case or, in some circumstances, to exclude evidence or to draw adverse inferences from the late introduction of an issue or evidence, are powers that are conferred by other legislation and under some other procedure rules.

> 7.4 In the case of *R (Kelly)* v *Warley Magistrates' Court* [2007] EWHC 1836 (Admin), the Administrative Court considered rules 3.5 and 3.10 of the Criminal Procedure Rules and held that the absence of any appropriate sanction within Part 3 rendered ineffectual the case management direction that was in issue in that case. Having considered that judgment, the Rule Committee has decided to amend rules 3.5 and 3.10, and the note to rule 3.5, to make the court's powers to impose sanctions explicit . . . .

The substituted Rule 3.10 provides:

> 3.10   In order to manage a trial or (in the Crown Court) an appeal:

> > (a) the court must establish, with the active assistance of the parties, what disputed issues they intend to explore; and

> > (b) the court may require a party to identify:

> > > (i)   which witnesses that party wants to give oral evidence,

> > > (ii)   the order in which that party wants those witnesses to give their evidence,

> > > (iii) whether that party requires an order compelling the attendance of a witness,

---

29   The Criminal Procedure (Amendment No.3) Rules 2007, SI 2007/3662.

(iv)   what arrangements are desirable to facilitate the giving of evidence by a witness,

(v)   what arrangements are desirable to facilitate the participation of any other person, including the defendant,

(vi)   what written evidence that party intends to introduce,

(vii) what other material, if any, that person intends to make available to the court in the presentation of the case,

(viii) whether that party intends to raise any point of law that could affect the conduct of the trial or appeal, and

(ix)   what timetable that party proposes and expects to follow.

A new case management power has been added as Rule 3.5(6):

(6)   If a party fails to comply with a rule or a direction, the court may:

(a)   fix, postpone, bring forward, extend, cancel or adjourn a hearing;

(b)   exercise its powers to make a costs order; and

(c)   impose such other sanction as may be appropriate.

The note to the new Rule 3.5 has also been expanded as follows:

At the end of the note after rule 3.5 (The court's case management powers), insert:

'See also rule 3.10. The court may make a costs order under:

(a)   section 19 of the Prosecution of Offences Act 1985, where the court decides that one party to criminal proceedings has incurred costs as a result of an unnecessary or improper act or omission by, or on behalf of, another party;

(b)   section 19A of that Act, where the court decides that a party has incurred costs as a result of an improper, unreasonable or negligent act or omission on the part of a legal representative;

(c)   section 19B of that Act, where the court decides that there has been serious misconduct by a person who is not a party.

Under some other legislation, including Parts 24, 34 and 35 of these Rules, if a party fails to comply with a rule or a direction then in some circumstances:

(a)   the court may refuse to allow that party to introduce evidence;

(b)   evidence that that party wants to introduce may not be admissible;

(c)   the court may draw adverse inferences from the late introduction of an issue or evidence.

See also:

> section 81(1) of the Police and Criminal Evidence Act 1984 and section 20(3) of the Criminal Procedure and Investigations Act 1996 (advance disclosure of expert evidence);

> section 11(5) of the Criminal Procedure and Investigations Act 1996 (faults in disclosure by accused); section 132(5) of the Criminal Justice Act 2003 (failure to give notice of hearsay evidence).'

The new Rules apply in cases in which the defendant is charged on or after 7 April 2008.

What is the effect of the new Rules? By virtue of the sanctions now available to it in the new Rule 3.5(6), a court which makes an order for disclosure under the substituted Rule 3.10, does not in so doing infringe LPP. Such an order merely sets conditions on the right to call live evidence.

Practitioners should therefore be aware that if an order has been made for prior disclosure relating to any of the categories set out in Rule 3.10, in the event that they wish to call live evidence, they must give serious consideration to the consequences of a failure to comply with the order before calling that evidence. Such failure could result in the court exercising its power to make a costs order,[30] for instance, if an adjournment is necessary for the prosecution to run criminal record checks on the witness. Other sanctions are also available, including the power to draw adverse inferences.

Whilst the court also has the power to exclude evidence, the Administrative Court in *Kelly* emphasised the need for sanctions to be 'proportionate' and 'no more than might reasonably be required for the proper working of such a regulation'. Mitting J stated 'I am inclined to think that the imposition of an effective sanction, such as a prohibition on relying on the evidence of a witness not previously identified, would require primary legislation'.[31]

Certificates of Readiness

Certificates of Readiness can and do cause problems. Questions such as 'have all necessary steps been taken to have the case ready for trial?', 'what remains to be done?', or 'is anything preventing the case being ready on time?' may bring to light the fact that the solicitor will not be ready for trial because of the defendant's fault; the fact of this state of unreadiness offends none of the defendant's rights, as set out above. It is suggested that any embarrassment to the solicitor's relationship with the client can be avoided by explicitly explaining to the client the duty of the

---

[30] See part 4 of this Practice Note for the principles to be applied.
[31] paragraph 37.

solicitor to the court in such circumstances. This can be done in the initial terms of business, which should be clearly set out in writing and accepted by the client at the start of the retainer.

However, solicitors must carefully consider questions such as 'Is the defendant in contact with his solicitors and has he confirmed that he will attend his trial?' Whilst the first part of the question is not objectionable, the second part could involve the disclosure of a privileged communication.

Non-attendance at trial

If a client tells the solicitor that he or she is not going to attend the trial, the solicitor is placed in an invidious position as far as the solicitor's duty to the court is concerned, for such information, in all likelihood, will be privileged; in which event the solicitor cannot waive the client's privilege, and nor can the court order him or her to do so.

The general guidance to Rule 11 indicates, in paragraph 5:

> If you are a solicitor you are an officer of the court and you should take all reasonable steps to assist in the smooth running of the court but only insofar as this is consistent with your duties to your client. Difficulties are likely to arise, for example, where the defendant client absconds in a criminal case. If the client does fail to attend:
>
> (a) in relation to your duty of confidentiality you may properly state that you are without instructions, but may not disclose information about the client's whereabouts; and
>
> (b) in relation to your duty to act in the client's best interests, you may consider it appropriate to withdraw from the hearing where, having regard to the client's best interests, you believe you cannot properly represent the client. There may be cases where you would be able to proceed in the absence of your client, for example, where you may infer that the defendant expects you to continue to represent them or where a legal point can be taken which would defeat the prosecution case.

A solicitor should therefore be careful to ensure that he or she advises the client in writing in the initial terms of business/retainer letter (and repeats such advice should it become apparent that the client is, or may be, contemplating non-attendance) that not only is the client under a legal duty to attend the trial, but in the event that without good reason he or she does not attend:

- he or she will commit an offence; and
- can be tried in their absence; and
- if convicted, the Court of Appeal may be slow to allow an appeal.

4.   The approach of the court towards solicitors under the CPR

In managing the case in accordance with the overriding objective, the court has a duty to deal with the defence 'fairly'.[32] Fairness in this context is to be viewed by reference to the reasoning of Lord Hobhouse in *Medcalf* v *Mardell*:

> It is fundamental to a just and fair judicial system that there be available to a litigant (criminal or civil), in substantial cases, competent and independent legal representation. The duty of the advocate is with proper competence to represent his lay client and promote and protect fearlessly and by all proper and lawful means his lay client's best interests. This is a duty which the advocate owes to his client but it is also in the public interest that the duty should be performed. The judicial system exists to administer justice and it is integral to such a system that it provide within a society a means by which rights, obligations and liabilities can be recognised and given effect to in accordance with the law and disputes be justly (and efficiently) resolved. The role of the independent professional advocate is central to achieving this outcome, particularly where the judicial system uses adversarial procedures.
>
> It follows that the willingness of professional advocates to represent litigants should not be undermined either by creating conflicts of interest or by exposing the advocates to pressures which will tend to deter them from representing certain clients or from doing so effectively. ... Unpopular and seemingly unmeritorious litigants must be capable of being represented without the advocate being penalised or harassed whether by the executive, the judiciary or anyone else. Similarly, situations must be avoided where the advocate's conduct of a case is influenced not by his duty to his client but by concerns about his own self-interest.[33]

Whilst these comments refer specifically to advocates in the criminal process, they were considered to have equal application to the 'instructing solicitor' by the Court of Appeal when Lord Hobhouse's reasoning was recently adopted by the Court in relation to solicitors in the context of the court's wasted costs jurisdiction:

> The role of the independent professional advocate in the administration of justice must be borne in mind and also the need not to undermine it by illegitimate pressures.[34]

---

[32]   See CPR 1.1(2)(b).
[33]   [2002] UKHL 27 paragraphs 51 and 52, [2003] 1 AC 120 at page 141.
[34]   Per Pill LJ in *Re: Mr Harry Boodhoo, Solicitor* [2007] EWCA Crim 14 at paragraph 49.

Withdrawing from a case

If a solicitor has to withdraw from a case, the court should be cautious in pressing the solicitor to explain the reasons for this, for to give such an explanation would require him or her to disclose privileged communications with their client. In *R* v *G & B* Lord Justice Rose said:

> ... it is for counsel and solicitors, not the court, to make that decision in the light of all the circumstances known to them, some of which may not, for reasons of legal privilege or otherwise, be known to the court.[35]

Requiring a solicitor to attend court

Similarly the court should be slow to order a solicitor to attend court to answer its questions, particularly if these can be adequately answered by letter. The Law Society is concerned at the practice apparently adopted by some courts which, after notification by a defence solicitor of a failure to take a procedural step required by the CPR, have 'ordered' the solicitor or a partner of the firm to attend court in person (expressly unpaid) to explain the reason for the failure. The Law Society considers such an approach to be unfair; not only is it extremely doubtful that the court actually has power to make such an 'order', the financial cost of complying for instance, by cancelling other appointments, could far exceed that of a wasted costs order, for which the Court of Appeal has set strict guidelines to ensure fairness to the solicitor.[36] The preferred approach should be for the solicitor to explain to the court in writing, as fully as his or her duty of confidentiality permits, the reason for the failure, and in the event that the court is not satisfied, it should then consider invoking its wasted costs powers.

In *R (on the application of Howe)* v *South Durham Magistrates' Court*[37] a witness summons was issued against a solicitor with a view to proving through him the identity of a defendant, charged with driving disqualified, for whom he acted, and for whom he had previously acted in the proceedings in which the defendant had been disqualified. Whilst in the specific circumstances the Court indicated that the justices were right to issue the witness summonses, Lord Justice Rose expressed the Court's concern that witness summonses should only be served on solicitors as a 'last resort'. Having referred to the speech of Lord Taylor of Gosforth in *R* v *Derby Magistrates' Court*, ex p. *B* (quoted above) on the fundamental importance of legal professional privilege to the administration of justice, Lord Justice Rose stated:

---

[35] See paragraph 19 of *R* v *G & B* [2004] 2 Cr App R 37, [2004] EWCA Crim 1368.
[36] See below.
[37] [2004] EWHC 362 (Admin), [2005] RTR 4.

More widely, outside the scope of legal professional privilege, *the maintenance of confidence between lawyer and client is of central importance in our administration of justice.* It is therefore important for prosecuting authorities and Justices[38] to note that applications for a summons to serve on a lawyer, with a view to proving the identity of a defendant for whom he or she previously acted, should not become a matter of routine in relation to offences of driving while disqualified, or indeed any other offence.

On the contrary, such a course should, in my judgment, be the route of last resort to be followed only when no other reasonably practicable means of proving identity exists.[39] (Emphasis added.)

Whilst these comments specifically refer to the service of a witness summons with a view to proving identity, they are, in the view of the Law Society, of wider application; for a solicitor to be served with a witness summons to explain a perceived failure to comply with the CPR is highly likely to strike at the 'maintenance of confidence between lawyer and client' which Rose LJ considered to be of such central importance in the administration of justice.

Questioning a solicitor

On the rare occasions that it is considered appropriate for the court to put questions to a solicitor in court, adopting the comments of Lord Justice Rose that the 'maintenance of confidence between lawyer and client is of central importance in our administration of justice', the Law Society would hope that when questioning a solicitor, courts should decide at an early stage whether a wasted costs order is contemplated. If it is contemplated, then the wasted costs procedures set out below should be adopted from thereon.

In summary:

- It is ultimately a matter for the solicitor, not the court, to decide whether he or she can properly continue to act.
- A solicitor cannot be ordered by the court to divulge privileged communications with a client.
- If the court wishes a solicitor to attend before it in the course of a trial, the issue of a witness summons should be the route of last resort, and only in circumstances in which he or she is required to provide material evidence and the court is of the opinion that he or she will not voluntarily attend as a witness.

---

[38] The Law Society is aware of no reason why this should not also apply to judges in the Crown Court.

[39] at paragraphs 41 and 42.

- If the court is considering making criticism of a solicitor, that solicitor should be invited to attend court and the wasted costs procedures adopted.

Wasted Costs Orders (WCO)

When a court is considering making a WCO it should follow the guidance set out in the provisions of the *Practice Direction (Costs: Criminal Proceedings).*[40] Practitioners should familiarise themselves with these provisions. Of particular importance are the following requirements:

- The court must formulate carefully and concisely the complaint and grounds upon which a WCO may be sought.
- The court should allow the solicitor to make representations. The solicitor should formally be told clearly what he or she is said to have done wrong and invited to comment.
- The solicitor alleged to be at fault should be given sufficient notice of a complaint made against him or her, and given a proper opportunity to respond to it.
- The court should make full allowance for the possible difficulty caused by client confidentiality/legal professional privilege for a legal representative in answering criticism.
- Where a legal representative is precluded by legal professional privilege from giving a full answer to any criticism, a court should not make such criticism unless, proceeding with extreme care, it is satisfied that there was nothing that the representative could say, if permitted, to answer the criticism and that it was in all of the circumstances fair to make such criticism.
- The court must be satisfied that there has been an improper, unreasonable or negligent act or omission and that, as a result, costs have been incurred by a party. A mere mistake is not sufficient to justify an order – there must be a more serious error. The primary object is not to punish but to compensate.
- The principles of the court's WCO jurisdiction (especially in relation to the solicitor's duties when a client fails to attend trial) have recently been reviewed by the Court of Appeal (Criminal Division) in *Re: Mr Harry Boodhoo, Solicitor,*[41] and practitioners are encouraged to read the Court's judgment.

---

[40] [2004] 2 All ER 1070, Part VIII.1: Costs against Legal Representatives.
[41] [2007] EWCA Crim 14.

Keeping the Law Society informed

The Law Society is aware of the difficulties that are being faced by practitioners whilst the CPR 'bed down'. Different practices are apparently being adopted at different courts. If solicitors encounter problems they are encouraged to bring these to the attention of the Law Society (phone 0207 242 1222) in the hope that a consistent approach can be achieved for all those on whom the burdens and duties imposed by the CPR fall.

Annex 4B

Virtual court first hearings practice note

17 November 2008

1. Introduction

1.1   Who should read this practice note?

Criminal solicitors taking instructions and advising at police stations and at Magistrates' Courts where the virtual first hearing system is in use.

1.2   What is the issue?

The Office of Criminal Justice Reform intends to conduct a widespread pilot of the virtual first hearing system, whereby the conduct of the first Magistrates' Court hearing will take place with the defendant appearing in court by a video link from the police station.

This practice note outlines what you should consider before advising a defendant to consent to proceed in this way.

1.3   Professional conduct

The following sections of the Solicitors' Code of Conduct 2007 [**www.rules.sra.org.uk**] are relevant to this issue:

*   Rule 1.04 – you must act in the best interests of your client
*   Rule 4.01 – you must keep the affairs of your client confidential

1.4   Legal and other requirements

*   s.57C Crime and Disorder Act 1998, as inserted by the Police and Justice Act 2006

1.5   Status of this advice

Practice notes are issued by the Law Society for the use and benefit of its members. They represent the Law Society's view of good practice in a particular area. They are not intended to be the only standard of good practice that solicitors can follow. You are not required to follow them, but doing so will make it easier to account to oversight bodies for your actions.

Practice notes are not legal advice, nor do they necessarily provide a defence to complaints of misconduct or of inadequate professional service. While care has been taken to ensure that they are accurate, up to date and useful, the Law Society will not accept any legal liability in relation to them.

For queries or comments on this practice note contact the Law Society's Practice Advice Service.

1.6   Terminology in this practice note

Must – a specific requirement in the Solicitor's Code of Conduct or legislation. You must comply, unless there are specific exemptions or defences provided for in the code of conduct or relevant legislation.

Should – good practice for most situations in the Law Society's view. If you do not follow this, you must be able to justify to oversight bodies why this is appropriate, either for your practice, or in the particular retainer.

May – a non-exhaustive list of options for meeting your obligations. Which option you choose is determined by the risk profile of the individual practice, client or retainer. You must be able to justify why this was an appropriate option to oversight bodies.

1.7   More information

1.7.1   Practice Advice Line

The Law Society provides support for solicitors on a wide range of areas of practice. Practice Advice can be contacted on 0870 606 2522 from 09.00 to 17.00 on weekdays.

1.7.2   Acknowledgements

The Law Society is grateful to Ian Kelcey, Chair of its Criminal Law Committee, for drafting this practice note.

2. What is a virtual first hearing?

In a virtual first hearing the defendant appears in the Magistrates' Court by a video link from the police station. The magistrates or District Judge and court staff will be at the court in the usual way, with the prosecutor and defence solicitor either at the police station, or the court. If the solicitor is at the court the defendant may need to provide instructions to their solicitor by phone or video link.

In order for a court to proceed by way of a virtual first hearing, the defendant must consent to appear in this way rather than in person. You must consider their circumstances and your ability to properly advise them before advising them to consent to a virtual hearing.

3. Your duty to the client

Consider your duties to the client when considering advising them to use the virtual court system.

3.1 Assessing the client's fitness

You have a duty to ascertain that your client is fit to take part in proceedings. You must assess whether they:

- are under the influence of drugs or alcohol, or suffering the effects of withdrawal;
- have cognitive, mental or physical health issues that may affect their rights while in police detention;
- have been subject to inappropriate police pressure.

3.2 Clients who require an appropriate adult or interpreter

If an appropriate adult is, or has been, present because of a client's mental health or learning disability you should be very cautious about advising them to consent to proceed by way of a virtual first hearing. We understand the virtual first hearing scheme will not be available in youth cases.

You must take into account that your ability to properly assess your client's mental state, or their level of understanding of the court process and the consequences of any decisions made, may be impaired if you are unable to take instructions from them in person.

It is extremely unlikely that you should advise the client to consent by virtual court hearing if they require an interpreter.

3.3 The client in the police station

Clients held in custody can often be in a vulnerable state in what may be the unfamiliar and frightening surroundings of a police station. It is your duty to help and represent their best interests at this stage.

You must:

- ensure that the police are conducting the investigation fairly and lawfully;
- assess the extent and nature of the evidence against the client;
- advise on whether the client should co-operate with the investigation, or exercise their right to silence.

You may also need to confirm your instructions in writing or agree a certain course of action in writing, particularly when you are advising in relation to plea or explaining issues relating to a bail application.

You must carefully consider whether this can properly be done by telephone or video link, or whether circumstances require you to attend in person at the police station.

You should only provide advice to your client in custody when confidentiality can be assured. In most cases, you should provide only very basic advice via the telephone, for example:

- the estimated time of your arrival;
- reminding the client of their right to silence.

You should not take instructions or provide advice in the presence of an appropriate adult, because the duty of confidentiality and legal professional privilege does not attach to the appropriate adult.

You should also exercise caution when using an interpreter provided by the police service. Further information:

- OCJR Revised National Agreement on the Use of Interpreters [**http://frontline.cjsonline.gov.uk**];
- Law Society operational guidance on defence interpreters issued in Criminal Practitioners' Newsletter number 46, October 2001 [search at **www.lawsociety.org.uk**].

3.4 The client once charged

Once the client has been charged, you have a duty to ensure that they understand the case against them, and their options regarding any plea.

You must:

- gather information about the case from the prosecution and from other witnesses;
- apply to the court for bail if necessary;
- advise the client in relation to their plea to the charge.

Again, you must carefully consider whether this can properly be done by telephone or video link, or whether circumstances require you to attend in person at the police station.

If the client decides to plead guilty, you must also:

- explain the likely sentence;
- gather information to use in submissions to the court in mitigation of sentence.

3.5   Advice on plea or surrender of rights

You should not give any advice that relates to the client's plea to the charge or results in the surrender of any of their rights, unless you are sure that the suspect can freely and confidentially acknowledge the advice given, and if necessary confirm any instruction or agreement to a course of action in writing.

3.6   Pre-charge advice by telephone for minor matters

Some pre-charge publicly funded advice may only be accessed by telephone through the Defence Solicitor Call Centre (DSCC) and CDS Direct. If the client has received such advice before your involvement in the case you should conduct an interview with your client in person to ensure that they have not given up any rights following the CDS Direct telephone advice.

For further information about the scope of telephone-only advice, see the Legal Services Commission's General Criminal Contract [**www.legalservices.gov.uk**].

Annex 4C

Withdrawing from a criminal case practice note

4 November 2008

1. Introduction

1.1 Who should read this practice note?

Solicitors practising in criminal law.

1.2 What is the issue?

Issues arise when you are considering either withdrawing from representing a defendant, or taking on a transferred case, close to or in the course of the trial.

Once the criminal trial process is engaged, you owe professional obligations both to the defendant/s for whom you act, but also to the court.

This practice note gives advice on these issues.

For contextual information see:

- *R* v *Ulcay* [2007] EWCA Crim 2379 [**www.bailii.org/ew/cases/ EWCA/Crim/2007/2379.html**]
- *R* v *B & G* [2004] EWCA Crim 1368 [**www.bailii.org/ew/cases/ EWCA/Crim/2004/1368.html**]

1.3 Professional conduct

The following sections of the Solicitors' Code of Conduct 2007 are relevant to this issue:

- Rule 2.01(2) Client relations – taking on clients
- Rule 3 Conflict of interest
- Rule 4 Confidentiality and disclosure
- Rule 11 Litigation and advocacy

1.4   Legal and other requirements

- Criminal Procedure Rules 2005 [**www.justice.gov.uk/about/ criminal-proc-rule-committee.htm**]
- Regulation 16 Criminal Defence Service (General) (No.2) Regulations [**www.opsi.gov.uk/si/si2001/20011437.htm**]

1.5   Status of this advice

Practice notes are issued by the Law Society for the use and benefit of its members. They represent the Law Society's view of good practice in a particular area. They are not intended to be the only standard of good practice that solicitors can follow. You are not required to follow them, but doing so will make it easier to account to oversight bodies for your actions.

Practice notes are not legal advice, nor do they necessarily provide a defence to complaints of misconduct or of inadequate professional service. While care has been taken to ensure that they are accurate, up to date and useful, the Law Society will not accept any legal liability in relation to them.

For queries or comments on this practice note contact the Law Society's Practice Advice Service.

1.6   Terminology in this advice

Must – a specific requirement in the Solicitor's Code of Conduct or legislation. You must comply, unless there are specific exemptions or defences provided for in the code of conduct or relevant legislation.

Should – good practice for most situations in the Law Society's view. If you do not follow this, you must be able to justify to oversight bodies why this is appropriate, either for your practice, or in the particular retainer.

May – a non-exhaustive list of options for meeting your obligations. Which option you choose is determined by the risk profile of the individual practice, client or retainer. You must be able to justify why this was an appropriate option to oversight bodies.

1.7   More information

1.7.1   Practice Advice Line

The Law Society provides support for solicitors on a wide range of areas of practice. Practice Advice can be contacted on 0870 606 2522 from 8am to 6pm on weekdays.

1.7.2   Practice note: Criminal Procedure Rules 2005

The Law Society has produced a practice note to help you understand your duties under the Criminal Procedure Rules 2005.

1.8   Acknowledgements

The Law Society is grateful to Christopher Murray of Kingsley Napley, former Chair of the Criminal Law Committee, for his assistance with the Law Society's intervention, at the invitation of the Court of Appeal, in *R* v *Ulcay*, and in subsequently drafting this practice note. It is also grateful to other members of the Committee for their input.

2.   Reasons to withdraw

You may withdraw from acting for a client in a criminal case, whether during the trial itself or during preparation for trial, where there are compelling reasons to do so.

2.1   Who determines whether there are compelling reasons?

The decision about whether compelling reasons to withdraw exist lies with you, not the court.

The Court in *R* v *Ulcay* agreed with the observations of Rose LJ in *R* v *G and B* when he said, at paragraph 14 of that case: 'We think it right, both in principle and pragmatically, that whether a solicitor or barrister can properly continue to act is a matter for him or her not the court, although of course the court can properly make observations on the matter.'

In *R* v *Ulcay* Judge LJ stated, at paragraph 30: 'The principle . . . remains clear. The court cannot oblige the lawyer to continue to act when he has made a professional judgement that he is obliged, for compelling reasons, to withdraw from the case'.

2.2   What are 'compelling reasons'?

You must withdraw from a case if you conclude that you are professionally embarrassed by continuing to act, in accordance with the Solicitors' Code of Conduct, and the professional obligations you owe to your client, and/or to the court [see **sra.org.uk/rules** or amendments as of 31 March 2009].

This is to avoid breaching the code, and also prevent risk of punishment by the court, whether through a wasted costs order or, in more serious cases, prosecution for an offence against public justice.

2.3 Examples of compelling reasons

2.3.1 Obligations to clients

Where you are acting for two defendants a conflict of interest may arise.

You must withdraw from at least one client where this has occurred. Continuing to act would be in breach of rule 3 of the Solicitors' Code of Conduct.

You must withdraw from both clients if, by continuing to act for the remaining client, you would breach your duty of confidentiality to your former client (rule 4).

2.3.2 Obligations to the court

You must withdraw from a case if a client changes instructions in such a manner that for you to continue would involve you misleading the court. Continuing to act would breach rule 11.

3. Withdrawal when the client wishes to change solicitor

The retainer is a contractual relationship and subject therefore to legal considerations. In principle, a client can end the retainer with you at any time and for any reason. However, when a client is a defendant in criminal proceedings, different practical considerations apply to the determination of the retainer and withdrawal depending on client funding.

3.1 Where the client is privately funded

You must withdraw from a case if the defendant is privately funded and they terminate the retainer. You have no further authority to represent them.

3.2 Where the client is publicly funded

If the defendant is funded by legal aid, regulation 16 of the Criminal Defence Service (General) (No.2) Regulations governs any application for a change of representation, and the court has the power to grant or refuse such an application.

The grounds for change are set out in regulation 16(2)(a)(i)–(iv). You must provide details of either:

- the nature of the duty which you consider obliges you to withdraw;
- the nature of the breakdown in your relationship with your client.

You must, however, take legal professional privilege (LPP) into consideration as this may limit the information that you can give without your client's consent.

4.   What should you tell the court when withdrawing?

You must inform the court of the reasons for your withdrawal, by providing enough explanation to enable the judge to decide how to proceed. However, in doing so you must not breach legal professional privilege (LPP).

This may mean that the court is not fully informed about the reasons for withdrawal or the nature of the breakdown between you and your client, but that cannot be avoided. Although the court can properly comment, the making of this decision rests solely with you.

For more information about LPP see the practice note on Criminal Procedure Rules.

5.   Making an informed decision to accept a transferred case

You may decide whether or not to accept a retainer from a new client, but once you have accepted the retainer you may not later withdraw for reasons of practical difficulty which may result from your obligation to comply with court orders.

You must therefore be satisfied that you are able to comply with any orders already made by the court, including the length of any adjournment, *before* accepting instructions to act.

5.1   Replacing a solicitor at short notice

When considering taking over a case from another solicitor at short notice, you should make full inquiries of the court, asking to be given all the relevant information it can provide.

You should do this before accepting the case to ensure that you can comply with the court's requirements.

5.2   Difficulties arising from compliance with an adjournment order

If the defendant has changed their legal team close to, or during, a trial it is the responsibility of the trial judge to decide whether to adjourn the trial to accommodate new legal team, and for how long. Once you have accepted the retainer and assumed conduct of criminal litigation you have a professional obligation, as an officer of the court, to comply with these orders and to do your best for the client under those circumstances.

In *R* v *Ulcay* the Court considered that a solicitor in such circumstances owes a duty to the court that requires them to 'soldier on'. If the trial judge's decision produces injustice or deprives the defendant of a fair trail, the remedy is to be sought in the Court of Appeal. See paragraphs 44 and 38 of the judgment.

5.3   How does compliance affect your professional obligation?

Complying with a court order which makes it impossible or difficult to achieve your normal standard of competence in looking after your client's interests does not put you in breach of the Solicitors' Code of Conduct, nor are you acting improperly or negligently.

Money laundering

In light of the Money Laundering Regulations 2007 (MLR 2007), what has the Law Society done to assist solicitors to comply with their obligations?

The Law Society has prepared practice notes on anti-money laundering (AML) (**Annex 5A**) and counter terrorist financing (CTF) (**Annex 5B**). The practice notes annexed to this chapter are correct at the time of going to print but it is recommended that you check the Law Society website as they are both regularly updated.

Further, the Law Society website sets out a number of AML services including the following:

- The Practice Advice Service (Tel: 0870 606 2522) can assist solicitors with navigating the practice notes and respond to general queries on AML compliance. It does not provide legal advice or advise on conduct issues, nor does it advise on compliance with the 2003 Regulations.
- The Solicitors' Regulation Authority's Professional Ethics Helpline (Tel: 0870 606 2577) can provide assistance with conduct issues relating to money laundering.
- The Anti-Money Laundering Directory – Solicitor's needing legal advice on AML compliance can access an online directory of solicitors who practise in this area and are willing to be contacted by other solicitors seeking legal advice. There is a link to this directory from the Law Society's website (**www.lawsociety.org.uk**).
- Law Society Publishing have published a book, Camp, P. (2008) *Solicitors and Money Laundering: A Compliance Handbook*, 3rd Edition, which is available from the Law Society's online bookshop (**www.lawsociety.org.uk/bookshop**).

I understand that the MLR 2007 refer to 'customer due diligence'. What is this?

Regulation 5 says that customer due diligence comprises:

- Identifying the client and verifying their identity on the basis of documents, data or information obtained from a reliable and independent source.

- Identifying where there is a beneficial owner who is not the customer, the beneficial owner and taking adequate measures, on a risk sensitive basis, to verify his identity so that you are satisfied that you know who the beneficial owner is. This includes understanding the ownership and control structure of a legal person, trust or similar arrangement.
- Obtaining information on the purpose and intended nature of the business relationship

Identification of a client or a beneficial owner is simply being told or coming to know a client's identifying details, such as their name and address. Verification is obtaining some evidence which supports this claim of identity.

For further information and definition of beneficial owner, please refer to Chapter 4 of the Law Society's Anti-money laundering practice note (**Annex 5A**).

When is 'customer due diligence' required for the purpose of complying with the MLR 2007?

Regulation 7 requires that you conduct customer due diligence when:

- Establishing a business relationship
- Carrying out an occasional transaction
- You suspect money laundering or terrorist financing
- You doubt the veracity or adequacy of documents, data or information previously obtained for the purposes of customer due diligence.

There is no obligation to conduct customer due diligence in accordance with the regulations for retainers involving non-regulated activities. (For details of non-regulated activities please see Chapter 1 of the Law Society's Anti-money laundering practice note).

For further information on customer due diligence, please refer to Chapter 4 of the Anti-money laundering practice note (**Annex 5A**).

Our new firm would like to prepare its policies and procedures in line with MLR 2007. Does the Law Society produce any sample/precedent client care letters?

You may wish to refer to the client care letters practice note (**Annex 7D**). Whilst the publication does not contain sample letters, it does provide solicitors with a client care checklist and includes sample paragraphs which you may wish to use as a basis for your client care letters.

For further guidance on precedent forms and policies please see Camp, *Solicitors and Money Laundering,* 3rd edition.

I am in the process of setting up a firm as a sole practitioner. I will be dealing with mainly conveyancing and probate matters. I am considering my obligations under the MLR 2007. Will I be required to appoint a nominated officer?

Regulation 20(2)(d)(i) requires that all firms within the regulated sector must have a nominated officer to receive disclosures under Part 7 of the Proceeds of Crime Act 2002 and the Terrorism Act 2000 and to make disclosures to the Serious Organised Crime Agency (SOCA).

Regulation 20(3) provides that there is no requirement to have a nominated officer in the regulated sector if you are an individual who provides regulated services but do not employ any people or act in association with anyone else.

For further information please see Chapter 3 of the Law Society's Anti-money laundering practice note (**Annex 5A**) and the Client care practice note (**Annex 7D**).

I act for a buyer in a domestic conveyancing matter and my client has come into the office with £20,000 cash to pay his deposit. Upon questioning the client it appears the money is from his own account but he did not want to pay the £30 bank fee for a bank cheque and hence the cash. Is there a limit upon the amount of cash firms can accept from clients?

Large payments made in actual cash may be a sign of money laundering. Although, the Law Society has not set a cash limit, the Law Society advises that as a matter of good practice you establish a policy on not accepting cash payments above a certain limit either at your office or into your bank account. The Law Society has steered clear of setting limits because cash tolerance will be different for every firm depending on the type of work done.

Chapter 11 of the Law Society's practice note on anti-money laundering looks at the importance for solicitors to look for warning signs. It is a matter for you when considering all the information at your disposal, whether you feel you have reasonable grounds for suspicion or knowledge of money laundering. Cash in itself is not an indicator of money laundering and should not necessitate an automatic report to SOCA but depending on the circumstances you may need to undertake further checks and customer due diligence to satisfy yourself that there are no grounds for making a report to SOCA.

My firm is concerned that in trying to comply with the MLR 2007 we will be incurring additional costs. Can my firm charge the client for checking the client's identity or if we need to make a report to SOCA, can we charge the client for that?

Compliance costs generally fall within a number of categories. The Law Society has considered the costs burden and its conclusions are as follows as applied to non-contentious business:

1. Compliance with Regulation 21 requires 'relevant employees' to be trained so that they are made aware of:

    (i) the provisions of the MLR 2007, Part 7 of the Proceeds of Crime Act 2002 (PoCA 2002), and sections 18 and 21A of the Terrorism Act 2000; and

    (ii) given training in how to recognise and deal with transactions which may be related to money laundering.

    The cost of staff training is normally treated as an overhead.

2. Solicitors must comply with the MLR 2007 when they conduct 'relevant business' as defined by Regulation 3(9). When the MLR 2007 apply they require solicitors to check the identity of their clients before forming a 'business relationship'. There is no rule/regulation preventing solicitors from charging their clients for checking identity provided the client is informed of the level and method of charging. Charges for identity checking are also subject to the normal constraints, including whether the charge is 'fair and reasonable.' Please see Article 3 of the Solicitors' (Non-Contentious Business) Remuneration Order 1994 (SI 1994/2616).

3. Another requirement of the MLR 2007 is for firms to employ systems to prevent and forestall money laundering. The Law Society suggests that solicitors approach additional 'know your client' checks on a risk basis. Often solicitors will make such checks without their client's knowledge, and certainly not upon their instructions. There does not appear to be any settled authority on whether solicitors can charge clients for such broader checking.

4. Compliance with PoCA 2002 and counter terrorism legislation also requires solicitors to make reports to SOCA. It is not possible to charge clients for work which is not in accordance with their instructions.

We are a niche litigation firm. We are unclear as to our obligations under the MLR 2007. Are we obliged to conduct customer due diligence on our clients? Are we also obliged to appoint a money laundering reporting officer?

Regulation 20 of the MLR 2007 requires the regulated sector to have certain systems in place.

The Treasury has confirmed that participation in litigation is an activity which is not covered by the MLR 2007 and you are therefore not obliged to identify and verify your clients. Nor are you obliged to appoint a money laundering reporting officer (see Chapter 1 of the Law Society's Anti-money laundering practice note).

However, you should still consider how these systems can assist you to comply with your obligations to report suspicious transactions in accordance with the Proceeds of Crime Act 2002 and the Terrorism Act 2000 (see Chapter 3 of the practice note).

As the firm specialises in litigation, you should also be familiar with the case of *Bowman* v. *Fels* [2005] EWCA Civ 226, further information on which is set out at Chapter 5 of the practice note.

We are in the process of setting up systems and procedures in compliance with Regulation 20 of the MLR 2007. We cannot find any guidance as to who in the firm is qualified to be a nominated officer. Further, is this the same as a money laundering reporting officer or do their roles vary?

A nominated officer is also commonly referred to as a money laundering reporting officer (see Definitions and Glossary section of the Law Society's Anti-money Laundering practice note).

There is no specific qualification criteria. Your nominated officer should be of sufficient seniority to make decisions on reporting which can impact your firm's business relations with your clients and your exposure to criminal, civil, regulatory and disciplinary sanctions. They should also be in a position of sufficient responsibility to enable them to have access to all of your firm's client files and business information to enable them to make the required decisions on the basis of all information held by the firm.

Firms authorised by the FSA will need to obtain the FSA's approval to the appointment of the nominated officer as this is a controlled function under section 59 of the Financial Services and Markets Act 2000.

For further information, please see Chapter 3 of the practice note.

My firm deals with commercial clients with complex structures and often receives funds from third parties. How far do we have to go to establish the source of funds in relation to fulfilling our obligations under the MLR 2007?

Accounts staff should monitor whether funds received from clients are from credible sources. For example, it is reasonable for monies to be received from a company if your client is a director of that company and has the authority to use company money for the transaction.

However, if funding is from a source other than your client, you may need to make further enquiries, especially if the client has not told you what they intend to do with the funds before depositing them into your account. If you decide to accept funds from a third party, perhaps because time is short, ask how and why the third party is helping with the funding.

You do not have to make enquiries into every source of funding from other parties. However, you must always be alert to warning signs and in some cases you will need to get more information.

In some circumstances, cleared funds will be essential for transactions and clients may want to provide cash to meet a completion deadline. Assess the risk in these cases and ask questions if necessary.

Please see Chapter 11 of the Law Society's Anti-money laundering practice note.

My firm regularly acts for a well known accountancy firm which is a partnership. Currently, the accountancy firm is acting in its capacity as an administrator for a UK company and my firm are undertaking the conveyancing of a piece of land that is being sold as part of the administration. For the purposes of fulfilling our obligations under the MLR 2007 who needs to be identified and how could we verify their identity?

The accountancy firm is your client and the transaction forms part of a business relationship. The work comes under the regulated sector. In order to verify your client's identity you may confirm the firm's existence and the trading address from a reputable professional directory or search facility with the relevant professional body. Otherwise, you should obtain evidence on the identity of at least the partner instructing you and one other partner, and evidence of the firm's trading address. Please see Chapter 4 of the Law Society's practice note on anti-money laundering.

Under the MLR 2007, you must consider who are the beneficial owners. As the accountancy firm is your client and not the company in administration, the beneficial owners are the partners of the accountancy firm and not the shareholders of the company in administration. While a beneficial owner only has to be identified under the MLR 2007 if they have ownership or control of more than 25 per cent of the entity, if you have obtained a list of all persons who could possibly be a beneficial owner, it is worth printing that list and putting it on file.

If you had not had previous dealings with this firm, it was not a well known firm or it came from a jurisdiction which was high risk then you should consider asking for the partnership agreement to determine in detail who exactly was a beneficial owner and to then consider undertaking electronic verification or requesting certified copies of passports.

Does the Law Society have any guidance for solicitors on the procedure for making a Suspicious Activity Report (SAR) under the MLR 2007?

Yes. Where a firm has a nominated officer, either they or their deputy will make the SAR to SOCA. The guidance requires you to make a disclosure as soon as you are suspicious or know of terrorist financing or money laundering (subject to privilege considerations). Swiftly made SARs avoid delays in fulfilling your client's instructions. You need not wait to ascertain whether or not a person is actually your client before making the disclosure. An SAR can be made about any person whom you suspect is involved in money laundering or terrorist financing.

Reports can either take the form of an SAR or limited intelligence value report (LIVR). SARs will generally be the normal method of reporting, particularly where consent is required; however, LIVRs may be appropriate where you know that a law enforcement agency already has an interest in a matter. SOCA has provided detailed information on when LIVRs should be used. If in doubt, complete an SAR form.

For further information please refer to Chapter 8 of the Law Society's Anti-money laundering practice note.

What information should be included in an SAR?

SOCA has provided information on completing the preferred SAR form. To speed up consideration of your SAR, it is recommended that you use SOCA's glossary of codes for each reason for the suspicion section of the report (see **www.soca.gov.uk**). Your regulation number is your firm's ID number.

SOCA has produced information on obtaining consent including a number of key points to remember (see SOCA website). You will only receive consent to the extent that you requested. For example:

> We seek consent to finalise an agreement for sale of property X into the name of [purchaser] and following payment of disbursements, pay the net proceeds of the sale of the property to [seller].

It is vital you clearly outline all the remaining steps in the transaction that could be a prohibited act.

For help on submitting an SAR and on consent issues the Financial Intelligence Helpdesk at SOCA can be contacted on 020 7328 8282.

For further information please refer to Chapter 8 of the Law Society's Anti-money laundering practice note.

I am employed by a public authority. Do the MLR 2007 apply to the activities I conduct?

You will need to refer to the MLR 2007 which came into force on 15 December 2007. For further information on this, please refer to the Law Society's Anti-money laundering practice note.

You will also need to consider whether or not you work in the 'regulated sector' having considered the most recent version of Schedule 9, Part 1 of the Proceeds of Crime Act 2002; it does not include solicitors employed by a public authority.

The Treasury Department has confirmed generally, that certain activities are not covered by the MLR 2007 which includes payment on account of costs to a solicitor or payment of a solicitor's bill, provision of legal services, publicly funded work and preparing a Home Information Pack.

If you are unsure whether or not the MLR 2007 apply to your work, you may consider seeking legal advice on your particular circumstances or alternatively, take the broadest approach.

I am my firms money laundering reporting officer. I have made a suspicious activity report (SAR) to SOCA requesting consent to proceed. When can I expect to hear from SOCA?

Consent decisions must be made within seven working days. The seven day notice period commences on the day after a disclosure is made. If nothing is heard within that time, then you can go ahead with an otherwise prohibited act without an offence being committed. If consent is withheld within the seven working days, then SOCA has a further 31 calendar days (known as the moratorium period) in which to take further action such as seeking a court order to restrain the assets in question. If nothing is heard after the end of the 31 day period, then you can proceed with the transaction without committing an offence.

If you need consent sooner, you should clearly state the reasons for the urgency in the initial report and perhaps contact Financial Intelligence Helpdesk at SOCA by telephone on 020 7238 8282 to discuss the situation. SOCA can sometimes give consent in a matter of hours.

Within the notice and 31 day period, you must not do a prohibited act. However, this will not prevent you taking other action on the file, such as writing letters and conducting searches.

SOCA will contact you by telephone to advise if consent has been issued and will then send you a follow up letter.

For further information, please refer to Chapter 8 of the Law Society's Anti-money laundering practice note. You may also wish to visit **www. soca.gov.uk.**

I suspect that my client is involving me in circumstances that may amount to committing one of the principal money laundering offences under PoCA 2002. Am I able to avoid all liability if I make a disclosure to SOCA?

Not necessarily. PoCA 2002 aims to deprive wrongdoers of the benefits of crime, not compensate the victims. The civil law provides an opportunity for victims to take action against wrongdoers and those who have assisted them, through a claim for constructive trusteeship. Victims often target the professional adviser in civil claims because they are more likely to be able to pay compensation, often by reason of their professional indemnity cover.

There is a risk of making a defensive disclosure to SOCA. Consent from SOCA only protects you from falling foul of the anti-money laundering regime. It will not defend you from civil liability. In fact, obtaining consent may create the very evidence on which a claimant can rely to found a civil liability.

It is therefore vital that you disclose to SOCA only those situations fulfilling the statutory tests in Part 7 of PoCA 2002; knowledge or suspicion of money laundering, or reasonable grounds to suspect money laundering. Please see Chapter 10 of the Law Society's Anti-money laundering practice note.

I act for a client in a commercial property transaction. Having considered my anti-money laundering obligations, I have come to the conclusion that legal professional privilege (LPP) prevents me from making a disclosure to SOCA. Can I ask my client to waive privilege?

When approaching your client for a waiver of privilege, you may feel less concerned about tipping off issues if your client is not the suspect party but is engaged in a transaction which involves criminal property. However, if you suspect that your client is implicated in the underlying criminal conduct, consider the tipping offence (Proceeds of Crime Act 2002, s.333A) and whether or not it is appropriate to discuss these matters openly with your client.

If you raise the matter with your client and they agree to waive privilege, you can make a disclosure to SOCA on your own or jointly with your client and seek consent if required.

If you are acting for more than one client on a matter, all clients must agree to waive privilege before you can make a disclosure to SOCA.

For further information, please refer to the Law Society's Anti-money laundering practice note.

My client is based in another part of the country and is unable to come to the office. Would I meet the customer due diligence (CDD) obligations under the MLR 2007 if I ask him to go to a solicitor local to him to certify a copy of his identification documents and send them to me?

No. There is a significant difference between certifying copies and 'reliance'. Reliance has a very specific meaning within the Regulations and relates to the process under Regulation 17 where you rely on another regulated person to conduct CDD for you. You remain liable for any failure in the client being appropriately identified. Reliance does not include:

- accepting information from others to verify a client's identity when meeting your own CDD obligations;
- electronic verification, which is outsourcing.

You need:

- the consent of the person on whom you rely for your reliance;
- agreement that they will provide you with the CDD material upon request;
- the identity of their supervisor for money laundering purposes. Consider checking the register of members for that supervisor, although a personal assurance of their identity may be sufficient where you have reasonable grounds to believe them.

You should ask the local solicitor what CDD enquiries have been undertaken to ensure that they actually comply with the MLR 2007, because you remain liable for non-compliance. This is particularly important when relying on a person outside the UK, and you should be satisfied that the CDD has been conducted to a standard compatible with the EU Third Directive, taking into account the ability to use different sources of verification and jurisdictional specific factors. It may not always be appropriate to rely on another person to undertake your CDD checks and you should consider reliance as a risk in itself.

With regard to obtaining certified copies, you may still need to carry out further CDD which could include the use of electronic verification and enhanced due diligence if you do not actually meet the client.

For further information on reliance, please refer to Chapter 4 of the Law Society's Anti-money laundering practice note.

Annex 5A

Anti-money laundering practice note

22 February 2008

DEFINITIONS AND GLOSSARY

Definitions

Beneficial owners	see – Chapter 4.7 [of this practice note]
Business relationship	a business, professional or commercial relationship between a relevant person and a customer, which is expected by the relevant person at the time when contact is established to have an element of duration
Customer due diligence	see – Chapter 4 [of this practice note]
Criminal conduct	conduct which constitutes an offence in any part of the UK or would constitute an offence in any part of the UK if it occurred there – see s.340(2) of POCA
Criminal property	property which is, or represents, a person's benefit from criminal conduct, where the alleged offender knows or suspects that it is such – see also the definition of property
Disclosure	a report made to SOCA under the Proceeds of Crime Act 2002 – also referred to as a suspicious activity report (SAR)
Insolvency practitioner	any person who acts as an insolvency practitioner within the meaning of section 388 of the Insolvency Act 1986 (as amended) or article 3 of the Insolvency (Northern Ireland) Order 1989 (as amended)

Inter vivos trust	a trust which takes effect while a person is alive
Legal professional privilege	see – Chapter 6.4 [of this practice note]
Nominated officer	a person nominated within the firm to make disclosures to SOCA under the Proceeds of Crime Act 2002 – also referred to as a money laundering reporting officer (MLRO)
Occasional transaction	a transaction (carried out other than as part of a business relationship) amounting to 15,000 euros or more, whether the transaction is carried out in a single operation or several operations which appear to be linked
Ongoing monitoring	see – Chapter 4.4 [of this practice note]
Overseas criminal conduct	conduct which occurs overseas that would be a criminal offence if it occurred in the UK
	does not include conduct which occurred overseas where it is known or believed on reasonable grounds that the relevant conduct occurred in a particular country or territory outside the UK, and such conduct was in fact not unlawful under the criminal law then applying in that country or territory
	that exemption will not apply to overseas criminal conduct if it would attract a maximum sentence in excess of 12 months imprisonment were the conduct to have occurred in the UK
	will always be exempt if the overseas conduct is such that it would constitute an offence under the Gaming Act 1968, the Lotteries & Amusements Act 1976 or s.23 or s.35 of the Financial Services and Markets Act 2000
	see s.102 of SOCPA
Politically exposed persons	see – Chapter 4.9.2 [of this practice note]
Privileged circumstances	see – Chapter 6.5 [of this practice note]
Property	all property whether situated in the UK or abroad, including money, real and personal property, things in action, intangible property and an interest in land or a right in relation to any other property

Regulated sector	activities, professions and entities regulated for the purposes of AML/CTF obligations – see Chapter 1 [of this practice note]
Tax adviser	a firm or sole practitioner who, by way of business, provides advice about the tax affairs of another person, when providing such services
Terrorist property	money or other property which is likely to be used for the purposes of terrorism, the proceeds of the commission of acts of terrorism and the proceeds of acts carried out for the purposes of terrorism
Trust or company service provider	a firm or sole practitioner who by way of business provides any of the following services to other persons –

1. forming companies or other legal persons
2. acting or arranging for another person to act
    1. as a director or secretary of a company;
    2. as a partner of a partnership; or
    3. in a similar position in relation to other legal persons;
3. providing a registered office, business address, correspondence or administrative address or other related services for a company, partnership or any other legal person or arrangement;
4. acting, or arranging for another person to act, as –
    1. a trustee of an express trust or similar legal arrangement; or
    2. a nominee shareholder for another person other than a company listed on a regulated market when providing such services.

Glossary

AIM	Alternative Investment Market
AML/CTF	Anti-money laundering/counter-terrorist financing

CDD	Customer due diligence
EEA	European Economic Area
FATF	Financial Action Task Force
FSA	Financial Services Authority
GRO	General Register Office
HMRC	Her Majesty's Revenue and Customs
IBA	International Bar Association
JMLSG	Joint Money Laundering Steering Group
LLPs	Limited Liability Partnerships
LPP	Legal professional privilege
PEPs	Politically exposed persons
POCA	Proceeds of Crime Act 2002
Regulations	Money Laundering Regulations 2007
SARs	Suspicious activity reports
SRA	Solicitors Regulation Authority
SOCA	Serious Organised Crime Agency
Terrorism Act	Terrorism Act 2000
Third directive	Third European Money Laundering Directive

Chapter 1 – Introduction

1.1 General comments

Solicitors are key professionals in the business and financial world, facilitating vital transactions that underpin the UK economy. As such, they have a significant role to play in ensuring their services are not used to further a criminal purpose. As professionals, solicitors must act with integrity and uphold the law, and they must not engage in criminal activity.

Money laundering and terrorist financing are serious threats to society, losing revenue and endangering life, and fuelling other criminal activity.

This practice note aims to assist solicitors in England and Wales to meet their obligations under the UK anti-money laundering and counter-terrorist financing (AML/CTF) regime.

1.2 Status of this practice note

This practice note replaces previous Law Society guidance and good practice information on complying with AML/CTF obligations.

The purpose of this practice note is to:

- outline the legal and regulatory framework of AML/CTF obligations for solicitors within the UK;
- outline good practice on implementing the legal requirements;
- outline good practice in developing systems and controls to prevent solicitors being used to facilitate money laundering and terrorist financing;
- provide direction on applying the risk-based approach to compliance effectively.

The Solicitors Regulation Authority (SRA) will take into account whether a solicitor has complied with this practice note when undertaking its role as regulator of professional conduct, and as a supervisory authority for the purposes of the regulations. This practice note is not mandatory but a solicitor may be asked by the SRA to justify a decision to deviate from it.

Some solicitors' firms are authorised and regulated by the FSA because they are involved in mainstream regulated activities, e.g. advising clients directly on investments such as stocks and shares. Those firms should also consider the Joint Money Laundering Steering Group's guidance [**www.jmlsg.org.uk**].

This practice note is not a substitute for the law, and compliance with it is not a defence to offences under POCA, the Terrorism Act or the regulations. However, courts will generally have regard to any good practice on a particular topic issued by a professional body when considering the standard of a professional's conduct and whether they acted reasonably, honestly and appropriately.

We are seeking Treasury approval of this practice note, which, in accordance with regulation 45(2), will require the court to consider compliance with its contents in assessing whether a person committed an offence or took all reasonable steps and exercised all due diligence to avoid committing the offence.

1.3   Definition of money laundering

Money laundering is generally defined as the process by which the proceeds of crime, and the true ownership of those proceeds, are changed so that the proceeds appear to come from a legitimate source. Under POCA, the definition is broader and more subtle. Money laundering can arise from small profits and savings from relatively minor crimes, such as regulatory breaches, minor tax evasion or benefit fraud. A deliberate attempt to obscure the ownership of illegitimate funds is not necessary.

There are three acknowledged phases to money laundering: placement, layering and integration. However, the broader definition of money laundering offences in POCA includes even passive possession of criminal property as money laundering.

1.3.1   Placement

Cash generated from crime is placed in the financial system. This is the point when proceeds of crime are most apparent and at risk of detection. Because banks and financial institutions have developed AML procedures, criminals look for other ways of placing cash within the financial system. You can be targeted because a solicitor's firm commonly deals with client money.

1.3.2   Layering

Once proceeds of crime are in the financial system, layering obscures their origins by passing the money through complex transactions. These often involve different entities like companies and trusts and can take place in multiple jurisdictions. You may be targeted at this stage and detection can be difficult.

1.3.3   Integration

Once the origin of the funds has been obscured, the criminal is able to make the funds reappear as legitimate funds or assets. They will invest funds in legitimate businesses or other forms of investment, often using you to buy a property, set up a trust, acquire a company, or even settle litigation, among other activities. This is the most difficult stage of money laundering to detect.

1.4   Legal framework

1.4.1   Financial Action Task Force (FATF)

This was created in 1989 by the G7 Paris summit, building on UN treaties on trafficking of illicit substances in 1988 and confiscating the proceeds of crime in 1990. In 1990, FATF released their 40 recommendations for fighting money laundering. Between October 2001 and October 2004 it released nine further special recommendations [**www.fatf-gafi.org**] to prevent terrorist funding.

1.4.2 European Union directives

1991 – First Money Laundering Directive

The European Commission issued this to comply with the FATF recommendations. It applied to financial institutions, and required member states to make money laundering a criminal offence. It was incorporated into UK law via the Criminal Justice Act 1991, the Drug Trafficking Act 1994 and the Money Laundering Regulations 1993.

[http://eur-lex.europa.eu/LexUriServ/LexUriServ.do?uri=CELEX:319 91L0308:EN:HTML]

2001 – Second Money Laundering Directive

This incorporated the amendments to the FATF recommendations. It extended anti-money laundering obligations to a defined set of activities provided by a number of service professionals, such as independent legal professionals, accountants, auditors, tax advisers and real estate agents. It was incorporated into UK law via the Proceeds of Crime Act 2002 and the Money Laundering Regulations 2003.

[http://eur-lex.europa.eu/LexUriServ/site/en/oj/2001/l_344/l_344200 11228en00760081.pdf].

2005 – Third Money Laundering Directive

This extended due diligence measures to beneficial owners, recognising that such measures can be applied on a risk-based approach, and required enhanced due diligence to be undertaken in certain circumstances. It is incorporated into UK law by the Money Laundering Regulations 2007 and the Terrorism Act 2000 ... and Proceeds of Crime Act 2002 (Amendment) Regulations 2007 ([TACT and] POCA Regulations 2007 [SI 2007/3398]) ...

[http://eur-lex.europa.eu/LexUriServ/site/en/oj/2005/l_309/l_309200 51125en00150036.pdf].

1.4.3 Proceeds of Crime Act 2002 (POCA)

Scope

POCA, as amended, establishes a number of money laundering offences including:

- principal money laundering offences;
- offences of failing to report suspected money laundering;

- offences of tipping off about a money laundering disclosure, tipping off about a money laundering investigation and prejudicing money laundering investigations.

The TACT ... and ... POCA Regulations 2007 [SI 2007/3398] repealed the s.333 POCA tipping off offence. It has been replaced by section 333A which creates two new offences. Section 342(1) has also been amended to reflect these new offences. Read more [at 5.8 of this practice note].

Application

POCA applies to all persons, although certain failure to report offences and the tipping off offences only apply to persons who are engaged in activities in the regulated sector.

The Proceeds of Crime Act 2002 (Business in the Regulated Sector and Supervisory Authorities) Order 2007 amended the Proceeds of Crime Act 2002, changing the definition of the regulated sector to bring it into line with the Money Laundering Regulations 2007.

Under Schedule 9 to POCA, key activities which may be relevant to you are the provision by way of business, in one of the following ways:

- advice about the tax affairs of another person by a firm or sole practitioner;
- legal or notarial services by a firm or sole practitioner involving the participation in financial or real property transactions concerning:

    - the buying and selling of real property or business entities;
    - the managing of client money, securities or other assets;
    - the opening or management of bank, savings or securities accounts;
    - the organisation of contributions necessary for the creation, operation or management of companies;
    - the creation, operation or management of trusts, companies or similar structures.

Chapters 5, 6, and 8 of this practice note provide more details on your obligations under POCA.

1.4.4   Terrorism Act 2000

Scope

The Terrorism Act 2000, as amended, establishes several offences about engaging in or facilitating terrorism, as well as raising or possessing funds for terrorist purposes. It establishes a list of proscribed organisations the

Secretary of State believes are involved in terrorism. The TACT and POCA Regulations 2007 entered into force on 26 December 2007 and introduced tipping off offences and defences to the principal terrorist property offences into the Terrorism Act 2000.

Read about these provisions in Chapter 7 [of this practice note].

Application

The Terrorism Act applies to all persons. There is also a failure to disclose offence and tipping off offences for those operating within the regulated sector.

The Terrorism Act 2000 (Business in the Regulated Sector and Supervisory Authorities) Order 2007 amended the Terrorism Act, changing the definition of the regulated sector to bring it into line with the Money Laundering Regulations 2007.

Chapters 7 and 8 [of this practice note] provide more detail on your obligations under the Terrorism Act.

1.4.5   The Money Laundering Regulations 2007

Scope

The Money Laundering Regulations 2007 repeal and replace the Money Laundering Regulations 2003 and implement the third directive. They set administrative requirements for the anti-money laundering regime within the regulated sector and outline the scope of customer due diligence.

The regulations aim to limit the use of professional services for money laundering by requiring professionals to know their clients and monitor the use of their services by clients.

Application

Regulation 3 states that the regulations apply to persons acting in the course of businesses carried on in the UK in the following areas:

- credit institutions;
- financial institutions;
- auditors, insolvency practitioners, external accountants and tax advisers;
- independent legal professionals;
- trust or company service providers;
- estate agents;
- high value dealers;
- casinos.

Independent legal professional

An independent legal professional includes a solicitor working in a firm or as a sole practitioner who by way of business provides legal or notarial services to other persons. It does not include solicitors employed by a public authority or working in-house.

The regulations only apply to certain solicitors' activities where there is a high risk of money laundering occurring. As such, they apply where solicitors participate in financial or real property transactions concerning:

- buying and selling of real property or business entities;
- managing of client money, securities or other assets;
- opening or management of bank, savings or securities accounts;
- organisation of contributions necessary for the creation, operation or management of companies;
- creation, operation or management of trusts, companies or similar structures.

You will be participating in a transaction by assisting in the planning or execution of the transaction or otherwise acting for or on behalf of a client in the transaction.

Activities covered by the regulations

In terms of the activities covered, note that:

- managing client money is narrower than handling it;
- opening or managing a bank account is wider than simply opening a solicitor's client account. It would be likely to cover solicitors acting as a trustee, attorney or a receiver.

Activities not covered by the regulations

The Treasury has confirmed that the following would not generally be viewed as participation in financial transactions:

- preparing a home information pack or any document or information for inclusion in a HIP – it is specifically excluded under regulation 4(1)(f);
- payment on account of costs to a solicitor or payment of a solicitor's bill;
- provision of legal advice;
- participation in litigation or a form of alternative dispute resolution;
- will-writing, although you should consider whether any accompanying taxation advice is covered;
- publicly funded work.

If you are uncertain whether the regulations apply to your work, seek legal advice on the individual circumstances of your practice or simply take the broadest of the possible approaches to compliance with the regulations.

Working elsewhere in the regulated sector

When deciding whether you are within the regulated sector for the purpose of the regulations, you also need to consider whether you offer services bringing you within the definitions of a tax adviser, insolvency practitioner, or trust or company service provider. You must also consider the full range of related services, such as tax planning.

You will also need to consider whether your firm undertakes activities falling within the definition of financial institution, particularly with respect to the list of operations covered by the banking consolidation directive, as contained in schedule 1 to the regulations. When considering those operations, you should note that a will is not a designated investment, so storing it is not a safe custody service, and is not covered by the regulations.

Being nominated as a trustee under a will does not amount to being a trust and company service provider, because the trust is not formed until the testator's death.

If you are an independent legal professional within the regulated sector and you also fall within another category, such as work regulated by FSA, this may affect your supervision under these regulations. You should contact the SRA for advice on any supervisory arrangements that they may have in place with other supervisory authorities.

1.5 Other Law Society services

We provide a number of other services to assist you in meeting your AML/CTF obligations:

- a monthly e-newsletter, Gatekeeper, providing updates on legislation and case law, highlighting emerging warning signs and criminal methodologies and detailing training opportunities;
- the Practice Advice Service, which can be contacted on 0870 606 2522 during office hours, which will help you to navigate the practice note and talk through general issues relating to compliance;
- the AML directory listing solicitors willing to give other solicitors thirty minutes of free advice on legal issues relating to compliance;
- training opportunities.

All of the Law Society's AML/CTF services can be accessed from **www. lawsociety.org.uk/moneylaundering**.

1.6   Acknowledgements

Many have had input into the preparation of this practice note. The members of the Money Laundering Task Force and others mentioned below deserve particular acknowledgement for both the time and energy they have committed to the development of the guidance.

Task force

Robin Booth	BCL Burton Copeland
Alison Matthews	Irwin Mitchell
Christopher Murray	Kingsley Napley
Peter Burrell	Herbert Smith
Stephen Gentle	Kingsley Napley
Nicola Boulton	Byrne and Partners
Louise Delahunty	Simmons and Simmons
Nick Cray	Lovells
Peter Rodd	Boys and Maugham
Chris McNeil	Freshfields Bruckhaus Deringer

Law Society staff

Che Odlum	Policy Adviser
Emma Oettinger	Policy Adviser
James Richards	E-communications Manager

Others

Richard Bark-Jones	Morecrofts
Daren Allen	DLA Piper
Sarah de Gay	Slaughter and May
Clive Cutbill	Withers
Johanna Waritay	Clifford Chance
Suzie Ogilvey	Linklaters
Elizabeth Richards	SRA

The Law Society would also like to specifically thank the following people for the generous provision of their time and expertise in assisting the Law Society with its campaign to ensure that the requirements regarding identification of beneficial owners were sufficiently clear and workable:

Richard Bark-Jones	Morecrofts
Toby Graham	Farrer & Co
Rabinder Singh QC	Matrix Chambers
Alex Balin	Matrix Chambers
Michael Furness QC	Wilberforce Chambers
Nicholas Le Poidevin	Lincolns Inn
Nicholas Green QC	Brick Court Chambers
Martyn Frost	STEP
Keith Johnston	STEP
Jacob Rigg	STEP

Chapter 2 – The risk-based approach

2.1 General comments

The possibility of being used to assist with money laundering and terrorist financing poses many risks for your firm, including:

- criminal and disciplinary sanctions for firms and individual solicitors;
- civil action against the firm as a whole and individual partners;
- damage to reputation leading to a loss of business.

These risks must be identified, assessed and mitigated, just as you do for all business risks facing your firm. If you know your client well and understand your instructions thoroughly, you will be better placed to assess risks and spot suspicious activities. Applying the risk-based approach will vary between firms. While you can, and should, start from the premise that most of your clients are not launderers or terrorist financers, you must assess the risk level particular to your firm and implement reasonable and considered controls to minimise those risks.

No matter how thorough your risk assessment or how appropriate your controls, some criminals may still succeed in exploiting you for criminal purposes. But an effective, risk-based approach and documented, risk-based judgements on individual clients and retainers will enable your firm to justify your position on managing the risk to law enforcement, courts and professional supervisors (oversight bodies).

The risk-based approach means that you focus your resources on the areas of greatest risk. The resulting benefits of this approach include:

- more efficient and effective use of resources proportionate to the risks faced;
- minimising compliance costs and burdens on clients;
- greater flexibility to respond to emerging risks as laundering and terrorist financing methods change.

2.2   Application

The Money Laundering Regulations 2007 permit a risk-based approach to compliance with customer due diligence obligations.

This approach does not apply to reporting suspicious activity, because POCA and the Terrorism Act lay down specific legal requirements not to engage in certain activities and to make reports of suspicious activities once a suspicion is held (see Chapters 5 and 7 [of this practice note]). The risk-based approach still applies to ongoing monitoring of clients and retainers which enables you to identify suspicions.

2.3   Assessing your firm's risk profile

This depends on your firm's size, type of clients, and the practice areas it engages in.

You should consider the following factors:

2.3.1   Client demographic

Your client demographic can affect the risk of money laundering or terrorist financing. Factors which may vary the risk level include whether you:

- have a high turnover of clients or a stable existing client base;
- act for politically exposed persons (PEPs);
- act for clients without meeting them;
- practise in locations with high levels of acquisitive crime or for clients who have convictions for acquisitive crimes, which increases the likelihood the client may possess criminal property;
- act for clients affiliated to countries with high levels of corruption or where terrorist organisations operate;
- act for entities that have a complex ownership structure;
- are easily able to obtain details of beneficial owners of your client or not.

2.3.2   Services and areas of law

Some services and areas of law could provide opportunities to facilitate money laundering or terrorist financing. For example:

- complicated financial or property transactions;
- providing assistance in setting up trusts or company structures, which could be used to obscure ownership of property;
- payments that are made to or received from third parties;

- payments made by cash;
- transactions with a cross-border element.

Simply because a client or a retainer falls within a risk category does not mean that money laundering or terrorist financing is occurring. You need to ensure your internal controls are designed to address the identified risks and take appropriate steps to minimise and deal with these risks. [See 3.5 of this practice note.]

Chapter 11 [of this practice note] provides more information on warning signs to be alert to when assessing risk.

2.4   Assessing individual risk

Determining the risks posed by a specific client or retainer will then assist in applying internal controls in a proportionate and effective manner.

You may consider whether:

- your client is within a high risk category;
- you can be easily satisfied the CDD material for your client is reliable and allows you to identify the client and verify that identity;
- you can be satisfied you understand their control and ownership structure;
- the retainer involves an area of law at higher risk of laundering or terrorist financing;
- your client wants you to handle funds without an underlying transaction, contrary to the Solicitors' Account Rules;
- there are any aspects of the particular retainer which would increase or decrease the risks.

This assessment helps you adjust your internal controls to the appropriate level of risk presented by the individual client or the particular retainer. Different aspects of your CDD controls will meet the different risks posed:

- If you are satisfied you have verified the client's identity, but the retainer is high risk, you may require fee earners to monitor the transaction more closely, rather than seek further verification of identity.
- If you have concerns about verifying a client's identity, but the retainer is low risk, you may expend greater resources on verification and monitor the transaction in the normal way.

Risk assessment is an ongoing process both for the firm generally and for each client, business relationship and retainer. In a solicitor's practice it is the overall information held by the firm gathered while acting for the client that will inform the risk assessment process, rather than sophisticated computer data analysis systems. The more you know your client and understand your instructions, the better placed you will be to assess risks and spot suspicious activities.

Chapter 3 – Systems, policies and procedures

3.1 General comments

Develop systems to meet your obligations and risk profile in a risk-based and proportionate manner. Policies and procedures supporting these systems mean that staff apply the systems consistently and firms can demonstrate to oversight bodies that processes facilitating compliance are in place.

3.2 Application

Regulation 20 of the Money Laundering Regulations 2007 requires the regulated sector to have certain systems in place. If you are in the regulated sector, failing to have those systems is an offence, punishable by a fine or up to two years' imprisonment. You must demonstrate your compliance to the SRA, as supervisor under the regulations.

If you are outside the regulated sector, you should still consider how these systems can assist you to comply with your obligations to report suspicious transactions in accordance with POCA and the Terrorism Act.

3.3 Nominated officers

3.3.1 Why have a nominated officer?

Regulation 20(2)(d)(i) requires that all firms within the regulated sector must have a nominated officer to receive disclosures under Part 7 of POCA and the Terrorism Act, and to make disclosures to SOCA.

Regulation 20(3) provides that there is no requirement to have a nominated officer in the regulated sector if you are an individual who provides regulated services but do not employ any people or act in association with anyone else.

Firms who do not provide services within the regulated sector should consider appointing a nominated officer, even though it is not required, because POCA and the Terrorism Act still apply. The Solicitors' Code of Conduct 2007 [**www.rules.sra.org.uk**] requires business management systems facilitating compliance with legal obligations.

3.3.2 Who should be a nominated officer?

Your nominated officer should be of sufficient seniority to make decisions on reporting which can impact your firm's business relations with your clients and your exposure to criminal, civil, regulatory and disciplinary sanctions. They should also be in a position of sufficient responsibility to enable them to have access to all of your firm's client files and business information to enable them to make the required decisions on the basis of all information held by the firm.

Firms authorised by the FSA will need to obtain the FSA's approval to the appointment of the nominated officer as this is a controlled function under section 59 of the Financial Services and Markets Act 2000.

3.3.3 Role of the nominated officer

Your nominated officer is responsible for ensuring that, when appropriate, the information or other matter leading to knowledge or suspicion, or reasonable grounds for knowledge or suspicion of money laundering is properly disclosed to the relevant authority. The decision to report, or not to report, must not be subject to the consent of anyone else. Your nominated officer will also liaise with SOCA or law enforcement on the issue of whether to proceed with a transaction or what information may be disclosed to clients or third parties.

The size and nature of some firms may lead to the nominated officer delegating certain duties regarding the firm's AML/CTF obligations. In some large firms, one or more permanent deputies of suitable seniority may be appointed. All firms will need to consider arrangements for temporary cover when the nominated officer is absent.

3.4 Risk assessment

You can extend your existing risk management systems to address AML and CTF risks. The detail and sophistication of these systems will depend on your firm's size and the complexity of the business it undertakes. Ways of incorporating your risk assessment of clients, business relationships and transactions into the overall risk assessment will be governed by the size of your firm and how regularly compliance staff and senior management are involved in day-to-day activities.

Issues which may be covered in a risk assessment system include:

- the firm's current risk profile;
- how AML/CTF risks will be assessed, and processes for re-assessment and updating of the firm's risk profile;

- internal controls to be implemented to mitigate the risks;
- which firm personnel have authority to make risk-based decisions on compliance on individual files;
- how compliance will be monitored and effectiveness of internal controls will be reviewed.

3.5   Internal controls and monitoring compliance

The level of internal controls and extent to which monitoring needs to take place will be affected by:

- your firm's size;
- the nature, scale and complexity of its practice;
- its overall risk profile.

Issues which may be covered in an internal controls system include:

- the level of personnel permitted to exercise discretion on the risk-based application of the regulations, and under what circumstances;
- CDD requirements to be met for simplified, standard and enhanced due diligence;
- when outsourcing of CDD obligations or reliance will be permitted, and on what conditions;
- how you will restrict work being conducted on a file where CDD has not been completed;
- the circumstances in which delayed CDD is permitted;
- when cash payments will be accepted;
- when payments will be accepted from or made to third parties;
- the manner in which disclosures are to be made to the nominated officer.

Monitoring compliance will assist you to assess whether the policies and procedures you have implemented are effective in forestalling money laundering and terrorist financing opportunities within your firm. Issues which may be covered in a compliance system include:

- procedures to be undertaken to monitor compliance, which may involve:

  - random file audits;
  - file checklists to be completed before opening or closing a file;
  - a nominated officer's log of situations brought to their attention, queries from staff and reports made;

- reports to be provided from the nominated officer to senior management on compliance;
- how to rectify lack of compliance, when identified;
- how lessons learnt will be communicated back to staff and fed back into the risk profile of the firm.

3.6 Customer due diligence

You are required to have a system outlining the CDD measures to be applied to specific clients. You should consider recording your firm's risk tolerances to be able to demonstrate to your supervisor that your CDD measures are appropriate.

Your CDD system may include:

- when CDD is to be undertaken [4.3.1 of this practice note];
- information to be recorded on client identity;
- information to be obtained to verify identity, either specifically or providing a range of options with a clear statement of who can exercise their discretion on the level of verification to be undertaken in any particular case;
- when simplified due diligence may occur [4.8 of this practice note];
- what steps need to be taken for enhanced due diligence [4.9 of this practice note];
- what steps need to be taken to ascertain whether your client is a PEP [4.9.2 of this practice note];
- when CDD needs to occur and under what circumstances delayed CDD is permitted [4.3.5 of this practice note];
- how to conduct CDD on existing clients [4.10 of this practice note];
- what ongoing monitoring is required [4.4 of this practice note].

For suggested methods on how to conduct CDD see Chapter 4 of this practice note.

3.7 Disclosures

Firms, but not sole practitioners, need to have a system clearly setting out the requirements for making a disclosure under POCA and the Terrorism Act. These may include:

- the circumstances in which a disclosure is likely to be required;
- how and when information is to be provided to the nominated officer or their deputies;

- resources which can be used to resolve difficult issues around making a disclosure;
- how and when a disclosure is to be made to SOCA;
- how to manage a client when a disclosure is made while waiting for consent;
- the need to be alert to tipping off issues.

For details on when a disclosure needs to be made see Chapters 5, 6 and 7 of this practice note. For details on how to make a disclosure see Chapter 8 of this practice note.

3.8   Record keeping

Various records must be kept to comply with the regulations and defend any allegations against the firm in relation to money laundering and failure to report offences. A firm's records system must outline what records are to be kept, the form in which they should be kept and how long they should be kept.

Regulation 19 requires that firms keep records of CDD material and supporting evidence and records in respect of the relevant business relationship or occasional transaction. Adapt your standard archiving procedures for these requirements.

3.8.1   CDD material

You may keep either a copy of verification material [4.3.3 of this practice note], or references to it. Keep it for five years after the business relationship ends or the occasional transaction is completed. Consider holding CDD material separately from the client file for each retainer, as it may be needed by different practice groups in your firm.

Depending on the size and sophistication of your firm's record storage procedures you may wish to:

- scan the verification material and hold it electronically;
- take photocopies of CDD material and hold it in hard copy with a statement that the original has been seen;
- accept certified copies of CDD material and hold them in hard copy;
- keep electronic copies or hard copies of the results of any electronic verification checks;
- record reference details of the CDD material sighted.

The option of merely recording reference details may be particularly useful when taking instructions from clients at their home or other locations away from your office. The types of details it would be useful to record include:

- any reference numbers on documents or letters;
- any relevant dates, such as issue, expiry or writing;
- details of the issuer or writer;
- all identity details recorded on the document.

Where you are relied upon by another person under regulation 17 for the completion of CDD measures, you must keep the relevant documents for five years from the date on which you were relied upon.

3.8.2 Risk assessment notes

You should consider keeping records of decisions on risk assessment processes of what CDD was undertaken. This does not need to be in significant detail, but merely a note on the CDD file stating the risk level you attributed to a file and why you considered you had sufficient CDD information. For example:

> This is a low risk client with no beneficial owners providing medium risk instructions. Standard CDD material was obtained and medium level ongoing monitoring is to occur.

Such an approach may assist firms to demonstrate they have applied a risk-based approach in a reasonable and proportionate manner. Notes taken at the time are better than justifications provided later.

Firms may choose standard categories of comment to apply to notes.

3.8.3 Supporting evidence and records

You must keep all original documents or copies admissible in court proceedings.

Records of a particular transaction, either as an occasional transaction or within a business relationship, must be kept for five years after the date the transaction is completed.

All other documents supporting records must be kept for five years after the completion of the business relationship.

3.8.4 Suspicions and disclosures

It is recommended that you keep comprehensive records of suspicions and disclosures because disclosure of a suspicious activity is a defence to criminal proceedings. Such records may include notes of:

- ongoing monitoring undertaken and concerns raised by fee earners and staff;
- discussions with the nominated officer regarding concerns;
- advice sought and received regarding concerns;
- why the concerns did not amount to a suspicion and a disclosure was not made;
- copies of any disclosures made;
- conversations with SOCA, law enforcement, insurers, supervisory authorities, etc. regarding disclosures made;
- decisions not to make a report to SOCA which may be important for the nominated officer to justify his position to law enforcement.

You should ensure records are not inappropriately disclosed to the client or third parties to avoid offences of tipping off and prejudicing an investigation, and to maintain a good relationship with your clients. This may be achieved by maintaining a separate file, either for the client or for the practice area.

3.8.5   Data protection

The Data Protection Act 1998 applies to you and SOCA. It allows clients or others to make subject access requests for data held by them. Such requests could cover any disclosures made.

Section 29 of the Data Protection Act 1998 states you need not provide personal data where disclosure would be likely to prejudice the prevention or detection of crime, or the apprehension or prosecution of offenders.

HM Treasury and the Information Commissioner have issued guidance which essentially provides that the section 29 exception would apply where granting access would amount to tipping off. This may extend to suspicions only reported internally within the firm.

If you decide the section 29 exception applies, document steps taken to assess this, to respond to any enquiries by the Information Commissioner.

- HM Treasury guidance [**www.hm-treasury.gov.uk**]
- Information Commissioner guidance [**www.ico.gov.uk**]

Note the definition of personal data.

3.9   Communication and training

Your staff members are the most effective defence against launderers and terrorist financers who would seek to abuse the services provided by your firm.

Regulation 20 requires that you communicate your AML/CTF obligations to your staff, while regulation 21 requires that you provide staff with appropriate training on their legal obligations and information on how to recognise and deal with money laundering and terrorist financing risks.

Rule 5 of the Solicitors' Code of Conduct also requires you to train your staff to a level appropriate to their work and level of responsibility.

3.9.1   Criminal sanctions and defences

Receiving insufficient training is a defence for individual staff members who fail to report a suspicion of money laundering. However, it is not a defence to terrorist funding charges, and leaves your firm vulnerable to sanctions under the regulations for failing to properly train your staff.

3.9.2   Who should be trained?

When setting up a training and communication system you should consider:

- which staff require training;
- what form the training will take;
- how often training should take place;
- how staff will be kept up to date with emerging risk factors for the firm.

Assessments of who should receive training should include who deals with clients in areas of practice within the regulated sector, handles funds or otherwise assists with compliance. Consider fee earners, reception staff, administration staff and finance staff, because they will each be differently involved in compliance and so have different training requirements.

Training can take many forms and may include:

- face-to-face training seminars;
- completion of online training sessions;
- attendance at AML/CTF conferences;
- participation in dedicated AML/CTF forums;
- review of publications on current AML/CTF issues;
- firm or practice group meetings for discussion of AML/CTF issues and risk factors.

Providing an AML/CTF policy manual is useful to raise staff awareness and can be a continual reference source between training sessions.

3.9.3 How often?

You are required to provide training at regular and appropriate intervals. In determining whether your training programme meets this require-ment, you should have regard to the firm's risk profile and the level of involvement certain staff have in ensuring compliance.

You should consider retaining evidence of your assessment of training needs and steps taken to meet such needs.

You should also consider:

* criminal sanctions and reputational risks of non-compliance;
* developments in the common law;
* changing criminal methodologies.

Some type of training for all relevant staff every two years is preferable.

3.9.4 Communicating with your clients

While not specifically required by the regulations, we consider it useful for you to tell your client about your AML/CTF obligations. Clients are then generally more willing to provide required information when they see it as a standard requirement.

You may wish to advise your client of the following issues:

* the requirement to conduct CDD to comply with the regulations;
* whether any electronic verification is to be undertaken during the CDD process;
* the requirement to report suspicious transactions.

Consider the manner and timing of your communications, for example whether the information will be provided in the standard client care letter or otherwise.

Chapter 4 – Customer due diligence

4.1 General comments

Customer due diligence (CDD) is required by the Money Laundering Regulations 2007 because you can better identify suspicious transactions if you know your customer and understand the reasoning behind the instructions they give you.

4.2 Application

You must conduct CDD on those clients who retain you for services regulated under the regulations (see Chapter 1 [of this practice note]). Rule 2 of the Solicitors' Code of Conduct is also relevant to all solicitors.

4.3 CDD in general

4.3.1 When is CDD required?

Regulation 7 requires that you conduct CDD when:

- establishing a business relationship;
- carrying out an occasional transaction;
- you suspect money laundering or terrorist financing;
- you doubt the veracity or adequacy of documents, data or information previously obtained for the purpose of CDD.

The distinction between occasional transactions and long-lasting business relationships is relevant to the timing [4.3.5 of this practice note] of CDD and the storage of records [4.5 of this practice note].

Where an occasional transaction is likely to increase in value or develop into a business relationship, consider conducting CDD early in the retainer to avoid delays later. As relationships change, firms must ensure they are compliant with the relevant standard.

There is no obligation to conduct CDD in accordance with the regulations for retainers involving non-regulated activities.

Existing business relationships before 15 December 2007

You must apply CDD measures at appropriate times to existing clients on a risk-sensitive basis. You are not required to apply CDD measures to all existing clients immediately after 15 December 2007. Where you have verified a client's identity to a previously applicable standard then, unless circumstances indicate the contrary, the risk is likely to be low. If you have existing high risk clients that you have previously identified you may consider applying the new CDD standard sooner than for low risk clients. Read more [at 4.10 of this practice note].

4.3.2 What is CDD?

Regulation 5 says that CDD comprises:

- identifying the client and verifying their identity on the basis of documents, data or information obtained from a reliable and independent source;
- identifying, where there is a beneficial owner who is not the client, the beneficial owner and taking adequate measures, on a risk-sensitive basis, to verify his identity so that you are satisfied that you know who the beneficial owner is. This includes understanding the ownership and control structure of a legal person, trust or similar arrangement;
- obtaining information on the purpose and intended nature of the business relationship.

Identification and verification

Identification of a client or a beneficial owner is simply being told or coming to know a client's identifying details, such as their name and address.

Verification is obtaining some evidence which supports this claim of identity.

A risk-based approach

Regulation 7(3) provides that you must:

- determine the required extent of customer due diligence measures on a risk-sensitive basis depending on the type of client, business relationship, product or transaction;
- be able to demonstrate to your supervisory authority that you took appropriate measures in view of the risks of money laundering and terrorist financing.

You cannot avoid conducting CDD, but you can use a risk-based approach to determine the extent and quality of information required and the steps to be taken to meet the requirements.

You need only obtain information on the purpose and intended nature of your client's use of your services when you are in a business relationship with them. However, it's good practice and required by rule 2 of the Solicitors' Code of Conduct to obtain such information to ensure you fully understand instructions and closely monitor the development of each retainer, even if it is for an occasional transaction or transactions below the threshold.

4.3.3   Methods of verification

Verification can be completed on the basis of documents, data and information which come from a reliable and independent source. This means that there are a number of ways you can verify a client's identity including:

- obtaining or viewing original documents;
- conducting electronic verification;
- obtaining information from other regulated persons.

Independent source

You need an independent and reliable verification of your client's identity. This can include materials provided by the client, such as a passport.

Consider the cumulative weight of information you have on the client and the risk levels associated with both the client and the retainer.

You are permitted to use a wider range of sources when verifying the identity of the beneficial owner and understanding the ownership and control structure of the client. Often only the client or their representatives can provide you with such information. Apply the requirements in a risk-based manner to a level at which you are satisfied that you know who the beneficial owner is.

Documents

You should not ignore obvious forgeries, but you are not required to be an expert in forged documents.

Electronic verification

This will only confirm that someone exists, not that your client is the said person. You should consider the risk implications in respect of the particular retainer and be on the alert for information which may suggest that your client is not the person they say they are. You may mitigate risk by corroborating electronic verification with some other CDD material.

When choosing an electronic verification service provider, you should look for a provider who:

- has proof of registration with the Information Commissioner's Office to store personal data;
- can link an applicant to both current and previous circumstances using a range of positive information sources;
- accesses negative information sources, such as databases on identity fraud and deceased persons;
- accesses a wide range of 'alert' data sources;

- has transparent processes enabling you to know what checks are carried out, the results of the checks, and how much certainty they give on the identity of the subject;
- allows you to capture and store the information used to verify an identity.

When using electronic verification, you are not required to obtain consent from your client, but they must be informed that this check will take place.

While we believe electronic verification can be a sufficient measure for compliance with money laundering requirements, there may be circumstances where it will not be appropriate. For example, the Council for Mortgage Lenders notes that electronic verification products may not be suitable for fraud prevention purposes, such as verifying that a person's signature is genuine.

4.3.4   Reliance and outsourcing

Reliance has a very specific meaning within the regulations and relates to the process under regulation 17 where you rely on another regulated person to conduct CDD for you. You remain liable for any failure in the client being appropriately identified. Reliance does not include:

- accepting information from others to verify a client's identity when meeting your own CDD obligations;
- electronic verification, which is outsourcing.

You need:

- the consent of the person on whom you rely for your reliance;
- agreement that they will provide you with the CDD material upon request;
- the identity of their supervisor for money laundering purposes. Consider checking the register of members for that supervisor, although a personal assurance of their identity may be sufficient where you have reasonable grounds to believe them.

We believe you should ask what CDD enquiries have been undertaken to ensure that they actually comply with the regulations, because you remain liable for non-compliance. This is particularly important when relying on a person outside the UK, and you should be satisfied that the CDD has been conducted to a standard compatible with the third directive, taking into account the ability to use different sources of verification and jurisdictional specific factors. It may not always be appropriate to rely on another person to undertake your CDD checks and you should consider reliance as a risk in itself.

Reliance in the UK

You can only rely on the following persons in the UK:

- a credit or financial institution which is an authorised person;
- a person in the following professions who is supervised by a supervisory authority:

    - auditor;
    - insolvency practitioner;
    - external accountant;
    - tax adviser;
    - independent legal professional.

Reliance in an EEA state

You can only rely on the following persons in an EEA state:
- a credit or financial institution;
- auditor, or EEA equivalent;
- insolvency practitioner, or EEA equivalent;
- external accountant;
- tax adviser;
- independent legal professional

if they are both:

- subject to mandatory professional registration recognised by law; and
- supervised for complying with money laundering obligations under Chapter 5, Section 2 of the third directive.

A person will only be supervised in accordance with the third directive if the third directive has been implemented in the EEA state. You can check on the International Bar Association's website on the progress of implementation across Europe [**www.anti-moneylaundering.org**].

Reliance in other countries

You can only rely on the following persons outside of the EEA:

- credit or financial institution, or equivalent;
- auditor, or equivalent;
- insolvency practitioner, or equivalent;

- external accountant;
- tax adviser;
- independent legal professional

if they are both:

- subject to mandatory professional registration recognised by law; and
- supervised for complying with money laundering obligations to a standard equivalent to that under Chapter 5, Section 2 of the third directive.

Consult a list of countries where CDD requirements and supervision of credit or financial institutions are considered equivalent to the European Economic Area [at **www.jmlsg.org.uk**].

Consult a list of national money laundering legislation around the world, and whether it applies to lawyers [at **www.anti-moneylaundering. org**].

Passporting clients between jurisdictions

Many firms have branches or affiliated offices ('international offices') in other jurisdictions and will have clients who utilise the services of a number of international offices. It is not considered proportionate for a client to have to provide original identification material to each international office.

Some firms may have a central international database of CDD material on clients to which they can refer. Where this is the case you should review the CDD material to be satisfied that CDD has been completed in accordance with the third directive. If further information is required, you should ensure that it is obtained and added to the central database. Alternatively, you could ensure that the CDD approval controls for the database are sufficient to ensure that all CDD is compliant.

Other firms may wish to rely on their international office to simply provide a letter of confirmation that CDD requirements have been undertaken with respect to the client. This will amount to reliance only if the firm can be relied upon under the terms of regulation 17 and the CDD is completed in accordance with that regulation.

Finally, firms without a central database may wish to undertake their own CDD measures with respect to the client, but ask their international office to supply copies of the verification material, rather than the client themselves. This will not be reliance, but outsourcing.

It is important to remember that one of your international offices may be acting for a client who is not a PEP [see 4.9.2 of this practice note] in that country, but will be when they are utilising the services of your office. As such, you will need to have in place a process for checking whether a person passported into your office is a PEP and, if so, undertake appropriate enhanced due diligence measures [4.9 of this practice note].

UK-based fee earners will have to undertake their own ongoing monitoring of the retainer [4.4 of this practice note], even if the international office is also required to do so.

4.3.5 Timing

When must CDD be undertaken?

Regulation 9 requires you to verify your client's identity and that of any beneficial owner, before you establish a business relationship or carry out an occasional transaction.

Regulation 11 provides that if you are unable to complete CDD in time, you cannot:

- carry out a transaction with or for the client through a bank account;
- establish a business relationship or carry out an occasional transaction.

  You must also:

- terminate any existing business relationship;
- consider making a disclosure to SOCA.

Evidence of identity is not required if a one-off transaction involves less than 15,000 or if two or more linked transactions involve less than 15,000 in total. This exception does not apply if there is any suspicion of money laundering or terrorist financing.

Exceptions to the timing requirement

There are several exceptions to the timing requirement and the prohibition on acting for the client.

However, you should consider why there is a delay in completing CDD, and whether this of itself gives rise to a suspicion which should be disclosed to SOCA.

Normal conduct of business

Regulation 9(3) provides that verification may be completed during the establishment of a business relationship (not an occasional transaction), where:

- it is necessary not to interrupt the normal conduct of business; and
- there is little risk of money laundering or terrorist financing occurring.

You must complete verification as soon as practicable after the initial contact.

Consider your risk profile when assessing which work can be undertaken on a retainer prior to verification being completed.

Do not permit funds or property to be transferred or final agreements to be signed before completion of full verification.

If you are unable to conduct full verification of the client and beneficial owners, then the prohibition in regulation 11 will apply.

Ascertaining legal position

Regulation 11(2) provides that the prohibition in 11(1) does not apply where:

> A lawyer or other professional adviser is in the course of ascertaining the legal position for their client or performing their task of defending or representing their client in, or concerning legal proceedings, including advice on instituting or avoiding proceedings.

The requirement to cease acting and consider making a report to SOCA when you cannot complete CDD, does not apply when you are providing legal advice or preparing for or engaging in litigation or alternative dispute resolution.

This exception does not apply to transactional work, so take a cautious approach to the distinction between advice and litigation work, and transactional work.

4.4   Ongoing monitoring

Regulation 8 requires that you conduct ongoing monitoring of a business relationship on a risk-sensitive and appropriate basis. Ongoing monitoring is defined as:

- scrutiny of transactions undertaken throughout the course of the relationship (including where necessary, the source of funds), to ensure that the transactions are consistent with your knowledge of the client, their business and the risk profile;
- keeping the documents, data or information obtained for the purpose of applying CDD up to date. You must also be aware of obligations to keep clients' personal data updated under the Data Protection Act.

You are not required to:

- conduct the whole CDD process again every few years;
- conduct random audits of files;

- suspend or terminate a business relationship until you have updated data, information or documents, as long as you are still satisfied you know who your client is, and keep under review any request for further verification material or processes to get that material;
- use sophisticated computer analysis packages to review each new retainer for anomalies.

Ongoing monitoring will normally be conducted by fee earners handling the retainer, and involves staying alert to suspicious circumstances which may suggest money laundering, terrorist financing, or the provision of false CDD material.

For example, you may have acted for a client in preparing a will and purchasing a modest family home. They may then instruct you in the purchase of a holiday home, the value of which appears to be outside the means of the client's financial situation as you had previously been advised in earlier retainers. While you may be satisfied that you still know the identity of your client, as a part of your ongoing monitoring obligations it would be appropriate in such a case to ask about the source of the funds for this purchase. Depending on your client's willingness to provide you with such information and the answer they provide, you will need to consider whether you are satisfied with that response, want further proof of the source of the funds, or need to discuss making a disclosure to SOCA with your nominated officer.

To ensure that CDD material is kept up to date, you should consider reviewing it:

- when taking new instructions from a client, particularly if there has been a gap of over three years between instructions;
- when you receive information of a change in identity details.

Relevant issues may include:

- the risk profile of the client and the specific retainer;
- whether you hold material on transactional files which would confirm changes in identity;
- whether electronic verification may help you find out if your clients' identity details have changed, or to verify any changes.

4.5 Records

You are required to keep records [3.8 of this practice note] of your CDD material.

4.6   CDD on clients

Your firm will need to make its own assessments as to what evidence is appropriate to verify the identity of your clients. We outline a number of sources which may help you make that assessment.

4.6.1   Natural persons

A natural person's identity comprises a number of aspects, including their name, current and past addresses, date of birth, place of birth, physical appearance, employment and financial history, and family circumstances.
Evidence of identity can include:

- identity documents such as passports and photocard driving licences;
- other forms of confirmation, including assurances from persons within the regulated sector or those in your firm who have dealt with the person for some time.

In most cases of face-to-face verification, producing a valid passport or photocard identification should enable most clients to meet the AML/CTF identification requirements.
It is considered good practice to have either:

- one government document which verifies either name and address or name and date of birth;
- a government document which verifies the client's full name and another supporting document which verifies their name and either their address or date of birth.

Where it is not possible to obtain such documents, consider the reliability of other sources and the risks associated with the client and the retainer. Electronic verification may be sufficient verification on its own as long as the service provider uses multiple sources of data in the verification process.
Where you are reasonably satisfied that an individual is nationally or internationally known, a record of identification may include a file note of your satisfaction about identity, usually including an address.

UK residents

The following sources may be useful for verification of UK-based clients:

- current signed passport;
- birth certificate;
- current photocard driver's licence;

- current EEA member state identity card;
- current identity card issued by the Electoral Office for Northern Ireland;
- residence permit issued by the Home Office;
- firearms certificate or shotgun licence;
- photographic registration cards for self-employed individuals and partnerships in the construction industry;
- benefit book or original notification letter from the DWP confirming the right to benefits;
- council tax bill;
- utility bill or statement, or a certificate from a utilities supplier confirming an arrangement to pay services on pre-payment terms;
- a cheque or electronic transfer drawn on an account in the name of the client with a credit or financial institution regulated for the purposes of money laundering;
- bank, building society or credit union statement or passbook containing current address;
- entry in a local or national telephone directory confirming name and address;
- confirmation from an electoral register that a person of that name lives at that address;
- a recent original mortgage statement from a recognised lender;
- solicitor's letter confirming recent house purchase or land registry confirmation of address;
- local council or housing association rent card or tenancy agreement;
- HMRC self-assessment statement or tax demand;
- house or motor insurance certificate;
- record of any home visit made;
- statement from a member of the firm or other person in the regulated sector who has known the client for a number of years attesting to their identity – bear in mind you may be unable to contact this person to give an assurance supporting that statement at a later date.

Persons not resident in the UK

Where you meet the client you are likely to be able to see the person's passport or national identity card. If you have concerns that the identity document might not be genuine, contact the relevant embassy or consulate.

The client's address may be obtained from:

- an official overseas source;
- a reputable directory;
- a person regulated for money laundering purposes in the country where the person is resident who confirms that the client is known to them and lives or works at the overseas address given.

If documents are in a foreign language you must take appropriate steps to be reasonably satisfied that the documents in fact provide evidence of the client's identity.

Where you do not meet the client, the regulations state that you must undertake enhanced due diligence measures [4.9 of this practice note].

Clients unable to produce standard documentation

Sometimes clients are unable to provide standard verification documents. The purpose of the regulations is not to deny people access to legal services for legitimate transactions, but to mitigate the risk of legal services being used for the purposes of money laundering. You should consider whether the inability to provide you with standard verification is consistent with the client's profile and circumstances or whether it might make you suspicious that money laundering or terrorist financing is occurring.

Where you decide that a client has a good reason for not meeting the standard verification requirements, you may accept a letter from an appropriate person who knows the individual and can verify the client's identity.

For example:

- Clients in care homes might be able to provide a letter from the manager.
- Clients without a permanent residence might be able to provide a letter from a householder named on a current council tax bill or a hostel manager, confirming temporary residence.
- A refugee might be able to provide a letter from the Home Office confirming refugee status and granting permission to work, or a Home Office travel document for refugees.
- An asylum seeker might be able to provide their registration card and any other identity documentation they hold, or a letter of assurance as to identity from a community member such as a priest, GP, or local councillor who has knowledge of the client.
- A student or minor might be able to provide a birth certificate and confirmation of their parent's address or confirmation of address from the register of the school or higher education institution.
- A person with mental health problems or mental incapacity might know medical workers, hostel staff, social workers, deputies or guardians appointed by the court who can locate identification documents or confirm the client's identity.

Professionals

Where other professionals use your services, you may consult their professional directory to confirm the person's name and business address. It will not be necessary to then confirm the person's home address. You may consult directories for foreign professionals, if you are satisfied it is a valid directory, e.g. one produced and maintained by their professional body, and you can either translate the information, or understand it already.

4.6.2 Partnerships, limited partnerships and UK LLPs

A partnership is not a separate legal entity, so you must obtain information on the constituent individuals.

Where partnerships or unincorporated businesses are:

- well-known, reputable organisations;
- with long histories in their industries; and
- with substantial public information about them, their principals, and controllers

the following information should be sufficient:

- name;
- registered address, if any;
- trading address;
- nature of business.

Other partnerships and unincorporated businesses which are small and have few partners should be treated as private individuals. Where the numbers are larger, they should be treated as private companies.

Where a partnership is made up of regulated professionals, it will be sufficient to confirm the firm's existence and the trading address from a reputable professional directory or search facility with the relevant professional body. Otherwise you should obtain evidence on the identity of at least the partner instructing you and one other partner, and evidence of the firm's trading address.

For a UK LLP, obtain information in accordance with the requirements for companies as outlined below.

4.6.3 Companies

A company is a legal entity in its own right, but conducts its business through representatives. So you must identify and verify the existence of the company. You should consider whether the person instructing you on behalf of the company has the authority to do so.

A company's identity comprises its constitution, its business and its legal ownership structure. The key identification particulars are the company's name and its business address, although the registration number and names of directors may also be relevant identification particulars.

Where a company is a well-known household name, you may consider that the level of money laundering and terrorist financing risks are low and apply CDD measures in a manner which is proportionate to that risk.

Where you commence acting for a subsidiary of an existing client, you may have reference to the CDD file for your existing client for verification of details for the subsidiary, provided that the existing client has been identified to the standards of the 2007 regulations.

You will also need to consider the identity of beneficial owners where simplified diligence [4.8 of this practice note] does not apply.

Public companies listed in the UK

Where a company is either:

- listed and its securities are admitted to trading on a regulated market; or
- a majority-owned and consolidated subsidiary of such a company

simplified due diligence [4.8 of this practice note] applies.

For a listed company, this evidence may simply be confirmation of the company's listing on the regulated market. Such evidence may be:

- a copy of the dated page of the website of the relevant stock exchange showing the listing;
- a photocopy of the listing in a reputable daily newspaper;
- information from a reputable electronic verification service provider or online registry.

For a subsidiary of a listed company you will also require evidence of the parent/subsidiary relationship. Such evidence may be:

- the subsidiary's last filed annual return;
- a note in the parent's or subsidiary's last audited accounts;
- information from a reputable electronic verification service provider or online registry.

The regulated market in the UK is the London Stock Exchange. AIM is not considered a regulated market within the UK, but under the risk-based approach you may feel that the due diligence process for listing on AIM gives you equivalent comfort as to the identity of the company under consideration.

Where further CDD is required for a listed company (i.e. when it is not on a regulated market) obtain relevant particulars of the company's identity.

Verification sources may include:

- a search of the relevant company registry (such as Companies House: **www.companieshouse.gov.uk**);
- a copy of the company's certificate of incorporation;
- information from a reputable electronic verification service provider.

You are still required to conduct ongoing monitoring [4.4 of this practice note] of the business relationship with a publicly listed company to enable you to spot suspicious activity.

Private and unlisted companies in the UK

Private companies are generally subject to a lower level of public disclosure than public companies. In general however, the structure, ownership, purposes and activities of many private companies will be clear and understandable.

The standard identifiers for private companies are:

- full name;
- business/registered address;
- names of two directors, or equivalent;
- nature of business.

Other sources for verifying corporate identification may include:

- certificate of incorporation;
- details from the relevant company registry, confirming details of the company and of the director, including the director's address;
- filed audited accounts;
- information from a reputable electronic verification service provider.

Public overseas companies

Simplified due diligence [4.8 of this practice note] applies when:

- a company or its subsidiary is listed on a regulated market subject to specified disclosure obligations.

Specified disclosure obligations are disclosure requirements consistent with specified articles of:

- the Prospectus Directive (2003/71/EC);
- the Transparency Obligations Directive (2004/109/EC);
- the Market Abuse Directive (2003/6/EC).

If a regulated market is located within the EEA, under a risk-based approach you may wish to simply record the steps taken to ascertain the status of the market. Consider a similar approach for non-EEA markets that subject companies to disclosure obligations which are contained in international standards equivalent to specified disclosure obligations in the EU.

Consult a list of countries where CDD requirements and supervision of credit or financial institutions are considered equivalent to the UK [**www.jmlsg.org.uk**].

Consult a list of regulated markets within the EU [**http:// ec.europa.int**].

Evidence of the company's listed status should be obtained in a manner similar to that for UK public companies. Companies whose listing does not fall within the above requirements should be identified in accordance with the provisions for private companies.

Private and unlisted overseas companies

Obtaining CDD material for these companies can be difficult, particularly regarding beneficial ownership.

You should apply the risk-based approach, looking at the risk of the client generally, the risk of the retainer and the risks presented as a result of the country in which the client is incorporated. Money laundering risks are likely to be lower where the company is incorporated or operating in an EEA state or a country which is a member of FATF.

The company's identity is established in the same way as for UK private and unlisted companies.

Where you are not obtaining original documentation, you may want to consider on a risk-sensitive basis having the documents certified by a person in the regulated sector or another professional whose identity can be checked by reference to a professional directory.

4.6.4   Other arrangements or bodies

Trusts

A trust is not a separate legal entity. Your client may be the settlor, the trustee(s) or occasionally the beneficiaries.

UK common law trusts are used extensively in everyday situations and often pose limited risk. They can become more risky if:

- the client requests a trust be used when there seems to be little reason to do so;
- the trust is established in a jurisdiction which has limited AML/CTF regulation.

In a higher risk situation you should consider either conducting further CDD or enhanced monitoring. This could include:

- conducting CDD on all the trustees, or on the settlor even after the creation of the trust;
- asking about the purpose of the trust and the source of the funds used to create it;
- obtaining the trust deed or searching an appropriate register maintained in the country of establishment.

Your client, whether they are the trustee(s), settlor or beneficiaries, must be identified in accordance with their relevant category (i.e. natural person, company, etc.). Where you are acting for more than one trustee it is preferable that you verify the identity of at least two of the trustees. Where the trustee is another regulated person, you may rely on their listing with their supervisory body.

You must consider beneficial ownership [4.7 of this practice note] issues where you are acting for the trustee(s).

Foundations

A foundation is the civil law equivalent to a common law trust and operates in many EEA countries. You should understand why your client is using a solicitor outside of the jurisdiction of establishment, and the statutory requirements for the establishment of the foundation. Then obtain similar information as you would for a trust.

Where the foundation's founder is anonymous, you may consider whether any intermediary or agent is regulated for AML/CTF and whether they can provide assurances on the identity of relevant persons involved with the foundation.

Foundations can also be a loose term for charitable institutions in the UK and the USA – where that is the case they must be verified in accordance with the procedures for verifying charities set out below.

Charities

Charities may take a number of forms. In the UK, you may come across five types of charities:

- small;
- registered;
- unregistered;
- excepted, such as churches;
- exempt, such as museums and universities.

For registered charities, you should take a record of their full name, registration number and place of business. Details of registered charities can be obtained from:

- the Charity Commission of England and Wales at **www.charity-commission.gov.uk**;
- the Office of the Scottish Charity Regulator at **www.oscr.org.uk**.

Other countries may also have charity regulators which maintain a list of registered charities. You may consider it appropriate to refer to these when verifying the identity of an overseas charity. Currently in Northern Ireland there is no regulator for charities.

For all other types of charities you should consider the business structure of the charity and apply the relevant CDD measures for that business structure. You can also generally get confirmation of their charitable status from HMRC. Further, in applying the risk-based approach to charities it is worth considering whether it is a well-known entity or not. The more obscure the charity, the more likely you are to want to view the constitutional documents of the charity.

Due to the increased interest in some charities and not-for-profit organisations from terrorist organisations you may want to also consult the Bank of England's sanctions list to ensure the charity is not a proscribed organisation.

Deceased persons' estates

When acting for the executor(s) or administrators of an estate, you should establish their identity using the procedures for natural persons or companies set out above. When acting for more than one executor or administrator, it is preferable to verify the identity of at least two of them. You should consider getting copies of the death certificate, grant of probate or letters of administration.

During the administration of the estate, regulation 6(8) provides that the beneficial owner is:

- the executor, original or by representation; or
- the administrator for the time being of a deceased person.

This definition is wide enough to cover you when you deal with foreign deceased estates that are in the course of administration.

If a will trust is created, and the trustees are different from the executors, the procedures in relation to trusts will need to be followed when the will trust comes into operation.

Churches and places of worship

Places of worship may either register as a charity or can apply for registration as a certified building of worship from the General Register Office (GRO) which will issue a certificate. Further, their charitable tax status will be registered with HMRC. As such, identification details with respect to the church or place of worship may be verified:

- as for a charity;
- through the headquarters or regional organisation of the denomination or religion.

For UK charities, identification details may be verified:

- with reference to the GRO certificate;
- through an enquiry to HMRC.

Schools and colleges

Schools and colleges may be a registered charity, a private company, an unincorporated association or a government entity and should be verified in accordance with the relevant category.

The Department for Education and Skills [now DCFS – Department for Children, Family and School] maintains lists of approved educational facilities which may assist in verifying the existence of the school or college.

Clubs and associations

Many of these bear a low money laundering risk, but this depends on the scope of their purposes, activities and geographical spread.

The following information may be relevant to the identity of the club or association:

- full name;
- legal status;
- purpose;
- any registered address;
- names of all office holders.

Documents which may verify the existence of the club or association include:
- any articles of association or constitutions;
- statement from a bank, building society or credit union;
- recent audited accounts;
- listing in a local or national telephone directory.

Pension funds

Regulation 13(7)(c) provides that simplified due diligence is permitted where:

> A pension, superannuation or similar scheme which provides retirement benefits to employees, where contributions are made by an employer or by way of deduction from an employee's wages and the scheme rules do not permit the assignment of a member's interest under the scheme (other than an assignment permitted by section 44 of the Welfare Reform and Pensions Act 1999 (disapplication of restrictions on alienation) or section 91(5)(a) of the Pensions Act 1995 (inalienability of occupational pension)).

So you only need evidence that the product is such a scheme and so qualifies for simplified due diligence. Such evidence may include:

- a copy of a page showing the name of the scheme from the most recent definitive deed;
- a consolidating deed for the scheme, plus any amending deed subsequent to that date.

Pension funds or superannuation schemes outside the above definition should be subject to CDD according to their specific business structure.

For information on how to conduct CDD on other funds please see the Joint Money Laundering Steering Group's guidance [**www.jmlsg.org.uk**].

4.6.5   Government agencies and councils

The money laundering and terrorist financing risks associated with public authorities varies significantly depending on the nature of the retainer and the home jurisdiction of the public authority. It may be simple to establish that the entity exists, but where there is a heightened risk of corruption or misappropriation of government monies, greater monitoring of retainers should be considered.

The following information may be relevant when establishing a public sector entity's identity:

- full name of the entity;
- nature and status of the entity;
- address of the entity;
- name of the home state authority;
- name of the directors or equivalent.

Simplified due diligence [4.8 of this practice note] applies to UK public authorities. Where simplified due diligence does not apply, you may get information verifying the existence of the public sector from:

- official government websites;
- a listing in a national or local telephone directory.

4.7 CDD on a beneficial owner

4.7.1 General comments

When conducting CDD on a client, you will need to identify any beneficial owners within the meaning of regulation 6 of the regulations. Note that this definition goes beyond the traditional understanding of the meaning of a beneficial owner.

To identify the beneficial owner, obtain at least their name and record any other identifying details which are readily available. You may decide to use records that are publicly available, ask your client for the relevant information or use other sources.

To assess which identity verification measures are needed, consider the client's risk profile, any business structures involved and the proposed transaction.

The key is to understand the ownership and control structure of the client. A prudent approach is best, monitoring changes in instructions, or transactions which suggest that someone is trying to undertake or manipulate a retainer for criminal ends. Simply ticking boxes is unlikely to satisfy the risk-based approach.

Appropriate verification measures may include:

- a certificate from your client confirming the identity of the beneficial owner;
- a copy of the trust deed, partnership agreement or other such document;
- shareholder details from an online registry;
- the passport of, or electronic verification on, the individual;
- other reliable, publicly available information.

4.7.2 Assessing the risk

Issues you may consider when assessing the risk of a particular case include:

- why your client is acting on behalf of someone else;
- how well you know your client;
- whether your client is a regulated person;
- the type of business structure involved in the transaction;
- where the business structure is based;
- the AML/CTF requirements in the jurisdiction where it is based;
- why this business structure is being used in this transaction;

- how soon property or funds will be provided to the beneficial owner.

Only in rare cases will you need to verify a beneficial owner to the same level that you would a client.

When conducting CDD on beneficial owners within a corporate entity or arrangement, you must:

- understand the ownership and control structure of the client as required by regulation 5(b);
- identify the specific individuals listed in regulation 6.

The level of understanding required depends on the complexity of the structure and the risks associated with the transaction. For example, it may be sufficient to review the trust deed or partnership arrangement and discuss the issue with your client. In the case of a company, you may obtain a company structure chart from your client directly, their website or their annual reports.

It is vital to understand in what capacity your client is instructing you to ensure that you are identifying the correct beneficial owners.

If for example you are acting for Bank A, which is a corporate entity, to purchase new premises for Bank A, then it would be the shareholders and controllers of Bank A who are the beneficial owners. However, if Bank A is a trustee for XYZ Trust and they have instructed you to sell trust property, then Bank A is instructing you on behalf of the arrangement which is XYZ Trust in their capacity as trustee. The beneficial owners in that transaction will be those with specified interests in and/or control of the XYZ Trust.

4.7.3 Agency

Regulation 6(9) says a beneficial owner generally means any individual who ultimately owns or controls the client or on whose behalf a transaction or activity is being conducted.

In these cases, it is presumed the client is himself the beneficial owner, unless the features of the transaction indicate they are acting on someone else's behalf. So you do not have to proactively search for beneficial owners, but to make enquiries when it appears the client is not the beneficial owner.

Situations where a natural person may be acting on behalf of someone else include:

- exercising a power of attorney. The document granting power of attorney may be sufficient to verify the beneficial owner's identity;
- acting as the deputy, administrator or insolvency practitioner. Appointment documents may be sufficient to verify the beneficial owner's identity;

- an appointed broker or other agent to conduct a transaction. A signed letter of appointment may be sufficient to verify the beneficial owner's identity.

You should be alert to the possibility that purported agency relationships are actually being utilised to facilitate a fraud. Understanding the reason for the agency, rather than simply accepting documentary evidence of such at face value, will assist to mitigate this risk. Where a client or retainer is higher risk, you may want to obtain further verification of the beneficial owner's identity in line with the suggested CDD methods to be applied to natural persons.

4.7.4   Companies

Regulation 6(1) defines the beneficial owner of a body corporate as meaning:
Any individual who:

- as respects any body other than a company whose securities are listed on a regulated market, ultimately owns or controls (whether through direct or indirect ownership or control, including through bearer share holdings) more than 25 per cent of the shares or voting rights in the body; or
- as respects any body corporate, otherwise exercises control over the management of the body.

This regulation does not apply to a company listed on a regulated market. It does apply to UK limited liability partnerships.

Shareholdings

You should make reasonable and proportionate enquiries to establish whether beneficial owners exist and, where relevant as determined by your risk analysis, verify their identity. These may include:

- getting assurances from the client on the existence and identity of relevant beneficial owners;
- getting assurances from other regulated persons more closely involved with the client, particularly in other jurisdictions, on the existence and identity of relevant beneficial owners;
- conducting searches on the relevant online registry;
- obtaining information from a reputable electronic verification service.

Where the holder of the requisite level of shareholding of a company is another company, apply the risk-based approach when deciding whether further enquiries should be undertaken.

A proportionate approach

It would be disproportionate to conduct independent searches across multiple entities at multiple layers of a corporate chain to see if, by accumulating very small interests in different entities, a person finally achieves more than a 25 per cent interest in the client corporate entity. You must simply be satisfied that you have an overall understanding of the ownership and control structure of the client company.

Voting rights are only those which are currently exercisable and attributed to the company's issued equity share capital.

Companies with capital in the form of bearer shares

These pose a higher laundering risk as it is often difficult to identify beneficial owners and such companies are often incorporated in jurisdictions with lower AML/CTF regulations. You should adopt procedures to establish the identities of the holders and material beneficial owners of such shares and ensure you are notified whenever there is a change of holder and/or beneficial owner. This may be achieved by:

* requiring that the shares be held by a regulated person;
* getting an assurance that either such a regulated person or the holder of the shares will notify you of any change of records relating to the shares.

Control

A corporate entity can also be subject to control by persons other than shareholders. Such control may rest with those who have power to manage funds or transactions without requiring specific authority to do so, and who would be in a position to override internal procedures and control mechanisms.

You should remain alert to anyone with such powers while you are obtaining a general understanding of the ownership and control structure of the corporate entity. Further enquiries are not likely to be necessary. Monitor situations within the retainer where control structures appear to be bypassed and make further enquiries at that time.

4.7.5   Partnerships

Regulation 6(2) provides that in the case of a partnership (but not a limited liability partnership) the following individuals are beneficial owners:

* any individual ultimately entitled to or who controls (whether directly or indirectly), more than 25 per cent of the capital or profits of the partnership or more than 25 per cent of the voting rights in the partnership; or

- any individual who otherwise exercises control over the management of the partnership.

Relevant points to consider when applying this regulation:

- the property of the entity includes its capital and its profits;
- control involves the ability to manage the use of funds or transactions outside of the normal management structure and control mechanisms.

You should make reasonable and proportionate enquiries to establish whether beneficial owners exist and, where relevant, verify their identity in a risk-based manner.
Enquiries and verification may be undertaken by:

- receiving assurances from the client on the existence and identity of relevant beneficial owners;
- receiving assurance from other regulated persons more closely involved with the client, particularly in other jurisdictions, on the existence and identity of relevant beneficial owners;
- reviewing the documentation setting up the partnership such as the partnership agreement or any other profit-sharing agreements.

4.7.6   Trusts

Regulation 6(3) sets out three types of beneficial owners of a trust:

- Part A: individual with specified interest – those with at least a 25 per cent specified interest in trust capital;
- Part B: class of persons to benefit – those in whose main interest the trust operates;
- Part C: individuals who control a trust.

You must identify persons within all relevant categories.

Non-individual beneficiaries

While generally the beneficiaries of a trust will be individuals, they may at times be a company, an entity or an arrangement, such as a charity.
Regulation 6(5) says you will have to apply regulation 6(1) to a beneficiary company to determine their beneficial owners. This means that:

- You should consider for all companies whether anyone exercises control over the beneficiary company outside of the normal management structures. Identify them as a beneficial owner of the client trust. You may ask the client if they are aware of any such person, as this information would not be on a publicly available register and it will generally not be proportionate for you to have direct dealings with the beneficiary company.

- Where the beneficiary company is a private or unlisted company, you should consider whether they have shareholders with more than a 25 per cent interest in the beneficiary company. This can be done by a simple search on Companies House or equivalent online registry.
- If you locate such a shareholder, you should note their identity as a beneficial owner of the client trust. You will have already verified the identity through the company register check. Where there is a tiered structure, e.g. where, through its shareholding in a such shareholder, another company has more than a 25 per cent interest in the beneficiary company enquire of the client why there is a tiered structure in use and make a risk-based decision, considering the risk of the client generally and the whole retainer, as to whether:

  - further identity enquiries are required;
  - you simply identify the second company as the beneficial owner of the client trust and then conduct closer monitoring of any transactions;
  - you have a suspicion warranting a disclosure to SOCA, and consider withdrawing from the retainer.

The further you look for beneficial owners within beneficial owners the smaller the interest and the harder it is to exercise control. Therefore the risk of laundering or terrorist financing is lower. Consider this when setting proportionate CDD.

If you do not find an individual within either of the above categories, then simply list the beneficiary company as the beneficial owner of the client trust.

Regulation 6(5)(a) does not apply to beneficiaries that are non-corporate entities or another trust. You should still identify them as a beneficial owner of the client trust and consider whether you need to know more about them.

Individual with specified interest (Part A)

A person has a specified interest if they have a vested interest of the requisite level in possession or remainder or reversion, defeasible or indefeasible.

Vested interest

This is an interest not subject to any conditions precedent. It is held by the beneficiary completely and inalienably, even if it is still under the control of the trustees at that time.

Contingent interest

This interest is subject to the satisfaction of one or more conditions precedent, such as attaining a specified age or surviving a specified person. Failure to satisfy all conditions precedent results in the failure of the interest.

Interest in possession

This interest is the right to enjoy the use or possession of the fund and under the regulations relates solely to an interest in the capital of the fund.

Interest in remainder

This is the beneficiary's right to the capital of the fund which is postponed to one or more prior interests in possession in the income of the fund.

Interest in reversion

This is the right of the settlor to receive any part of the fund at the end of the trust. It occurs in cases including when the trust fails because all of the beneficiaries die or a life interest terminates and there are no remainder beneficiaries.

Defeasible interest

An interest is defeasible if it can be terminated in whole or in part, without the consent of the beneficiary, by the happening of an event, such as the failure of a condition subsequent or the exercise by the trustees of a power to terminate or vary the interest.

Indefeasible interest

An interest is indefeasible if it cannot be terminated in whole or in part without the consent of the beneficiary by the happening of any event.

Defeasible and indefeasible interests are included, so that you consider the beneficiaries who are going to get the property as at the time you are instructed, and conduct CDD on them.

Class of persons to benefit (Part B)

Part B of the definition in regulation 6(3) covers any trust that includes persons who do not fit within Part A. Within Part B, you must identify the class of persons in whose main interest the trust operates. All discretionary trusts will fall within Part B.

Note: If a trust has one or more persons who are individuals with a 25 per cent specified interest, as well as other beneficiaries, identify the individuals who fit within the first part of the definition, then consider the rest of the beneficiaries as a class under Part B.

Identification of a class is by description, such as:

- the grandchildren of X;
- charity Y;
- pension holders and their dependants.

When considering in whose main interest a trust is set up or operates, and there are several classes of beneficiary, consider which class is most likely to receive most of the trust property. For example:

- Where a trust is for the issue of X, then the class is the issue of X as there is only one class.
- Where a trust is for the children of X, if they all die, for the grandchildren of X and if they all die, for charity Y, then the class is likely to be the children of X as it is unlikely that they will all die before the funds are disbursed.
- Where a discretionary trust allows for payments to the widow, the children, their spouses and civil partners, the grandchildren, and their spouses and civil partners, then all interests are equal and all classes will need to be identified.

Where in doubt about which class has the main interest, you should identify all classes.

Note: Interests in parts of the trust property can change significantly between retainers, particularly with discretionary trusts. So it is good practice to obtain an update on any changes from the trustees with each set of new retainers your firm receives in relation to a discretionary trust.

Control of the trust (Part C)

Control is defined as a power, either:

- exercisable alone;
- jointly with another person;
- with the consent of another person

under the trust instrument or by law to either:

- dispose of, advance, lend, invest, pay or apply trust property;
- vary the trusts;
- add or remove a person as a beneficiary or to a class of beneficiaries;
- appoint or remove trustees;
- direct, withhold consent to or veto the exercise of a power such as is mentioned in the options above.

The definition of control can include beneficiaries acting collectively where they have the power to take or to direct action.

Regulation 6(5)(b) specifically excludes from the definition of control:

- the power exercisable collectively at common law to vary or extinguish a trust by all of the beneficiaries – see *Saunders* v *Vautier* [1841] EWHC Ch J82 [**www.bailii.org/ew/cases/EWHC/Ch/1841/ J82.html**];
- the power of members of a pension fund to influence the investment of the fund's assets;
- the power to consent to advancement implied to a person with a life interest under section 32(1)(c) of the Trustee Act 1925;
- the powers of beneficiaries to require the appointment or retirement of trustees under Trusts of Land and Appointment of Trustees Act 1996.

Identifying trust beneficial owners in practice

You are only required to make reasonable and proportionate enquiries to establish whether beneficial owners exist and, where relevant, verify their identity. If unsure whether a beneficiary or other person is a beneficial owner, you may consider taking legal advice from a trust practitioner, or identify them and consider whether verification is required.

Enquires and verification may be undertaken by:

- getting assurances from trustees on the existence and identity of beneficial owners;
- getting assurances from other regulated persons more closely involved with the client, particularly in other jurisdictions, on existence and identity of beneficial owners;
- reviewing the trust deed;
- obtaining information from a reputable electronic verification service on details of identified beneficiaries.

View practical examples of how various interests and powers of control may appear [at 4.12 – Annex A of this practice note].

4.7.7   Other arrangements and legal entities

Regulation 6(6) provides that where you are dealing with a client who is not a natural person, nor a corporate entity or a trust, then the following individuals are beneficial owners:

- where the individuals who benefit from the entity or arrangement have been determined, any individual who benefits from at least 25 per cent of the property of the entity or arrangement;
- where the individuals who benefit from the entity or arrangement have yet to be determined, the class or persons in whose main interest the entity or arrangement is set up or operates;
- any individual who exercises control over at least 25 per cent of the property of the entity or arrangement.

Unincorporated associations and foundations are examples of entities and arrangements likely to fall within this regulation.

When applying this regulation relevant points to consider are:

- the property of the entity includes its capital and its profits;
- determined benefits are those to which an individual is currently entitled;
- contingent benefits or where no determination has been made should be dealt with as a class as benefit has yet to be determined;
- a class of persons need only be identified by way of description;
- an entity or arrangement is set up for, or operates in, the main interest of the persons who are likely to get most of the property;
- control involves the ability to manage the use of funds or transactions outside the normal management structure and control mechanisms;
- where you find a body corporate with the requisite interest outlined above, you will need to make further proportionate enquiries as to the beneficial owner of the body corporate.

You should make reasonable and proportionate enquiries to establish whether beneficial owners exist and, where relevant, verify their identity in a risk-based manner.

Enquires and verification may be undertaken by:

- asking the client and receiving assurances as to the existence and identity of beneficial owners;
- asking other regulated persons more closely involved with the client (particularly in other jurisdictions) and receiving assurances as to the existence and identity of beneficial owners;
- reviewing the documentation setting up the entity or arrangement such as its constitution or rules.

4.8 Simplified due diligence

Regulation 13 permits simplified due diligence to be undertaken in certain circumstances.

4.8.1 What is simplified due diligence?

You simply have to obtain evidence that the client or products provided are eligible for simplified due diligence. You will not need to obtain information on the nature and purpose of the business relationship or on beneficial owners. You will need to conduct CDD and ongoing monitoring where you suspect money laundering.

4.8.2 Who qualifies for simplified due diligence?

The following clients and products qualify:

- a credit or financial institution which is subject to the requirements of the money laundering directive [**http://eur-lex.europa.eu/ LexUriServ/site/en/oj/2005/l_309/l_30920051125en00150036.pdf**];
- a credit or financial institution in a non-EEA state which is supervised for compliance with requirements similar to the money laundering directive;
- companies listed on a regulated EEA state market or a non-EEA market which has similar disclosure requirements to European Community legislation;
- beneficial owners of pooled accounts held by a notary or independent legal professional, i.e. financial services firms are not required to apply CDD to the third party beneficial owners of omnibus accounts held by solicitors, provided the information on the identity of the beneficial owners is available upon request;
- UK public authorities;
- a non-UK public authority which:

    - is entrusted with public functions pursuant to the treaty on the European Union or the Treaties on the European Communities, or Community secondary legislation;
    - has a publicly available, transparent and certain identity;
    - has activities and accounting practices which are transparent;
    - is accountable to a community institution, the authorities of an EEA state or is otherwise subject to appropriate check and balance procedures;

- certain insurance policies, pensions or electronic money products;

- products where:

    - they are based on a written contract;
    - related transactions are carried out through a regulated credit institution;
    - they are not anonymous;
    - they are within relevant maximum thresholds;
    - realisation for the benefit of a third party is limited;
    - investment in assets or claims is only realisable in the long term, cannot be used as collateral and there cannot be accelerated payments, surrender clauses or early termination.

For further details on the requirements for qualification for simplified due diligence, see regulation 13 of and Schedule 2 to the regulations.

Consult a list of countries where CDD requirements and supervision of credit or financial institutions are considered equivalent to the UK [**www.jmlsg.org.uk**].

Consult a list of national money laundering legislation around the world, and whether they apply to lawyers [**www.anti-moneylaundering. org**].

4.9   Enhanced due diligence

Regulation 14 provides that you will need to apply enhanced due diligence on a risk-sensitive basis where:

- the client is not dealt with face to face;
- the client is a politically exposed person (PEP) [4.9.2 of this practice note];
- there is any other situation which can present a higher risk of money laundering or terrorist financing.

The regulations do not set out what will be enhanced due diligence for the last option.

In applying the risk-based approach to the situation you should consider whether it is appropriate to:

- seek further verification of the client or beneficial owner's identity;
- obtain more detail on the ownership and control structure of the client;
- request further information on the purpose of the retainer or the source of the funds; and/or
- conduct enhanced ongoing monitoring.

4.9.1 Non face-to-face clients

A client who is not a natural person can never be physically present for identification purposes and will only ever be represented by an agent. The mere fact that you do not have face-to-face meetings with the agents of an entity or arrangement does not automatically require that enhanced due diligence is undertaken. You should consider the risks associated with the retainer and the client, assess how well standard CDD measures are meeting those risks and decide whether further CDD measures are required.

Where a client is a natural person and they are not physically present for identification purposes, you must undertake enhanced due diligence.

Regulation 14(2) outlines possible steps which can be taken above standard verification procedures to compensate for the higher risk of non face-to-face transactions. The regulations suggest the following options, although this list is not exhaustive:

- Using additional documents, data or information to establish identity. This may involve using electronic verification to confirm documents provided, or using two or three documents from different sources to confirm the information set out in each.
- Using supplementary measures to verify or certify the documents supplied or obtain confirmatory certification by a credit or financial institution which is subject to the money laundering directive. You may consider electronic verification to confirm the documents provided. Alternatively consider getting certified copies of documents:

  - When dealing with foreign passports or identity cards, check the requirements for that country with the relevant embassy or consulate.
  - With all other documents, consider whether the certifying person is regulated with respect to the regulations or is otherwise a professional person subject to some sort of regulation or fit and proper person test, who can easily be independently contacted to verify their certification of the documents. Such persons include bank managers, accountants, or local GPs. You may also consider accepting documents certified by the Post Office-provided Identity Checking Service.

- Ensuring the first payment in the retainer is through an account opened in the client's name with a credit institution. EU regulation 1781/2006 says credit institutions must provide the payers name, address and account number with all electronic fund transfers. It entered force on 1 January 2007 and is directly applicable to all member states. Use this to further verify your client's identity.

Further details see Part II – Wire transfers of the JMLSG guidance [**www.jmlsg.org.uk**].

If such information is not included on the electronic fund transfer, discuss this with the relevant financial or credit institution. Consider taking up the matter with the FSA, if the institution refuses to give you written confirmation of the details. Take other steps to verify your client's identity.

4.9.2   Politically exposed persons

You must take the following steps to deal with the heightened risk posed by having a client who is a PEP:

- Have senior management approval for establishing a business relationship with a PEP.
- Take adequate measures to establish the source of wealth and source of funds which are involved in the business relationship or occasional transaction.
- Conduct closer ongoing monitoring of the business relationship.

You are not required to actively investigate whether beneficial owners of a client are PEPs. However, where you have a beneficial owner who you know is a PEP, you should consider on a risk-based approach what extra measures, if any, you need to take when dealing with that client.

Further, merely doing work for a non-UK public authority does not mean that you are in a business relationship with a PEP. You should however ensure that you have considered the risks associated with the particular public authority and taken steps to address those risks.

Who is a PEP?

A person who has been entrusted within the last year with one of the following prominent public functions by a state other than the UK, a Community institution or an international body:

- heads of state, heads of government, ministers and deputy or assistant ministers;
- members of parliament;
- members of supreme courts, of constitutional courts, or of other high-level judicial bodies whose decisions are not generally subject to further appeal, except in exceptional circumstances;
- members of courts of auditors or of the boards of central banks;
- ambassadors, chargés d'affaires and high-ranking officers in the armed forces;

- members of the administrative, management or supervisory bodies of state-owned enterprises.

In addition to the primary PEPs listed above, a PEP also includes:

- family members of a PEP – spouse, partner, children and their spouses or partners, and parents;
- known close associates of a PEP – persons with whom joint beneficial ownership of a legal entity or legal arrangement is held, with whom there are close business relationships, or who is a sole beneficial owner of a legal entity or arrangement set up by the primary PEP.

The regulations only apply to persons appointed by governments and authorities outside the UK, but it may be appropriate, on a risk-based approach to apply some or all of the enhanced due diligence requirements to a person appointed in the UK, who would have been a PEP had they been appointed outside the UK.

How to identify PEPs

You are not required to conduct extensive investigations to establish whether a person is a PEP. Just have regard to information that is in your possession or publicly known.

To assess your PEP risk profile, you should consider your existing client base, taking into account the general demographic of your client base, and how many clients you currently know would be a PEP.

If the risk of you acquiring a PEP as a client is low, you may simply wish to ask clients whether they fall within any of the PEP categories. Where they say no, you may reasonably assume the individual is not a PEP unless anything else within the retainer, or that you otherwise become aware of, makes you suspect they may be a PEP.

Where you have a higher risk of having PEPs as clients or you have reason to suspect that a person may actually be a PEP contrary to earlier information, you should consider conducting some form of electronic verification. You may find that a web-based search engine will be sufficient for these purposes, or you may decide that it is more appropriate to conduct electronic checks through a reputable international electronic verification provider.

Note: The range of PEPs is wide and constantly changing, so electronic verification will not give you 100 per cent certainty. You should remain alert to situations suggesting the client is a PEP. Such situations include:

- receiving funds in the retainer from a government account;
- correspondence on official letterhead from the client or a related person;
- general conversation with the client or person related to the retainer linking the person to a PEP;
- news reports which actually come to your attention suggesting your client is a PEP or linked to one.

Where you suspect a client is a PEP but cannot establish that for certain, you may consider on a risk-sensitive basis applying aspects of the enhanced due diligence procedures.

Senior management approval

The regulations do not define senior management, so your firm must decide who that is, on a risk-sensitive basis. Senior management may be:

- the head of a practice group;
- another partner who is not involved with the particular file;
- the partner supervising the particular file;
- the nominated officer;
- the managing partner.

In any case, it is recommended that you advise those responsible for monitoring risk assessment that a business relationship with a PEP has begun, to help their overall monitoring of the firm's risk profile and compliance.

Establishing source of wealth and funds

Generally this simply involves asking questions of the client about their source of wealth and the source of the funds to be used with each retainer. When you know a person is a PEP, their salary and source of wealth is often publicly available on a register of their interests. This may be relevant for higher risk retainers.

Enhanced monitoring

You should ensure that funds paid into your client account come from the account nominated and are for an amount commensurate with the client's known wealth. Ask further questions if they are not.

4.10   Existing clients

Regulation 7(2) states you must apply CDD measures to an existing customer at other appropriate times and on a risk-sensitive basis, repealing the previous exemption for customers with whom you had a business relationship prior to 1 March 2004.

You do not have to ensure all existing clients have been identified and verified by 15 December 2007, nor update all current identification in accordance with the new requirements by that date.

Factors that may trigger a need for CDD include:

- a gap in retainers of three years or more;
- a client instructing on a higher risk retainer;
- where you develop a suspicion of money laundering or terrorist financing by the client;
- an existing high risk client.

For all clients, you should ensure ongoing monitoring of the business relationship to identify any suspicious activity.

When conducting CDD on existing clients or a subsidiary of an existing client, you may consider information already on your files which would verify their identity or publicly available information to confirm the information you hold, rather than approaching the client to provide that information initially. It may be appropriate for a fee earner or partner who has known the client for long time to place a certificate on the file providing an assurance as to identity.

4.11   FATF counter measures

Regulation 18 states that the Treasury may direct you not to:

- enter into a business relationship;
- carry out an occasional transaction;
- proceed further with a business relationship or occasional transaction;
- when the client is from a country subject to FATF counter measures.

Your CDD measures will need to ascertain whether your client, and in high risk situations key beneficial owners, are subject to such directions.

The HM Treasury website [**www.hm-treasury.gov.uk**] contains a consolidated list of persons and entities internationally and in the UK to whom financial sanctions apply. You can register for updates of a publication of a financial sanctions release.

4.12   Annex A – Examples of beneficial ownership for a trust

4.12.1   Example 1

Details

A's will provides that after payment of legacies and testamentary expenses his residuary estate passes to his children in equal shares. Three children survive A, one of whom (B) is under 18.

Application

On A's death each of the children have a vested interest in one third of the residuary estate, notwithstanding that B will not receive his share until he is 18 as he cannot give a valid receipt to the executors, and none of them will be entitled to receive anything until the conclusion of the administration of the estate.

As such all three children should be identified under Part A, after the estate ceases to be in administration.

4.12.2   Example 2

Details

C executed an inter vivos trust in 2000 'for the benefit of my grand-children who shall be born before 31/12/2020'. At the time he had two grandchildren. C died in 2006, and in 2007 your firm is instructed to act for the trustees. There are now four grandchildren.

Application

Each of the grandchildren has a vested interest in possession in one quarter of the trust fund, notwithstanding that further grandchildren may be born before 31/12/2020 and their shares may be reduced. Therefore each grandchild has a specified interest in at least 25 per cent of the capital of the trust property and should be identified under Part A.

Development

In 2015 new trustees are appointed, at which point there are five grand-children, each of whom has a specified interest in 20 per cent of the fund.

Application

Your firm will have to apply CDD to the new trustees (either as part of the client CDD or a person who has control) and to the class of beneficiaries under Part B, which will be the grandchildren of C.

4.12.3   Example 3

Details

C's will provides that after payment of legacies and testamentary expenses his residuary estate passes to 'such of my children as shall survive me and attain the age of 21 years'. Three children survive C, one of whom (D) is under 21.

Application

While the estate is in administration, it is the personal representative who will be the beneficial owner. The two elder children will have been paid out following completion of the administration of the estate, as they have absolute vested interests. D's interest in the one third of the estate is not a specified interest, being subject to a contingency and therefore not vested. As D also does not have control, this leaves you to apply CDD under Part B to the class of one, constituted by D.

4.12.4   Example 4

Details

E executes an inter vivos trust on 31/01/2007, creating a life interest in income for his wife, with remainder to such of their children as shall be living at his wife's death. At the time he has two children.

Application

The wife has a vested interest in possession, but it is in income, not in the capital of the trust. Therefore she is not a beneficial owner under Part A. As s.32(1)(c) of the Trustee Act 1925 is excluded from being defined as control over the trust, she is not a beneficial owner under Part C either.

The children have an interest in the remainder, but it is contingent on them surviving their mother and does not vest until their mother's death. Therefore they should be identified as a class under Part B.

The settlor would be identified under Part A as he also has a vested interest in reversion as he has not provided for the situation which will arise if all of the children pre-decease their mother. Should this happen there will be a total failure of the trust, which will revert to E, or if he has predeceased his wife, to his estate.

The trustees would also be identified under Part C as a result of their control over the trust.

4.12.5   Example 5

Details

F's will provides for a life interest for his wife, with remainder to his children in equal shares. One of the children dies prior to the wife.

Application

The wife is not a beneficial owner (see example 4).

The child who has pre-deceased his mother has a vested interest in the remainder as there is no condition precedent that he must survive his mother. Therefore the interest survives him and is capable of being bequeathed by his will or passing under his intestacy.

It will depend on the number of children as to the level of interest each has. If it is under 25 per cent then it would simply be under Part B. If each has at least 25 per cent then they will need to be individually identified under Part A and enquiries will need to be made of the trustee as to who is now entitled to the deceased child's interest.

4.12.6   Example 6

Details

I's will provides for a life interest in favour of his wife, with remainder to his four children in equal shares. The trustee is given express power to vary the shares, in whole or in part.

Application

This means that the interests of the children are vested but are defeasible. Until the trustee exercises their power to vary the interest, all of the children will be identified under Part A. Once the trustee exercises their power, any children with an interest remaining at 25 per cent or more will continue to be identified under Part A, while the others will be identified under Part B. The trustees will be identified under Part C. The wife is not a beneficial owner (see example 4).

4.12.7 Example 7

Details

J by his will created a life interest in favour of his wife, with the remainder to his three children in equal shares. The trustees are given a power, during the life of the widow, to appoint an interest in all or part of the capital of the fund, without her consent, in favour of such charities as they may select.

Application

Until the power of appointment is exercised all three children have a vested interest in the remainder and should be identified under Part A.

If for example the power of appointment is exercised and 50 per cent of the fund is to be paid to one specified charity – prior to the distribution it is recommended that the charity be identified under Part A and the children under Part B. After the distribution is made, the children will then return to having a one-third share each and be identified under Part A. As such it is important to obtain updated information when taking on a new retainer for such a trust.

4.12.8 Example 8

Details

N creates an inter vivos trust for his three named grandchildren subject to attaining 21, with substitution for their issue, reserving to himself the power to appoint or remove trustees.

Applications

The three grandchildren have contingent interests and so will be identified under Part B. N has control and should be identified under Part C due to the power to appoint or remove trustees.

4.12.9 Example 9

Details

O creates an inter vivos trust for his three named grandchildren subject to attaining 21, with substitution for their issue, appointing a protector (P) with power to veto any advancement of capital by the trustees under s.32 of the Trustee Act 1925 and to appoint or remove trustees.

Application

The grandchildren have contingent interests and are identified under Part B. Both P and the trustees have control over the trust and should be identified under Part C.

4.12.10   Example 10

Details

Q's will creates discretionary trusts of which his wife and issue are the beneficiaries. He gives his trustees the power, with the consent of his children, to add beneficiaries from amongst the spouses and civil partners of his issue.

Application

Both the trustees and the children have control of the trust and are subject to identification under Part C, while the wife and all of the issue are discretionary beneficiaries and are to be identified as a class under Part B.

Chapter 5 – Money laundering offences

5.1   General comments

The Proceeds of Crime Act 2002 (POCA) created a single set of money laundering offences applicable throughout the UK to the proceeds of all crimes. It also creates a disclosure regime, which makes it an offence not to disclose knowledge or suspicion of money laundering, but also permits persons to be given consent in certain circumstances to carry out activities which would otherwise constitute money laundering.

5.2   Application

POCA applies to all solicitors, although some offences apply only to persons within the regulated sector, or nominated officers.

5.3   Mental elements

The mental elements which are relevant to offences under Part 7 of POCA are:

- knowledge;
- suspicion;
- reasonable grounds for suspicion.

These are the three mental elements in the actual offences, although the third one only applies to offences relating to the regulated sector. There is also the element of belief on reasonable grounds in the foreign conduct defence to the money laundering offences. A person will have a defence to a principal offence if they know or believe on reasonable grounds that the criminal conduct involved was exempt overseas criminal conduct.

For the principal offences of money laundering the prosecution must prove that the property involved is criminal property [see POCA s.340(2)]. This means that the prosecution must prove that the property was obtained through criminal conduct and that, at the time of the alleged offence, you knew or suspected that it was.

For the failure to disclose offences, where you are acting in the regulated sector, you must disclose if you have knowledge, suspicion or reasonable grounds for suspicion; while if you are not in the regulated sector you will only need to consider making a disclosure if you have actual, subjective knowledge or suspicion.

These terms for the mental elements in the offences are not terms of art; they are not defined within POCA and should be given their everyday meaning. However, case law has provided some guidance on how they should be interpreted.

5.3.1 Knowledge

Knowledge means actual knowledge. There is some suggestion that wilfully shutting one's eyes to the truth may amount to knowledge. However, the current general approach from the criminal courts is that nothing less than actual knowledge will suffice.

5.3.2 Suspicion

The term 'suspects' is one which the court has historically avoided defining; however because of its importance in English criminal law, some general guidance has been given. In the case of *Da Silva* [2006] EWCA Crim 1654 [**www.bailii.org/ew/cases/EWCA/Crim/2006/1654.html**], which was prosecuted under the previous money laundering legislation, Longmore LJ stated:

> It seems to us that the essential element in the word 'suspect' and its affiliates, in this context, is that the defendant must think that there is a possibility, which is more than fanciful, that the relevant facts exist. A vague feeling of unease would not suffice.

There is no requirement for the suspicion to be clear or firmly grounded on specific facts, but there must be a degree of satisfaction, not necessarily amounting to belief, but at least extending beyond speculation.

The test for whether you hold a suspicion is a subjective one.

If you think a transaction is suspicious, you are not expected to know the exact nature of the criminal offence or that particular funds were definitely those arising from the crime. You may have noticed something unusual or unexpected and after making enquiries, the facts do not seem normal or make commercial sense. You do not have to have evidence that money laundering is taking place to have suspicion.

Chapter 11 of this practice note contains a number of standard warning signs which may give you a cause for concern; however, whether you have a suspicion is a matter for your own judgement. To help form that judgement, consider talking through the issues with colleagues or with the Law Society. You could take legal advice, possibly from another solicitor on the Law Society's AML directory [**www.lawsociety.org.uk/ choosingandusing/findasolicitor/moneylaunderingdirectory**]. Listing causes for concern can also help focus your mind.

If you have not yet formed a suspicion but simply have cause for concern, you may choose to ask the client or others more questions. This choice depends on what you already know, and how easy it is to make enquiries.

If you think your own client is innocent but suspect that another party to a transaction is engaged in money laundering, you may still have to consider referring your client for specialist advice regarding the risk that they may be a party to one of the principal offences.

5.3.3   Reasonable grounds to suspect

The issues here for the solicitor conducting regulated activities are the same as for the mental element of suspicion, except that it is an objective test. Were there factual circumstances from which an honest and reasonable person, engaged in a business in the regulated sector should have inferred knowledge or formed the suspicion that another was engaged in money laundering?

5.4   Principal money laundering offences

5.4.1   General comments

Money laundering offences assume that a criminal offence has occurred in order to generate the criminal property which is now being laundered. This is often known as a predicate offence. No conviction for the predicate offence is necessary for a person to be prosecuted for a money laundering offence.

The principal money laundering offences apply to money laundering activity which occurred on or after 24 February 2003 as a result of the Proceeds of Crime Act 2002 (Commencement No.4, Transitional Provisions & Savings) Order 2003.

If the money laundering occurred or started before 24 February 2003, the former legislation will apply. If the money laundering occurred or started before 24 February 2003, the former legislation will apply – see the second edition of Money Laundering Legislation: Guidance for Solicitors 2002.

However if the money laundering took place after 24 February 2003, the conduct giving rise to the criminal property can occur before that date.

When considering the principal money laundering offences, be aware that it is also an offence to conspire or attempt to launder the proceeds of crime, or to counsel, aid, abet or procure money laundering.

5.4.2 Section 327 – concealing

A person commits an offence if he conceals, disguises, converts, or transfers criminal property, or removes criminal property from England and Wales, Scotland or Northern Ireland.

Concealing or disguising criminal property includes concealing or disguising its nature, source, location, disposition, movement, ownership or any rights connected with it.

5.4.3 Section 328 – arrangements

A person commits an offence if he enters into, or becomes concerned in an arrangement which he knows or suspects facilitates the acquisition, retention, use or control of criminal property by or on behalf of another person.

What is an arrangement?

Arrangement is not defined in Part 7 of POCA. The arrangement must exist and have practical effects relating to the acquisition, retention, use or control of property.

An agreement to make an arrangement will not always be an arrangement. The test is whether the arrangement does in fact, in the present and not the future, have the effect of facilitating the acquisition, retention, use or control of criminal property by or on behalf of another person.

What is not an arrangement?

Bowman v *Fels* [2005] EWCA Civ 226 [**www.bailii.org/ew/cases/EWCA/Civ/2005/226.html**] held that s.328 does not cover or affect the ordinary conduct of litigation by legal professionals, including any step taken in litigation from the issue of proceedings and the securing of injunctive relief or a freezing order up to its final disposal by judgment.

Our view, supported by Counsel's opinion, is that dividing assets in accordance with the judgment, including the handling of the assets which are criminal property, is not an arrangement. Further, settlements, negotiations, out of court settlements, alternative dispute resolution and tribunal representation are not arrangements. However, the property will generally still remain criminal property and you may need to consider referring your client for specialist advice regarding possible offences they may commit once they come into possession of the property after completion of the settlement.

The recovery of property by a victim of an acquisitive offence will not be committing an offence under either s.328 or s.329 of the Act.

Sham litigation

Sham litigation created for the purposes of money laundering remains within the ambit of s.328. Our view is that shams arise where an acquisitive criminal offence is committed and settlement negotiations or litigation are intentionally fabricated to launder the proceeds of that separate crime.

A sham can also arise if a whole claim or category of loss is fabricated to launder the criminal property. In this case, money laundering for the purposes of POCA cannot occur until after execution of the judgment or completion of the settlement.

Entering into or becoming concerned in an arrangement

To enter into an arrangement is to become a party to it.

To become concerned in an arrangement suggests a wider practical involvement such as taking steps to put the arrangement into effect.

Both entering into and becoming concerned in, describe an act that is the starting point of an involvement in an existing arrangement.

Although the Court did not directly consider the conduct of transactional work, its approach to what constitutes an arrangement under section 328 provides some assistance in interpreting how that section applies in those circumstances.

Our view is that *Bowman* v *Fels* supports a restricted understanding of the concept of entering into or becoming concerned in an arrangement, with respect to transactional work. In particular:

- entering into or becoming concerned in an arrangement involves an act done at a particular time;
- an offence is only committed once the arrangement is actually made; and
- preparatory or intermediate steps in transactional work which does not itself involve the acquisition, retention, use or control of property will not constitute the making of an arrangement under s.328.

If you are doing transactional work and become suspicious, you have to consider:

- whether an arrangement exists and, if so, whether you have entered into or become concerned in it or may do so in the future;
- if no arrangement exists, whether one may come into existence in the future which you may become concerned in.

5.4.4   Section 329 – acquisition, use or possession

A person commits an offence if he acquires, uses or has possession of criminal property.

5.5   Defences to principal money laundering offences

You will have a defence to a principal money laundering offence [5.4 of this practice note] if:

- you make an authorised disclosure prior to the offence being committed and you gain appropriate consent (the consent defence);
- you intended to make an authorised disclosure but had a reasonable excuse for not doing so (the reasonable excuse defence).

In relation to s.329 you will also have a defence if you received adequate consideration for the criminal property (the adequate consideration defence [5.5.2 of this practice note]).

5.5.1   Authorised disclosures

Section 338 authorises you to make a disclosure regarding suspicion of money laundering as a defence to the principal money laundering offences.

It specifically provides that you can make an authorised disclosure either:

- before money laundering has occurred, and if you have the appropriate consent;
- while it is occurring but as soon as you suspect;
- after it has occurred, if you had good reason for not disclosing earlier and make the disclosure as soon as practicable.

If a disclosure is authorised, it does not breach any rule which would otherwise restrict it, such as rule 4 of the Solicitors' Code of Conduct [**www.rules.sra.org.uk**] relating to client confidentiality.

Where your firm has a nominated officer, you should make your disclosure to the nominated officer. The nominated officer will consider your disclosure and decide whether to make an external disclosure to SOCA. If your firm does not have a nominated officer, you should make your disclosure directly to SOCA.

Appropriate consent

If you have a suspicion that a retainer you are acting in will involve dealing with criminal property, you can make an authorised disclosure to SOCA via your nominated officer and seek consent to undertake the further steps in the retainer which would constitute a money laundering offence.

For further information on how to make an authorised disclosure to SOCA and the process by which consent is gained, see Chapter 8 of this practice note.

Reasonable excuse defence

This defence applies where a person intended to make an authorised disclosure before doing a prohibited act, but had a reasonable excuse for not disclosing. Reasonable excuse has not been defined by the courts, but the scope of the reasonable excuse defence is important for legal professional privilege.

You must make an authorised disclosure where you intend to deal with property in one or more of the ways specified in the money laundering offences, but know or suspect that the property is criminal property.

However, you are prevented from disclosing if your knowledge or suspicion is based on privileged information, and legal professional privilege is not excluded by the crime/fraud exception. You will have a reasonable excuse for not making an authorised disclosure and will not commit a money laundering offence.

Read more about legal professional privilege [at 6.4 of this practice note].

There may be other circumstances which would provide a reasonable excuse, however these are likely to be narrow. You should clearly document the reason for not making a disclosure on this ground.

Where you suspect part way through

It is not unusual for a transactional matter to seem legitimate early in the retainer, but to develop in such a way as to arouse suspicion later on. It may be that certain steps have already taken place which you now suspect facilitated money laundering; while further steps are yet to be taken which you also suspect will facilitate further money laundering.

Section 338(2A) provides that you may make an authorised disclosure in these circumstances if:

- at the time the initial steps were taken they were not a money laundering offence because you did not have good reason to know or suspect that the property was criminal property; and
- you make a disclosure of your own initiative as soon as practicable after you first know or suspect that criminal property is involved in the retainer.

In such a case you would make a disclosure seeking consent for the rest of the transaction to proceed, while fully documenting the reasons why you came to know or suspect that criminal property was involved and why you did not suspect this to be the case previously.

5.5.2 Adequate consideration defence

This defence applies if there was adequate consideration for acquiring, using and possessing the criminal property, unless you know or suspect that those goods or services may help another to carry out criminal conduct.

The Crown Prosecution Service guidance for prosecutors [www.cps.gov.uk] says the defence applies where professional advisors, such as solicitors or accountants, receive money for or on account of costs, whether from the client or from another person on the client's behalf. Disbursements are also covered. The fees charged must be reasonable, and the defence is not available if the value of the work is significantly less than the money received.

The transfer of funds from client to office account, or vice versa, is covered by the defence.

Returning the balance of an account to a client may be a money laundering offence if you know or suspect the money is criminal property.

In that case, you must make an authorised disclosure and obtain consent to deal with the money before you transfer it.

Reaching a matrimonial settlement or an agreement on a retiring partner's interest in a business does not constitute adequate consideration for receipt of criminal property, as in both cases the parties would only be entitled to a share of the legitimately acquired assets of the marriage or the business. This is particularly important where your client would be receiving the property as part of a settlement which would be exempted from s.328 [5.4.3 of this practice note] due to the case of *Bowman* v *Fels*.

The defence is more likely to cover situations where:

- a third party seeks to enforce an arm's length debt and, unknown to them, is given criminal property in payment for that debt;
- a person provides goods or services as part of a legitimate arm's length transaction but unknown to them is paid from a bank account which contains the proceeds of crime.

5.6   Failure to disclose offences – money laundering

5.6.1   General comments

The failure to disclose provisions in sections 330, 331 and 332 apply where the information on which the knowledge or suspicion is based came to a person on or after 24 February 2003, or where a person in the regulated sector has reasonable grounds for knowledge or suspicion on or after that date.

If the information came to a person before 24 February 2003, the old law applies.

In all three sections, the phrase 'knows or suspects' refers to actual knowledge or suspicion – a subjective test. However, solicitors and nominated officers in the regulated sector will also commit an offence if they fail to report when they have reasonable grounds for knowledge or suspicion – an objective test. On this basis, they may be guilty of the offence under ss.330 or 331 if they should have known or suspected money laundering.

For all failure to disclose offences you must either:

- know the identity of the money launderer or the whereabouts of the laundered property; or
- believe the information on which your suspicion was based may assist in identifying the money launderer or the whereabouts of the laundered property.

5.6.2 Section 330 – failure to disclose: regulated sector

A person commits an offence if:

- he knows or suspects, or has reasonable grounds for knowing or suspecting, that another person is engaged in money laundering; and
- the information on which his suspicion is based comes in the course of business in the regulated sector; and
- he fails to disclose that knowledge or suspicion, or reasonable grounds for suspicion, as soon as practicable to a nominated officer or SOCA.

Our view is that delays in disclosure arising from taking legal advice or seeking help from the Law Society may be acceptable provided you act promptly to seek advice.

5.6.3 Section 331 – failure to disclose: nominated officer in the regulated sector

A nominated officer in the regulated sector commits a separate offence if, as a result of an internal disclosure under s.330, he knows or suspects, or has reasonable grounds for knowing or suspecting, that another person is engaged in money laundering and he fails to disclose as soon as practicable to SOCA.

5.6.4 Section 332 – failure to disclose: nominated officer in the non-regulated sector

An organisation which does not carry out relevant activities and so is not in the regulated sector, may decide on a risk-based approach to set up internal disclosure systems and appoint a person as nominated officer to receive internal disclosures.

A nominated officer in the non-regulated sector commits an offence if, as a result of a disclosure, he knows or suspects that another person is engaged in money laundering and fails to make a disclosure as soon as practicable to SOCA.

For this offence, the test is a subjective one: did you know or suspect in fact?

5.7 Exceptions to failure to disclose offences

There are three situations in which you have not committed an offence for failing to disclose:

- You have a reasonable excuse.
- You are a professional legal adviser and the information came to you in privileged circumstances.
- You did not receive appropriate training from your employer.

The first defence is the only one which applies to all three failure to disclose offences; the other two defences are only specifically provided for persons in the regulated sector who are not nominated officers.

All of the failure to disclose sections also reiterate that the offence will not be committed if the property involved in the suspected money laundering is derived from exempted overseas criminal conduct.

5.7.1 Reasonable excuse

No offence is committed if there is a reasonable excuse for not making a disclosure, but there is no judicial guidance on what might constitute a reasonable excuse.

However, as with reasonable excuse under the principal money laundering offences, where common law legal professional privilege has not been expressly excluded, following the reasoning in *Bowman* v *Fels*, it is considered that the decision not to make a disclosure because the information came to the person in privileged circumstances would be a reasonable excuse.

You should carefully document any reasons for not making a disclosure under this section.

5.7.2 Privileged circumstances

No offence is committed if the information or other matter giving rise to suspicion comes to a professional legal adviser in privileged circumstances.

You should note that receipt of information in privileged circumstances is not the same as legal professional privilege [6.4 of this practice note]. It is a creation of POCA designed to comply with the exemptions from reporting set out in the European directives.

Privileged circumstances means information communicated:

- by a client, or a representative of a client, in connection with the giving of legal advice to the client; or
- by a client, or by a representative of a client, seeking legal advice from you;
- by a person in connection with legal proceedings or contemplated legal proceedings.

The exemption will not apply if information is communicated or given to the solicitor with the intention of furthering a criminal purpose.

The Crown Prosecution Service guidance for prosecutors indicates that if a solicitor forms a genuine, but mistaken, belief that the privileged circumstances exemption applies (for example, the client misleads the solicitor and uses the advice received for a criminal purpose) the solicitor will be able to rely on the reasonable excuse defence.

For a further discussion of privileged circumstances see Chapter 6 [of this practice note].

5.7.3   Lack of training

Employees within the regulated sector who have no knowledge or suspicion of money laundering, even though there were reasonable grounds for suspicion, have a defence if they have not received training from their employers. Employers may be prosecuted for a breach of the Money Laundering Regulations 2007 if they fail to train staff.

5.8   Tipping off

The offences of tipping off for money laundering are contained in the Proceeds of Crime Act 2002 as amended by the [Terrorism Act 2000 and] Proceeds of Crime Act 2002 (Amendment) Regulations 2007 (TACT and POCA Regulations 2007).

There are also tipping off offences for terrorist property in the Terrorism Act 2000, as amended by the TACT [and POCA] Regulations 2007.

5.8.1   Offences

Tipping off – in the regulated sector

There are two tipping off offences in s.333A of POCA. They apply only to business in the regulated sector.

- Section 333A(1) – disclosing a suspicious activity report (SAR). It is an offence to disclose to a third person that a SAR has been made by any person to the police, HM Revenue and Customs, SOCA or a nominated officer, if that disclosure might prejudice any investigation that might be carried out as a result of the SAR. This offence can only be committed:

    - after a disclosure to SOCA or a nominated officer;
    - if you know or suspect that by disclosing this information, you are likely to prejudice any investigation related to that SAR;

- [if] the information upon which the disclosure is based came to you in the course of business in the regulated sector.

- Section 333A(3) – disclosing an investigation. It is an offence to disclose that an investigation into a money laundering offence is being contemplated or carried out if that disclosure is likely to prejudice that investigation. The offence can only be committed if the information on which the disclosure is based came to the person in the course of business in the regulated sector. The key point is that you can commit this offence, even where you are unaware that a SAR was submitted.

Prejudicing an investigation – outside the regulated sector

Section 342(1) contains an offence of prejudicing a confiscation, civil recovery or money laundering investigation, if the person making the disclosure knows or suspects that an investigation is being, or is about to be conducted. Section 342(1) was amended by paragraph 8 of the TACT and POCA Regulations 2007. The offence in s.342(2)(a) only applies to those outside the regulated sector. The offence in s.342(2)(b) applies to everyone.

You only commit the offence in s.342(2)(a) if you knew or suspected that the disclosure would, or would be likely to prejudice any investigation.

5.8.2 Defences

Tipping off

The following disclosures are permitted:

- s.333B – disclosures within an undertaking or group, including disclosures to a professional legal adviser or relevant professional adviser;
- s.333C – disclosures between institutions, including disclosures from a professional legal adviser to another professional legal adviser;
- s.333D – disclosures to your supervisory authority;
- s.333D(2) – disclosures made by professional legal advisers to their clients for the purpose of dissuading them from engaging in criminal conduct.

A person does not commit the main tipping off offence if he does not know or suspect that a disclosure is likely to prejudice an investigation.

Section 333b – Disclosures within an undertaking or group, etc.

It is not an offence if an employee, officer or partner of a firm discloses that a SAR has been made if it is to an employee, officer or partner of the same undertaking.

A solicitor will not commit a tipping off offence if a disclosure is made to another lawyer either:

- within a different undertaking, if both parties carry on business in an EEA state;
- in a country or territory that imposes money laundering requirements equivalent to the EU and both parties share common ownership, management or control.

Section 333c – Disclosures between institutions, etc.

A solicitor will not commit a tipping off offence if all the following criteria are met:

- The disclosure is made to another lawyer in an EEA state, or one with an equivalent AML regime.
- The disclosure relates to a client or former client of both parties, or a transaction involving them both, or the provision of a service involving them both.
- The disclosure is made for the purpose of preventing a money laundering offence.
- Both parties have equivalent professional duties of confidentiality and protection of personal data.

Section 333d(2) – Limited exception for professional legal advisers

A solicitor will not commit a tipping off offence if the disclosure is to a client and it is made for the purpose of dissuading the client from engaging in conduct amounting to an offence. This exception and the tipping off offence in s.333A apply to those carrying on activities in the regulated sector.

Prejudicing an investigation

Section 342(4) – Professional legal adviser exemption

It is a defence to a s.342(1) offence that a disclosure is made by a legal adviser to a client, or a client's representative, in connection with the giving of legal advice or to any person in connection with legal proceedings or contemplated legal proceedings.

5.8.3   Making enquiries of a client

You should make preliminary enquiries of your client, or a third party, to obtain further information to help you to decide whether you have a suspicion. You may also need to raise questions during a retainer to clarify such issues.

There is nothing in POCA which prevents you making normal enquiries about your client's instructions, and the proposed retainer, in order to remove, if possible, any concerns and enable the firm to decide whether to take on or continue the retainer.

These enquiries will only be tipping off if you disclose that a SAR has been made to SOCA or a nominated officer or that a money laundering investigation is being carried out or contemplated. The offence of tipping off only applies to the regulated sector.

It is not tipping off to include a paragraph about your obligations under the money laundering legislation in your firm's standard client care letter.

Chapter 6 – Legal professional privilege

6.1   General comments

Solicitors are under a duty to keep the affairs of their clients confidential, and the circumstances in which they are able to disclose client communications are strictly limited.

However, sections 327–329, 330 and 332 of POCA contain provisions for disclosure of information to be made to SOCA.

Solicitors also have a duty of full disclosure to their clients. However, sections 333A and 342 of POCA prohibit disclosure of information in circumstances where a SAR has been made and/or where it would prejudice an existing or proposed investigation.

This chapter examines the tension between a solicitor's duties and these provisions of POCA. Similar tensions also arise with respect to the Terrorism Act and you should refer to the Law Society's practice note on anti-terrorism in those circumstances.

This chapter should be read in conjunction with Chapter 5 of this practice note and if you are still in doubt as to your position, you should seek independent legal advice. The Law Society's AML directory may be of assistance in locating a solicitor who practises in this area of law.

6.2   Application

This chapter is relevant to any solicitor considering whether to make a disclosure under POCA.

6.3 Duty of confidentiality

A solicitor is professionally and legally obliged to keep the affairs of clients confidential and to ensure that his staff do likewise. The obligations extend to all matters revealed to a solicitor, from whatever source, by a client, or someone acting on the client's behalf. See Solicitors' Code of Conduct – rule 4.

In exceptional circumstances this general obligation of confidence may be overridden. See Solicitors' Code of Conduct rule 4 – note 10. However, certain communications can never be disclosed unless statute permits this either expressly or by necessary implication. Such communications are those protected by legal professional privilege (LPP).

6.4 Legal professional privilege

6.4.1 General overview

LPP is a privilege against disclosure, ensuring clients know that certain documents and information provided to lawyers cannot be disclosed at all. It recognises the client's fundamental human right to be candid with his legal adviser, without fear of later disclosure to his prejudice. It is an absolute right and cannot be overridden by any other interest.

LPP does not extend to everything lawyers have a duty to keep confidential. LPP protects only those confidential communications falling under either of the two heads of privilege – advice privilege or litigation privilege.

For the purposes of LPP, a lawyer includes solicitors and their employees, barristers and in-house lawyers. It does not include accountants.

6.4.[2] Advice privilege

Principle

Communications between a lawyer, acting in his capacity as a lawyer, and a client, are privileged if they are both:

- confidential;
- for the purpose of seeking legal advice from a solicitor or providing it to a client.

Scope

Communications are not privileged merely because a client is speaking or writing to you. The protection applies only to those communications which directly seek or provide advice or which are given in a legal context, that involve the lawyer using his legal skills and which are directly related to the performance of the lawyer's professional duties (*Passmore on Privilege* 2nd edition 2006).

Case law helps define what advice privilege covers.

Communications subject to advice privilege:

- a solicitor's bill of costs and statement of account (*Chant* v *Brown* (1852) 9 Hare 790);
- information imparted by prospective clients in advance of a retainer will attract LPP if the communications were made for the purpose of indicating the advice required (*Minster* v *Priest* [1930] AC 558 per Lord Atkin at 584).

Communications not subject to advice privilege:

- notes of open court proceedings (*Parry* v *News Group Newspapers* (1990) 140 New Law Journal 1719) are not privileged, as the content of the communication is not confidential;
- conversations, correspondence or meetings with opposing lawyers (*Parry* v *News Group Newspapers* (1990) 140 New Law Journal 1719) are not privileged, as the content of the communication is not confidential;
- a client account ledger maintained in relation to the client's money (*Nationwide Building Society* v *Various Solicitors* [1999] PNLR 53);
- an appointments diary or time record on an attendance note, time sheet or fee record relating to a client (*R* v *Manchester Crown Court*, ex p. *Rogers* [1999] 1 WLR 832 [**www.bailii.org/ew/cases/EWHC/Admin/1999/94.html**];
- conveyancing documents are not communications so not subject to advice privilege (*R* v *Inner London Crown Court*, ex p. *Baines & Baines* [1988] QB 579).

Advice within a transaction

All communications between a lawyer and his client relating to a transaction in which the lawyer has been instructed for the purpose of obtaining legal advice are covered by advice privilege, not withstanding that they do not contain advice on matters of law and construction, provided that they are directly related to the performance by the solicitor of his professional duty as legal adviser of his client (*Three Rivers District Council and Others* v *Bank of England* [2004] UKHL 48 at 111).

This will mean that where you are providing legal advice in a transactional matter (such as a conveyance) the advice privilege will cover all:

- communications with;
- instructions from; and
- advice given to

the client, including any working papers and drafts prepared, as long as they are directly related to your performance of your professional duties as a legal adviser.

6.4.3 Litigation privilege

Principle

This privilege, which is wider than advice privilege, protects confidential communications made after litigation has started, or is reasonably in prospect, between either:

- a lawyer and a client;
- a lawyer and an agent, whether or not that agent is a lawyer;
- a lawyer and a third party.

These communications must be for the sole or dominant purpose of litigation, either:

- for seeking or giving advice in relation to it;
- for obtaining evidence to be used in it;
- for obtaining information leading to obtaining such evidence.

6.4.4 Important points to consider

An original document not brought into existence for these privileged purposes and so not already privileged, does not become privileged merely by being given to a lawyer for advice or other privileged purpose.

Further, where you have a corporate client, communication between you and the employees of a corporate client may not be protected by LPP if the employee cannot be considered to be 'the client' for the purposes of the retainer. As such some employees will be clients, while others will not (*Three Rivers District Council* v *The Governor and Company of the Bank of England (No.5)* [2003] QB 1556).

It is not a breach of LPP to discuss a matter with your nominated officer for the purposes of receiving advice on whether to make a disclosure.

6.4.5 Crime/fraud exception

LPP protects advice you give to a client on avoiding committing a crime (*Bullivant* v *Att-Gen of Victoria* [1901] AC 196) or warning them that proposed actions could attract prosecution (*Butler* v *Board of Trade* [1971] Ch 680). LPP does not extend to documents which themselves form part of a criminal or fraudulent act, or communications which take place in order to obtain advice with the intention of carrying out an offence (*R* v *Cox & Railton* (1884) 14 QBD 153). It is irrelevant whether or not you are aware that you are being used for that purpose (*Banque Keyser Ullman* v *Skandia* [1986] 1 Lloyd's Rep 336).

Intention of furthering a criminal purpose

It is not just your client's intention which is relevant for the purpose of ascertaining whether information was communicated for the furtherance of a criminal purpose. It is also sufficient that a third party intends the lawyer/client communication to be made with that purpose (e.g. where the innocent client is being used by a third party) (*R* v *Central Criminal Court*, ex p. *Francis & Francis* [1989] 1 AC 346).

Knowing a transaction constitutes an offence

If you know the transaction you're working on is a principal offence [see 5.4 of this practice note], you risk committing an offence yourself. In these circumstances, communications relating to such a transaction are not privileged and should be disclosed.

Suspecting a transaction constitutes an offence

If you merely suspect a transaction might constitute a money laundering offence, the position is more complex. If the suspicions are correct, communications with the client are not privileged. If the suspicions are unfounded, the communications should remain privileged and are therefore non-disclosable.

Prima facie evidence

If you suspect you are unwittingly being involved by your client in a fraud, the courts require prima facie evidence before LPP can be displaced (*O'Rourke* v *Darbishire* [1920] AC 581). The sufficiency of that evidence depends on the circumstances: it is easier to infer a prima facie case where there is substantial material available to support an inference of fraud. While you may decide yourself if prima facie evidence exists, you may also ask the court for directions (*Finers* v *Miro* [1991] 1 WLR 35).

The Crown Prosecution Service guidance for prosecutors indicates that if a solicitor forms a genuine, but mistaken, belief that the privileged circumstances exemption (see 6.5 below) applies (for example, the client misleads the solicitor and uses the advice received for a criminal purpose) the solicitor will be able to rely on the reasonable excuse defence. It is likely that a similar approach would be taken with respect to a genuine, but mistaken, belief that LPP applies.

We believe you should not make a disclosure unless you know of prima facie evidence that you are being used in the furtherance of a crime.

6.5   Privileged circumstances

Quite separately from LPP, POCA recognises another type of communication, one which is given or received in 'privileged circumstances'. This is not the same as LPP, it is merely an exemption from certain provisions of POCA, although in many cases the communication will also be covered by LPP.

The privileged circumstances exemptions are found in the following places:

- POCA – section 330(10) and (11);
- POCA – section 333D(2) (repealing and replacing s.333(3));
- POCA – section 342(4);
- Terrorism Act – section 19(3) and (5);
- Terrorism Act – section 21A(8);
- Terrorism Act – section 21G(2).

Although the wording is not exactly the same in all these sections, the essential elements of the exemption are:

- you are a professional legal adviser;
- the information or material is communicated to you:

    - by your client or their representative in connection with you giving legal advice;
    - by the client or their representative in connection with them seeking legal advice from you;
    - by any person for the purpose of/in connection with actual or contemplated legal proceedings;

- the information or material cannot be communicated or given to you with a view to furthering a criminal purpose.

The offence of prejudicing an investigation was amended by section 342(3)(ba) to restrict to work outside the regulated sector. Therefore the privileged circumstances defence only applies to solicitors who are conducting work that falls outside the regulated sector.

The term professional legal adviser includes solicitors, their non-solicitor partners and their employees (see s.330(7A) of POCA), barristers and in-house lawyers.

The Society believes that the definition of a representative can be interpreted broadly.

Consider the crime/fraud exception when determining what constitutes the furthering of a criminal purpose.

Finally, section 330(9A) protects the privilege attaching to any disclosure made to a nominated officer for the purposes of obtaining advice about whether or not a disclosure should be made.

6.6   Differences between privileged circumstances and LPP

6.6.1   Protection of advice

When advice is given or received in circumstances where litigation is neither contemplated nor reasonably in prospect, except in very limited circumstances communications between you and third parties will not be protected under the advice arm of LPP.

Privileged circumstances, however, exempt communications regarding advice to be provided to representatives, so this may include communications with:

- a junior employee of a client;
- other professionals assisting in a transaction such as surveyors or estate agents.

6.6.2   Losing protection by dissemination

Under common law, privileged information can be shared within law firms without losing the protection of LPP and this can include other persons with a common interest, such as co-defendants (*Gotha City* v *Sotheby's (No.1)* [1998] 1 WLR 114). As such under common law, privileged material can be put into a data room for the purposes of a transaction and will remain privileged if it is stipulated that privilege is not waived.

For the privileged circumstances exemption to apply, the information must actually be exchanged for the purpose of giving or seeking legal advice. As such the protection is likely to be lost if information is put in a data room and viewed by the other side.

6.6.3   Vulnerability to seizure

It is important to correctly identify whether communications are protected by LPP or if they are merely covered by the privileged circumstances exemption. This is because the privileged circumstances exemption exempts you from certain POCA provisions. It does not provide any of the other LPP protections to those communications. Therefore a communication which is only covered by privileged circumstances, not LPP, will still remain vulnerable to seizure or production under a court order or other such notice from law enforcement.

6.7   When do I disclose?

If the communication is covered by LPP and the crime/fraud exception does not apply, you cannot make a disclosure under POCA.

If the communication was received in privileged circumstances and the crime/fraud exception does not apply, you are exempt from the relevant provisions of POCA, which include making a disclosure to SOCA.

If neither of these situations applies, the communication will still be confidential. However, the material is disclosable under POCA and can be disclosed, whether as an authorised disclosure, or to avoid breaching section 330. Section 337 of POCA permits you to make such a disclosure and provides that you will not be in breach of your professional duty of confidentiality when you do so.

Chapter 7 – Terrorist property offences

7.1   General comments

Terrorist organisations require funds to plan and carry out attacks, train militants, pay their operatives and promote their ideologies. The Terrorism Act 2000 (as amended) criminalises not only the participation in terrorist activities but also the provision of monetary support for terrorist purposes.

7.2   Application

All persons are required to comply with the Terrorism Act. The principal terrorist property offences in ss.15–18 apply to all persons and therefore to all solicitors. However, the specific offence of failure to disclose and the two tipping off offences apply only to persons in the regulated sector.

The definition of business in the regulated sector was amended by the Terrorism Act 2000 (Business in the Regulated Sector and Supervisory Authorities) Order 2007 to reflect changes brought about by the third money laundering directive. There are similar changes to the definition of business in the regulated sector in the Proceeds of Crime Act 2002.

7.3   Principal terrorist property offences

7.3.1   Section 15 – fundraising

It is an offence to be involved in fundraising if you have knowledge or reasonable cause to suspect that the money or other property raised may be used for terrorist purposes. You can commit the offence by:

- inviting others to make contributions;
- receiving contributions;
- making contributions towards terrorist funding, including making gifts and loans.

It is no defence that the money or other property is a payment for goods and services.

7.3.2   Section 16 – use or possession

It is an offence to use or possess money or other property for terrorist purposes, including when you have reasonable cause to suspect they may be used for these purposes.

7.3.3   Section 17 – arrangements

It is an offence to become involved in an arrangement which makes money or other property available to another if you know, or have reasonable cause to suspect it may be used for terrorist purposes.

7.3.4   Section 18 – money laundering

It is an offence to enter into or become concerned in an arrangement facilitating the retention or control of terrorist property by, or on behalf of, another person including, but not limited to the following ways:

- by concealment;
- by removal from the jurisdiction;
- by transfer to nominees.

It is a defence if you did not know, and had no reasonable cause to suspect, that the arrangement related to terrorist property.

Read about arrangements under POCA in Chapter 5 [of this practice note].

7.4 Defences to principal terrorist property offences

The TACT [and POCA] Regulations 2007 of 26 December 2007 introduced three new defences to the main offences in ss.15–18. These defences are contained in ss.21ZA–21ZC.

- Prior consent defence – you make a disclosure to an authorised person before becoming involved in a transaction or an arrangement, and the person acts with the consent of an authorised officer.
- Consent defence – you are already involved in a transaction or arrangement and make a disclosure, so long as there is a reasonable excuse for failure to make a disclosure in advance.
- Reasonable excuse defence – you intended to make a disclosure but have a reasonable excuse for failing to do so. See 5.7.1 [of this practice note] on reasonable excuse.

Read Chapter 8 [of this practice note] for more information on how to make a disclosure and gaining consent.

There are further defences relating to co-operation with the police in s.21. You do not commit an offence under ss.15–18 in the following further circumstances:

- You are acting with the express consent of a constable, including civilian staff at SOCA.
- You disclose your suspicion or belief to a constable or SOCA after you become involved in an arrangement or transaction that concerns money or terrorist property, and you provide the information on which your suspicion or belief is based. You must make this disclosure on your own initiative and as soon as reasonably practicable.

The defence of disclosure to a constable or SOCA is also available to an employee who makes a disclosure about terrorist property offences in accordance with the internal reporting procedures laid down by the firm.

7.5 Failure to disclose offences

7.5.1 Non-regulated sector

Section 19 provides that anyone, whether they are a nominated officer or not, must disclose as soon as reasonably practicable to a constable, or SOCA, if they know or suspect that another person has committed a terrorist financing offence based on information which came to them in the course of a trade, profession or employment. The test is subjective.

7.5.2   Regulated sector

Section 21A, inserted by the Anti-Terrorism Crime and Security Act 2001, creates a criminal offence for those in the regulated sector who fail to make a disclosure to either a constable or the firm's nominated officer where there are reasonable grounds for suspecting that another person has committed an offence. This was further expanded by the TACT [and POCA] Regulations 2007 to cover failure to disclose an attempted offence under sections 15–18.

7.6   Defences to failing to disclose

The following are defences to failure to disclose offences under both section 19 and section 21A. Either:

- you had a reasonable excuse for not making the disclosure; or
- you received the information on which the belief or suspicion is based in privileged circumstances, without an intention of furthering a criminal purpose.

The TACT [and POCA] Regulations 2007 introduced an additional defence for those in the regulated sector. A person has a defence where they are employed or are in partnership with a solicitor to provide assistance and support and they receive information concerning terrorist property in privileged circumstances.

Read about privileged circumstances in 5.7.2 [of this practice note].

It is also a defence under section 19 if you made an internal report in accordance with your employer's reporting procedures.

7.7   Section 21D tipping off offences: regulated sector

- Section 21D(1) – disclosing a suspicious activity report (SAR). It is an offence to disclose to a third person that a SAR has been made by any person to the police, HM Revenue and Customs, SOCA or a nominated officer, if that disclosure might prejudice any investigation that might be carried out as a result of the SAR. This offence can only be committed:

    - after a disclosure to SOCA or a nominated officer;
    - if you know or suspect that by disclosing this information, you are likely to prejudice any investigation related to that SAR;
    - [if] the information upon which the disclosure is based came to you in the course of business in the regulated sector.

- Section 21D(3) – disclosing an investigation. It is an offence to disclose that an investigation into allegations relating to terrorist property offences is being contemplated or carried out if that disclosure is likely to prejudice that investigation. The offence can only be committed if the information on which the disclosure is based came to the person in the course of business in the regulated sector. The key point is that you can commit this offence, even where you are unaware that a SAR was submitted.

7.8   Defences to tipping off

7.8.1   Section 21E – disclosures within an undertaking or group, etc.

It is not an offence if an employee, officer or partner of a firm discloses that a SAR has been made if it is to an employee, officer or partner of the same undertaking.

A solicitor will not commit a tipping off offence if a disclosure is made to another lawyer either:

- within a different undertaking provided that both parties carry on business in an EEA state;
- in a country or territory that imposes money laundering requirements equivalent to the EU, and both parties share common ownership, management or control.

7.8.2   Section 21F – other permitted disclosures

A solicitor will not commit a tipping off offence if all the following criteria are met:

- The disclosure is made to another lawyer in an EEA state, or one having an equivalent AML regime.
- The disclosure relates to a client or former client of both parties, or a transaction involving them both, or the provision of a service involving them both.
- The disclosure is made for the purpose of preventing a money laundering offence.
- Both parties have equivalent professional duties of confidentiality and protection of personal data.

7.8.3   Section 21G – limited exception for professional legal advisers

A solicitor will not commit a tipping off offence if the disclosure is to a client and it is made for the purpose of dissuading the client from engaging in conduct amounting to an offence. This exception and the tipping off offence in section 21D apply to the regulated sector.

7.9   Other terrorist property offences in statutory instruments

The Al Qaida and Taliban (United Nations Measures) Order 2006 and the Terrorism (United Nations Measures) Order 2006 create offences of providing funds or economic resources to terrorists. Terrorists can be funded from legitimately obtained income, including charitable donations, so it is difficult to know at what stage legitimate earnings become terrorist assets.

It may be helpful to consult:

- **www.hm-treasury.gov.uk** – the consolidated sanctions list of the names of suspected terrorists maintained by HM Treasury;
- **www.homeoffice.gov.uk** – a list of proscribed organisations maintained by the Home Office.

7.10   Making enquiries of a client

You will often make preliminary enquiries of your client, or a third party, to obtain further information to help you to decide whether you have a suspicion. You may also need to raise questions during a retainer to clarify such issues.

These enquiries will only amount to tipping off if you disclose that a suspicious activity report has been made, or that an investigation into allegations relating to terrorist property offences is being carried out or contemplated.

Chapter 8 – Making a disclosure

8.1   General comments

The disclosure regime for money laundering and terrorist financing is run by the financial intelligence unit within the Serious Organised Crime Agency (SOCA). SOCA was created on 3 April 2006 by the Serious Organised Crime and Police Act 2005. It is a law enforcement body devoted to dealing with organised crime within the UK and networking with other law enforcement agencies to combat global organised crime.

For full details on SOCA and their activities view their website at: **www.soca.gov.uk**.

8.2   Application

All persons within the regulated sector and nominated officers have obligations under POCA to make disclosures of suspicions of money laundering.

In addition any person may need to make an authorised disclosure about criminal property.

All persons are required to make disclosures to SOCA of suspected terrorist financing.

8.3   Suspicious activity reports

8.3.1   What is a SAR?

A suspicious activity report (SAR) is the name given to the making of a disclosure to SOCA under either POCA or the Terrorism Act.

8.3.2   Who discloses?

Where a firm has a nominated officer, either they or their deputy will make the SAR to SOCA.

8.3.3   When?

You must make a SAR as soon as you are suspicious or know of terrorist financing or money laundering (subject to privilege considerations). Swiftly made SARs avoid delays in fulfilling your client's instructions.

You do not need to wait to ascertain whether or not a person is actually your client before making the disclosure. A SAR can be made about any person whom you suspect is involved in money laundering or terrorist financing.

8.3.4   Types of disclosures

Reports can either take the form of a SAR or a limited intelligence value report (LIVR). SARs will generally be the normal method of reporting, particularly where consent is required; however, LIVRs may be appropriate where you know that a law enforcement agency already has an interest in a matter. SOCA has provided detailed information [**www.soca.gov.uk/ downloads/LIVGuidance.pdf**] on when LIVRs should be used. If in doubt, complete a SAR form.

8.3.5   How to disclose

Forms

SOCA has issued a preferred form to be completed when making a SAR, which is likely to become mandatory in the near future. Criminal penalties will apply for its non-use. We encourage you to start using the preferred form now.

SARs online

You should use SARs online where you have computer access. This securely encrypted system provided by SOCA allows you to:

- register your firm and relevant contact persons;
- submit a SAR at any time of day;
- receive e-mail confirmations of each SAR submitted.

Post or fax

SARs can still be submitted in hard copy, although they should be typed and on the preferred form. You will not receive acknowledgement of any SARs sent this way. Where you require consent you should send by fax not by post.

Hard copy SARs should be sent to:
Fax: 020 7238 8256
Post: UK FIU
PO Box 8000
London SE11 5EN

8.3.6   Information to include

SOCA has provided information on completing the preferred SARs form [**www.soca.gov.uk**].

To speed up consideration of your SAR, it is recommended that you use SOCA's glossary of codes for each reason for suspicion section of the report.

Your regulator number is your firm's ID number. Find this at **www. solicitors-online.com** or by calling the Solicitors Regulation Authority on 0870 606 2555.

8.3.7   Getting consent from SOCA to proceed

You will often be asking SOCA for consent to undertake acts which would be prohibited as a principal money laundering offence. From 26 December 2007, the Terrorism Act 2000 and Proceeds of Crime Act 2002 (Amendment) Regulations 2007 enter force, introducing a consent defence to sections 15–18 of the Terrorism Act 2000. The Regulations introduce s.21ZA, which provides a defence if you made a disclosure to an authorised person before becoming involved in a transaction or an arrangement, and the person acts with the consent of an authorised officer.

While SOCA has produced information on obtaining consent, here are a number of key points to remember:

- You only receive consent to the extent to which you asked for it. So it is vital you clearly outline all the remaining steps in the transaction that could be a prohibited act. For example:

  > We seek consent to finalise an agreement for sale of property X and to then transfer property X into the name of (purchaser) and following payment of disbursements, pay the proceeds of the sale of the property to (seller).

- The initial notice period is seven working days after the SAR is made, and if consent is refused, the moratorium period is a further 31 calendar days from the date of refusal. If you need consent sooner, you should clearly state the reasons for the urgency in the initial report and perhaps contact SOCA to discuss the situation. SOCA can sometimes give consent in a matter of hours.
- Within the notice and moratorium period you must not do a prohibited act. However this will not prevent you taking other actions on the file, such as writing letters, conducting searches, etc.
- SOCA will contact you by telephone to advise that consent has been provided and will then send a follow up letter.

8.3.8   Talking to a SOCA representative

The Financial Intelligence Helpdesk can be contacted on 020 7238 8282. You can contact SOCA on this number for:

- help in submitting a SAR or with the SARs online system;
- help on consent issues;
- assessing the risk of tipping off so you know whether disclosing information about a particular SAR would prejudice an investigation.

8.3.9   Confidentiality of SARs

SOCA is required to treat your SARs confidentially. Where information from a SAR is disclosed for the purposes of law enforcement, care is taken to ensure that the identity of the reporter and their firm is not disclosed to other persons.

If you have specific concerns regarding your safety if you make a SAR, you should raise this with SOCA either in the report or through the helpdesk.

If you fear the confidentiality of a SAR you made has been breached call the SARs confidentiality breach line on 0800 234 6657. In addition, you can e-mail the Law Society at antimoneylaundering@ lawsociety.org. uk, so that we can continue to monitor this issue for discussion with SOCA.

8.4   Feedback on SARs

SOCA provides some feedback on the value of SARs they have received, although such feedback will always be anonymised to protect the confidentiality of those who submitted it. Feedback is provided:

* on their website;
* in their annual reports;
* during SOCA legal sector seminars, details of which are advertised in the Law Society's AML newsletter – Gatekeeper.

Chapter 9 – Enforcement

9.1   General comments

The UK AML/CTF regime is one of the most robust in Europe. Breaches of obligations under the regime are backed by disciplinary and criminal penalties.

Law enforcement agencies and regulators are working co-operatively with the regulated sector specifically and solicitors generally to assist compliance and increase understanding of how to effectively mitigate risks. However, be in no doubt of the seriousness of the sanctions for a failure to comply, nor the willingness of supervisory and enforcement bodies to take appropriate action against non-compliance.

9.2 Supervision under the regulations

Regulation 23 [of the Money Laundering Regulations 2007] provides for several bodies to be supervisory authorities for different parts of the regulated sector.

Where a person in the regulated sector is covered by more than one supervisory authority, either the joint supervisory authorities must negotiate who is to be the sole supervisor of the person, or they must co-operate in the performance of their supervisory duties.

A supervisory authority must:

- monitor effectively the persons it is responsible for;
- take necessary measures to ensure their compliance with the requirements of the regulations;
- report to SOCA any suspicion that a person it is responsible for has engaged in money laundering or terrorist financing.

9.2.1 Solicitors Regulation Authority

The supervisory authority listed in the regulations for solicitors in England and Wales is the Law Society of England and Wales. This responsibility has been delegated in practice to the Solicitors Regulation Authority (SRA).

9.2.2 Other supervisors

Other supervisory authorities which may be of relevance to some solicitors include:

- the Financial Services Authority – **www.fsa.org.uk**;
- the Insolvency Practitioners Association – **www.insolvency-practitioners.org.uk**;
- the Council of Licensed Conveyancers – **www.theclc.gov.uk**;
- the Chartered Institute of Taxation – **www.tax.org.uk**.

Where the SRA reaches agreement with another supervisor about who is to be the supervisory authority for the solicitor, this agreement will be made known to the solicitor in accordance with regulation 23(3).

In all other cases of supervisory overlap, and where you have questions about AML supervision, contact the SRA.

The SRA will be publishing information for trust and company service providers who are regulated by the SRA and are authorised persons. Details will appear on the SRA's website at **www.sra.org.uk**, and the Law Society's website at **www.lawsociety.org.uk/moneylaundering**.

The Joint Money Laundering Steering Group (JMLSG) provides guidance to the financial sector which the FSA considers when assessing compliance with AML/CTF obligations.

9.2.3   Enforcement powers under the regulations

Part 5 of the regulations gives designated authorities a variety of powers for performing their functions under the regulations. They can also impose civil penalties for non-compliance.

The powers are:

- regulation 37: power to require information from, and attendance of, relevant and connected persons without a warrant;
- regulation 38: power to enter and inspect without a warrant;
- regulation 39: power to obtain a warrant to do things under regulations 37 and 38;
- regulation 40: power to obtain a court order requiring compliance with regulation 37.

HM Treasury has stated that designated authorities may use these powers in their role as supervisor, and only on those relevant persons they supervise.

9.3   Disciplinary action

Conduct which fails to comply with AML/CTF obligations may also be a breach of rule 5 of the Solicitors' Code of Conduct 2007, and result in disciplinary action by the SRA.

For further information on the Solicitors' Code of Conduct go to **www.sra.org.uk** or contact the professional ethics helpline on 0870 606 2577 (inside the UK), 1100 to 1300 and 1400 to 1600, Monday to Friday.

9.4   Offences and penalties

Not complying with AML/CTF obligations puts you at risk of committing criminal offences. Below is a summary of the offences and the relevant penalties. In addition to the principal offences, you could also be charged with offences of conspiracy, attempt, counselling, aiding, abetting or procuring a principal offence, depending on the circumstances.

9.4.1 POCA

Section	Description	Penalty
327	Conceals, disguises, converts, transfers or removes criminal property	On summary conviction – up to six months' imprisonment or a fine or both
		On indictment – up to 14 years' imprisonment or a fine or both
328	Arrangements regarding criminal property	
329	Acquires, uses or has possession of criminal property	
330	Failure to disclose knowledge, suspicion or reasonable grounds for suspicion of money laundering – regulated sector	On summary conviction – up to six months' imprisonment or a fine or both
		On indictment – up to five years' imprisonment or a fine or both
331	Failure to disclose knowledge, suspicion or reasonable grounds for suspicion of money laundering – nominated officer in the regulated sector	
332	Failure to disclose knowledge or suspicion of money laundering – nominated officer in non-regulated sector	
333	Tipping off – before 26 December 2007	On summary conviction – up to six months' imprisonment or a fine or both
333A	Tipping off – regulated sector	On summary conviction – up to three months' imprisonment or a fine not exceeding level 5 or both
		On conviction on indictment – up to two years' imprisonment or a fine or both
342	Prejudicing an investigation	On indictment – up to five years' imprisonment or a fine or both

9.4.2   Terrorism Act

Section	Description	Penalty
15	Fundraising	On summary conviction – up to six months' imprisonment or a fine or both
		On indictment – up to 14 years' imprisonment or a fine or both
16	Use and possession	
17	Funding arrangements	
18	Money laundering	
19	Failure to disclose	
21A	Failure to disclose – regulated sector	
21	Tipping off – regulated sector	On summary conviction – up to three months' imprisonment or a fine not exceeding level 5 on the standard scale, or both
		On conviction on indictment – up to two years' imprisonment, or a fine or both

9.4.3   Regulations

Regulation 45 [of the Money Laundering Regulations 2007] lists a number of sections, the breach of which is an offence.

Section	Description	Penalty
7(1)	Applying CDD to new customers	On summary conviction – a fine
		On indictment – up to two years' imprisonment or a fine or both
7(2)	Applying CDD to existing customers	
7(3)	Determining extent of CDD on a risk-sensitive basis and being able to demonstrate this to the SRA	
8(1)	Conducting ongoing monitoring	
8(3)	Determining extent of ongoing monitoring on a risk-sensitive basis and being able to demonstrate this to the SRA	
9(2)	Verification prior to the establishment of a business relationship or carrying out of an occasional transaction	
11(1)(a)	Not use a bank account without CDD	
11(1)(b)	Not establish a business relationship or carry out an occasional transaction if no CDD	

Section	Description	Penalty
11(1)(c)	Terminate existing relationship or occasional transaction if no CDD	
14(1)	Conduct enhanced due diligence	
15(1)	Relates to financial and credit institutions	
15(2)		
16(1)		
16(2)		
16(3)		
16(4)		
19(1)	Keep your own records	
19(4)	Keep records others have relied on	
19(5)	Be prepared to provide records others have relied on	
19(6)	Ensure those you rely on are willing to provide records	
20(1)	Establish policies and procedures	
21	Train relevant employees	
26	Does not relate to solicitors	
27(4)		
33		
Directions under 18	Not to act where Treasury makes a direction	

9.5   Joint liability

Regulation 47 provides that offences under the regulations can be committed by a firm as a whole, whether it is a body corporate, partnership or unincorporated association.

However, if it can be shown that the offence was committed with the consent, contrivance or neglect of an officer, partner or member, then both the firm and the individual can be liable.

9.[6]   Prosecution authorities

The Crown Prosecution Service is a prosecuting authority for offences under POCA, the Terrorism Act and the regulations.

The Revenue and Customs Prosecutions Office is a prosecuting authority for offences under POCA and the regulations.

The FSA is a prosecuting authority under POCA and the regulations as a result of section 402 of the Financial Services and Markets Act 2000.

The Office of Fair Trading, the Local Weights and Measures Authority and the Department of Enterprise, Trade and Investment in Northern Ireland are all prosecuting authorities for breaches of the regulations.

Chapter 10 – Civil liability

10.1   General comments

The Proceeds of Crime Act 2002 aims to deprive wrongdoers of the benefits of crime, not compensate the victims. The civil law provides an opportunity for victims to take action against wrongdoers and those who have assisted them, through a claim for constructive trusteeship. Victims often target the professional adviser in civil claims because they are more likely to be able to pay compensation, often by reason of their professional indemnity cover.

If you believe that you may have acted as a constructive trustee, you should seek legal advice.

10.2   Constructive trusteeship

Constructive trusteeship arises as a result of your interference with trust property or involvement in a breach of fiduciary duty. These are traditionally described respectively as knowing receipt and knowing assistance.

Your liability in either case is personal, an equitable liability to account, not proprietary. A constructive trustee has to restore the value of the property they have received or compensate the claimant for the loss resulting from the assistance with a breach of trust or fiduciary duty. See Lord Millett in *Dubai Aluminium Co Ltd* v *Salaam* [2002] 3 WLR 1913, 1933.

The state of your knowledge is key to this liability. Records of CDD [3.8 of this practice note] measures undertaken and disclosures or your notes provide evidence of your knowledge and intentions.

10.3   Knowing receipt

Liability for knowing receipt will exist where a person receives property in circumstances where the property is subject to a trust or fiduciary duty and contrary to that trust applies the property for their use and benefit. Considering each element in turn:

10.3.1   Receipt

- You must have received the property in which the claimant has an equitable proprietary interest.
- The property must be received:

- – in breach of trust;
- – in breach of a fiduciary duty; or
- – legitimately, but then misapplied.

10.3.2 For your use and benefit

When you receive money, e.g. as an agent, or, as in the case of a solicitor's client account, as a trustee of a bare trust, then you are not liable for knowing receipt as it is not received for your use or benefit. You may however still be liable for knowing assistance.

Receiving funds that you apply in satisfaction of your fees will however be beneficial receipt and could amount to knowing receipt.

10.3.3 You must be at fault

What constitutes fault here is the subject of some debate. The Court of Appeal in *BCCI* v *Akindele* [2001] Ch 437 held that the test is whether you acted unconscionably. The test is a subjective one which includes actual knowledge and wilful blindness. The factors the court identified were that:

1. You need not have acted dishonestly. It is enough to know a fiduciary or trust duty has been breached.

2. Your knowledge of funds' provenance should be such that it was unconscionable for you to retain any benefit.

It's unclear whether a reckless failure to make enquiries a reasonable person would have made would be sufficient to establish liability. In *Dubai Aluminium Co Ltd* v *Salaam* [2002] 3 WLR 1913, 1933 Lord Millett described knowing receipt as dishonest assistance. However, that may well have been specific to the particular facts he was considering.

10.4 Knowing assistance

If you help in a breach of fiduciary or trust duties then you are personally liable for the damage and loss caused. See *Twinsectra* v *Yardley* [2002] WLR 802.

The requirements to establish liability of this kind are:

10.4.1 Assistance in a breach of trust or fiduciary duty

The breach need not have been fraudulent (see *Royal Brunei Airlines* v *Tan* [1995] 2 AC 378), and you do not need to know the full details of the trust arrangements you help to breach, nor the obligations incumbent on a trustee/fiduciary.

You assist if you either:

- know that the person you are assisting is not entitled to do the things that they are doing;
- have sufficient ground for suspicion of this.

10.4.2   You must be at fault

There must be dishonesty, not just knowledge. The test for dishonesty is objective. The Privy Council in *Eurotrust* v *Barlow Clowes* [2006] 1 All ER stated that the test is whether your conduct is dishonest by the standards of reasonable and honest people, taking into account your specific characteristics and context, i.e. your intelligence, knowledge at the relevant time, and your experience.

Conscious impropriety is not required; it is enough to have shown wilful blindness by deliberately failing to make the enquiries that a reasonable and honest person would make.

10.5   Making a disclosure to SOCA

10.5.1   Risk of defensive disclosure to SOCA

Where you suspect or know your clients are involving you in circumstances that could amount to one of the principal money laundering offences, you must disclose your suspicions to SOCA, subject to the constraints of LPP, and obtain their permission before allowing the transaction to proceed.

Consent from SOCA only protects you from falling foul of the anti-money laundering regime. It will not defend you from civil liability. In fact, obtaining consent may create the very evidence on which a claimant can rely to found a civil liability.

It is therefore vital that you only disclose to SOCA those situations fulfilling the statutory tests in Part 7 of POCA; knowledge or suspicion of money laundering, or reasonable grounds to suspect money laundering.

10.5.2   While awaiting consent from SOCA

Your position can be difficult. While the client will be expecting you to implement their instructions, you may be unable to do so, or give explanations, as you may risk a tipping off offence.

The client may seek a court order for the return of the funds on the basis that you are breaching their retainer.

Case law provides no direct authority on the point, but a recent ruling on the obligations of banks is helpful in suggesting the courts' likely view of the obligations imposed on solicitors. In *K v NatWest* [2007] 1 WLR 311 the Court of Appeal ruled that a bank's contract with the customer was suspended whilst the moratorium period was in place, so the customer had no right to an injunction for return of monies. The court also said that as a matter of discretion, the court would not force the bank to commit a crime.

The Court of Appeal also approved the use of a letter to the court from the bank as evidence of its suspicion. Provision of evidence in these circumstances is permitted under s.333(2)(b) of Proceeds of Crime Act as an exception to the tipping off provisions.

10.5.3   Where SOCA consents

In continuing with a transaction you will have to show that either:

*   Although you had sufficient suspicion to justify a disclosure to SOCA, your concerns were not such as to render them accountable on a constructive trustee basis. Courts are likely to take into account the fact that you will generally operate in the regulated sector, and assume a degree of sophistication as a result of anti-money laundering training. Solicitors are expected to be able to account for decisions to proceed with transactions.
*   Your suspicions were either removed or reduced by subsequent information or investigations.

The courts have provided limited assistance in this area. *Bank of Scotland v A Limited* [2001] 1 WLR 751 stated that complying with a client's instructions was a commercial risk which a bank had to take. While the court gave some reassurance on the unlikelihood of any finding of dishonesty against an institution that had sought guidance from the court and did not pay funds away, this is of limited assistance because it is for the positive act of paying away funds that protection will be needed.

Such protection is not readily available. In *Amalgamated Metal Trading v City of London Police* [2003] 1 WLR 2711 the court held that while a court could make a declaration on whether particular funds were the proceeds of crime, a full hearing would be required with both the potential victim and the client participating. There would have to be proof on the balance of probabilities that the funds were not the proceeds of crime. In practice this is highly unlikely to be practical.

10.6   Notify your professional indemnity insurers

You must notify your insurers at the earliest opportunity of any circumstances that might give rise to a claim. You should consider notifying your insurers whenever you make a disclosure to SOCA. In particular:

- you may be unable to follow clients' instructions, e.g.:

    - where consent has not been given by SOCA;
    - where you judge you may be exposing yourself to a civil claim, so may face a claim from the client for failure to meet the terms of your retainer;

- SOCA has given consent, but where you fear civil liability. Consider whether to not proceed with the transaction.

Any disclosure made to insurers should clearly state any money laundering issues, that a disclosure has been made to SOCA and, if known, SOCA's response.

Chapter 11 – Money laundering warning signs

11.1   General comments

The Money Laundering Regulations 2007 require you to conduct ongoing monitoring of your business relationships and take steps to be aware of transactions with heightened money laundering or counter-terrorist financing risks.

The Proceeds of Crime Act 2002 requires you to report suspicious transactions.

This chapter highlights a number of warning signs for solicitors generally and for those working in specific sectors, to help you decide whether you have reasons for concern or the basis for a disclosable suspicion.

11.2   General warning signs

Because money launderers are always developing new techniques, no list of examples can be fully comprehensive; however, here are some key factors which may heighten a client's risk profile or give you cause for concern.

11.2.1 Secretive clients

While face-to-face contact with clients is not always necessary, an excessively obstructive or secretive client may be a cause for concern.

11.2.2 Unusual instructions

Instructions that are unusual in themselves, or that are unusual for your firm or your client, may give rise to a cause for concern.

Instructions outside your firm's area of expertise

Taking on work which is outside your firm's normal range of expertise can be risky because money launderers might use such firms to avoid answering too many questions. An inexperienced solicitor might be influenced into taking steps which a more experienced solicitor would not contemplate. Be wary of instructions in niche areas of work in which your firm has no background, but in which the client claims to be an expert.

If your client is based a long way from your offices, consider why you have been instructed. For example, have your services been recommended by another client or is the matter based near your firm? Making these types of enquiries makes good business sense as well as being a sensible anti-money laundering check.

Changing instructions

Instructions or cases that change unexpectedly might be suspicious, especially if there seems to be no logical reason for the changes.

The following situations could give rise to a cause for concern. Consider the Solicitors' Accounts Rules [**www.sra.org.uk/accounts-rules**] if appropriate.

- A client deposits funds into your client account but then ends the transaction for no apparent reason.
- A client tells you that funds are coming from one source and at the last minute the source changes.
- A client unexpectedly asks you to send money received into your client account back to its source, to the client or to a third party.

Unusual retainers

Be wary of:

- disputes which are settled too easily as this may indicate sham litigation;
- loss-making transactions where the loss is avoidable;

- dealing with money or property where you suspect that either is being transferred to avoid the attention of a trustee in a bankruptcy case, HMRC, or a law enforcement agency;
- settlements paid in cash, or paid directly between parties – for example, if cash is passed directly between sellers and buyers without adequate explanation, it is possible that mortgage fraud or tax evasion is taking place;
- complex or unusually large transactions;
- unusual patterns of transactions which have no apparent economic purpose.

11.2.3   Use of client accounts

Only use client accounts to hold client money for legitimate transactions for clients, or for another proper legal purpose. Putting dirty money through a solicitor's client account can clean it, whether the money is sent back to the client, on to a third party, or invested in some way. Introducing cash into a banking system can become part of the placement stage of money laundering. Therefore, the use of cash may be a warning sign.

Solicitors should not provide a banking service for their clients. However, it can be difficult to draw a distinction between holding client money for a legitimate transaction and acting more like a bank.

For example, when the proceeds of a sale are left with your firm to make payments, these payments may be to mainstream loan companies, but they may also be to more obscure recipients, including private individuals, whose identity is difficult or impossible to check.

Establish a policy on handling cash

Large payments made in actual cash may also be a sign of money laundering. It is good practice to establish a policy of not accepting cash payments above a certain limit either at your office or into your bank account.

Clients may attempt to circumvent such a policy by depositing cash directly into your client account at a bank. You may consider advising clients in such circumstances that they might encounter a delay in completion of the final transaction. Avoid disclosing your client account details as far as possible and make it clear that electronic transfer of funds is expected.

If a cash deposit is received, you will need to consider whether you think there is a risk of money laundering taking place and whether it is a circumstance requiring a disclosure to SOCA.

Source of funds

Accounts staff should monitor whether funds received from clients are from credible sources. For example, it is reasonable for monies to be received from a company if your client is a director of that company and has the authority to use company money for the transaction.

However, if funding is from a source other than your client, you may need to make further enquiries, especially if the client has not told you what they intend to do with the funds before depositing them into your account. If you decide to accept funds from a third party, perhaps because time is short, ask how and why the third party is helping with the funding.

You do not have to make enquiries into every source of funding from other parties. However, you must always be alert to warning signs and in some cases you will need to get more information.

In some circumstances, cleared funds will be essential for transactions and clients may want to provide cash to meet a completion deadline. Assess the risk in these cases and ask questions if necessary.

Disclosing client account details

Think carefully before you disclose your client account details. They allow money to be deposited into your accounts without your knowledge. If you need to provide your account details, ask the client where the funds will be coming from. Will it be an account in their name, from the UK or abroad? Consider whether you are prepared to accept funds from any source that you are concerned about.

Keep the circulation of client account details to a minimum. Discourage clients from passing the details on to third parties and ask them to use the account details only for previously agreed purposes.

11.2.4   Suspect territory

While there are no longer any countries currently listed on the FATF non co-operative and compliant territories list, this does not mean that all have anti-money laundering standards equivalent to those in the UK. Retainers involving countries which do not have comparative money laundering standards may increase the risk profile of the retainer. The International Bar Association provides a summary of money laundering legislation around the world at: **www.anti-moneylaundering.org**.

Consider whether extra precautions should be taken when dealing with funds or clients from a particular jurisdiction. This is especially important if the client or funds come from a jurisdiction where the production of drugs, drug trafficking, terrorism or corruption is prevalent.

You can also check whether your client is a proscribed person on the HM Treasury's sanctions lists [**www.hm-treasury.gov.uk**].

Transparency International provides a corruption perception index [**www.transparency.org**] which may help when you are considering dealing with clients from other countries.

11.3   Private client work

11.3.1   Administration of estates

The administration of estates is a regulated activity. A deceased person's estate is very unlikely to be actively utilised by criminals as a means for laundering their funds; however, there is still a low risk of money laundering for those working in this area.

Source of funds

When you are acting either as an executor, or for executors, there is no blanket requirement that you should be satisfied about the history of all of the funds which make up the estate under administration; however you should be aware of the factors which can increase money laundering risks.

Consider the following when administering an estate:

- where estate assets have been earned in a foreign jurisdiction, be aware of the wide definition of criminal conduct in POCA and the provisions relating to overseas criminal conduct;
- where estate assets have been earned or are located in a suspect territory, you may need to make further checks about the source of those funds.

The wide nature of the offences of 'acquisition, use and possession' in section 329 of POCA may lead to a money laundering offence being committed at an early point in the administration. The section 328 offence may also be relevant.

Be alert from the outset and monitor throughout so that any disclosure can be considered as soon as knowledge or suspicion is formed and problems of delayed consent are avoided. A key benefit of the *Bowman* v *Fels* judgment is that a solicitor who makes a disclosure is now able to continue work on the matter, so long as they do not transfer funds or take any other irrevocable step.

How the estate may include criminal property

An extreme example would be where you know or suspect that the deceased person was accused or convicted of acquisitive criminal conduct during their lifetime.

If you know or suspect that the deceased person improperly claimed welfare benefits or had evaded the due payment of tax during their lifetime, criminal property will be included in the estate and so a money laundering disclosure may be required. Information on the financial thresholds for benefits can be obtained from **www.dwp.gov.uk** or **www.hmrc.gov.uk**.

While administering an estate, you may discover or suspect that beneficiaries are not intending to pay the correct amount of tax or are avoiding some other financial charge (for example, by failing to disclose gifts received from the deceased less than seven years before death). Although these matters may not actually constitute money laundering (because no criminal conduct has yet occurred so there is no 'criminal property'), you should carefully consider their position in conduct terms with respect to rule 1.01 of the Solicitors' Code of Conduct.

Grant of probate

A UK grant of probate may be required before UK assets can be released, while for overseas assets the relevant local laws will apply. Remain alert to warning signs, for example if the deceased or their business interests are based in a suspect territory.

If the deceased person is from another jurisdiction and a lawyer is dealing with the matter in the home country, it may be helpful to ask that person for information about the deceased to gain some assurances that there are no suspicious circumstances surrounding the estate. The issue of the tax payable on the estate may depend on the jurisdiction concerned.

11.3.2 Trusts

Trust work is a regulated activity.

Trusts can be used as a money laundering vehicle. The key risk period for trusts is when the trust is set up, as if the funds going into the trust are clean, it is only by the trustees using them for criminal purposes that they may form the proceeds of crime.

When setting up a trust, be aware of general money laundering warning signs and consider whether the purpose of the trust could be to launder criminal property. Information about the purpose of the trust, including why any unusual structure or jurisdiction has been used, can help allay concerns. Similarly information about the provider of the funds and those who have control of the funds, as required by the Money Laundering Regulations 2007, will assist.

Whether you act as a trustee yourself, or for trustees, the nature of the work may already require information which will help in assessing money laundering risks, such as the location of assets and the identity of trustees. Again, any involvement of a suspect jurisdiction, especially those with strict bank secrecy and confidentiality rules, or without similar money laundering procedures, may increase the risk profile of the retainer.

If you think a money laundering offence has, or may have, been committed that relates to money or property which already forms part of the trust property, or is intended to do so, consider whether your instructions involve you in a section 328 arrangement offence. If they do, consider the options for making a disclosure.

11.3.3   Charities

In common with trusts, while the majority of charities are used for legitimate reasons, they can be used as money laundering/terrorist financing vehicles.

If you are acting for a charity, consider its purpose and the organisations it is aligned with. If you are receiving money on the charity's behalf from an individual or a company donor, or a bequest from an estate, be alert to unusual circumstances including large sums of money.

There is growing concern about the use of charities for terrorist funding. The Bank of England maintains a list of individuals and organisations for whom you may not provide regulated services [**www.hm-treasury. gov.uk/financialsanctions**].

11.3.4   Powers of attorney/deputyship

Whether acting as, or on behalf of, an attorney or deputy, you should remain alert to money laundering risks.

If you are acting as an attorney you may learn financial information about the donor relating, for example, to non-payment of tax or wrongful receipt of benefits. You will need to consider whether to make a disclosure to SOCA.

Where the public guardian has an interest – because of a deputyship or registered enduring power of attorney – consider whether the Office of the Public Guardian (OPG) needs to be informed. Informing the OPG is unlikely to be tipping off because it is unlikely to prejudice an investigation.

If you discover or suspect that a donee has already completed an improper financial transaction that may amount to a money laundering suspicion, a disclosure to SOCA may be required (depending on whether legal professional privilege applies). However, it may be difficult to decide whether you have a suspicion if the background to the information is a family dispute. You can get legal advice on this through the Law Society's AML directory.

11.4   Property work

11.4.1   Ownership issues

Properties owned by nominee companies or multiple owners may be used as money laundering vehicles to disguise the true owner and/or confuse the audit trail.

Be alert to sudden or unexplained changes in ownership. One form of laundering, known as flipping, involves a property purchase, often using someone else's identity. The property is then quickly sold for a much higher price to the same buyer using another identity. The proceeds of crime are mixed with mortgage funds for the purchase. This process may be repeated several times.

Another potential cause for concern is where a third party is providing the funding for a purchase, but the property is being registered in someone else's name. There may be legitimate reasons for this, such as a family arrangement, but you should be alert to the possibility of being misled about the true ownership of the property. You may wish to undertake further CDD measures [Chapter 4 of this practice note] on the person providing the funding.

11.4.2   Methods of funding

Many properties are bought with a combination of deposit, mortgage and/or equity from a current property. Usually, as a solicitor, you will have information about how your client intends to fund the transaction, and will expect to be updated if those details change, for example if a mortgage falls through and new funding is obtained.

This is a sensible risk assessment measure which should help you decide whether you need to know more about the transaction.

Private funding

Usually purchase funds comprise some private funding, with the majority of the purchase price being provided via a mortgage. Transactions that do not involve a mortgage have a higher risk of being fraudulent.

Look out for:

- large payments from private funds, especially if your client has a low income;
- payments from a number of individuals or sources.

If you are concerned:

- Ask your client to explain the source of the funds. Assess whether you think their explanation is valid – for example, the money may

have been received from an inheritance or from the sale of another property.
- Consider whether the beneficial owners were involved in the transaction

Remember that payments made through the mainstream banking system are not guaranteed to be clean.

Funds from a third party

Third parties often assist with purchases, for example relatives often assist first time home buyers. You may be asked to receive funds directly from those third parties. You will need to decide whether, and to what extent, you need to undertake any CDD measures in relation to the third parties.

Consider whether there are any obvious warning signs and what you know about:

- your client;
- the third party;
- their relationship;
- the proportion of the funding being provided by the third party.

Consider your obligations to the lender in these circumstances – you are normally required to advise lenders if the buyers are not funding the balance of the price from their own resources.

Direct payments between buyers and sellers

You may discover or suspect that cash has changed hands directly, between a seller and a buyer, for example at a rural auction.

If you are asked to bank the cash in your client account, this presents a problem because the source of the cash is not your client and so checks on the source of the funding can be more difficult. The auction house may be able to assist because of checks they must make under the regulations. However, you may decide to decline the request.

If you suspect that there has been a direct payment between a seller and a buyer, consider whether there are any reasons for concern (attempted avoidance of tax for example) or whether the documentation will include the true purchase price.

A client may tell you that money is changing hands directly when this is not the case. This could be to encourage a mortgage lender to lend more than they would otherwise, because they believe that private funds will contribute to the purchase. In this situation, consider your duties to the lender.

11.4.3   Valuing

An unusual sale price can be an indicator of money laundering. While you are not required to get independent valuations, if you become aware of a significant discrepancy between the sale price and what you would reasonably expect such a property to sell for, consider asking more questions.

Properties may also be sold below the market value to an associate, with a view to obscuring the title to the property while the original owner still maintains beneficial ownership.

11.4.4   Lender issues

You may discover or suspect that a client is attempting to mislead a lender client to improperly inflate a mortgage advance – for example, by misrepresenting the borrower's income or because the seller and buyer are conspiring to overstate the sale price. Transactions which are not at arm's length may warrant particularly close consideration.

However, until the improperly obtained mortgage advance is received there is not any criminal property for the purposes of disclosure obligations under POCA.

If you suspect that your client is making a misrepresentation to a mortgagee you must either dissuade them from doing so or consider the ethical implications of continuing with the retainer. Even if you no longer act for the client you may still be under a duty to advise the mortgage company.

If you discover or suspect that a mortgage advance has already been improperly obtained, consider advising the mortgage lender.

If you are acting in a re-mortgage and discover or suspect that a previous mortgage has been improperly obtained, you may need to advise the lender, especially if the re-mortgage is with the same lender. You may also need to consider making a disclosure to SOCA as there is criminal property (the improperly obtained mortgage advance).

Legal professional privilege

If your client has made a deliberate misrepresentation on their mortgage application it is likely that the crime/fraud exemption [6.4.5 of this practice note] to legal professional privilege [6.4 of this practice note] will apply, meaning that no waiver to confidentiality will be needed before a disclosure is made.

However, you will need to consider matters on a case-by-case basis and if necessary, seek legal advice, possibly by contacting a solicitor in the AML directory.

Tipping off offences

You may be concerned that speaking to the lender client conflicts with tipping off offences. A key element of these offences is the likelihood of prejudicing an investigation. This may be a small risk when making disclosures to reputable lenders, and if the lender is your client the legal professional privilege exemption may apply to such a disclosure.

11.4.5   Tax issues

Tax evasion of any type, whether committed by your client or the other party to a transaction, can result in you committing a section 328 arrangements offence.

Abuse of the Stamp Duty Land Tax procedure may also have money laundering implications, for example if the purchase price is recorded incorrectly.

If a client gives you instructions which offend the Stamp Duty Land Tax procedure, you must consider your position under rule 1.10 of the Solicitors' Code of Conduct [**www.rules.sra.org.uk**]. If you discover the evasion after it has occurred, you are obliged to make a disclosure, subject to any legal professional privilege [6.4 of this practice note].

11.5   Company and commercial work

The nature of company structures can make them attractive to money launderers because it is possible to obscure true ownership and protect assets for relatively little expense. For this reason solicitors working with companies and in commercial transactions should remain alert throughout their retainers, with existing as well as new clients.

11.5.1   Forming a new company

If you work on the formation of a new company, be alert to any signs that it might be misused for money laundering or terrorist financing.

If the company is being formed in a foreign jurisdiction, it may be helpful to clarify why this is the case. In countries where there are few anti-money laundering requirements, you should make particularly careful checks.

If you are in doubt, it may be better to refuse the retainer.

11.5.2   Holding of funds

If you wish to hold funds as stakeholder or escrow agent in commercial transactions, consider the checks you wish to make about the funds you intend to hold, before the funds are received and whether it would be appropriate to conduct CDD measures [Chapter 4 of this practice note] on all those on whose behalf you are holding funds.

Consider any proposal that you collect funds from a number of individuals, whether for investment purposes or otherwise. This could lead to wide circulation of your client account details and payments being received from unknown sources.

11.5.3   Private equity

Law firms could be involved in any of the following circumstances:

- the start-up phase of a private equity business where individuals or companies seek to establish a private equity firm (and in certain cases, become authorised to conduct investment business);
- the formation of a private equity fund;
- ongoing legal issues relating to a private equity fund;
- execution of transactions on behalf of a member of a private equity firm's group of companies (a private equity sponsor), that will normally involve a vehicle company acting on its behalf (newco).

Who is the client?

Start-up phase

In this phase, as you will be approached by individuals or a company seeking to become established (and in certain cases authorised) your client would be the individuals or company and you would therefore conduct CDD accordingly.

Formation of private equity funds

Your client is likely to be the private equity sponsor or it may be an independent sponsor.

You will rarely, if ever, be advising the fund itself and, unless you are instructed directly by an investor, you will not be considered to be advising the investors in the fund.

You should therefore identify who your client is and apply the CDD measures according to their client type as set out in 4.6 [of this practice note].

Where the client is a newco, you will need to obtain documentation evidencing the establishment of the newco and consider the issue of beneficial ownership.

Generally private equity work will be considered at low risk of money laundering or terrorist financing for the following reasons:

- Private equity firms in the UK are also covered by the Regulations as a financial institution and they are regulated by the FSA.
- Investors in private equity funds are generally large institutions, some of which will also be regulated for money laundering purposes. They will have long established relationships with the private equity firm, usually resulting in a well-known investor base.
- Where the private equity sponsor or fund manager is regulated in the UK, EEA or a comparable jurisdictions, it is likely to have followed CDD processes prior to investors being accepted.
- The investment is generally illiquid and the return of capital is unpredictable.
- The terms of the fund documentation generally strictly control the transfer of interests and the return of funds to investors.

Factors which may alter this risk assessment include:

- where the private equity sponsor or an investor is located in a jurisdiction which is not regulated for money laundering to a standard which is equivalent to the third directive;
- where the investor is either an individual or an investment vehicle itself (a private equity fund of funds);
- where the private equity sponsor is seeking to raise funds for the first time.

JMLSG has prepared detailed advice on CDD measures for private equity businesses in Part II of its guidance, which you may wish to consider [**www.jmlsg.org.uk**].

The following points should be considered when undertaking CDD measures in relation to private equity work:

- Where your client qualifies for simplified due diligence [4.8 of this practice note] you do not have to identify beneficial owners unless there is a suspicion of money laundering.
- Where simplified due diligence does not apply you need to consider the business structure of the client and conduct CDD on the client in accordance with that structure.
- Where there is an appropriately regulated professional closely involved with the client who has detailed knowledge of the beneficial owners of the client, you may consider relying on them in accordance with regulation 17.
- Whether an unregulated private entity firm, fund manager or other person involved with the transaction is an appropriate source of information regarding beneficial ownership of the client should be determined on a risk-sensitive basis; issues to consider include:

- the profile of the private equity sponsor, fund manager (if different), or such other person;
- their track record within the private equity sector;
- their willingness to explain identification procedures and provide confirmation that all beneficial owners [4.7 of this practice note] have been identified.

- Where you are using another person as an information source for beneficial owners, where there are no beneficial owners within the meaning of regulation 6, the source may simply confirm their actual knowledge of this, or if beneficial owners do exist, the source should provide you with the identifying details of the beneficial owner or an assurance that the beneficial owners have been identified and that the details will be provided on request.
- Where there is a tiered structure, such as a feeder fund or fund of funds structure, you must identify the beneficial owner but you may decide having made enquiries that no such beneficial owners exist even though you have got to the top of the structure.
- Where it is envisaged that you will be acting for a newco which is to be utilised at a future point in a flotation or acquisition, it is only once they are established and signed up as a party to the transaction that you need to commence CDD measures on the newco. However once you start acting for a newco, you will need to consider identification for it, and its beneficial owner. You may therefore wish to commence the process of identifying any beneficial owner in advance.

11.5.4 Collective investment schemes

Undertaking work in relation to retainers involving collective investment schemes may pose similar problems when undertaking CDD as for private equity work.

The risk factors with respect to a collective investment scheme will be decreased where:

- the scheme is only open to tax exempt institutional investors;
- investment managers are regulated individuals or entities;
- a prospectus is issued to invite investment.

Factors which will increase the risks include where:

- the scheme is open to non-tax exempt investors;
- the scheme or its investors are located in a jurisdiction which is not regulated for money laundering to a standard which is equivalent to the third directive;
- neither the scheme nor the investment managers are regulated and do not conduct CDD on the investors.

JMLSG have also issued guidance which touches on the area of collective investment schemes, which you may wish to have regard to.

In addition to the points to consider outlined for private equity work, where a collective investment scheme has issued a prospectus it is advisable to review a copy of the prospectus to understand the intended structure of the investment scheme.

Chapter 12 – Offences and reporting examples

12.1   General comments

Chapters 5 and 6 of this practice note worked through the theory of the law relating to when a money laundering offence [5.4 of this practice note] has occurred, the requirements for making a disclosure and when you are unable to make a disclosure because of LPP [6.4 of this practice note] or are exempted from making a disclosure due to privileged circumstances [6.5 of this practice note].

This chapter contains:

- flowcharts to give an overview of how all the obligations link together;
- examples to help put the theory into context.

This chapter does not replace application of the legislation to your situation; nor should it be viewed without reference to the detailed discussion of the law in the rest of the practice note.

Further examples may be added to future editions of this practice note.

Do I have a suspicion that a principal money laundering offence is occurring?

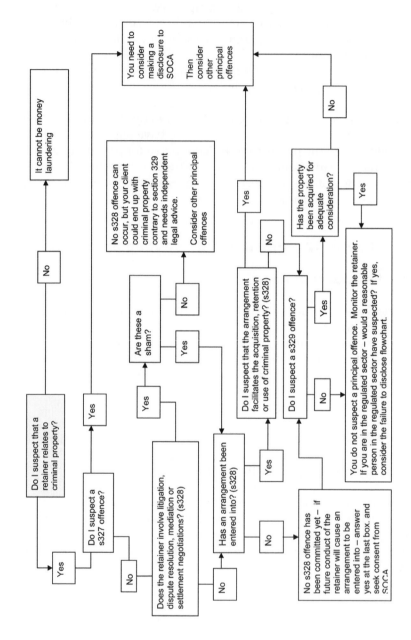

12.2   **Principal offences**

If you suspect that property involved in a retainer is criminal property, offences under section 327 and section 329 are relatively straightforward to assess. However, an arrangement offence under section 328 may be more complicated, particularly with transactional matters.

12.2.1   Do I have an arrangement?

Under section 328, an arrangement must be created at a particular point in time. If you have formed a suspicion, first consider whether an arrangement already exists. For example, a client may instruct you to act for them in the purchase of a property, including the drafting of the contract and transfer documents. When you are instructed there will already an arrangement between the vendor and the purchaser, but not yet an arrangement for the purposes of section 328.

If an arrangement within section 328 already exists, any steps you take to further that arrangement will probably mean you are concerned in it. In this case, you would immediately need to consider making a disclosure.

12.2.2   No pre-existing arrangement

If there is no pre-existing arrangement, the transactional work you carry out may bring an arrangement under section 328 into existence. You may become concerned in the arrangement by, for example, executing or implementing it, which may lead you to commit an offence under section 328, and possibly under section 327 or 329.

Consider whether you need to make an authorised disclosure [5.5.1 of this practice note] to:

- obtain consent to proceed with the transaction;
- provide yourself with a defence to the principal money laundering offences.

If you are acting within the regulated sector, consider whether you risk committing a failure to disclose offence, if you do not make a disclosure to SOCA.

The following two flowcharts show the issues to consider when deciding whether to make a disclosure to SOCA.

I suspect continuation of a retainer will lead to me being a party to a principal offence. Do I have a defence?

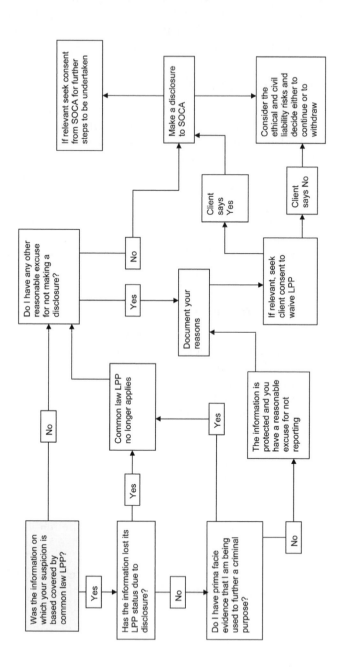

I suspect someone else of a principal offence, or should reasonably suspect them, and am concerned I may commit a failure to disclose offence. Do I have a defence?

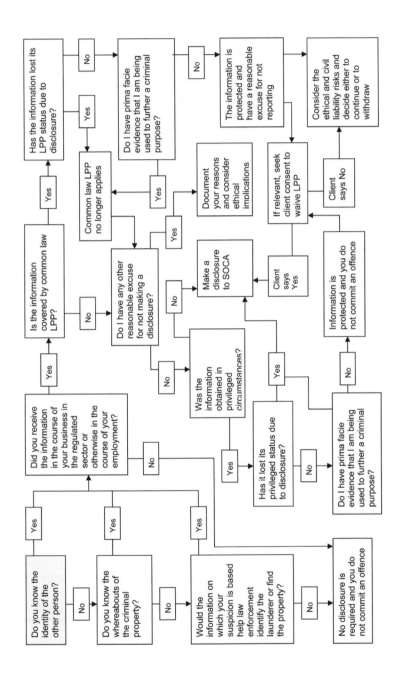

12.3   Should I make a disclosure?

12.3.1   Property transactions

Considering further the earlier example of a suspect contract for the purchase of a property, the following issues will be relevant when considering the disclosure requirements under POCA.

- If the information on which your suspicion is based is covered by LPP and the crime/fraud exception [6.4.5 of this practice note] does not apply, you cannot make a disclosure under POCA.
- If the information was received in privileged circumstances and the crime/fraud exception does not apply, you are exempt from the relevant provisions of POCA, which include making a disclosure to SOCA.
- If neither of these situations applies, the communication will still be confidential. However, the material is disclosable under POCA and an authorised disclosure should be made.

You have the option of withdrawing from the transaction rather than making an authorised disclosure, but you may still need to make a disclosure to avoid committing a failure to disclose offence.

What if I cannot disclose?

If you decide that either you cannot make a disclosure due to LPP or you are exempt from making a disclosure due to privileged circumstances, you have two options:

- you can approach the client for a waiver of privilege to make a disclosure and obtain consent to carry out the prohibited act; or
- you should consider your ethical obligations and whether you need to withdraw from the transaction.

Waiver of privilege

When approaching your client for a waiver of privilege, you may feel less concerned about tipping off issues [5.8 of this practice note] if your client is not the suspect party but is engaged in a transaction which involves criminal property. However, if you suspect that your client is implicated in the underlying criminal conduct, consider the tipping off offence and whether it is appropriate to discuss these matters openly with your client.

If you raise the matter with your client and they agree to waive privilege, you can make a disclosure to SOCA on your own or jointly with your client and seek consent if required.

If you are acting for more than one client on a matter, all clients must agree to waive privilege before you can make a disclosure to SOCA.

Refusal to waive privilege

Your client, whether sole or one of a number for whom you act, may refuse to waive privilege, either because he does not agree with your suspicions or because he does not wish a disclosure to be made. Unless your client provides further information which removes your suspicions, you must decide whether you are being used in a criminal offence, in which case neither LPP nor privileged circumstances apply.

If your client refuses to waive privilege but accepts that in proceeding with the transaction he may be committing an offence, you might conclude that you are being used in a criminal offence in which case neither exemption applies. In such circumstances it is not appropriate to tell the client that you are making the disclosure, as the risks of tipping off are increased.

If you are unable to make a disclosure, consider the ethical and civil risks [Chapter 10 of this practice note] of continuing in the retainer and consider withdrawing.

Consent and progressing the retainer

If you make a disclosure and consent is needed, consider whether you can continue working on the retainer before you receive that consent.

This will depend on whether an arrangement already exists or whether the further work will bring the arrangement into existence. Provided there is no pre-existing arrangement [5.4 of this practice note] you should be free to continue your preparatory activities. However, the arrangement/prohibited act should not be finalised without appropriate consent.

12.3.2 Company transactions

Criminal property in a company

The extent of the regulatory and legal obligations affecting companies and businesses means that there is an increased possibility that breaches will have been committed by your client that constitute criminal conduct and give rise to criminal property under POCA.

For example, the Companies Act 1985 contains many offences which will give rise to criminal property as defined by POCA. There does not need to be a criminal conviction, nor even a prosecution underway. If criminal conduct has (or is suspected to have) taken place, and a benefit has been achieved, the result is actual or notional criminal property.

For a number of offences, the only benefit to your client (for the purposes of POCA) is saved costs. For example, it is criminal conduct to fail to notify the Information Commissioner that a company will be processing 'personal data'. The saved notification fee should be treated as criminal property for the purposes of POCA.

It may be difficult to establish whether property or funds which are the subject of the transactions are the 'saved costs' in whole or in part and are therefore tainted. If you are dealing with the whole of a company's business or assets, no distinction is necessary. In other cases, it would be wrong to assume that because some assets are tainted, they all are, or that you are dealing with the tainted ones.

In most cases, unless there is some basis for suspecting that the assets in question result from saved costs, no disclosure/consent may be required in respect of the principal offence. However a disclosure may still be required in respect of the failure to disclose offences.

Mergers and acquisitions

In typical corporate merger/acquisition/sale/take-over transactions, there are a number of issues to consider.

Solicitors acting in company transactions will be acting in the regulated sector and so will have dual disclosure obligations, under the failure to disclose offence and in respect of the principal offences.

Different tests have to be applied to determine whether a disclosure can be made. When you are considering whether you are obliged to make a disclosure to avoid committing a failure to disclose offence, either LPP or privileged circumstances may apply.

When you are considering whether you must make a disclosure as a defence to the principal offences, only LPP is relevant.

For example, when you are acting for a vendor, you may receive information from the client about the target company which is protected under LPP and exempt from disclosure due to privileged circumstances. However, you may receive information from other representatives of the client (such as other professional advisers) which may only be exempt due to privileged circumstances. If information received is initially privileged, you need to consider whether the privilege is lost in the course of the transaction.

The information may be put into a data room and the purchaser, as part of the due diligence inquiries, may raise questions of the vendor's solicitors which, in effect, result in the information being received again by the vendor's solicitor.

That second receipt from the purchaser, or their solicitor, would not be protected by privileged circumstances. It will lose its exemption from disclosure unless the information was also subject to LPP which had not been waived when it was placed in the data room (e.g. a letter of advice from a solicitor to the vendor).

Consider whether privilege is removed by the crime/fraud exception. You may suspect, or have reasonable grounds to suspect someone of money laundering (which may simply mean they possess the benefits of a criminal offence contrary to section 329). Where the information on which the suspicion is based could be protected by LPP or exempted due to privileged circumstances, consider whether the crime/fraud exception applies.

This may depend on:

- the nature of the transaction;
- the amount of the criminal property;
- the strength of the evidence.

These factors are considered in more detail below with respect to specific types of company sales.

Asset sales

In the case of an asset sale, all or some of the assets of the business may be transferred. If any asset transferred to a new owner is criminal property, a money laundering offence may be committed:

- The vendor may commit a section 327 offence by transferring the criminal property.
- Both the vendor and purchaser may be entering into an arrangement contrary to section 328.
- The purchaser may be committing a section 329 offence by possessing the criminal property.

Adequate consideration defence

When looking at the purchaser's position, you will need to consider whether there would be an adequate consideration defence [5.5.2 of this practice note] to a section 329 possession offence. This is where the purchase price is reasonable and constitutes adequate consideration for any criminal property obtained. In such a case, should the purchaser effectively be deprived of the benefit of that defence by section 328?

It is a question of interpretation whether sections 328 and 329 should be read together such that, if the defence under section 329 applies, an offence will also not be committed by the vendor under section 328. You should consider this point and take legal advice as appropriate.

Disclosure obligations after completion

As well as making disclosures relating to the transaction, vendors and purchasers will need to consider disclosure obligations in respect of the position after completion.

The purchaser will, after the transaction, have possession of the assets and may be at risk of committing a section 329 offence (subject to the adequate consideration defence outlined above).

The vendor will have the sale consideration in their possession. If the amount of the criminal property is material, the sale consideration may indirectly represent the underlying criminal property and the vendor may commit an offence under section 329.

Whether the criminal property is material or not will depend on its impact on the sale price. For example, the sale price of a group of assets may be £20m. If the tainted assets represent 10 per cent of the total, and the price for the clean assets alone would be £18m, it is clear that the price being paid is affected by, and represents in part, the criminal property.

If a client commits one of the principal money laundering offences, whether you are acting for the vendor or purchaser, you will be involved in a prohibited act. You will need to make a disclosure along with your clients and obtain appropriate consent.

When considering whether to advise your client about their disclosure obligations, remember the tipping off offences.

- Am I prevented from reporting due to LPP?
  Where you are acting for either the purchaser or vendor and conclude that you may have to make a disclosure and seek consent, first consider whether LPP applies. As explained above, this depends on how you received the information on which your suspicion is based.

  Generally, when acting for the purchaser, if the information comes from the data room, LPP will not apply. When acting for the vendor, LPP may apply if the information has come from the client for the purpose of obtaining legal advice.

- The crime/fraud exception
  Where LPP applies, you will also need to consider whether the crime/fraud exception applies. The test is whether there is prima facie evidence that you are being used for criminal purposes.

  Whether the crime/fraud exception applies will also depend on the purpose of the transaction and the amount of criminal property involved. For example, if a company wished to sell assets worth £100m, which included £25 of criminal assets, it would be deemed that the intention was not to use solicitors for criminal purposes but to undertake a legitimate transaction. However, if the amount of criminal property was £75m, the prima facie evidence would be that the company did intend to sell criminal property and the exception would apply to override LPP.

Real cases will not all be so clear-cut. Consider the parties' intentions. If you advise your client of money laundering risks in proceeding with a transaction and the client decides, despite the risks, to continue without making a disclosure, you may have grounds to conclude that there was prima facie evidence of an intention to use your services for criminal purposes and therefore that privilege may be overridden.

Remember that for the purposes of the crime/fraud exception, it is not just the client's intention that is relevant.

Where LPP applies and is not overridden by the crime/fraud exception, it is nonetheless possible for your client to waive the privilege in order for a disclosure to be made.

Share sales

A sale of a company by way of shares gives rise to different considerations to asset sales. Unless shares have been bought using the proceeds of crime they are unlikely to represent criminal property, so their transfer will not usually constitute a section 327 offence (for the vendor), or a section 329 offence (for the purchaser).

However the sale of shares could constitute a section 328 offence, depending on the circumstances, particularly if the criminal property represents a large percentage of the value of the target company. Consent may be needed if:

- the benefit to the target company from the criminal conduct is such that its share price has increased;
- as part of the transaction directors will be appointed to the board of the target company and they will use or possess criminal property;
- the purpose of the transaction is to launder criminal property. That is, it is not a genuine commercial transaction.

Is the share value affected by criminal property?

If a company has been used to commit criminal offences, some or all of its assets may represent criminal property. The value of the shares may have increased as a result of that criminal activity. When the shares are then sold, by converting a paper profit into cash, the vendor and the purchaser have both been involved in a prohibited arrangement.

For example, if 10 per cent of the profits of a company are earned from criminal activity, it is likely that the share price would be lower if only the legitimate profits were taken into account.

However, if the value of the criminal property is not sufficient to affect the purchase/sale price, the transaction is unlikely to be considered a prohibited arrangement since the vendor does not benefit from the company's criminal conduct. For example, a company is being purchased for £100m and within it is £25 of saved costs. If the costs had been paid by the company, it is unlikely that the price would be £99,999,975. The business is still likely to be valued at £100m.

Where criminal property is immaterial

Even if the value of criminal property is very small and immaterial to the purchase price, purchasers still need to consider their position after the acquisition. While shareholders do not possess a company's assets, the target company and directors may subsequently transfer, use or possess the assets for the purposes of the principal money laundering offences in sections 327 and 329.

If as part of the transaction, the purchaser proposes appointing new directors to the board of the target company, those directors may need to make a disclosure and seek consent so that they may transfer use or possess and use the criminal property.

In this case, you, and the vendors and the existing and new directors, may still need to make a disclosure (subject to LPP issues), and seek consent, because they will be involved in an arrangement which involves the acquisition, use or control of criminal property by the new directors contrary to section 328.

In summary, the position may be as follows where the amount of the criminal property is immaterial:

- The target company will possess the proceeds of criminal conduct and may need to make a disclosure. If you discover this in privileged circumstances or it is protected by LPP, you cannot make a disclosure unless the fraud/crime exception applies.
- Those individuals or entities which, as a result of the transaction, will be in a position after completion to possess and use criminal property will need to make a disclosure and seek consent before completion.
- The solicitors acting on the transaction and the vendor may also need to make a disclosure if they are involved in an arrangement which facilitates the acquisition or use of criminal property.
- Whenever a disclosure must be made, you must first consider whether privilege applies and, if applicable, whether the fraud/crime exception applies.

Shareholders

Generally in a purchase or sale transaction, you will act for the company, not for its shareholders. However it is possible for shareholders to become involved in an arrangement prohibited by section 328. This is most likely to happen when the transaction requires a Class I or Class II circular to shareholders under the listing rules.

Firstly, consider whether the shareholders are, or may become, aware – perhaps through the risk warnings in the circular – of the risk of criminal conduct. Unless they are so aware, they are unlikely to have the necessary suspicion to be at risk of committing a money laundering offence.

Secondly, where shareholders are aware of the criminal conduct, consider whether the amount of criminal property is material to the transaction. That is, would it have an impact on the price or terms? If it is material, by voting in favour of it the shareholders will become concerned in a prohibited arrangement and will be required to make a disclosure and seek consent.

Also consider, in the context of an initial public offering, what risk warnings to include in any prospectus. You may need to give shareholders notice of their disclosure obligations via such a risk warning.

It is good practice to discuss the issue with SOCA to ensure that there are no tipping off concerns if details of the risks are set out in the public circular.

When each shareholder requires consent from SOCA, their express authority to make the disclosure will be required. It may be simplest to ask the shareholders to authorise the board of the vendor to make a disclosure and seek consent on their behalf at the same time as asking them to give conditional approval for the transaction.

Overseas conduct

Where your suspicion of criminal conduct relates in whole or in part to overseas conduct, be aware of the wide definition of criminal conduct.

For example, you might discover or suspect that a company or its foreign subsidiary has improperly manipulated its accounting procedures so that tax is paid in a country with lower tax limits. Or you might form a concern about corrupt payments to overseas commercial agents which might be illegal in the UK.

Even where the conduct is lawful overseas, in serious cases it will still be disclosable if the money laundering is taking place in the UK and the underlying conduct would be criminal if it had occurred in the UK.

In some cases the only money laundering activity in the UK may be your involvement in the transaction as a UK solicitor.

AMENDMENTS TO PRACTICE NOTE – FEBRUARY 2008

Introduction

This is a summary of changes made to the AML/CTF practice note in the 22 February 2008 version. It has been updated with advice on recent changes to tipping off offences. The government has substantially changed the tipping off offences in POCA 2002, and introduced new tipping offences and consent defences into the Terrorism Act 2000.

The summary of changes highlights the main changes to assist firms in adapting their policies and procedures. It is not an exhaustive list of amendments nor a detailed explanatory guide to the reasons behind the various amendments.

Chapter 1

1.4.3

Changes to scope and application sections to reflect changes to POCA due to the [TACT and] POCA . . . Regulations 2007.

1.4.4

Changes to the scope and application of the Terrorism Act 2000 due to the TACT [and POCA] Regulations 2007.

1.4.5

Changes to clarify that solicitors should contact the SRA in case of any questions concerning supervision.

Chapter 5

5.8

There are substantial changes to explain the new tipping off offences that have been introduced through the TACT and POCA . . . Regulations 2007.

5.8.1

Changes include a full description of the offences and a new section 5.8.1.2 dealing with the offence of prejudicing an investigation (s.342(1)). This offence applies to those outside the regulated sector.

5.8.2

Changes to the section on making enquiries. It reflects the position under the two new tipping off offences.

5.8.3.1–5.8.3.4

These are new sections to reflect the new defences introduced under the TACT and POCA . . . Regulations 2007.

Chapter 6

6.5

Changes to include the new exemption of dissuading a client from engaging in criminal activity.

Chapter 7

7.2

Changes to include information about the tipping off offences relating to the TACT and POCA . . . Regulations 2007.

7.4

Changes to include information on the consent defences.

7.7

A new section explaining the tipping off offences.

7.8

A new section explaining the defences to tipping off.

7.10

A new section about making enquiries of clients.

Chapter 9

9.2.2

Changes to explain that cases of supervisory overlap should be addressed to the SRA.

Deleted sentence stating that when the standards differ should comply with the higher standard.

9.2.3

Deletion of information on visits to firms by officers of designated authorities.

9.4.1

Changes to the penalties for tipping off resulting from the TACT and POCA . . . Regulations 2007.

Annex 5B

Anti-terrorism practice note – the conflicting duties of maintaining confidentiality and reporting terrorism

19 July 2007

Introduction

The Law Society recognises the tension that can exist when the duty of solicitors to advance the interests of their clients may conflict with the interests of the public as a whole. There is a potential for this tension to emerge where solicitors are representing people charged with, or suspected of, serious crime, and in particular, in relation to suspected terrorists.

The right of persons suspected of a criminal offence to communicate in confidence with their legal adviser is a fundamental aspect of their right to have a fair trial. The importance of legal professional privilege has been described thus:

> ... there is a clear policy justification for singling out communications between lawyers and their clients from other professional communications. The privilege belongs to the client, but it attaches both to what the client tells his lawyer and to what the lawyer advises his client to do. It is in the interests of the whole community that lawyers give their clients sound advice, accurate as to the law and sensible as to their conduct. The client may not always act upon that advice (which will sometimes place the lawyer in professional difficulty, but that is a separate matter) but there is always a chance that he will. And there is little or no chance of the client taking the right or sensible course if the lawyer's advice is inaccurate or unsound because the lawyer has been given an incomplete or inaccurate picture of the client's position.'[1]

However, The Law Society also recognises that everyone has a public duty, reinforced by the notification offence provisions under consideration in this practice note, to co-operate with the authorities in preventing future acts which could result in serious harm to others. Solicitors should never knowingly assist others to commit, or cover up, future crimes.

---

[1] Per Baroness Hale in *Three Rivers District Council* v *Bank of England (No.6)* [2004] 3 WLR 1274 at paragraph 61, [2005] 1 AC 610

Disclaimer

This practice note is not intended to constitute legal advice. Practitioners are strongly recommended to consult specialist lawyers and take full advice on the issues raised in this practice note as applicable to themselves and their practices.

Purpose of the practice note

This practice note explains the nature of the solicitor's duty of confidentiality to a client, and how the anti-terrorism 'failure to disclose' offence provisions affect this duty.

Put in stark terms, does a solicitor risk imprisonment for failure to disclose information about terrorism that is gained in the course of their professional duties?

Failure to disclose information about terrorism – the offences

There are three provisions of the Terrorism Act 2000 ('TA 2000'), which penalise, with the threat of imprisonment, persons who fail to disclose varying degrees of knowledge, belief or suspicion of the commission by others of terrorist offences.

'Disclosure of information: duty' – s.19 TA 2000

Under this section it is an offence for a person not to 'disclose to a constable as soon as reasonably practicable' his or her belief or suspicion, and the information on which it is based, that another person has committed an offence under sections 15 to 18 of the TA 2000,[2] when that belief or suspicion is based on information coming to him or her in the course of a trade, profession, business or employment.

'Failure to disclose: regulated sector' – s.21A TA 2000[3]

If a person knows or suspects, or has reasonable grounds for knowing or suspecting, that another person has committed an offence under sections 15 to 18 of the TA 2000, and the information, or other matter upon which that

---

[2]   Offences of fund raising (s.15), use and possession of terrorist property (s.16), funding arrangements (s.17) and money laundering (s.18)

[3]   For full money laundering guidance on these provisions, reference should be made to the money laundering guidance published by the Money Laundering Task Force of the Law Society at **www.lawsociety.org.uk**

knowledge, suspicion, reasonable belief is based, came to him or her during the course of business in the regulated sector, the person commits an offence if he or she does not disclose the information or other matter to a constable (or nominated officer) as soon as practicable after it comes to him or her.

'Information about acts of terrorism' – s.38B TA 2000

If a person has information which he or she 'knows or believes might be of material assistance in (a) preventing the commission by another person of an act of terrorism or, (b) in securing the apprehension, prosecution or conviction of another person, in the UK, for an offence involving the commission, preparation or instigation of an act of terrorism,' he or she commits an offence if he does not disclose the information to police as soon as reasonably practicable.

The solicitor's duty of client confidentiality

A solicitor is under a professional and legal obligation to keep the affairs of clients confidential and to ensure that all members of his or her staff do likewise.[4] This duty of confidence is fundamental to the fiduciary relationship that exists between solicitor and client. It extends to all matters divulged to a solicitor by a client, or on his or her behalf, from whatever source.

Overriding confidentiality

In certain circumstances confidentiality can be overridden. For solicitors the most relevant instances will arise when:

- a court order, or a statutory obligation, requires them to disclose by compulsion of law; or
- an exception to the duty of confidentiality arises from the public interest.[5]

Compulsion of law

A court has the power to compel the disclosure of confidential information held by a solicitor. The most common examples of this are the statutory

---

[4] Practice Rule 16E of the Solicitors' Practice (Confidentiality and Disclosure) Amendment Rule 2004, in effect since April 2006. NB: when the new Solicitors' Code of Conduct comes into effect on 1 July 2007 this rule will be incorporated into the Code as rule 4, and will cease to have effect as a separate Practice Rule

[5] Confidentiality and Disclosure Guidance – Explanatory notes not forming part of Rule 16E, paragraphs 9–20

powers exercised by judges to compel production of confidential ('special procedure') material under Schedule 1 to the Police and Criminal Evidence Act 1984 (PACE), and in certain circumstances, the issuing of witness summonses under the Criminal Procedure (Attendance of Witnesses) Act 1965.

A duty to the public to disclose

The circumstances in which a solicitor may make disclosure on grounds related to issues of public interest are very limited. Essentially a solicitor may reveal confidential information only to the extent necessary to prevent the client, or a third party, committing a criminal act that is reasonably believed to be likely to result in serious bodily harm, and in cases of continuing or anticipated child abuse if disclosure is in the public interest.

Confidentiality and legal professional privilege

Certain confidential communications, however, can never be revealed without the consent of the client; they are privileged against disclosure. This protection is called legal professional privilege ('LPP').

In two recent cases, the House of Lords has underlined the policy behind LPP, its necessity and its nature.

> The policy of legal professional privilege requires that the client should be secure in the knowledge that protected documents and information will not be disclosed at all.[6]

> . . . it is necessary in our society, a society in which the restraining and controlling framework is built upon a belief in the rule of law, that communications between clients and lawyers, whereby the clients are hoping for the assistance of the lawyers' legal skills in the management of their (the clients') affairs, should be secure against the possibility of any scrutiny from others, whether the police, the executive, business competitors, inquisitive busy bodies or anyone else . . .[7]

> . . . (LPP is) a fundamental human right long established in the common law. It is a necessary corollary to the right of any person to obtain skilled advice about the law. Such advice cannot be effectively obtained unless the client is able to put all the facts before the adviser without fear that they may afterwards be disclosed and used to his prejudice.[8]

---

[6]   Per Lord Hoffmann in *R (Morgan Grenfell & Co Ltd)* v *Special Commissioner of Income Tax and Another* [2002] UKHL 21 at paragraph 30, [2003] 1 AC 563
[7]   Per Lord Scott in *Three Rivers District Council* v *Bank of England* (ibid) at paragraph 34
[8]   Per Lord Hoffmann in *Morgan Grenfell* (ibid) at paragraph 7

What communications are privileged?

Not everything that lawyers have a duty to keep confidential is privileged. Only those confidential communications falling under either of the two heads of privilege – 'advice privilege' or 'litigation privilege' – are protected by LPP.

Who is a 'lawyer' for such purposes?

This includes solicitors and their employees, barristers, in-house lawyers, but does not include accountants, even if they give legal advice (subject to one very limited exception).

'Advice privilege'

Communications between a lawyer (acting in his or her capacity as a lawyer) and a client are privileged if they are confidential and for the purpose of seeking legal advice from a lawyer or providing legal advice to a client.

For example:

- conveyancing documents are not communications;[9]
- neither is a client account ledger maintained in relation to the client's moneys;[10]
- nor is an appointments diary or time record on an attendance note, time-sheet or fee record relating to a client;[11]
- a solicitor's bill of costs and statement of account may, in certain circumstances, be privileged;[12]
- but notes of open court proceedings,[13] or conversations, correspondence or meetings with opposing lawyers[14] are not privileged, as the content of the communication is not confidential.

Merely because a client is speaking or writing to his or her solicitor does not make that communication privileged – it is only those communications

---

[9] *R v Inner London Crown Court*, ex p. *Baines & Baines* [1988] QB 579
[10] *Nationwide Building Society* v *Various Solicitors* [1999] PNLR 53. Such entries are not created for the purpose of giving legal advice to a client but are internal records maintained, in part, to discharge a solicitor's professional and disciplinary obligations under the Solicitors' Accounts Rules
[11] *R v Manchester Crown Court*, ex p. *Rogers* [1999] 1 WLR 832
[12] *Chant* v *Brown* (1852) 9 Hare 790
[13] *Parry* v *News Group Newspapers* (1990) 140 New Law Journal 1719
[14] *Parry* (ibid)

between the solicitor and the client relating to the matter in which the solicitor has been instructed for the purpose of obtaining legal advice that will be privileged. Such communications do not need to 'contain advice on matters of law or construction, provided that they are directly related to the performance by the solicitor of his professional duty as legal adviser of his client'.[15]

'Litigation privilege'

Under this head the following are privileged:

Confidential communications made, after litigation has started, or is 'reasonably in prospect', between:

- a lawyer and a client;
- a lawyer and an agent (whether or not that agent is a lawyer); or
- a lawyer, or his or her client, and a third party

for the sole or dominant purpose of litigation, whether:

- for seeking or giving advice in relation to it; or
- for obtaining evidence to be used in it; or
- for obtaining information leading to obtaining such evidence.

Pre-existing documents

An original document, which is not brought into existence for either of these privileged purposes and so is not already privileged, does not acquire privileged status merely by being given to a lawyer for advice or otherwise for a privileged purpose.

Fraud or illegality – the crime/fraud exception

It is proper for a lawyer to advise a client on how to stay within the law and avoid committing a crime,[16] or to warn a client that proposed actions could attract prosecution,[17] and such advice will be protected by privilege.

LPP does not, however, exist in respect of documents which themselves form part of a criminal or fraudulent act, or communications

---

[15] Per Lord Carswell in *Three Rivers DC* v *Governor of the Bank of England* [2004] (ibid) at paragraph 111

[16] *Bullivant* v *Attorney-General of Victoria* [1901] AC 196

[17] *Butler* v *Board of Trade* [1971] Ch 680 14; *R* v *Cox & Railton* (1884) 14 QBD 153

which take place in order to obtain advice with the intention of carrying out an offence.[18] It is irrelevant whether or not the lawyer is aware that he or she is being used for that purpose.[19] If the lawyer suspects that he or she is unwittingly being involved by their client in a fraud, before they can consider themselves released from the duty of confidentiality, the courts require there to be strong prima facie evidence before LPP can be displaced.[20] Whilst the lawyer may release himself or herself if such evidence exists, he or she may also raise the issue with the court for an order authorising him or her to make disclosure to the victim.[21]

The general 'crime/fraud exception' principle is restated in the Police and Criminal Evidence Act 1984 ('PACE')[22] at section 10(2), where items held with the intention of furthering a criminal purpose are declared not to be items subject to LPP. It is important to note that the intention to further a criminal purpose need not be that of the client (or the lawyer) – it is sufficient that a third party intends the lawyer/client communication to be made with that purpose (e.g. where the innocent client is being 'used' by a third party).[23]

Overriding privilege

By statute

LPP is a fundamental human right; Parliament can of course legislate contrary to fundamental principles of human rights. However, the House of Lords in *Morgan Grenfell* stressed that a parliamentary intention to override rights, such as LPP, must be expressly stated in the statute or appear by necessary implication.[24]

Public duty

Unlike the position in relation to confidential material (see above), there is no public interest exception to LPP. It is therefore prima facie unlawful for a solicitor to disclose a communication if to do so would involve a breach of LPP.

---

[18] *R v Cox & Railton* (ibid)
[19] *Banque Keyser Ullman v Skandia* [1986] 1 Lloyd's Rep 336
[20] *O'Rourke v Darbishire* [1920] AC 581
[21] *Finers v Miro* [1991] 1 WLR 35
[22] It is also reflected in numerous other criminal statutes – including the Proceeds of Crime Act 2002 s.330 (failure to disclose) and s.333 (tipping off)
[23] *R v Central Criminal Court*, ex p. *Francis & Francis* [1989] 1 AC 346
[24] See also *R v Secretary of State for the Home Department*, ex p. *Simms* [2000] 2 AC 115

Do sections 19 and 21A of the Terrorism Act 2000 override LPP?

Section 19(5) does not require disclosure by a 'professional legal adviser' of either information which he or she obtains 'in privileged circumstances', or a belief or suspicion based on information which he or she obtains in 'privileged circumstances'.

Section 21A(5) provides that a person does not commit an offence under the section if he or she is a 'professional legal adviser' and the information or other matter came to him or her in 'privileged circumstances'.

Under both provisions, 'privileged circumstances' effectively mirror LPP at common law, and both are subject to the caveat that it will not cover communications in furtherance of a criminal purpose.

A solicitor does not therefore, subject to the caveat, breach these sections of the TA 2000 if he or she fails to disclose information which has come to him or her in privileged circumstances.

Does section 38B of the Terrorism Act 2000 override LPP?

Whilst there is no equivalent provision in this section to that relating to 'professional legal advisers' as in sections 19 and 21A TA 2000, in order to override LPP the statute must do so expressly or by necessary implication.

No express words are used overriding LPP; therefore, only if there is a 'necessary implication' can LPP be overridden.

What is meant by 'a necessary implication'?

Lord Millett expressed the test in *B v Auckland District Law Society*:[25]

> A useful test is to write in the words 'not being privileged documents' and ask, not 'does that produce a reasonable result' or 'does it impede the statutory purpose for which production may be required?' but 'does that produce an inconsistency?' or 'does it stultify the statutory purpose?' The circumstances in which such a question would receive an affirmative answer would be rare.

This provides helpful assistance in the absence of specific judicial interpretation of s.38B TA 2000. It would seem unlikely that it could be successfully argued that the statutory purpose of s.38B would be stultified if it was to read (adopting the wording in the earlier sections and adapting Lord Millett's formula), 'the person commits an offence if he does not disclose the information unless it was obtained in privileged circumstances as soon as reasonably practicable . . .'.

In these circumstances, therefore, the Law Society considers that LPP is not overridden by s.38B TA 2000 and that information of the kind

---

[25] [2003] 3 WLR 859

referred to in the section, if received in privileged circumstances, cannot be disclosed without the authority of the client.

It is crucial, however, that a solicitor, when in receipt of such information, should be absolutely satisfied that the client's purpose in supplying that information has been for the obtaining of legal advice and is directly related to the performance by the solicitor of his or her professional duty as the legal adviser of the client.

If it is not, then it is not protected by LPP.

It will, however, remain confidential.

The only defence available to an offence under s.38B is that the person charged has a reasonable excuse for not making a disclosure. Is confidentiality a 'reasonable excuse'?

There is a clear duty owed by the solicitor to the public to disclose confidential information to prevent the client, or a third party, committing a criminal act that is reasonably believed to be likely to result in serious bodily harm.

If there is a public duty to disclose in such circumstances, it would seem likely that confidentiality would not amount to a reasonable excuse for non-disclosure under s.38B TA 2000, and that a solicitor prosecuted for failing to disclose such information would have no defence.

It is The Law Society's view that the solicitor must disclose such confidential information as soon as reasonably practicable.

Oaths and affidavits

What is the difference between an oath and an affirmation?

The Law Society's *Guide to Oaths and Affirmations* explains the difference by reference to a person's belief in divine mercy or vengeance. As such, an oath imprecates divine vengeance if the person does not speak the truth, whereas an affirmation is a solemn affirmation of the truth without reference to anything divine. It follows that an affirmation may be appropriate in cases where the person is an atheist or agnostic and where statutory provision permits such use.

This book is now out of print but copy extracts can be obtained from the Law Society's library (0870 606 2511). Please also see Anderson and Warner (2008) *Execution of Documents*, 2nd Edition, Law Society Publishing which is available from the Law Society's online bookshop (**www.law society.org.uk/bookshop**).

How much should I charge for swearing an oath and is this charge mandatory?

Section 2 of the Commissioners for Oaths (Fees) Order 1993, SI 1993/2297, states that the following fees 'shall' be charged: £5.00 for taking an affidavit, declaration or affirmation, for each person making the same and, in addition, £2.00 for each exhibit or schedule referred to. For further information on oaths and affirmations see Anderson and Warner, *Execution of Documents*.

Is it true that the fee for swearing oaths has risen to £10.00?

Under the Commissioners for Oaths (Fees) Order 1993, SI 1993/2297 and the Commissioner of Oaths (Authorised Persons)(Fees) Order 1993, SI 1993/2298, the swear fees for solicitors remains at £5.00 per deponent and £2.00 for exhibits.

Under the Magistrates Courts Fees Order 2008, SI 2008/1052 and the Civil Proceedings Fees Order 2008, SI 2008/1053, the courts now charge between £10.00 and £25.00 for a swear fee whereas it used to be a free service.

As a practising assistant solicitor on a busy high street, I am asked to swear numerous oaths, affidavits and to take declarations. I charge the usual fee of £5.00 for the swear and £2.00 for any exhibits which my firm allows me to keep. Are these charges subject to VAT?

No. By agreement between the Law Society and H M Revenue & Customs oath fees retained personally by associate or assistant solicitors are not subject to VAT unless the associate or assistant solicitor is:

(a) registered or liable to register for VAT as a result of the aggregate of taxable supplies made to their own account; or

(b) required to account to their firm for oath fees received in which case the fees should be dealt with as part of the firm's taxable turnover.

Please see Anderson and Warner, *Execution of Documents* for more details.

I am a sole practitioner and am concerned about VAT implications for oath fees.

Oath fees earned by sole practitioners or partners remain part of the turnover of the 'taxable person' and liable to VAT.

If you are liable to VAT, then the fees prescribed by the Commissioners for Oaths (Fees) Order 1993 (SI 1993/2297) are inclusive of VAT. If the deponent is also a taxable person, and asks for a tax invoice, the invoice can be of the less detailed kind described in paragraph 53 of Customs & Excise Notice 700. At the end of each accounting period, you should account to HM Revenue & Customs for the appropriate fraction of the fees received. Please see **www.hmrc.gov.uk**.

I am on the roll of solicitors but do not have a current practising certificate. Can I administer an oath?

No. Section 81 of the Solicitors Act 1974 extends the right of commissioners for oaths to all solicitors with practising certificates. Only a solicitor with a current practising certificate is able to administer oaths.

My client is abroad on business and urgently needs to swear an affidavit for use in court proceedings here. Can I send the affidavit to him for swearing abroad?

Yes. He can swear it before any person who has authority to administer an oath in that place (Commissioners for Oaths Act 1889, s.3(1)).

Alternatively, s.6 (as amended) of that Act empowers every British ambassador, envoy, minister, consul and other officials exercising their functions abroad to administer oaths there.

Please see Anderson and Warner, *Execution of Documents* for more details.

I have been asked to administer an oath to a document intended for use in court proceedings in a foreign country. Can I do this?

It depends on the law of that country. Do not take it for granted that the country concerned will accept the signature of a Commissioner authorised to take oaths under the law of England and Wales.

You should suggest that the prospective deponent makes enquiries with his lawyers abroad. In case of doubt, he can be referred to a Notary Public whose authority to administer oaths is recognised internationally.

I am a solicitor with a practising certificate, does this mean that I am also regarded as a Notary Public?

No. Admission as a solicitor does not automatically mean that you are a Notary Public. The main regulations are contained in the Notaries (Qualifications) Rules 1998. If you wish to qualify as a notary please contact the Court of Faculties, Faculty Office, 1 The Sanctuary, Westminster, London SW1P 3JT (Tel: 020 7222 5381).

Details of the Faculty Office and all the rules governing the qualification and admission of notaries can be found at their website (**www.facultyoffice.org.uk**).

I have been asked to administer an oath where the deponent is a child. Am I able to do this and if so is there a special form of oath to be used?

Yes, so long as you are a solicitor with a current practising certificate you are able to administer an oath to any deponent including a child. There is no special form of oath prescribed for a deponent who is a child and no obligation upon a solicitor to ascertain the age of any person who seeks to take the oath. In the case of a person obviously of tender years the commissioner ought to satisfy himself so far as practicable that the child understands that he is about to swear the truth of the contents of the document. See Anderson and Warner, *Execution of Documents* for more details.

I have been asked to swear an affidavit. I am a newly qualified solicitor and am unsure of the wording which a deponent must use when I administer the oath. Please could you assist?

The form of words customarily adopted is:

> I swear by Almighty God that this is my name and handwriting and that the contents of this my affidavit are true [and that these are the exhibits referred to therein].

I am a newly qualified solicitor, and have been asked to swear a statutory declaration for the first time. What is the wording of the oral declaration to be made by the declarant?

The form of wording is as follows:

> I solemnly and sincerely declare that this is my name and handwriting and that the contents of this my declaration are true [if there are exhibits add and that this/these is/are the exhibit/s referred to].

I am a trainee solicitor and wish to administer oaths and take declarations. Can I do this?

No. Only the following people can administer an oath, take an affirmation or take a declaration:

- Commissioners for Oaths;
- solicitors (holding a current practising certificate);
- barristers;
- Notaries Public;
- licensed conveyancers;
- Fellows of the Institute of Legal Executives (if they pay a full subscription to the Institute; but not retired Fellows);
- certain officials of the High Court;
- circuit judges or district judges;
- justices of the peace; and
- certain officials of any county court appointed by the judge of that court for the purpose.

I need to prepare an affidavit which includes a number of attachments. How should these be dealt with?

Documents or things such as physical objects which are referred to in the affidavit are referred to as 'exhibits'. These are to be kept separate from the affidavit but must be produced at the same time as the affidavit before the Commissioner. Such exhibits need to be marked with an identifying initial and number matching that found in the relevant place in the affidavit.

Each of the exhibits can be marked as follows:

> This is the (specify attachment/exhibit) marked [initials/number referred to in affidavit] referred to in the annexed affidavit of [name of deponent] sworn/affirmed before me this [day] day of [month] [year]
>
> (Signature of Commissioner)
> A [Commissioner for Oaths] [solicitor empowered to administer oaths]

In practice this form of words might be written by hand on the attachment/ exhibit.

What is a statement of truth?

The statement of truth has replaced the affidavit (or affirmation) as the main means of verifying the contents of a document in litigation save in a few cases.

A statement of truth is a statement that the party putting forward the document (other than a witness statement) believes the facts stated in the document are true (Civil Procedure Rules (CPR) 22.1(4)). If the document is a witness statement, it is a statement that its maker believes that the facts stated within it are true.

My client is paralysed and she now needs to swear an affidavit. She is physically incapable of signing the affidavit. How do I deal with this?

If your client is incapable of making any distinguishable mark whatsoever to the affidavit, then the jurat may read as follows:

> Sworn by the above-named deponent, AB, at ____ in the county of ____ this ____ day of ____ 20__ without the deponent affixing hereto any mark or signature, she being physically incapable of doing so.

Please see *Oaths and Affirmations*, 2nd Edition by D Boland, copy extracts of which can be obtained from the Law Society's library (telephone

0870 606 2511). Alternatively see Anderson and Warner, *Execution of Documents*.

I have been asked to administer an oath, however, the deponent has already signed the affidavit. Is there any requirement for her to sign the affidavit in my presence?

No, however, you should clarify that the signature is that of the Deponent.

Is there any information on administering oaths in relation to different religious beliefs?

When dealing with deponents of different religions the following points should be considered.

- Religious practices in relation to oath taking should be dealt with sensitively not as though they are an inconvenience.
- Not everyone from ethnic minority communities is religious: some may prefer to affirm.
- Sikh, Hindu and Muslim women may prefer to affirm if having to give evidence during menstruation or shortly after childbirth.
- Requests to wash hands, feet or other body parts before taking the oath should be treated sympathetically.
- Some witnesses may want to remove shoes or cover their heads or bow with folded hands.
- Holy books should be covered in cloth or velvet bags at all times when not in use. When uncovered, they should only be touched by the person taking the oath, not by the Commissioner. They should not be marked inside or out.

I represent a client on an application for a search order. I need to prepare an affidavit. Are there any drafting requirements that I need to consider?

Yes. Practice Direction 32 on Written Evidence that supplements CPR 32 sets out the required format of an affidavit. This includes the form of heading, body, jurat, type of paper, together with the manner in which the affidavit should be set out. A copy of the Practice Direction is available on the Ministry of Justice website (**www.justice.gov.uk**) in the Civil Procedure Rules section.

I have been asked to administer an affidavit. The deponent is Turkish and is unable to speak English. What do I need to consider?

If the deponent is unable to speak or understand the English language, an interpreter must be employed. The interpreter will translate the text of the affidavit (or swear or affirm that she has already done so) and the words of the oath or the affirmation to the deponent, after having been herself duly sworn.

Practice management

Does the Law Society have any information on computer software for solicitors?

Yes, in February 2009 the Law Society launched the 2009 edition of the Software Solutions Guide at the Legal IT show in Islington, London. The Law Society sent a copy of the Software Solutions Guide to all partners in firms with 10 or fewer partners, and to the senior partners of larger firms. The aim of the guide is to help firms to select software packages suitable for their needs. The suppliers featured in the Software Solutions Guide have all taken part in a rigorous vetting procedure by the Law Society selection panel in terms of product strategy, financial health and feedback from existing users of their systems. The Software Solutions Guide is currently on the Law Society website (see **www.it.lawsociety.org.uk**).

What are the usual quarter days?

These are March 25 (Lady Day), June 24 (Midsummer Day), September 29 (Michaelmas Day) and December 25 (Christmas Day).

I have just completed my training contract during which period I was paid the Law Society's recommended minimum salary. Does the Law Society recommend a minimum salary for newly qualified solicitors entering private practice?

There is no recommended minimum salary for qualified solicitors. However, the Strategic Research Unit at the Law Society has published a factsheet entitled 'Private Practice Solicitors' Salaries' which is based on research conducted in 2007 and is available online at **www.research. lawsociety.org.uk**. Alternatively, you may wish to contact a local legal recruitment agency.

I am a partner in a firm of solicitors and have been summoned for jury service. My understanding is that solicitors are exempt from this particular civic duty. Is this correct?

No. Pursuant to section 321 (Schedule 33) of the Criminal Justice Act 2003 and the Criminal Justice Act 2003 (Commencement No.3 and Transitional Provisions) Order 2004 which commenced on 5 April 2004 solicitors are now eligible for jury service.

Jury service which usually lasts for up to ten working days is compulsory for all registered electors in England and Wales, aged between 18 and 70, who have lived in the UK, Channel Islands or Isle of Man for a continuous period of at least five years since the age of 13.

The Law Society has issued guidance which can be found in the Criminal Practitioner's Newsletter, Issue 62, October 2005. This can be found on the Law Society website (**www.lawsociety.org.uk**) under News/ Newsletters.

My firm has paid the fee for my practising certificate. Do I have to declare this on my income tax return form?

No. Under section 343 of the Income Tax (Earnings and Pensions Act) 2003, where an employer has paid an employee's professional subscription to a recognised body no benefit is deemed to accrue to the employee and this does not have to be recorded on his income tax return. This applies to solicitors in private practice and those solicitors in-house who are required by rule 2.02 of the Code of Conduct (**www.sra.org.uk/ solicitors/code-of-conduct/207.article**) to hold a practising certificate.

I am a solicitor and would like to qualify as a notary. How do I go about this?

Qualifying as a notary is regulated by the Faculty Office of the Archbishop of Canterbury under the direction of the Master of Faculties. The rules governing the qualification and admission of Notaries can be found at **www.facultyoffice.org.uk**. The main regulations are contained in the Notaries (Qualification) Rules 1998.

Although some exemptions may be available, you must obtain a Postgraduate Diploma in Notarial Practice from the University of the Cambridge Institute of Continuing Education. The diploma is primarily offered through distance learning with required attendance at an induction day and a notarial practice weekend. Candidates must then acquire a 'Faculty' from the Master of Faculties who must be satisfied that the candidate is of good standing.

For further information on qualifying as a Notary please see the Notary Society's website (**www.thenotariessociety.org.uk**).

I am aware of the requirement in rule 2.02 of the Solicitors' Code of Conduct 2007 that firms give clients details of the status of the fee earner who is dealing their particular matter, but I would also like to know the name of the case that states this?

The case is *Pilbrow* v. *Pearless de Rougement* [1999] 3 All ER 355. For a copy of the case please contact the Law Society Library Enquiry Service on 0870 606 2511.

How long should I retain my closed files in storage?

There is no specific Law Society guidance stating how long a file should be retained in storage. Firms therefore need to decide how long they wish to store closed files taking into account relevant statutory provisions such as limitation periods.

In your client care letter, you should advise the client how long you will retain the file and outline what will happen to the file after that time.

You should also advise the client of any costs relating to any of the following:

(a) storage;

(b) retrieval; and

(c) additional copies of papers requested by the client.

If you intend to store documents in an electronic format, you should first consider whether the absence of paper documents will be detrimental to the client's interests before you agree such storage methods with your client.

You should also consider any file retention requirements of your professional indemnity insurers when assessing the appropriate length of time to retain files.

For further information on:

(a) wills, deeds and douments, see the Law Society's File retention practice note (**Annex 7G**).

(b) retention of client due diligence files, see paragraph 3.8 of the Law Society's Anti-money laundering practice note (**Annex 5A**).

(c) please see the Law Society's Client care letters practice note (**Annex 7C**).

I work as a practice manager at a firm that deals predominantly with wills and probate matters. The firm is in the process of reviewing its file retention policy. Is there any information on retaining client files and papers?

Yes. You may wish to refer to the Law Society's practice note on file retention on wills and will files. The Wills and Equity Committee of the Law Society has set out information in order to help practitioners identify issues that should be considered before relevant files are 'weeded' or 'destroyed'. To see a copy of the Law Society's practice note entitled 'File retention: records management – retention and wills, deeds and documents together with supporting data', please see **Annex 7G**.

Can I charge my client for storage, copying or production of old records and documents?

Your retainer should set out any charges you propose making for storage, copying the file or producing a document from storage. You might consider reminding the client that there is a cost to your business for storage and retrieval of documents from deep storage, particularly where the material is kept off site. For further information see the Law Society's practice notes on file retention (**Annex 7G**) and client care letters (**Annex 7C**).

Our firm has just merged and some of our old will files have gone astray. What issues should I consider?

Loss of a file may amount to inadequate professional service or negligence where deeds are lost, so you may need to contact your professional indemnity insurer to record the loss. You should consider contacting the client to discuss what remedial action can be taken, if any, where original papers such as wills have been lost. If a claim arises in relation to lost papers, the courts will weigh the available evidence to assess your part in the matter. For further information see the Law Society's practice note on file retention (**Annex 7G**).

Does the Law Society provide any guidance with complying with the Data Protection Act (DPA) 1998 in relation to information held on clients?

Yes. You must comply with the DPA 1998 with respect to information held on your clients. You should include reference as to how you comply with the DPA in your terms of business. For further information please see the Law Society's practice note on data protection (**Annex 7F**) and also, for an example of a clause which could be used in your terms of business, see the Law Society's practice note on client care letters (**Annex 7C**).

Please also see Carey, P. (ed.) (2008) *Data Protection Handbook*, 2nd Edition, Law Society Publishing, which is available from the Law Society's online bookshop (**www.lawsociety.org.uk/bookshop**).

Does my practice need to register with the Information Commissioner's Office (ICO) under the DPA 1998 and, if so, how much does it cost to register?

The DPA 1998 will usually apply. However, there are certain exceptions when you may not need to register and you should look at the provisions of DPA 1998 to see whether or not these apply to your firm.

If you are required to comply with DPA 1998:

- You must give notification to the ICO. Notification is a statutory requirement to be given to the ICO that you are processing personal information (failure to notify is a criminal offence).
- You must process personal information in accordance with the eight principles of DPA 1998. For more information see the Law Society's practice notes on data protection (**Annex 7F**) and information security (**Annex 7I**).
- You must answer subject access requests received from individuals.

An annual fee of £35 (not subject to VAT) is payable to the ICO (see **www.ico.gov.uk**).

I am a partner at a six partner firm that deals with immigration matters. I am encountering problems within the partnership and have concerns about my own financial position. What assistance can the Law Society provide?

You may wish to contact the Law Society's Pastoral Care Helpline on 020 7320 5795. You will be referred to the most suitable helpline(s) for guidance and assistance. For further information on Law Society helplines please see the Law Society website (**www.lawsociety.org.uk**) and **Useful contacts**.

Annex 7A

Banking crisis practice note

8 January 2009

1. Introduction

1.1 Who should read this practice note?

All solicitors handling client accounts.

1.2 What is the issue?

In the event of a bank's collapse, client funds could be lost. This practice note gives interim advice on mitigating any risk of liability for these funds.

1.3 Professional conduct

- The Solicitors' Accounts Rules 1998
- Rule 10.05 of the Solicitors' Code of Conduct on undertakings and its related guidance [see **rules.sra.org.uk**]

1.4 Status of this practice note

This is interim advice. It may be updated as economic events change and in light of any legal advice provided to the Law Society. Neither the Society nor the Solicitors Regulation Authority (SRA) can provide financial or legal advice. The law in this area is uncertain because it has never been tested, so consider this advice in light of that. This advice supersedes previous advice on this issue.

Practice notes are issued by the Law Society for the use and benefit of its members. They represent the Law Society's view of good practice in a particular area. They are not intended to be the only standard of good practice that solicitors can follow. You are not required to follow them, but doing so will make it easier to account to oversight bodies for your actions.

Practice notes are not legal advice, nor do they necessarily provide a defence to complaints of misconduct or of inadequate professional service. While care has been taken to ensure that they are accurate, up to date and useful, the Law Society will not accept any legal liability in relation to them. For queries or comments on this practice note contact the Law Society's Practice Advice Service.

1.5 Terminology in this practice note

Must – a specific requirement in the Solicitors' Code of Conduct or legislation. You must comply, unless there are specific exemptions or defences provided for in the code of conduct or relevant legislation.

Should – good practice for most situations in the Law Society's view. If you do not follow this, you must be able to justify to oversight bodies why this is appropriate, either for your practice, or in the particular retainer.

May – a non-exhaustive list of options for meeting your obligations. Which option you choose is determined by the risk profile of the individual practice, client or retainer. You must be able to justify why this was an appropriate option to oversight bodies.

You – a practice.

1.6 More information

1.6.1 Practice Advice Line

The Law Society provides support for solicitors on a wide range of areas of practice. Practice Advice can be contacted on 0870 606 2522 from 09.00 to 17.00 on weekdays.

www.lawsociety.org.uk/practiceadvice

1.6.2 Solicitors Regulation Authority

The Solicitors Regulation Authority regulates solicitors in England and Wales. It makes and enforces the Solicitors' Code of Conduct.

www.sra.org.uk

2. Liability for client money if a bank collapses

It is unlikely that you will be liable in negligence if client money is lost if a bank collapses, as long as you have placed the money in accordance with the Solicitors' Accounts Rules. However, any final decision on this is for the courts. If you have made any express undertakings to pay money, you must honour these even if the bank has collapsed.

You may update your terms of business to limit any liability, provided you follow rule 2.07 of the code of conduct [see **www.rules.sra.org.uk** for recent amendments]. You may also state in your terms of business that, if you make a claim under the Financial Services Compensation Scheme (FSCS) in respect of client money on your clients' behalf, you will, subject to their consent, give certain client information to the FSCS to help them identify clients and amounts to which clients are entitled in client accounts.

3.   Solicitors' Accounts Rules 1998 (SARs)

You must place client money in a client account at a bank or building society, as defined in section 87 of the Solicitors Act 1974.

- Banks must have permission from the FSA to accept deposits.
- A client account must be held at a branch or a head office in England and Wales – Rule 14(4).

Read the Solicitors' Account Rules (SARs) [at **www.sra.org.uk**].
    The SARs do not prevent you from:

- dividing money among separate client accounts;
- distributing client money in different banks.

4.   Financial Services Compensation Scheme (FSCS)

The FSCS has confirmed that the scheme applies to client money as to other banking deposits. Therefore the scheme covers deposits belonging to clients who are individuals or small businesses up to £50,000, per client, per authorised deposit-taking institution.

Read more about deposit claims [at **www.fscs.org.uk/consumer/ faqs/deposit_claims_faqs/**].

You do not need to write to the bank to confirm that an account was opened on behalf of multiple clients. Banks will know this from your application to open the account, particularly as the account must have the word 'client' in its title according to Rule 14(3) SARs.

If a bank collapses, you should contact the FSCS with details of all clients whose money is held in the account and the amount in the account to which they are entitled, with supporting evidence. You must seek the consent of your clients before doing so. If an individual client does not give consent, the FSCS will still need to know the account balances, but you may withhold the identity of the client. In this latter case, the client will not be able to receive compensation from the FSCS.

The FSCS will then contact the clients directly.

4.1 Multiple client accounts

It is likely to be difficult to identify whose money is in which account if you hold client money in several different general client accounts with different banks. You need to be able to identify the total amounts held on behalf of each of your clients even though you will not know in which bank the individual's money is held.

If one of those banks fails, you should notify the FSCS of all client money held in all the general client accounts with that bank and the entitlement of clients to those funds. The FSCS will need to be satisfied as to the entitlement of individual clients to funds held in the client account. If funds are pooled between a number of different banks and it is not possible to identify which clients' funds are held in which bank, you will need to let the FSCS have the full picture of the money held in all the accounts.

You may need to seek additional funds from clients according to the proportion of the total funds held in the failed bank if you are to complete transactions for them before they receive compensation.

4.2 Accounts in foreign banks

You may move funds to foreign banks provided that the client's bank account is held at a branch in England and Wales under Rule 14(4) of the SARs.

You can check whether the bank is registered with the FSA by looking at the FSA online listing [at **www.fsa.gov.uk**].

The FSCS distinguishes between UK subsidiaries of overseas banks and UK branches of overseas banks. For UK subsidiaries of overseas banks, the FSCS will compensate for loss in the same way as for UK banks. For branches of overseas banks, you should normally make an application to any relevant scheme in the home country.

Some overseas EEA banks with branches in the UK have arrangements with the FSCS to top up any difference, e.g. as to the level of compensation between the branch's home state scheme and FSCS (up to the £50,000 UK limit). These branches are listed on the FSCS website.

5. What you should tell your client

You should explain to the client how their money is held by doing all of the following:

1. Explain that it is unlikely that you will be held liable for losses resulting from a banking failure.

2. Tell them the name of the bank in which their money is held.

3. Explain that the £50,000 FSCS limit applies to the individual client, and so if they hold other personal monies themselves in the same bank as your client account, the limit remains £50,000 in total.

4. Tell them that some deposit taking institutions have several brands, i.e. where the same institution is trading under different names. Clients should check either with their bank, the FSA or a financial adviser for more information.

5. Seek consent for the disclosure to FSCS of client details in the event of a bank failure.

6.   Qualified undertakings

Some solicitors have asked whether they can offer qualified undertakings.

You are free to decide whether to offer or accept an undertaking, so long as to do so is not against the client's interests. You do not need to give an undertaking simply because it is in the client's interests to do so. You may also negotiate the terms of their undertakings, where this is in the best interests of clients.

However, in residential conveyancing transactions, it is highly unlikely that buyers' solicitors could properly accept offers of a limited undertaking in their clients' best interest. Also, offering such an undertaking may breach the obligations of sellers' solicitors to their clients, depending on the terms of their retainer.

For further information on conveyancing undertakings to discharge mortgages see both:

*   rule 10.05 of the Solicitors' Code of Conduct [**www.rules.sra.org.uk**];
*   the *Conveyancing Handbook*, 15th edition. The relevant sections are section E.3, F.4 and the guidance on accepting undertakings after *Patel* v *Daybells* [2001] EWCA Civ 1229 in Appendix IV.7.

7.   Interest rates

You should ensure that your clients gain a rate of interest on their money consistent with the need to invest cautiously. At a time of volatile interest rates, you should check the interest rates paid on client accounts. You should change bankers if you consider that there is a better deal available elsewhere.

8. **Useful links**

- Solicitors' Accounts Rules [**www.sra.org.uk**]
- Financial Services Authority / FSA money made clear [**www.fsa.gov.uk**]
- HM Treasury [**www.hm-treasury.gov.uk**]
- Financial Services Compensation Scheme [**www.fscs.org.uk**]
- FSA Handbook [**http://fsahandbook.info/FSA/html/handbook**]

Annex 7B

Business continuity practice note

29 January 2009

1.   Introduction

1.1   Who should read this practice note?

Managing partners, practice managers and all staff concerned with the management and day-to-day operation of practices.

1.2   What is the issue?

Solicitors' practices need effective business continuity management (BCM) so they can handle their clients' business if something goes wrong.

This practice note outlines the essentials of BCM for solicitors and contains links to further help.

2.   What is business continuity management (BCM)?

BCM is not just about IT systems recovery. The British Standard for BCM, BS 25999, describes it as a management process that:

1.   identifies threats and impacts;

2.   builds the capacity for an effective response.

Its objective is to protect:

*   stakeholders;
*   reputation;
*   brand;
*   value-creating activities.

3.   Good practice for BCM

Practices should do all of the following:

1. Allocate overall responsibility for BCM to a partner, or staff members of equivalent seniority.

2. Conduct a risk assessment leading to risk improvement and increased resilience.

3. Create a written business continuity plan fully supported by necessary recovery provisions.

4. Conduct a programme of testing.

5. Implement a process of maintenance.

6. Communicate the BCM plan to staff.

The Department for Business, Enterprise and Regulatory Reform provides extensive guidance to assist firms in implementing business continuity management.

4.   Professional rules and statutory provision

Implementing BCM arrangements will help your practice to comply with the following:

4.1   Rule 5: Business management in England and Wales

Rule 5 deals with:

*   the supervision and management of a firm's in-house practice;
*   the maintenance of competence;
*   the internal business arrangements essential for the proper delivery of services to clients.

5.01(1)(k) requires provision for 'the continuation of the practice of the firm in the event of temporary absences and emergencies, with the minimum of disruption to clients' business'.

5.01(1)(l) requires provision for 'the management of risk'.

4.2   The Data Protection Act 1998 (DPA)

The seventh data protection principle in Schedule 1 to the Data Protection Act 1998 (DPA) requires data controllers to take appropriate technical and organisational measures against:

- unauthorised or unlawful processing of personal data;
- accidental loss or destruction of, or damage to, personal data.

5. More information

5.1 Status of this practice note

Practice notes are issued by the Law Society as a professional body for the benefit of its members. They represent the Law Society's view of good practice in a particular area. They are not intended to be the only standard, nor do they necessarily provide a defence to complaints of misconduct or of inadequate professional service. Solicitors are not required to follow them.

They do not constitute legal advice and, while care has been taken to ensure that they are accurate, up to date and useful, the Law Society will not accept any legal liability in relation to them.

For queries or comments on this practice note contact the Law Society's Practice Advice Service [**www.lawsociety.org.uk/practiceadvice**].

5.2 Terminology in this practice note

Must – a specific requirement in the Solicitors' Code of Conduct or legislation. You must comply, unless there are specific exemptions or defences provided for in the code of conduct or relevant legislation.

Should – good practice for most situations. If you deviate from this, you must be able to justify why this is appropriate, either for your firm, or in the particular retainer.

May – a non-exhaustive list of options for meeting your obligations. Which option you choose is determined by the risk profile of the individual firm, client or retainer. You must be able to justify why this was an appropriate option to oversight bodies.

5.3 Other products

5.3.1 Law Society practice note on information security

Managing information security within your practice.

5.3.2 Law Society training and events

Lexcel accredited training and development in BCM implementation.

5.3.3 Lexcel Practice Excellence Kit, 4th edition

Provides template procedures to enable firms to draft and enforce policies.

Annex 7C

Client care letters practice note

3 July 2008

1. Introduction

1.1 Who should read this practice note?

This practice note is relevant to all those who are required to prepare client care letters.

1.2 What is the issue?

Many clients are not regular users of legal services provided by solicitors. In addition, a solicitor is often instructed while the client is experiencing a stressful situation. The primary issue for the client is a successful resolution of their legal problem or completion of their transaction. Specific details around costs and what services you will provide to them can often be considered as secondary by the client until a problem arises.

A vital tool for helping to focus the client on the exact parameters of a retainer is the initial letter to the client, often called the client care letter, and any attached terms of business. They may also be used as evidence against complaints of insufficient information or inadequate professional service.

Even with knowledgeable or regular users of legal services, you should still ensure the exact scope of the retainer is recorded to limit the potential for disputes.

1.3 Professional conduct

The following sections of the Solicitors' Code of Conduct 2007 [**www.rules.sra.org.uk**] (code of conduct) are relevant to the information which has to be provided in writing to the client at the outset of the retainer:

- Rule 2.02 Client care
- Rule 2.03 Information about the cost

1.4   Status of this practice note

Practice notes are issued by the Law Society for the use and benefit of its members. They represent the Law Society's view of good practice in a particular area. They are not intended to be the only standard of good practice that solicitors can follow. You are not required to follow them, but doing so will make it easier to account to oversight bodies for your actions.

Practice notes are not legal advice, nor do they necessarily provide a defence to complaints of misconduct or of inadequate professional service. While care has been taken to ensure that they are accurate, up to date and useful, the Law Society will not accept any legal liability in relation to them.

The examples in this practice note are not the only way of meeting rule 2 of the code of conduct, and we recognise that many practices have already considered this issue in detail and implemented bespoke templates.

For queries or comments on this practice note, contact the Law Society's Practice Advice Service: **www.lawsociety.org.uk/practiceadvice**.

1.5   Terminology

Must – a specific requirement in the Solicitors' Code of Conduct or legislation. You must comply, unless there are specific exemptions or defences provided for in the code of conduct or relevant legislation.

Should – good practice for most situations in the Law Society's view. If you do not follow this, you should be able to justify to oversight bodies why the alternative approach you have taken is appropriate, either for your practice, or in the particular retainer.

May – a non-exhaustive list of options for meeting your obligations. Which option you choose is determined by the risk profile of the individual practice, client or retainer. You must be able to justify why this was an appropriate option to oversight bodies.

1.6   More information and products

1.6.1   Law Society

- Practice Advice Service
- Practice Advice Service costs booklets
- Training – regular programmes on client care and complaints management

- Lexcel – our practice management standard, awarded only to practices meeting the highest management and client care standards
- Law Management Section – join for support and training
- Law Society publications – order from our bookshop:

  - *Practice Management Handbook*
  - *Companion to the Solicitors' Code of Conduct 2007*
  - *The Solicitor's Handbook*
  - *Lexcel Office Procedures Manual*
  - *Excellent Client Service*

1.6.2 Other

- Solicitors Regulation Authority's Professional Ethics Helpline for advice on conduct issues.
- Legal Complaints Service (LCS) – investigates complaints about inadequate professional services. It runs Lawyerline, a telephone helpline for solicitors to assist with responding to client complaints. Call 0870 606 2588. Opening hours: 09.00 to 17.00, Monday to Friday.

2. Communication

2.1 Principles of effective communication

The code of conduct outlines a number of issues that must be communicated in writing to the client at the outset of the retainer. It does not specify a format for providing this written information, but states that it should be provided in a clear and readily accessible manner.

To communicate well, you should:

- make sure that the information you need to communicate is presented in a clear and straightforward manner. Complicated forms and overly legalistic language will act as a barrier to understanding;
- be alert to communication challenges which clients face, such as hearing difficulties, disability, learning difficulties, language barriers or other cross-cultural issues, and look at ways to overcome those challenges;
- consider your client demographic when deciding how to present information. For example, you may provide information in a language other than English, if you have a large client base from a particular ethnic group for whom English is a second language.

As people understand information differently, you may explain to your client the importance of the client care letters and the terms of business.

You should also provide the opportunity to explain any parts of the documents they do not understand or have questions about.

2.2   Length and style

Many clients complain about being given large documents containing lots of legal language in small print by their solicitors. Often these documents are not read or understood.

You should adopt the following style in your client care letters to help clients understand them:

- Prepare separate terms and conditions if the client care letter will exceed three pages once all of the required information is included. This ensures important information is not overlooked.
- Use a clear font such as Arial or Times New Roman, in no smaller than 11 point. Use at least single line spacing.
- Make use of headings and bullet points to break up blocks of text and highlight points.
- Use plain language.
- Only include terms and conditions which actually apply to the specific retainer.
- Include a table of contents, if the terms and conditions are longer than five pages.

3.   Client care letters

3.1   Who is the client?

While not a regulatory requirement, your client care letter should clearly identify who you understand your client to be and what capacity they are acting in. This is particularly relevant when acting for more than one person, for a trustee, an agent or for a legal entity.

3.2   Client's instructions

Rule 2.02 provides that you must both:

- clearly identify the client's objectives in relation to the work to be done for the client;
- give the client a clear explanation of the issues involved and the options available to them.

Confirming this in writing will create a contemporaneous record of the scope of the relevant retainer. This will be one relevant factor in resolving complaints of failing to comply with instructions.

You should also include information about any limitations or specific exclusions from the retainer. For example, you may need to advise the client that standard local authority searches on a conveyance may not guarantee that the land is not contaminated and so they may wish to seek the advice of an environmental consultant.

3.3   Agree the next steps

Rule 2.02 provides that you must agree with your client at the outset the next steps to be taken [**www.rules/sra.org.uk** for most recent version].

Confirming this in writing will provide a clear record for you and the client of what will happen next. You should include information about timescales for completing these next steps where possible, to manage the client's expectations and provide yourself with a timetable to help limit delay.

3.4   Who will be handling the retainer?

You must give the client the name and status of the person dealing with the matter and the name of the person responsible for its overall supervision.

You should advise who in your office will be able to access the client's file and answer routine queries when you are out of the office.

You should also set out how the client is best able to contact you. For example: 'I can usually be contacted by telephone after [*time*] each day.'

3.5   Costs

The failure to provide adequate costs information is one of the areas most likely to result in a client complaint.

Rule 2.03 of the code of conduct provides that you must give your client the best information possible about the likely overall cost of a matter at the outset and at other appropriate times. You must also discuss with them whether the likely outcome of the matter will justify the risks involved.

The client needs to thoroughly understand the cost implications of proceeding with a matter before they can make an informed decision on whether to proceed and whether to retain your firm. You should communicate all costs information in plain language and in a way which makes it clear to the client exactly what they are paying for.

You must provide all costs information in writing.

For further advice on providing costs information see:

- rule 2.03 and related guidance in the code of conduct;
- Practice Advice Service booklets.

3.5.1   Best possible information

To give the best information possible, you may:

- agree a fixed fee;
- give a realistic estimate;
- give a forecast within a possible range of costs;
- explain why overall costs cannot be fixed or realistically estimated – instead give best information possible about the cost of the next stage of the matter.

3.5.2   Providing details of charges

You must make it clear how charges are calculated. You must outline:

- the basis for the fixed fee or the relevant hourly rates and an estimate of the time to be charged;
- whether rates may be increased during the period of the retainer;
- expected disbursements and likely timeframes for these being due;
- potential liability for others' costs, where relevant;
- VAT liability.

3.5.3   Method of payment

You must confirm with the client how and when any costs are to be paid. In doing so, you must consider whether the client may:

- be eligible for legal aid and should apply for it;
- be offered a conditional fee agreement;
- have insurance that may cover another party's costs – if they do not, you should consider whether to advise the client to seek after-the-event insurance to cover such costs;
- seek payment of the costs from another person such as an employer or trade union.

3.5.4   Other points

You must provide costs information to the client even where the client will not themselves be paying for your services, e.g. if they are publicly funded, covered by insurance or instructing you under a conditional fee agreement.

You must outline the circumstances in which the client may be liable for the costs of other parties, including where they are successful and obtain an award for costs.

You must advise your client that you can exercise a lien over their papers for unpaid costs. This may be done in the letter or in the terms of business with respect to terminating the retainer.

You should outline your standard billing arrangements and discuss any requirements for receiving funds on account.

You should, in appropriate cases, explain that the client may set an upper limit on the costs the firm may incur without obtaining further authority and that you will contact them in writing when this limit is being approached to discuss the issue of costs further.

3.6   Complaints

You must advise clients in writing of their right to complain, and the process for doing so. You should include a simple prominent paragraph in the client care letter.

For example:

Complaints

[Practice name] is committed to high quality legal advice and client care. If you are unhappy about any aspect of the service you have received, please contact [Name] on [phone number and e-mail] or by post to our [place] office.

For further information on managing complaints effectively, see the Law Society's complaints management practice note [**www.lawsociety.org.uk/ productsandservices/practicenotes/complaintsmgnt.page** and **Annex 7D**].

3.7   Terms of business

Where you have separate terms of business, you should make reference to their existence and explain their importance.

If there is a significant aspect of service or another unusual aspect of the retainer specifically agreed with the client that forms part of your usual terms of business, you should consider whether to simply amend the terms of business, or include it separately in the client care letter.

3.8   Client's acknowledgement

While not a regulatory requirement, you should get your client to sign and date a copy of the client care letter and any attached terms of business. This helps you if there is a complaint from the client that they were not provided with the relevant information or that it was not sufficiently clear.

Under rule 48.8 of the Civil Procedure Rules, if the client has not agreed your terms of business in a contentious matter in the County Court, you will be unable to claim any more costs from the client than the client is entitled to recover from the other side.

4.   Terms of business

4.1   General terms

4.1.1   Service standards

At the outset of the retainer you must agree an appropriate level of service with the client. You should confirm this in writing.

Service standards may include:

We will update you [by telephone or in writing] with progress on your matter [regularly, fortnightly, monthly, following agreed events] – the Law Society believes this should occur at least every six weeks, unless agreed to the contrary.

- We will communicate with you in plain language.
- We will explain to you [by telephone or in writing] the legal work required as your matter progresses.
- We will update you on the cost of your matter [monthly, three monthly, six monthly, at agreed events] – the Law Society believes this should occur at least every six months.
- We will update you on whether the likely outcomes still justify the likely costs and risks associated with your matter whenever there is a material change in circumstances.
- We will update you on the likely timescales for each stage of this matter and any important changes in those estimates.
- We will continue to review whether there are alternative methods by which your matter can be funded.

4.1.2   Responsibilities

You must explain to the client the respective responsibilities of the solicitor and the client in relation to the particular retainer. You should confirm these in writing.

Your responsibilities may include:

- We will review your matter regularly.
- We will advise you of any changes in the law.
- We will advise you of any circumstances and risks of which we are aware or consider to be reasonably foreseeable that could affect the outcome of your matter.

The client's responsibilities may include:

- You will provide us with clear, timely and accurate instructions.
- You will provide all documentation required to complete the transaction in a timely manner.
- You will safeguard any documents which are likely to be required for discovery.

4.1.3   Hours of business

You should advise the client of your practice's normal opening hours and the details of any out-of-hours or emergency service you provide.

4.1.4   Equality and diversity

Rule 6.03 of the code of conduct provides that you must have an equality and diversity policy and make it available where requested. You should make sure that client's are aware that such a policy exists and that they can ask for a copy.

You may wish to highlight your policy in your terms of business. For example:

[*Practice name*] is committed to promoting equality and diversity in all of its dealings with clients, third parties and employees. Please contact us if you would like a copy of our equality and diversity policy.

4.1.5   Data protection

You must comply with the Data Protection Act 1998 with respect to information held on your client. You should include reference to how you comply with the Data Protection Act in your terms of business.

For example:

We use the information you provide primarily for the provision of legal services to you and for related purposes including:

- updating and enhancing client records;
- analysis to help us manage our practice;
- statutory returns;
- legal and regulatory compliance.

Our use of that information is subject to your instructions, the Data Protection Act 1998 and our duty of confidentiality. Please note that our work for you may require us to give information to third parties such as expert witnesses and other professional advisers. You have a right of access under data protection legislation to the personal data that we hold about you.

We may from time to time send you information which we think might be of interest to you. If you do not wish to receive that information please notify our office in writing.

4.1.6   Storage of documents

You should advise the client how long you will retain the file and outline what will happen to the file after that time.

You should advise the client of costs related to all of the following:

- storage;
- retrieval;
- additional copies.

If you intend to store documents in an electronic format, you should first consider whether the absence of paper documents will be detrimental to the client's interests, before you agree to such storage methods with your client.

You should also consider any file retention requirements of your indemnity insurers when assessing the appropriate length of time to retain client files.

For further information on storage of files, particularly in relation to wills and probate files, see the Law Society's file retention practice note [**www.lawsociety.org.uk/productsandservices/practicenotes/filereten-tion.page**].

For further information on retention of client due diligence files, see paragraph 3.8 of the Law Society's anti-money laundering practice note

[www.lawsociety.org.uk/productsandservices/practicenotes/aml/386.
article].

For example:

After completing the work, we will be entitled to keep all your papers and documents while there is still money owed to us for fees and expenses.

We will keep our file of your papers for up to [x] years, except those papers that you ask to be returned to you. We keep files on the understanding that we can destroy them [x] years after the date of the final bill. We will not destroy documents you ask us to deposit in safe custody.

If we take papers or documents out of storage in relation to continuing or new instructions to act for you, we will not normally charge for such retrieval. However we may charge you both for:

- time spent producing stored papers that are requested;
- reading, correspondence or other work necessary to comply with your instructions in relation to the retrieved papers.

4.1.7   Outsourcing of work

Where you outsource work on client files, there is a risk your outsourced provider may breach client confidentiality.

Drawing attention to this risk may mitigate any breach of confidentiality which then occurs, but you still risk a finding of misconduct or inadequate professional service. You should ensure that you have a confidentiality agreement with your suppliers.

In your terms and conditions you should:

- advise the client if the practice outsources work and the type of work it outsources;
- alert the client to the potential risks in relation to preserving client confidentiality;
- ask the client to tell you if they object to this practice.

For example:

Sometimes we ask other companies or people to do [typing/photocopying/other work] on our files to ensure this is done promptly. We will always seek a confidentiality agreement with these outsourced providers. If you do not want your file to be outsourced, please tell us as soon as possible.

4.1.8 Vetting of files and confidentiality

Where your files are required to be produced to assessors or others as part of an audit or quality check you should advise your client of this.

For example:

External firms or organisations may conduct audit or quality checks on our practice. These external firms or organisations are required to maintain confidentiality in relation to your files.

4.1.9 Limiting liability

Rule 2.07 of the code of conduct allows you to limit your practice's liability under certain circumstances. You must ensure that you advise the client of any limitation of liability in writing and specifically draw their attention to it.

Where your practice is a LLP you should also explain any limitation on personal liability for the members, directors and employees of the practice.

For further details on restrictions in relation to the limitation of liability, see the guidance to rule 2.07.

For example:

Our liability to you for a breach of your instructions shall be limited to £X, unless we expressly state a higher amount in the letter accompanying these terms of business. We will not be liable for any consequential, special, indirect or exemplary damages, costs or losses or any damages, costs or losses attributable to lost profits or opportunities.

We can only limit our liability to the extent the law allows. In particular, we cannot limit our liability for death or personal injury caused by our negligence.

Please ask if you would like us to explain any of the terms above.

4.1.10 Applicable law

You may specifically state that the law of England and Wales applies to any disputes over the terms and conditions, particularly if there is any international aspect to the retainer.

For example:

Any dispute or legal issue arising from our terms of business will be determined by the law of England and Wales, and considered exclusively by the English and Welsh courts.

4.1.11   *Terminating the retainer*

You should clearly state the manner in which a client can terminate your retainer and the consequences of them doing so. You should also outline the circumstances under which you can terminate the retainer, in accordance with rule 2.01. This may be an appropriate place to mention your right to a lien for unpaid costs.

For example:

You may end your instructions to us in writing at any time, but we can keep all your papers and documents while there is still money owed to us for fees and expenses.

We may decide to stop acting for you only with good reason, e.g. if you do not pay an interim bill or there is a conflict of interest. We must give you reasonable notice that we will stop acting for you.

If you or we decide that we should stop acting for you, you will pay our charges up until that point. These are calculated on [an hourly basis plus expenses/by proportion of the agreed fee] as set out in these terms and conditions.

4.2   Money laundering and terrorist financing

Your anti-money laundering obligations depend on whether you are providing services to this client within the regulated sector [1.4.5 of the anti-money laundering practice note (**Annex 5A**)].

If you are providing a client with regulated services, you must conduct client due diligence and monitor your client's retainer for warning signs of money laundering or terrorist financing.

If you are not providing a client with regulated services, you must still monitor your client's retainer for warning signs of money laundering or terrorist financing.

If you provide both regulated and non-regulated services, you may wish to apply the higher level of obligations to all clients. However, you should consider the cost implications of doing so.

For advice on whether you are providing services within the regulated sector and other anti-money laundering requirements, see the Law Society's anti-money laundering practice note [**www.lawsociety.org.uk/ productsandservices/practicenotes/aml/386.article** and **Annex 5A**].

For further advice on your counter terrorist financing obligations, see the Law Society's anti-terrorism practice note [**www.lawsociety.org.uk/ productsandservices/practicenotes/antiterrorism.page** and **Annex 5A**].

4.2.1   Client due diligence

For more information on how to conduct CDD, see Chapter 4 of the Law Society's anti-money laundering practice note [**www.lawsociety.org.uk/ productsandservices/practicenotes/aml/386.article** and **Annex 5A**].

While you may have already obtained CDD material before sending out the client care letter, you should still include information in the terms and conditions about your CDD obligations.

You should cover all of the following points in your terms and conditions:

- The Money Laundering Regulations 2007 require you to:

  - obtain information about a client's identity and to verify that information;
  - obtain identity information about people related to the client (beneficial owners), where relevant, and at times verify that information;
  - continue to monitor the transaction and keep identity information up to date.

- There are a number of processes by which you may verify a client's identity. You should state your practice's preferred method of verification, e.g. passport.
- You should state any fees being passed on to clients for the purposes of conducting CDD. The photocopying of a passport or similar activities would come within normal administration costs, but search fees charged by external providers may be charged to the client as a disbursement.
- If the client has difficulty providing the information you requested, you should ask them to contact you to discuss other ways to verify their identity.

For example:

The law requires solicitors to get satisfactory evidence of the identity of their clients and sometimes people related to them. This is because solicitors who deal with money and property on behalf of their client can be used by criminals wanting to launder money.

To comply with the law, we need to get evidence of your identity as soon as possible. Our practice is to [insert your standard practice]. The fee for these searches is £[x] and will appear on your bill under expenses.

If you cannot provide us with the specific identification requested, please contact us as soon as possible to discuss other ways to verify your identity.

4.2.2   Making a disclosure

If you suspect a client is engaged in money laundering or terrorist financing, you may risk committing a principal money laundering or terrorism offence or an offence of failing to disclose your suspicions to relevant authorities.

For further information on your legal options in these circumstances, see Chapter 5 of the Law Society's anti-money laundering practice note [**www.lawsociety.org.uk/productsandservices/practicenotes/aml/457. article** and **Annex 5A**].

Making a disclosure may require you to either temporarily cease work on the client's retainer or to withdraw completely. It is not tipping off to include a paragraph about your obligations under the money laundering legislation in your terms of business.

For example:

We are professionally and legally obliged to keep your affairs confidential. However, solicitors may be required by statute to make a disclosure to the Serious Organised Crime Agency where they know or suspect that a transaction may involve money laundering or terrorist financing. If we make a disclosure in relation to your matter, we may not be able to tell you that a disclosure has been made. We may have to stop working on your matter for a period of time and may not be able to tell you why.

4.3   Mortgage fraud

Where you are acting for both the lender and the purchaser you should highlight the lender's requirements that you fully disclose to them relevant facts affecting their decision to make the loan. If you specifically draw this term to your client's attention and have them sign their acceptance of this term, then you may rely on this as consent from the client to make the disclosures to the lender.

For example:

We are also acting for your proposed lender [Name of bank/building society] in this transaction. We have a duty to fully reveal to your lender all relevant facts about the purchase and mortgage. This includes:

- any differences between your mortgage application and information we receive during the transaction;
- any cash back payments or discount schemes that a seller is giving you.

4.4   Fees and costs-related matters

4.4.1   Introductions and referrals

Rule 9.02 of the code of conduct [**www.rules.sra.org.uk**] provides that you must advise the client about any relationship you have with a third party, such as a funder, fee-sharer or introducer that affects steps you can take on the client's behalf. You must provide full disclosure regarding the extent of any payments made between yourself and the third party.

For example:

We have a financial relationship with [firm name] regarding your case/transaction. As a result of this relationship we:

- (Option A) Pay [practice name] £[x] for them to refer your case/transaction to us];
- (Option B) Receive £[x] from [practice name] to provide you with [service name(s)]. You will be required to pay £[x] to [practice name] for these services].

Despite this financial relationship with [practice name], we will provide you with independent advice and you are able to raise questions with us about any aspect of your case/transaction.

Any information you provide to us during your case/transaction will not be shared with [practice name] unless you agree. However, because we are acting both for you and [practice name] in your case/transaction, we may have to stop acting for both of you if there is a conflict of interest.

4.4.2   Payment of commissions

You must not make secret profit from your relationship with your client. Rule 2.06 of the code of conduct provides that you must pay any commission over £20 to your client unless you have told them the amount and they agree to you keeping this.

The guidance to rule 2.06 provides that you should put the agreement regarding the retention of the commission in writing and that agreement must be obtained prior to receiving the commission. The Law Society believes you should have a separate written agreement for the commission, rather than simply including the details in your client care letter or terms of business.

If the commission relates to activities regulated by the FSA then you must obtain permission from the client even if the commission is valued under £20.

4.4.3   Payment of interest

The Solicitor's Accounts Rules [**www.sra.org.uk/accounts-rules**] provide that you must account to the client for any interest earned on client monies. You should advise the client of any circumstances where interest will be payable to them, and how and when you will account to them for it.

For example:

Any money received on your behalf will be held in our client account. Interest will be calculated and paid to you at the rate set by [name of bank and relevant accounts]. That of course may change. The period for which interest will be paid normally runs from the date(s) when funds are received by us until the date(s) on the cheque(s) issued to you. The payment of interest is subject to certain minimum amounts and periods of time set out in the Solicitors' Accounts Rules 1998.

4.4.4   Distance selling

If you have not met the client, you must consider whether the Consumer Protection (Distance Selling) Regulations 2000 apply. These regulations provide for a period during which the client can cancel their instructions without cost. You should include information about this right in the terms of business.

For example:

We have not met with you, so the Consumer Protection (Distance Selling) Regulations 2000 apply to this file. This means you have the right to cancel your instructions to us within seven working days of receiving this letter. You can cancel your instructions by contacting us by post or by fax to this office.

Once we have started work on your file, you may be charged if you then cancel your instructions. If you would like us to commence work on your file within the next seven working days, please:

- sign these terms and conditions;
- tick the box marked 'commence work now';
- return it to this office by post or fax.

For further information on distance selling requirements, see the Office of Fair Trading website [**www.oft.gov.uk**].

4.4.5   Financial arrangements with clients

You should tell clients how you will receive funds from them and make payments to them. This is due to the strict requirements for client accounts, and the risk that clients may try to use your client account to launder money.

For example:

Our practice's policy is [not to accept cash from clients/to only accept cash up to £X].

If you try to avoid this policy by depositing cash directly with our bank, we may decide to charge you for any additional checks we decide are necessary to prove the source of the funds.

Where we have to pay money to you, it will be paid by cheque or bank transfer. It will not be paid in cash or to a third party.

4.5   Financial services

If your practice is authorised by the Financial Services Authority (FSA), you must ensure you comply with the requirements of the FSA as to status disclosure statements in your terms of business.

4.5.1   *Providing exempt financial services*

If you are not authorised by the FSA, as a solicitor you are still entitled to carry out exempt regulated activities under the regulation of the SRA, as part of the Designated Professional Body regime. You must include a disclosure in your terms and conditions which clearly states your regulatory status.

You must tell your client in writing in a manner which is clear, fair and not misleading:

*   that you are not authorised under the Financial Services and Markets Act nor are you regulated by the FSA;
*   the nature of the exempt regulated activities you will be carrying out and that they are limited in scope;
*   that you are regulated by the Law Society as the designated professional body, while outlining the role of the Solicitor's Regulation Authority and the Legal Complaints Service.

If the exempt regulated activities involve insurance mediation activity, there is a separate paragraph which must be included – see section 4.5.2 below.

For further information on exempt regulated activities see the FSA handbook [**http://fsahandbook.info/FSA/html/handbook**].

For example:

We are not authorised by the Financial Services Authority. If, while we are acting for you, you need advice on investments, we may have to refer you to someone who is authorised to provide the necessary advice.

However, we may provide certain limited investment advice services where these are closely linked to the legal work we are doing for you. This is because we are members of the Law Society of England and Wales, which is a designated professional body for the purposes of the Financial Services and Markets Act 2000.

The Solicitors Regulations Authority is the independent regulatory arm of the Law Society. The Legal Complaints Service is the independent complaints-handling arm of the Law Society. If you are unhappy with any investment advice you receive from us, you should raise your concerns with either of those bodies.

4.5.2   *Providing exempt insurance mediation*

You must register with the Financial Service Authority's Exempt Professional Firm's register to engage in insurance mediation work.

Insurance mediation work includes advising on and/or arranging an insurance policy. Common examples include advising on and/or arranging defective title indemnity insurance in conveyancing matters, or after-the-event insurance in litigation.

If you carry out any insurance mediation activities, you must advise the client in writing in a manner which is clear, fair and not misleading, what your regulated status is.

The FSA provides that the following statement must be included in your terms and conditions:

We are not authorised by the Financial Services Authority. However, we are included on the register maintained by the Financial Services Authority so that we may carry on insurance mediation activity, which is broadly the advising on, selling and administration of insurance contracts. This part of our business, including arrangements for complaints or redress if something goes wrong, is regulated by the Solicitors Regulation Authority. The register can be accessed via the Financial Services website at **www.fsa.gov.uk/ register**.

The Law Society of England and Wales is a designated professional body for the purposes of the Financial Services and Markets Act 2000. The Solicitors Regulation Authority is the independent regulatory arm of the Law Society. The Legal Complaints Service is the independent complaints-handling arm of the Law Society. If you are unhappy with any insurance advice you receive from us, you should raise your concerns with either of those bodies.

Annex 7D

Complaints management practice note

9 April 2008

Chapter 1 – Introduction

1.1 Who should read this practice note?

This practice note is relevant to managing partners, practice managers and all employees involved in responding to complaints.

1.2 What is the issue?

Rule 2 of the Solicitors' Code of Conduct 2007 requires that all practices have a process for responding to client complaints. However, there are several further reasons why good quality complaints management is essential for a practice wanting to remain competitive in today's legal market.

1.2.1 Enhanced accountability

An effective complaints management process enables individual solicitors and practices to demonstrate how they discharge their professional obligations and meet reasonable client expectations. Solicitors are held to account by regulators and clients for how they conduct themselves, both in terms of technical legal skills and client care.

1.2.2 Accepting that complaints will occur

Complaints are a business risk which cannot be avoided, but must instead be managed. However high your standard of client care, you cannot keep all clients, and others contacting your practice, happy all the time.

1.2.3   All feedback is useful

While praise is preferable, complaints are crucial feedback on how to improve your practice. An effective complaints management process is an integral aspect of quality client care. It allows you to continually improve business practices, retain clients, enhance your reputation and remain competitive.

1.3   Professional conduct

The following sections of the Solicitors' Code of Conduct 2007 (code of conduct) are relevant to complaints management:

• Rule 2.05 Complaints Handling [**www.rules.sra.org.uk**].

1.4   Status of this practice note

Practice notes are issued by the Law Society as a professional body for the benefit of its members. They represent the Law Society's view of good practice in a particular area. They are not intended to be the only standard, nor do they necessarily provide a defence to complaints of misconduct or of inadequate professional service. Solicitors are not required to follow them.

They do not constitute legal advice and, while care has been taken to ensure that they are accurate, up to date and useful, the Law Society will not accept any legal liability in relation to them.

For queries or comments on this practice note contact the Law Society's Practice Advice Service (**www.lawsociety.org.uk/practiceadvice**).

1.5   Terminology

Must – a specific requirement in the Solicitors' Code of Conduct or legislation. You must comply, unless there are specific exemptions or defences provided for in the code of conduct or relevant legislation.

Should – good practice for most situations. If you deviate from this, you must be able to justify why this is appropriate, either for your practice, or in the particular retainer.

May – a non-exhaustive list of options for meeting your obligations. Which option you choose is determined by the risk profile of the individual practice, client or retainer. You must be able to justify why this was an appropriate option to oversight bodies.

1.6   More information and products

Many have had input into the preparation of this practice note. The members of the Money Laundering Task Force and others mentioned below deserve particular acknowledgement for both the time and energy they have committed to the development of the guidance.

1.6.1   Law Society

- Practice Advice Service
- Practice Advice Service booklet: Your Client – Your Business
- Training – regular programmes on client care and complaints management
- Lexcel – our practice management standard, awarded only to practices meeting the highest management and customer care standards
- Law Management Section – join for support and training
- Law Society publications – order from our bookshop:
  - *Practice Management Handbook*
  - *Companion to the Solicitors' Code of Conduct 2007*

1.6.2   Other

- Solicitors Regulation Authority's Professional Ethics Helpline for advice on conduct issues.
- Legal Complaints Service (LCS) – investigates complaints about inadequate professional services. It runs Lawyerline, a telephone helpline for solicitors to assist with responding to client complaints. Call 0870 606 2588. Opening hours: 08.00 to 16.00 Tuesday to Thursday, and 07.00 to 15.00 on Fridays.
- Law Management Section – join for support and training.

1.7   Acknowledgements

To ensure the quality of this practice note, the Law Society has reviewed guidance published by a number of complaints bodies and the International Standards Organisation. Specific reference has been made to:

- ISO 10002: 'Quality management – Customer satisfaction – Guidelines for complaints handling in organizations';
- Queensland Ombudsman: 'Effective complaints management' – fact sheets;
- Financial Ombudsman Service UK: 'A guide for complaints handlers';
- The Commission for Local Administration in England: 'Running a complaints system';

- Law Society publications: 'Your Client – Your Business' (2007) and *Handling Complaints Effectively* (2006).

Chapter 2 – Principles of complaints management

2.1   Visibility

Information on how and where to complain should be well publicised to clients.

2.2   Accessibility

A complaints management process should be easy to access for all clients and free of charge. Make information available on how to make a complaint and how it will be resolved. The process and supporting information should be easy to understand and use. You should consider formats for information in light of your client demographic and principles of equality.

2.3   Responsiveness

The timeliness of your response is as important as its tone, in reassuring your client that they are being taken seriously. Acknowledge receipt of each complaint to the client and address the complaint promptly. Treat clients courteously and update them on the progress of their complaint through the complaints management process.

2.4   Objectivity

It is important to see a complaint as an opportunity for improvement in client care rather than as a personal attack on your practice. Address all complaints in an equitable, objective and unbiased manner through the complaints management process.

2.5   Confidentiality

As with any information received from the client during a retainer, you should treat the information received through the complaints management process with confidentiality. Only make personally identifiable information about the client available where needed, for the purposes of addressing the complaint within the practice.

Details of staff involvement should also be treated with discretion.

2.6   Client-focused approach

Your clients are the future of the practice. A satisfied client can recommend up to five new clients, but a dissatisfied client can lose the practice up to 23 new clients. You should adopt a client-focused approach, be open to feedback including complaints, and show commitment to resolving complaints by taking action. You should remain sensitive to the individual differences and needs of your client.

2.7   Accountability

You should set clear accountability within the practice for responding to complaints, deciding on action, and reporting on these decisions.

2.8   Communication

Good communication is essential to both high quality client care and effective complaints management. Poor communication will result in clients feeling that they have not been understood, taken seriously or valued, which in turn is likely to lead them to raise their complaints in another forum. Effective communication can help to resolve disputes quickly and build greater client loyalty.

To communicate well, you should:

- make sure that the information you need to communicate is presented in a clear and straightforward manner. Complicated forms and overly legalistic language will act as a barrier to clients seeking to resolve their concerns directly with you, and instead encourage them to seek other avenues of redress;
- be alert to communication challenges which clients face, such as hearing difficulties, disability, language barriers or other cross-cultural issues, and look at ways to overcome those challenges;
- genuinely listen to the client and seek to understand the situation from their point of view. Clients who feel that they have been genuinely listened to are more confident that they are being taken seriously and will be more open to resolving the situation through your practice, rather than seeking external intervention;

- keep clients updated on the progress of their complaint and outline what the next step in the process is and the likely timeframes.

Address the specific issues raised by the complaint, rather than simply providing a stock standard response. Even if you decide that the complaint is not justified or that you are unable to provide the client with the remedy they seek, be polite and professional in your response. Clients are more likely to respect the decision you have made if it has been explained clearly and has been delivered in a respectful manner.

Chapter 3 – Framework

3.1   Types of complaints

Rule 2 specifically requires that practices respond to complaints from clients. However, complaints can come from a range of other sources, including:

- people connected with the client, such as family members, carers and guardians;
- solicitors representing the other side of the dispute or transaction;
- barristers involved in the retainer;
- those involved in the justice system such as judges, court officials and prison officials.

Rule 1 says you must not behave in a way that diminishes the trust the public places in you or the profession. Complaints from any source can undermine the reputation of the practice. A well-developed complaints management process should be able to adapt to resolve complaints from all of these sources.

A complaint is any expression of dissatisfaction made to a practice in relation to the legal services, client care or complaints management processes provided by the practice, where a response or resolution is explicitly or implicitly expected.

The general principles in this practice note apply to any category of complaint. However, you must consider whether the complaint involves matters which you can resolve internally, or whether you need to notify any other agencies of the complaint.

Complaints will generally fall within one or more of the following four categories:

3.1.1 Inadequate professional service

Any aspect of client care falling below that which could be reasonably expected. These complaints may be considered by the Legal Complaints Service.

3.1.2 Negligence

A failure to provide legal services to the standard provided by a reasonably competent solicitor. These complaints may involve your insurers or the courts.

3.1.3 Misconduct

A breach of the Solicitors' Code of Conduct. These complaints may be investigated by the Solicitors Regulation Authority. Rule 20.04 requires that you must report serious misconduct to the SRA.

3.1.4 Criminal conduct

On rare occasions allegations of criminal conduct may be made. These may warrant the involvement of the police.

3.2 Models

A complaints management process is a structured process for receiving, recording, investigating and responding to complaints. A good system will be simple, transparent and timely. It should complement your practice's values and be integral to the way your practice conducts its practice.

The code of conduct allows practices to determine the form of their complaints management system. This will depend on the size and structure of the practice and the volume and nature of complaints received.

Components of a complaints management process include:

3.2.1 An initial client service stage

Frontline staff members should be designated and trained for receiving complaints. They should have the authority to deal with specified low-level client complaints, such as apologising for failing to respond to a letter and preparing and sending the response. This stage should include complaint registration and attempted resolution.

3.2.2   An internal investigation or review stage

This stage applies where:

- the complaint is more serious and requires investigation;
- the complaint raises allegations of repeated and systemic poor service;
- the client seeks an internal review of a decision.

Any investigation or review should be undertaken by someone in the practice uninvolved with the retainer resulting in the complaint. This person should be at least as senior as the person complained about or the person who initially responded to the complaint.

3.2.3   An external investigation stage

Where a practice cannot resolve a complaint directly with the client, an independent third party may be required. You may offer the client the opportunity to involve an independent mediator to assist with resolving the complaint. For inadequate professional service matters, the client should be advised of their right to raise their concerns with the Legal Complaints Service.

3.2.4   Continuous improvement features

An effective complaints management process will feed into continuous improvement of your practice's practices. Record relevant complaints data and analyse it for both the causes of individual complaints and trends in complaints. You should use this information to help enhance business processes and employee training.

3.3   Policy

Rule 2 provides that practices must have a document on complaints management, which outlines in clear and concise terms the general processes which will be followed when a complaint is made. This is the document which must be made available to clients and other interested parties upon request, in accordance with rule 2.05.

Read a sample complaints management policy [at Annex 1 to this practice note] which you may wish to adapt for your practice.

Internally, depending on the size of your practice, you may require more detailed procedures. These should comply with the public policy, but will outline:

- how complaints are to be recorded and filed;
- who needs to be notified, internally and externally, about different types of complaints;
- who has authority for dealing with complaints;
- timescales for investigating the complaint and responding to the client;
- circumstances in which complaints should be escalated within the practice;
- circumstances in which no action will be taken on complaints or communication with a complainant will cease;
- guidelines on appropriate remedies;
- training requirements for staff on complaints management.

3.4   Management commitment

Rule 2 of the code of conduct is specifically directed at practice principals, recognising the crucial role which management commitment plays in developing a culture of client care and effective complaints management.

Senior management must be supportive of the complaints management process, and encourage a workplace culture that embraces accountability and opportunities for continual improvement.

A complaints management process will be most effective when the practice as a whole commits to:

- encouraging both positive and negative feedback from clients;
- accepting the right of clients to complain;
- acknowledging the benefits of an effective complaints management process;
- approaching complaint resolution in a non-defensive, open and proactive way;
- providing remedies that meet the client's needs;
- promoting accountability for effective complaints management within the practice;
- using complaints information to continually improve business practices and levels of client care.

To effectively build a positive complaints culture in your practice, senior management should:

- raise awareness among staff of the complaints management process;
- appropriately resource the process;
- model good complaints management behaviour.

3.5   Ensuring visibility and access

You must advise clients in writing of their right to complain, and the process for doing so, at the start of a retainer. You should include a simple prominent paragraph in the client care letter or your standard terms and conditions.

For example:

Complaints

> [Practice name] is committed to high quality legal advice and client care. If you are unhappy about any aspect of the service you have received please contact [Name] on [phone number and e-mail] or by post to our [place] office.

Additional options for ensuring high visibility of the complaints management process may include:

- including contact details for complaints as a footer in all client correspondence or fee notes;
- a feedback section with contact details on your website;
- a sign in the office reception highlighting your commitment to client care and listing complaint contact details.

Consider your client demographic when deciding how to present information. For example, you may provide information in a language other than English, if you have a large client base from a particular ethnic group for whom English is a second language.

3.6   Resources

A complaints management process needs resources to be effective. This includes both people and equipment. While it is up to each practice to decide the appropriate levels of resources to be allocated, a complaints management process should:

- ensure complaints receive an appropriate response in a timely manner;
- enable lessons learnt from the complaint to be incorporated into continuous business improvement.

To decide on allocation of resources, you should consider:

- the size of your practice;
- the number and severity of the complaints received;
- the flexibility of existing resources.

3.6.1   Personnel

Rule 2 provides that all staff must to be aware of:

- your complaints management process;
- what information to provide to clients;
- the importance of recording relevant information about the complaint.

You may employ a complaints manager to oversee the complaints management process. Such a role may be combined with responsibilities for business development, risk management, regulatory compliance or other relevant areas.

Even if the role is shared between existing staff, you should be clear on who has authority to:

- make decisions on complaints;
- internally review such decisions.

You should ensure these staff members clearly understand their authority and the scope of their role and provide this information to other staff members.

You should make complaints management policies, procedures and forms easily accessible for all staff. You should provide the relevant staff with regular training on the practice's complaints management process. Staff who actually manage the practice's complaints may benefit from training on communication skills, negotiation, stress management and problem solving.

You should encourage staff to be involved in the complaints management process to help them develop a greater awareness of client service issues. They will then feel involved in developing and maintaining strong client relationships. A supportive environment focusing on appropriate accountability and learning, rather than blame, will greatly enhance staff support of the complaints management process.

3.6.2   Equipment

Your practice should be able to receive complaints in any format in which you communicate with clients. This may include mail, fax, telephone and e-mail.

Systems for recording complaints information and tracking the progress of a complaint may be electronic or paper based. Whichever option is chosen, the process should ensure that:

- every complaint is recorded;
- key information about the complaint is captured in a central repository;
- the status of each complaint and the response provided can be identified;
- complaints are periodically reviewed to limit recurrence of the situations which led to the complaint and enhance business practices.

Chapter 4 – The complaints management process

4.1   Receiving and recording

You should have processes in place to receive complaints by telephone or in writing. You may also provide an e-mail address or a web-based form for submission of complaints.

You should record the following information on receipt, to ensure complaints are responded to promptly and that relevant information is captured to assist with business improvement:

- the client's contact details;
- a short summary of the complaint, attaching any supporting documentation received;
- specific issues complained about;
- any remedy requested;
- date for a response;
- who will prepare the response;
- any immediate action taken.

It should be possible to track the complaint through the practice, and for updates to be provided to the client on request, or at pre-determined times.

4.2   Acknowledgement

You should acknowledge each complaint promptly, preferably in writing, even if it was received by telephone. Prompt acknowledgement will increase the client's perception that you are taking the matter seriously and are seeking a resolution.

The code of conduct does not set a specific timeframe for acknowledgement of a complaint. However, we believe acknowledgement within three working days is reasonable in most cases. It may be more effective to send a letter by e-mail or fax to ensure prompt receipt. This may be as well as, or instead of, mail.

The acknowledgement letter is a key opportunity to demonstrate your responsiveness to the client and to narrow the issues of dispute. It should contain:

- a statement of your understanding of the complaint;
- a request for any further information or material you require to consider the complaint and a timeframe for providing it to you;
- if no remedy has been sought, ask the client to outline what remedy they would like and a timeframe for informing you;
- the contact details of the person dealing with the complaint;
- when you will next contact the client and what information you will provide at that time.

Attach a copy of your public policy on complaints management, which will include details of the full complaints management process and general timeframes.

The following further details should be included in your acknowledgement letter, according to the guidance to rule 2 of the code of conduct [**www.sra.org.uk/rule2**].

- contact details for the Legal Complaints Service (LCS) including their website and postal address;
- advice that the LCS can review the matter at the end of the consideration of the complaint by the practice;
- the time limits for complaint to the LCS.

You do not need to duplicate this in the letter, if it is already in your public policy document attached to the letter.

4.3   Assessment

Your initial assessment will shape the way a complaint is resolved.

4.3.1 Treat each complaint seriously and consider it objectively

You should respond to all complaints, even where you ultimately decide they are frivolous or vexatious. Objectively considering the complaint ensures you are better able to respond in a measured and professional way.

4.3.2 Understand what the client is complaining about

You should clearly itemise the issues that your client is complaining about, if they have not already done so. If you are unsure or need more information, contact them for clarification. Clients will quickly lose faith in a practice's complaints management abilities if you fail to specifically address their concerns or address issues they have not raised.

4.3.3 Consider the complexity and seriousness of the complaint

The complexity and seriousness will influence the extent of any investigations required and who is the appropriate person in the practice to deal with the complaint. In particular cases it may be appropriate for a manager or a partner to immediately intervene in the conduct of a case to mitigate damage to the client and the practice.

4.3.4 Identify remedies sought and consider the range of remedies you could offer

Clients may still expect action, even where they do not specifically mention what outcome they would like. You may contact the client and ask what outcome they want.

Compensation may not be the most appropriate solution if the client just wants an apology and improved future service. However, compensation may be relevant, if they have borne extra expense or lost money as a result of your practice's action or inaction. In discussion with the client, they may be able to quantify this, enabling you to suggest reasonable compensation.

The level or type of remedy requested or to be considered may determine the appropriate person within the practice who should manage the complaint or approve any final decision. You should remember that the effectiveness of certain remedies may be tied to how quickly they are provided, as some remedies may not be available if certain time limits have elapsed. You should consider expediting your response where the likely remedies require it.

4.4   **Action**

The action taken depends on the outcome of the assessment stage. The level of the investigation of the relevant circumstances of the complaint should be proportionate to the seriousness, frequency and severity of the complaint.

4.4.1   Timeframes

The complaint's complexity will drive the required time for investigating a complaint. You should always deal with a matter promptly as delays diminish the value of the final resolution.

For most service complaints, we believe 21 days to be a reasonable amount of time to either:

• conduct a preliminary investigation and provide interim feedback to a client; or
• reach a conclusion and offer relevant remedies.

Where complex issues are likely to take more than 21 days to investigate, you should agree a realistic, fair timeframe for responding to the client, to manage their expectations.

If complaints are consistently taking longer than this to resolve, you should consider why this is the case and seek to make your complaints management processes more timely.

4.4.2   Gathering evidence

It is a point of natural justice that both clients and staff members involved in the complaint should be given an opportunity to provide their account of the situation and respond to any allegations made by the other.

The seriousness of the complaint will drive whether you should either:

• simply ask the relevant staff members to explain their conduct of the retainer; or
• ask another staff member not involved with the retainer to independently review the file or the account information, before asking the relevant staff members for their explanation.

You should offer to support staff during the investigation, although this should not encroach on the objectivity or robustness of the investigation.

4.4.3   Records

You should document any steps taken to investigate the complaint. Where meetings are held with either or both parties, you should at least make a note of what was discussed at the meetings and give the parties to the meeting the opportunity to comment on and sign a copy of the note.

You should keep a copy of any documents relied upon for resolving the complaint, or at least a detailed reference of where the original is.

4.5   Remedies

After an appropriate investigation, you will decide on the practice's response to the complaint. Where the complaint is justified, you should quickly offer an apology and an appropriate remedy. The goodwill generated by such remedies will be diminished by unreasonable delays or fraught negotiations.

Even if you decide the complaint is unjustified or that the problem is not a result of your practice's actions, you should still consider taking action to enhance the client relationship and change any perception that they have been treated poorly by your practice.

You should consider your duty to notify your insurer about the complaint and the proposals for its remedy.

4.5.1   Options for remedies

Options for remedies can include:

- an apology where the complaint is justified;
- an expression of sympathy for the client's situation, or their perception of it, even if your practice has found that it is not at fault;
- fixing the specific problem;
- improving the aspect of service that led to the problem;
- offering to meet and explain again the service being provided, if the client is confused or misunderstands the service;
- offering compensation for either specific losses or general inconvenience;
- offering to reduce the bill or to undertake the work to rectify the situation free of charge.

You should be clear about who in your practice can authorise certain remedies.

4.5.2   Discussing remedies with the client

You should consider the remedies your client has requested, while being clear about what remedies are available to manage the client's expectations.

Remain open to reasonable requests for financial compensation. Client may have suffered legitimate financial loss through your practice's actions. Where the client seeks unfeasible or unreasonable remedies, you should clearly say why you are unable or unwilling to provide remedies.

4.5.3   Guidelines on remedies

You should consider the remedies and compensation levels for inadequate professional service recommended by the Legal Complaints Service [**www.legalcomplaints.org.uk**].

Accumulated experience within the practice will help you develop your own set of guidelines on reasonable remedies in particular situations.

4.6   Providing feedback

4.6.1   The response

Promptly communicate any decision or action to the client. The tone and timing of your feedback is as important as its content. You should continue to be professional, accountable and client-focused in your communications. A well-drafted response should:

- re-state the details of the complaint;
- outline the investigations undertaken to consider the complaint;
- state the findings resulting from the investigation;
- make any offers of remedy and explain how they can accept those remedies;
- explain any improvements the practice has made as a result of the complaint;
- re-affirm the client's value to the practice and the practice's commitment to good client service;
- outline appeal avenues if they remain dissatisfied.

4.6.2   Interim feedback

If the complaint cannot be immediately resolved, you should do all of the following:

- deal with the complaint in a manner intended to lead to its effective resolution as soon as possible;
- keep the client informed of progress, and likely timeframes for resolution;
- provide prompt remedies for parts of the complaint where possible, rather than waiting for the final resolution of the complaint.

4.6.3   Keep staff informed

Keeping staff informed fosters a culture within the practice of openness and accountability.

4.7   Closing the complaint

If the client accepts the proposed decision or action, then the decision or actions should be carried out and recorded.

If the client rejects the proposed decision or action, then the complaint should remain open. The client's decision should be recorded. If the client has asked for an internal review, you should proceed to that step. If they do not request an internal review, you should advise them again of their appeal options.

The practice should continue to monitor the progress of the complaint until all reasonable internal and external appeal options are finalised or the client is satisfied.

4.8   Unmeritorious or vexatious complaints

Some clients make complaints without merit or use the practice's complaints management process in a vexatious manner. You should treat these clients with respect and professionalism. You should treat all complaints seriously and properly assess them. Even clients who are known to be difficult, or have difficulty expressing themselves may still have a legitimate grievance.

4.8.1   Unmeritorious complaints

If you decide that the complaint is without merit, you should explain politely and clearly why you will not be taking any further action following the complaint and what the appropriate appeal options are. This will help assure the client that they have been given a fair hearing. You may still express sympathy for either the client's situation or their perception of their situation, without it being an admission of fault.

4.8.2   Ceasing correspondence

You may cease correspondence with a client in relation to a complaint where they continue to correspond with you about it, even though you have dealt with it fully.

This would be where their complaint has been fully considered by the practice, a decision has been made, remedies offered if appropriate and appeal options either taken up or ignored.

You should be willing to correspond with them about the outcome of your consideration on more than one occasion, before considering this option.

If you decide to cease corresponding with a client in relation to a complaint you should write to them, doing all of the following:

*   outline briefly the details of their complaint;
*   re-state what decision has been made and why, or what remedies were offered;
*   explain that in the absence of new evidence in relation to that complaint, you will not continue to correspond with them on the matter and that you regard the complaint as closed.

You should monitor any further correspondence for new evidence or areas of complaint not previously considered and make a note of your consideration. If further evidence or areas of complaint are raised you must assess this information and consider appropriate action.

4.8.3   Ongoing relationship with the client

If a client seeks to re-instruct you or to continue with a retainer where matters remain unresolved, you should consider whether you can continue to act under the circumstances. Can you effectively quarantine the dispute from the rest of the retainer, or has the relationship so broken down that you should not continue to act for the client? For advice on refusing or ceasing to act for a client, call the Solicitors Regulation Authority's Professional Ethics Helpline.

Chapter 5 – Appeals

5.1   Receiving and recording

Depending on the size of your practice, you may be able to offer an internal review of a complaint decision.

Where an internal appeal process exists, the person conducting the appeal should be more senior than the person who is the subject of the complaint and who conducted the first investigation.

The internal reviewer should receive all of the complaint and investigation material, and any representations from the client on why the initial decision was incorrect. The reviewer should be able to conduct further investigations if they consider that the initial investigation was insufficient.

You should send the client a further acknowledgement letter giving:

- the contact details of the reviewer;
- the process to be followed;
- timeframes for the appeal.

Once the internal review is complete, you should tell the client what the decision is and what the external appeal options are.

5.2   Mediation

You may consider offering a complaint to an independent mediator, especially where:

- a senior partner was already involved in the initial investigation – common in smaller practices;
- the relationship with the client is particularly deteriorating.

Involving a third party may reassure the client that the matter has been considered objectively. It also allows a practice to show that they are being proactive in resolving the complaint and may relieve them of the perceived or actual conflict faced in judging their own conduct. You may contact the SRA for a referral to the Local Conciliations Officer scheme in your area.

Using an independent mediator will not preclude a client from going on to raise the complaint with an external agency. But the mediation and its outcome would be relevant to the external agency's consideration of how the practice tried to resolve the complaint.

You should make the following clear at the start of the process:

- the mediation terms;
- how feedback from the mediation will be given;
- timeframes for accepting the outcome of the mediation.

5.3   External referral

Depending on the type of complaint, the client may refer a matter to an external agency. This is not part of the practice's internal complaints management process, but you should advise the client of how to appeal and relevant contact details. You should sufficiently document your internal processes to be able to appropriately respond to such an appeal.

Chapter 6 – Monitoring and continual improvement

You should use the lessons from complaints to continually improve you practice's business practices. This brings a dividend on the time and money spent managing complaints.

6.1   Monitoring

You should consistently record relevant complaints information centrally to enable effective monitoring. You should review information regularly with senior management. The timetable depends on your practice's size and the number of complaints it receives, but a quarterly review should generally be considered reasonable.

Relevant information should include all of the following:

- summary of the key information documented on receipt. See 4.1 [of this practice note];
- the outcomes of any investigation;
- details of remedies provided;
- a note about complaints externally reviewed and the outcomes.

By regularly reviewing this information, you can:

- identify trends in complaints and areas of service needing improvement;
- assess whether policy or procedure changes are reducing the level of complaints;
- assess the effectiveness of your complaints management process in resolving complaints internally;
- build up an understanding of what are appropriate remedies in particular complaints.

6.2 Continual improvement

You should keep reviewing your complaints management process and consider how to update and improve it. You should encourage innovation and recognise good quality complaints management behaviour within the practice.

You should consider whether any failures in service are one off, or a part of a wider systemic issue. With systemic issues, you should go beyond the retainer in hand to get the most out of your complaints management process. You should consider:

- training on compliance with procedures;
- changing high level procedures in light of new situations;
- changing specific work practices to avoid repeating a problem.

When considering changes, you should involve staff members who implement procedures or work practices to fully understand the practical implications.

Annex 1 – Sample complaints procedure

[Firm's Name]

Complaints Handling Policy

Our complaints policy

We are committed to providing a high-quality legal service to all our clients. When something goes wrong, we need you to tell us about it. This will help us to improve our standards.

If you have a complaint, please contact us with the details.

What will happen next?

1. We will send you a letter acknowledging receipt of your complaint within three days of receiving it, enclosing a copy of this procedure.

2. We will then investigate your complaint. This will normally involve passing your complaint to our client care partner, [name], who will review your matter file and speak to the member of staff who acted for you.

3. [Name] will then invite you to a meeting to discuss and hopefully resolve your complaint. S/he will do this within 14 days of sending you the acknowledgement letter.

4. Within three days of the meeting, [name] will write to you to confirm what took place and any solutions s/he has agreed with you.

5. If you do not want a meeting or it is not possible, [name] will send you a detailed written reply to your complaint, including his/her suggestions for resolving the matter, within 21 days of sending you the acknowledgement letter.

6. At this stage, if you are still not satisfied, you should contact us again and we will arrange for [another partner . . . or . . . someone uncon-nected with the matter at the firm . . . or, for a sole practitioner: [name] to review his/her own decision . . . or . . . appropriate alterna-tive such as review by another local solicitor or mediation] to review the decision.

7. We will write to you within 14 days of receiving your request for a review, confirming our final position on your complaint and explaining our reasons.

8. If you are still not satisfied, you can then contact the Legal Complaints Service at Victoria Court, 8 Dormer Place, Leamington Spa, Warwickshire CV32 5AE about your complaint. Any complaint to the Legal Complaints Service must usually be made within six months of the date of our final decision on your complaint but for further information, you should contact the Legal Complaints Service on 0845 608 6565 or at **www.legalcomplaints.org.uk**.

If we have to change any of the timescales above, we will let you know and explain why.

Annex 7E

Continuing professional development practice note

29 January 2009

1.   Introduction

1.1   Who should read this practice note?

All solicitors in legal practice or employment in England or Wales.

1.2   What is the issue?

All solicitors and registered European lawyers (RELs) in legal practice or employment in England and Wales must comply with the Solicitors Regulation Authority's continuing professional development scheme (CPD scheme).

This practice note gives advice on getting the most from the CPD scheme, by choosing activities most suited to you as a practitioner and to your practice as a business.

2.   What is CPD?

CPD is a course, lecture, seminar or other programme or method of study, whether requiring attendance or not. To qualify as CPD, it must be relevant to the needs and professional standards of solicitors and comply with guidance issued from time to time by the Law Society.

All solicitors and RELs in their first CPD year and in each subsequent year must complete 16 hours of CPD per year. The year runs from 1 November to 31 October.

Read more about compliance with the CPD scheme at **www.sra. org.uk**, including:

- compulsory participation in the Law Society Management Course Stage 1;

- differing levels of requirements for newly qualified solicitors, part-time solicitors and RELs;
- suspensions and waivers that may be applicable;
- completion of training records.

Visit the SRA's website [**www.sra.org.uk**].

3.   Planning for your CPD

You should link your individual training needs to the objectives of your practice to get the most from your CPD activities. You should:

- identify and analyse your training needs;
- discuss these needs with your firm.

Resources on the SRA website:

- training needs analysis form;
- training and development plan.

4.   Getting the most out of the CPD scheme

You must meet the requirements of the CPD scheme, but the scheme offers flexibility on how you do this. You can take advantage of the wide range of activities the scheme offers, staying up to date with changes in the law and the profession that are relevant to your practice. Participation in the CPD scheme enhances the credibility of you and your practice, and allows your practice to remain commercially competitive.

The basics:

- At least 25 per cent of your CPD requirement must be met by partici-pating in accredited courses which require attendance for one hour or more.
- The remaining 75 per cent of your CPD may be met by participating in a wide range of other activities, some of which you may already be involved in.

An accredited course is one that:

- is offered by providers authorised by the SRA;
- requires attendance for one hour or more.

It can include:

- a distance learning course involving assessment by dissertation and written examination;
- a face-to-face coaching or mentoring session, accredited under an authorisation agreement, of one hour or more.

Read more about the basics:

- Find a CPD provider [**www.sra.org.uk/solicitors/cpd/find-cpd-providers.page**]
- Continuing professional development – Solicitors Regulation Authority (SRA) requirements [**www.sra.org.uk/documents/solicitors/cpd/guidance-for-solicitors/cpd-requirements.pdf**]

For the 75 per cent of your CPD requirement that does not need to be on accredited courses, your options include:

- participation in non-accredited courses;
- working towards professional qualifications;
- coaching and/or mentoring sessions of under an hour;
- work shadowing;
- listening to or watching audio/visual material produced by an authorised provider;
- distance learning;
- writing on law or practice;
- research;
- production of a dissertation counting towards an SRA recognised qualification;
- development of specialist areas of law;
- preparing and delivering training courses forming part of the process of qualification or post-admission training;
- work towards a National Vocational Qualification (NVQ);
- work towards the Training and Development Lead Body Units D32, D33 and D34 relating to assessing and verifying the achievement of National Vocational Qualifications (NVQs).

4.1 Participation in accredited courses

You may claim CPD hours for preparing, delivering and/or attending complete courses of more than 30 minutes. Accredited CPD courses are offered by providers authorised by the SRA. Accredited courses can be run externally or in-house, where a firm is authorised by the SRA.

A list of accredited CPD providers [can be found at **www.sra.org.uk/solicitors/cpd/find-cpd-providers.page**].

4.2 Participation in non-accredited courses

You may claim CPD hours for preparing, delivering and/or attending courses that are of particular relevance and benefit to your area of work. Courses must be more than 30 minutes in length.

4.3 Working towards professional qualifications

You may claim CPD hours for this only if you take examinations. However, you may claim both study and examination time.

4.4 Coaching and/or mentoring

You may claim CPD hours for participating in coaching and/or mentoring sessions if the sessions:

- are structured;
- involve professional development;
- are more than 30 minutes long;
- have written aims and objectives;
- are documented showing an outcome;
- are accredited under an authorisation agreement.

Sessions may be face to face or delivered from a distance. Face-to-face sessions of over an hour that meet the above requirements will qualify as an accredited course.

4.5 Work shadowing

You may claim CPD hours for participation in work shadowing schemes. Work shadowing is where you shadow or follow someone in their work role for a period of time, for the purpose of enhancing your performance and that of the person you shadow.

To qualify, work shadowing must:

- be structured;
- have clear aims and objectives;
- require feedback or reflection on the shadowing activity.

4.6 Participation in distance-learning courses

You may claim CPD hours for participation in distance learning where there is provision for answering enquiries or for discussion.

A list of providers of accredited distance-learning courses [can be found at **www.sra.org.uk/documents/solicitors/cpd/find-cpd-providers/distance_learn.pdf**].

4.7 Writing on law or practice

You may claim CPD hours for writing on law or practice for publication. Examples include:

- law books and journals;
- publications for clients;
- clients' own publications;
- newspapers and magazines, whether legal publications or not;
- the internet.

4.8 Research

You may claim CPD hours for research that relates to legal topics or has relevance to your practice/organisation. Research must result in some form of written document, precedent, memorandum, questionnaire or survey, etc.

4.9 Development of specialist areas of law

You may claim CPD hours for participating in the development of specialist areas of law and practice by attending meetings of specialist committees and/or working parties of relevant professional or other competent bodies charged with such work. Time spent at meetings may be claimed.

4.10 Work towards the achievement of a National Vocational Qualification (NVQ)

NVQs may be achieved in any business-related area and at any level. You may claim CPD hours for time spent building a portfolio of evidence and/or attending lectures, workshops, etc.

4.11 Work towards the Training and Development Lead Body Units D32, D33 and D34 relating to assessing and verifying the achievement of National Vocational Qualifications (NVQs)

You may claim CPD hours for time spent building a portfolio of evidence and/or attending lectures, workshops, etc.

5. Case studies of CPD compliance in practice

The following case studies demonstrate how you may meet your CPD requirements by participating in a mixture of accredited and non-accredited activities, and by choosing activities that are relevant to both you and your firm.

5.1 A 1 year PQE solicitor

The Insolvency team get most of their CPD points twice a year through an organisation called Insolvency Network UK. This is run by Insolvency Lawyers from different regional firms and they present to each other on different topics. One of my colleagues earned CPD points giving a presentation on directors disqualification at the last meeting.

I also attended an accredited CPD course called Corporate Insolvency For Beginners; watched some internal video training sessions; and attended a SESCA Enterprises course. SESCA is the professional training subsidiary of the South Eastern Society of Chartered Accountants and provides legal lectures.

5.2 A senior associate

A senior associate met his CPD obligations by:

- preparing for an hour-long session as part of a day-long seminar for in-house lawyers at his group's client organisations on his area of technical expertise. To help with his group's business development he sat in on all of the sessions at the seminar. (Preparation time – 6 accredited CPD hours; delivery – 1 accredited CPD hour; course attendance – 6 accredited CPD hours);
- in advance of the seminar, completing the firm's e-learning course on Presentation Skills (0.75 unaccredited CPD Hours) and then attended an in-house course on advanced presentation skills to help him practice his talk (3 accredited CPD hours);
- attending a day-long public course on his area of technical expertise (6 accredited CPD hours);
- preparing for and presenting a 30–minute talk as part of his group's induction programme for their new trainees (Preparation time – 1.5 accredited CPD hours; presentation time – 0.5 accredited CPD hours);
- writing a practice note on a new legal development for his group's know how bank (6 unaccredited CPD hours);
- preparing and presenting a seminar on the restructuring process during the credit crisis (6 accredited CPD hours).

5.3 A partner

In addition to having training responsibility, I am the partner in my firm who mentors compliance with SRA rules. As well as attending a course myself on the Solicitors' Code of Conduct, I gave a talk on the subject to our own staff. At the time I had delivered the talk to the staff, I felt that I had had a real opportunity to come to grips with it. So I got two benefits: a detailed understanding of the code of conduct as well as CPD credit for my talk.

I have also given lectures, either to selected clients or to groups of clients, on particular subjects in which I am interested. Over the years, that has generated a reasonable amount of CPD hours in preparation and presentation time.

5.4 A junior solicitor

A junior solicitor met her CPD obligations by:

- attending some of her group's monthly lunchtime technical sessions, each one hour, at which partners led discussions of the law and practice relevant to current deals, or of recent developments in their field of practice (7 accredited CPD hours over the year);
- researching and co-writing with a partner a technical article on a new legal development (10 unaccredited CPD hours);
- completing a half day in-house course on effective business communication (3 accredited CPD hours).

6. More information

6.1 Professional conduct

- The Training Regulations 1990
- Solicitors' Code of Conduct 2007, rule 5.01(1)(l): Supervision and management responsibilities

6.2 Status of this practice note

Practice notes are issued by the Law Society for the use and benefit of its members. They represent the Law Society's view of good practice in a particular area. They are not intended to be the only standard of good practice that solicitors can follow. You are not required to follow them, but doing so will make it easier to account to oversight bodies for your actions.

Practice notes are not legal advice, nor do they necessarily provide a defence to complaints of misconduct or of inadequate professional service. While care has been taken to ensure that they are accurate, up to date and useful, the Law Society will not accept any legal liability in relation to them.

For queries or comments on this practice note contact the Law Society's Practice Advice Service.

6.3 Terminology in this practice note

Must – a specific requirement in the Solicitors' Code of Conduct or legislation. You must comply, unless there are specific exemptions or defences provided for in the code of conduct or relevant legislation.

Should – good practice for most situations in the Law Society's view. If you do not follow this, you should be able to justify to oversight bodies why the alternative approach you have taken is appropriate, either for your practice, or in the particular retainer.

May – a non-exhaustive list of options for meeting your obligations. Which option you choose is determined by the risk profile of the individual practice, client or retainer. You must be able to justify why this was an appropriate option to oversight bodies.

CPD – Continuing Professional Development.

REL – Registered European Lawyer.

SRA – Solicitors Regulation Authority.

6.4 Other products

6.4.1 Practice Advice Service

The Law Society provides support for solicitors on a wide range of areas of practice. Practice Advice can be contacted on 0870 606 2522 from 09.00 to 17.00 on weekdays.

www.lawsociety.org.uk/practiceadvice

6.4.2 SRA

The SRA regulates solicitors in England and Wales. It makes and enforces the Solicitors' Code of Conduct.

www.sra.org.uk

6.4.3 Law Society CPD Online

Provides two online CPD courses based on the Solicitors' Code of Conduct 2007, and risk management.

www.lawsocietycpd.org.uk

6.4.4 Law Society training and events

CPD and non-CPD events and training seminars.

www.lawsociety.org.uk/events

Annex 7F

Data protection practice note

18 February 2009

1. Introduction

1.1 Who should read this practice note?

Managing partners, practice managers and all staff concerned with the management and day-to-day operations of practices.

1.2 What is the issue?

Processing personal data is fundamental to the work of a solicitor. The Data Protection Act 1998 (DPA) regulates the processing of information relating to individuals. Solicitors must comply with the DPA. Failure to do so may constitute a criminal offence.

This practice note sets out how solicitors can comply with the Act.

2. What does the Data Protection Act cover?

You must comply with the Act if you or your staff process personal data.

'Personal data' means data which relate to a living individual who can be identified either:

- from those data; or
- from those data and other information which is in your possession, or is likely to come into your possession, and includes any expression of opinion about the individual and any indication of your intentions or those of any other person in respect of the individual.

If in doubt you should consult the Information Commissioner's Technical Guidance on determining personal data [**www.ico.gov.uk/about_us/ news_and_views/current_topics/what_is_personal_data.aspx**].

3.   Good practice for compliance

Practices should undertake the following activities to ensure data are adequately protected.

3.1   Appointing someone to be responsible for compliance

Firms should appoint someone with appropriate authority to take the lead on data protection. This person should:

- familiarise themselves with the Act, guidance and relevant case law and keep abreast of changes;
- notify the Information Commissioner, keep the notification up to date and renew it annually;
- regularly 'audit' the firm's use of personal data and check compliance;
- draw up a written data protection policy and ensure that other members of staff are aware of, understand and comply with it;
- take the lead to ensure that data subject access and other legitimate DPA requests are handled in a timely manner.

Larger firms are likely to appoint a specialist data protection officer who may report to a senior partner.

3.2   Notifying the Information Commissioner (IC)

The Information Commissioner oversees the DPA. You must not process personal data until you have provided the IC with both:

1.   your 'registrable details';

2.   a general description of the security measures you will take to protect personal data.

Registrable details include:

- your name and address;
- a description of personal data;
- the purposes for which the data is being processed.

This information is then entered into on the Public Register of Data Controllers. The register is available via the ICO website [**www.ico. gov.uk**].

3.2.1 Notification process

You must complete a form to provide notification. You may do this in one of three ways:

1. Complete the online form. You must print off and sign a copy.

2. Telephone the notification helpline: 01625 545740. An advisor will assist you and the completed form will be sent to you.

3. Postal submission. You may request a form by writing to: The Information Commissioner's Office, Wycliffe House, Water Lane, Wilmslow, Cheshire, SK9 5AF.

A fee of £35 is charged for notification. Annual renewal costs an additional £35.

Further information, form templates and a step-by-step guide are available at the Commissioner's website.

The Information Commissioner has issued warnings about fake data protection agencies offering to complete the notification process. Firms should be aware of the Commissioner's advice.

3.2.2 Failure to notify

Processing personal data without notifying the IC is an offence. Failure to notify may result in a fine. In 2008 there were at least three prosecutions of solicitors who did not comply.

You should note that the Information Commissioner does not have to inform you, or remind you, of this obligation.

3.3 Audit your use of personal data

You should understand the ways in which you are managing personal data. You may achieve this by creating a basic model of the personal data you are processing. The notification process will provide you with a starting point, but you should also understand and identify:

1. the different categories of individual about whom you process personal information, for example: clients, business partners, etc.;

2. whether you receive that information directly from the individual themselves or indirectly through other people;

3. where the information is kept, for example: on a central data store, on local machines, in e-mail accounts, etc.;

4. what is done with the data, for example: who has access to it, who it is shared with, etc.

Constructing a formal model is not a requirement of the Act. However, keeping rough notes and/or diagrams that help you understand the way you use personal data may help when checking compliance with the DPA. It should also help to ensure that you haven't missed any categories of data processing from your compliance check.

3.4   Check compliance against the data protection principles

The Act sets out eight data protection principles with which you must comply. Check your data processing against each principle. (See section 4 [of this practice note]: Principles.)

You should read carefully the principles and their interpretation which can be found in the DPA Schedule 1, Part I (principles) and Part II (interpretation).

3.5   A written data protection policy

A written data protection policy is not a requirement of the DPA. Drawing one up will however ensure a systematic approach to compliance. Additionally, if you have staff, it will help to inform them about their own duties under the Act.

A typical data protection policy should cover the following:

- the general principles of the Act and the obligation of all members of the firm to help ensure full compliance;
- contact details of the person/s responsible for taking the lead on compliance and the circumstances in which they should be contacted or consulted;
- procedures for dealing with both internal and external access requests. Usually it should only be necessary for staff to recognise an access request, before passing it on to whoever is responsible for compliance;
- staff responsibility for personal data;
- information security procedures – this may involve cross-referencing to an information security policy document

4.   The data protection principles

There are eight principles with which you must comply under the DPA.

4.1   First principle: fair and lawful processing

The first data protection principle states that personal data shall be processed 'fairly and lawfully', and shall not be processed unless:

- at least one of the conditions in Schedule 2 is met;
- in the case of sensitive personal data, at least one of the conditions in Schedule 3 is also met.

You should therefore list all the data you process and check that conditions for Schedule 2 have been met in each case, and in Schedule 3 where appropriate.

4.1.1   Sensitive personal data

'Sensitive personal data' is defined as information consisting of a person's:

(a) racial or ethnic origin;

(b) political opinions;

(c) religious beliefs or other beliefs of a similar nature;

(d) membership of any trade union;

(e) physical or mental health or condition;

(f) sexual life;

(g) commission or alleged commission of any offence, including details of:

- any proceedings for any offence committed or alleged to have been committed by him;
- the disposal of such proceedings;
- the sentence of any court in such proceeding.

4.1.2   Other considerations

You should also consider the following in order to comply with the first principle:
1. Have you misled anyone?

    You should look at:

    - how the data has been obtained;
    - whether the person from which the information was obtained has been deceived or misled as to the purpose or purposes for which the data will be processed.

2. How you have satisfied basic information requirements?

    Consider whether you have informed the data subjects of:

    - your identity;

- the purpose or purposes for which the data are intended to be processed;
- anything else which you think is necessary in order to make the processing fair.

3. Have you complied with any additional, special, rules?

Special rules apply to the collection and processing of personal information by e-mail, etc. and, in particular, unsolicited electronic marketing communications. These are covered by the Privacy and Electronic Communications (EC Directive) Regulations 2003.

4.2   Second principle: processing for limited purposes

The second data protection principle states that personal data:

1. shall be obtained only for one or more specified and lawful purposes;
2. shall not be further processed in any manner incompatible with that purpose or those purposes.

The importance of 'purpose' is stated throughout the Act and reinforced most clearly in this principle. You should do the following to comply:

1. Check whether or not a purpose for obtaining the data has been specified – generally, the person concerned should have been informed of this purpose in order to comply with the first principle.
2. Ensure the specified purpose is lawful.

If 'further processing' does not fall within the specified purpose, you must identify whether it is compatible with the original processing of the data. If so, you may continue with further processing.

4.3   Third principle: adequate, relevant and not excessive

The third data protection principle states that, in relation to the purpose or purposes for which they are processed, personal data shall be:

- adequate;
- relevant;
- not excessive.

You should therefore check that any personal data you are holding meets these criteria.

4.4   Fourth principle: accurate and up to date

The fourth data protection principle states that personal data must be accurate and, where necessary, kept up to date.

The Act defines inaccurate data as 'incorrect or misleading as to any matter of fact'.

Inaccurate data that accurately record the information you have been given do not contravene the fourth principle if:

- you have taken reasonable steps to ensure their accuracy – 'reasonable' depends on the purpose of the processing; and
- you include in the data any notification of inaccuracy made by the data subject.

4.5   Fifth principle: not kept for longer than is necessary

The fifth data protection principle states that personal data processed for any purpose or purposes must not be kept for longer than is necessary for that purpose or those purposes.

You should set up data retention and review schedules for categories of personal data to help you to comply with this principle. After a set period of time the data should be reviewed, and destroyed when they no longer need to be retained.

4.6   Sixth principle: processed in line with subjects' rights

The sixth data protection principle requires that personal data be processed in accordance with the rights of data subjects under the Act.

The DPA gives data subjects a number of rights, the foremost of which is the right to have access to their personal data where permitted under the Act.

Data subject rights also include:

- prevention of processing for direct marketing purposes;
- rights related to automated decision-taking;
- prevention of processing which is likely to cause damage or distress.

4.7   Seventh principle: security

The seventh data protection principle requires data controllers to take appropriate technical and organisational measures against:

1.   unauthorised or unlawful processing of personal data;
2.   accidental loss or destruction of, or damage to, personal data.

This principle is complemented by the obligation to inform the Information Commissioner about security measures to protect personal data (see section 3.1 [of this practice note]).

You should consider all of the following to determine the appropriateness of your security measures:

- implementation cost;
- technological developments;
- nature of the data: note that sensitive personal data will merit particular attention;
- harm that might result from unauthorised or unlawful processing, or from accidental loss destruction and damage to the data.

These factors must be balanced and a risk-based approach to compliance is appropriate.

You must also take reasonable steps to ensure the reliability of any employees who have access to personal data.

4.7.1 Data processors

Special rules apply to contractors and others who are not employees but who are processing personal data on your behalf. The Act refers to them as 'data processors'.

In order to comply with the seventh principle you must only use a data processor who can:

- provide sufficient guarantees in respect of the technical and organisational security measures governing the processing to be carried out;
- take 'reasonable steps' to ensure compliance with those measures.

You will not be regarded as compliant with the seventh principle unless this work is carried under a contract which:

- is made or evidenced in writing;
- states that the data processor is to act only on instruction from you;
- requires the data processor to comply with obligations equivalent to those imposed on you by the seventh principle.

4.8 Eighth principle: not transferred to other countries without adequate protection

The eighth data protection principle states that personal data shall not be transferred to a country or territory outside the European Economic Area (EEA) unless that country or territory ensures an adequate level of protection for the rights and freedoms of data subjects in relation to the processing of personal data.

The EEA encompasses the European Union (EU) along with Iceland, Liechtenstein and Norway. EU findings of adequacy have been made in respect of Switzerland, Hungary and (partially) Canada. 'Safe Harbor' arrangements with individual companies in the United States (US) have been in operation since 2000. The scheme is enforced by the US Federal Trade Commission.

You should consult more detailed guidance if you are considering transferring personal data overseas.

5.   Exceptions: manual data

If you do not use computers to process personal data you should consult the Information Commissioner's guidance on manual data.

See also the Information Commissioner's guidance on what constitutes personal data.

6.   Rules of professional conduct

Rule 5: Business management in England and Wales [**www.sra.org.uk/ rules**].

Rule 5 deals with:

- the supervision and management of a firm or in-house practice;
- the maintenance of competence; and
- the internal business arrangements essential to the proper delivery of services to clients.

5.01(1)(k) requires provision for 'the continuation of the practice of the firm in the event of temporary absences and emergencies, with the minimum of disruption to clients' business'.

5.01(1)(l) requires provision for 'the management of risk'.

7.   Statutory provisions

Data Protection Act 1998.

8.   More information

8.1   Status of this practice note

Practice notes are issued by the Law Society as a professional body for the benefit of its members. They represent the Law Society's view of good practice in a particular area. They are not intended to be the only standard, nor do they necessarily provide a defence to complaints of misconduct or of inadequate professional service. Solicitors are not required to follow them.

They do not constitute legal advice and, while care has been taken to ensure that they are accurate, up to date and useful, the Law Society will not accept any legal liability in relation to them.

For queries or comments on this practice note contact the Law Society's Practice Advice Service: **www.lawsociety.org.uk/practiceadvice**.

8.2   Terminology in this practice note

Must – a specific requirement in the Solicitors' Code of Conduct or legislation. You must comply, unless there are specific exemptions or defences provided for in the code of conduct or relevant legislation.

Should – good practice for most situations. If you deviate from this, you must be able to justify why this is appropriate, either for your firm, or in the particular retainer.

May – a non-exhaustive list of options for meeting your obligations. Which option you choose is determined by the risk profile of the individual firm, client or retainer. You must be able to justify why this was an appropriate option to oversight bodies.

8.3   Other products

- The Law Society's information security practice note
- *Data Protection Handbook* 2nd edition
- *Freedom of Information Handbook* 2nd edition
- *Intellectual Property Law Handbook*

Annex 7G

File retention practice note

11 September 2007

File retention: records management – retention and wills, deeds and documents together with supporting data

Status of this practice note

Practice notes are issued by the Law Society for the use and benefit of its members. They represent the Law Society's view of good practice in a particular area. They are not intended to be the only standard of good practice that solicitors can follow. You are not required to follow them, but doing so will make it easier to account to oversight bodies for your actions.

Practice notes are not legal advice, nor do they necessarily provide a defence to complaints of misconduct or of inadequate professional service. While care has been taken to ensure that they are accurate, up to date and useful, the Law Society will not accept any legal liability in relation to them.

For queries or comments on this practice note contact the Law Society's Practice Advice Service.

1.1. The information set out below has been developed by the Wills & Equity Committee of the Law Society in order to help practitioners identify issues that should be considered before relevant files are 'weeded' or destroyed.

Aims

1.2.   The aims of this exercise are:

(a) to remind the profession of the possible circumstances in which a challenge to the practice of the firm is more likely to succeed if protective measures are not put in place;

(b) to encourage the profession to offer and maintain a high level of service to clients by adopting some of the practice management suggestions set out below.

The background to the project

1.3.   The December 1986 guidance under Annex 12A of the Guide to the Professional Conduct of Solicitors has now been superseded by the new solicitors' Code of Conduct, which does not contain guidance published in the same format. It should be noted that rule 5 (business management) in the new Code of Conduct – which came into force on 1 July 2007 – requires principals in a firm to make arrangements for the effective management of their firm and these arrangements must include, amongst a list of other things, the safekeeping of documents as assets entrusted to the firm [see **www.rules.sra.org.uk** for most recent updates].

1.4.   Following the splitting of regulation of the profession from representation in January 2006 and after the coming into force of the new code, on 1 July 2007, there is an information gap that could and should be filled by the representative part of the Society producing advice as necessary, although the Professional Ethics helpline (0870 606 2577) of the regulatory part of the Law Society will still be able to advise practitioners on matters in this area.

1.5.   The Wills & Equity Committee takes the view that the former 12A guidance does not contain sufficient good practice information to allow it to be used as a ready reference source by solicitors on a day-to-day basis, since it operates more at the level of principle rather than practicality. The Wills & Equity Committee hopes that the attached good practice information can be used as a practical source on a day-to-day basis.

1.6.   It is hoped that the good practice advice and information set out below will be of practical help to solicitors: it is not, nor is intended to be definitive guidance on the possible options available to the profession.

General position in relation to storage and destruction of wills and will files

1.7. For how long should the original will be retained?

With will related material you need to bear in mind that an original will stored by you is the property of the client and after the client's death, it is the property of the estate. On this basis you should consider storage of the original until after the death of the client, or until you are able to return the original to the client.

Some firms store the will indefinitely, while others have a policy of holding the original will for fifty years from the date of its creation. There is no absolute rule, but it is suggested that solicitors should err on the side of caution, even if the firm believes or knows that a later will has been made.

At some point the firm may consider destroying the original will, after consultation with the client, if you know or have been told by the client that a new will has been made. You should consider and inform the client that occasionally the validity of the subsequent will might be challenged and then a prior will might be proved as the last will of the deceased. It is also possible that in cases where undue influence is alleged or where an Inheritance (Provision for Family and Dependants) Act 1975 claim is made an earlier revoked will may be produced as evidence of a settled or disturbed pattern of behaviour or thought by the testator. If a will is revoked you may wish to consider keeping a copy in your records.

With wills the limitation period does not start to run until the testator has died (see discussion of limitation periods in 1.26 below) and so the general six year limitation from the time the case is concluded is of little relevance.

1.8. How long should will files and supporting documentation be retained?

When framing a policy on storage and disposal of will related documentation a firm should consider a number of matters.

The file belongs to the client, subject to a limited number of documents which can be removed and which belong to the firm. Documents which come into existence during the retainer fall into four broad categories: (i) documents prepared by you for the client and which have been paid for by the client belong to the client; (ii) documents prepared for the firm's own benefit or protection for which the client has not been charged belong to the firm; (iii) documents and letters written by the client to you where property passes to you on despatch belong to the firm; (iv) documents prepared by a third party during the course of the retainer and paid for by the client belong to the client (see *Cordery on Solicitors* for more detail).

If the client cannot be contacted or is unable to respond or make a decision, the firm will have to make a risk assessment before destruction of any such material, including consideration of whether the firm's insurer's should be consulted.

For will files and related material you need to bear in mind that the limitation period does not start to run until the testator has died (see discussions of limitation periods in 1.26 below). The general limitation period applicable in will related cases is 6 years from the date of death of the testator.

Therefore consider:

(a) storing the file and any other supporting documentation for as long as the will is stored;

(b) editing the file and supporting documents so that the most important material is kept. You will have to decide whether to edit soon after the file is closed, or several years thereafter. An advantage of editing the file soon after the end of the transaction is that the relevant issues will be fresh in your mind. If the file is left to be edited at a later stage bear in mind that your memory of issues may have dimmed and that you may no longer be working at the firm, leaving editing to be carried out by someone unfamiliar with the matter;

(c) keeping an abstract with the original will setting out significant matters.

Editing information

In order to help you decide how to handle a will file containing material such as instructions, retainer letters, general correspondence, drafts and attendance notes, you should assess if there are any unusual circumstances or disposals (see 1.9 below) that might be questioned by for example, a disappointed beneficiary.

You may decide that it is worth keeping the whole file, or selected material recording instructions or attendance notes of advice you gave to the client warning of matters such as a possible Inheritance (Provision for Family and Dependants) Act 1975 claims, or an abstract setting out how the matter was handled.

If you retain the original will while destroying the file, you may decide keep a note of the destruction with the will, so the absence of papers can be explained at a later stage (see reference to *Larke* v *Nugus* immediately below) to show that the destruction was carried out in accordance with good business practice.

Even where you might know or suspect that a client has made a new will, it is still possible that the validity of a subsequent will could be challenged so you should consider making a risk assessment of whether originals should be destroyed or copies kept where the original has been sent to the client. You might also think of advising the client that all supporting papers will be destroyed unless claimed and then keep a record of this notice.

Prior to destruction of papers you should consider *Larke* v *Nugus* [2000] WTLR 1033 and established guidance from Professional Ethics that where there is a dispute about the circumstances in which a will was made, and where requested, a solicitor should make available a statement of evidence regarding the execution of the will and the circumstances surrounding it, to anyone who asks the solicitor for such a statement, whether or not the solicitor acted for the person making the request.

Coding your files

It may be worth the firm building subject coding into the filing system for stored wills and files to enable staff to check which clients have particular provision in their wills related to, for example taxation of trusts; this should help identify all clients with circumstances that may be affected by a subsequent change in the law.

Your retainer should set out if you have any obligation to advise a client of a legal or taxation regime change, but even where there is no obligation to advise the client you may decide to inform clients of a change so that they have the option of coming back to you for a review of their affairs.

Money laundering rules – 'relevant business'

The Money Laundering Regulations 2003 require that for 'relevant business', evidence of identity is to be retained for at least five years after the business relationship ends and for details of a transaction to be kept for a five-year period from the date on which all activities taking place in the course of the transaction were completed.

Note that will-writing is not treated as relevant business

Note that trust and probate work is relevant business for the purposes of money laundering rules.

Destruction of files where there have been lifetime disposals/transfers of property at an undervalue

1.9.   What sort of transactions related to the work I've done for my will client should I think of keeping with the will or recording on the will file?

Listed below is the sort of transactions where you need to consider retaining the file regardless of the standard conveyancing or other general firm policy on limitation periods.

(1) Deeds of gift

(2) Gifts of land

(3) Transfers at an undervalue

(4) Right to buy where funds came from someone other than the purchasing tenant/s

(5) Lifetime gifts

Such transactions might be challenged in the future by someone alleging that there were, for example, capacity issues or that undue influence, fraud, negligence or, mistake was in play around the time a will was made or property disposed of. A disappointed beneficiary might ask why a hoped for share of an estate is non-existent or reduced and your files may be called for. Therefore you should consider keeping records (see reference to *Larke* v *Nugus* at 1.8 above) with the will that could explain why, for example there was a conveyance at an undervalue, and recording that appropriate advice was offered to the client at the time. You should bear in mind that memories fade with time and that relevant staff may not be around at the time of a challenge who were around when the transaction happened or the will is challenged, so without adequate records you may not be able to defend the advice given by the firm.

If related transactions are undertaken by a separate department such as the Property department there is a risk that the relevant records will be kept in property files and that the Property department may have a policy of file destruction after a shorter period of time (i.e. 6–12 years). You should consider how you can best ensure that all relevant documents, advice and information about the affairs of a will client are preserved in an accessible form (also see 1.15–1.21 [of this practice note] discussing storage of electronic data).

Remember that a standard 6–year limitation period may not protect you in will related cases where, for example, undue influence is alleged and note that in *Humphreys* v *Humphreys* [2005] 1 FCR 712 (Ch D) there was a successful challenge thirteen years after the transaction.

1.10. How should retention of general files and related property transactions be dealt with?

Your firm may have different policies on the appropriate time for storing property transactions and wills files. Where a transfer of land has been made which could have a bearing on the dispositions in a will you should try to ensure that the link is noted and that a record is kept on the will file (which may be retained for longer than the property file) particularly if advice about the effect and consequences of the transfer has been given by other colleagues in the firm (the information could concern the sale of shares in a family company or business or agricultural property).

You may also keep a general file recording contact with a particular client which is not related to any major transaction, but which contains pertinent information about, for example, family dynamics or the intentions of the client. You should not overlook such files when assessing what should be retained with the will (see also the discussion in 1.8 and 1.9 above).

Practical problems – on the terms of the retainer, storage, production of documents, charges and client consent to destruction

1.11 How soon can I destroy information and documents on the file at the end of a will transaction?

Your retainer may have set out what will happen to papers, however bear in mind that the original will and certain other papers are not your property and should not be destroyed without written permission from the client.

If nothing has been agreed at the outset in your retainer, you should seek to contact your client and return any papers that you do not intend to retain.

If you cannot contact your client for some reason then you should document your efforts to trace the client and then carry out a review before deciding whether to retain or destroy material. You may wish to consider passing very old documents to a local authority archive as an alternative to destruction, but note the position regarding client confidentiality or legal privilege if the client may still be alive or recently dead (see 1.13–1.14 [of this practice note]). The National Archives recommends that where personal data needs to be stored for the life of the relevant individual and the date of death is not known it should be held until that individual would have reached 100 years.

You may also wish to take note of the appropriate limitation period (see question 1.26 [of this practice note]) before deciding when to destroy the file and what if anything from the file you should retain, whether as an original or a copy. Consider that certain papers such as attendance notes and copy e-mails may later help to explain why certain actions were taken. You may wish to refer to the facts of *Larke* v *Nugus* (1.8 above) and *Humphreys* v *Humphreys* [2005] 1 FCR 712 (Ch D).

You may need your client's permission if you wish to put records of documents they own on microfilm, and so it may be worth dealing with such questions in your retainer letter as a matter of routine.

The requirement under Schedule 11, paragraph 6(3) of the Value Added Tax Act 1994 should also be taken into account. This says that records and papers relevant to VAT liability have to be kept for six years.

Also note the anti-money laundering requirements set out in 1.8 above.

1.12   Can I charge my client for storage, copying or production of old records and documents?

Your retainer should set out charges for storage, if any, and charges for copying the file or producing a document from storage. You might consider reminding the client that there is a cost to your business for storage and retrieval of documents from deep storage, particularly where the material is kept off site.

Confidentiality and legal professional privilege

1.13   Are family members or beneficiaries entitled to disclosure of family papers?

Confidentiality – After the client's death, the right to confidentiality will pass to the client's executors and it can only be waived by them. If the family members are personal representatives, it will be their decision whether to disclose information to beneficiaries.

There is an exception in cases where the validity of the will is in dispute. In such a case, the solicitor who prepared the will should make available a statement of his or her evidence regarding the execution of the will, and the circumstances surrounding it, regardless of whether or not the solicitor is acting for those named as executors in the will. The statement should be available to anyone who is a party to probate proceedings or whom the solicitor believes has a reasonable claim under the will (*Larke* v *Nugus* – 1.8 above).

Privilege – 'Legal advice privilege' protects a client's communications to and from his lawyer made for the purpose of seeking legal advice or assistance. Legal privilege belongs to the client, and only he/she can waive it. Privilege of the client passes to the personal representatives on death.

1.14 Does confidentiality or legal privilege prevent me from providing information about the circumstances in which a trust was established, to beneficiaries under that trust?

Confidentiality – Yes. The information will be confidential to the settlor during his lifetime. On his death the duty to keep matters confidential will pass to his/her personal representatives. An executor's powers derive from the will, whereas an administrator's powers derive from the grant of representation. Accordingly, if the client died intestate, the administrator's authority to waive confidentiality will date from the issue of the grant.

Privilege – Privilege prevents any information being given to the beneficiaries during the settlor's lifetime unless the settlor waives privilege. On death of the settlor the right to assert privilege passes to the settlor's successors in title (the personal representatives – see 1.11 above).

Data protection and electronic storage

This information highlights some of the basic issues concerning data protection. More extensive information on all aspects of data protection is available from the Information Commissioner at: **www.ico.gov.uk**.

1.15 Do I treat electronic data the same as paper based information?

The same issues of principle arise with electronic data as with other material, so you always need to consider limitation periods, ownership, confidentiality, privilege and make an adequate risk assessment, etc., prior to destruction. However electronic data is subject to further regulatory safeguards as set out in the Data Protection Act 1998.

1.16 Does the Data Protection Act 1998 require me to destroy personal data on beneficiaries and family members shortly after the will has been made?

The Data Protection Act 1998 allows you to retain personal data stored in an office the information on file without breaching the Act for as long as necessary for one or more specified lawful purposes (see further information).

1.17 Are my paper files subject to the Data Protection Act 1998?

Personal data contained within files in paper format are subject to the Act only if they are held in a relevant filing system (*Durant* v *FSA* 2003).

1.18 How does the Data Protection Act 1998 affect electronically stored information?

See 1.15–1.16 above. All personal data which are held in electronic format, including scanned documents which were formerly held in hard copy form, are subject to the Act.

1.19 Is electronic storage of all file material safe, or could the material be corrupted?

It is much easier to corrupt electronic data, whether by accident or design, than paper. Systems need to be in place to safeguard the authenticity, reliability, accessibility and security of all electronic material.

1.20 Is storing relevant e-mails containing relevant advice and discussion of cross-departmental issues on one matter safe?

E-mail is both unreliable and an insecure medium. If necessary, encryption should be used to safeguard the confidentiality of information transmitted via e-mail. E-mail should not be relied upon as a storage medium. Information should be stored in a system, whether paper or electronic, which manages it according to its function and content, not its format.

1.21 The firm is upgrading its IT systems in a few weeks. What issues should I keep in mind when thinking of how to transfer electronically stored data?

It is a mistake to treat all data as though it were of equal value. Only business critical data or data of clear reference value should be migrated to new systems; the remainder should be destroyed according to an agreed retention and disposal policy prior to any migration occurring. This is particularly important where personal data is concerned, since migration is a form of processing and should therefore not be undertaken if there is no longer any need to retain the data.

Migration of large quantities of data is additionally a costly process and can also result in loss or corruption of data elements. Before data transfer to a new system, the firm should consider whether or not data is likely to be corrupted by the migration process.

Storage issues in relation to file transfer within firms, use of external storage facilities, firm merger and office relocation

1.22   Our firm has moved to new offices where there is no longer as much storage room for old files. My partners have asked me to rationalise the private clients departments' files and to dispose of a target of 50% to reduce the cost of paying for external storage. The other partners think that there are few issues involved in disposing of files beyond the usual 6-year limitation period. What should I tell my partners?

You should refer your partners to the sections of this good practice advice on limitation periods (1.26 and 1.8 which looks at owner-ship of papers), so that they are aware of the risks of disposing of will related files where a claim could well be brought far beyond the normal six-year period.

1.23   Our firm has just merged and some of our old will files have gone astray. What are the issues I should consider?

Loss of a file may amount to inadequate professional service or negligence where deeds are lost, so you may need to contact your insurer to record the loss and you should consider contacting your client to discuss what remedial action can be taken, if any, if original papers such as wills have been lost. If a claim arises in relation to lost papers the courts will weigh the available evidence to assess your part in the matter.

Family solicitors and advice where you feel you have a particular understanding of the needs of the client

1.24   I have been advising the family for years and feel I understand what they all want. I do not think the lifetime transfers I have been involved with will be challenged. Do I need to make/keep records of why the transfer/will was made?

A solicitor should always keep a proper note of the advice that was given to the client together with details of the execution of the will/transfer if the solicitor was involved regardless of whether or not the solicitor believes that there may be a subsequent challenge.

In cases where you have a good relationship with a number of members of a family, you might think that you understand how they will react. However even in these circumstances you should consider that you may not have the complete picture of family dynamics and finances. Where there is an unusual disposal such as a gift at an undervalue, or where the will leaves unequal shares to children, it would be prudent to keep detailed records of the instructions and your advice . . . indefinitely in case of a later challenge. Challenges could come after a breakdown in family relations long after you made the will or as a result of changing fortunes of family members. It is impossible to predict when such situations will arise so it is important to be prepared for such possibilities.

1.25 Should storage of powers of attorney or living wills be linked to storage of will related material?

Powers of attorney

The original power of attorney belongs to the client and so the power of attorney should not be destroyed without the client's prior consent or until you are satisfied that actual revocation has taken place or that the client is dead. Where a later power of attorney is made it cannot automatically be assumed that revocation of an earlier power of attorney has taken place. See *Re E* [2000] 1 FLR 882.

Alternatively the power could be given to the client and you will have to make a risk assessment if you then consider destroying the file and copies of the power.

Even where a new power has been created bear in mind that the validity of the later document could be challenged so the earlier power may be required. In addition you should note that the different types of power of attorney can run concurrently. An ordinary power of attorney is not automatically revoked by the creation (applicable until October 2007) or existence of an unregistered enduring power of attorney or from October 2007 the creation of a registered lasting power of attorney, where capacity of the donor has not yet been lost.

Bearing this in mind you must be cautious about destroying both original powers of attorney and related files. You must also consider if you wish to store documents, files or abstracts linked to the creation of a power of attorney with will related material so that your firm holds a complete picture of the client's affairs and wishes during life.

Living wills

If the client chooses to store a living will with your firm rather than with a doctor, you may wish to consider keeping the living will with the will, power of attorney and other such papers since the terms may have some bearing on the client's general wishes during life. However note that the living will must be readily accessible since production may be required at very short notice.

Limitation periods

1.26   Which limitation periods need to be applied when destroying old files?

The limitation period may vary depending on the type of work

Wills files

When considering whether a file should be destroyed you should note that in wills cases successful claims can be brought well after the usual contractual period of 6 years from the end of the retainer or time the work was completed/applicable in many other matters. In wills cases the limitation period does not start to run until the client dies and the will comes into effect.

Trusts

For breach of trust the normal limitation period under the Limitation Act 1980, s.21 is six years from the date of the breach or the time the breach is discovered (subject to special provisions for fraud and for a trustee in possession of trust property).

Personal representatives

For claims against personal representatives the limitation period is twelve years from the date on which the right to receive the property accrues (Limitation Act 1980, s.22(a)) or from the date the right to receive the share accrued which may be from the end of the executors' year rather than the date of death.

Discoverability

Under s.32 of the Limitation Act 1980 the limitation period does not start to run until the claimant discovers the mistake, fraud or concealment or could have discovered it with reasonable diligence.

Disability/undue influence

Note that the limitation period, whichever applies, may not start to run until a claimant, deemed to have been under a disability (for example a minor child, a person with capacity problems, or someone suffering undue influence) has become free of that disability. So, for example, where a cause of action is apparent, a minor child will have 6 years from the date of attaining 18 years to take action.

Annex 7H

Initial interviews practice note

15 May 2008

1. Introduction

1.1 Who should read this practice note?

This practice note is relevant to all solicitors who conduct initial interviews with clients.

1.2 What is the issue?

Many clients will seek an initial interview with a practice to explore their legal options in a given situation.

This is a good opportunity to understand what services your client wants and to agree with the client the terms and conditions for providing your services. Effective communication during the initial client interview reduces the chances of disputes arising later in the retainer.

1.3 Professional conduct

The following sections of the Solicitors' Code of Conduct 2007 (the code of conduct) are relevant to an initial interview [see **www.rules.sra.org.uk** for most recent updates]:

- Rule 2.01 Taking on clients
- Rule 2.02 Client care
- Rule 2.03 Information about the cost
- Rule 3 Conflict of interests
- Rule 4 Confidentiality and disclosure

1.4 Status of this practice note

Practice notes are issued by the Law Society for the use and benefit of its members. They represent the Law Society's view of good practice in a particular area. They are not intended to be the only standard of good practice that solicitors can follow. You are not required to follow them, but doing so will make it easier to account to oversight bodies for your actions.

Practice notes are not legal advice, nor do they necessarily provide a defence to complaints of misconduct or of inadequate professional service. While care has been taken to ensure that they are accurate, up to date and useful, the Law Society will not accept any legal liability in relation to them.

For queries or comments on this practice note contact the Law Society's Practice Advice Service: **www.lawsociety.org.uk/practiceadvice**.

1.5   Terminology

Must – a specific requirement in the Solicitors' Code of Conduct or legislation. You must comply, unless there are specific exemptions or defences provided for in the code of conduct or relevant legislation.

Should – good practice for most situations in the Law Society's view. If you do not follow this, you should be able to justify to oversight bodies why the alternative approach you have taken is appropriate, either for your practice, or in the particular retainer.

May – a non-exhaustive list of options for meeting your obligations. Which option you choose is determined by the risk profile of the individual practice, client or retainer. You must be able to justify why this was an appropriate option to oversight bodies.

1.6   More information and products

1.6.1   Law Society

- Practice Advice Service
- Training – regular programmes on client care and complaints management
- Lexcel – our practice management standard, awarded only to practices meeting the highest management and customer care standards
- Law Management Section – join for support and training
- Law Society publications – order from our [online] bookshop:

  - *Practice Management Handbook*
  - *Companion to the Solicitors' Code of Conduct 2007*

1.6.2   Other

- Solicitors Regulation Authority's Professional Ethics Helpline for advice on conduct issues.

- Legal Complaints Service (LCS) – investigates complaints about inadequate professional services. It runs Lawyerline, a telephone helpline for solicitors to assist with responding to client complaints. Call 0870 606 2588. Opening hours: 09.00 to 17.00, Monday to Friday.

2.   Basis on which initial interviews are conducted

Many practices will offer new clients an initial interview to discuss their legal requirements, discover what assistance the practice can provide and outline the likely costs.

Existing clients seeking to re-instruct the practice may also be offered an initial interview to discuss the new retainer.

These initial interviews may be offered free of charge, for a fixed fee or for a reduced rate.

Marketing material advertising these interviews, or staff offering them to prospective or existing clients should be clear on all of the following:

- who can take advantage of these interviews;
- the purpose and scope of the interviews;
- the basis for costing, if any, of the interview.

3.   Initial information obtained from the client

3.1   Conflict information

You should obtain information from the client before the interview to check for conflicts with existing clients. Occasionally, clients will use the initial interview process to deliberately create conflicts and prevent you continuing to act in a matter.

When an appointment is made in advance, even if it is a meeting out of the office, the following information should be obtained from the client:

- name, address and telephone number;
- field of law involved, e.g. matrimonial or crime;
- name of the opponent or others involved in the matter if applicable.

This information will enable you to conduct a conflict check and to cancel the interview if there is a conflict.

If your practice provides interviews on a walk-in basis, then these checks should be done before the interview takes place and if the checks reveal a conflict, no interview should take place.

3.2   Identity information

Conducting conflict checks will provide you with some identity information from the client. The anti-money laundering regulations require that if the client wants you to act in matters involving regulated activities, you must also obtain evidence to verify that identification information.

The general position is that you must obtain evidence of identity before commencing a business relationship or carrying out an occasional transaction in relation to regulated activities. However, this may be delayed where you are merely ascertaining the legal position of the client, or if the matter is low risk and is necessary to avoid interrupting the normal conduct of business.

As such, you may conduct the initial interview without verifying the client's identity in relation to regulated activities as long as you are only providing legal advice and not conducting transactional work.

If you continue with the retainer, you should follow your practice's processes for obtaining evidence of identity before undertaking any transactional work on the file. Some practices may choose to ask clients to bring evidence of their identity with them to the initial interview to reduce delays in proceeding with the retainer.

For further information on verification of a client's identity, see the Law Society's anti-money laundering practice note.

4.   Initial information given to the client

4.1   Pro forma information

When the client attends the interview the following information must be explained to them and confirmed in writing:

- name and status of the solicitor or other person conducting the interview;
- information on the costs for the interview (see section 4.2 [below]);
- details of who to contact if they have a complaint.

This information can be prepared in a pro forma document in advance. You should take the client through the information and ask them to sign and date the document to acknowledge receipt. You should make a copy of the signed document to retain on your files.

It may be useful for the client to have information about your practice's area of practice and relevant contact details. You may include this in the pro forma document because the client will be taking this away with them.

4.2   Costs of the initial interview

The written information provided to the client must clearly state the basis for the costs in relation to the interview. Examples include:

- The interview is free.
- The cost of the whole interview is £x.
- The cost of the interview is at a reduced cost of £x per hour pro rata.
- The first y minutes are free, and thereafter they will be charged pro rata at the rate of £x per hour.

When receiving the fees from the initial interview:

- If you have an agreed fee, i.e. the cost of the whole interview is £x, this is office money and must be paid into the office account in accordance with rule 19(5) of the Solicitors' Accounts Rules 1998.
- If you do not have an agreed fee, then this is money paid on account of costs. It is thus client money and must be paid into the client account.

5.   Non face-to-face interviews

Some initial interviews may be conducted by telephone or video conference link. This may require you to alter your normal procedures for initial interviews.

You can still conduct conflict checks as you would for a face-to-face interview. In relation to identity checks you should refer to our anti-money laundering practice note for extra requirements where you do not meet your client face-to-face.

In relation to the initial information about the interview and its costs to be provided to the client, you should consider:

- e-mailing or faxing the information to the client before the interview and seeking a return e-mail or fax confirming their acceptance;
- discussing these matters during the interview, obtaining their acceptance of the terms and making a contemporaneous note of this.

6.   Confidentiality

The duty of confidentiality in rule 4 of the code of conduct applies to information obtained in the initial interview, even if the matter goes no further.

7. The interview – main areas to cover

7.1 Client's objectives

Rule 2.02 provides that you must identify your client's objectives. You should take the time to understand what your client really wants and needs. This will enable you to tailor your services in a way that increases efficiency and client satisfaction.

7.2 Your role

Many clients will rarely engage a solicitor, so will be unfamiliar with how the relationship between a solicitor and a client operates, or the legal processes which apply to their situation.

You should take time to explain your role and the relevant services you provide or do not provide. You must also advise the client of any relationships you have with third parties, such as an introducer or fee sharer, that affect the steps you can take on the client's behalf. See rule 2.02 in the code of conduct.

7.3 Your advice

Rule 2 of the code of conduct provides that you must explain to the client:

- the issues involved with their matter;
- the options available to them;
- your responsibilities;
- whether the outcomes to be achieved are worth the risk and expense.

You should outline in clear terms the general process that will apply to their situation. For example, outline the steps which take place in a conveyance or the stages in litigating a personal injuries case.

When providing this overview, you should include information on:

- likely complications which commonly arise in relation to the particular type of matter;
- the different ways a particular matter could progress.

For example:

- When completing a conveyance, it may be common to find that certain extensions on the property do not have planning approval and if this occurs there will be a new set of options for the client to consider.

- A personal injuries case may settle once you make the claim, or after mediation, or it may require a full trial.

Providing this information at an early stage [will mean that] the client is more likely to understand that this is a normal part of the legal process, rather than assuming you did not handle the matter properly.

You should also provide general timeframes within which the client can expect completion of the transaction or resolution of the case. The client will then feel more involved in the process, reducing the chance that they complain about delay or a lack of information.

When discussing the issue of risk, you should make it clear that any assessment of risk provided is a realistic estimate based on the information the client has provided you. You should make a record of the risk estimate provided, so that if the retainer proceeds, you can monitor developments in the risk levels and update your client accordingly.

7.4   The costs of the retainer

Failure to provide adequate costs information is one of the areas most likely to result in a client complaint.

Rule 2.03 of the code of conduct provides that you must give your client the best information possible about the likely overall cost of a matter at the outset. You must also discuss with them whether the likely outcome of the matter will justify the risks involved.

The client needs to really understand the cost implications of proceeding with a matter, before they can make an informed decision on whether to proceed and whether to retain your practice. To promote this level of understanding you should communicate all costs information in plain English and in a way which makes it clear to the client exactly what they will be getting for the money they will pay. The information provided must not be inaccurate or misleading.

You must provide detailed written costs information to the client if the retainer proceeds. During the interview you should provide a simple overview of the likely costs. You should consider the points outlined in the rest of section 7.4 in developing this overview.

For further advice on providing costs information see:

- rule 2.03 and related guidance in the code of conduct;
- Law Society Practice Advice Service booklets.

7.4.1   Best information possible

Giving the best information possible includes:

- agreeing a fixed fee;
- giving a realistic estimate;

- giving a forecast within a possible range of costs;
- explaining why overall costs cannot be fixed or realistically estimated – instead give the best information possible about the cost of the next date of the matter.

7.4.2   Providing details of charges

You must make it clear how charges are calculated. You should provide advice during the interview on:

- relevant hourly rates and an estimate of the time to be charged;
- whether rates may be increased during the period of the retainer;
- expected disbursements and likely timeframes for these being due;
- potential liability for others' costs (where relevant);
- VAT liability.

7.4.3   Method of payment

You should discuss with the client how and when any costs are to be paid. In doing so, you should consider whether the client may:

- be eligible for legal aid and should apply for it;
- be offered a conditional fee agreement;
- have insurance that may cover another party's costs – if they do not, you should consider whether to advise the client to seek after-the-event insurance to cover such costs;
- seek payment of the costs from another person such as an employer or trade union.

7.4.4   Other points

You must provide costs information to the client even where the client will not themselves be paying for your services. For example, if they are publicly funded, covered by insurance or instructing you under a conditional fee agreement.

If the matter is contentious, you must outline the circumstances in which the client may be liable for the costs of other parties, including where they are successful and obtain an award for costs.

You should outline your standard billing arrangements and discuss any requirements for receiving funds on account.

You should, in appropriate cases, explain that the client may set an upper limit on the costs which the practice may incur without further authority and that you will contact them in writing when this limit is being approached to discuss the issue of costs further.

8. Terminating the retainer

Throughout the initial interview you need to be alert to any circumstances that would require you to terminate the retainer. Such circumstances include:

- There is a conflict of interest which precludes you from acting under rule 3 of the code of conduct [**www.rules.sra.org.uk**].
- You are being asked to breach the law or the code of conduct if you fulfil the retainer.
- Your practice does not have the experience or the resources to fulfil the retainer.
- You believe the instructions are provided under duress or as a result of undue influence and do not represent the true wishes of the client.

9. Follow-up after the interview

You should write to the client confirming the discussions held during the initial interview if:

- you agreed to do so during the initial interview;
- you want to record the advice you have given so that there can be no misunderstanding;
- you agree to act further for the client.

If you are continuing with the retainer, you should ensure that specific items agreed during the interview are included in any written terms and conditions sent to the client.

10. Records

Following the interview, your notes should be kept with the copy of the information form that the client signed. These documents will form the basis of the client file if you agree to act further for the client. If the retainer is not proceeding, you should still file these documents as a record of the interview.

You should retain these documents in accordance with your practice's file retention policy.

Annex 71

Information security practice note

11 September 2008

1. Introduction

1.1 Who should read this practice note?

- Sole practitioners and all solicitors responsible for developing information security policies in practices.
- In-house solicitors, partners and others, including non-qualified staff, with an interest in information security.

1.2 What is the issue?

Solicitors are increasingly vulnerable to the risk of the loss, damage or destruction of important data through theft, malicious intent or accident. This risk is growing as computers and the internet are increasingly used to process and transmit confidential client and business information.

1.3 Professional conduct

The following sections of the Solicitors' Code of Conduct 2007 (code of conduct) [**www.rules.sra.org.uk**] are relevant to information security:

- Rule 1 Core duties
- Rule 4 Duty of confidentiality
- Rule 5 Supervision and management responsibilities

1.4 Legal and other requirements

The following legislation is relevant to information security:

- Data Protection Act 1998
- Regulation of Investigatory Powers Act 2000
- Computer Misuse Act 1990

1.5   Status of this practice note

Practice notes are issued by the Law Society for the use and benefit of its members. They represent the Law Society's view of good practice in a particular area. They are not intended to be the only standard of good practice that solicitors can follow. You are not required to follow them, but doing so will make it easier to account to oversight bodies for your actions.

Practice notes are not legal advice, nor do they necessarily provide a defence to complaints of misconduct or of inadequate professional service. While care has been taken to ensure that they are accurate, up to date and useful, the Law Society will not accept any legal liability in relation to them.

For queries or comments on this practice note contact the Law Society's Practice Advice Service [**www.lawsociety.org.uk/practiceadvice**].

1.6   Terminology in this practice note

You – solicitors' practices.

Must – a specific requirement in the Solicitors' Code of Conduct or legislation. You must comply, unless there are specific exemptions or defences provided for in the code of conduct or relevant legislation.

Should – good practice for most situations. If you deviate from this, you must be able to justify why this is appropriate, either for your firm, or in the particular retainer.

May – a non-exhaustive list of options for meeting your obligations. Which option you choose is determined by the risk profile of the individual firm, client or retainer. You must be able to justify why this was an appropriate option to oversight bodies.

1.7   More information

- Information Commissioner's website [**www.ico.gov.uk**]
- Information security advice: Department for Business, Enterprise & Regulatory Reform [**www.berr.gov.uk/whatwedo/sectors/infosec/index.html**]
- Protective security advice: Centre for Protection of National Infrastructure [**www.cpni.gov.uk**]
- Warning Advice and Reporting Points (WARPs) [**www.warp.gov.uk**]

2.   Rules of professional conduct

2.1   Rule 4 – duty of confidentiality

Rule 4 of the code of conduct sets out a general requirement of confidentiality:

You and your firm must keep the affairs of clients and former clients confidential except where disclosure is required or permitted by law or by your client (or former client).

You must not put a client's confidentiality at risk by acting for another client.

The rule also sets out 'proper arrangements' to protect client confidentiality when acting for two or more clients whose interests are 'adverse' and where 'material' confidential information is held. However, these arrangements are designed with large firms and corporate clients in mind. We expect that most firms would rarely, if ever, be in a position to set up such arrangements. The guidance to rule 4 explains the situations and requirements for information barriers.

You should consider rule 4 in the wider context of the code of conduct as a whole. Two rules in particular set that context:

- Rule 1 Core duties;
- Rule 5 Supervision and management responsibilities.

2.2   Rule 1 – core duties

Rule 1 (core duties) requires solicitors to act with integrity, in the best interests of each client and to provide a good standard of service. It also requires a solicitor not to behave in a way that is likely to diminish the trust the public places in the solicitor or the profession. All these core duties could potentially be breached by a firm which did not operate effective information security arrangements.

2.3   Rule 5 – supervision and management responsibilities

This rule requires a principal in a firm to make arrangements for the effective management of the firm as a whole. These arrangements are detailed in the rule and explained further in the guidance to the rule. They include exercising appropriate supervision over all staff. This will include:

- setting up appropriate information security arrangements and ensuring they are implemented;
- training staff in your practice to a level of competence appropriate to their work and level of responsibility;
- managing risk;
- ensuring documents and assets entrusted to the firm are kept safe;
- ensuring the practice can continue with minimum interruption to clients' business in the event of absences and emergencies.

3.   Statutory provisions

3.1   The Data Protection Act 1998 (DPA)

The DPA contains 8 data protection principles. The seventh principle in Schedule 1 to the DPA requires data controllers to take appropriate technical and organisational measures against both:

- unauthorised or unlawful processing of personal data; and
- accidental loss or destruction of, or damage to, personal data.

To determine the appropriateness of security measures, you should consider all of the following:

- implementation costs;
- technological developments;
- the nature of the data – sensitive personal data will merit particular attention;
- the harm that might result from unauthorised or unlawful processing or from accidental loss destruction and damage to the data.

You should adopt a risk-based approach to compliance, giving appropriate weight to each of these factors. This is discussed in more depth in section 5 of this practice note.

You must also take reasonable steps to ensure the reliability of any employees who have access to the personal data. Special rules apply to contractors or others who process personal data on your behalf. See DPA Schedule 1 for guidance.

3.2   Regulation of Investigatory Powers Act 2000

If you monitor or store the electronic communications of fee-earners and other staff for business/security reasons you must comply with the relevant provisions of:

- the Regulatory and Investigatory Powers Act 2000;
- the Lawful Business Practice Regulations 2000.

You should also consult Part 3 of the Information Commissioner's consolidated Employment Practices Data Protection Code. The code gives guidance for businesses on monitoring or recording e-mails in the workplace.

3.3   The Computer Misuse Act 1990 (CMA)

The Computer Misuse Act 1990 creates three computer misuse offences:

- s.1: Unauthorised access to computer material;
- s.2: Unauthorised access with intent to commit or facilitate the commission of further offences;
- s.3: Unauthorised modification of computer material.

A programme of information security awareness can help you to highlight these provisions within your firm.

4.   Good practice for information security

The following good practice recommendations offer a foundation relevant to all practice sizes and types in developing their own, risk-based policies and procedures for information security.

4.1   Written policy

You should set out your information security practices in a written policy. The policy should reflect solicitors' professional and legal obligations. You should supplement this with implementation procedures. You should monitor these and review them at least annually.

4.2   Responsibility

You should appoint a senior member of staff to own the policy and procedures and ensure implementation.

4.3   Reliable people

You should implement and maintain effective systems to ensure the continuing reliability of all persons, including non-employees, with access to information held by the firm.

4.4   General awareness

You should ensure that all staff and contractors are aware of their duties and responsibilities under the firm's information security policy. This includes understanding how different types of information may need to be managed.

4.5   Effective systems

You should identify and invest in suitable organisational and technical systems to manage and protect the confidentiality, integrity and availability of the various types of information you hold.

5.   Risk assessment

In addition to the good practice above, you may carry out a risk-based assessment of your information security requirements to develop detailed policies and procedures that will satisfy the overall objectives of [the firm's] information security policy.

A risk-based approach to information security involves identifying:

* the firm's information assets;
* threats to those assets, and their likelihood and impact;
* ways to reduce, avoid or transfer risk.

A comprehensive risk-based assessment can be a complex task, so you may need expert advice.

Where resources do not permit a comprehensive risk-based information security assessment firms may nevertheless benefit from carrying out a basic, high-level exercise. This may help to identify any areas in which [the firm's] information security is particularly weak or non-existent.

Annex 7J

Job seeking practice note

19 December 2008

1. Introduction

This practice note gives advice on seeking a job in the legal profession.

2. Applying for jobs

2.1 Self assessment

Before applying for a job, you should look at your knowledge, experience and skills, and ask yourself the following questions:

- What are your strengths?
- What are your weaknesses and how can these be improved?
- What skills and characteristics do you have, e.g. language skills?
- What kind of qualities can you as a person bring to a prospective employer?
- What makes you different from other candidates?
- What are your activities outside of your work that bring transferable skills?
- What positions of responsibility have you held?
- Where do you want to work in light of the wide range of opportunities available?

2.2 Sources of information

The Law Society *Gazette*, the weekly publication available from the Law Society, has weekly advertisements of vacancies. You can access these in the magazine, or online at **www.lawgazettejobs.co.uk**, where you can sign up for job alerts and apply online direct.

Some newspapers have a particular day for legal vacancies:

- Tuesday – *The Times*
- Wednesday – *The Guardian*
- Thursday – *The Independent*

Do some research for other legal publications available online, and for publications used by potential employers in your area and by organisations involved with the area of law you wish to practise in.

2.3   Recruitment agencies

Many recruitment agencies specialise in legal positions. You should keep in contact with agencies because the jobs available through them change regularly. Even if they cannot help now, they may be able to in future.

You should discuss your CV with a recruitment consultant. They may be prepared to draft a CV for you and circulate it to employing organisations and firms. Ask their advice, even if they do not have a vacancy that immediately suits you.

2.4   Networking

Networking is a good way of finding out about vacancies and letting as many people as possible know that you are seeking work. You should make a list of all your contacts including former and existing colleagues, former bosses, business acquaintances, professional advisers, friends, relations and members of professional associations and groups.

Arrange meetings with as many of your contacts as possible to ask for advice about your career. During the meeting ask your contact to identify two other people you could approach to help you with your search. This helps build up a network of potential opportunities. The more people who know you are looking for work, the higher the chances will be that you will hear of something.

2.5   Speculative applications

If you are uncertain about your prospects or you have not seen any vacancies that meet your needs, you may apply speculatively to certain firms or organisations. To do this, you should draw up a shortlist of firms or organisations in your area doing the kind of work in which you have an expertise or interest. You should also read the national and local press to find out if the firms or organisations you are approaching have any new development in your area. You may well be at an advantage if you can apply before they start to advertise any vacancies.

When applying speculatively, you should always explain why you have approached that firm or organisation.

If you are interested in a particular area of law, the local Citizen's Advice Bureau will be able to provide details of which firms in your locality deal with your field.

2.6   Careers service

The careers services at universities are a valuable source of information and advice. You should contact the careers services to enquire about the assistance available to you. Local authorities also provide career services.

3.   Curriculum vitae

This is the first contact with the employer, so you should make the best possible impression and market yourself as effectively as possible in your CV and covering letter.

You should:

- include all the relevant information about you, because the person reading the CV will know nothing else about you;
- avoid careless mistakes;
- revise your CV carefully before sending it to employers, especially if you have not changed it for a long time.

3.1   Top tips on CV writing

3.1.1   Things you should do

1. Keep it short: your CV should be 2–3 pages in length at most.

2. Make it easy to read by choosing a clear typeface and font size.

3. Print it on good quality paper. Use black ink on white paper, and use identical stationery on covering letters.

4. Use positive language and a confident tone.

5. Put enough personal details on the first page for any potential employer to contact you easily.

6. Arrange education and experience clearly starting with the most recent first.

7. Keep dates down one side of the page: left or right.

8. Highlight key skills relevant to the job, ensuring bullet points and headings contain reasonable detail and do not read simply as a checklist.

9. Leave out any irrelevant or negative information.

10. List all your professional memberships and relevant qualifications.

11. Put relevant information demonstrating suitability for the post nearer the beginning.

12. Ensure your career history explains your role, status and achievements, giving examples of interesting and relevant matters that demonstrate your skills.

13. Ask someone else to read your CV to give you their impressions.

3.1.2   Things to avoid

1. Binding your CV – it makes it difficult to copy or scan. If your CV is over a page long, use a paper clip.

2. Lying – this can lead to instant dismissal if discovered. Past employers may give a different picture if contacted.

3. Jokes – not everyone will share your sense of humour.

4. Writing your whole life story.

5. Leaving unexplained gaps in your career history. It may seem like you are trying to hide something. State whether travelling, taking a career break, etc.

6. Writing bland profile/objective sections. Statements such as 'highly motivated team player' can be better demonstrated through examples in the body of your CV.

7. Listing interests unless they are current. Think carefully about the impression they will give the reader. Only include those interests that demonstrate positive skills that the company may be looking for.

3.2   Typical CV outline

3.2.1   Contact details

You should put your contact details at the top of the first page. It's not necessary to give the document a heading i.e. 'Curriculum Vitae'. Instead, use your name as the heading. Use a larger type in bold.

To save space, include your address on the line below your name. In this section, you should also include contact telephone numbers and an e-mail address.

3.2.2 Education and qualifications

You should lay these out with the most recent first, and include:

- all professional memberships and general academic achievements;
- anything you are currently studying at the top of the list with anticipated result;
- the name of the establishment and the dates you attended there.

3.2.3 Work experience

Show the most recent job first and include the following information.

1. Dates, placed vertically in either the left-hand or right-hand margin.

2. Organisation and location, giving a brief description about the business that allows the reader to quickly compare the size and complexity of organisations.

3. Job title, with a description underneath of what you were employed to do that is no more than five lines long. Be selective and mention the role's principal tasks and responsibilities. Include those things you enjoy and are good at, leaving out things you enjoy less, unless they are crucial parts of the job you are targeting.

4. Achievements – these set you apart from the competition. You should include what you did, the results of your actions, and whether you worked independently or as part of a team. Write achievements as short, punchy, bullet-point statements of fact.

If you are newly qualified, you should also include details of the practice areas that you were involved in during your training contract, including skills you acquired and your achievements. If the practice where you did your training contract is similar to the one that you are applying to, then point this out. You should list any work experience that demonstrates attributes, qualities and skills.

You do not need to provide salary details or reasons for leaving on your CV.

3.2.4 IT skills

You should give an impression of your familiarity with computers, listing any software packages you can use that would be relevant to the job and your level of proficiency. Examples are Microsoft Word or Excel.

3.2.5 Interests and activities

Employers are looking for evidence of team working and social skills outside work. You should list involvement in sporting teams and other organisations and highlight positions of responsibility you have held. Avoid giving irrelevant activities/interests that do not demonstrate any skills to the firm/organisation such as reading, or listening to music.

3.2.6 Referees

You must get agreement from referees to act in this capacity before you submit your CV. You should not give the identities of your referees on the CV, and wait until an employer requests them.

You are responsible for referee management. When references are requested, you should contact referees to describe the role you are applying for, and the skills the employer is interested in, enabling a relevant, constructive conversation between referee and employer/recruiter.

3.2.7 Covering letter

You should always accompany a CV with an individually prepared covering letter that includes:

- why you are applying for the position advertised;
- particular skills you have;
- reference to particularly salient items on your CV you want the employer to note.

You may add items or explain gaps or any areas which they may question. For example, you could explain how you benefited from periods travelling or gaps looking after children.

If you are applying speculatively and do not know if a vacancy exists, you should explain why you have targeted that firm/organisation and what you have to offer.

3.3 Top tips on covering letters

3.3.1 Research

Before putting pen to paper, you should:

- read the firm/organisation's literature or information;
- find out as much as you can about them. You will then be in a better position to compose a letter about why you are suited to them;
- consider the firm/organisation's requirements and decide what they are looking for;

- consider whether you have the skills, abilities and qualities required, and, if so, how these can be best conveyed;
- check your CV covers all the necessary points. If it does, highlight the points for employers to note. If not, you should revise it.

3.3.2   The letter

The letter must:

- encourage the employer to take your CV seriously;
- set the reader's expectations of what will be in the CV;
- persuade the employer that you are a suitable candidate for the job;
- indicate evidence for the claims you make about yourself.

The letter should include:

- the purpose of the letter;
- the reasons why you are applying to that firm/organisation;
- (highlighted) the best three things you can offer the firm/organisation;
- a positive signing off.

3.3.3   Presentation

First impressions are important, so you should:

- make your letter an attractive document, well laid out on an A4 sheet;
- ensure that there are no spelling mistakes or other errors;
- address your letter to an individual, where possible, and consider telephoning to find out the correct name and title;
- capture the reader's attention;
- express what you need to say as concisely as you can;
- convey a positive attitude and reasonable confidence.

3.3.4   Format

Like every good story, your letter should have a beginning, middle and an end.

Beginning – an introduction. Provide a brief introduction of:

- who you are;
- which job you are applying for;
- where you saw the advertisement;
- why you decided to apply.

State that your CV is enclosed.

Middle – cover in more depth why you are applying, why you are interested in the job and in this firm/organisation. You should show that you understand the requirements of the role and that you know about the firm/organisation. Then explain why you are right for the role and highlight your achievements and experiences that are particularly relevant to it.

Once you have identified what the employer is likely to be looking for, you should:

- refer them to your CV to indicate that you would meet their requirements;
- demonstrate your strengths and why you are a suitable candidate;
- indicate what sort of contribution you could make and be clear about what you have to offer;
- tailor the letter to the specific job and firm/organisation to fit their interests or needs and show you have done your research.

End – you should end the letter on a positive note, saying when you will be available for interview and that you look forward to hearing from them. Don't forget to sign your letter.

4.   Interviews

You should consult the numerous books and articles that advise on recruitment interviews.

4.1   Top tips for interviews

4.1.1   Preparation

Interviews can be a very stressful and traumatic process. The best way to allay interview fears is to prepare.

You should ask yourself the following questions before an interview:

- Why do you want a career in the law?
- What areas of law are you most interested in and why?
- Are your sights set on a commercial firm, a general firm or a high street firm?
- Why did you choose the firm/organisation to which you are applying?
- What can you offer that firm/organisation?

If you want to work in law because you enjoy a challenge and like getting a deal done, then you may say just that, but try to give examples of comparative achievements in your past. You should tell your interviewer briefly of the challenges you faced and your sense of satisfaction at having got the job done. This will reveal something unique in your personality to your interviewer.

Obviously, one of the reasons for wanting a job is to make money, but your interviewer already knows this and knows that every other candidate wants the same thing. So instead, concentrate on the things that make you stand out from the crowd.

You should find out as much as you can about the firm/organisation before arriving for an interview. Most have websites and are also happy to send brochures to interview candidates. You can also search the websites of the legal press for a more objective view. You should try to get a feeling of the ethos of the firm/organisation – what are their buzz words, do they put most value in ambitious, confident people, or instead prefer communicative team players.

If you know who will be interviewing you, then you may find out a little about them. If they have published articles then try and get hold of them. Remember firms/organisations have personalities which you should find out about and compare to its competitors – why did you choose to apply to firm/organisation A over firm/organisation B? You can then work out what you and your chosen firm/organisation have in common.

The purpose of your preparation is to ensure you are making the right choice, and can be confident at interview.

The final rule on preparation is knowing when to stop. No interviewer expects you to know everything about the firm/organisation. They simply want to know that your application is carefully considered.

4.1.2   Typical questions

- Tell me about yourself.
- Why did you decide on a career in law?
- What do you consider your strengths/weaknesses?
- Why do you want to be a solicitor?
- What are your main achievements to date?
- Have you ever had a position of responsibility?
- How do you manage your time?
- How well do you work under pressure? Give examples.
- Where do you expect to be in five years' time?
- Why do you want to work for this company?
- What do you know about this company?
- What are your salary expectations?
- Are you flexible to move/travel?
- Are you applying for other jobs?
- Tell me about a time when you had to deal with a personality conflict with a colleague.

- Tell me about a time you handled a stressful situation well.
- Tell me about a time you built a rapport with a difficult person.
- Describe a time when you worked with a colleague to finish a project on time.
- Give an example of a time when you showed initiative.
- What's the biggest challenge you've ever had?
- Give me an example of a time when you were particularly creative in solving a problem.
- How would you go about generating business for the firm?
- What's your view on . . .? (current affairs question)
- Have you any questions to ask me?

4.1.3   Finding the right answers

An employer will choose criteria that you must fulfil and the interview is the chance to prove that you possess them. Such criteria will be different for each firm/organisation, but examples include:

- drive and initiative;
- influencing skills;
- personal qualities;
- analytical skills;
- flexibility;
- technical skills;
- organisational skills.

You should back up your answers with one or two examples from your life. There follow some guidelines for answering some of those difficult questions.

- How well do you work under pressure?
  You should emphasise that you work as well under pressure as you do at any other time but that you prioritise tasks so that your workload is manageable. Point out your ability to leave work at the office and find time and ways to relax.
- Are you applying to other companies?
  You need to show that you have not just been applying indiscriminately, so only mention firms/organisations with similar attributes to the one you are at an interview for. You should also demonstrate a particular interest in and commitment to that firm/organisation.
- Tell me about yourself
  Be prepared for open-ended questions, the interviewer not only wants to hear your answer but how you answer. This is a test of your verbal communication skills. Do not waffle or tell them your life story. Concentrate on a brief summary, recent experiences and major

relevant achievements. You can then ask if they would like you to expand on any area.

- What salary are you looking for?

  Part of your pre-interview research should be to find the firm/organisation's salary range. Say that you expect to be within that range. Think about the whole package including pensions and healthcare, not just salary.

- What is your greatest weakness?

  A good approach is to admit a real weakness that does not impact on the job, then describe how you overcome it by using strengths which are relevant to the job. For example, overcoming nervousness at public speaking by extensive preparation and organisation. Be prepared for the possibility that they may ask for several weaknesses, so have several answers prepared.

- How would you go about generating business for the firm?

  The key issue when answering this question is your ability to network and have a social life outside the firm. Another issue to consider is the quality of service you provide when you secure a client, to make sure they return in the future.

- Why do you want to work for us?

  This is something you should have thought about in your preparation. It could be the excellence of the firm/organisation, their size, their training, their specialisation, etc.

  Try to find a fit between your strengths, values and interests and those of the firm/organisation. Try to emphasise what you can do for them, not just what they can do for you.

4.1.4 At the interview

Remember that the profession you have chosen involves a good deal of client contact and the solicitor–client relationship requires the client to place their complete confidence in the solicitor. You must put an interviewer at ease and convince him/her of your professionalism to give them the confidence you can manage their clients.

Areas the interviewer will note at interview:

- your appearance – be business-like;
- whether you are a serious, committed candidate;
- whether your interest in law is genuine;
- the sort of temperament/ personality you reveal;
- whether you are articulate and able to think on your feet;
- how you will get on with the rest of their staff;
- whether you would fit in to their particular organisational structure and culture;

- whether your responses correspond or conflict with those on your CV or application form;
- whether you use your initiative;
- whether you display intellectual, analytical and reasoning ability;
- your attitude to working alone or under supervision;
- how you seem able to cope with pressure and deadlines;
- whether you are organised and able to manage your time;
- how self-aware you are;
- whether you have a sense of humour.

4.1.5   General tips

- Dress smart.
- Walk through the door smiling, make eye contact with your interviewer(s), and offer a firm handshake.
- Sit upright. Leaning slightly forward indicates interest and engagement. Also hold you hands together – this stops you fidgeting and also appears attentive and interested.
- If there is more than one interviewer present then try to address your answers equally to each of those present.
- Do not let your eyes wander around the room to avoid appearing uninterested and disrespectful.
- Be succinct and to the point whilst also ensuring you sell yourself.
- Do not attempt to fill silences while the interviewer is looking at your CV or a list of questions in front of them.
- Listen carefully to the questions you are asked in their entirety and answer them precisely. Remember that this is what your clients will expect of you as a solicitor. Remember to adapt your pre-prepared answers to the precise question asked.
- If you do not understand something you are asked or told, ask your interviewer(s) to explain.
- Feel free to ask a couple of questions yourself, and think about them in advance.
- Thank your interviewer(s) for seeing you, shake hands and smile.
- Remember to say goodbye.

4.1.6   Your questions

At the end of the interview, the interviewer will commonly ask if you have any questions. This is a good opportunity for you to show off your interest in the job and the firm/organisation. Avoid asking questions that have been answered for you in the course of the interview. Do not ask anything you should already know from details they have sent you, or about salary, holidays, etc.

Good topics to ask about are:

- the organisation – strategic goals, challenges they are facing, why does/do the interviewer(s) enjoy working there, most significant recent developments in the firm/organisation, etc.;
- the working conditions – opportunities, career development, how is performance evaluated, etc.;
- the process – what happens next, how many people are being interviewed, do they fill open positions from within the firm/organisation first, etc.

4.1.7   After the interview

- Think about what you have learned and your impressions of the employer. The interview is your opportunity to decide if you want to work for them.
- Reflect on the interview. Make a note of the questions they asked. Were you satisfied with your answers, or could you do better next time?
- If they do not contact you when they said they would or if it has been a long time since the interview (more than two weeks), try ringing to check the situation.
- If you are rejected, try ringing to ask if they could tell you the main reasons.

5.   Applications

5.1   Top tips for applications

Some organisations argue that there is not enough detail on a CV to select you for interview and are opting to use application forms or the online application process.

An application is your chance to demonstrate your written communication skills – be clear and concise. Employers are looking to see early evidence of this skill.

As with all applications preparation is the key to making any good application. Find out as much as you can about the company and its recruitment criteria. Information can be found on their website or any promotional literature.

Many application forms are designed to test your powers of summarising briefly. At first glance, the spaces provided for your answers do not appear big enough. Application forms are designed for this purpose. Gauge your answer by the size of the space provided.

Use each section's specified word count as a guide to how much detail they want from you.

Read through the form carefully and follow instructions. Do not attach extra information to your application, such as your CV. Applications are carefully designed to extract the right amount of information to make a decision to select or reject you. Any additional information will usually be ignored. Consider adding it only if the form invites you to do so or if the form is inadequate and gives you no space at all to sell yourself.

Do a draft of your answers first, preferably on a photocopy of the form, so that you can be sure they are going to fit in the boxes.

Make your application a pleasure to read. Any form that is easy to read and the product of intelligent thought will have an immediate advantage. You are wasting your time if it does not look visually decent. Under no circumstances should you resort to tiny writing to cram more in.

Knowing the ethos of a company puts you in a much better position to explain why you are right for them. This is most relevant for the skills or achievement-based questions.

Have a clear idea of what the selection criteria are and what matching skills, knowledge and experience you have. When answering questions that ask about how you have demonstrated teamwork or found original ways to solve a problem, choose examples from different parts of your life and be as specific as possible when describing them. Concentrate on your personal contribution to whatever it is you are writing about and stress achievements and outcomes.

Ensure that your answers are tailored to the particular section of the application you are completing and that questions are addressed directly and succinctly.

Do not leave gaps in your life. It is always a better idea to explain what happened, i.e. travelling or a gap year.

Choose your referees with care – reliable people who have agreed to help. Your offer of employment will be subject to receiving references.

6.   Setting up in practice

You may be considering setting up your own practice rather than seeking employment in an already existing firm/organisation or changing your career pattern.

The Law Society offers a free toolkit for sole practices, small firms and solicitors thinking of setting up in business. It helps practitioners understand how to set up in business, successfully manage their practices and prepare for retirement.

Download the toolkit [at **www.lawsociety.org.uk/documents/downloads/pm_toolkit_v1_3_final.pdf**]

You must give very careful consideration to taking this important step because there is much legislation and many rules and regulations affecting the setting up of a new practice. Contact the Solicitors Regulation Authority for more information after reading the Society's toolkit.

7.   Alternative careers for solicitors

Being a solicitor is not the only career in law. The opportunities to transfer the skills picked up in the study of law and practising as a solicitor into other employment areas are endless. A law degree, professional qualification and experience gained working as a solicitor are valuable commodities that are sought after by a wide variety of employers. The skills a legal education develops are vast and these skills and abilities are valued in the general career market. They include:

- the ability to research;
- the ability to collect and analyse large amounts of information;
- the ability to weigh-up points and counter points;
- the ability to create a logical argument and reasoned conclusion from a set of facts;
- the ability to communicate clearly with the public and the profession alike;
- discretion;
- the ability to handle and work under pressure;
- a first-class memory.

Below is a selection of roles for which little or no further training is required. This list is not exhaustive.

- Consultant to firms
- Court reporter
- Law centre worker
- Law costs draftsmen
- Law firm manager
- Law firm researcher
- Law firm trainer
- Legal executive
- Legal journalist
- Legal secretary
- Licensed conveyancer
- Locum solicitor
- Magistrates' clerk
- Paralegal
- Solicitor within a charity
- Solicitor within a company
- Solicitor within local government

8. More information

8.1 Useful contacts

8.1.1 Law Society Pastoral Care Helpline

Referral service for solicitors who need help with personal, financial, professional or employment problems.

Telephone: 020 7320 5795
Lines are open from 09.00 to 17.00, Monday to Friday.

8.1.2 Solicitors' Assistance Scheme

Provides free initial legal advice, including advice on employment issues, to solicitors, their families and their staff.

www.thesas.org.uk
Telephone: 020 7117 8811

8.1.3 Solicitors Benevolent Association

Charity providing financial assistance in times of hardship for solicitors and their dependants.

www.sba.org.uk
Telephone: 020 8675 6440

8.1.4 Association of Women Solicitors

Offering support to female trainees and qualified solicitors. The group has a well-established mentoring scheme.

www.womensolicitors.org.uk
Telephone: 020 7320 5793

8.1.5 The Law Society's Junior Lawyers Division

Support, advice and networking opportunities for students, trainees and newly qualified solicitors up to five years' PQE.

www.lawsociety.org.uk/juniorlawyers
Confidential helpline – 09.00 to 21.00
Freephone: 08000 856 131
E-mail: juniorlawyershelpline@lawsociety.org.uk

8.1.6   *LawCare*

Confidential free advisory and support service for lawyers, their staff and their immediate families to deal with health problems such as depression and addiction, and related emotional difficulties.

www.lawcare.org.uk
Telephone: 0800 279 6888 09.00 to 19.30 weekdays, 10.00 to 16.00 weekends

8.1.7   *Law Gazette Jobs*

Law Gazette Jobs has a careers zone for finding employment and provides access to the latest legal jobs. You are able to sign up for job alerts and will be e-mailed when new vacancies arrive that match your criteria.

www.lawgazettejobs.co.uk

8.1.8   *Law Society Publishing books*

For practical coverage of employment law, see our latest book: *Employment Law Handbook*, 4th edition.

For more employment related titles: **www.lawsociety.org.uk/ bookshop.**

8.1.9   *Law Society Practice Advice Service*

Help for solicitors and their staff with issues of legal practice, policy and procedure from experienced solicitors.

Telephone: 0870 606 2522
Lines are open from 09.00 to 17.00, Monday to Friday.

8.1.10   *Solicitors Regulation Authority Contact Centre*

Assists solicitors with enquiries relating to practising certificates, continuing professional development (CPD) and other general enquiries.

www.sra.org.uk
Telephone: 0870 606 2555

8.1.11   *Status of this practice note*

Practice notes are issued by the Law Society for the use and benefit of its members. They represent the Law Society's view of good practice in a particular area. They are not intended to be the only standard of good practice that solicitors can follow. You are not required to follow them, but doing so will make it easier to account to oversight bodies for your actions.

Practice notes are not legal advice, nor do they necessarily provide a defence to complaints of misconduct or of inadequate professional service. While care has been taken to ensure that they are accurate, up to date and useful, the Law Society will not accept any legal liability in relation to them.

Annex 7K

Redundancy practice note

19 December 2008

1. Introduction

1.1 Who should read this practice note?

Solicitors who are, or may be, facing redundancy.

1.2 What is the issue?

The prospect of redundancy can be unsettling, this practice note contains general advice for solicitors facing redundancy and also signposts where to find comprehensive information and further assistance.

2. Circumstances for redundancy

Redundancy usually occurs when:

- the job you were hired to do no longer exists;
- your employer needs to cut costs or reduce staff numbers;
- the employer has ceased or intends to cease operations either in a particular location or a particular legal field.

3. Employer obligations

Your employer has certain legal responsibilities surrounding redundancy.

3.1 Fair selection

Your employer must select those for redundancy in a fair, objective and non-discriminatory manner. Workers are protected from being chosen unfairly for redundancy by the Employment Rights Act 1996.

[View the] Employment Rights Act 1996 on the Office of the Public Sector website [at **www.opsi.gov.uk**].

3.2   Consulting with you

Employers must both:

- notify individuals concerned of the possibility of redundancy;
- consult with them before reaching a definite decision regarding dismissal.

The consultation should include all of the following factors:

- why the firm/organisation has decided that it is necessary to make redundancies;
- how the firm/organisation identified the selection pools;
- the selection criteria and how [they are] applied;
- why your position has been provisionally selected for redundancy;
- the terms on which any redundancy would take place;
- possibilities for alternative employment within the firm/organisation;
- any ideas you may have for avoiding redundancy or reasons why you think the firm/organisation should not select you for redundancy.

3.3   Redundancy pay

Statutory redundancy pay is only awarded where you have had at least two years' continuous service with your employer, including time spent under a training contract. See section 4 for more information.

3.4   Notice periods

The length of your notice period will appear in your contract of employment and must not be less than the minimum periods. If your contractual notice is less than the statutory minimum, the statutory minimum will prevail. The minimum periods are:

- at least one week's notice if you have been employed for between one month and two years;
- one week's notice for each year if employed for between two and twelve years;
- twelve weeks' notice if employed for twelve years or more.

3.5   Considering alternatives to redundancy

Employers must take reasonable steps to avoid redundancies. This includes taking steps to redeploy affected employees.

3.6 Maternity

Employees on maternity leave have special protection under regulation 10 of the Maternity and Parental Leave Regulations 1999 relating to suitable alternative employment. This includes an express statutory right to any suitable alternative vacancy that exists.

[View the] Maternity and Parental Leave Regulations 1999 on the Office of the Public Sector website [at **www.opsi.gov.uk**].

3.7 Collective redundancy

A collective redundancy situation arises when an employer proposes to dismiss twenty or more employees in one establishment over a period of ninety days. Collective redundancy triggers specific requirements for:

- notification;
- information provision;
- consultation.

You should take legal advice if you believe that your redundancy falls into this category. Find out more on the BERR website [**www.berr.gov.uk**].

4. Issues for trainee solicitors

Trainee solicitors may have their training contract terminated by redundancy because either:

- the firm/organisation has ceased doing business; or
- the requirements for employees to do trainee work have ceased or diminished.

4.1 Your rights

You should check the terms of your employment contract to ensure that the firm/organisation is not in breach of any clauses in making you redundant. These terms are separate from your training contract. You should consult an employment law solicitor if you feel your employment contract has been breached in any way.

Where a genuine situation of redundancy has been identified, practices must make an application to the SRA for termination of the training contract.

Trainees do not generally have an automatic right to a redundancy payment as the statutory scheme requires two years of continuous employment with an employer. You may however have this qualifying service period if you worked with the firm/organisation before undertaking your training contract, for example as a paralegal.

To discuss training contract issues, contact the SRA [**www.sra.org.uk**].

4.2 Notifying the SRA

You should notify the SRA of the status of your training contract via a TC3 form. Your firm/organisation can obtain these from the SRA, to be signed by both you and the firm/organisation you are leaving. This will enable you to suspend your training contract and bank the time you have worked.

It is your responsibility to find another firm/organisation who will enable you to complete your training with them. The TC3 form should be signed by the new firm/organisation when you resume your training contract.

5. Your redundancy package

There is no basic right to a redundancy package beyond the statutory minimum payment for eligible employees. Employers do however have discretion to make ex gratia payments to all employees and you should check your firm/organisation's redundancy policy or contractual redundancy terms. You should consider negotiating a redundancy package but your approach should depend on both:

* your perception of the firm/organisation's position;
* the reasons for the redundancy.

For example, options will be limited if your employer is insolvent.

5.1 Statutory pay

Statutory redundancy pay is awarded where you have had at least two years' continuous service with your employer. It is based upon your age and length of service.

The Employment Equality (Age) Regulations 2006 which came into force on 1 October 2006 removed the previous upper and lower age limits of 65 and 18 for statutory redundancy payments.

[View the] Employment Equality (Age) Regulations 2006 on the Office of the Public Sector website [at **www.opsi.gov.uk**].

5.2   Calculating the statutory minimum

This produces the number of weeks' pay that you are entitled to, this is then multiplied by your gross weekly pay, subject to an annually reviewed cap.

You can calculate your statutory redundancy amount using the BERR online calculator [**www.berr.gov.uk**].

5.3   Negotiating a package

You should discuss the terms of your redundancy with your firm/organisation if you feel that there is room for negotiation. This may form part of the redundancy consultation procedure, but you may also request the meeting directly. This will give you the opportunity to consider your situation and the proposed terms. A generous package may be available beyond statutory pay.

The amount of redundancy payment depends on both:

- your length of continuous employment with the firm/organisation;
- your years of service relative to your age band.

You should separate any negotiated compensation from other monies due, for example for expenses claims or payment in lieu of notice or holiday.

If you receive benefits such as a car or assistance with child care provision, you may consider negotiating the continuation of these for a limited period or until you have found another position.

You could also ask your employer to pay for the renewal of your practising certificate. A current practising certificate may help you with finding locum work until a permanent position is obtained.

You should ask your employer to provide full references which explain why you were made redundant and confirming that the decision was not a reflection of your work but changes in client demands, or the economy for example. It is important to have a letter from your employer confirming the position, otherwise you could lose your entitlement to state benefits.

You may consider continuing to receive the firm/organisation's updating materials.

5.4   Tax

You do not have to pay tax on statutory redundancy payment. However, any additional redundancy payments you receive from your employer may be taxable.

See the table below for examples:

Payment	Is tax payable?	Is national insurance payable?
Redundancy payment	Only above £30,000	No
Unpaid salary	Yes	Yes
Bonus payment	Yes	Yes
Occupational pension	Yes	No

Anything else you receive that is not money is converted into a cash value for tax and national insurance contribution purposes. If these items were given to compensate for your redundancy, the cash value counts towards the £30,000 tax free limit.

Payment in lieu of notice is usually subject to tax and national insurance contributions as normal. However, you may be able to get this paid tax free if there is no clause entitling your employer to make this payment in your contract of employment. You should take specialist legal advice on this point.

[See the] Redundancy factsheet (PDF) on the HM Revenue & Customs website [**www.hmrc.gov.uk/guidance/redundancy-factsheet.pdf**].

5.5   State benefits

Statutory redundancy payments have no effect on your entitlement to contribution-based Jobseeker's Allowance. If you have lost your job through redundancy you normally qualify for Jobseeker's Allowance. You cannot claim Income Support or Income-based Jobseeker's Allowance if your personal resources, including redundancy pay or unfair dismissal compensation, exceed £8,000. You may however, qualify for contribution-based allowance. Contribution-based Jobseeker's Allowance depends on the status of the worker's national insurance contributions. You will need to have paid national insurance contributions for one of the last two complete benefit years before the tax year in which the allowance is claimed, and have contributions or credits for both benefit years. Jobseeker's Allowance is paid for six months, maximum.

[See the] Details of benefits and eligibility (PDF) on the Job Centre Plus website [**www.jobcentreplus.gov.uk**].

6.   Personal considerations

6.1   Working notice periods

You should consider with your employer whether you are to work the period of notice. If you are, remember that your employer should allow you reasonable time off to look for an alternative position. Legislation does not specify what is reasonable as this would vary depending on circumstances.

6.2   CPD requirements

When you are made redundant you may suspend your CPD requirement. You do not need to make an application to the Solicitors Regulation Authority. You should make a note in your personal training record of the date and reason for any suspension. You then can resume once you are back in legal employment. You must ensure that you record this information correctly because the Solicitors Regulation Authority is able to call for your training record at any time. If you choose not to suspend, you will be expected to meet your CPD requirements in full.

You will be required to declare that you have satisfied your CPD requirement when you next apply for your practising certificate, so you must make a decision whether or not to suspend and record details of the suspension.

Further information can be obtained from the Solicitors Regulation Authority. See 8.12 [below] SRA Contact Centre.

6.3   Practising certificate requirements

If you hold a practising certificate at the time of being made redundant your certificate will be up for renewal on 31 October. You then have a choice to renew the certificate or to allow it to lapse. If you wish to renew your certificate, you must complete a RF3 application form and submit the relevant fees and application to the Solicitors Regulation Authority. If you do not apply to renew your certificate by March/April you will be sent a KR1 application form to keep your name on the Roll. The fee is currently £20 per year.

If you have not held a practising certificate for more than twelve months, you will become subject to section 12C of the Solicitors Act 1974. This means that if you wish to apply for a practising certificate, you will be required to notify the Solicitors Regulation Authority six weeks in advance of your intention. You must complete form RFs12, and return it with the appropriate fee to the Solicitors Regulation Authority. There are no special conditions that apply, nor are there any compulsory courses, other than the normal continuing professional development requirements (CPD).

6.4   Finances

You must notify your creditors, in particular Banks and Building Societies, if you feel that you are unable to make normal payments. If possible, you should arrange a meeting so that you are able to speak face to face.

If redundancy leaves you in a difficult financial situation the Solicitors Benevolent Association (SBA) [**www.sba.org.uk**] may be able to help, particularly if you have dependants or unusual financial problems.

You may also benefit from seeking independent legal advice. The Solicitors' Assistance Scheme (SAS) [**www.thesas.org.uk**] offers confidential legal advice to fellow solicitors with the initial consultation being free.

You may consider the availability of all state benefits.

- Contact your local Department for Work and Pensions (DWP) office on the DWP website [**www.dwp.gov.uk**].
- Obtain e-mailed assistance from a benefits adviser on the Directgov website [**www.direct.gov.uk**].

You may consider the possibility of being entitled to a tax rebate. Consult the HMRC fact sheet on redundancy (PDF) for details [**www.hmrc.gov.uk/guidance/redundancy-factsheet.pdf**].

You should avoid hasty decisions about pension contributions.

6.5 Keeping in touch

It is important to keep in touch with the profession even though you may be out of the work place. You may consider:

- maintaining contact with friends in practice;
- developing or maintaining contacts with your local Law Society;
- attending local and special interest groups' meetings;
- signing up to relevant mailing lists to keep up to date with events; and
- notifying the *Law Society Gazette* of your current address.

You may keep your name on the Roll of Solicitors even if you do not keep up your practising certificate. The cost of this is £20 per year.

If your name is removed from the Roll, you must refer to yourself as a former solicitor, not a solicitor. To reinstate your name to the Roll you must complete a KR4 form and pay a £20 fee.

If you remove your name and then find employment that requires you to both be on the Roll and hold a practising certificate, it will take approximately 21 to 28 days to have your name reinstated. You may not apply for a practising certificate until your name is included on the Roll.

7. Moving on

Redundancy is no reflection of your legal ability. You shouldn't take it personally; the job was deemed redundant and not you. You will likely experience a range of emotions, and it helps to talk this through to deal with your response. Your employer may provide counselling services. For alternative assistance contact LawCare who offer a confidential free advisory and support service for lawyers who are suffering from work-related difficulties [**www.lawcare.org.uk**].

For information on job seeking, read the Society's job seeking practice note.

8.   More information

8.1   Employment rights, pay, fair selection and consultation

www.direct.gov.uk
www.adviceguide.org.uk
www.acas.org.uk

8.2   Practice Advice Service

The Law Society provides support for solicitors on a wide range of areas of practice. Practice Advice can be contacted on 0870 606 2522 from 09.00 to 17.00 on weekdays.

8.3   The Solicitors' Assistance Scheme

www.thesas.org.uk

8.4   Junior Lawyers Division of the Law Society

Support, advice and networking opportunities for students, trainees and newly qualified solicitors.

www.lawsociety.org.uk/juniorlawyers

8.5   Junior Lawyers Division confidential helpline

Free phone: 08000 856 131
Lines are open 09.00–21.00, Monday to Friday.

8.6   LawCare

Telephone: 0800 279 6888
Lines are open 09.00–19.30, Monday to Friday, and 10.00–16.00 at weekends.

www.lawcare.org.uk

8.7 Law Gazette Jobs

www.lawgazettejobs.co.uk

8.8 Law Society Publishing books

For practical coverage of employment law and employment tribunals, see our latest books:

Employment Law Handbook, 4th edition;
Employment Tribunals, 2nd edition.

Visit **www.lawsociety.org.uk/bookshop** for more employment related titles.

8.9 Law Society Pastoral Care Helpline

Referral service for solicitors who need help with personal, financial, professional or employment problems.

Telephone: 020 7320 5795
Lines are open 09.00–17.00, Monday to Friday.

8.10 Solicitors' Assistance Scheme

Provides free initial legal advice, including on employment issues, to solicitors, their families and their staff.

www.thesas.org.uk
Telephone: 020 7117 8811

8.11 Solicitors Benevolent Association

Charity providing financial assistance in times of hardship for solicitors and their dependants.

www.sba.org.uk
Telephone: 020 8675 6440

8.12 Solicitors Regulation Authority Contact Centre

Assists solicitors with enquiries relating to practising certificates, continuing professional development (CPD) and other general enquiries.

www.sra.org.uk
Telephone: 0870 606 2555

8.13   Status of this advice

Practice notes are issued by the Law Society for the use and benefit of its members. They represent the Law Society's view of good practice in a particular area. They are not intended to be the only standard of good practice that solicitors can follow. You are not required to follow them, but doing so will make it easier to account to oversight bodies for your actions.

Practice notes are not legal advice, nor do they necessarily provide a defence to complaints of misconduct or of inadequate professional service. While care has been taken to ensure that they are accurate, up to date and useful, the Law Society will not accept any legal liability in relation to them.

For queries or comments on this practice note contact the Law Society's Practice Advice Service.

8.14   Terminology in this advice

Must – a specific requirement in the Solicitor's Code of Conduct or legislation. You must comply, unless there are specific exemptions or defences provided for in the code of conduct or relevant legislation.

Should – good practice for most situations in the Law Society's view. If you do not follow this, you must be able to justify to oversight bodies why this is appropriate, either for your practice, or in the particular retainer.

May – a non-exhaustive list of options for meeting your obligations. Which option you choose is determined by the risk profile of the individual practice, client or retainer. You must be able to justify why this was an appropriate option to oversight bodies.

Tax and VAT

My client is based overseas and is purchasing a property in the UK. Will he be liable to pay VAT on his legal costs?

Yes. The supply of legal services in relation to UK land is always subject to UK VAT at the standard rate wherever the client is based. HM Revenue and Customs (HMRC) takes the view that land related services include all services that relate directly to specific sites or property. This would include conveyancing services, advice on the sale, disposal, transfer or surrender of an interest in or right over land or buildings, advice on title and advice on applying for or challenging the refusal of planning permission.

HMRC does not regard the administration of a deceased's estate that includes property situated in the UK as a land related service. In order to fall outside the land related category, the legal services must primarily involve some other area, for example a company acquisition to which the land element is incidental – in such a case a single composite bill would also help to support an argument that the legal services were not land related.

A colleague has informed me that I must personally complete the stamp duty land tax (SDLT) forms on behalf of my client. Is this true?

The current stamp duty regime became effective on 1 December 2003. Although it is not mandatory, the Law Society advises that it is good practice for solicitors to complete the form on behalf of the client as most clients are likely to require guidance when completing it themselves and may go to accountants instead for assistance. Clients are however responsible for signing the returns. Furthermore, if you are also acting on behalf of a lender, then the lender is likely to insist that you take responsibility for completing the form. The Law Society recommends that you charge the client for time spent completing the form.

If you choose to complete the content of the form on behalf of your client, then you should inform him that it is his obligation to notify 'liability to tax' within the defined period (i.e. within 30 days from the effective date of transaction) and pay the tax due. You should inform the client that he remains ultimately responsible for the accuracy of the information and for the consequences of delay on his part and the implications for registering the property as a result. Where you are acting for the lender, you should be aware that the failure of the client to co-operate in completing the form could lead to a conflict of interest. It is advisable to inform your client of the penalties, which may be incurred if the form is returned late.

My firm has paid the fee for my Practising Certificate. Do I have to declare this on my income tax return form?

No. Under section 343 of the Income Tax (Earnings and Pensions Act) 2003, where an employer has paid an employee's professional subscription to a recognised body no benefit is deemed to accrue to the employee and this does not have to be recorded on his income tax return. This applies to solicitors in private practice and those solicitors in-house who are required by rule 2.02 of the Code of Conduct (**www.sra.org.uk/solicitors/code-of-conduct/207.article**) to hold a practising certificate.

I am a sole practitioner and am concerned about VAT implications for oath fees.

Oath fees earned by sole practitioners or partners remain part of the turnover of the 'taxable person' and liable to VAT.

If you are liable to VAT, then the fees prescribed by the Commissioners for Oaths (Fees) Order 1993, SI 1993/2297, are inclusive of VAT. If the deponent is also a taxable person, and asks for a tax invoice, the invoice can be of the less detailed kind described in paragraph 53 of Customs & Excise Notice 700. At the end of each accounting period, you should account to HMRC for the appropriate fraction of the fees received. Until January 2010 the standard rate of VAT is 15 per cent for which the fraction is 7/47ths. Please see **www.hmrc.gov.uk** for updates.

For further information please see Anderson, M. and Warner, V. (2008) *Execution of Documents* (2nd Edition), Law Society Publishing, which is available from the Law Society's online bookshop (**www.lawsociety. org.uk/bookshop**).

My client is buying a house and has asked me to complete the Stamp Duty Land Tax form on his behalf. Must I obtain his National Insurance (NI) number to enable me to complete the form?

No, the NI number is not essential. HMRC has produced some useful guidance entitled 'How to complete your Land Transaction Return' (see paragraph 50) which is available at **www.hmrc.gov.uk/sdlt6/index.htm**

Can I delay accounting for and paying VAT to HMRC on clients' bills until I have received payment from the client?

No. The effect of HMRC Notice 700 is to make unlawful and ineffective the practice of a solicitor writing to a client to inform them of the fees but not issuing a VAT invoice until payment has been received.

The tax point for services is usually the date on which their performance is completed. VAT becomes payable on that date irrespective of when the bill is delivered.

There is an exception for solicitors in that if a tax invoice is issued within three months of the basic tax point, the date of the invoice becomes the actual tax point. VAT is therefore payable by a solicitor when the work is completed or when the bill is delivered provided that this is within three months of the completion of the work (HMRC Notice 700 and the Value Added Tax Act 1994, s.6(6)). It is an offence for a solicitor not to quantify the charges within three months of completing a matter for the purposes of calculating and paying VAT.

I act for a tenant who is required to pay his landlord's legal costs. Will my client be able to recover the VAT charged on the bill?

HMRC Notice 742 (Land and Property) points out that payment by a tenant of a landlord's costs incurred in respect of the grant of a lease or licence would be regarded as part of the consideration for the supply by the landlord to the tenant. If the supply to the tenant is a taxable supply then the landlord should issue a VAT invoice addressed to the tenant for the amount of the legal costs plus VAT (N.B. the landlord's solicitor should not invoice the tenant for the legal costs as the tenant is not the recipient of the supply by the solicitor). As the paying party, if your client is registered for VAT, he will be able to recover the whole or part of the VAT charged to him.

The ability to recover VAT will depend on whether the landlord has elected to waive exemption from VAT in relation to the property (usually referred to as the option to tax).

If no option to tax has been made, the landlord would not be entitled to an input tax credit on his costs, so your client would be required to pay the gross costs including the VAT element. There will have been no taxable supply to your client, so he will not receive a VAT invoice and will be unable to recover as input tax the amount representing VAT on the landlord's costs which he has paid to the landlord.

If the landlord has opted to tax so that VAT is payable in respect of the rent or premium, the landlord can recover the VAT element of the costs he pays to his solicitor. Your client will only be required to pay the net amount of the landlord's costs, but to that net amount the landlord will add a VAT charge in respect of the supply he makes to the tenant.

In effect, the amount paid by the tenant would be the same whether or not the landlord has opted to tax: but only if the landlord has done so will the tenant receive a VAT invoice from the landlord and be able to recover the VAT element if the tenant is a registered taxable person.

Please see the Law Society VAT Guide 1996 available at **www.law society.org.uk**.

We are a new legal aid practice. Has the Law Society issued any guidance on how we should account for VAT on legal aid payments. In particular, when does the VAT tax point arise?

Yes, the Law Society has issued a practice note on VAT on legal aid work (**Annex 8D**).

As regards the VAT tax point, this is based on the normal VAT rules as they apply to solicitors. When the VAT tax point arises is a question of fact to be decided on a case-by-case basis. The basic tax point arises when the supply of services is known to be completed. This is the basic occasion of charge. You must account to HM Revenue and Customs for the tax due on the consideration payable for your services at the end of the quarter in which the tax point falls. This consideration is the total amount payable to you, including taxable disbursements. (For further information please see the practice note.)

My firm has a legal aid contract with the Legal Services Commission (LSC). At what point does VAT become payable?

VAT is due on regular payments to the extent that they represent either:

- advance payment for cases not yet started; or
- cases started but not yet completed.

The proper application of the VAT regulations for solicitors is consistent with the way other businesses account for VAT. Under the regulations, two possible scenarios arise:

- Where the claim submitted to the LSC is for a sum greater than the regular payment amount, VAT is payable on the amount of the submitted claim.
- Where the claim submitted to the LSC is for a sum less than the regular payment amount, VAT is payable on the full amount of the regular payment.

Regular payments are initially calculated on the expected level of work for the coming year, subject to review by the Legal Services Commission. The LSC might adjust payments to take account of fluctuations in the level of cases actually undertaken.

As individual cases are completed, you must both:

- bill the fees, disbursements and VAT to the client's ledger; and
- withdraw the funds from the LSC contract ledger account and post them to the client's ledger account.

This means that the amounts received from the LSC may exceed or fall short of the value of completed cases at any given time, depending on the progress of individual cases.

Regular payments are consideration for services to be supplied, or already supplied, to clients qualifying for legal aid funding.

The payments include a VAT element and fall within the scope of VAT when the payment is received, unless VAT is already accounted for because the case has been completed. The only exception is where you can show that an element of the payment is for non-vatable disbursements.

To do this, and provide a more accurate representation of the VAT accountable to HMRC, you must both:

- discharge any non-vatable disbursement as it becomes liable and is rightfully due
- post out the payment from the relevant LSC contract ledger account once payment has been drawn and debited against the client's ledger account

This ensures any residual over or under payment balance remaining on the LSC contract ledger account would relate to pure costs, vatable disbursements and VAT itself.

Please see the Law Society's practice note VAT on legal aid work (**Annex 8D**).

Annex 8A

Tax payment difficulties

9 February 2009

1. Introduction

1.1 Who should read this practice note?

Solicitors who anticipate future financial difficulties, particularly in relation to their tax returns due in January 2009 and other tax liabilities.

1.2 What is the issue?

Many practices are experiencing financial difficulties due to the economic downturn.

HM Revenue and Customs (HMRC) have introduced a Business Support Service to help you weather the current economic conditions by assisting both large and small businesses unable to pay their tax. The service was launched on 24 November 2008, and deals with all values of debts that are *becoming due*, although some larger and more complex cases may need to be referred to a specialist to deal with. Debts which are *overdue* may also have to be referred to a specialist who will contact you within four working days.

The service is primarily available to self-employed people and companies but can be used by anyone who is having difficulty in meeting their tax liabilities. It covers most taxes and duties including income tax, corporation tax, VAT, PAYE and national insurance.

2. Who is eligible for deferral?

To qualify for deferral, you will need to be:

- in genuine difficulty;
- unable to pay your tax on time;
- likely to be able to pay your tax if HMRC allowed you more time.

HMRC undertakes to be flexible and agree time to pay arrangements on a case-by-case basis to bring your business back up to date within an agreed timescale.

3.   How to apply

When you call the Business Support Service, you will need to provide all of the following:

1.   your tax reference number;

2.   details of which tax you are, or will have, difficulty paying;

3.   the amount of debt, or anticipated debt;

4.   why you are in difficulties;

5.   how long you will need to pay;

6.   basic details of your business' income and outgoings.

Most applicants will be given a decision over the phone. More complex cases are referred to another office, the turnaround for which is around four days.

You can call HMRC's Business Payment Support Line seven days a week on 0845 302 1435. The lines are open:

Monday–Friday: 08.00 to 20.00
Weekends: 08.00 to 16.00

Or visit their website: **www.hmrc.gov.uk**.

4.   How to avoid surcharges

If you contact HMRC before the payment is due and agree a payment arrangement:

*   You will not be charged VAT default surcharges.
*   Entering into such an agreement will not be treated as a default so it will not extend the twelve-month rolling period.
*   The default percentage will not increase because of the arrangement.

The above remains true provided, and as long as you adhere to the terms of the arrangement.

If you become unable to keep to an arrangement entered into with HMRC, or this becomes likely, you should contact HMRC straight away and certainly before missing a payment. In such cases, HMRC will look to see if it can reschedule the payments or extend the agreement, provided your business remains viable.

5.   Interest on tax deferral arrangement

The interest charged, where it applies, will be at the HMRC's published rate which is currently between 2.5% and 3.5% depending on the tax that has been deferred.

6.   More information

6.1   Status of this practice note

This is interim advice. Practice notes are issued by the Law Society for the use and benefit of its members. They represent the Law Society's view of good practice in a particular area. They are not intended to be the only standard of good practice that solicitors can follow. You are not required to follow them, but doing so will make it easier to account to oversight bodies for your actions.

Practice notes are not legal advice, nor do they necessarily provide a defence to complaints of misconduct or of inadequate professional service. While care has been taken to ensure that they are accurate, up to date and useful, the Law Society will not accept any legal liability in relation to them.

For queries or comments on this practice note contact the Law Society's Practice Advice Service.

6.2   Practice Advice Service

The Law Society provides support for solicitors on a wide range of areas of practice. Practice Advice can be contacted on 0870 606 2522 from 09.00 to 17.00 on weekdays.

Read more about the Practice Advice Service [at **www.lawsociety. org.uk/practiceadvice**].

6.3   Acknowledgements
*   HMRC Business Support Service
*   Law Society Tax Law Committee

Annex 8B

VAT change practice note

11 December 2008

1. Introduction

1.1 Who should read this practice note?

Solicitors dealing with invoicing, making and receiving payments which include VAT.

1.2 What is the issue?

In his Pre-Budget Report on 24 November 2008, the Chancellor of the Exchequer announced a cut in the standard rate of value added tax (VAT) from 17.5 per cent to 15 per cent, as of 1 December 2008. This new rate will apply until 31 December 2009, after which HMRC has advised that it will revert to 17.5 per cent on 1 January 2010.

This practice note provides an overview of the changes with advice on applying the correct rates.

1.3 Legal and other requirements

Value Added Tax Act 1994, section 2(2) [**www.statutelaw.gov.uk**].

1.4 Status of this advice

Practice notes are issued by the Law Society for the use and benefit of its members. They represent the Law Society's view of good practice in a particular area. They are not intended to be the only standard of good practice that solicitors can follow. You are not required to follow them, but doing so will make it easier to account to oversight bodies for your actions.

Practice notes are not legal advice, nor do they necessarily provide a defence to complaints of misconduct or of inadequate professional service. While care has been taken to ensure that they are accurate, up to date and useful, the Law Society will not accept any legal liability in relation to them.

For queries or comments on this practice note contact the Law Society's Practice Advice Service.

1.5 Terminology in this advice

Must – a specific requirement in the Solicitor's Code of Conduct or legislation. You must comply, unless there are specific exemptions or defences provided for in the code of conduct or relevant legislation.

Should – good practice for most situations in the Law Society's view. If you do not follow this, you must be able to justify to oversight bodies why this is appropriate, either for your practice, or in the particular retainer.

May – a non-exhaustive list of options for meeting your obligations. Which option you choose is determined by the risk profile of the individual practice, client or retainer. You must be able to justify why this was an appropriate option to oversight bodies.

HMRC – Her Majesty's Revenue and Customs.

1.6 Acknowledgements

The Society acknowledges the contributions of Her Majesty's Revenue & Customs CT & VAT Directorate, and the Tax Law Committee in developing this practice note.

1.7 More information

1.7.1 Practice Advice Service

The Law Society provides support for solicitors on a wide range of areas of practice. Practice Advice Service can be contacted on 0870 606 2522 from 9am to 5pm on weekdays.

1.7.2 HMRC

- VAT rate change guide (PDF) [**www.hmrc.gov.uk/vat/vat-rate-change.pdf**]
- Business Payment Support Service [**www.hmrc.gov.uk/pbr2008/business-payment**]
- HMRC website [**www.hmrc.gov.uk**]

1.7.3 Other Law Society materials

Practice note on legal aid VAT.

2. VAT rates and tax points

You should apply the following tax rates when raising an invoice for VAT purposes:

- Matters completed before 1 December 2008 will be charged at the old rate of 17.5 per cent.
- Matters completed on or after 1 December 2008 will be charged at the new rate of 15 per cent.

A VAT invoice is normally raised when the service is completed. However, in circumstances where work is yet to be completed, the rate of VAT to be charged will depend on the date at which the supply of service, the tax point, occurs.

2.1 The basic tax point

The basic tax point for the supply of service is the date the service is performed. The basic tax point can be overridden by the actual tax point.

2.2 The actual tax point

The actual tax point occurs *earlier* than the basic tax point when a VAT invoice is raised or payment is made before the performance or completion of a service. The actual tax point is the date at which either:

- the invoice is issued; or
- payment is received,

whichever occurs first.

The actual tax point occurs *later* than the basic tax point when an invoice is issued or payment received after the basic tax point. This is known as the 14–day rule.

2.3 The 14-day rule for all services

The 14-day rule enables you to issue a VAT invoice within 14 days of the basic tax point. The date of the invoice is the tax point, and this overrides the basic tax point.

HMRC has agreed, by concession, to extend the 14-day period to 30 days for the supply of services made between 18 November and 30 November. See below for illustrative examples.

2.3.1   Further extension for legal services only

A further extension applies when the fee for a legal service was not ascertained or ascertainable at the time the service was performed. This extends the 14-day period to three months. You may issue the VAT invoice no later than three months after completion of your services. The date of the invoice will be the tax point.

You should be aware that failure to issue a VAT invoice within the extended period will cause the actual tax point to revert to the basic tax point.

See the HMRC website for further information on VAT invoice extensions.

2.3.2   Illustrative examples

1.   Work completed from 18–30 November 2008

You must charge VAT at 17.5 per cent if an invoice is issued or payment received for this work before 1 December 2008.

You should charge VAT at 15 per cent if no invoice is issued nor payment received until 1 December or after. The VAT invoice must be issued no later than 30 days following completion of the work.

2.   Work completed on or before 17 November 2008

The VAT rate is 17.5 per cent if:

* the fee was agreed with the client on or before 17 November; and
* the work is completed by this date.

However, if the fee has not been agreed at the time the work is completed, VAT will be payable at 15 per cent, provided the VAT invoice is issued no later than three months after completion of the performance of the service.

3.   Applying the correct rate

3.1   Disbursements

The rate of VAT charged in respect of disbursements depends on the tax point. This is the date on which the invoice is issued, regardless of when the disbursement was incurred.

3.2 Work in progress

A tax point is created each time:

- an invoice is issued; or
- a payment is received.

You must calculate the VAT at 15 per cent for interim invoices issued by your office for work that is ongoing and due to be completed on or after 1 December.

For interim invoices sent out prior to 1 December, you can elect to charge either:

- 17.5 per cent; or
- 15 per cent.

If you elect to charge 15 per cent, you should issue a new invoice. If the client has already paid 17.5 per cent, you must issue the client with a VAT credit note. This must be issued within 45 days of 1 December. You must adjust your VAT return.

Interim invoices may be resubmitted at your discretion. HMRC has advised that there is no requirement to apportion pre and post rate changes for continuous supplies.

3.3 Counsel's fees

The tax point for supplies of legal services by barristers is the earliest of the following:

- the date of receipt of payment;
- the date of issue of a VAT invoice;
- the date the barrister ceases to practise.

You will be charged VAT at 17.5 per cent if you pay counsel's fees before 1 December 2008.

You must charge your client the precise amount if you treat counsel's fees as a disbursement for VAT purposes. This includes VAT that you pay to counsel. You must not:

- charge your own client VAT on the disbursement;
- recover as input tax the VAT that you pay to counsel.

3.4   What happens if I make a mistake?

HMRC recognises that this change could lead to errors or mistakes in the first VAT return following the change, and they will take this into account when assessing the VAT return.

You should, however, refer to HMRC for further guidance on specific issues. For the latest information see the HMRC website.

4.   Legal Services Commission

The Legal Services Commission (LSC) makes payments to providers using fixed fee and non-fixed fee charging schemes on the following basis:

*   All claims for work with a case concluded date before 1 December will attract a 17.5 per cent VAT rate.
*   All claims for work with a case concluded date on or after 1 December will attract a 15 per cent VAT rate.

This applies to:

*   claims;
*   claim forms;
*   all areas of LSC funded work.

4.1   Standard monthly payments (SMP)

The VAT treatment of SMP from the Legal Services Commission (LSC) for legal aid work depends on the extent to which each payment relates to completed cases. The tax point for regular payments is the date the payment is received.

SMP may create tax points before 1 December for uncompleted cases or work that has not commenced. These may be recalculated with VAT at 15 per cent if the cases to which the payments are eventually allocated are completed on, or after, that date.

For more information on SMP, please refer to the Law Society's VAT guide for legal aid work.

4.2   LSC Online

LSC Online users who enter cases individually should not include those that concluded on or after 1 December in their December submission. Any which are included will be incorrectly credited with VAT at 17.5 per cent.

This does not apply where:

- you have yet to relaunch LSC Online; or
- you load your monthly submissions directly from your case management or bulkload system.

For more information, please refer to the LSC website [**www.legalservices. gov.uk**].

4.3 Advocate Graduated Fee Scheme and Solicitor Standard Fee claims

The VAT rate change applies to cases that conclude on or after 1 December in respect of:

- litigators' claims; and
- payments made on or after 1 December, for barristers' and solicitor advocates' claims.

The CREST IT system calculates and adds VAT automatically to VAT-registered claimants. The system will be upgraded to reflect the new rate, but this will not be in place for 1 December.

Pending the upgrade courts will continue to process and pay claims at the former rate of 17.5 per cent. Individual payees may resolve overpayments of VAT with HMRC where necessary. Following the upgrade CREST will apply 15 per cent VAT to all claims.

Crown Court managers have been made aware of the situation.

5. VAT on leases for the purposes of Stamp Duty Land Tax (SDLT)

The changes will affect calculation of the net present value (NPV) of rent payable under a lease, where VAT is charged on the rent.

In calculating VAT, the tax point for rental payments is either:

- the date on which a VAT invoice is issued; or
- a payment is received,

whichever is the earlier.

The rate that is in force at the tax point will be the rate that applies.

5.1   Calculating NPV

If the effective date of the grant of a lease is on or after 1 December 2008, VAT will be 15 per cent up to and including 31 December 2009.

When the rate changes back to 17.5 per cent on 1 January 2010 it will apply to all leases with an effective date on or after 1 January of that year.

5.2   Repayments of tax paid on rent

HMRC will view the effect of the VAT changes as rendering such rents variable or uncertain. HMRC will treat such rent as becoming certain when the VAT rate returns to 17.5 per cent again on 1 January 2010.

HMRC will therefore consider repayments of overpaid tax in light of the Finance Act 2003 Schedule 17A paragraph 8, which deals with cases where rents cease to be uncertain. You may submit a claim for an overpayment due to the VAT rate being calculated at 17.5 per cent, if the amount of rent payable becomes certain within the first five years of the term of the lease.

5.2.1   Making an SDLT claim

HMRC do not intend to make any repayments before 1 January 2010.

However, if the end of the fifth year of the lease falls on or before 31 December 2009, any claim for repayment of overpaid tax should be made within 30 days of the date when the rents for the first five years of the term become certain.

It is unlikely that claims for SDLT repayment will be for large sums; for example, an estimate repayment on an annual rent of £1m would be less than £250. Interest will be paid on such repayments on the usual basis. Claims should be made in writing to the Birmingham Stamp Office.

For further information see the HMRC website.

Annex 8C

VAT on disbursements practice note

19 February 2009

1. Introduction

1.1 Who should read this practice note?

Solicitors dealing with invoicing, making and receiving payments that include disbursements and VAT.

1.2 What is the issue?

Within your practice, many solicitors refer to a variety of costs related to providing your service as disbursements, such as travelling expenses. But these costs might not qualify as disbursements for VAT purposes.

You must charge your client VAT when billing if an item is not a disbursement for VAT purposes.

This practice note seeks to clarify this issue to help you identify what is or is not a disbursement for VAT purposes. It is complementary to HMRC's guidance.

2. VAT on qualifying disbursements

If HMRC considers a payment to be a disbursement for VAT purposes, the item is deemed to have been provided directly to the client.

Therefore VAT on disbursements is:

- not charged to the client by the solicitor;
- not reclaimed from HMRC by the solicitor;
- only reclaimable by clients who are VAT registered and have obtained a valid VAT invoice, and this reclamation is subject to the usual conditions.

3. Qualifying disbursements

HMRC considers a disbursement for VAT purposes to be a payment made to a third party by a supplier on behalf of a client, as the client's agent. Any payments you make to third parties on behalf of a client can be treated as disbursements for VAT purposes.

Therefore you do not charge VAT when billing your client for that item.

To qualify as a disbursement, the following criteria must be met:

- You acted as the agent of your client when you paid the third party.
- You charged your client the precise amounts you paid out, e.g. without any mark-up for profit.
- Your client authorised you to make the payment on their behalf.
- Your client knew that the goods or services would be provided by a third party.
- Your client actually received and used the goods or services provided by the third party.
- Your client was responsible for paying the third party, e.g. estate duty or stamp duty.
- The item was separately itemised when you invoiced your client.

However, costs incurred by suppliers/solicitors in the course of making their own supply to the client cannot be treated as disbursements. These must be included in the value of those supplies when VAT is calculated.

Costs that can be treated as disbursements for VAT purposes include:

- medical fees, reports, records, expert opinions;
- expert services, such as an interpreter;
- surveyor's fees.

You must consider who received the benefit of the services provided to decide whether expenditure on such services qualifies as a disbursement for VAT purposes.

An invoice for an interpreter can be a disbursement if:

- the interpreter is needed so that the client can communicate with you, or for them to understand court proceedings. Here, the supply will be to the client;
- you receive an invoice from the interpreter.

An invoice for a translator cannot be a disbursement if the translation was commissioned to enable you to understand a document and advise the client accordingly: the client did not directly receive the benefit of the supply.

4. Payments or disbursements not qualifying

Normal costs incurred in performing a service as part of your business cannot be treated as disbursements for VAT purposes. If an item is not a disbursement for VAT purposes, you must charge the client VAT when billing.

For example, HMRC considers postal charges as an integral part of a solicitor's service, reflected in fee rates, so not a disbursement for VAT purposes.

Costs that cannot be treated as disbursements for VAT purposes include:

- costs incurred or services provided by you in the course of providing a service to your clients, e.g. account administration;
- business expenses, such as travelling and subsistence costs, telephone bills, postage costs and other office costs;
- bank transfer fees to or from your own professional account;
- royalty or licence fees incurred in providing goods or services to your client.

Such costs should either be included in the price of your services on which you charge VAT, or invoiced or charged separately and VAT charged on those items.

5. VAT on counsel's fees

HMRC allows you to choose whether to treat counsel's fees as qualifying as a disbursement for VAT purposes or not. You may either:

1. treat counsel's fees as not being a disbursement for VAT purposes. To do this, you should show fees as inclusive of VAT and levy your bill in the usual way, claiming counsel's fees as part of your services to your client; or

2. treat counsel's fees as a disbursement for VAT purposes. To do this, you should insert on the fee note your client's name and the word 'per' immediately before your name, or cross out your name and insert the name of your client. In this case the supply is deemed to have been made direct to your client.

6. Advantages to your client of disbursements

Treating a payment as a disbursement for VAT purposes means you do not add VAT to the disbursement when you bill your client. This helps save money for any clients not registered for VAT, or otherwise not entitled to reclaim VAT on these costs either directly from you or from the third party.

7. Keeping records of disbursements

You must keep records to show:

- you were entitled to exclude the payment from the value of your own services to your client;
- you did not reclaim VAT on the goods or services provided by the third party.

Such records should include order forms and copy invoices.

8. More information

8.1 Professional conduct

In addition to considering whether costs are disbursements for VAT purposes, you may need to consider whether a payment is a disbursement, and if so, the type of disbursement, for the purposes of the Solicitors' Accounts Rules 1998.

8.2 Further products and support

8.2.1 Practice Advice Service

The Law Society's practice advice service provides support for solicitors on a wide range of areas of practice. Practice Advice can be contacted on 0870 606 2522 from 09.00 to 17.00 on weekdays.

8.2.2 Law Society publications

- *Solicitors' Accounts Manual* – 10th edition
- *Solicitors and the Accounts Rules*

8.3 Status of this practice note

Practice notes are issued by the Law Society for the use and benefit of its members. They represent the Law Society's view of good practice in a particular area. They are not intended to be the only standard of good practice that solicitors can follow. You are not required to follow them, but doing so will make it easier to account to oversight bodies for your actions.

Practice notes are not legal advice, nor do they necessarily provide a defence to complaints of misconduct or of inadequate professional service. While care has been taken to ensure that they are accurate, up to date and useful, the Law Society will not accept any legal liability in relation to them.

For queries or comments on this practice note contact the Law Society's Practice Advice Service.

www.lawsociety.org.uk/practiceadvice

8.4   Terminology in this practice note

Must – a specific requirement in the Solicitor's Code of Conduct or legislation. You must comply, unless there are specific exemptions or defences provided for in the code of conduct or relevant legislation.

Should – good practice for most situations in the Law Society's view. If you do not follow this, you must be able to justify to oversight bodies why this is appropriate, either for your practice, or in the particular retainer.

May – a non-exhaustive list of options for meeting your obligations. Which option you choose is determined by the risk profile of the individual practice, client or retainer. You must be able to justify why this was an appropriate option to oversight bodies.

8.5   Acknowledgements

HM Revenue and Customs.

Annex 8D

VAT on legal aid work practice note

4 July 2008

1. Introduction

1.1 Who should read this practice note?

All solicitors and their legal cashiers who account for VAT on payments received under a legal aid contract or certificate.

1.2 What is the issue?

The legal aid contracting system has evolved since monthly payment arrangements were first introduced by the Legal Services Commission (LSC), including the terminology used. The system now refers to regular payments rather than standard monthly payments (SMPs).

The new rule 21(2) of the Solicitors' Accounts Rules 1998 changed the treatment of these regular payments. This new rule came into effect on 1 May 2005. You must now pay these into your office account, rather than choosing to pay them into either your client or office account.

There is now a simplified method of accounting for VAT.

1.3 Status of this practice note

HM Revenue and Customs has endorsed this practice note.

The best practice advice in this practice note replaces the Society's 2001 interim guidance.

Practice notes are issued by the Law Society for the use and benefit of its members. They represent the Law Society's view of good practice in a particular area. They are not intended to be the only standard of good practice that solicitors can follow. You are not required to follow them, but doing so will make it easier to account to oversight bodies for your actions.

Practice notes are not legal advice, nor do they necessarily provide a defence to complaints of misconduct or of inadequate professional service.

While care has been taken to ensure that they are accurate, up to date and useful, the Law Society will not accept any legal liability in relation to them.

For queries or comments on this practice note contact the Law Society's Practice Advice Service.

1.4   Terminology

Must – a specific requirement in the Solicitors' Code of Conduct or legislation. You must comply, unless there are specific exemptions or defences provided for in the code of conduct or relevant legislation.

Should – good practice for most situations. If you deviate from this, you must be able to justify why this is appropriate, either for your firm, or in the particular retainer.

May – a non-exhaustive list of options for meeting your obligations. Which option you choose is determined by the risk profile of the individual firm, client or retainer. You must be able to justify why this was an appropriate option to oversight bodies.

1.5   Acknowledgements

The Society acknowledges the considerable assistance received from the Institute of Legal Cashiers and Administrators in updating the advice given in this practice note and the co-operation from HM Revenue and Customs (HMRC).

1.6   More information and products

1.6.1   Law Society

- The Law Society's VAT Guide 1996
- Practice Advice Service
- Law Society publications – order from our [online] bookshop [**www.lawsociety.org.uk/bookshop**]:

  - *Solicitors' Accounts Manual* – 10th edition
  - *Solicitors and the Accounts Rules: A Compliance Handbook*
  - *Understanding Legal Aid: A Practical Guide to Public Funding*
  - *Making a Success of Legal Aid: Better Days for the Practitioner*

1.6.2   Others

- HM Revenue and Customs [**www.hmrc.gov.uk**]
- Institute of Legal Cashiers and Administrators [**www.icla.org.uk**]

2.   Types of legal aid

There are several types of public funding – one of these is legal aid. In essence, there are two types of legal aid:

- licensed – often referred to as certificated work;
- contract.

A basic understanding of these two types of legal aid is required to account for these payments.

2.1   Licensed

The Legal Services Commission (LSC) issues a public funding certificate after a successful application to them. Claims are paid twice a month via a statement for the following payments:

- disbursements;
- billed costs;
- on account of costs.

Most certificated work claims relate to billed costs.

2.2   Contract

There are two types of contract: criminal and civil. It is possible to have both or either contracts. Both provide regular payments, called standard monthly payments (SMPs).

3.   VAT tax point

This is based on the normal VAT rules as they apply to solicitors. When the VAT tax point arises is a question of fact to be decided on a case-by-case basis. The basic tax point arises when the supply of services is known to be completed. This is the basic occasion of charge. You must account to HMRC for the tax due on the consideration payable for your services at the end of the quarter in which the tax point falls. This consideration is the total amount payable to you, including taxable disbursements.

3.1   Licensed work

This is relatively simple:

- The tax point date arises once the matter is concluded.
- You must then raise a CLS CLAIM 1 and submit this to the LSC.
- The LSC will pay a few weeks later.

3.2 Contract work

VAT is due on regular payments to the extent that they represent either:

- advance payment for cases not yet started;
- cases started but not yet completed.

The proper application of the VAT regulations for solicitors is consistent with the way other businesses account for VAT. Under the regulations, two possible scenarios arise:

- Where the claim submitted to the LSC is for a sum greater than the regular payment amount, VAT is payable on the amount of the submitted claim.
- Where the claim submitted to the LSC is for a sum less than the regular payment amount, VAT is payable on the full amount of the regular payment.

Regular payments are initially calculated on the expected level of work for the coming year, subject to review by the Legal Services Commission. The LSC might adjust payments to take account of fluctuations in the level of cases actually undertaken.

As individual cases are completed, you must both:

- bill the fees, disbursements and VAT to the client's ledger;
- withdraw the funds from the LSC contract ledger account and post them to the client's ledger account.

This means that the amounts received from the LSC may exceed or fall short of the value of completed cases at any given time, depending on the progress of individual cases.

Regular payments are consideration for services to be supplied, or already supplied, to clients qualifying for legal aid funding.

The payments include a VAT element and fall within the scope of VAT when the payment is received, unless VAT is already accounted for because the case has been completed. The only exception is where you can show that an element of the payment is for non-vatable disbursements.

To do this, and provide a more accurate representation of the VAT accountable to HMRC, you must both:

- discharge any non-vatable disbursement as it becomes liable and is rightfully due;
- post out the payment from the relevant LSC contract ledger account once payment has been drawn and debited against the client's ledger account.

This ensures any residual over or under payment balance remaining on the LSC contract ledger account would relate to pure costs, vatable disbursements and VAT itself.

4. Accounting treatment

Rule 19(4) of the Solicitors' Accounts Rules 1998 (the accounts rules) [www.sra.org.uk/accounts-rules] says you must generally hold money paid on account of costs in a client account. For a privately paying client, VAT is not payable until the work has been completed and billed. This is because you are in effect holding money on your client's behalf. This money is likely to include money for several purposes other than payment of the solicitor's fees, such as paying stamp duty taxes and buying property.

HMRC says money held in this way cannot be said to have been received by you until the accounts rules permit you to transfer them to the office account. Until then, it is as if the money were held in the client's own bank account. However, HMRC says that regular payments you receive under a contract with the LSC do not fall into this category. This is because regular payments are intended to represent consideration for work to be undertaken under the contract from the outset. So, receiving regular payment amounts to the receipt of a payment for VAT purposes.

Under rule 21(2)(a) of the accounts rules, you must pay regular payments into an office account at a bank or building society in England and Wales. These payments are office money and you must record them on the office side of a client ledger account. As with all types of work, you must both:

- open a ledger account for each client;
- open an LSC ledger account to record regular payments received under your contract. See rule 32(4) and note (v) to rule 32.

Below is an example ledger card which would be opened to record regular payments relating to a general criminal contract.

Client name: Legal Services Commission
Client matter: General criminal contract

		Office account			Client account		
Date	Narrative	DR	CR	Balance	DR	CR	Balance

4.1 Licensed work

You should raise an invoice once work is concluded, as with private paying work. The LSC will send you a statement detailing the number of payments made to you in the one combined sum. You must pay this money directly into the client's ledger account, where the bills should already be waiting for payment.

Rule 21(1)(b) of the accounts rules says you may pay money for costs from the LSC into an office account at a bank or building society in England and Wales, if you either:

- transfer all money for paying disbursements to a client account within 14 days of receipt;
- pay the disbursements within 14 days of receipt.

4.2 Contracted criminal work

A regular payment is received each month. You must record them on the office account side of your LSC client ledger account. You must then report the following to the LSC each month:

- who you have represented;
- the work undertaken;
- the costs you are claiming.

This gives the LSC a record of the expenditure level under the contract.

You must account for VAT on completed cases at the basic tax point. This is the date when the supply of services is completed.

To account for the correct VAT amount, you must determine whether the payment received is a fixed fee that is inclusive or exclusive of VAT.

You must raise a bill in accordance with the actual value of the claim due against the criminal contract and posted to the client's individual ledger card.

To pay the bill, you must allocate money from the LSC contract ledger account to the client's individual ledger account. This will clear the recorded time and disbursements from the firm's work in progress figures.

Posting of the bill will also automatically post the correct amount of VAT for that matter to the system VAT Output Account. This is because VAT will be charged on profit costs and disbursements, such as travel, which are subject to VAT. Similarly, billing disbursements will automatically adjust the VAT liability where they are either:

- treated as disbursements for VAT purposes, such as court fees;
- a vatable disbursement being treated by the firm on the agency basis.

Example:

A firm has had a criminal contract for some time and is currently holding a balance of £2,365. They receive another regular payment under their general criminal contract for £1,175. The firm subsequently has claims for three clients:

Mr Jones' case concluded on 4 Jan for £269.45.

Mr Smith's case concluded on 8 Jan for £89.45.

Mrs Thomas' case concluded on 12 Jan for £121.44.

Example accounting entries for those transactions:

Client name: Legal Services Commission Client matter: General criminal contract					File No: 4000		
		Office account			Client account		
Date	Narrative	DR	CR	Balance	DR	CR	Balance
Balance c/fwd				2,365 CR			
03/01/XX	Recd LSC		1,175.00	3,540 CR			
04/01/XX	Jnl to 1234/ Jones	269.45		3,270.55 CR			
08/01/XX	Jnl to 1235/ Smith	89.45		3,181.10 CR			
12/01/XX	Jnl to 1 236/ Thomas	121.44		3,059.66 CR			

Client name: Jones AN Client matter: Crime					File No: GG/1234		
		Office account			Client account		
Date	Narrative	DR	CR	Balance	DR	CR	Balance
04/01/XX	Our charges	229.32		229.32 DR			
04/01/XX	VAT	40.13		269.45 DR			
04/01/XX	Jnl from LSC – Crime		269.45	Nil			

Client name: Smith AB Client matter: Crime					File No: GG/1235		
		Office account			Client account		
Date	Narrative	DR	CR	Balance	DR	CR	Balance
08/01/XX	Our charges	76.13		76.13 DR			
04/01/XX	VAT	13.32		89.45 DR			
04/01/XX	Jnl from LSC – Crime		89.45	Nil			

Client name: Thomas AA Client matter: Crime					File No: CD/1236		
		Office account			Client account		
Date	Narrative	DR	CR	Balance	DR	CR	Balance
12/01/XX	Our charges	103.36		103.36 DR			
04/01/XX	VAT	18.08		18.08 DR			
04/01/XX	Jnl from LSC – Crime		121.44	Nil			

With a criminal contract, the amount of VAT you report each month to the LSC is the same value you account to the HMRC. Once the work has been completed, you should then submit this amount collectively to the LSC on a monthly basis.

4.3   Contracted civil work

As with the criminal contract, a regular payment is received each month. You must record them on the office account side of your LSC client ledger account. You must then report the following to the LSC each month:

* who you have represented;
* the work undertaken;
* the costs you are claiming.

This gives the LSC a record of the expenditure level under the contract.

You must account for VAT on completed cases at the basic tax point. This is the date when the supply of services is completed.

A civil contract has a fixed fee allocated to specific categories and levels of work. The amount paid for each case under this scheme is called a tailored fixed fee (TFF). The TFF is paid regardless of the value of work actually undertaken. Although you report to the LSC the actual value of work undertaken, a bill is only raised for the value of the TFF. So sometimes you will have done more or less work than the value of the TFF.

The TFF is published on the LSC's website [**www.legalservices. gov.uk**]. You should refer to this to be able to reconcile the contract correctly.

To pay the bill, you must allocate money from the LSC contract ledger account to the client's individual ledger account. This will clear the recorded time and disbursements from the firm's work in progress figures. Posting of the bill will also automatically post the correct amount of VAT for that matter to the system VAT Output Account. This is because VAT will be charged on profit costs and disbursements, such as travel, which are subject to VAT. Similarly, billing disbursements will automatically adjust the VAT liability where they are either:

* treated as disbursements for VAT purposes, such as court fees; or
* a vatable disbursement being treated by the firm on the agency basis.

Example:

A firm has had a civil contract for some time and is currently holding a balance of £1,587. It receives another regular payment under its general civil contract for £587, and subsequently has claims for three clients:

- Mr Moore's case concluded on 5 Jan and has a reported value of £196.79, although the TFF for this particular case of work is £94, excluding VAT.
- Mr Howells' case concluded on 10 Jan and has a reported value of £72.18, although a TFF for this particular case of work is £221, excluding VAT.
- Mrs Picton's case concluded on 20 Jan and has a reported value of £589.62, including a disbursement of £5. A TFF for this particular case of work is £370.

The accounting entries would look similar to this:

Client name: Legal Services Commission Client matter: Unified civil contract					File No: AB/5000		
		Office account			Client account		
Date	Narrative	DR	CR	Balance	DR	CR	Balance
Balance c/fwd				1,587 CR			
03/01/XX	Recd LSC		587.00	2,174 CR			
05/01/XX	Jnl to AB/5001	110.45		2,063.55 CR			
10/01/XX	Jnl to AB/5002	259.67		1,803.88 CR			
20/01/XX	Jnl to 1 236/	121.44		1,369.13 CR			

Client name: Moore G Client matter: Matrimonial					File No: AB/5001		
		Office account			Client account		
Date	Narrative	DR	CR	Balance	DR	CR	Balance
05/01/XX	Our charges	94.00		94.00 DR			
05/01/XX	VAT	16.45		110.45 DR			
04/01/XX	Jnl from LSC – Civil		110.45	Nil			

Client name: Howells AB Client matter: Divorce					File No: AB/5002		
		Office account			Client account		
Date	Narrative	DR	CR	Balance	DR	CR	Balance
10/01/XX	Our charges	221.00		221.00 DR			
10/01/XX	VAT	38.67		259.67 DR			
04/01/XX	Jnl from LSC – Civil		259.67	Nil			

Client name: Picton J Client matter: Children					File No: CD/5003		
		Office account			Client account		
Date	Narrative	DR	CR	Balance	DR	CR	Balance
12/07/XX	Copy birth certificate	5.00		5.00 DR			
20/01/XX	Our charges	365.75		370.75 DR			
10/01/XX	VAT	64.00		434.75 DR			
20/01/XX	Jnl from LSC – Civil		434.75	Nil			

Under the civil contract you must report the following:

- to the LSC – the value of work undertaken;
- to HMRC – the amount actually received under the tailored fixed fee (TFF) scheme.

4.4 Accounting for VAT – contract

The tax point for regular payments is the date the payment is received. Some of the regular payments include payment for work already completed. Before you complete your VAT return, you must therefore calculate your liability for any additional output tax.

Example:

Using the example given under the accounting treatment for contracted criminal work in section 4.2, we will examine the VAT implications arising from those transactions in January. The following invoices were raised and you should have recorded the VAT listed below in your VAT journal as output tax due to HMRC.

04 Jan 08	Jones	£40.13
08 Jan 08	Smith	£13.32
12 Jan 08	Thomas	£18.08
		£71.53

In addition, you received a regular payment from the LSC on 3 Jan for £1,175. This has triggered a tax point, so there is potential VAT liability of £175, even though you have not raised an invoice for this sum as a total. There are two ways of calculating this liability to HMRC:

1. Subtract the amount you have already accounted for in your VAT journal (£71.53) from what you know is due to HMRC as a result of your regular payment (£175). £175 less £71.53 = £103.47. You must pay over to HMRC this additional £103.47 when you complete your VAT return.

2. You received £1,175 in payment on your crime contract. The three invoices you have raised total £480.34 (£269.45 plus £89.45 plus £121.44). £1,175 less £480.34 gives you a net unbilled balance of £694.66. This is not currently reflected in your VAT journal as output VAT. When you complete your VAT return you must pay over to HMRC the VAT element of £694.66, which is **£103.46**.

You may either:

- manually adjust your VAT calculation; or
- raise an invoice for the amount so that your VAT journal balances to the amount being paid over to HMRC.

Either way, you must remember to reverse the entries before completing your next VAT return.

Example:

31.12 XX	Total VAT for quarter ending 31 Dec XX	£36,422.00
31.12.XX	*Adjustment for contract payments*	*£103.47*
01.01.XX	Total amount paid to HMRC	(£36,523.47)
01.01.XX	*Adjustment contra*	*(£103.47)*
31.03.XX	Quarter ending 31 Mar XX	£42,118.00
31.03.XX	*Adjustment for contract payments*	*£694.00*
01.04.XX	Total amount paid to HMRC	(£42,812.00)
01.04.XX	*Adjustment contra*	*(£694.00)*

The above scenario is based on the commencement of a contract. Where a contract passes its first VAT quarter, an additional calculation may be required. You must also calculate the VAT element to be paid over on this balance if you still have an excess, i.e. a credit, on your contract ledger card. In this case, divide it by 47 and multiply it by 7.

There are two ways of calculating the liability to HMRC:

1. £175 is due to HMRC as a result of the regular payment. You have already accounted for £71.53 in your VAT journal. You still have a credit balance of £382 not allocated to costs from the previous quarter. The VAT element included in this is £56.89. Add together the amount due from the regular HMRC payment to the VAT element of the credit balance. Then subtract the money already accounted for in your VAT journal. This is £175 + 56.89 – £71.53 = £160.36. You must pay **£160.36** to HMRC when you complete your VAT return.

2. You received £1,175 in payment of your crime contract. You should subtract the three invoices you have raised (£269.45, £89.45 and £121.44). This gives a net balance of £694.66, which has not been billed. You should add this to your current balance of £382 on your crime contract. Neither figure is currently reflected as output VAT in your VAT journal. These figures added together are £1,076.66. When you complete your VAT return you must pay the VAT element of £1,076.66 = **£160.36** to HMRC.

Example:

31.12 XX	Total VAT for quarter ending 31 Dec XX	£36,422.00
31.12.XX	*Adjustment for contract payments*	*£160.36*
01.01.XX	Total amount paid to HMRC	(£36,523.47)
01.01.XX	*Adjustment contra*	*(£160.36)*
31.03.XX	Quarter ending 31 Mar XX	£42,118.00
31.03.XX	*Adjustment for contract payments*	*£694.00*
01.04.XX	Total amount paid to HMRC	(£42,812.00)
01.04.XX	*Adjustment contra*	*(£694.00)*

5.   Refunds

If you must repay some, or all, of a regular payment to the LSC, e.g. where the amount of work undertaken falls, then the amount refunded ceases to be consideration for a supply. You may adjust accordingly at that time the VAT previously accounted for on the amount to be refunded.

In addition to a refund, you may also find your regular payments are insufficient to cover the work undertaken. You should therefore make no adjustment before your VAT return.

Example:

31.12 XX	Total VAT for quarter ending 31 Dec XX	£36,422.00
31.12.XX	Adjustment for contract payments	£103.47
01.01.XX	Total amount paid to HMRC	(£39,621.00)
01.01.XX	Adjustment contra	(£103.47)
31.03.XX	Quarter ending 31 Mar XX	£42,118.00
31.03.XX	*No adjustment required*	
01.04.XX	*No adjustment contra required*	

6.   Cash accounting scheme

To use this, you must meet the conditions for the scheme as explained in VAT notice 731 – cash accounting [**www.hmrc.gov.uk**].

Wills and probate/private client/family

What is a *Larke* v *Nugus* letter?

A letter requesting information about the circumstances in which a will was made has come to be known as a *Larke* v *Nugus* letter pursuant to the case *Larke* v *Nugus* [2000] WTLR 1033.

This type of letter may request some or all of the following information:

- How long you had known the deceased.
- Who introduced you to the deceased.
- The date you received instructions from the deceased.
- Contemporaneous notes of all meetings and telephone calls including an indication of where the meeting took place and who else was present at the meeting.
- How the instructions were expressed.
- What indication the deceased gave that he knew he was making a will.
- Whether the deceased exhibited any signs of confusion or loss of memory.
- Whether and to what extent earlier wills were discussed and what attempts were made to discuss departures from the deceased's earlier will-making pattern; what reasons the testator gave for making any such departures.
- How the provisions of the will were explained to the deceased
- Who, apart from the attesting witnesses, were present at the execution of the will and where, when and how this took place.

As long ago as 1959, the Law Society Council stated that a solicitor who acted for a testator in drawing up his will should, if the will becomes the subject matter of a dispute after the testator has died, make available a statement of evidence regarding the execution of the will and the circumstances surrounding it to anyone who is a party to probate proceedings or whom the solicitor believes has a reasonable claim under the will whether or not the solicitor acted for those propounding the will.

This recommendation was considered by the Court of Appeal in the above case. For further guidance please see the Law Society's Disputed will practice note (**www.lawsociety.org.uk**).

I have drafted a will for my client, who is illiterate and therefore incapable of signing it. How do I deal with this?

Although section 9 of the Wills Act 1837 requires that the will be 'signed by the testator or by some other person in his presence and by his direction', signature is given a wide meaning: a mark, an initial, and even a thumb print have all been held to suffice. Although an attestation clause, confirming that the will was read over to the testator who understood and approved it, is not required by section 9, the inclusion of such a clause will normally avoid the necessity of providing the registrar with an affidavit of due execution.

I have taken instructions from an elderly lady in relation to making a will. My client has asked if she is entitled to any public funding. What is the position?

The making of wills and matters of trust law are services that cannot normally be publicly funded as part of the Community Legal Services scheme. However, the Lord Chancellor issued a direction under the Access to Justice Act 1999, s.6(8) authorising the Legal Services Commission (LSC) to fund certain areas of work which would normally be excluded.

In relation to wills, the Lord Chancellor has permitted the LSC to fund Legal Help where the client is:

(a) aged 70 or over; or

(b) a disabled person within the meaning of the Disability Discrimination Act 1995; or

(c) the parent of a disabled person (as defined in (b) above) who wishes to provide for that person in a will, or

(d) the parent of a minor who is living with the client but not with the other parent, and where the client wishes to appoint a guardian for the minor in a will.

Applications for funding under this direction must still satisfy all relevant criteria in the Legal Service's Commission Funding Code and Regulations.

Is it correct that if a solicitor-executor witnesses a client's will, which includes a charging clause, this precludes him from later charging for the legal services rendered as solicitor-executor?

No, section 28 of the Trustee Act 2000 provides that a charging clause is not regarded as a gift for the purposes of the Wills Act 1837, s.15.

Therefore, solicitors who witness wills which allow them to charge for their services do not forfeit the benefit of the charging clause.

A client wishes to revoke their will. Will mental capacity be an issue?

The capacity to revoke a will was considered in the case of *Re Sabatini* (1970) 114 SJ 35, which established that a person who intends to revoke his or her will must have the same degree of understanding as when he or she made the will. The person must therefore be capable of:

(a) understanding the nature of the act of revoking a will;

(b) understanding the effect of revoking the will (this might even involve a greater understanding of the operation of the intestacy rules than is necessary for the purpose of making a will, although there is no direct authority on the point and it would be extremely difficult to prove this retrospectively);

(c) understanding the extent of his or her property; and

(d) comprehending and appreciating the claims to which he or she ought to give effect.

Please see Bielanska et.al (2004) *Elderly Client Handbook*, 3rd Edition, Law Society Publishing.

The partners in our firm have been appointed as executors in a will. However, we no longer carry out probate work and wish to renounce the appointment. Can we do this?

Yes. Where all the partners were appointed executors, rule 37(2A) of the Non-Contentious Probate Rules 1987 allows two partners to renounce probate (and administration with will annexed) on behalf of and with the authority of the other partners. The renunciation must recite the authority of the other partners. The executors must not have assumed a duty or performed an act which would normally only be attributable to a person assuming the executorship.

My client died a few days ago. I need to obtain a grant of probate urgently. Can a grant be issued immediately?

In general, a grant of probate will not be issued from the probate registry within seven days of the date of death and a grant of letters of administration will not be issued within fourteen days of the date of death. In exceptional cases, a district judge or probate registrar may give leave for the grant to be issued earlier but the applicant will first have to explain the need for expedition by way of a letter accompanying the application (Non-Contentious Probate Rules 1987 (SI 1987/2024), Rule 6(2)).

I am acting for three executors under a will. There has been a lot of animosity between them and now one of the executors has instructed another firm to act on his behalf. I understand that the Law Society did issue some guidelines as to costs when the personal representatives (PRs) are separately represented. Where can I find this?

The guidance was originally published in the Law Society *Gazette* on 3 September 1986. You can access it by searching the *Gazette*'s archive at **www.lawgazette.co.uk/archive.law**. Alternatively, the guidance is reproduced in King, *Probate Practitioner's Handbook*.

I am acting in a probate matter where a number of the beneficiaries are children. The PRs are concerned about who can give a good receipt on behalf of the children. Is there anything I should consider?

Yes, first look at the will to see whether it authorises parents or guardians to give a good receipt on behalf of the minor or whether it authorises the minor to give a good receipt at a specified age (often age 16). The Society of Trust and Estate Practitioners (STEP) provisions allow payment of income to a minor beneficiary's parent or guardian, or to the child itself if over 16. Even in the absence of such authority PRs do not need to hold the legacy until the minor is 18. If the legacy is contingent, there will usually be trustees appointed who can hold the legacy. If it is absolute, the PRs can appoint trustees under the Administration of Estates Act 1925, s.42 to hold the legacy.

I act for a residuary beneficiary in the administration of an estate. I cannot trace the executor of the will. What should I do?

Where there are appropriate circumstances, the court can pass over the persons entitled to a grant and appoint such person(s) as the court deems necessary. This form of application is particularly helpful where those entitled to a grant cannot be traced or where it is desired to appoint some person who is not interested in the estate as beneficiary or creditor.

The application is made ex parte under the Non-Contentious Probate Rules 1987, Rule 52, to a district judge or probate registrar supported by an affidavit. It is possible to pay a fee of £5.00 to have the affidavit approved by the registrar.

See King, *Probate Practitioner's Handbook* for further guidance.

I am dealing with the administration of an estate, and before I distribute I wish to advertise for any further creditors and potential beneficiaries who have a claim against the estate but who I am unable to trace. When and where should I place an appropriate advertisement?

Section 27 of the Trustee Act 1925 requires you to consider advertising for creditors and potential beneficiaries before starting to distribute the estate. The advertisement gives notice of your intention to distribute to those who may have claims against the estate. The point during the administration at which the advertisement is inserted will depend on a number of factors, varying with each estate.

A suitably worded advertisement may be inserted in the London Gazette and in a newspaper circulating in any area where the deceased lived or owned land. In addition, you should also consider advertising elsewhere if there are any special factors affecting the estate. The advertisements must give claimants at least two months to notify you of their claim.

After the advertisements have been inserted, and assuming that no claimants have come forward in the two month period, you may distribute the estate with reference only to claims known to you at the time of distribution (see King, L. (ed.) (2006) *Probate Practitioner's Handbook*, 5th edition, Law Society Publishing).

I am a probate solicitor and have just been instructed by a client in the administration of his late wife's estate. The deceased had assets in France. How do I proceed with the distribution of her estate?

If the deceased died domiciled in England and Wales, but with assets in another country, a foreign will may have been made. A lawyer of that country may have to be instructed. It is usually necessary to extract the grant in England and Wales and then send it accompanied by a sealed and certified copy of the will to a local practitioner. If the French assets include real property, then French law will determine what happens to it, rather than any English will.

Various publications dealing with property in foreign jurisdictions may be of interest, those dealing with conveyancing often contain a section on wills and probate. Please also see King, *Probate Practitioner's Handbook*.

I am acting as executor in the administration of an estate where the only residuary beneficiary is a charity. The charity is unhappy with my firm's costs and has requested a remuneration certificate. I have provided the charity with a client care letter and information on costs, even though they are strictly speaking not my 'clients'. Am I obliged to comply with their request? My final bill of costs is less than £50,000.

Yes. As the charity is an entitled third party, Article 2 of the Solicitors' (Non-Contentious Business) Remuneration Order 1994 permits a residuary beneficiary absolutely and immediately (not contingently) entitled to an inheritance to request a remuneration certificate where the only personal representatives are:

*   solicitors (whether or not acting in a professional capacity); or
*   solicitors acting jointly with partners or employees in a professional capacity.

I am acting on a probate matter where a claim has been made under the Inheritance (Provision for Family & Dependants) Act 1975. How should I proceed with the administration of the estate?

If a claim has been issued, personal representatives (PRs) should be cautious about how they administer the estate. Broadly speaking, PRs faced with a claim should pay debts and funeral expenses and collect in the assets of the estate. However they should not distribute until the claim has been resolved. For further information please see King, *Probate Practitioner's Handbook*.

I understand that there is a practice guidance for the resolution of probate and trust disputes. Where can I obtain this?

A practice guidance for the resolution of probate and trust disputes has been produced by the Association of Contentious Trusts and Probate Specialists. This can be obtained from their website (**www.actaps.com**).

I have just received instructions from the widow of a former client to obtain a grant of probate. The deceased had assets in this country but had been domiciled abroad for many years. Will it be necessary for me to obtain a grant in England?

Yes, if the deceased died domiciled outside England and Wales, but left assets in England and Wales (unless the Colonial Probates Act 1892 applies, or the deceased was domiciled in Scotland or Northern Ireland), it will be necessary to obtain a grant in England and Wales: see Non-Contentious Probate Rules 1987 Rule 30.

For further guidance see King, *Probate Practitioner's Handbook*.

I am a probate solicitor and understand that I can now send a death verification form to banks and building societies instead of the original death certificate. Is this correct and, if so, where can I get a copy of the form, and can I reproduce it on my word processor?

That is correct. The Law Society has agreed a protocol with the British Bankers Association, the Building Societies Association and the Association of British Insurers. The death verification form, which must be signed by a partner of the firm, gives a guarantee that you have in your possession and inspected an original.

A protocol letter has also been agreed, and you can reproduce both the letter and the form electronically. The form must remain unaltered although you can modify the letter.

Copies of the form and letter are available online (**www.lawsociety. org.uk**) and have been published in King, *Probate Practitioner's Handbook*.

I am an in-house solicitor for a Local Authority and have obtained letters of administration for the estate of a deceased person as we are creditors. Are we entitled to our expenses?

Yes. A creditor who obtains a grant may reimburse himself out of the estate for the expense he has been put to in obtaining the grant.

What is the interest rate payable on legacies?

Legacies should be paid with due diligence and usually within the executor's year. Practice Direction 40 of the Civil Procedure Rules states:

> Where an account of legacies is directed by any judgement, then, subject to –
>
> (a) any directions contained in the will or codicil in question;
>
> (b) and any order made by the court,
>
> interest shall be allowed on each legacy at the basic rate payable for the time being on funds in court or at such other rate as the court shall direct, beginning one year after the testator's death

The current rate payable on legacies can be checked on the Court Funds Office website (**www.officialsolicitor.gov.uk/cfo/investments_interest. htm**).

I have been instructed to prepare a will on behalf of a client who is adamant that she does not want to make provision for her daughter. I am concerned that the daughter may have a claim under the Inheritance (Provision for Family and Dependants) Act 1975 (IPFDA 1975). What should I do?

If you fear a claim under IPFDA 1975 but your client does not wish to make provision for any potential claimant, she should be encouraged to leave a memorandum with the will explaining why no provision was made, unless your client's reason s are unreasonable in which case the memorandum could do more harm than good.

There appears to be a trend in IPFDA 1975 actions towards the introduction of parallel claims – proprietary estoppel, declarations as to beneficial interests, mutual will obligations, claims based on a contractual relationship with the deceased – to bolster inheritance claims. Such claims are based on a combination of the deceased's intentions and of fact. The claim will only be made after the deceased's death. Often there are no independent witnesses so the surviving claimant is free to give their version of the deceased's intentions, unchallenged.

With this in mind, it may well be appropriate for a detailed attendance note of the initial instructions to be copied to the client with the draft will. The client should be asked to confirm the attendance note details are correct when confirming instructions to engross the will. The attendance note should be kept, as with any memorandum, with the will. At least then there is an accurate record of the testator's intention.

Following the Mental Capacity Act 2005 (MCA), is there a prescribed form to be used for a client wishing to make an Advance Decision to refuse treatment?

There is no prescribed form and in fact there are no particular formalities about the format of an Advance Decision; it can be written or verbal – unless it deals with life-sustaining treatment, in which case it must be written and specific rules apply.

Chapter 9 of the MCA Code of Practice provides specific guidance on this and it does suggest that a written document may be helpful in all cases to prove that an Advance Decision exists. The Code of Practice can be found on the Office of the Public Guardian website (**www.publicguardian.gov.uk**).

An Advance Decision should not be confused with an Advance Statement which allows a person to set out their wishes about future care and treatment and must be in writing.

My client wishes to enter into an enduring power of attorney. Is this possible now that the Mental Capacity Act 2005 is in force?

No. The enduring power of attorney should have been created before 1 October 2007. Your client would now have to consider entering into a lasting power of attorney (LPA) under the new regime. A property and affairs LPA can be used to appoint attorneys to make a range of decisions – including the buying and selling of property, operating a bank account, dealing with tax affairs and claiming benefits. A personal welfare LPA might authorise the attorneys to make decisions about where the donor should live, consenting to or refusing medical treatment on the donor's behalf and day to day care, including diet and dress.

For more information please see the practice note on LPAs (**Annex 9B**).

My client's business has failed and he faces bankruptcy. He executed an enduring power of attorney (EPA) before 1 October 2007 and a lasting power of attorney (LPA) in respect of personal welfare on 3 October 2007. Are they affected?

1. An EPA, whether registered or unregistered, is revoked if either the donor or any of his attorneys become bankrupt (Mental Capacity Act 2005, Schedule 4, Part 12(7)).

2. As the LPA is in relation to personal welfare it is not revoked (Mental Capacity Act 2005, s.13(3)). If the LPA was in respect of property and affairs it would be revoked.

Please see the website of the Office of the Public Guardian at **www. publicguardian.gov.uk** and the Law Society's practice note for solicitors on lasting powers of attorney (**Annex 9B**).

I am preparing a lasting power of attorney (LPA) for an elderly client. The form requires the certificate provider to confirm that he or she is acting independently of the donor and in particular is not a person listed in the disqualification criteria. Does this mean I am not regarded as independent and so cannot provide the certificate?

The Law Society's view is that regulation 8(3) of the Lasting Power of Attorney, Enduring Powers of Attorney and Public Guardian Regulations 2007, SI 2007/1253, sets out the disqualification criteria. This does not include the person who assisted in the preparation of the LPA. Our interpretation is that as long as the solicitor is not a donee of the LPA and is not within the disqualification criteria of regulation 8(3) then they can be the certificate provider. It is also our view that if it had been intended that a solicitor should not perform both roles, it is highly likely that there would have been something to this effect in the Regulations.

We therefore interpret the reference to an 'independent' person in relation to the categories in regulation 8(3) as someone who is unconnected with the donor in terms of family relationship and is not a donee of the power or associated as an employee/director/partner/care home staff of a donee of the power, i.e. is independent of the person(s) exercising the power.

We have also received confirmation that the Public Guardian would treat such an LPA as valid unless there is a court decision to the contrary (i.e. if someone successfully objects to its validity on that ground).

The Law Society has prepared a practice note on LPAs which you may find useful (see **Annex 9B**).

An elderly client for whom I have acted for many years has asked me to draft what she describes as a 'living will' setting out her wishes for her future care and treatment. Is there a prescribed form which I should use?

There is no prescribed form for a client who wishes to make an 'Advance Decision' as it is referred to under the Mental Capacity Act 2005.

An Advance Decision enables a person aged over 18, while still capable, to refuse specified medical treatment at a time in the future when they may lack the capacity to consent to or refuse that treatment. They must say exactly what treatment they want to refuse and they can cancel their decision or any part of it at any time. If the Advance Decision refuses life-sustaining treatment, it must be in writing, be signed and witnessed and state clearly that the decision applies even if life is at risk.

You may wish to suggest that the client sends a copy of the completed Advance Decision to her GP.

For further information, please refer to Chapter 9 of the Code of Practice issued by the Lord Chancellor in April 2007 which accompanies the Mental Capacity Act 2005 and is available at **www.direct.gov.uk**.

You may also be interested in the Law Society's practice note on lasting powers of attorney (**Annex 9B**) and Greaney, N. et al. (2008) *Mental Capacity: A Guide to the New Law*, 2nd edition, Law Society Publishing.

I work as practice manager at a firm that deals predominantly with wills and probate matters. The firm is in the process of reviewing its file retention policy. Is there any information on retaining client files and papers?

Yes. You may wish to refer to the Law Society's practice note on file retention on wills and will files. The Wills and Equity Committee of the Law Society has set out information in order to help practitioners identify issues that should be considered before relevant files are 'weeded' or 'destroyed'. For details of the Law Society's practice note entitled 'File retention: records management – retention and wills, deeds and documents together with supporting data', please see **Annex 7G**.

In order to proceed with my client's case, I need to access her GP and hospital health records, and understand that there is a form approved by the Law Society and the British Medical Association to request the records. From where can I get a copy of this form?

The consent form, which has been agreed by the BMA and the Law Society, can be obtained online (**www.lawsociety.org.uk**). The form is aimed at improving protection for the public when they agree to release their health records and will demonstrate that the patient's informed consent has been gained before health records are disclosed.

I understand that the Law Society has produced a Family Law Protocol. When was this launched and where can I obtain it?

The Protocol was launched on 7 March 2002 and was revised in 2006. The second edition is available to download from **www.lawsociety.org.uk**. It can also be purchased in a bound format at the Law Society's online bookshop (**www.lawsociety.org.uk/bookshop**).

In a family matter, with the agreement of my client at the outset, can I charge extra if she is awarded a financial settlement which exceeds her expectations?

No. This arrangement would constitute a Conditional Fee Agreement which is prohibited in family matters under section 58A of the Courts and Legal Services Act 1990 as substituted by section 27 of the Access to Justice Act 1999.

Annex 9A

Estate administration with banks

18 January 2008

[Introduction]

This practice note is relevant to any solicitor involved in the administration of estates.

Solicitors often experience difficulty and delay during the estate administration process in relation to assets held by banks.

This practice note contains protocols that set out procedures agreed with banks to clarify and speed up the estate administration process. This is a joint initiative with the Society of Trust and Estate Practitioners (STEP).

These are the first in a series of agreements with the major banks, aimed at helping the profession negotiate the different administrative procedures of each bank, where the bank holds assets and the practitioner is seeking to wind-up an estate.

The following protocols have already been agreed. The Law Society is working on further protocols with other banks.

- Lloyds TSB protocol – 18 January 2008
- HSBC protocol – 26 March 2008

Note that these do not address professional conduct or legal requirements.

Further help

Practice Advice Service

The Practice Advice Service is a dedicated support line for members of the Law Society, which is able to help solicitors with a wide range of practice and procedure issues. The service is staffed by experienced solicitors with access to a wide range of information sources. The Practice Advice Service can be contacted on 0870 606 2522 from 09.00 to 17.00 on weekdays.

www.lawsociety.org.uk/practiceadvice

Solicitors Regulation Authority

The Solicitors Regulation Authority regulates solicitors in England and Wales. It makes and enforces the Solicitors' Code of Conduct.

www.sra.org.uk

Legal Complaints Service

The Legal Complaints Service investigates inadequate professional service complaints about solicitors in England and Wales.

www.legalcomplaints.org.uk

Banking practices protocol between Lloyds TSB, the Law Society of England and Wales and the Society of Trust and Estate Practitioners

This protocol has been agreed between Lloyds TSB, the Law Society of England and Wales and the Society of Trust and Estate Practitioners [STEP]. The purpose is to bring clarity to probate-related dealings between advisers and Lloyds TSB.

Set out below is the information that Lloyds TSB will require from the solicitor/STEP member on first contact or shortly afterwards. If this information is provided, delays in dealing with the account or investments will be reduced.

1. Death certificate/death certificate verification form.

2. Date of death.

3. List of the deceased's names, such as maiden names, in which accounts were held or may have been held, and last address of the deceased prior to death or admission to hospital/nursing home etc.

4. Account numbers of relevant accounts if known.

5. Verification of the status of the solicitor/probate practitioner. The verification procedure for STEP members who are not solicitors must be agreed direct between STEP and Lloyds TSB. To verify non-solicitor STEP members please contact the Membership Department at STEP Worldwide on tel 020 7838 4890.

6. Correct address for correspondence in connection with the accounts of the deceased.

Set out below is the information that the solicitor/STEP member is likely to require from Lloyds TSB and also an outline of how Lloyds TSB might respond to such requests.

7. The numbers of all accounts, including internet accounts, in the name of the deceased, including those held jointly. This information will be provided automatically by Lloyds TSB subject to full name and address disclosure by the solicitor/STEP member, but note that where the deceased is the second named on the account, disclosure is not automatic and additional enquiries may be necessary.

8. Details of the balance on all accounts in the deceased's name (including joint accounts) at the date of death and, where appropriate, the amount of accrued interest to the date of death.

9. Confirmation that the current account balance will be placed on deposit, pending closure on production of the grant of probate. The solicitor/STEP member must specifically request this information. Lloyds TSB can 'place funds on deposit on request' only via specified 'executor accounts'. The solicitor/executor/STEP member will be asked to complete an application form and the process will be subject to Lloyds TSB's 'know your customer/anti-money laundering rules'.

10. Full details of any items the bank is holding in safe custody on behalf of the deceased. The solicitor/STEP member must specifically request this information. Note that Lloyds TSB staff may not know the nature of items being held, so the solicitor/STEP member or an agreed agent may need to visit to inspect and value the items.

11. A certificate showing any interest paid and tax deducted during the period from 6 April last to the date of death (and for the previous tax year). The solicitor/STEP member must specifically request this information.

12. Any dividend or interest counterfoils which the bank is holding. The solicitor/STEP member must specifically request this information. Note that Lloyds TSB operates a BACS system so is unlikely to hold many counterfoils.

13. Details of all standing orders and direct debits in force at the date of death and confirmation that a stop has been placed on them. Note that the solicitor/STEP member should consider the effect of a stop being put on certain payments if someone remains resident at the former address of the deceased.

14. Confirmation that the bank will allow the balance on accounts to be used before production of the grant of probate for payment of inheritance tax, settlement of funeral expenses and payment of probate fees.

15. Confirmation that the correct address for correspondence has been noted on all accounts in the name of the deceased.

16. Where available, details of any transfers over £3,000 which have taken place in the last seven years. The solicitor/STEP member must specifically request this information. Note that Lloyds TSB is unlikely to retain information beyond six years.

17. Correct address for correspondence in connection with the accounts of the deceased.

18. Where possible, details of the accounts held in the name of the deceased across the Lloyds TSB group. The solicitor/STEP member must specifically request this information.

Account closure

19. On closing an account Lloyds TSB is to confirm that the account has been closed; the closing balance will be sent within a reasonable time.

20. Bank statements for the period from the date of death to closure, and the closing balance, is to be sent to the solicitor/STEP member and not the lay executor.

21. When a deceased holds both credit and debit balances on accounts with Lloyds TSB, the bank will apply set-off rules and clear any Lloyds TSB debts, providing the solicitor/STEP member with settlement on the net figure. The solicitor will be advised of the net balance via an assets and liabilities pro forma. The type of accounts included in calculating a net balance will include: savings accounts, current accounts, unsecured loan accounts and credit card accounts.

22. The time periods suggested in relation to account closures are:

    a. information to be sent no more than fifteen working days after receipt of the request;

    b. closing balance to be sent no more than ten working days after receipt of grant of probate (although it may not be possible to supply this information in the case of shares and investments);

    c. closing balance statement to be sent no more than ten working days from closure of the account.

Banking practice protocol between HSBC, the Law Society of England and Wales and the Society of Trust and Estate Practitioners

This protocol has been agreed between HSBC, the Law Society of England and Wales and the Society of Trust & Estate Practitioners. The purpose is to bring clarity to probate-related dealings between advisers and HSBC.

Set out below is the information HSBC will require from the solicitor/STEP member on first contact or shortly afterwards. If this information is provided, delays in dealing with the account or investments will be reduced.

What information will the bank require from the solicitor/probate practitioner on a first approach? We suggest the following may be useful:

1. Death certificate/death certificate verification form.

2. Date of death.

3. List of names, such as maiden names, in which accounts were held.

4. Verification of the status of the solicitor/probate practitioner to include confirmation of authority to act on behalf of the executors/next of kin (and in the case of solicitors a letter on headed paper with the Law Society roll number quoted should ensure that delay is kept to a minimum).

5. Correct address for correspondence in connection with the accounts of the deceased.

6. Approximate value of the estate.

7. Information regarding the will to confirm the existence of the will and the names of the executors.

Set out below is the information that the solicitor/STEP member is likely to require from HSBC and also an outline of how HSBC might respond to such requests.

Please confirm that the bank will be able to supply the following once the solicitor/probate practitioner has supplied the information listed above.

8. Confirmation of the numbers of all accounts in the name of the deceased (including those held jointly).

9. Details of the balance on all accounts in the deceased's name (including joint accounts) at the date of death and, where appropriate, the amount of accrued interest to the date of death.

10. Confirmation that the current account balance will be placed on deposit pending closure on production of the grant of probate.

11. Full particulars of any items the bank is holding in safe custody on behalf of the deceased.

12. Full particulars of any items the bank is holding as security on behalf of the deceased.

13. A certificate showing any interest paid and tax deducted during the period from 6 April last to the date of death (and for the previous tax year).

14. Any dividend or interest counterfoils which the bank is holding.

15. Details of all standing orders and direct debits in force at the date of death and confirmation that a stop has been placed on them.

16. Confirmation that the bank will allow the balance on accounts to be used before production of the grant of probate for payment of inheritance tax, settlement of funeral expenses and payment of probate fees.

17. Confirmation that the correct address for correspondence has been noted on all accounts in the name of the deceased.

18. Correct address for correspondence in connection with the accounts of the deceased.

Account closure

On closing an account please confirm that information and the closing balance will be sent within a reasonable time. We suggest the following time periods:

19. Information sent no more than fifteen working days after receipt of the request.

20. Closing balance sent no more than ten working days after receipt of grant of probate.

21. Closing balance statement sent no more than ten working days from closure of the account.

22. Without a grant a signed indemnity may be required to release over £5,000, but with a grant there is no limit on the amount that can be released.

Lasting powers of attorney practice note

24 September 2007

Status of this practice note

Practice notes are issued by the Law Society for the use and benefit of its members. They represent the Law Society's view of good practice in a particular area. They are not intended to be the only standard of good practice that solicitors can follow. You are not required to follow them, but doing so will make it easier to account to oversight bodies for your actions.

Practice notes are not legal advice, nor do they necessarily provide a defence to complaints of misconduct or of inadequate professional service. While care has been taken to ensure that they are accurate, up to date and useful, the Law Society will not accept any legal liability in relation to them.

For queries or comments on this practice note contact the Law Society's Practice Advice Service.

1. Introduction

1.1 The following practice note is intended to assist solicitors in advising clients who wish to draw up a Lasting Power of Attorney (LPA), as well as solicitors who are acting as an attorney under an LPA. It also covers the ongoing arrangements for Enduring Powers of Attorney (EPA).

1.2 LPAs were created by the Mental Capacity Act 2005 (MCA 2005). The MCA 2005 covers England and Wales and provides a statutory framework for adults who lack capacity to make decisions for themselves, or who have capacity and want to make preparations for a time when they may lack capacity in the future. Everyone working with and caring for adults who lack capacity, including solicitors, health and social care professionals, families and other carers, must comply with the MCA 2005.

1.3   The Mental Capacity Act 2005 Code of Practice (the Code of Practice) supports the MCA 2005 and provides guidance and information to all those working under the legislation. Certain categories of people are required to have regard to the relevant guidance in the Code of Practice, including the attorney under an LPA and anyone acting in a professional capacity – such as a solicitor.

1.4   An LPA enables a person aged 18 or over (the donor) to appoint another person or persons (their donee or attorney) to act on their behalf, following the principles of the MCA 2005, if they subsequently lose capacity. This has replaced the EPA as the type of power of attorney that can operate after a person ceases to have capacity. Unlike EPAs, a person can choose to delegate decisions affecting their personal welfare – including healthcare and medical treatment decisions – as well as decisions concerning their property and financial matters to their attorney(s).

1.5   Any solicitor intending to give advice about an LPA or act as an attorney under an LPA must be aware of the provisions in the MCA 2005 and the Code of Practice. Solicitors should also be familiar with the relevant guidance produced by the Office of the Public Guardian.

1.6   The MCA 2005 repealed the Enduring Powers of Attorney Act 1985 and it is no longer possible to create a new EPA. However, EPAs which were executed before the MCA 2005 came into force on 1 October 2007, whether they have been registered or not, will continue to be valid. The result is that for the foreseeable future there will be two distinct regimes catering for those who lack capacity. EPAs are considered in section 14 of this practice note.

1.7   Ordinary Powers of Attorney can still be created but they will become invalid if the donor loses capacity to make decisions within the scope of the particular power of attorney.

2.   General overview: property and affairs LPAs and personal welfare LPAs

2.1   Property and affairs LPAs can be used to appoint attorneys to make a range of decisions – including the buying and selling of property, operating a bank account, dealing with tax affairs, and claiming benefits (see paragraphs 7.32–7.39 of the Code of

Practice). A personal welfare LPA might authorise the attorney(s) to make decisions about where the donor should live, consenting to or refusing medical treatment on the donor's behalf, and day-to-day care, including diet and dress (see paragraphs 7.21–7.31 of the Code of Practice).

2.2   There are two separate prescribed forms, one for a property and affairs LPA and one for a personal welfare LPA. Both forms are divided into three parts:

PART A – Donor's statement

This part of the form includes: the donor's details; details of the attorney(s) being appointed and how they are to act; details of the persons to be notified when an application to register the LPA is made; and a number of statements which must be confirmed by the donor.

PART B – Certificate provider's statement

This part must be completed by an independent third party (known as the certificate provider) after he or she has discussed the contents of the LPA with the donor without, if possible, anyone else present. The certificate provider must confirm that in his or her opinion: the donor understands the purpose and scope of the LPA; no undue pressure or fraud is involved in the decision to make the LPA; and there is nothing else to prevent the LPA being created.

Part C – Attorney's statement

Each attorney named in Part A of the LPA must complete a separate statement confirming that he or she understands their duties and obligations as an attorney. Both LPA forms also include the pre-scribed information which must be read by the donor, certificate provider and attorney(s).

2.3   The LPA must be registered with the Office of the Public Guardian before it can be used. A property and affairs LPA can be used while the donor still has capacity, unless it specifies that it can't, while a personal welfare LPA can only be used when the donor no longer has capacity to make the particular decision affecting their health or personal welfare.

3.   Who is the client?: property and affairs LPAs and personal welfare LPAs

3.1   Where a solicitor is instructed to prepare an LPA, the donor is the client.

A solicitor should not accept instructions where he or she has reasonable grounds to suspect that those instructions have been given by a client under duress or undue influence – until the solicitor is satisfied that they represent the client's wishes (Solicitors Regulation Authority, Solicitors' Code of Conduct 2007, Rule 2.01) [see **www.rules.sra.org.uk**].

When asked to prepare an LPA on written instructions alone, a solicitor should always consider carefully whether these instructions are sufficient, or whether he or she should see the client to discuss them.

3.2   A solicitor should be instructed by the client. Where instructions for the preparation of an LPA are given by someone other than the client, a solicitor should not proceed without checking that the client agrees with the instructions given (ibid., Rule 2.01). In any case of doubt the solicitor should attempt to see the client alone or take other appropriate steps, both to confirm the instructions with the donor personally after offering appropriate advice, and also to ensure that the donor has the necessary capacity to make the power (see section 4 below).

3.3   Once the LPA has been registered and the donor lacks the capacity to make the relevant decision, instructions may be accepted from the attorney(s) but the solicitor continues to owe his or her duties to the donor. In the case of a property and affairs LPA being used as an Ordinary Power of Attorney, instructions may be accepted from the attorney(s) after the LPA has been registered.

4.   Capacity to make an LPA: property and affairs LPAs and personal welfare LPAs

4.1   The solicitor should be satisfied that, on the balance of probabilities, the donor has the mental capacity to make an LPA. Some LPAs may be made when the donor is already losing capacity and consequently he or she could be unaware of the implications of their actions and more likely to be vulnerable to exploitation.

4.2   A valid LPA must include a certificate completed by an independent third party known as the certificate provider (who can be a solicitor) confirming that 'the donor understands the purpose of the LPA and the scope of the authority under it' and that no fraud or undue pressure is being used (see sections 6.5 and 6.6 below).

4.3   Section 2 of the MCA 2005 provides the core definition of incapacity that applies to decisions made under this Act:

> . . . a person lacks capacity in relation to a matter if at the material time he is unable to make a decision for himself in relation to the matter, because of an impairment of, or a disturbance in the functioning of, the mind or brain.

4.4 There is however no specific definition or test of what level of capacity is required to make an LPA. It is assumed that a court if asked to make a declaration on this point would use the principles of the MCA 2005 as a starting point – and in particular the following principles:

> A person must be assumed to have capacity unless it is established that he lacks capacity. (s.1(3))

> A person is not to be treated as unable to make a decision merely because he makes an unwise decision. (s.1(4))

It is likely that the courts will also consider established case law on EPAs.

4.5 If there is any doubt about the donor's capacity, a medical opinion should be considered. In cases where the LPA is being contested, for example by a family member, it may be necessary for the matter to be decided by the Court of Protection if the dispute cannot be resolved by other means. See Chapter 15 of the Code of Practice for guidance on resolving disputes and disagreements.

4.6 Solicitors assessing a client's capacity to create an LPA should refer to sections 2 and 3 of the MCA 2005 and Chapters 2–4 of the Code of Practice. Further guidance can be obtained from Assessment of Mental Capacity: Guidance for doctors and lawyers issued by the Law Society and the British Medical Association.

5. Risk of abuse: property and affairs LPAs and personal welfare LPAs

5.1 When advising clients of the benefits of LPAs, the solicitor should also inform them of the risks of abuse, particularly the risk that the attorney(s) could misuse the power. Throughout this practice note, an attempt has been made to identify possible risk areas and to suggest ways of preventing abuse, which the solicitor should discuss with the donor (see for example sections 6.14 and 13 below). Written information for clients on both the benefits and risks of LPAs, whether in a brochure or correspondence, may also be helpful.

5.2 During the initial stages of advising a client, the solicitor should consider that there may be circumstances when an LPA may not be appropriate, and a later application to the Court of Protection for deputyship, with the oversight of the Office of the Public Guardian, may be preferable. This may be advisable, for example:

- where there are indications of persistent family conflicts suggesting that an LPA may be contested; or

- where the assets are more substantial or complex than family members are accustomed to handle; or

- in cases where litigation may lead to a substantial award of damages for personal injury.

6.   Taking instructions for an LPA: property and affairs LPAs and personal welfare LPAs

The solicitor should take full and careful instructions from the donor, and ensure that the following matters, where applicable, are considered by the donor when giving instructions.

Please note that this section of the practice note covers issues common to both property and affairs LPAs and personal welfare LPAs. For issues specific to property and affairs LPAs see section 7 below. For issues specific to personal welfare LPAs see section 8 below.

6.1   Choice of attorney(s)

The choice of attorney(s) is clearly a personal decision for the donor, but it is important for the solicitor to advise the donor of the various options available, and to stress the need for the attorney(s) to be absolutely trustworthy (see section 5 above). The donor should be advised that the appointment of a sole attorney, whether this be for a property and affairs LPA or a personal welfare LPA, may provide greater opportunity for abuse and exploitation than appointing more than one attorney (see section 6.2 below).

The solicitor should ask questions about the donor's relationship with the proposed attorney(s) including any replacement attorney (see section 6.11 below) and, depending on which type of LPA is being created, whether the attorney(s) has the skills required to manage the donor's property and financial affairs or to make decisions about the donor's personal welfare. The donor should also consider the suitability of appointing a family member or someone independent of the family, or a combination of both.

If the donor wishes to create both a property and affairs LPA and a personal welfare LPA then they should consider whether they wish to appoint different attorneys for each LPA.

6.2   More than one attorney

Where more than one attorney is to be appointed for a property and affairs LPA or for a personal welfare LPA, they must be appointed to act 'jointly', 'jointly and severally', or 'jointly in respect of some matters and jointly and severally in respect of others' (s.10(4), MCA 2005). The LPA forms do not use these legal terms but instead refer to attorneys working 'together', 'together and independently' or 'together in respect of some matters and together and independently in respect of others'.

One of these alternatives must be ticked by the donor in the prescribed form. If more than one attorney has been appointed and it is not stated whether they are appointed jointly or jointly and severally, then when the LPA is registered they will be treated on the basis that they are appointed jointly. This default position however does not extend to EPAs and failure to specify on the prescribed form whether the attorneys should act jointly or jointly and severally invalidates the instrument as an enduring power.

The differences between a 'joint' and 'joint and several' appointment should be explained to the donor.

- In addition to the explanatory information in the prescribed form to the effect that joint attorneys must all act together and cannot act separately, the donor should be advised that an LPA with joint attorneys will terminate if any one of the attorneys: disclaims; dies; becomes bankrupt (this only applies to property and affairs LPAs); or lacks capacity. It will also terminate with the dissolution or annulment of the marriage or civil partnership between the donor and the attorney (unless it specifically states otherwise in the LPA). However, joint appointments may provide a safeguard against possible abuse, since each attorney will be able to oversee the actions of the other(s).
- Similarly, in addition to the explanatory information in the prescribed form to the effect that joint and several attorneys can all act together but can also act independently if they wish, the donor should be advised that, where there is a joint and several appointment, the LPA will not be automatically terminated by the: disclaimer; death; bankruptcy; dissolution/annulment of marriage/civil partnership; or incapacity of one attorney. In these circumstances the LPA would continue and the remaining attorney(s) can continue to act.

See also section 6.11 below regarding replacement attorneys.

(I)   The donor may have to make difficult choices as to which member(s) of the family or others to appoint as his or her attorney. This may partly depend on the type of LPA being created and the different types of decisions that can be taken under a property and affairs LPA and a personal welfare LPA. It is possible to allow some flexibility, for example the donor may wish to appoint:

(II) A family member and a professional to act jointly and severally with, perhaps, the family member dealing with day-to-day matters, and the professional dealing with more complex decisions. However the donor and the attorneys should consider the potential for conflict that could arise from this arrangement. A professional attorney will have a higher duty of care and usually will be remunerated, and this could create tension between the attorneys: for example, if the professional wishes to take a cautious approach and perhaps seek a court declaration or medical opinion – which would result in costs being incurred.

(III) His or her spouse or civil partner as attorney, with their adult child(ren) appointed as replacement attorneys (see section 6.11 below) should the spouse or civil partner die or become incapacitated. Alternatively, the donor could appoint everyone to act jointly and severally, with an informal understanding that the children will not act while the spouse or civil partner is able to do so.

(IV) His or her three adult children as attorneys to act jointly and severally, with a proviso that anything done under the power should be done by at least two of them. This could be achieved by careful wording of the LPA document.

(V) His or her three adult children to act in respect of some decisions as joint attorneys and as joint and several attorneys in respect of other decisions. However the donor should consider that this arrangement may be confusing for the attorneys and third parties, such as banks and healthcare professionals, and could prove difficult to administer in practice. The prescribed form includes a large text box for the donor to explain how this should work and it is important that this is drafted clearly and precisely to avoid confusion.

Solicitors should be aware that time may be needed to explain the benefits and drawbacks of requiring specific decision to be made jointly, jointly and severally, or jointly in respect of some matters and jointly and severally in respect of others as it may be confusing for the donor and attorneys.

6.3 General or limited authority

The donor must be clear whether the LPA is to be a general power, giving the attorney(s) authority to manage all the donor's property and affairs or to make all personal welfare decisions, or whether any restrictions and/or conditions are to be placed on their power (see also sections 7.1 and 8.1

below). Any restrictions and/or conditions should be carefully drafted and clearly set out in the prescribed form.

In relation to a personal welfare LPA the solicitor should emphasise that a general power will include all healthcare decisions, except: giving or refusing consent to life sustaining treatment (unless the LPA document expressly authorises this); where the donor has made a valid advance decision; refusing or consenting to medical treatment for mental disorder where the donor is detained under the Mental Health Act 1983; or where the donor is subject to guardianship under the Mental Health Act 1983 (see sections 8.1–8.3 below).

The solicitor should also discuss with the donor what arrangements should be made for the management of those property and financial affairs or personal welfare decisions that are not covered by the LPA. The donor should be advised that if they leave a 'gap' it may be necessary for the Court of Protection to intervene and appoint a deputy— or for other people to make 'best interests' decisions on the donor's behalf under section 4 of the MCA 2005.

Where the donor wishes to give discretionary powers to their attorney(s) – such as discretionary investment management powers or authority to disclose the donor's will if necessary, then these should be included in the 'restrictions and/or conditions' section of the prescribed form.

6.4   Guidance

As well as placing restrictions and/or conditions on the attorney(s), the prescribed forms for both property and affairs LPAs and personal welfare LPAs also allows guidance to be provided to the attorney(s) when making decisions in the donor's best interests. Any restrictions or conditions if deemed valid will be binding on the attorney(s) whereas the guidance, although clearly pertinent, is not binding on the attorney(s). It is important that a solicitor advising the client makes clear the distinction and difference between restrictions/conditions and guidance. It will also be important that the drafting of this section of the prescribed form reflects this distinction and that the language used does not suggest that any guidance is binding.

The solicitor could also explain to the donor and the attorney(s) that because guidance is not binding on the attorney(s) a situation could occur where even after taking into account the guidance in the LPA, the attorney(s) might still come to the conclusion that it would be in the overall best interests of the donor – having used the 'best interests check-list' set out in section 4 of the MCA 2005 – to do something different from that suggested in the guidance section of the LPA. However it should also be stressed that the guidance would be relevant in assessing the best interests of the donor.

6.5 The certificate

A valid LPA – whether it be a property LPA and affairs or personal welfare LPA – must include a certificate completed by an independent third party known as the 'certificate provider' confirming that in his or her opinion:

- the donor understands the purpose of the LPA and the scope of the authority under it;
- no fraud or undue pressure is being used to induce the donor to create the LPA; and
- there is nothing else that would prevent the LPA being created.

The donor must be clear that choosing a suitable certificate provider is an important safeguard and without their statement the LPA cannot be registered and used. The choice of certificate provider is clearly a personal decision for the donor, but it is important for the solicitor to advise the donor of the various options available. It may also be important to advise on the quality of the options available – for example where a family dispute may lead to the certificate being challenged, the solicitor may need to advise on the most suitable choice of certificate provider, taking into account the individual circumstances of the case (see also section 6.6 below).

There are two types of certificate provider: a knowledge-based certificate provider who is someone who knows the donor personally and has done so for the previous two years – or a skills-based certificate provider who has the relevant professional skills and expertise to certify the LPA. A skills-based certificate provider must fit into one of the following categories:

- a registered healthcare professional (including GP);
- a registered social worker;
- a barrister, solicitor or advocate;
- an Independent Mental Capacity Advocate;
- someone who considers they have the relevant professional skills and expertise to be a certificate provider.

A certificate provider cannot be:

- under 18;
- a member of the donor's or attorney's family;
- a business partner or paid employee of the donor or attorney(s);
- an attorney appointed in this or another LPA or any EPA made by the donor;
- the owner, director, manager or an employee of a care home in which the donor lives or their family member or partner;
- an employee of a trust corporation appointed as attorney in this LPA (this only applies to someone certifying a property and affairs LPA).

A person who signs an LPA as a certificate provider will also need to be able to demonstrate:

- they understand what is involved in making an LPA;
- they understand the effect of making an LPA;
- that they have the skills to assess that the donor understands what an LPA is and what is involved in making an LPA;
- that they can assess that the donor also understands the contents of their LPA and what powers they are giving to the attorney(s);
- that they can verify that the donor is under no undue pressure by anyone to make the LPA;
- that they have sufficient knowledge and understanding of the donor's affairs to able to be satisfied that no fraud was involved in the creation of the LPA.

The donor should also be advised of the benefits of appointing a certificate provider who has the appropriate knowledge or experience of issues relating to mental capacity and in particular the provisions of the MCA 2005 including the core principles.

6.6   Solicitors providing a certificate

6.6.1   A skills-based certificate

Solicitors are one of the professional groups specifically listed in the prescribed form as capable of providing a skills-based certificate. The role of the certificate provider is a vital safeguard against the abuse of vulnerable adults and it is crucial that anyone agreeing to be a certificate provider fully comprehends the significance.

A solicitor must ensure that they do not fall into one of the categories of people who cannot provide a certificate (see section 6.5 above). In particular, a solicitor cannot provide a certificate if he or she is:

- a business partner or paid employee of the attorney; or
- an attorney appointed under any LPA or EPA made by the donor. This would mean for example that a solicitor could not provide a certificate if in the past the client executed an EPA in favour of the solicitor, even though the EPA was never used or registered and was perhaps even revoked.

However a solicitor could be the certificate provider if he or she is a business partner or paid employee of the attorney of an EPA or another LPA.

A solicitor signing such a certificate will need to have taken a suitably detailed personal and financial history from the donor, and if necessary insist on seeing them on their own, to satisfy the requirements concerning undue pressure and fraud. This may have both time and costs implications.

The solicitor should also be aware that if, for example, a family member objects to the LPA at the point when it is registered then the certificate provider may be called to the Court of Protection to account for their opinion.

The certificate provider's duty of care is to the donor. In cases where the attorney is a solicitor and another solicitor from a different firm is to act as the certificate provider, then the client will be a client of both solicitors and separate client care letters should be sent by each.

6.6.2   A knowledge-based certificate

A solicitor may be approached by clients, former clients, friends or acquaintances asking them to provide a certificate on the basis that the solicitor has known them personally over the last two years. It is recommended that a solicitor should exercise caution before providing a certificate on this basis.

According to the LPA notes 'personally' means that that the donor is known to the certificate provider as more than a passing acquaintance. In addition the certificate provider cannot be related to the donor or to any of the attorneys – and must not fall into any of the other categories of people who cannot provide a certificate (see section 6.5 above).

A knowledge-based certificate provider has the same responsibilities as a skills-based certificate provider, for example they must discuss the contents of the LPA with the donor without, if possible, anyone else present. He or she must also confirm that: the donor understands the LPA they are making and that they are not being forced into making it (see section 6.5 above). In order to do this a detailed personal and financial history may need to be taken from the donor – however a fee cannot be charged for providing a knowledge-based certificate.

A knowledge-based certificate provider may also be called to the Court of Protection to account for their opinion if, for example, a family member objects to the LPA. The Court may impose a higher standard of care and skill if the knowledge-based certificate has been provided by a solicitor and the donor is their client or former client.

6.6.3   Referral arrangements

A solicitor may wish to refer a client to another solicitor in order to provide the certificate – or to provide a second certificate where the donor decides not to include anyone to be notified (see section 6.8 below). The solicitor must however ensure that there is no breach of rule 1 of the Solicitor's Code of Conduct or any other applicable provision of these rules.

6.7   Registration of the LPA

The donor must understand that the LPA cannot be used until it has been registered with the Office of the Public Guardian. The LPA can be registered anytime after it has been completed and signed by all those who are required to sign (see section 10 below).

It is important that the solicitor clearly explains to the donor the implications of not registering the LPA shortly after it has been made. For example if the donor of an unregistered personal welfare LPA faced a medical emergency their attorney(s) would not be authorised to act on their behalf until the power is registered, which at the very least would take between five and six weeks (see section 11.5 below).

Once registered, a property and affairs LPA can be used while the donor still has capacity, unless it specifies that it can't, while a personal welfare LPA can only be used when the donor no longer has capacity to make the particular decision affecting their healthcare or personal welfare.

6.8   Notification of intention to register the LPA

Solicitors should explain to the donor that they can name up to five people to be notified when an application to register the LPA is made. An attorney of the LPA cannot be specified as a named person. If the donor decides not to include anyone to be notified then a second person will be needed to provide an additional certificate (see section 6.5 above). The donor should be clear that including a named person is an important safeguard because if he or she lacks capacity at the time of registration they will be relying on these people to raise concerns.

The donor should be advised to make their named person(s) aware of the LPA, whether it is a property and affairs LPA or personal welfare LPA and what is required of them when an application to register is made, before the LPA is completed. This will ensure that where a person does not wish to take on this role, someone else can be appointed. The donor may also want to tell his or her named person(s) who they have appointed as attorney(s). This will allow them to raise any queries or concerns with the donor and may reduce unfounded objections being made when the application to register the LPA is made, avoiding extra costs and lengthy delays to the process.

6.9   The LPA register and disclosure of information

The Office of the Public Guardian is responsible for maintaining a register of all LPAs – as well as a register of EPAs and of court appointed deputies. Clients should be aware that once their LPA is registered certain basic information about their LPA will be available to anyone who applies to search the register and pays a fee – such as:

- the donor's name (and previous names) and date of birth;
- whether it is a property and affairs LPA or a personal welfare LPA but not the contents;
- the date the LPA was created and registered;
- the name(s) of the attorney(s);
- the nature of the appointment (joint or joint and several);
- whether the LPA contains any restrictions, conditions or guidance but not the details of the restrictions, conditions or guidance; and
- whether or not a note has been attached to the LPA, but no details of what the note says.

Clients should also be aware that anyone can also, on application and payment of a fee, undertake a 'second tier search' for further information about their LPA. This will require the applicant to explain in greater detail to the Office of the Public Guardian why they require the information and to demonstrate that the request is in the donor's best interests.

6.10   Delegation by the attorney

It is a basic principle of the law of agency that an attorney cannot delegate his or her authority. Alternatively, this could be expressed as a duty on the part of an agent to perform his or her functions personally. Such a duty is imposed because of the discretion and trust reposed in the attorney(s) by the donor.

There are exceptions to this general rule and, like any other agent, an attorney acting under an LPA has an implied power in certain circumstances to delegate:

- any functions which are of a purely administrative nature and do not involve or require the exercise of discretion;
- any functions which the donor would not expect the attorney to attend to personally; or
- through necessity or unforeseen circumstances.

Any wider power of delegation must be expressly provided for in the LPA itself.

6.11   Substitute appointments

Whilst an LPA cannot provide for an attorney to make a substitute or successor appointment, it can appoint a replacement attorney to act if one or any of the attorneys cannot continue to act.

If the donor of a property and affairs LPA or a personal welfare LPA wants to appoint a replacement attorney he or she can appoint as many replacements as they like. It will be important that the donor sets out clearly how they are to be appointed and how they are to act, for example solely or jointly (see section 6.2 above). If the donor has more than one attorney, he or she can specify who the replacement attorney can replace and who they cannot replace. If no restrictions are put in place by the donor then the first replacement will replace the first attorney who needs replacing. The donor can only appoint a replacement attorney for the original attorneys.

The solicitor should advise that when considering whether a replacement attorney should be appointed, it is important that the donor chooses someone they know well and trust to make decisions in their best interests in the same way as would be the case for their first choice attorney(s).

6.12   Solicitor-attorneys

Where a solicitor is appointed as the attorney of an LPA it is recommended that their current terms and conditions of business (including charging rates and the frequency of billing) are discussed with and approved by the donor at the time of granting the power.

The prescribed forms for both property and affairs LPAs and personal welfare LPAs include a section where the donor can confirm that they have agreed for their attorney to be paid a fee and set out the arrangements which have been agreed. It is recommended that any decisions about payments should be recorded with the appropriate level of detail necessary.

A solicitor acting as an attorney of a property and affairs LPA must be aware of their money laundering compliance requirements (see section 7.7 below).

Further information on making decisions under an LPA and the implications for solicitors is provided in section 12 below.

6.13   Medical evidence

It may be worth asking the donor to give advance consent in writing authorising the solicitor to contact the donor's GP or any other medical practitioner if the need for medical evidence should arise at a later date to assess whether the donor has capacity to make a particular decision.

6.14   Safeguards against abuse

Solicitors should discuss with the donor appropriate measures to safeguard against the power being misused or exploited. This could include notifying other family members or friends (who are not named on the prescribed form as someone to be notified) of the existence of the power, why they have chosen the attorney(s) and how the donor intends it to be used. This may help to guard against the possibility of abuse by an attorney and may also reduce the risk of conflict between family members at a later stage.

The solicitor could also consider offering an auditing service, by inserting a clause into the power requiring the attorney to produce to the solicitor, on a specified date each year, an account of his/her actions as attorney during the last 12 months. If the attorney failed to render a satisfactory account, the solicitor could contact the Office of the Public Guardian (see section 13 below). Again a charging procedure for this auditing service must be agreed with the donor in advance.

7.   Taking instructions – property and affairs LPAs

This section of the practice note covers issues specific to property and affairs LPAs. For issues common to both property and affairs LPAs and personal welfare LPAs see section 6 above. For issues specific to personal welfare LPAs see section 8 below.

7.1   Scope

A registered property and affairs LPA can be used whilst the donor retains capacity as an Ordinary Power of Attorney. Alternatively the LPA can specify that it can only be used when the donor no longer has capacity.

The LPA could enable the attorney(s) to take a wide range of actions such as – the buying, selling, or mortgaging of property or dealing with the donor's tax affairs, or claiming benefits on behalf of the donor (paragraph 7.36 of the Code of Practice provides a more extensive list). The donor can limit the power of the LPA by specifying that the LPA only grants authority to the attorney(s) to execute certain specific tasks – or it can include a general authority to act (see section 6.3 above).

7.2   Gifts

Section 12 of the MCA 2005 gives the attorney(s) limited authority to make gifts of the donor's money or property:

- The recipient of the gift must be either an individual who is related to or connected with the donor (including the attorney(s)), or a charity to which the donor actually made gifts or might be expected to make gifts if he or she had capacity.
- The timing of the gift must occur within the prescribed parameters. A gift to charity can be made at any time of the year, but a gift to an individual must be of a seasonal nature, or made on the occasion of

a birth or marriage/civil partnership, or on the anniversary of a birth or marriage/civil partnership.
- The value of the gift must be not unreasonable having regard to all the circumstances and in particular the size of the donor's estate.

The donor cannot confer wider authority on the attorney than that specified in section 12, but it is open to the donor to restrict or exclude the authority which would otherwise be available to the attorney(s) under that subsection. This should be considered by the donor, since improper gifting in relation to EPAs was a widespread form of abuse in attorneyship. The donor may wish to specify in the power the circumstances in which the attorney(s) may make gifts of money or property.

The Court of Protection can authorise the attorney(s) to act so as to benefit themselves or others, otherwise than in accordance with section 12, provided that there are no restrictions in the LPA itself and the court is satisfied that this would be in the donor's best interests (s.23(4), MCA 2005).

Solicitors must also take account of Rule 3.04 of the Solicitors' Code of Conduct 2007 concerning gifts from clients [see **www.rules.sra.org.uk** for most up to date version].

7.3 Investment business

Unless the power is restricted to exclude investments as defined by the Financial Services and Markets Act 2000, the attorney(s) may need to consider the investment business implications of his/her appointment. A solicitor who is appointed as the attorney under an LPA is likely to be conducting investment business and if so, will need to be authorised under the Financial Services and Markets Act 2000. In addition, the solicitor will need to consider whether the Solicitors' Financial Services (Scope) Rules 2001 apply.

7.4 Trusteeships held by the donor

The solicitor should ask whether the donor holds:

- any trusteeships; and
- any property jointly with others.

Under the Trustee Delegation Act 1999 the general rule is that any trustee functions delegated to an attorney (whether under an ordinary power or an enduring/lasting power) must comply with the provisions of section 25 of the Trustee Act 1925, as amended by the 1999 Act.

However, section 1(1) of the 1999 Act provides an exception to this general rule. An attorney can exercise a trustee function of the donor if it relates to land, or the capital proceeds or income from land, in which the donor has a beneficial interest. This is, of course, subject to any provision to the contrary contained in the trust instrument or the power of attorney itself.

7.5   The donor's property and affairs

It may be helpful for solicitors to record and retain information relating to the donor's property and affairs, even where they are not to be appointed as an attorney themselves. The Law Society's Personal Assets Log, which is sometimes used when taking will-drafting instructions, could be suitably adapted for this purpose. In addition, there are certain requirements under the Solicitors' Financial Services (Conduct of Business) Rules 2001 where solicitors safeguard and administer documents of title to investments e.g. share certificates.

7.6   Disclosure of the donor's will

Solicitors are under a duty to keep their clients' affairs confidential (Solicitors Regulation Authority, Solicitors' Code of Conduct 2007, Rule 4). However, the attorney(s) may need to know about the contents of the donor's will in order to avoid acting contrary to the testamentary intentions of the donor (for example, by the sale of an asset specifically bequeathed, when other assets that fell into residue could be disposed of instead).

The question of disclosure of the donor's will should be discussed at the time of making the LPA, and instructions should be obtained as to whether disclosure is denied, or the circumstances in which it is permitted – which should be incorporated into the LPA. For example, the donor may agree that the solicitor can disclose the contents of the will to the attorney(s), but only if the solicitor thinks that disclosure of the will is necessary or expedient for the proper performance of the attorney's functions. This type of discretionary power would need to be included in section 6 of the prescribed form under 'restrictions and/or conditions'.

The attorney(s) also has a common law duty to keep the donor's affairs (including the contents of a will) confidential.

7.7   Money laundering

The preparation of an LPA for clients does not itself constitute a 'financial transaction' for the purposes of the Money Laundering Regulations 2007. However, a solicitor acting for an attorney, or as an attorney themselves, is likely to be undertaking 'relevant business'. Guidance is available to help solicitors understand their money laundering compliance requirements (see **www.moneylaundering.lawsociety.org.uk**) and help may also be obtained from the Law Society's Practice Advice Service.

7.8   Statutory wills

An attorney cannot execute a will on the donor's behalf because the Wills Act 1837 requires a will to be signed by the testator personally or by someone in his or her presence and at his or her direction.

Where a person lacks testamentary capacity, the Court of Protection can order the execution of a statutory will on his or her behalf. The Court's will-making jurisdiction is conferred by section 18 of the MCA 2005.

8.   Taking instructions – personal welfare LPAs

This section of the practice note covers issues specific to personal welfare LPAs. For issues common to both property and affairs LPAs and personal welfare LPAs see section 6 above. For issues specific to property and affairs LPAs see section 7 above.

8.1   Scope

Solicitors should make their clients aware that a registered personal welfare LPA only becomes operative once the donor has lost capacity to make the specific personal welfare decision which is required at the material time.

Clients should also be informed that, unless the donor adds restrictions or conditions, the attorney(s) of a personal welfare LPA will have authority to make all personal welfare, including healthcare, decisions, except for:

- decisions relating to life sustaining treatment, unless the LPA expressly authorises this (see section 8.2 below);
- where the donor has made a valid advance decision to refuse the proposed treatment (see section 8.3.1 below);
- consent or refusal of medical treatment for a mental disorder where the donor is detained under the Mental Health Act 1983; and
- decisions about where a donor subject to guardianship under the Mental Health Act 1983 is to reside, nor any other decisions which conflict with those of a guardian.

Although the MCA 2005 does not define 'personal welfare', Chapter 7 of the Code of Practice gives some guidance and suggests that a personal welfare LPA might include decisions about:

- where the donor should live and who they should live with;
- the donor's day-to-day care, including diet and dress;
- who the donor may have contact with;

- consenting to or refusing medical examination and treatment on the donor's behalf;
- arrangements needed for the donor to be given medical, dental or optical treatment;
- assessments for and provision of community care services;
- whether the donor should take part in social activities, leisure activities, education or training;
- the donor's personal correspondence and papers;
- rights of access to personal information about the donor;
- complaints about the donor's care and treatment.

A personal welfare LPA could be a very powerful document because of the wide-ranging decisions that could be made on behalf of the donor and therefore clients need to make an informed decision about the scope of the power. Clients should be encouraged to consider this carefully and may want to discuss the scope of authority with their prospective attorney(s) and, where appropriate, their GP or any relevant health or social care professionals.

The personal welfare LPA could of course be limited to specific decisions and it may be helpful to create a checklist of questions and a range of suggested clauses which the client might wish to include when creating a personal welfare LPA. For example, a clause could be included to restrict the power to accommodate the donor at another location without consulting specific members of the family.

Clients can also set out their wishes and preferences for personal care, including healthcare, which are not legally binding but which their attorney(s) will take into account in deciding best interests by completing the guidance for attorney(s) at section 8 of the prescribed form (see also section 6.4 above).

Possible points for the client to consider when deciding whether to make a personal welfare LPA could include:

- Do you want your attorney to be able to decide where you will live?
- Do you want the attorney to be able to decide whether other members of your family or your friends can visit you?
- Do you want your attorney to be able to make all types of health and medical decisions on your behalf including giving consent to have an operation?
- Do you want your attorney to decide whether or not you receive life sustaining treatment?
- Do you want to limit the scope of the decision-making and leave decisions to the medical team treating you at that time?

Solicitors will need to exercise care in drafting so that the client's instructions are clear to any health or social care professional who inquires as to the scope of the attorney's authority under the LPA.

8.2   Life sustaining treatment

Decisions to give or refuse life sustaining treatment can only be made by the attorney(s) if the donor has specifically confirmed this in section 6 of the prescribed form – in the presence of a witness. The witness must be over 18 and cannot be the attorney (see also section 10.2 below).

Life sustaining treatment is defined in section 4(10) of the MCA 2005 as 'treatment which in the view of a person providing healthcare for the person concerned is necessary to sustain life'. Further guidance is provided in paragraphs 5.29–5.36 of the Code of Practice.

8.3   Relationship with advance decisions and advance statements

8.3.1   Advance decisions

Some clients may ask about making a 'living will' – which is described in the MCA 2005 as an 'advance decision' – and whether they should make an advance decision rather than a personal welfare LPA or vice versa.

An advance decision allows a person with capacity to refuse specified medical treatment at a point in the future when he or she lacks the capacity to consent to that treatment. If an advance decision is both valid and applicable in the particular circumstances, it has the same effect as a contemporaneous refusal of treatment by a person with capacity. This means that the treatment specified in the decision cannot lawfully be given. Further information and guidance is provided in Chapter 9 of the Code of Practice.

It will be prudent for the solicitor to be prepared with perhaps an information sheet about the differences between a personal welfare LPA and an advance decision together with more detailed clauses which might be included in a personal welfare LPA.

Possible points for the client to consider when choosing between an advance decision and personal welfare LPA include:

- A personal welfare LPA allows a donor to give general authority for the attorney(s) to consent or refuse life sustaining treatment where Option A, section 6, of the prescribed form is completed. Unlike an advance decision it is not necessary to specify a particular treatment. This of course requires a high degree of trust by the donor towards the attorney(s).
- Under a personal welfare LPA the attorney(s) must make decisions in the donor's best interests – and follow the checklist in section 4 of the MCA 2005 which includes consultation with those close to the person who lacks capacity. Where an advance decision is being followed the best interests principle does not apply – and it must be carried out even if the healthcare professionals think it goes against the person's best interests.

- There are stringent requirements for completing and registering an LPA – whereas the MCA 2005 does not impose any particular formalities concerning advance decisions except for decisions relating to life sustaining treatment. This relative informality may be attractive for some clients but it can also lead to uncertainty over whether an advance decision exists or is valid.

Clients should be made aware that where a person makes a personal welfare LPA (regardless of whether it provides authority to consent/refuse life sustaining treatment) and subsequently makes an advance decision, which is valid and applicable in the circumstances, the advance decision takes priority. An LPA made after an advance decision will make the advance decision invalid, if the LPA gives the attorney authority to make decisions about the same treatment.

The solicitor should also advise that the law relating to euthanasia and assisted suicide has not been changed, and the introduction of personal welfare LPAs and statutory advance decisions does not legitimise euthanasia.

8.3.2   Advance statements

The client should also be aware that the MCA 2005 provides for creation of an 'advance statement', which enables a person with capacity to set out their wishes and feelings in writing about the care and treatment they would like to receive should they lose capacity in the future. Advance statements are not legally binding but should be taken into account by decision makers – including attorney(s) – when making best interests decisions under section 4 of the MCA 2005. A client could decide to make an advance statement as a separate exercise to providing guidance for their attorney in section 8 of the prescribed form.

Further information on advance statements is provided in paragraphs 5.37–5.45 of the Code of Practice.

9.   Drawing up the LPA – property and affairs LPAs and personal welfare LPAs

9.1   The prescribed forms

The LPA must be in the form prescribed by the Lasting Powers of Attorney, Enduring Powers of Attorney and Public Guardian Regulations 2007 (SI 2007/1253) (the regulations).

Solicitors should be aware that new regulations may be issued in the future and ensure that the LPA is in the form prescribed by the regulations in force at the time of execution by the donor.

Where the instrument differs from the prescribed form in an imma-terial respect, the Office of the Public Guardian may treat it as sufficient (Schedule 1, Part 1, para.3(1) to the MCA 2005).

The Court of Protection has the power to treat an LPA as valid even if it is not in the prescribed form, if it is satisfied 'that the persons exe-cuting the instrument intended it to create a lasting power of attorney' (Schedule 1, Part 1, para.3(2) to the MCA 2005).

9.2   Completing the form

Solicitors should be aware that the prescribed LPA forms are significantly longer than the previous EPA forms – the property and affairs LPA is 25 pages long and the personal welfare LPA is 24 pages long – and this will have implications for both the time spent with clients and the cost.

The donor of the LPA must have read (or have read to him or her) the prescribed information about the LPA and will need to sign a statement in the LPA to that effect. Any solicitor preparing an LPA should consider the time and cost implications of this obligation.

It may take time to provide the client with the appropriate informa-tion for him or her to decide whether they want to 'tick the box' to dis-pense with the provision to notify anyone when the power is registered (see section 6.8 above).

The attorney(s) will have to file a statement confirming that they have read the relevant information, or part of it, and understand the duties imposed on the attorney of an LPA with particular reference to section 1 of the MCA 2005 (the principles) and the duty to have regard to the Code of Practice. This again may have cost implications as explaining these provisions could take time – and simply sending or arranging for the attorney(s) to sign the document is unlikely to be sufficient.

There is space on the prescribed form to provide details of two attor-neys. Where it is intended to appoint more than two attorneys, their details may be included on a separate sheet which must be attached securely at the back of the LPA. Where more than two attorneys are to be appointed, details of the first two attorneys should be given in the main document, followed by the words

'and (see additional names on attached sheet)'

and the details given on a sheet to be attached to the main document marked clearly 'Part A, section 3: Names of additional attorneys'. This should be also be signed and dated.

The prescribed form also contains space to appoint a replacement attorney (see section 6.11 above). If the donor wishes to appoint more than one replacement attorney, the above paragraph applies in that the details given on the separate sheet must be attached to the main document and marked clearly.

An LPA may be refused registration because of a defect in the form or the wording of the instrument. In some cases, registration may be possible after the filing of further evidence to overcome the defect. Solicitors who have assisted a donor in drawing up an LPA which is subsequently refused registration because of a defect that is material may be liable for the additional costs of deputyship, since at that point the donor may not have the capacity to execute a new LPA.

10.   Executing the LPA – property and affairs LPAs and personal welfare LPAs

10.1   The regulations require that an LPA must be executed by the donor, the certificate provider and the attorney(s) in the following sequence:

- the donor must read (or have read to him/her) the prescribed information;

- the donor must complete and sign (in the presence of a witness) Part A of the document;

- the certificate provider(s) must complete Part B and sign it;

- the attorney(s) must read (or have read to him/her) the prescribed information;

- the attorney(s) must complete and sign (in the presence of a witness) Part C of the document.

This sequence is necessary because the certificate provider must confirm that they have read Part A and because the attorney(s) cannot accept a power which has not yet been conferred.

Execution by the donor, certificate provider and attorney(s) need not take place simultaneously – however the regulations require that each stage outlined above must take place as soon as reasonably practicable after the previous stage.

(Note, that section 6 of a personal welfare LPA must be signed and witnessed simultaneously, see section 8.2 above.)

10.2   Execution by the donor and the attorney(s) must take place in the presence of a witness (but not necessarily the same witness) who must sign Part A or Part C of the prescribed form, as the case may be, and give his or her full name and address. There are various restrictions as to who can act as a witness, and in particular:

- the witness must be at least 18;

- the donor and attorney must not witness each other's signature;

- it is not advisable for the donor's spouse or civil partner to witness his or her signature – this is because of the rules of evidence relating to compellability; and

- at common law, a blind person cannot witness another person's signature.

10.3   If the donor is physically disabled and unable to sign, he or she may leave a mark. Alternatively, the donor may authorise another person to sign the LPA at his or her direction, in which case it must be signed by that person in the presence of the donor and two witnesses.

Similarly an attorney who is unable to sign can leave a mark or authorise another person to sign at his or her direction in the presence of two witnesses. A certificate provider can leave a mark but cannot authorise someone to sign at his or her direction.

11.   The registration process – property and affairs LPAs and personal welfare LPAs

11.1   A key difference between LPAs and the old EPA procedure is that an LPA is not created unless the instrument conferring authority has been registered with the Office of the Public Guardian. So even if the LPA has been correctly filled in and properly signed it will have no authority until it is registered.

11.2   There is no time limit for making the application to register the LPA (however see section 6.7 above). The application can be made by the donor, or all the attorneys if the LPA is a joint power, or if a joint and several power by any of the attorneys.

11.3   The donor or the attorney(s) making the application to register must give notice to everyone named by the donor in the LPA as a person who should be notified, of an application to register using the prescribed form of notice (LPA001).

It may be helpful for the donor or attorney(s) to send the notice with an accompanying letter explaining the circumstances because, in the absence of such an explanation, there may be cause for concern. Giving an appropriate explanation and information at this stage may prevent the application from becoming contentious.

Although there is no statutory requirement to do so, a copy of the LPA could also be sent to the named person(s), in view of the fact that one of the grounds on which they can object to registration is that the power purported to have been created by the instrument is not valid as a lasting power.

11.4   When the application to register is made by the attorney(s), the Office of the Public Guardian will notify the donor that the application has been received – using the prescribed form of notice (LPA003B). Where 'it appears there is good reason to do so' the Office of the Public Guardian will inform the donor personally.

When the application is made by the donor, the Office of the Public Guardian will notify the attorney(s) using the prescribed form of notice (LPA003A). The attorney(s) is not obliged to inform the donor of their intention to register the LPA but it is recommended that the donor should be informed either in writing or in person. This should if possible take place at the same time as the named person(s) are notified.

11.5   There is a prescribed period of 5 weeks during which objections can be raised with the Public Guardian. The grounds for objecting include:

- the LPA has been revoked;

- the requirements to make an LPA have not been met;

- fraud or undue pressure was used to create the LPA;

- the attorney has behaved or is behaving in a way that contravenes his or her authority or is not in the best interests of the donor or proposes to behave in a way that would contravene his authority or would not be in the donor's best interests.

Where there are no objections or defects, the Office of the Public Guardian must register the power within 6 weeks of the date the notices were sent to the named persons.

11.6   The donor should be told that a fee will be payable for the registration of the LPA. A separate fee will be charged for a property and affairs LPA and for a personal welfare LPA – even if they have been made by the same donor.

11.7   The registered LPA document will be stamped on every page by the Office of the Public Guardian. A copy of the instrument is retained by the Office of the Public Guardian and the original will be returned to the person(s) who applied for registration. A prescribed notice of registration is sent to the donor and the attorney(s) (LPA004).

11.8   Following registration the existence of an LPA can be proved by the original stamped instrument, an office copy or a certified copy. If there is any doubt, a third party may search the register of LPAs which is maintained by the Office of the Public Guardian (see section 6.9 above).

12.   Decision-making under an LPA – property and affairs LPAs and personal welfare LPAs

12.1   The functional and time-specific test of incapacity and best interests

Unlike the old EPA regime where registration demonstrates to a third party that the attorney has responsibility and the authority to make financial decisions involving the donor's assets, the MCA 2005 does not have such a readily identifiable point where the attorney(s) takes over.

This is because section 2 of the MCA 2005 sets out a 'functional and time-specific' test of incapacity, which means capacity will vary according to the particular decision to be taken at the particular time. For example, a donor may be able to make decisions about household spending but not about selling his or her home. One month later their capacity to make these decisions may have changed – either improved or become worse. This means that there will not generally be any one point where a person loses capacity to make all decisions and therefore there is no one point when the donor stops acting and the attorney(s) takes over.

Instead, the MCA 2005 sets out a joint approach where the attorney and the donor work together. The starting assumption must always be that a donor has the capacity to make a decision, unless it can be established that they lack capacity (s.1(1), MCA 2005) and a donor should not be treated as unable to make a decision unless all practical steps to help him or her to do so have been taken without success (s.1(3), MCA 2005). Further guidance is provided in Chapters 2 and 3 of the Code of Practice.

Where it is established that the donor lacks the capacity to make a particular decision, section 4 of the MCA 2005 requires the attorney to act in the donor's 'best interests'. The MCA 2005 sets out a checklist of factors that should always be considered by a person deciding what is in the best interests of a person who lacks capacity. This includes, amongst other considerations, consulting, where appropriate, with the relatives, carers and others who have an interest in the donor's welfare. It also includes, where reasonably practical, permitting and encouraging the donor to participate as fully as possible or improving their ability to participate in making the decision – which could involve deferring making a decision or setting up further assistance in order to enable the donor to make a decision. This may be particularly relevant in relation to personal welfare

LPAs as these will only operate where the person lacks capacity to make the decision. Further guidance on best interests is provided in Chapter 5 of the Code of Practice.

The functional and time-specific test of incapacity and determining the donor's best interests under section 4 of the MCA 2005 are likely to prove challenging for solicitors acting as attorneys, and the increased cost implications for the client as well as for firms will need to be considered.

12.2   Duties and responsibilities of attorneys

An attorney has a duty to act within the scope of his or her powers set out in the LPA – but the authority conferred by the LPA is also subject to the provisions of the MCA 2005, in particular section 1 (the principles) and section 4 (best interests). The MCA 2005 also places a specific obligation on attorneys and anyone acting in a professional capacity to have regard to the Code of Practice.

Attorneys also have a duty:

* of care;
* to carry out the donor's instructions;
* not to take advantage of the position of the attorney;
* not to delegate unless authorised to do so;
* of good faith;
* of confidentiality;
* to comply with directions of the Court of Protection;
* not to disclaim without complying with the relevant guidance.

In relation to property and affairs LPA there is also a duty to:

* keep accounts;
* keep the donor's money and property separate from their own.

Solicitors acting as attorneys under an LPA are also required to display a higher standard of care and skill. According to paragraph 7.59 of the Code:

> If attorneys are being paid for their services, they should demonstrate a higher degree of care and skill.

> Attorneys who undertake their duties in the course of their professional work (such as solicitors or corporate trustees) must display professional competence and abide by their own professional rules and standards.

Further guidance on the duties and responsibilities of attorneys is provided in Chapter 7 of the Code of Practice.

12.3   Relationship between property and affairs and personal welfare LPAs

The attorney(s) has a duty to act within the extent of his powers, so a property and affairs LPA does not give the attorney(s) power to make personal welfare decisions – and vice versa. An attorney will however be expected, if practical and appropriate, to consult with the attorney(s) of any other LPA made by the donor, whenever his or her best interests are being considered (s.4(7)(c), MCA 2005 and paragraph 5.55 of the Code of Practice). It is also likely that EPA attorney(s) would also be consulted (see section 14.5 below).

Attorneys should also be aware that the demarcation between decisions made under a property and affairs LPA and a personal welfare LPA may not always be clear. For instance the choice of nursing home may have both welfare and financial implications for the donor. It will be important in these types of cases for the attorneys to consult each other and seek to reach agreement. If there are conflicts then an application could be made to the Court of Protection to resolve the issue but this will in itself have cost implications and should only be considered as a last resort.

12.4   Disclaiming an appointment

An attorney or proposed attorney can disclaim his or her appointment by completing the prescribed form (LPA005) which must be sent to the donor and copied to the Office of the Public Guardian and any other attorney(s) appointed under the power.

12.5   Support for attorneys

Section 22 of the MCA 2005 provides that the Court of Protection can determine questions about the validity and revocation of LPAs (both registered and unregistered), and can direct that the instrument should not be registered, or where it has been registered and the donor lacks capacity, that it should be revoked.

However, the Court should not be seen as being available to 'hold the hand' of the attorney, who should in normal circumstances be able to act in the best interests of the donor, taking advice where necessary from a solicitor or other professional adviser. It should be noted that, although the Court may interpret the terms of an LPA or give directions as to its exercise, it does not have power to extend or amend the terms of the LPA as granted by the donor.

13.   Where abuse is suspected – property and affairs LPAs and personal welfare LPAs

If solicitors suspect that an attorney may be misusing an LPA or acting dishonestly they should contact the Office of the Public Guardian immediately. They should also contact the police if they suspect physical or sexual abuse, theft or serious fraud. It may also be necessary – particularly in cases involving personal welfare LPAs – to refer the matter to local adult protection authorities. Further guidance is provided in paragraphs 7.69–7.74 and Chapter 14 of the Code of Practice.

14.   Enduring Powers of Attorney

14.1   The Enduring Powers of Attorney Act 1985 was repealed by the MCA 2005, but it is reintroduced almost in its entirety, in Schedule 4 to the MCA 2005. The amendments take account of the changes to the Court of Protection and the new role of the Office of the Public Guardian in the registration process. It is not possible to make new EPAs, although the operation of existing EPAs made before 1 October 2007 will fall under Schedule 4 to the MCA 2005.

14.2   Schedule 4 paragraph 1(1) to the MCA 2005 specifically excludes the principles of the MCA 2005 applying to the EPA attorney. However under the law of agency, the EPA attorney has certain duties towards the donor (these are listed in section 12.2 above and further guidance is provided in paragraphs 7.58–7.68 of the Code of Practice).

14.3   According to paragraph 7.5 of the Code of Practice, EPA attorneys do not have a legal duty to have regard to the Code – but the Code's guidance will still be helpful to them.

A solicitor acting as an EPA attorney may still be considered to have a duty to have regard to the Code of Practice since he or she will be acting in a 'professional capacity' for the purposes of section s.42(4)(e)of the MCA 2005. However, Schedule 4 to the MCA 2005 retains the EPA concept that there is one point in time when a person is deemed to lack capacity and that the power must be registered with the Office of the Public Guardian when the attorney believes that the donor is becoming or has become incapable of managing his or her financial affairs. This is different to the concept of incapacity used in the rest of the MCA 2005 which is both function and time-specific (see section 12.1 above). It would appear to be the case that the effect of this is that the Code will selectively apply to the professional EPA attorney as there will not be a requirement to assess capacity on each and every decision being made.

14.4   Under an EPA the attorney is under a common law duty to act in the donor's best interests. This does not apply where the client has capacity and the EPA is unregistered and being used as an Ordinary Power of Attorney – although the normal duties under the law of agency apply.

14.5   The attorney of an EPA is not specifically named as a person to be consulted when a decision maker is making a best interests determination under section 4 of the MCA 2005. However it is likely that in the majority of cases any EPA attorney will be considered to be a person who is 'interested in his welfare' for the purposes of section 4(7)(b) of the MCA 2005, and therefore would be consulted. This appears to be confirmed in paragraph 5.55 of the Code of Practice.

14.6   The Office of the Public Guardian is responsible for maintaining a register of EPAs which can be searched by any person on payment of a fee (see section 6.9 above).

15.   Further advice

Solicitors may obtain further help on matters relating to professional ethics from the Solicitors Regulation Authority's Professional Ethics helpline (0870 606 2577) and on practice issues from the Law Society's Practice Advice Service (0870 606 2522).

Information and advice (but not legal advice) can also be obtained from the Office of the Public Guardian (0845 330 2900).

Annex 9C

Gifts of property: Implications for future liability to pay for long term care

Guidelines for solicitors prepared by the Law Society's Mental Health and Disability Committee – Revised April 2000

1. Elderly people or those nearing retirement may seek advice from solicitors as to the advantages and disadvantages of transferring their home or other property to relatives, even though in some cases they still intend to live in the home. The solicitor's advice will of course vary, according to the individual circumstances of the client, their motivation for making such a gift, and what they are hoping to achieve by it.

2. The following guidelines are designed to assist solicitors, both to ensure that their clients fully understand the nature, effects, benefits, risks and foreseeable consequences of making such a gift, and also to clarify the solicitor's role and duty in relation to such transactions. In particular, consideration is given to the implications of making gifts of property on possible future liability for the payment of fees for residential or nursing home care. This area of law is still under review by the Government, so solicitors should be aware that the law may change.

3. Whilst these guidelines generally refer to the making of 'gifts' they apply with equal force to situations where the disposal of property at a significant undervalue is contemplated.

The need for legal advice

4. The Law Society is aware of a number of non-solicitor legal advice services which are marketing schemes for elderly people to effect a gift of property with the intention of avoiding the value of that property being taken into account to pay for residential care. Some make unjustified claims as to the effectiveness of the schemes, or fail to take into account the individual circumstances of clients. Seldom do these schemes highlight

the other risks involved in making a gift of the home to members of the family.

5.   These guidelines are also intended to assist solicitors to stress the need for clients to obtain proper legal advice, and to highlight the risks of using unqualified advisers.

Who is the client?

6.   The solicitor must first be clear as to who s/he is acting for, especially where relatives purport to be giving instructions on behalf of an elderly person. In most cases, it will be the elderly person who owns the home or property so if the solicitor is to act in a transfer the elderly person will be the client. This will be the assumption for the purpose of these guidelines. It is important to recognise that there is an inevitable conflict of interest between the elderly person and anyone who stands to gain from the transaction, so the elderly person should receive independent advice (see also paras.30–31 below).

7.   The solicitor acting for the elderly person should see the client alone, to satisfy him/herself that the client is acting freely, to confirm the client's wishes and intentions, and to gauge the extent, if any, of family or other influence [. . .]. It may be necessary to spend some time with the client, talking about wider issues, in order to evaluate these aspects, clarify the family circumstances, and assess whether the client has the mental capacity to make the gift (see Appendix A [of these guidelines] for details of the relevant test of capacity).

8.   If the client is not already known to the solicitor, it may also be advisable to check whether another solicitor has previously acted for the client, and if so, to seek the client's consent to contact that solicitor, in case there are factors to be taken into account which are not immediately apparent.

The client's understanding

9.   It is important to ensure that the client understands the nature of a gift, that this is what is intended and the long-term implications. Before making any such gift clients should in particular understand:

- that the money or property they intend to give away is theirs in the first place;
- why the gift is being made;
- whether it is a one-off, or part of a series of gifts;
- the extent of the gift in relation to the rest of their money and property;

- that they are making an outright gift rather than, say, a loan or acquiring a share in a business or property owned by the recipient;
- whether they expect to receive anything in return and, if so, how much, or on what terms (for example: someone who is giving away their house might expect to be able to carry on living there rent free for the rest of their life: but who pays for the insurance and upkeep?);
- whether they intend the gift to take effect immediately, or at a later date perhaps when they die, or go into residential care;
- that, if the gift is outright, they can't assume that the money or property would be returned to them on request;
- the effect that making the gift could have on their future standard of living;
- the effect that the gift could have on other members of the family who might have expected eventually to inherit a share of the money or property;
- the possibility that the recipient could die first, or become involved in divorce or bankruptcy proceedings, in which case the money or property given away could end up belonging to somebody else;
- that the donor and recipient could fall out and even become quite hostile to one another;
- whether they have already made gifts to the recipient or other people; and
- any other foreseeable consequences of making or not making the gift (some of which are considered below).

The client's objectives

10. The solicitor should establish why the gift of property is being contemplated, and whether the client's objectives will in fact be achieved by the making of the gift or could be achieved in some other way. In establishing the client's objectives, the following matters may be relevant:

(i) If the objective is to ensure that a particular relative (e.g. a child) inherits the client's home rather than someone else, this can equally well be achieved by making a will.

(ii) If the objective is to avoid inheritance tax on the death of the client, a rough calculation should be made of the client's likely estate to assess the amount of tax which may be payable, and whether other tax saving measures could be considered. The client might not appreciate that the value of the property, together with the remainder of the estate, may not exceed the level at which inheritance tax becomes payable.

The client might also not be aware that if s/he intends to continue living in the home after giving it away, there may be no inheritance tax saving because of the 'reservation of benefit' rules. The consequence might also be to increase the liability to inheritance tax on the death of the relative to whom the gift has been made if s/he dies before the client. Again, other schemes to mitigate these vulnerabilities should be considered.

(iii) If the objective is to relieve the elderly client of the worry and responsibility of home ownership, other ways of achieving this should be discussed, such as making an Enduring Power of Attorney.

(iv) If the client volunteers that a significant part of his/her objective is to try to avoid the value of the home being taken into account in various forms of means-testing, the implications and possible consequences should be explained to the client. These matters are considered in the following paragraphs in relation to liability to pay for long-term care. Alternative measures should also be discussed. The solicitor may also need to consider her/his own position (see paras.28–31 below).

Other reasons for transferring the home

11. There may, of course, be good reasons for transferring the home, or a share in the home, to a relative or another person quite apart from the desire to avoid means-testing. If such reasons exist the transfer should be effected sooner rather than later and it would be worthwhile reciting the reason in the transfer deed. For example:

(a) the home has not been vested in the appropriate names in the first place (e.g. it was funded in whole or in part by a son or daughter but vested in the name of the parent);

(b) a daughter has given up a well paid job to live in the home and care for an infirm parent in the expectation of inheriting the home on the death of the parent;

(c) the parent has for some years been unable to meet the outgoings or pay for alterations or improvements to the home and these have been funded by a son in the expectation of inheriting the home on the death of the parent;

(d) the home comprises part of a family business (e.g. a farm) which would no longer be viable if the home was 'lost'.

12. If the home is already vested in the joint names of the infirm elderly person and another occupier, or can for justifiable reasons be transferred by the elderly person into joint names, the beneficial interest of the elderly person may, on a means assessment, have little value when subject to the continued rights of occupation of the co-owner.

Severance of a joint tenancy

13. If the home is vested in the joint names of an elderly couple it may be worth considering a severance of the joint tenancy with a view to preserving at least a one-half share for the family. Each spouse can then make a will leaving his or her one-half share to the children. This provides some protection in the event that a caring spouse dies before an infirm spouse but there may be vulnerability to a claim under the Inheritance (Provision for Family and Dependants) Act 1975. It is possible to sever the joint tenancy even after the infirm spouse has become mentally incapable.

Implications of making the gift

14. A proper assessment of the implications of making a gift of the home, both for the client and for her/his relative(s) can best be achieved by listing the possible benefits and risks. These may include the following:

Possible benefits

- A saving of inheritance tax, probate fees and costs on the death of the client. Although in most cases the existence of a potential liability for inheritance tax will mean that a gift of the home by itself will not avoid vulnerability to means-testing, the high value of homes particularly in London may create this situation.
- Avoiding the need to sell the home to pay for charges such as residential care or nursing home fees, thus securing the family's inheritance.
- Avoiding the value of the home being taken into account in means-testing for other benefits or services.

Possible risks

- The value of the home may still be taken into account under the anti-avoidance measures in relation to means-testing (see paras.15–27).
- The capital gains tax owner-occupier exemption will apply to the gift, but may be lost thereafter and there will be no automatic uplift to the market value of the home on the client's death.
- The client may never need residential or nursing home care (it has been estimated that less than 6% of people aged 75–85 need residential care), so the risks of giving away the home may outweigh any potential benefits to be achieved.
- If the client does eventually need residential or nursing home care but no longer has the resources to pay the fees him/herself because of the gift, the local authority may only pay for a basic level of care (e.g.

a shared room in a home of its choice), so the client may be dependent on relatives to top up the fees if a better standard of care is desired.

- The relatives to whom the gift has been made may fail to keep their side of the understanding, whether deliberately or through no fault of their own. For example, they may:

  - fail to support the client (e.g. by not topping up residential care fees);
  - seek to move the client prematurely into residential care in order to occupy the home themselves or to sell it;
  - die suddenly without making suitable provision for the client;
  - run into financial difficulties because of unemployment or divorce or become bankrupt and in consequence be unable to support the client.

- The home may be lost on the bankruptcy, divorce or death of the relative to whom it has been given, resulting in the client being made homeless if s/he is still living there.
- There may be no inheritance tax saving whilst the client continues to live in the home, yet there could be a liability for inheritance tax if the relative dies before the client.
- The relative to whom the home has been gifted may lose entitlement to benefits and/or services (e.g. social security benefits, legal aid) due to personal means-testing if not living in the home.
- The local authority may decide, having regard to the client's owner-ship of the notional capital value of the home, rather than the property itself (see paras.18–19 below), that s/he is not entitled to certain community care services, or even to be funded at all for residential care should this be needed.

Anti-avoidance measures

15. The client can be given no guarantees that there is a fool-proof way of avoiding the value of the home being taken into account in means-testing, since the anti-avoidance measures in the law enable some gifts to be ignored by the authorities and even set aside by the court. Not only are these measures subject to change from time to time, but it is also unclear how far the authorities will go in order to pursue contributions they believe to be owing to them.

16. In most cases, the intention behind making the gift is the most important factor. Where the intention is clearly to create or increase entitlement to financial support from the local authority, measures can

be taken to impose a charge on the asset given away in the hands of the recipients or even to recover the asset itself. However, it is necessary that the authority concerned believe that this was a 'significant' part of the client's intention in making the gift. Using one of the marketed schemes (see para.4 above) which have been advertised specifically to help people to avoid local authority means-testing may make clear the client's intention.

Charges for residential and nursing home care

17. At present, a major cause for concern among many older clients is the fear of having to sell their homes in order to pay for residential or nursing home care in the future, and they may wish to take steps to protect their families' inheritance. In giving advice on this matter, it is important that solicitors are familiar with the key points summarised in Appendix B [of these guidelines], including:

- the eligibility criteria for NHS funded nursing home care;
- the charging and funding arrangements by local authorities for residential and nursing home care (when applicable);
- when care must be provided free of charge; and
- if charges may be made, the means-testing rules which apply.

Implications of the 'notional capital' rule

18. Where the local authority believe that property has been given away by the client with the intention of creating or increasing entitlement to help with residential care fees, or nursing home fees where these are payable, then it may decide that the client has 'notional capital' equivalent in value to that of the property given away. If that notional capital value exceeds the capital cut off (currently £16,000, see Appendix B [of these guidelines]) the authority may decide that the client is not entitled to any assistance (or any continuing assistance) with the home care fees.

19. In such cases it would be the client who then had to take action if s/he wished to challenge the decision. This may involve the use of the local authority's complaints procedures, as well as the Ombudsman or a judicial review. These may all entail significant legal expense and anxiety for the client as the outcome could not be guaranteed. If a judicial review is necessary it would be the client who had to establish that the authority's decision was *Wednesbury* unreasonable (i.e. the burden of proof would be on the client). See *Robertson* v *Fife* (Court of Session) 12/1/2000 [http://www.scotscourt.gov.uk/index1.htm].

Enforcing payment of fees for residential and nursing home care

20. Having assessed someone as being in need of residential or nursing home care and then provided that care, the local authority cannot withdraw that provision simply because the resident does not pay assessed contributions. However, where charges may legally be made, the authority can take steps to recover contributions, and in assessing ability to pay, may take into account property that has been given away for the purpose of avoiding means-testing.

21. The enforcement provisions available to local authorities are as follows:

(i)   taking proceedings in the Magistrates' Court to recover sums due as a civil debt (section 56 National Assistance Act 1948);

(ii) imposing a charge on any property belonging to the resident, with interest chargeable from the day after death (sections 22 and 24 HAS-SASSA Act 1983 [Health and Social Services and Social Security Adjudications Act 1983]);

(iii) imposing a charge on property transferred by the resident within 6 months of going to residential care, or whilst in care, with the intention of avoiding contributions (section 21 HASSASSA Act 1983).

22. Once the debt for unpaid contributions reaches £750, insolvency proceedings could be taken to declare the resident bankrupt, whereupon transactions at an undervalue may be set aside within 2 years, or within 5 years if the person made bankrupt was insolvent at the time of the transaction, which is unlikely (sections 339–341 Insolvency Act 1986).

23. Under other provisions, a gift may be set aside without time limit and without bankruptcy, if the court is satisfied that the transfer was made for the purpose of putting assets beyond the reach of a potential creditor or otherwise prejudicing the creditor's interests (sections 423–425 Insolvency Act 1986). This provision is exceptionally wide, and the court has extensive powers to restore the position to that which it would have been had the gift not been made.

24. Although some local authorities have threatened to use insolvency proceedings, few have actually done so, perhaps because of lack of expertise or the prospect of bad publicity. However, with increasing pressures on local authority resources to provide community care services, there is no guarantee they will not do so in the future.

25. The burden of proof remains on the local authority to establish that the purpose behind the gift of the property was to avoid means-testing. But it may be difficult for the donor or his/her relatives to give evidence

as to the donor's intentions, and if another purpose of the gift cannot be established or indicated the judge may conclude that it must have been to avoid means-testing.

26. The purpose of the gift will have been discussed in advance with the solicitor, and it would be prudent for the solicitor to retain evidence of the advice given in order to protect him/herself in the event of a subsequent family dispute or professional negligence claim. The file notes and correspondence will normally be covered by legal professional privilege or at least by the duty of confidentiality. The court will not usually order discovery of a solicitor's file unless there is prima facie evidence of fraud, but has done so in similar circumstances on the basis of public policy considerations (*Barclays Bank plc* v *Eustice* [1995] 1 WLR 1238). It is possible that a trustee in bankruptcy, or a local authority bringing proceedings under the Insolvency Act 1986, sections 423–425, may persuade the court to override privilege.

27. In *Yule* v *South Lanarkshire Council* [1999] 1 CCLR 546 Lord Philip held that a local authority was entitled to take account of the value of an elderly woman's home transferred to her daughter over 18 months before the woman entered residential care. The Court held that there was no time limit on local authorities when deciding whether a person had deprived themselves of assets for the purposes of avoiding residential care fees.

The solicitor's duty

28. The solicitor's role is more than just drawing up and registering the necessary deeds and documents to effect the making of the gift. S/he has a duty to ensure that the client fully understands the nature, effect, benefits, risks and foreseeable consequences of making the gift. The solicitor has no obligation to advise the client on the wisdom or morality of the transaction, unless the client specifically requests this.

29. The Professional Ethics Division of the Law Society has advised that the solicitor should follow his/her client's instructions, provided that by doing so, the solicitor will not be involved in a breach of the law or a breach of the principles of professional conduct. Reference is made to [Principle 12.02 of the *Guide to the Professional Conduct of Solicitors* (1999), see **sra.org.uk/rules** for latest regulation] which indicates when instructions must be refused. Solicitors will want to satisfy themselves in each individual case that no breach of the law is involved in the proposed transaction. Having advised the client as to the implications and possible consequences of making the gift, the decision whether or not to proceed remains with the client.

30. Solicitors must also be aware of the possible conflict of interest, or significant risk of such a conflict, between the donor and recipient of a gift. While there is no general rule of law that a solicitor should never act for both parties in a transaction where their interests might conflict, [Principle 15.01 of the *Guide to the Professional Conduct of Solicitors*] states: [see **sra.org.uk/rules** for latest regulation] 'A solicitor or firm of solicitors should not accept instructions to act for two or more clients where there is a conflict or a significant risk of a conflict between the interests of the clients'. Given the potentially vulnerable position of an elderly client, the solicitor will have to consider carefully whether he can act for the donor and the recipient or whether there is an actual or significant risk of conflict. If the solicitor has initially advised the donor alone as to all the implications of the gift and is satisfied that there is no undue influence and that the donor has capacity, the solicitor may be able to act for both clients in the conveyancing.

31. If the solicitor is asked to act for both parties, the solicitor should make them both aware of the possibility of a conflict of interest and advise one of them to consider taking independent advice. S/he should also explain that as a result of any conflict of interest, a solicitor acting by agreement for both parties may be unable to disclose all that s/he knows to each of them or to give advice to one of them which conflicts with the interests of the other and may have to cease acting for both. Both parties must be content to proceed on this basis, be competent to do so and give their consent in writing. However, if any doubt remains, the solicitor would be advised not to act for both parties.

Further reading

. . .

Appendix A:

Capacity to make a gift

The relevant test of capacity to make a gift is set out in the judgment in *Re Beaney (Deceased)* [1978] 1 WLR 770. In that case a 64–year-old widow with three grown up children owned and lived in a three-bedroom semi-detached house. Her elder daughter lived with her. In May 1973, a few days after being admitted to hospital suffering from advanced dementia, the widow signed a deed of gift transferring the house to her elder daughter. The widow died intestate the following year, and her son and younger daughter applied successfully to the court for a declaration that the transfer of the house was void and of no effect because their mother was mentally incapable of making such a gift. The judge in the case set out the following criteria for capacity to make a lifetime gift:

> The degree or extent of understanding required in respect of any instrument is relative to the particular transaction which it is to effect. . . . Thus, at one extreme, if the subject matter and value of a gift are trivial in relation to the donor's other assets, a low degree of understanding will suffice. But, at the other, if its effect is to dispose of the donor's only asset of value and thus, for practical purposes, to pre-empt the devolution of his estate under [the donor's] will or . . . intestacy, then the degree of understanding required is as high as that required for a will, and the donor must understand the claims of all potential donees and the extent of the property to be disposed of.

It is arguable that, when someone makes a substantial gift, a further point should be considered, namely, the effect that disposing of the asset could have on the donor for the rest of his or her life.

(Adapted from British Medical Association/Law Society, *Assessment of Mental Capacity: Guidance for Doctors and Lawyers* (1995) BMA.)

Appendix B:

Paying for residential and nursing home care

Charges

Individuals who can afford to pay for a place in a residential care or nursing home may arrange this independently, though it is advisable to seek a 'needs' assessment prior to entering residential or nursing care in order to achieve continuity if local authority funding may be needed in future:

- if met with a refusal to assess in advance, point out that the assessment of need for care provision does not depend upon the need for funding;
- it may also be wise to ensure that the particular home is willing to accommodate residents on local authority funding.

Local authority

Those who enter such a home through an arrangement made by the local authority must pay or contribute to the cost, whether the authority provides or buys in the accommodation:

- each authority must fix a standard weekly charge for its own homes which should represent the true economic cost of providing the accommodation – many have a standard scale of fees geared to their eligibility criteria;
- where the authority purchases a place from an independent home the weekly charge to the resident should represent the cost of the place to the authority;
- residents must generally contribute in accordance with their resources up to the appropriate charge, but no one will be required to pay more;
- the authority either:

  - pays the full fee to the home and collects the resident's contribution; or
  - pays its share whilst the resident and any third party pay the balance;

- a contract with the authority or the home should state what is included in the charge and what are extras.

Health authority

Where a health authority arranges a place in a nursing home under a contractual arrangement the individual remains an NHS patient and no charge is made but social security benefits may be withdrawn or reduced.

It is important to ascertain whether a move from hospital to a private nursing home also involves a transfer of responsibility from the health authority to social services.

Means-testing

When the resident cannot afford the full charge an assessment is made of ability to pay and this is reviewed annually but a resident should ask for re-assessment at any time if this would be beneficial:

- The assessment relates to both income and capital:

  - since April 1993 assessment has been brought largely into line with that for income support, though local authorities retain some discretion;
  - the capital cut-off point is £16,000 but capital above £10,000 will result in a tariff income (an attempt to apply a lower financial threshold before acknowledging need failed in *R v Sefton*

Metropolitan Borough Council, ex p. *Help the Aged* [1997] 1 CCLR 57, CA);
– notional capital and notional income rules apply as for income support.

• Assessment relates only to the means of the resident (unlike for income support where spouses and partners are generally assessed together):

– there is no power to oblige a spouse/partner to take part but spouses are liable to maintain each other (National Assistance Act 1948, s.42) and court action may be taken against a liable relative (s.43);
– jointly owned property may be deemed to be owned in equal shares (but query whether it has a value if a home is occupied by the joint owner);
– since 1996 one-half of occupational and private pensions of the resident are re-routed back to the non-resident spouse.

• The value of the resident's home is disregarded during a temporary stay or:

– if occupied by a spouse/partner, or a relative who is aged 60 or over or incapacitated;
– if occupied by someone else and the local authority exercises its discretion.

• There is a minimum charge payable by all residents and the assessment determines what should be paid above this, but all residents retain a personal expenses allowance (revised annually):

– to be used by the resident for expenditure of personal choice such as stationery, personal toiletries, treats (e.g. sweets, drinks, cigarettes) and presents;
– the authority has a discretion to increase the amount, but it should not be used for top-up to provide more expensive accommodation.

• Authorities should carry out a benefits check because they have an incentive to ensure that people in homes are receiving maximum state benefits:

– this should only be with the informed consent of the resident;
– income support will include a residential allowance (not for local authority homes).

Power to charge?

In two main situations (see *R* v *North and East Devon Health Authority*, ex p. *Coughlan* [1999] 2 CCLR 285; *R* v *Borough of Richmond*, ex p. *Watson* [1999] 2 CCLR 402) no charges may be made for the care of an individual:

- where, following discharge from detention under one of the longer treatment sections of the Mental Health Act 1983 (usually s.3 or s.37), he or she requires residential or nursing home care as a result of mental disorder:

    - no charge may be made for care as this is deemed 'aftercare' service provision under Mental Health Act 1983, s.117;
    - that section places a joint duty on the health and local authorities to provide the services required free of charge, unless it is decided by both that the person is no longer in need of these by virtue of their mental disorder;

- (only applicable to placements in nursing homes) where his or her need is primarily a health care need:

    - the health authority must fund the entire cost of the placement and the local authority has no power to purchase such care and pass the costs to the client;
    - the only exception is where the nursing care is 'merely ancillary or incidental to the provision of the accommodation' in a nursing home. This will depend on the level and type of care. Most nursing homes placements will be the responsibility of the NHS because a client will not be placed there unless their primary need is for nursing care, i.e. health care.

Regulations and guidance

National Assistance (Assessment of Resources) Regulations 1992 as amended

Circular LAC (99)9 'Charging for Residential Accommodation Guide' (CRAG) (copies available from the Department of Health, PO Box 777, London SE1 6XH; Fax: 01623 724 524; e-mail: doh@prologistics)

(Adapted from Gordon R. Ashton, *The Elderly Client Handbook: The Law Society's Guide to Acting for Older People* (Second edition, 2000) The Law Society.)

Annex 9D

Debt relief orders

1. Introduction

1.1 Who should read this practice note?

Solicitors who provide debt advice.

1.2 What is the issue?

The Tribunals, Courts and Enforcement Act 2007 introduced a new form of debt relief called a 'Debt Relief Order' (DRO) which is expected to come into force on the 6 April 2009.

This practice note explains the procedure for DRO applications.

2. What are Debt Relief Orders?

Debt Relief Orders are an alternative to bankruptcy for clients who have:

- less than £15,000 in unsecured debt
- less than £300 in assets and
- less than £50 per month disposable income after they have met all their essential expenditure.

Creditors who are included in the DRO will be prevented from taking any action to recover their debts from the client.

Generally the debts of the client will be discharged at the end of one year.

More information about eligibility for DROs can be found on the Insolvency website (**www.insolvency.gov.uk/insolvencyprofessionand legislation/DebtRelief.htm**).

3. How is a DRO application made?

Debt advisers act as 'intermediaries' and help debtors to apply online for a DRO via the Insolvency Service website.

A practising certificate is not sufficient to help a client make a DRO application. You must first be approved as an intermediary.

3.1. What is an intermediary?

An intermediary is a trained debt advisor who has been approved to make DRO applications by a 'competent authority'.

3.2. What is a competent authority?

A competent authority is a body authorised by the Secretary of State to approve intermediaries.

3.3. Where can I apply to become an intermediary?

Six organisations have been given interim approval to act as competent authorities. The Solicitors Regulation Authority is not registered as a competent authority so holding a practising certificate is not sufficient to act as an intermediary.

Five of these organisations will only consider applications from their own employees or volunteers.

However, members of the Institute of Money Advisers (IMA) can apply for approved intermediary status. Membership is open to those who provide free money advice, including legal aid solicitors and solicitors who carry out pro bono debt advice.

You can apply to become a member of the IMA on their website (**www.i-m-a.org.uk/membership.html**).

Details of all competent authorities can be found on the Insolvency Service website (**www.insolvency.gov.uk/insolvencyprofessionand legislation/DebtRelief.htm**).

3.4 What training do I need to become an intermediary?

Competent authorities will decide individually how intermediaries are best trained.

Training is free to all members of the IMA and is carried out by the Money Advice Trust.

Information about training to become an intermediary can be found on the IMA website (**www.i-m-a.org.uk/debt-relief-orders.html**).

4. Debt Relief Orders and the Legal Services Commission (LSC)

The LSC's recent consultation on the Civil Bid Round for 2010 proposed that any provider with a debt contract should offer clients access to at least one approved intermediary.

This is still in the consultation stages but gives an indication of the LSC's approach to DROs.

Download the consultation documentation. The relevant sections are 4.45 and 4.46 (**https://consult.legalservices.gov.uk/inovem/consult.ti/ 2010Contracts/listdocuments**).

5. More information

5.1 Professional conduct

The following sections of the Solicitors' Code of Conduct 2007 are relevant to this issue:

Rule 1.01 Justice and the rule of law: You must uphold the rule of law and the proper administration of justice

5.2 Further products and support

5.2.1 Practice Advice Line

The Law Society provides support for solicitors on a wide range of areas of practice. Practice Advice can be contacted on 0870 606 2522 from 09:00 to 17:00 on weekdays.

5.3 Status of this practice note

Practice notes are issued by the Law Society for the use and benefit of its members. They represent the Law Society's view of good practice in a particular area. They are not intended to be the only standard of good practice that solicitors can follow. You are not required to follow them, but doing so will make it easier to account to oversight bodies for your actions.

Practice notes are not legal advice, nor do they necessarily provide a defence to complaints of misconduct or of inadequate professional service. While care has been taken to ensure that they are accurate, up to date and useful, the Law Society will not accept any legal liability in relation to them.

For queries or comments on this practice note contact the Law Society's Practice Advice Service: **www.lawsociety.org.uk/practiceadvice**

5.4   Terminology in this practice note

Must – a specific requirement in the Solicitor's Code of Conduct or legislation. You must comply, unless there specific exemptions or defences provided for in the code of conduct or relevant legislation.

Should – good practice for most situations in the Law Society's view. If you do not follow this, you must be able to justify to oversight bodies why this is appropriate, either for your practice, or in the particular retainer.

May – a non-exhaustive list of options for meeting your obligations. Which option you choose is determined by the risk profile of the individual practice, client or retainer. You must be able to justify why this was an appropriate option to oversight bodies.

Useful contacts

LAW SOCIETY

General enquiries – 0207 242 1222

JLD Helpline – 0800 085 6131
For junior lawyers who want to talk to someone about a pastoral or career related problem. Lines are open from 09.00 to 21.00, Monday to Friday.

Lawyerline – 0870 606 2588
Now run by the Law Society, this service provides advice on client care and complaints handling. Lines are open from 09.00 to 17.00, Monday to Friday. E-mail: lawyerline@lawsociety.org.uk.

Library – 0870 606 2511
Assistance for solicitors and their staff with legal information enquiries. Free to members. We can supply copies of published material by e-mail for a small charge. Lines are open from 09.00 to 18.00, Monday to Thursday; 09.00 to 17.00 on Fridays.

Pastoral Care Helpline – 020 7320 5795
The Law Society's Pastoral Care Helpline offers help with personal, financial, professional and employment problems. This service refers you to the most suitable helpline for your needs. Lines are open from 09.00 to 17.00, Monday to Friday.

Practice Advice Service – 0870 606 2522
Advice for solicitors and their staff from our team of experienced solicitors on legal practice issues, Law Society policy and Law Society practice notes. Advice is available on complying with the anti-money laundering regulations and navigating the anti-money laundering practice note. Lines are open from 0900 to 1700, Monday to Friday. E-mail: practiceadvice @lawsociety.org.uk.

PASTORAL CARE HELPLINES

LawCare – 0800 279 6888

Support for members of the legal profession and their families on issues relating to stress, depression, addiction and other health problems. Lines are open from 09:00 to 19:30 weekdays and 10:00 to 16:00 on weekends and bank holidays.

Maternity and Paternity Helpline – 0870 043 4844

Advice for solicitors, men as well as women, on their rights in relation to childcare issues.

Solicitors' Assistance Scheme – 020 7117 8811

Confidential legal advice for solicitors, trainee solicitors and the staff and family of solicitors, on professional and personal difficulties.

Solicitors Benevolent Association – 020 8675 6440

The Solicitors Benevolent Association (SBA) is the principal nationwide charity for solicitors in England and Wales. The aim of the Association is to assist solicitors and their dependants who are in need.

SOLICITORS REGULATION AUTHORITY

Contact Centre – 0870 606 2555

Provided by the Solicitors Regulation Authority to assist solicitors with enquiries relating to practising certificates, continuing professional development (CPD) and other general enquiries.

Ethics helpline –0870 606 2577

Provided by the Solicitors Regulation Authority.

Record changes – operations@sra.org.uk

Record changes to solicitors' employment details, and to practice and firm registration.

Further resources

Further reading

Please note that all Law Society Publishing and other key legal titles are available from the Law Society's online bookshop (**www.lawsociety. org.uk/bookshop**).

Anderson, M. and Warner, V. (2008) *Execution of Documents,* 2nd Edition, Law Society Publishing

Bielanska et.al (2004) *Elderly Client Handbook*, 3rd Edition, Law Society Publishing.

Brazell, L. (ed.) (2008) *Intellectual Property Law Handbook*, Law Society Publishing

Burdge, P. (2006) *Civil Costs Assessment Handbook*, 2nd edition, Law Society Publishing

Burn, S. (2007) *Civil Litigation Handbook,* 2nd edition, Law Society Publishing

Camp, P. (2009) *Companion to the Solicitors' Code of Conduct 2007*, 2nd Edition, Law Society Publishing

Camp, P. (2009) *Solicitors and the Accounts Rules: A Compliance Handbook*, 2nd Edition, Law Society Publishing

Camp, P. (2008) *Solicitors and Money Laundering: A Compliance Handbook*, 3rd Edition, Law Society Publishing

Carey, P and Turle, M. (eds.) (2008) *Freedom of Information Handbook,* 2nd edition, Law Society Publishing

Cook, M. (2009) *Cook on Costs*, 2009 edition, LexisNexis Butterworths

Ede, R. and Edwards, A. (2008) *Criminal Defence*, 3rd Edition, Law Society Publishing

Edwards, A. and Savage, J. (2009) *Sentencing Handbook*, Law Society Publishing

Greaney, N. et al. (2008) *Mental Capacity: A Guide to the New Law*, 2nd edition, Law Society Publishing.

Hayden, T. and Hanney, J. (2005) *Licensing for Conveyancers: A Practical Guide*, Law Society Publishing

King, L. (ed.) (2006) *Probate Practitioner's Handbook*, 5th edition, Law Society Publishing

Madge, N., McConnell, D., Gallagher, J. & Luba, J. (2006) *Defending Possession Proceedings*, 6th edition, LAG Books

Manley, I. and Heslop, E. (2008) *Employment Tribunals*, 2nd edition, Law Society Publishing

Scott, P. (ed.) (2009) *Practice Management Handbook*, 2nd edition, Law Society Publishing

Scrope, H. and Barnett, D. (2008) *Employment Law Handbook*, 4th edition, Law Society Publishing

Silverman, F. (ed.) (2008) *Conveyancing Handbook*, 15th edition, Law Society Publishing

Sime, S. and French, D. (2008) *Blackstone's Civil Practice 2009*, 2009 edition, Oxford University Press

Solicitors Regulation Authority (2009) *Solicitors' Accounts Manual*, 11th edition, Law Society Publishing

Underwood, K. (2006) *Fixed Costs,* 2nd edition, LexisNexis Butterworths

Wignall, G. & Green, S. (eds.) (2008) *Conditional Fees*, 3rd Edition, Law Society Publishing

Law Society's *Litigation Funding* magazine (subscriptions available from 0207 841 5523)

Websites

Academy of Experts (online directory) –
 www.academy-experts.org

Acas   –
 www.acas.org.uk

Association of Contentious Trusts and Probate Specialists –
www.actaps.com

Association of Women Solicitors –
www.womensolicitors.org.uk

British and Irish Legal Information Institute –
www.bailii.org

Centre for Protection of National Infrastructure –
www.cpni.gov.uk

Charity Commission of England and Wales –
www.charity-commission.gov.uk;

Chartered Institute of Taxation –
www.tax.org.uk

Claims Management Regulation (part of Ministry of Justice) –
www.claimsregulation.gov.uk/search.aspx

Citizens Advice Bureau –
www.adviceguide.org.uk

Civil Justice Council –
www.civiljusticecouncil.gov.uk

Code of Conduct *see* Solicitors' Code of Conduct

Council for Licensed Conveyancers –
www.conveyancer.org.uk

Council of Mortgage Lenders –
www.cml.org.uk

Courts Service *see* HM Courts Service

Crown Prosecution Service –
www.cps.gov.uk

Department of Work and Pensions –
www.dwp.gov.uk

Department for Business, Enterprise & Regulatory Reform –
www.berr.gov.uk

European Union law –
http://eur-lex.europa.eu/

Expert Witness Institute –
www.ewi.org.uk

Faculty Office of the Archbishop of Canterbury –
www.facultyoffice.org.uk

Financial Action Task Force (FATF)
www.fatf-gafi.org

Financial Services Authority –
www.fsa.org.uk

Financial Services Compensation Scheme –
www.fscs.gov.uk

Find a solicitor (Law Society's online directory) –
www.solicitors-online.com

Gambling Commission –
www.gamblingcommission.gov.uk

Gazette *see* Law Society *Gazette*

HM Courts Service –
www.hmcourts-service.gov.uk

HM Revenue & Customs –
www.hmrc.gov.uk

HM Treasury –
www.hm-treasury.gov.uk

Information Commissioner –
www.ico.gov.uk

Insolvency Practitioners Association –
www.insolvency-practitioners.org.uk

International money laundering legislation –
www.anti-moneylaundering.org

Joint Money Laundering Steering Group –
www.jmlsg.org.uk

Land Registry –
www.landregistry.gov.uk

LawCare –
www.lawcare.org.uk

Law Society costs resources –
www.costs.lawsociety.org.uk

Law Society Dispute Resolution Section –
www.lawsociety.org.uk/disputeresolution

Law Society events and training –
www.lawsociety.org.uk/events

Law Society *Gazette* –
www.lawgazette.co.uk

Law Society Home Information Packs resources –
www.hips.lawsociety.org.uk

Law Society International Division –
www.lawsociety.org.uk/international

Law Society Junior Lawyers Division –
www.lawsociety.org.uk/juniorlawyers

Law Society Law Management Section –
www.lawsociety.org.uk/lawmanagement

Law Society money laundering resources –
www.lawsociety.org.uk/moneylaundering

Law Society Practice Advice Service –
www.lawsociety.org.uk/practiceadvice

Law Society Probate Section –
www.lawsociety.org.uk/probate

Law Society Property Section –
www.lawsociety.org.uk/property

Law Society strategic research unit–
www.research.lawsociety.org.uk

Legal Complaints Service –
www.legalcomplaints.org.uk

Legal Services Commission –
www.legalservices.gov.uk

Lexcel –
www.lawsociety.org.uk/lexcel

Metropolitan Police Service (fees for copy documentation in civil proceedings) –
www.met.police.uk/fees/index.htm

Ministry of Justice –
www.justice.gov.uk

National Land Information Service –
www.nlis.org.uk

Office of Court Funds, Official Solicitor and Public Trustee –
www.officialsolicitor.gov.uk

Office of Public Sector Information –
www.opsi.gov.uk

Office of the Public Guardian –
www.publicguardian.gov.uk

Office of the Scottish Charity Regulator –
www.oscr.org.uk

Regulatory requirements in relation to referrals –
www.referrals.sra.org.uk

Sentencing Guidelines Council –
www.sentencing-guidelines.gov.uk

Serious Organised Crime Agency –
www.soca.gov.uk

Software Solutions Guide –
www.it.lawsociety.org.uk

Solicitors Accounts Rules –
www.sra.org.uk/accounts-rules

Solicitors' Assistance Scheme –
www.thesas.org.uk

Solicitors Benevolent Association –
www.sba.org.uk

Solicitors' Code of Conduct –
www.sra.org.uk/rules

Solicitors Regulation Authority –
www.sra.org.uk

Statute Law Database –
www.statutelaw.gov.uk

Transparency International (corruption perception index) –
www.transparency.org

Index